THE NEW INSTITUTIONAL ECONOMICS AND DEVELOPMENT

Theory and Applications to Tunisia

CONTRIBUTIONS
TO
ECONOMIC ANALYSIS

183

Honorary Editor:
J. TINBERGEN

Editors:
D. W. JORGENSON
J. WAELBROECK

NORTH-HOLLAND
AMSTERDAM • NEW YORK • OXFORD • TOKYO

THE NEW INSTITUTIONAL ECONOMICS AND DEVELOPMENT

Theory and Applications to Tunisia

Edited by:

Mustapha K. NABLI
University of Tunis
Tunisia

Jeffrey B. NUGENT
University of Southern California
Los Angeles, CA, U.S.A.

1989

NORTH-HOLLAND
AMSTERDAM • NEW YORK • OXFORD • TOKYO

ELSEVIER SCIENCE PUBLISHERS B.V.
Sara Burgerhartstraat 25
P.O. Box 211, 1000 AE Amsterdam, The Netherlands

Distributors for the United States and Canada:

ELSEVIER SCIENCE PUBLISHING COMPANY INC.
655 Avenue of the Americas
New York, N.Y. 10010, U.S.A.

Library of Congress Cataloging-in-Publication Data

The New institutional economics and development : theory and
  applications to Tunisia / edited by Mustapha K. Nabli, Jeffrey B.
  Nugent.
       p.   cm. -- (Contributions to economic analysis ; 183)
     Includes bibliographical references.
     ISBN 0-444-87487-9
     1. Tunisia--Economic policy. 2. Institutional economics.
  3. Social groups. 4. Economic development.   I. Nabli, Mustapha K.
  II. Nugent, Jeffrey B.   III. Series.
  HC820.N49   1989
  338.9611--dc20   89-16371
                                                             CIP

ISBN: 0 444 87487 9

PRINTED IN THE NETHERLANDS

INTRODUCTION TO THE SERIES

This series consists of a number of hitherto unpublished studies, which are introduced by the editors in the belief that they represent fresh contributions to economic science.

The term "economic analysis" as used in the title of the series has been adopted because it covers both the activities of the theoretical economist and the research worker.

Although the analytical methods used by the various contributors are not the same, they are nevertheless conditioned by the common origin of their studies, namely theoretical problems encountered in practical research. Since for this reason, business cycle research and national accounting, research work on behalf of economic policy, and problems of planning are the main sources of the subjects dealt with, they necessarily determine the manner of approach adopted by the authors. Their methods tend to be "practical" in the sense of not being too far remote from application to actual economic conditions. In additon they are quantitative.

It is the hope of the editors that the publication of these studies will help to stimulate the exchange of scientific information and to reinforce international cooperation in the field of economics.

The Editors

PREFACE

This book is about the New Institutional Economics (NIE) and its possible application to Development Economics. Numerous theoretical links between NIE and Development Economics are identified and then illustrated in empirical case studies of the Tunisian economy. The book is self-contained; it includes both theory and empirical applications. Both are presented in such a way as to be accessible to each of the following types of readers: (1) development economists and practitioners, (2) readers interested in institutions and institutional economics, (3) regional specialists and others with particular interest in the experiences of countries like Tunisia, and (4) general readers including those interested in political economy.

With these different kinds of audiences in mind, the book is organized in such a way that the relevant portions of the book can be efficiently read by each different type of reader. Hence, it is expected that development economists and practitioners would want to read primarily Parts I and IV and those case studies of Parts II and III dealing with subjects of particular interest to them. Likewise, it is expected that those interested in institutions and institutional economics would be primarily interested in the case studies of Parts II and III. Indeed, since even within this group, specialization of interests would seem likely, it is expected that those interested in transaction cost and contractual choice issues would want to read Chapters 1 and 2 of Part I and the case studies of Part II whereas those interested primarily in public choice and collective action issues would want to read Chapters 1 and 3 of Part I and Part III. Regional specialists and others interested in the Tunisian experience would be most interested in the case studies of Parts II and III. General readers on the other hand might be primarily interested in Chapter 1, some of the individual case studies of Parts II and III, and Part IV.

As revealed in the list of contributors, the book is the result of a relatively extensive collaboration among scholars at the University of Southern California (USC) and the University of Tunis which in turn arose from an agreement of collaboration between the two universities. As such, this book would not have been possible without the initiative of Deans Moncef Ben Slama and Abdeljabbar Bsaies of the Faculté des Sciences Economiques et de Gestion de Tunis and Deans Irwin C. Lieb and subsequently William G. Spitzer of USC's College of Letters, Arts and Sciences in getting the project started and giving priority in it to the collaborative research program on applying the NIE to Tunisian institutions. Indeed, the encouragement and the very considerable attention of Dean Ben Slama throughout the project have been instrumental to the completion of the present outcome. The research has also benefitted from financial support from the United States Information Agency, the National Science Foundation, Tunisia's Ministry of Higher Education, the Occidental Petroleum Corporation and the two universities. This support is gratefully acknowledged. Also, we thank the fine fingers of Virginia Krocker, Naomi Smith and Sharon Koga. Without them this book could not have seen the light of day.

We also gratefully acknowledge the permissions of *World Development,* the *Journal of Theoretical and Institutional Economics* and The China Land Reform Association to publish in Chapters 1, 4 and 6 revised versions of papers published in these sources.

While we are grateful to all our collaborators for their interest, cooperation and hard work throughout the project, our debt to Timur Kuran who developed a special graduate course on institutions and development is especially great. His contribution to the volume extends well beyond that of the papers he has authored.

List of Contributors

MONGI AZABOU, Assistant Professor, Faculté des Sciences Economiques et de Gestion de Tunis, University of Tunis.

MOHAMED Z. BECHRI, Assistant, Faculté des Sciences Economiques et de Gestion de Tunis and University of Southern California.

LOTFI BOUZAÏANE, Assistant, Faculté des Sciences Economiques et de Gestion de Tunis, University of Tunis.

ABDELJABBAR BSAIES, Professor and Dean, Faculté des Sciences Economiques et de Gestion de Tunis, University of Tunis.

SAMAR K. DATTA, Director, Agro-economic Research Centre, Visva-Bharati University, India, and Adjunct Associate Professor, University of Southern California.

LAMINE DOGHRI, Associate Professor, Faculté des Sciences Economiques et de Gestion de Tunis, University of Tunis.

ABDESSATAR GRISSA, Professor, Faculté des Sciences Economiques et de Gestion de Tunis, University of Tunis.

BRUCE H. HERRICK, John F. Hendon Professor and Head of Economics, Washington and Lee University.

TIMUR KURAN, Associate Professor, Department of Economics, University of Southern California.

MOHAMED S. MATOUSSI, Associate Professor, Faculté des Sciences Economiques et de Gestion de Tunis, University of Tunis.

MUSTAPHA K. NABLI, Professor, Faculté des Sciences Economiques et de Gestion de Tunis, University of Tunis.

JEFFREY B. NUGENT, Professor, Department of Economics, University of Southern California.

ABDERRAZAK ZOUARI, Associate Professor, Faculté des Sciences Economiques et de Gestion de Sfax, University of the South, Tunisia.

TABLE OF CONTENTS

Contents

List of Figures

List of Tables

PART ONE

THE NEW INSTITUTIONAL ECONOMICS:

ISSUES AND APPLICATIONS

The purpose of this part of the book is to alert the reader to what is meant by the New Institutional Economics (NIE), its principal components and the relationships between them, the principal unsettled issues, its strengths and weaknesses, the relevant empirical evidence and what has and has not been learned to date. Although this part of the book is designed to prepare the reader for the case studies in subsequent parts of the book, since it is self-contained and of more general interest, it can also be used independently.

In Chapter 1 we identify the principal contributions to the literature on the NIE and divide them into two principal components, transaction (and information) costs and the theory of collective action. The domain and scope of each component is described and the interrelationships between them identified. The chapter concludes with a discussion concerning the relevance of such theories to development.

Chapter 2 by Datta and Nugent provides a unifying transaction cost framework for explaining choices among different forms of contract. Most applications to the explanation of contractual choices have been concerned with a rather narrow range of contractual choices and have focused almost exclusively on agriculture and labor-shirking as the single form of opportunistic behavior to which contracts may be vulnerable. This literature as well as empirical evidence on the choice among contracts is reviewed, beginning with agriculture and followed by mining, fishing, and transportation. The non-agricultural experience reveals the importance of the largely neglected asset-misuse form of opportunistic behavior. The results suggest that rather different conclusions are likely to be drawn once this and other sources of opportunistic behavior are considered.

Chapter 3 by Nabli and Nugent performs a similar function with respect to the theory of collective action. Its importance lies in the fact that collective action is generally required for the production and maintenance of public goods. The chapter begins with the definition of public goods and the identification of the free-rider problem which so often plagues attempts at collective action. Numerous factors hypothesized to affect the likelihood of success in collective action in general are identified and briefly explained. These include the type of public goods, group characteristics, environmental considerations, expectations and other dynamic factors. This is followed by a more detailed discussion of the theory and its applications relevant to different types of collective action problems. The relationships between collective action and the state on the one hand and between collective action and development on the other are examined. The chapter is concluded with a review of some of the principal unresolved issues of relevance to development. This review underscores the need for more dynamic analyses.

Chapter 1

THE NEW INSTITUTIONAL ECONOMICS
AND ECONOMIC DEVELOPMENT:
AN INTRODUCTION*

Mustapha K. Nabli and Jeffrey B. Nugent

Several remarkable developments have taken place in the social sciences in the last two decades. Conspicuous among them are those which highlight the shortcomings of the (traditional) neoclassical economics paradigm and provide original and powerful insights into how institutions are created. Disparate in origin and differing in form, these developments have coalesced into what Williamson (1975, 1985) and others have dubbed the New Institutional Economics (NIE).

The pioneering contributions that constitute the NIE are noteworthy on several grounds. First, the institutions and their determinants that are the subject matter of NIE have long served as a battleground among the alternative leading paradigms, namely Marxian, neoclassical, and sociobiological. Second, NIE represents the culminating intersection of a number of different lines of investigation, each interesting in its own right, including the analysis of behavioral norms, the integration of persons with different tastes and preferences into voting coalitions, interest group formation, the problems of and prerequisites for (successful) collective action, transaction costs, organization theory, limitations on the rationality of human behavior, the emergence of rules of thumb for firm decision-making, the determinants of firm structure, coordination problems, rent-seeking behavior, technological change and its relationship to institutional change and the determinants and effects of property rights. Third, many of these individual lines of investigation within the NIE are interdisciplinary, allowing for cross-fertilization and mutual stimulation among historians, sociologists, political scientists, psychologists, lawyers and, of course, economists.

Because of the field's rapid and multidirectional growth, it would be a monumental task indeed to synthesize it in its entirety. Even if it were possible to do so in a single volume of relatively modest size, it should be stressed that

*The authors gratefully acknowledge the useful comments of David Feeny, Bruce Herrick, Timur Kuran, Ruud Picavet and the participants of seminars at Cornell University and Tilburg University at which earlier versions of this introduction were presented. Portions of an earlier version were published in *World Development* (September, 1989) by Pergamon Journals, Oxford, U.K.

this is not our purpose here. For recent expositions of many of the elements of the NIE, the reader is referred to specialized journals like the *Journal of Economic Behavior and Organization*, the *Journal of Institutional and Theoretical Economics*, *Public Choice*, the *Journal of Law, Economics and Organization*, the *Journal of Law and Economics*, the *Journal of Economic Issues* and to several recent books [Mueller, ed. (1983), Eliasson, ed. (1986) and Langlois, ed. (1986)]. Instead, our purpose is to relate some of the most important strands of analysis that constitute the NIE both to one another and to the economics of development.

Of course, the importance of institutions to economic development has been mentioned frequently. It has been stressed not only in classic works such as Adam Smith's *Wealth of Nations*, and in the work of the institutionalists of the early 20th century, but also in the literature of modern development economics, ranging from the qualitative, such as Myrdal (1968), and the semi-quantitative, such as Morawetz (1981), to the highly quantitative, e.g., Adelman and Morris (1967) and Morris and Adelman (1986). Institutions and their importance to development have also been made the exclusive subject of at least one development textbook [Gannagé (1966)], and an important feature of several others, including one of the most modern [Basu (1984)]. Both these textbooks and Myrdal's monumental book make a plea for the importance of understanding the local environment, and in particular the relevant institutions, for the proper design of development policy. Myrdal and numerous others describe the institutions in developing countries (LDCs), and Adelman and Morris identify some statistical correlations between the level of development and various social, political and institutional indicators. Similarly, Scully (1988) demonstrates the statistical significance of the elements of an institutional framework on economic growth during the period 1960-80 in a cross section of 115 countries.

As recently as 1985, still another leading development economist, Henry Bruton (1985), called attention to the importance of institutions in development but without even a single mention of the NIE or any of its elements.

As Theodore Schultz observed some years ago, economists are quick to preach the merits of appropriate institutional changes but in their analytical models they generally leave no room for or even make mention of institutions. "It is a neat trick, but it cannot hide the fact that, in thinking about institutions, the analytical cupboard is bare..." [Schultz (1968, p. 1113)].

In the absence of a theoretical structure,[1] there does not yet exist any

---

[1]This is not meant to imply that there are as yet no attempts to explain insti-

systematic attempt to apply the NIE as a whole to development.[2] In short, the impact on the economics of development has thus far been extremely limited. Moreover, without such an impact, the economics of development may be in serious trouble as the following statement of Sir Arthur Lewis suggests:

> Development Economics will certainly die if they (Ph.D. students) come to think, rightly or wrongly, that work on economic institutions will not count for distinction in Ph.D. exams [Lewis (1984, p. 8)].

In view of the *many* applications of the NIE to fields such as industrial organization, health economics, macroeconomics and international trade within economics (to name only a few) and even to international relations and politics, the *dearth* of published applications to development economics is rather surprising. Furthermore, because the process of economic development is a long term one in which institutions change and hence cannot safely be assumed to remain constant as in some of these other areas of economics, the shortage of applications (with the notable exceptions indicated below) of the new institutional analysis to development is not only surprising but also quite disturbing.

Objectives and Scope of the Study

This study has three objectives. The first is to show the relevance of the principles and insights of the NIE to the analysis of the problems of LDCs. By choosing a wide range of institutional forms and issues in the applications, we emphasize the breadth of scope and fruitfulness of the approach. By concentrating our attention on a single country, Tunisia, we can both draw

---

tutions in LDCs. Indeed, very recently there have been two as yet unpublished conferences, one at Cornell University in November 1986 and another at Indiana University, and several widely scattered published contributions. Most of these, however, deal with one particular element of NIE, the applications of which are confined to a very few subjects such as sharecropping, caste, the choice of policy regimes, interlinking of markets and overgrazing. Naturally, most of these individual studies will be discussed in Chapters 2 and 3 which attempt to synthesize the most relevant elements of NIE and demonstrate their application to LDCs and their development problems. Several of the more scattered studies on rural institutions in India have been brought together by Bardhan [Bardhan (1984a, 1984b, forthcoming)].

[2]Note the absence of such a treatment in the most important textbooks in development, e.g., Bruton (1965), Donaldson (1983), Gillis, Perkins, Roemer and Snodgrass (1987), Hagen (1986), Herrick and Kindleberger (1983), Meier (1984), Myint (1971), Nafziger (1984), Todaro (1981), and Yotopoulos and Nugent (1976). Basu (1984) and Hill (1986) criticize the theory of development in large part precisely for its failure to incorporate an institutional framework.

upon several different elements in the NIE and realize the complementarities
between them. Although it might have been interesting to draw on studies
of, realize applications to, and make comparisons with, other LDCs, given
the time and resources available, this is not attempted here.

Second, the study makes it possible to evaluate the degree to which the
various elements of the NIE, which have been developed mostly in the context
of the advanced industrial economies (DCs), may need to be adapted, completed or modified in order to be applicable to the rather differing conditions
of Tunisia or any other LDC.

Third, the study provides yet another set of applications and empirical
investigations of the NIE in general. The need for empirical and applied
work on the NIE, particularly in different contexts, is well recognized and
recommended by such authors as Matthews (1986). Such applications and
empirical investigations are critically important for the further testing and
sharpening of the various hypotheses that have been advanced.

Since the case studies and applications presented in this volume draw
heavily on the theoretical and methodological insights of the NIE, we deem it
worthwhile to survey them along with the existing applications in Chapters
2 and 3 in Part I of the volume. Chapter 2 deals with the transactions and
information costs approach and Chapter 3 with the theory of collective action.
As we shall see below, broadly defined these two sets of approaches encompass
most of the important contributions to the field.

In order to reach as broad an audience as possible, in presenting the principles of the NIE and suggesting insights that might be useful in development
economics, we minimize the use of technical jargon and avoid mathematics.
This is especially true in this introduction and the two remaining chapters of
Part I.

Tunisia provides an interesting and useful case to study for several reasons. First, Tunisia has witnessed an interesting variety of very fundamental
institutional changes in its recent history. In particular, its status changed
from a dependency of the Ottoman Empire to a semi-autonomous state in
the late 18th century, and then to a French protectorate by the 1880's. After independence in 1956, the country passed through a phase as a relatively
inward-oriented "socialistic" and public sector-dominated economy, but, since
the late 1960's has become an increasingly open, private enterprise-oriented
market economy.[3] Second, Tunisia is in many ways, including its size, income

---

[3] For some useful references to Tunisian history, in general, and its economic
history, in particular, see Brown (1974), Kraïem (1973), Mahjoub (1983), and
Valensi (1969, 1970).

level, high level of dependence on a particular country (France) for its imports and exports, its import-substituting policy orientation, the dualistic character of its economy, and its relative resource endowment, a rather typical LDC. At least, it is more typical than the few very large LDCs, like India, China, Brazil and Mexico, or the very small star economic performers of East Asia, such as Hong Kong, Singapore and Taiwan, which have been more frequently and thoroughly studied.

Defining Institutions

The consensus on the centrality of institutions to development has not been matched by one on its definition. Different authors have used quite different definitions, each emphasizing quite different aspects or characteristics of the more general phenomenon. Among the characteristics or aspects of institutions which vary are the degree to which they are (a) organizational, i.e., the extent to which organizations and institutions coincide, (b) formal, (c) created at a specific time and place by a specific means (as opposed to having evolved from more diffuse sources), (d) embedded in (as opposed to differentiated from) other institutions, (e) universal (as opposed to particularistic) in the interests they serve, (f) creating (as opposed to simply maintaining) a certain public good, and (g) technology-linked.

For Schotter "a social institution is a regularity in social behavior that is agreed to by all members of society, specifies behavior in specific recurrent situations, and is either self-policed or policed by some external authority" [Schotter (1981, p. 11)]. He goes on to insist that "institutions are properties of equilibria of games and not properties of the games' description" [Schotter (1981, p. 155)]. As such they are seen as regularities in behavior that would emerge from a set of rules. Heiner (1983, p. 573) adopts a similar definition, as does Uphoff (1986) for whom "institutions are complexes of norms of behavior that persist over time, by serving collectively valued purposes" [Uphoff (1986, p. 9)] and Adelman and Head (1983, p. 2) who define institutions as patterned forms of interaction among human beings.

In contrast to the preceding definitions, the more usual ones put emphasis on the "rules" aspect of institutions, which are considered as precedents for the evolution of behavioral norms. For instance, for Douglass North, "institutions are rules, enforcement characteristics of rules, and norms of behavior that structure repeated human interaction" [North (1986b, p. 6)]. In a similar vein, for Ruttan and Hayami "institutions are the rules of a society or of organizations that facilitate coordination among people by helping them form expectations which each person can reasonably hold in dealing with others" [Ruttan and Hayami (1984, p. 204)].

The difference between the two kinds of definitions would seem to be related to the level and sequence of analysis. For example, at a relatively "low" level of analysis, e.g., that of contractual arrangements, the rules characteristic may dominate but at a relatively "high" level of analysis, such as that of cultural values and mores, the behavioral norms definition may seem more relevant. Similarly with respect to sequence, while at a given point in time the rules and norms that characterize institutions may be considered as given and independent of individual or group behavior, over time they may well evolve as a result of the preceding experience. Over time, therefore, we may observe dynamic chains going from rules to behavioral regularities to rules, etc. In any case, in most definitions there appear to be three more or less explicitly stated characteristics which may be considered basic to the concept of a social institution.

The first such characteristic is the rules and constraints nature of institutions. Elinor Ostrom (1986) has defined these rules and constraints as "prescriptions commonly known and used by a set of participants to order repetitive, interdependent relationships. Prescriptions refer to which actions are required, prohibited or permitted" [Ostrom (1986, p. 5)]. It is important in terms of institutional analysis to consider configurations of rules rather than single rules separately. It is as sets or configurations that rules are considered as basic characterisitics of institutions.

The second characteristic of institutions is the ability of their rules and constraints characteristic to govern the relations among individuals and groups. Whether they are "voluntarily" accepted through custom or tradition, or are enforced and policed through an external authority and a coercive incentive system, to serve an institutional role these rules and constraints have to be applicable in social relations.

The third characteristic of institutions is their predictability. The rules and constraints have to be understood, at least in principle, as being applicable in repeated and future situations. Agents should expect these rules and constraints to have some degree of stability; otherwise, they would not have an institutional character.

For present purposes an institution is defined as a set of constraints which governs the behavioral relations among individuals or groups. Formal organizations, such as labor unions and employers' organizations are institutions because they provide sets of rules governing the relationships both among their members and between members and non-members. Likewise, markets, be they stock exchanges, labor markets, credit markets, wholesale markets or traditional bazaars (suqs), are institutions because they embody rules and regulations, formal or informal, which govern their operation. Contracts, explicit or implicit, are also institutions in that they lay down rules which govern specified activities involving the parties to such contracts. Similarly, cultural rules and codes of conduct are institutions in so far as they, too, can constrain the relationships between different individuals and/or groups.

It is the purpose of the NIE not only to explain the determinants of institutions and their evolution over time but also to evaluate their economic efficiency and distributional implications. Since institutions generally attempt to satisfy certain goals and adopt structures such as incentives, the division of labor, rules for entry, exit, decision-making and external relations, all such aspects of institutions should be considered in explaining institutions and their effects.

Themes in the NIE

In mainstream neoclassical economics, four main types of constraints have received considerable attention: individual preferences, technological opportunities, physical and human capital endowments and market opportunities. In such analyses the institutional framework has almost invariably been taken as given, and in many cases has even been altogether omitted. The consequence of taking the institutional framework as given has been to leave the analysis of institutional constraints to non-economists (typically political scientists, lawyers, sociologists, and anthropologists). While the analyses of non-economists are rich in descriptive detail, and while they contain numerous useful insights, they tend to be relatively light in their ability to provide either reliable generalizations or a sound logical basis for policy choices. Without a place to fit such insights into their framework, most economists have unfortunately remained oblivious to the results of such analyses. The explicit or implicit assumption of given institutions is, of course, especially unrealistic and limiting in the context of economic development, a process whereby institutions generally undergo substantial change.

The goal of the NIE is to overcome these important limitations of mainstream neoclassical economics. Like most other intellectual developments, the NIE has evolved from earlier ideas. In particular, one important forerunner was Marxian analysis in which institutions were relatively exclusively determined by technology. Institutional changes, however, would necessarily arise from internal contradictions i.e., a dialectic process which may be anything but smooth and comfortable [deJanvry (1981)]. Marxists identify these processes with class struggles but fail to provide "micro-foundations" of just how they work. Significantly, however, this challenge has recently been taken up with collective action theory by several Marxian scholars, such as Elster

(1985), Offe (1985) and Roemer (1978). Sociobiologists have tended to emphasize that differences in biological and environmental forces have triggered different kinds of social and cultural responses which eventually solidify into institutions [Jones (1981) and Norgaard (1981)]. As shall be subsequently demonstrated, economic historians, such as North (1981), Feeny (1982) and Ruttan and Hayami (1984), have made even more direct contributions to the NIE in noting correlations between institutional, technological and other changes. Another important forerunner to and motivator of NIE was the Institutionalist School which included such eloquent contributors as Thorstein Veblen, John R. Commons, Wesley Mitchell and Clarence Ayres. Indeed, the NIE resembles the earlier or "old" Institutionalist School in several important respects. Both are extremely broad in scope and replete with many interesting and diverse perspectives. More importantly, the two schools share a strong criticism of neoclassical economics for (a) its lack of attention to institutions and hence also non-budgetary constraints, (b) its overemphasis on the rationality of decision-making, (c) its excessive concentration on equilibrium and statics as opposed to disequilibrium and dynamics and (d) its denial that preferences can change or that behavior is repetitive or habitual.

The NIE departs from the earlier Institutionalist School in that its critique of mainstream economics is a largely positive one. The NIE attempts to modify or broaden the mainstream toolkit and then to use this broadened analytical framework to explain phenomena that had previously seemed impenetrable. As Langlois (1986 p. 5) puts it, "the problem with many of the early Institutionalists is that they wanted an economics with institutions but without theory; the problem with many neoclassicists is that they want economic theory without institutions; what NIE tries to do is to provide an economics with both theory *and* institutions.[4]

The NIE is not, however, a homogeneous and monolithic body of knowledge. While it is essentially micro-economic in perspective, it includes various approaches, each with its own techniques and concepts and advantages and disadvantages, for analyzing institutions. While there is as yet no consensus on what is included in the NIE, we find that two broad and general approaches are salient, namely transaction and information costs, on the one hand, and the theory of collective action, on the other.

While Chapters 2 and 3 which follow provide concise expositions of the main concepts, methods and results of each of these approaches, to give the

---

[4]While in the light of the review by Coats (1986) of the Langlois, ed., (1986) volume it is clear that some economists and other social scientists are likely to deem this presumptuous, we still feel that this generalization is a fair one.

reader a feel for what lies ahead the main issues and hypotheses are identified below. We then point out the complementarities between the two approaches and their relevance to development economics. The Tunisian case studies which constitute Parts II and III of this volume, the former dealing with transaction and information costs and the latter with collective action, draw heavily on these theoretical and methodological introductions.

Transaction and Information Costs

The first general approach, is that of "transaction costs" and "information costs," which contains several different but interrelated themes.[5] One such theme is concerned with the role of transaction costs in economic organization. It has been stimulated by the influential work of Oliver Williamson (1975, 1979, 1985) who has combined the concepts of bounded rationality and opportunistic behavior. The general hypothesis is that institutions are transaction cost-minimizing arrangements which may change and evolve with changes in the nature and sources of transaction costs and the means for minimizing them.[6]

A second theme is the property rights approach which is associated with the law and economics literature. Based on the pioneering work of Alchian (1959, 1961), Coase (1960) and Demsetz (1967), this approach explains how technological and other conditions including apparent externalities can give rise to the kinds of institutional mechanisms for internalizing externalities known as property rights. The existence of property rights may reduce conflicts and facilitate cooperation, in both cases resulting in a reduction in transaction costs. In this way, along with technology and other traditional constraints, institutional constraints enter into the decision processes of individuals. In the presence of transactions costs, different systems of property rights yield solutions of differing efficiency. What is efficient in the presence of transaction costs may be quite different from that which is efficient in the traditional neoclassical economics without transactions costs. As such, the property rights approach is closely related to that dealing with transaction costs and their role in determining both the form of organization of firms and the relative importance of the market, on the one hand, and hierarchical authority, on the other. A key proposition in the property rights approach

---

[5]For instance, Matthews (1986) considers that the economics of institutions includes the following transaction cost-related themes: property rights, conventions, types of contract, and authority. See also North (1981, 1986a).

[6]For some limitations on this hypothesis as well as a more complete discussion see Akerlof (1970, 1976), Basu (1984), Field (1981), Dow (1987) and Chapter 2 below.

associated with Coase (1960) is that, in the absence of transaction costs at least, the assignment of property rights would lead to efficient contractual outcomes through bargaining and negotiation. However, as has been stressed by Farrell (1987), the proposition is valid only when all the relevant information is public knowledge. When this is not the case, efficient outcomes are no longer guaranteed and the outcome of bargaining may be inefficient.

This leads to a third theme which is concerned with incomplete information and asymmetries in information in particular. While this theme has developed quite separately from the first, and the analysis to which it has given rise is more mathematically oriented, the two themes are intimately related. Indeed, information problems can be considered as one particular source of transaction costs.[7] The problems of "adverse selection" and "moral hazard," which will be defined in Chapter 2 below and which were first identified in the context of insurance markets, have been found to be relevant for a large class of problems where asymmetries of information are present between the parties to a contract. These problems, moreover, may lead to "market failure" unless incentive mechanisms capable of overcoming them such as appropriate forms of contract, are developed.[8]

It should be clear, therefore, that asymmetries of information are closely related to opportunistic behavior and transaction costs. When the information set available to one party to a contract involving two parties is not identical to that available to the other party, one of the parties may be able to engage in opportunistic behavior so as to increase that party's benefits at the expense of the other's. However, the latter may engage in monitoring or information search activities in order to minimize his (her) loss. These activities, however, are costly and have to be matched with their expected benefits.

Both the economics of transaction costs and that of costly information have recognized the existence of a general "agency problem" in contractual arrangements. Jensen and Meckling (1976) and Williamson (1975, 1985) have applied the agency concept to managerial behavior and the ownership structure of firms. Moreover, it can readily be generalized so as to be applied to any situation where contracts are incomplete and/or information is asymmetric and the action of one individual, the "agent," affects another individual, the "principal." Problems in corporate management, labor markets, govern-

---

[7]See also Stiglitz (1985) who argues that information costs are a special case or form of transaction costs.

[8]For some recent applications of relevance to agriculture and LDCs, see Akerlof (1970), and Greenwald and Glasspiegel (1983).

ment procurement, insurance and credit contracts can be analyzed using the agency framework.

The general approach of "transaction and information cost economics" has proved to be particularly useful for the analysis of contractual choice. One such area of application is that dealing with contracts between different owners of the inputs used in production. If all economic agents were equally well endowed in the resources relevant to productive activities, and there were no economies of scale, production could very conceivably take place without recourse to contracts among the owners of the productive inputs. Every individual would constitute a Robinson Crusoe-type economy. However, since economic resources are not distributed in this way and scale and specialization economies are frequently important, there is almost inevitably a need for contractual relationships. Those agents relatively better endowed in some resources, such as land and capital, can contract to sell some of these resources to those agents better endowed in other respects, such as labor, human capital and experience, and/or to buy from the latter.

Regardless of the specific nature of the economic activity in which the different productive inputs are combined, the forms of contract virtually always turn out to be one or another variant or mix of the following: (a) fixed rent contracts, (b) wage contracts, and (c) share contracts. While this nomenclature is appropriate only for contracts involving exchanges among the owners of inputs into the production process, there are parallels with regard to contractual relationships involving exchange of the outputs within the production process. For example, when the producing firm is forward-integrated into retail markets, and hires its own marketing people, it uses a wage contract. Likewise, when the producer sells directly to separate retailers, this is the counterpart to a fixed rent contract. Finally, if the producer does not sell to the retailer but rather the retailer sells on behalf of the producer on a consignment basis, this is the counterpart to a share contract. Important opportunities to test hypotheses about the determinants of such contractual mixes arise because these contractual mixes vary over both time and space.

Another area of application concerns the identification of the factors affecting the relative importance of market and non-market activities and institutions in the course of economic development. What factors distinguish what is done via "arms-length" market transactions between households and firms, or among different firms, from what is done within households, on the one hand, or within vertically or horizontally integrated firms, on the other? How do these factors change with modernization and development?

In this respect, social scientists have over the years offered numerous different explanations for the rise of the market. Particularly rich in insights has been the work of Williamson (1975, 1985) emphasizing the role of efficiency tradeoffs between the economies of specialization and market transactions, on the one hand, and those of intrafirm coordination and control or hierarchy, on the other hand. While both market transactions and internal hierarchy involve transaction costs, according to Williamson the choice between them depends largely on their relative magnitudes.

Collective Action

The second general approach in the NIE, and which is therefore distinct from either the transaction or information cost approaches, concerns collective action and the elimination of "the free-rider problem." The key issue in the collective action literature is to "explain collective outcomes in terms of individual motivation" [Hardin (1982), p. 2], or, to put it differently, to explain the likelihood of success or failure of a given set of self-interested individuals in undertaking actions that may benefit them collectively.

The theory of collective action has been concerned with public or collective goods not only of physical character, such as pollution, highways, parks and the like, but also and more interestingly of an abstract character, such as a higher wage rate, a higher price, a tariff or quota, a regulation, a lower tax rate or a policy rule. The public or collective goods aspect of collective action gives rise to the free-rider problem inasmuch as the self-interested individuals may find it preferable *not* to participate in the provision of the public good and/or to reveal false preferences about its value to them. This problem derives from two characteristics inherent in public goods, namely that, once the goods are provided, individuals can no longer be excluded from their benefits and that their value to existing beneficiaries is not reduced by increasing the number of beneficiaries. The incentive to free-ride analyzed by Olson (1965), Hardin (1968) and others tends to result in inefficient collective outcomes in that public goods are under-provided. The theory of collective action has been concerned not only with the explanations for how optimizing behavior on the part of individuals can result in non-cooperation but also with the identification of conditions under which cooperation can be achieved. An extensive literature — theoretical, empirical, and experimental — has evolved, showing that cooperative outcomes in which the free-rider problem is overcome can be and actually are reached.

One segment of this literature, namely that concerning the emergence of behavioral norms and rules [Ullman-Margalit (1977), Schotter (1981) and Brennan and Buchanan (1985)], has remained almost entirely theoretical. In the case of the emergence of interest groups and organizations, however, the theory of collective action has gone well beyond the realm of pure theory. This work has been spearheaded by the publication of two remarkable books by Mancur Olson [Olson (1965, 1982)], and a synthesis by Hardin (1982). In Olson's analysis considerable attention in the explanation of success in collective action is given to the nature of the group, such as its size, its age and its purpose, and the extent to which group characteristics are shared among group members, such as homogeneity in origin and in goals, and the role of selective incentives in the realization of collective action and the overcoming of free-rider problems. Such incentives may take the form of positive "joint product" benefits to members who participate in group activities or of penalties imposed on those who fail to contribute to the collective action.

In addition to the group characteristics emphasized by Olson and his followers, a number of other factors have been identified that are likely to enhance the prospects for collective action. The availability of political entrepreneurs [Hardin (1982)] and psychological attitudes such as relative deprivation among group members [Brenner (1983)] can explain why certain groups become organized even if on the basis of Olson's group characteristics they would appear to be weak. Succcess in collective action may also be affected by the tolerance on the part of other groups, and by the quality of communication and organizational skills and the knowledge of the technology of collective action among group members and particularly among the leadership. Also the concepts of "exit" and "voice" provided by Hirschman (1970) are useful not only in distinguishing between success and failure in collective action but also in identifying the nature of any collective action taken. Specifically, the members of any organization or group who may be dissatisfied with the functioning or performance of the organization or group have two choices, namely, to remain in the group but to express their dissatisfaction through "voice," e.g., by criticizing the group and trying to reform it by taking political action within it, or to "exit," i.e., to leave the organization or group. When the latter is relatively costless, exit is likely to be chosen over voice, thereby undermining the possibilities of collective action.

The principles of collective action have been applied to a large number of problems, including the formation of labor unions [Olson (1982)], squatter communities [Hirschman (1984), Jimenez (1985)], development projects [Hirschman (1967)], environmental groups [Hardin (1982)], and agricultural policies [Bates (1981)]. The application of greatest relevance to the LDCs and which has managed to sustain interest for the longest period of time is the issue of peasant rebellion [Scott (1976), Popkin (1979, 1981) and especially Feeny (1983)].

Another major field of investigation in the theory and application of collective action concerns the use of a common pool of resources and the so-called "tragedy of the commons" that frequently arises in such cases [G. Hardin (1968)]. In this type of problem the public or collective goods considered are subject to a significant degree of congestion. The principles of collective action seem to imply that the joint use of common-pool resources, such as bodies of water, pools of oil, grazing land, parks or fishing areas, is likely to be problematic, at least in the absence of a system of individual property rights. This is because each user would have the incentive to overuse the resource, eventually leading to its depletion and destruction.

As a result, policy prescriptions usually emphasize the need for the external imposition of a system of private property rights or the strict enforcement of rules designed to avoid the problems of communal ownership by an external authority such as the government. However, recent studies by Blomquist and Ostrom (1985), Ostrom (1985), Runge (1981, 1986) and Wade (1987) have shown that special institutional arrangements including customs and social conventions designed to induce cooperative solutions can overcome the collective action difficulties and help achieve efficiency in the use of such resources.

The relationship between interest groups and the state is also receiving increasing attention in the collective action literature. When the state can be considered as playing only a mediating role in collective action, passively responding to interest group pressures, the various principles discussed above can be used to assess the relative influence of different groups over policy. Frequently, however, the state and its agents are not merely neutral and passive bystanders in the process of group interaction. This has given rise to the positive theory of rent-seeking which is concerned with the means that interest groups use for getting what they want, i.e., by affecting voting patterns, legislation and regulatory agencies, administrative budgets, rules and/or judicial decisions.[9] Empirical applications of rent-seeking include the determination of trade protection and of income transfers to farmers. The normative theory of rent-seeking, however, suggests the importance not only of the costs of creating new institutions but also of the distinctions both between profit-seeking and rent-seeking and between competitive and noncompetitive rent-seeking.[10]

Since the theory of rent-seeking has been developed and applied mostly

[9] Among the important contributions by economists to these issues are those of Stigler (1971), Olson (1965, 1982), McCormick and Tollison (1981), Peltzman (1976), Becker (1983) and Kalt and Zupan (1984).
[10] See especially Krueger (1974), Buchanan, Tollison and Tullock, eds. (1980), Bhagwati (1982), Bhagwati and Srinivasan (1982), Tollison (1982), Colander, ed. (1984) and Appelbaum and Katz (1987).

to DCs within an institutional framework of representative government but LDCs are generally characterized by autocratic governments and bureaucracies, this raises the question of the extent to which the theory and its predictions can be transfered to LDCs.

While most of the aforementioned elements of collective action theory are essentially static in character, in the last few years collective action theory has become more concerned with dynamic issues which are of major relevance to institutional change in general and development in particular. These considerations will be discussed below.

Complementarities between Transaction and Information Costs and Collective Action

While the two main branches of the NIE identified here, namely, the analysis of transaction costs, information costs and contractual choices, on the one hand, and the analysis of collective action and pressure groups, on the other hand, have developed quite separately, they are by no means independent or unrelated. In fact, many issues and approaches in the NIE are at the confluence of these two approaches, thereby constituting interesting subjects for further study, and justifying their joint treatment in this volume.

First, there are important similarities in the frameworks themselves and the axioms upon which they are based. For example, as in the analysis of transaction costs, collective action is analysed from the point of view of self-interest and bounded rationality, including opportunism.

Second, both transaction costs and collective action may be affected by the same factors. For example, caste, ethnicity and family loyalty may affect the contractual relations among members of an economic organization by reducing transaction costs [Ben Porath (1980), Pollak (1985), Nugent (1985)], but also may either facilitate collective action by their members by helping to solve the free-rider problems which plague such action or retard such action by increasing the transaction costs of change [Akerlof (1976), Basu (1986), and Basu, Jones and Schlicht (1986)]. Both transaction costs and the likelihood of collective action may also be affected by changes in commodity and factor prices, risk and expectations.

Third, because the role of government is emphasized in both the transaction cost and collective action components of NIE, they have to be interrelated and complementary. On the one hand, government decisions affect the transaction and information costs of the different economic agents and thereby their choices of organizational form and type of contract. On the other hand, the different agents or groups have the incentive to organize themselves in such a way as to influence these government decisions in the protection of their interests.

Fourth, since governments as a whole or the branches thereof (legislatures, ministries or public enterprises) are also organizations plagued with internal sources of inefficiency arising from transaction and information costs, these objects of collective action are at the same time subject to transaction and information costs.[11]

Fifth, even when voluntary, actual contractual choices are typically made within contexts in which various other institutions or "macro rules" are given. Among the given institutions are the systems of property rights and "transaction rights" [Blau (1964), Posner (1980), Witt (1987)], the family (and the complex set of reciprocal responsibilities that family participation entails), other social norms and conventions, community bonds, ethnicities, local and national laws and regulations and the judicial and penal systems. The existence of norms and conventions facilitates coordination and cooperation and protects expectations. In some cases, certain changes in these macro rules can significantly reduce transaction costs and thereby stimulate economic development, but not necessarily unambiguously.

When any individual or group finds that, at least from his (its) own perspective, the existing contractual alternatives and existing "macro rules" or other institutions are inefficient, inequitable or both, that individual or group is a potential candidate for engaging in collective action to change the contracts, macro rules or both in such a way as to improve the outcome for himself (itself).

Since in this sense collective action can be said to begin where contractual choices based on the principles of transaction costs leave off, the two perspectives are obviously complementary. Both have a lot to do with explaining institutions and changes therein. Moreover, one approach may provide a solution to the problem of the other. For example, if existing contracts are inefficient, collective action to initiate a change may be the solution. Likewise, one means of attaining collective action, and hence of solving the free-rider problem inherent in it, may be a contractual one designed to overcome free riding.

One hypothesis that may be advanced in the light of this dynamic interaction is that the transaction cost analysis of existing contractual arrangements is relevant when such costs are not so prohibitive as to prevent their

---

[11]Wolf (1986) calls attention to the parallel between "market failure" and "government failure." Crain, Leavens and Tollison (1986), on the other hand, call attention to the relevance and importance of transaction and information costs in the organization of government and the rules which it adopts in making decisions.

formation. But when the costs of transacting are very high, strategic behavior becomes rampant and collective action becomes necessary in order to find a solution. Similarly, the two approaches may be used simultaneously in order to explain some dynamic institutional interactions. For instance, the formation, functioning and evolution of some organizations may be fruitfully analysed in terms of both transactions costs and collective action. Hence, the relative position, power and composition of sub-groups in an organization, may be explained in terms of collective action theory but then the determination of the structure of authority within it may be fruitfully analysed in terms of transaction costs. Inversely, the internal structure and the costs of organization may affect the relative position of the sub-groups.[12]

The X-efficiency theory of Leibenstein (1966) provides another example of potential complementarity between transactions costs and collective action principles. Leibenstein hypothesizes that firms and other non-market organizations fail to use the resources available to them as efficiently or as fully as they could and identifies some of the factors responsible for this. De Alessi (1983) shows how the basic postulates and axioms of the X-efficiency theory are rooted in transaction cost considerations. In particular, the postulates of selective rationality, the existence of inert areas, and incomplete contracts, which imply that effort is a discretionary variable, can be interpreted as following from rational choice in the presence of transactions costs. Moreover, Leibenstein (1986) shows how a major facet of X-efficiency theory, the less-than-maximum effort by the individual agents, can be understood to arise because of free-rider and collective action problems.

In general, therefore, it would seem highly desirable that the two approaches be brought together so as to allow the analyst the opportunity to take advantage of their complementarities.

The NIE and Development

The dearth of systematic attempts (with the exceptions noted above and in more detail later on, most of which are confined to agriculture) to apply the NIE to development, in spite of the fact that potentially it would seem that the approach could be most useful in the LDC context and for problems of development, has been noted above. While in Chapter 15 of this volume, Bruce Herrick addresses the issue of the relevance and likely impact of NIE on the theory of economic development from a general and epistemological perspective, we deem it important to identify here some major

---

[12]Indeed, such an analysis is applied to Tunisian labor unions in Chapter 11 below.

areas of potential use of the NIE in the context of development.

It has long been recognized that traditional neoclassical economics, by taking institutions as given or failing to recognize their relevance for the analysis of economic problems, has been unable to provide satisfactory explanations for a wide range of conditions commonly found in LDCs. For example, neither general references to market imperfections and distortions nor detailed analyses of their welfare consequences help explain either the pervasiveness of these imperfections and distortions or the considerable difficulties in removing them.

Marxists and neo-Marxists, of course, have been quick to fault neoclassical economics for these failures and asserted their own explanations based on class relations which in turn depend on the relations of production. Frequently also, they criticize these existing institutions for their coercive character and their impeding effects on development and distribution. Some common examples that have been prominent in the development literature are sharecropping and the interlinking of credit and labor (credit of the labor-tying variety).[13]

Marxists have typically asserted these to be feudal, semi-feudal or pre-capitalist in origin and exploitative and regressive in effect. As Bardhan (1980, 1988, forthcoming) asserts, however, such authors have unfortunately overlooked various possible micro-economic explanations for these relationships.

Stiglitz (1985, 1986), Bardhan (1984a, 1988, forthcoming) and many other authors whose work will be referred to in Chapter 2 have shown how the economics of information and transaction costs can be useful in understanding these same institutions. Much of this work has been strictly theoretical in nature. The relatively rare empirical studies reviewed in Chapter 2 below have involved cross-sectional comparisons among different individuals or groups at a single point in time rather than over time. As a result, they have generally been unable to separate the influence of transaction or information cost differences from those of cultural and other differences. Moreover, virtually no applications have been attempted in LDCs outside of agriculture.

As explained above, one of the purposes of this study is to evaluate the extent to which the various approaches utilized are applicable to the rather differing conditions of an LDC. The absence or underdevelopment of various markets, such as those for finance, insurance and future transactions of commodities, skilled workers and managers, is itself a subject of interest that may be analyzed in institutional terms. Quite naturally, the degree to

---

[13]See, e.g., Bhaduri (1973, 1983).

which well developed and efficiently functioning markets of these sorts exist has a considerable effect on the reliability of information, the nature and extent of opportunistic behavior and the means of monitoring such behavior. In other words, the transaction costs of various market institutions have to be examined critically since in LDCs their nature and magnitudes might well be very different from those in DCs where the existence of such markets generally can be taken for granted. Moreover, the pervasive role of government in LDCs, itself an institutional feature demanding an explanation, should also be taken into account. By being party to contracts and being able to set rules and constraints, LDC governments can change the nature and role of transaction costs and information costs, either reducing their importance or magnifying them and thereby creating additional sources of opportunistic behavior.

While again Marxists and neo-Marxists have been quick to blame pre-capitalist, neo-colonial or capitalist-controlled LDC governments for adopting policies inimical to social progress and equity in distribution, they have generally been unable to explain how this comes about. As shall be pointed out below, the theory of collective action is capable of explaining why the poor are frequently unable to organize themselves and hence likely to remain weak and poor. But, as Bardhan (1988) points out, this useful connection between Marxian analysis of development policy and collective action has yet to be made.

Whether for this or other reasons, the numerous specific hypotheses inherited from the existing literature on collective action, which have been formulated and even in many cases tested on the basis of experience in DCs, have not yet been seriously investigated or empirically tested in LDCs.[14] Since the environmental conditions, including the channels of communication, the form of government, the focus of policy making, and the extent and nature of government regulation of economic activity in LDCs are quite different than in DCs, the determinants of interest group formation and the ability of different interest groups to overcome free-rider and other problems could be quite different. To what extent will analytical modifications be required in order to treat such issues in the Tunisian context? If modifications are necessary, how can they be characterized?

Institutional change[15] can be considered to be at the heart of the long

---

[14]Srinivasan (1985) has pointed out the relevance of these contributions to the study of economic development and in particular to trade policies.

[15]Ruttan and Hayami (1984) present some elements of a theory of the determinants of institutional change and innovation as applied to agriculture.

run process of economic development, providing the missing link between development and growth. Although it is commonly stated that economic development can be defined as economic growth accompanied by structural change, it has proved difficult both to operationalize structural change and to identify its determinants and effects on development. Since institutions can be considered as part of this economic structure, an analysis of their determinants and effects may well constitute an important component of the relation between growth and development. Indeed, it might be appropriate to define economic development as economic growth accompanied by "efficient" institutional change. Numerous interrelationships between institutions and economic growth can be identified. On the one hand, economic growth can and frequently does trigger changes in institutions and, on the other hand, institutions can profoundly influence the level and rate of economic growth.

With respect to the effect of institutions on economic growth, the preceding discussion of the NIE shows that, by affecting transaction costs and coordination possibilities, institutions can have the effect of either facilitating or retarding economic growth. The choice of appropriate political institutions, rules and policies enhances economic growth. Moreover, by affecting resource mobility and the incentives for innovation and accumulation, institutions may induce or hinder economic efficiency in the allocation of resources and growth. Institutions affect growth also through their effects on expectations, social norms and preferences. Expectations are, of course, subjective, calling attention to the importance of perceptions and the way in which they are formed rather than only to the objective factors that are included in traditional economic analysis. Social norms can also play an important role in affecting the extent to which growth-enhancing activities can take place. For example, religious norms may either encourage or inhibit money lending and entrepreneurial activities. This calls attention to the role of preferences in institutional change and development. Enhancing some preferences or changing them may have an effect similar to that of setting norms or rules in helping to resolve free-rider problems and reducing transaction costs.

On the other hand, with respect to the effects of economic growth on institutions and, as noted above, running through all the principal themes of the NIE is the notion that economic growth may have profound impacts on institutions. Economic growth may well induce changes in contractual choices, the relative importance and character of markets, the extent of private property rights, the relative importance of different constraints, the relative position and power of interest groups and organizations, the relative importance of what is done within households and within firms (as opposed to the relations between them), technological choices (and hence the need for specific kinds of institutions), the costs and benefits of internal monitoring, and the degree of internationalization of the economy (and hence the degree to which any particular country's national authorities have the ability to enforce the relevant contracts and laws). Economic growth can render some existing institutions, such as norms, rules and policies, redundant and require others to come into existence.

Improved economic opportunities, in turn, may increase the mobility of workers, capitalists and merchants both geographically and sectorally. Greater mobility, however, may tend to undermine both the efficiency of the family, clan and community as sources of information with respect to trustworthiness, reliability, willingness to work and so on, and the effectiveness of such groups in exerting the kinds of positive and negative incentives that encourage the adherence to social norms. As confidence in the adherence to these norms and/or the reliability of expectations concerning anticipated behavior declines, this may require the development of new institutions for dealing with these issues such as new laws and regulations and a system of national justice, including the means of policing the laws and of imposing penalties on those transgressing the laws, and also new forms of insurance such as social security.

The dynamic interaction between institutions and economic growth poses the problem of institutional change and its relation to economic development, and in particular calls attention to the "efficiency of institutions."

Some practitioners of the NIE have assumed that competition — actual or potential — among alternative institutions would assure the emergence of efficient institutions at any point in time. As Matthews (1986) has pointed out, in such a case institutions are in continual and quick adaptation, and institutional change is a necessary concomitant of economic growth. If so, however, it would not be meaningful to consider institutional change as an independent "determinant" of economic growth.

The opposing view considers that institutions may not always evolve "efficiently"; indeed institutional rigidities, inertia and so on may set in, thereby preventing, even for long periods of time, institutional adaptations to the various environmental changes and causing institutions to be inefficient. Citing a number of historical examples, Basu, Jones and Schlicht (1987) have suggested that it is quite possible that some institutional alternatives are eliminated from the feasible set by historical precedent, the forces exerted by existing institutions being one of the major forces impacting on the institutional choices of subsequent periods. Since efficient solutions may not be known, or even if known, may be ruled out by the idiosyncracies of a given society's historical "endowment", there is no reason to believe that such an assumption of institutional efficiency is generally justified. Even if it were, its imposition would tend to make the analysis tautological, i.e., "what exists is efficient, therefore it exists."

Another reason for doubting that an existing institution is necessarily efficient is that its existence may be so much taken for granted that its efficiency and appropriateness go unquestioned and unchallenged. People may simply go on accepting the status quo without investigating its efficiency relative to that of the potential alternatives.

Even if people should question the appropriateness of an institution, and indeed should realize its inefficiency, they may not have sufficient motivation to do anything about it. Akerlof (1976) and Basu, Jones and Schlicht (1987) cite the continued practice of the caste system and the excessive modesty and the abstinance from consumption displayed by Indian widows as examples. Institutions which benefit no one may be retained if each member of society fears being penalized (by ostracism or otherwise) for not adhering to the institutional rules. If institutional inertia can persist even when *no* member of society benefits from it, it should not be surprising that such inertia could frequently exist when only some members of society are disadvantaged by it. Even if the benefits of institutional change are known to be sufficiently large that, at least potentially, those who would benefit from it could compensate those who would be hurt by it, this does not mean that they will do so.

Another obstacle to institutional change is the difficulty of identifying and obtaining agreement on the best among the various possible means of accomplishing such compensation. The implementation of a compensation mechanism can be further impeded when such a mechanism conflicts with social convention. Naturally also, uncertainties about the magnitude of the potential benefits and costs and their distribution (which would be expected to be more substantial in LDCs) may further compound the problems by increasing the information and transaction costs of institutional change. Quite conceivably, frustrated groups may eventually be induced to resort to physical force either in promoting institutional change or in impeding it, quite possibly inducing violent counteraction by opposing group(s). All such actions would of course have the effect of further adding to the social costs of institutional change and lowering the likelihood that existing institutions would be efficient.

Explanations of the status-quo and the failure of societies to adapt to changing circumstances has been given prominence in the "critical mass" models which feature interdependencies among the preferences of different individuals [Granovetter (1978)]. Collective action in such analyses requires that a critical minimum or threshold number of individuals engage in it. Once the process is started, it feeds on itself through a bandwagon effect. The analysis can be generalized to introduce the phenomenon of preference falsification [Kuran (1987)] which may further amplify the process.

The propensity to adapt its institutions to fit changing circumstances quite naturally may vary from one society to another. Why and how? What are the factors that affect it? To what extent will economic growth be retarded by the inability to innovate institutionally? These are problems of the utmost importance in economic development and which are yet to be satisfactorily answered.

Of course, not all institutional changes are beneficial. Since, in the way we have defined them above, institutional changes involve substituting new constraints for old ones, the new ones may introduce distortions leading to static and dynamic efficiency losses. Additional social losses may be involved in the transition from one set of institutions to another, including the costs of designing and implementing the new institutions. Moreover, since a basic and valuable characteristic of institutions is predictability and the preservation of expectations, if such transitions are either too rapid or too frequent, they can undermine predictability and thereby impose social losses.

Since NIE explanations of existing institutional arrangements and their functions may well yield rather different policy implications than those derived from traditional approaches, the application of the NIE to development policy could lead to significant new policy initiatives in LDCs. Stiglitz (1985) has illustrated this possibility with respect to policies for dealing with urban unemployment such as wage subsidies, unemployment compensation or shadow wage evaluation, and the design and extent of land reforms in rural areas of LDCs. These suggestions, however, have been made rather casually for illustrative purposes, not as serious propositions. Even taken altogether, the use that has been made of the NIE barely scratches the surface of its potential for development policy.

Organization of the Volume and its Case Studies

Following this introduction, Part I of the volume is completed with Chapters 2 and 3 which introduce the main concepts and hypotheses of the two major approaches of the NIE. Chapter 2 presents the theory of transaction and information costs and applications to this theory to contractual choice and organizational form that would seem relevant to development. In Chapter 3 the problem of collective action is posed and factors distinguishing success from failure identified. Applications of the theory to explain the emergence of organizations, the relative importance of interest groups and their influence over policies and their relationship with the state are reviewed and analysed. Also discussed are the special collective action problems arising from the use of common property resources and the relationships among collective action, institutional change and development.

The case studies applying these theories to Tunisian institutions are presented in Parts II and III. As the definition of an institution adopted above and the scope of the NIE make clear, the range of choice for institutions that could be studied is potentially extremely wide. In narrowing the range of choice and in selecting an institution for inclusion in the present study the following criteria were used: (1) the importance of the institution either in the past or at present, (2) the relevance of the institution to developmental problems and current policy choices in Tunisia and other LDCs, (3) the promise of complementarity in the analysis and the implications thereof among the selected studies, (4) the manageability of achieving a satisfactory understanding of the selected institution with the resources available and within the specified time horizon of the study (about three years), and (5) the relevance of the analysis of the particular Tunisian institution chosen to answer certain questions that remain unanswered in the existing literature on institutions in general and on Tunisian institutions in particular.

The studies included in this volume deal with a variety of institutions such as contracts (in agriculture, fishing, and tax collection), markets (wholesale markets, credit markets and the traditional bazaars or suks), organizations (labor unions and producer organizations), firms (public and private) and systems such as banking and education. While it would have been possible to organize the presentation of these case studies according to such distinctions in the type of institution, we deem it more efficient and fruitful to do so according to the particular component of the NIE utilized.

Specifically, the papers of Part II relate to contractual choice problems and are based on transaction and information cost considerations. This section begins in Chapter 4 with a study by Matoussi and Nugent which uses transaction costs to explain the switch to sharecropping from wage and fixed rent contracts in a very fertile region of Tunisia known as Medjez-el-bab. This is followed in Chapter 5 by a study by Azabou, Bouzaïane and Nugent which again uses transaction cost economics to explain not only the dominance of share contracts in Tunisian fishing but also the exceptional cases in which, in some segments of the industry at least, wage and rent contracts are, or have been, observed. In Chapter 6, Azabou and Nugent explain the usefulness of fixed rent forms of contract (known as tax farming) in collecting taxes in Tunisia's periodic markets (most of which are weekly in occurance and rural in location). Part II of the volume is completed in Chapter 7 with a paper by Nabli, Nugent and Doghri in which the principles of transaction costs are drawn upon to explain the size and ownership form choices of private firms in various sectors of Tunisian manufacturing.

Part III is concerned with the application of the principles of collective action. This section begins in Chapter 8 with an historical and institutional account of a case of institutional atrophy, namely that of the amin in the craft guilds of Tunis by Kuran. This is followed in Chapter 9 by an institutional explanation for the failure to introduce modern secular education in the country during the 19th and early 20th centuries by Bsaies. The principles of collective action are subsequently applied in Chapters 10 and 11 to Tunisia's producer organizations by Nugent, and labor unions by Zouari. The degeneration in the wholesale market of Tunis and the role of the porters' union in that process are analyzed in Chapter 12 by Azabou, Kuran and Nabli. In Chapter 13 Bechri uses the theory of interest groups to analyze the functioning of the credit market in general and interest rate determination in particular. In Chapter 14 Grissa takes up the problem of public enterprises.

Part IV includes two chapters. Chapter 15 by Herrick, as indicated above, examines the relevance and use of the NIE with respect to the theory of economic development, particularly from the epistemological point of view. The final chapter, Chapter 16, presents some concluding remarks and some suggestions both for further research and for policy.

References

Adelman, Irma and Cynthia Taft Morris, 1967, *Society, Politics and Economic Development.* Baltimore: Johns Hopkins University Press.

_____, and Thomas F. Head, 1983, "Promising Developments for Conceptualizing and Modeling Institutional Change," Berkeley, Giannini Foundation Working Paper No. 259.

Akerlof, George, 1970, "The Market for Lemons: Qualitative Uncertainty and the Market Mechanism," *Quarterly Journal of Economics* 84 (August), 488-500.

_____, 1976, "The Economics of Caste and of the Rat Race and Other Woeful Tales," *Quarterly Journal of Economics* 90, 599-617.

Alchian, A.A., 1959, "Private Property and the Relative Cost of Tenure," in Philip D. Bradley (ed.), *The Public Stake in Union Power.* Charlottesville: University of Virginia Press, 350-371.

_____, 1961, "Some Economics of Property." Santa Monica: Rand Corporation.

Appelbaum, E. and E. Katz, 1987, "Seeking Rents by Setting Rents: The

Political Economy of Rent-Seeking," *Economic Journal* 97, (September), 685-699.

Bardhan, Pranab K., 1980, "Interlocking Factor Markets and Agrarian De-velepmont: A Review of Issues," *Oxford Economic Papers* 32 (March), 82-95.

——————, 1984a, *Land, Labor and Rural Poverty: Essays in Develop-ment Economics.* New York: Columbia University Press.

——————, 1984b, *The Political Economy of Development in India.* Oxford: Basil Blackwell.

——————, 1988, "Alternative Approaches to Development Economics: An Evaluation," ch. 3 in H.B Chenery and T.N. Srinivasan, (eds.), *Hand-book of Development Economics.*

——————, forthcoming, "Alternative Approaches to the Theory of In-stitutions in Economic Development" in P. Bardhan, (ed.), *The Theory of Agrarian Institutions.* New York: Oxford University Press.

Basu, Kaushik, 1984, *The Less Developed Economy: A Critique of Contem-porary Theory.* Oxford: Basil Blackwell.

——————, 1986, "Markets, Power and Social Norms in a Develop-ment Context." East Lansing: Michigan State University, Center for Advanced Study in International Development, Occasional Paper No. 9.

——————, Eric Jones and Ekkehart Schlicht, 1987, "The Growth and Decay of Custom: The Role of the New Institutional Economics in Eco-nomic History," *Explorations in Economic History 24.*

Bates, Robert M. 1981, *Markets and States in Tropical Africa: The Political Basis of Agricultural Policies.* Berkeley: University of California Press.

Becker, Gary S., 1983, "Competition among Pressure Groups for Political Influence," *Quarterly Journal of Economics* 98 (August), 371-400.

Ben Porath, Y., 1980, "The F-Connection: Families, Friends and Firms and the Organization of Exchange," *Population and Development Review* 6 (March), 1-30.

Bhaduri, Amit, 1973, "A Study in Agricultural Backwardness Under Semi-feudalism," *Economic Journal,* 83: 120-137.

——————, 1983, *The Economic Structure of Backward Agriculture.* London: Academic Press.

Bhagwati, J.N., 1982, "Directly Unproductive Profit-Seeking (DUP) Activi-ties," *Journal of Political Economy* 99, no. 5 (October), 988-1002.

——————, and T.N. Srinivasan, 1982, "The Welfare Consequences of Directly Unproductive Profit-Seeking (DUP) Lobbying Activities: Price Versus Quantity Distortions," *Journal of International Economics* 3, no. 1/2 (August), 33-44.

Blau, Peter M., 1964, *Exchange and Power in Social Life.* New York: John Wiley.

Blomquist, W.H. and Elinor Ostrom, 1985, "Institutional Capacity and the Resolution of a Commons Dilemma." *Policy Studies Review* 5 (Novem-ber): 383-393.

Brennan, Geoffrey and James M. Buchanan, 1985, *The Reason of Rules.* Cambridge: Cambridge University Press.

Brenner, Reuven, 1983, *History - The Human Gamble.* Chicago: University of Chicago Press.

Brown, L. Carl, 1974, *The Tunisia of Ahmad Bey,* 1837-1855. Princeton: Princeton University Press.

Bruton, Henry J., 1965, *Principles of Development Economics*. Englewood Cliffs: Prentice Hall.

_____, 1985, "The Search for a Development Economics," *World Development* 13, No. 10/11, 1099-1124

Buchanan, James M., Robert D. Tollison and Gordon Tullock, (eds.), 1980, *Toward a Theory of Rent-Seeking Society*. College Station: Texas A & M University Press.

Coase, R.H., 1960, "The Problem of Social Cost," *Journal of Law and Economics* 3 (October), 1-44.

Coats, A.W., 1986, "Review of Langlois, Richard N. (ed.) Economics as a Process Essays in the New Institutional Economics" in *Kyklos* 39 (Fasc. 4), 628-630.

Colander, David C. (ed.), 1984, *Neoclassical Political Economy: The Analysis of Rent-Seeking and DUP Activity*. Cambridge, Mass: Balinger.

Crain, W. Mark, Donald R. Leavens and Robert D. Tollison, 1986, "Final Voting in Legislatures," *American Economic Review* 76, no. 4 (September): 833-841.

De Alessi, L., 1983, "Property Rights, Transactions Costs, and X-Efficiency: An Essay in Economic Theory," *American Economic Review* 73, no. 1 (March), 64-81.

de Janvry, Alain, 1981, *The Agrarian Question and Reformism in Latin America*. Baltimore: Johns Hopkins University Press.

Demsetz, Harold, 1967, "Toward a Theory of Property Rights," *American Economic Review* 57 (May): 347-359.

Donaldson, Lorraine, (1984), *Economic Development: Analysis and Policy*, West Publishing Company.

Dow, Gregory K., 1987, "The Function of Authority in Transaction Cost Economics," *Journal of Economic Behavior and Organization* 8 (March): 13-38.

Eliasson, Gunnar, ed., 1986, *The Economics of Institutions and Markets*. Stockholm: Industrial Institute for Economic and Social Research.

Elster, Jon, 1985, *Making Sense of Marx*. London: Cambridge University Press.

Farrell, Joseph, 1987, "Information and the Coase Theorem," *Journal of Economic Perspectives* 1, no. 2, 113-130.

Feeny, David, 1982, *The Political Economy of Productivity*. Vancouver: University of British Columbia Press.

_____, 1983, "The Moral or the Rational Peasant? Competing Hypotheses of Collective Action," *Journal of Asian Studies*,42 (August): 769-789.

Field, Alexander James, 1981, "The Problem with Neocalssical Institutional Economics A Critique with Special Reference to the North/Thomas Model of Pre-1500 Europe," *Explorations in Economic History* 18, 174-198.

Gannagé, Elias, 1966, *Institutions et Developpement*, Paris: Presses Universitaires de France.

Gillis, Malcolm, Dwight H. Perkins, Michael Roemer and Donald R. Snodgrass, 1987, *Economics of Development*. New York: W.W. Norton, Second Edition.

Granovetter, Mark, 1978, "Threshold Models of Collective Behavior," *American Journal of Sociology* 83, 1620-1443.

Greenwald, Bruce C. and Robert R. Glasspiegel, 1983, "Adverse Selection in the Market for Slaves: New Orleans, 1830-1860," *Quarterly Journal of Economics* (August), 479-499.

Hagen, Everett E., 1986, *The Economics of Development*, Fourth Edition, Homewood, Illinois: Irwin.

Hardin, Garrett, 1968, "The Tragedy of the Commons," *Science* 162 (December), 1243-1248.

Hardin, Russell, 1982, *Collective Action*, Washington, D.C., Resources for the Future.

Heiner, Ronald A., 1983, "The Origin of Predictable Behavior," *The American Economic Review* 73, no. 4, 560-595.

Herrick, Bruce and Charles P. Kindleberger, 1983, *Economic Development*, Fourth Edition.

Hill, Polly, 1986, *Development Economics on Trial*. London: Cambridge University Press.

Hirschman, Albert O., 1967, *Development Projects Observed*. Washington: Brookings Institution.

——————————, 1970, *Exit, Voice and Loyalty: Responses to Decline in Firms, Organizations and States*. Cambridge: Harvard University Press.

——————————, 1984, *Getting Ahead Collectively: Grassroots Experiences in Latin America*. New York: Pergamon Press.

Jensen, Michael C. and William H. Meckling, 1976, "Theory of the Firm: Managerial Behavior, Agency Costs and Ownership Structure," *Journal of Financial Economics* 3, no. 4 (October). 305-360.

Jimenez, Emanuel, 1985, "Urban Squatting and Community Organization in Developing Countries," *Journal of Public Economics* 27: 69-92.

Jones, Eric, 1981, *The European Miracle: Environments, Economics, and Geo-politics in the History of Europe and Asia*. Cambridge: Cambridge University Press.

Kalt, Joseph and Mark Zupan, 1984, "Capture and Ideology in the Economic Theory of Politics," *American Economic Review* 74 (June): 279-300.

Kraïem, Mustapha, 1973, *La Tunisie Précoloniale*. Tunis: Societé Tunisienne de Diffusion.

Krueger, Anne O., 1974, "The Political Economy of the Rent-Seeking Society," *American Economic Review* 64 (June), 297-303.

Kuran, Timur, 1987a, "Chameleon Voters and Public Choice," *Public Choice* 53, no. 1: 53-78.

Langlois, Richard N., 1986, "The New Institutional Economics: An Introductory Essay," in Langlois, ed., *Economics as a Process: Essays in the New Institutional Economics*. New York: Cambridge University Press.

——————————, (ed.), 1986, *Economics as a Process: The New Institutional Economics*. New York: Cambridge University Press.

Leibenstein, H., 1966, "Allocative Efficiency vs. 'X-Efficiency'," *American Economic Review* 56, (June), 392-415.

——————————, 1986, "Organizational Economics and Institutions as Missing Elements in Economic Development Analysis," Cornell University Conference on the Role of Institutions in Economic Development.

Lewis, W. Arthur, 1984, "The State of Development Theory," *American Economic Review* 74 (March), no. 1, 1-10.

Mahjoub, Azzam, 1983, *Industrie et Accumulation du Capital en Tunisie: Premiere Partie: de la Fin du XVIIIe Siècle Jusquà la Deuxième Guerre*

Mondiale. Tunis: Bibliothèque de Droit et de Sciences Politiques et Economiques. C.E.R.P.

Matthews, R.C.O., 1986, "The Economics of Institutions and the Sources of Growth," *Economic Journal* 96 (December), 903-918.

McCormick, Robert E. and Robert D. Tollison, 1981, *Politicians, Legislation and the Economy: An Inquiry into the Interest Group Theory of Government.* Boston: Martinus Nijhoff.

Meier, Gerald M., 1984, *Leading Issues in Economic Development,* Fourth Edition. New York: Oxford University Press.

Morawetz, David, 1981, *Why the Emperor's New Clothes Are Not Made in Colombia.* New York: Oxford University Press.

Morris, Cynthia Taft and Irma Adelman, 1986, "Economic Development and Institutional Change in the 19th Century." paper presented to the conference on Institutions and Development, Cornell University, November 1986.

Mueller, Dennis C., (ed.), 1983, *The Political Economy of Growth.* New Haven: Yale University Press.

Myint, H., 1971, *Economic Theory and the Underdeveloped Countries.* New York, London: Oxford University Press.

Myrdal, Gunnar, 1968, *Asian Drama: An Inquiry into the Poverty of Nations.* New York, Twentieth Century Fund.

Nafziger, E. Wayne, 1984, *The Economics of Developing Countries.* Belmont: Wadsworth.

Norgaard, Richard B., 1981, "Sociosystem and Ecosystem Coevolution in the Amazon," *Journal of Environmental Economics and Management* 8: 238-254.

North, Douglass C., 1981, *Structure and Change in Economic History.* New York: Norton.

_____, 1986a, "The New Institutional Economics," *Journal of Institutional and Theoretical Economics* 142 (1): 230-237.

_____, 1986b, "Institutions and Economic Growth: An Historical Introduction," Cornell University Conference on the Role of Institutions in Economic Development, Ithaca, New York.

Nugent, Jeffrey B., 1985, "The Old-age Security Motive for Fertility," *Population and Development Review* 11 (March), 75-97.

Offe, C., ed. 1985, *Disorganized Capitalism, Contemporary Transformation of Work and Politics.* London: Cambridge University Press.

Olson, Mancur, 1965, *The Logic of Collective Action.* Cambridge: Harvard University Press.

_____, 1982, *The Rise and Decline of Nations: Economic Growth, Stagflation and Social Rigidities.* New Haven: Yale University Press.

Ostrom, Elinor, 1986, "An Agenda for the Study of Institutions," *Public Choice* 48, 3-25.

_____, 1988, "Institutional Arrangements for Resolving the Commons Dilemma: Some Contending Approaches," in Vincent Ostrom, David Feeny and Hartmut Picht, eds., *Rethinking Institutional Analysis and Development: Issues, Alternatives and Choices.* San Francisco: The Institute for Contemporary Studies, 101-139.

Peltzman, Sam, 1976, "Toward a More General Theory of Regulation," *Journal of Law and Economics* 2 (August), 211-240.

Pollak, Robert A., 1985, "A Transaction Costs Approach to Families and Households," *Journal of Economic Literature* 23 (June): 581-608.

Popkin, Samuel L., 1979, *The Rational Peasant: The Political Economy of Rural Society in Vietnam*. Berkeley: University of California Press.

_____, 1981, "Public Choice and Rural Development – Free Riders, Lemons, and Institutional Design," in C.S. Russell and N.K. Norman, eds., *Public Choice and Rural Development*, Washington, D.C.: Resources for the Future, 43-80.

Posner, Richard A., 1980, "A Theory of Primitive Society with Special Reference to Law," *Journal of Law and Economics* 23 (April), 1-53.

Roemer, John, 1978, "Neoclassicism, Marxism and Collective Action" *Journal of Economic Issues* 12 (1): 147-161.

Runge, Carlisle Ford, 1981, "Common Property Externalities: Isolation, Assurance and Depletion in a Traditional Grazing Context," *American Journal of Agricultural Economics* 63 (November), 595-606.

_____, 1986, "Common Property and Collective Action in Economic Development," *World Development* 14 (June), 623-635.

Ruttan, V.M. and Y. Hayami, 1984, "Toward a Theory of Induced Institutional Innovation," *Journal of Development Studies* 20 (July), 203-223.

Schotter, Andrew, 1981, *The Economic Theory of Social Institutions*. New York: Cambridge University Press.

Schultz, Theodore W., 1968, "Institutions and the Rising Economic Value of Man," *American Journal of Agricultural Economics* 50, (December): 1113-1122.

Scott, James C., 1976, *The Moral Economy of the Peasant: Rebellion and Subsistence in Southeast Asia*. New Haven: Yale University Press.

Scully, Gerald W., 1988, "The Institutional Framework and Economic Development," *Journal of Political Economy* 96, no. 3, 652-662.

Srinivasan, T.N., 1985, "Neoclassical Political Economy, the State and Economic Development," *Asian Development Review* 3, no.2, 38-58.

Stigler, George, 1971, "The Theory of Economic Regulation," *Bell Journal of Economics* 2 (Spring), no. 1, 3-21.

Stiglitz, Joseph E., 1985, "Economics of Information and the Theory of Economic Development," *Revista de Econometria*.

_____, 1986, "The New Development Economics," *World Development* 14, no. 2, 257-265.

Todaro, Michael P., 1981, *Economic Development in the Third World*, Second Edition. New York: Longman.

Tollison, Robert D., 1982, "Rent-Seeking: A Survey," *Kyklos* 35, Fasc. 4, 575-602.

Ullman-Margalit, Edna, 1977, *The Emergence of Norms*. Oxford: Clarendon Press.

Uphoff, N., 1986, *Local Institutional Development*, Kumarian Press.

Valensi, Lucette, 1969, "Islam et Capitalisme: Production et Commerce des Chechias en Tunisie et en France aux XVIII et XIX Siècles," *Revue d'Histoire Moderne et Contemporaine* 16:376-406.

_____, 1970, "La Conjuncture Agraire en Tunisie au XVIIIe et XIXe Siècle," *Revue Historique* 494 (Av-Juin).

Wade, Robert, 1987, "The Management of Common Property Resources: Finding a Cooperative Solution," *World Bank Research Observer* 2 (July), 229-234.

Williamson, Oliver E., 1975, *Markets and Hierarchies: Analysis and Antitrust Implications*. New York: Free Press.

_____, 1979, "Transaction-Cost Economics: The Governance of Contractual Relations," *Journal of Law and Economics* 22 (October), no. 2, 233-261.

_____, 1985, *The Economic Institutions of Capitalism*. New York: Free Press.

Witt, Ulrich, 1987, "How Transaction Rights are Shaped to Channel Innovativeness," *Zietschrift für die Gesamte Staatswissenschafl* 143.

Wolf, Charles, Jr., 1986, "Markets or Governments: Choosing between Imperfect Alternatives." Santa Monica: Rand Corp., Rand note no. 2505-SF.

Yotopoulos, Pan A. and Jeffrey B. Nugent, 1986, *Economics of Development: Empirical Investigations*. New York: Harper and Row.

Chapter 2

TRANSACTION COST ECONOMICS
AND CONTRACTUAL CHOICE:
THEORY AND EVIDENCE*

Samar K. Datta and Jeffrey B. Nugent

This chapter is intended to serve as an introduction to the analysis of organizational form and contracts. While there exist several different types of theories for explaining organizational and contractual forms, including those which stress power, risk and uncertainty, transaction costs and cultural and ethnic factors, at present we focus on the role of transaction cost theory as developed in large part by Williamson (1975, 1981, 1985).

While in much of the literature transaction costs have been considered to be merely one among several alternative explanations for choices among contracts,[1] we define transaction costs sufficiently broadly for the theory of transaction costs to serve as a unifying framework for analyzing such choices. In contrast to both the formal models (including principal-agent models)[2] which are generally abstract and not always realistic[3] and the less formal surveys[4] (most of which pertain to very specific sectors and settings), this chapter identifies the general issues involved in organizational form and contract choices by taking advantage of a broad spectrum of the historical and contemporary experience with such choices.

---

*The authors gratefully acknowledge the useful comments of Lee Alston, David Feeny, Bruce Herrick, Timur Kuran, Mustapha Nabli, Keijiro Otsuka, Jean-Philippe Platteau, Murray Wolfson and numerous participants of the University of Warwick's Seminar in Economic Development held in July 1986 on earlier versions of this paper.
[1] An early advocate of such a position was Cheung (1969).
[2] For an unusually serious attempt to illustrate the applicability of this body of theory to the choice of contracts over time and space, see Townsend (1984). See also Ross (1973) and Grossman and Hart (1983).
[3] While there are some analyses which deal with more realistic conditions, e.g., Nalebuff and Stiglitz (1983), Sappington and Demski (1983), Rogerson (1983), Sappington (1983), Lewis (1984), these analyses are generally less able to offer clearcut advantages for certain types of contracts. Nevertheless, familiarity with these analyses can be extremely useful in the practical analysis of contractual choices.
[4] See especially Otsuka and Hayami (1986) and Quibria and Rashid (1984, 1986).

The presentation is divided into the following sections: Section I explains the origin and consequences of contracting and the important and interrelated roles of "opportunistic" behavior and transaction and information costs. Section II alerts the reader to the most important criticisms which have been raised concerning the analysis of transaction costs. With the help of a simple graphical model, Section III identifies the main alternative forms of contract and the different forms of opportunistic behavior to which each form of contract is vulnerable. Section IV discusses the role of transaction costs in various kinds of institutional changes. Section V illustrates the use of the transaction cost approach to contractual choices in a variety of sectors. Some concluding comments are presented in Section VI.

I. The Origins and Consequences of Contracting and the Roles of Risk, Culture, Ethnicity, and Transaction Costs

At any given point in time and, hence, at any given state of technology, in most sectors at least, the ability to substitute one primary input or "factor" (like capital) for another (such as labor), even for sizeable changes in factor prices, is likely to be rather limited, especially in the short run. Given both the inflexibility of factor proportions and the unevenness of relative factor endowments (including information) across households (some households being relatively well endowed in capital and others in labor), it is important to provide appropriate incentives for the different factor owners to trade with each other so that economic activities can be efficiently undertaken. These incentives also have to deal with any informational asymmetries which may arise when the seller of any factor is in a better position to judge its quality than the buyer. Naturally, the very same needs for exchange and the problem of information asymmetries arise in the case of commodity markets. The purpose of contracting is to provide the incentives for both efficient trade in, and effective coordination of, factor services and commodities.

While the need for contracting and the role of transaction costs, therefore arise in any transaction, for simplicity of exposition in what follows we shall make reference primarily to transactions for factor services. Since the desired factor proportions vary considerably from one economic activity to another, changes in demand patterns, opportunities for trade and exchange and, of course, technology can create disequilibria between existing contractual forms and the requirements of efficient production and exchange. Although the time required for the elimination of such disequilibria may vary considerably (perhaps in proportion to the social costs of such changes), in general and in the long run, the competition (actual or potential) among alternative contractual forms can be counted upon to restore equilibrium.[5]

Over time and in the process of development, activities such as manufacturing, in which the opportunities for factor substitution are especially low, become more important. Even in activities such as agriculture in which factor substitution is easier, technology tends to change in such a way as to decrease the degree of substitutability [Yotopoulos and Nugent (1976, Ch. 9) and Sundrum (1983, Ch. 9, 10)]. Not only do factor proportions become more rigid over time but also the number of different inputs required and the opportunities for the division of labor [Leijonhufvud (1986) and North (1986a, 1986b)] tend to increase. Taste changes, new products and the greater emphasis on product quality associated with rising income and wealth also contribute to the same trends. Still another characteristic of secular change is the increasing importance of "asset specificity," wherein the productive inputs embody use-specific investments that increase the scope for bargaining by widening the productivity differential between the use in question and the next best alternative. All such changes raise the importance of identifying those forms of contract which minimize the costs of transactions.

Another conspicuous characteristic of the real world is risk. Risks vary both in form and by origin. They can arise from factors like fluctuations in price, power failures, breakdowns of equipment, human disability and death, human error, dramatic changes in weather or external market conditions, and luck, which may be considered external to or exogenous to the individual contracting agents. Risks can also arise from endogenous sources such as the vulnerability of the different economic agents to what Williamson (1975, 1985) has referred to as "opportunistic behavior."[6] The existence of exogenous sources of risk, moreover, may well make it more difficult for any particular party to a contract to distinguish between the output shortfalls attributable to purely exogenous factors and those of endogenous origin arising from shirking

---

[5]See especially Hayami (1971), Ruttan and Hayami (1984), Binswanger and Ruttan, ed. (1978), Hayami and Kikuchi (1982) and Hayami and Ruttan (1985). But, as noted below, various impediments to such adjustments can arise.

[6]"Opportunistic" behavior in the sense of Williamson (1975, 1985) occurs when one party to a contract has the incentive to bend, get around or violate the terms of the contract at the expense of one or more other parties to the contract. One can think of it as "cheating" on the agreement explicit or implicit but, opportunism doesn't have to be as blatant as that. Just the self-interest on the part of one of the parties to the contract to not perform to the maximum, whether or not he or she is conscious of it, can therefore constitute opportunistic behavior. A worker, for example, may practice opportunistic behavior on his employer by working less than he is supposed to, i.e., by "shirking" in his application of labor.

in the quantity or quality of the inputs on the part of their suppliers. As a result, the likelihood of endogenous risk and the consequences of opportunistic behavior on the part of the different agents is likely to rise with the importance of exogenous risk. Indeed, when the consequences of these various risks are sufficiently great, the result can be "market failure," i.e., a condition in which a particular market fails to come into existence or to function effectively.

Since the ability to bear these various risks is likely to vary rather considerably from one agent to another, the bearing of any such risk is similar to the provision and use of an additional input.[7] Thus risk adds to the number of inputs to be contracted, to the number of contingencies to be considered and frequently also to the number of parties to the contract(s).

Contracting necessarily involves costs. These include the *direct costs* of (a) obtaining the information that the various parties to the contract need in order to assess the relevant quantities and qualities of what is transacted and more generally the benefits and costs of the contract (*vis-à-vis* the relevant alternatives), (b) negotiating among the parties to reach agreement on the provisions of the contract, and (c) communicating all such provisions to all the relevant agents. But contracting costs also, and more importantly, include the *indirect costs* arising from the opportunistic behavior induced by the involvement of multiple agents in contexts in which various sources of risk are present. Among these indirect costs are those of monitoring and enforcing the terms and conditions of the contracts.

It is also useful to distinguish between *ex ante* and *ex post* transaction costs. Among the former are the direct and indirect costs arising from the contract selection process, including those of generating the relevant information and of drafting, negotiating and safeguarding the agreement. The *ex ante* costs would also include those arising from "adverse selection," the principle (from the literature on health or life insurance) wherein, for any given insurance program and specified premium, those with the incentive to accept it would be primarily those with insurance risks exceeding the stated premium. Adverse selection can therefore add to the costs of any given insurance program and tend to undermine its financial viability.

If contracts were self-enforcing and capable of dealing with all possible aspects of human action and all possible contingencies, *ex post* transaction costs would not exist. Since in reality (because of bounded rationality and other considerations) contracts are typically grossly incomplete, and by no means self-enforcing, *ex post* transaction costs *do* arise. These costs include the costs of (a) formal legal action with respect to disputes and the establishment and

---

[7] For a detailed explanation, see Cheung (1978).

operation of governance procedures, (b) dealing with the maladaptation of the actual provisions of the contract, including the renegotiation of contracts, (c) monitoring the contracts, and (d) bonding the parties of the contract to continue to work together. The *ex post* transaction costs include also those arising from behavior of the "moral hazard" type which, again in the context of insurance, occurs when someone who is insured against the consequences of risk becomes less vigilant in adhering to safety rules or in other words displays riskier behavior.

Both the adherence to contracts and the efficiency of performance can be affected by perceptions about the fairness and legitimacy of contractual arrangements. Since these factors, in turn, can be affected by ideology, ideology can also play an important role in reducing transaction costs. Not surprisingly, large business organizations and governments maintain public relations departments to influence ideology and popular notions about the legitimacy and fairness of existing contractual arrangements. By getting people to adhere more closely to expected norms, thereby reducing opportunistic behavior and transaction costs, ideology can increase the economies associated with the greater division of labor. At the same time, however, ideology can increase the transaction costs of changing contractual forms and terms and thereby also the inefficiency of institutions in the long run.

Most of the literature on contracts has focused on the *ex-ante* side of contracts and assumes that the agreed upon *ex ante* alignment of incentives or property rights is implemented efficaciously. Since in reality the *ex post* transaction costs may well be larger than the *ex ante* transaction costs, in our opinion, considerably more attention should be given to *ex post* transaction costs. If nothing more, transaction costs should be defined sufficiently broadly so as to include those of both types.

Descriptive analyses reveal that the forms of contract which are dominant in one context may not be observed in others, even in the same activities. For example, while until its formal abolition slavery was dominant in agriculture of the American South and of the West Indies, it was not dominant in agriculture of the American North and West even when and where slavery was legal. Likewise, whereas share contracts are dominant in certain agricultural activites in LDCs, they are no longer common in the same activities in the DCs.[8] Theories of contractual choice arise to explain these variations.

One type of explanation is that such differences are based on tastes and preferences which vary by country, ethnicity and sector.[9]

---

[8]See, e.g., Day (1967).
[9]A rather outspoken proponent of this view was Boeke (1953) but it has

As shall be demonstrated below, however, different ethnic groups or countries may also differ with respect to environmental conditions including market prices and relative factor endowments, suggesting that the latter factors may be the more fundamental ones explaining the observed differences across ethnic and other groups. Moreover, since information networks often work better and reputations are more meaningful and better communicated within ethnic groups and within local communities than between them, the greater incentives for reputation-enhancing good performance may help explain why economic activities are frequently undertaken entirely by members of particular communities or ethnic groups even if wage or other cost differentials would favor the use of resources from outside these groups.[10] Hence, ethnicity and community integrity may play a very significant role in reducing transaction costs. These arguments do not necessarily imply that differences in preferences among different groups are unimportant in explaining contractual choices. Indeed, in the longer run, preferences and thereby contracts may be affected by ideology, transaction costs and actual or past contractual choices.

Despite the relevance of individual identities, ethnicity and contracting to most real world economic activities and the likely sizable magnitude of the associated transaction costs, such considerations have been ignored in standard economic analysis. As Samuelson (1957) put it, standard economic analysis and its results are indifferent both to the way the inputs are put together and to the identities of the various agents who provide the inputs and coordinate their use. As it has with other institutions, standard economic analysis has taken contracts as given.

The purpose of transaction cost analysis is to provide a simple yet powerful analytical framework for explaining contractual choices. The basic proposition of such analysis is that, although these various components of transaction costs can be distinguished, what is generally relevant to contractual choice is only their total. Therefore, for convenience, rather than dealing separately with the costs of information, negotiation, bonding, etc., our analysis is in terms of aggregate transaction costs.

The skyrocketing costs of medical care, legal services, insurance and military procurement, strikes and lockouts, the widely acclaimed contribution

---

also cropped up in the work of Myrdal, e.g., Myrdal (1957, 1968). Some proponents of this view have even gone so far as to say that underdevelopment is due to the dominance of backward, tradition-laden forms of contracts.

[10]See, for example, Doeringer, Moss and Terkla (1986), Datta and Nugent (1985) and Wells (1984).

of smooth contractual relationships between labor and management to the success of East Asian economies in achieving rapid economic growth, and the virtually universal plight of public enterprises, have all helped demonstrate the importance of transaction and information costs and the need to reduce them. As a result, considerable progress is finally being made on the application of transaction and information costs to the design and administration of effective forms of contracting for health services, defense materials, insurance and management [Pauly (1986), Harris and Raviv (1978, 1979), Spulber (1988)]. Nevertheless, especially with respect to applications to economic development issues and to LDCs more generally, with the exception of agrarian issues and institutions and in particular sharecropping which has been frequently studied from a transaction cost perspective e.g., [Lucas (1979), Alston and Higgs (1982), Bardhan (1980, 1983a, forthcoming), Braverman and Stiglitz (1982), Braverman and Guasch (1986), and Eswaran and Kotwal (1985a, 1985b, 1985c)], there remains a considerable distance to go before it can be said that all the relevant features and aspects of transaction costs and contractual choice are fully integrated into the economics of development.

II. Criticisms of the Theory of Transaction Costs

Before going further in our application of transaction costs to the choice among contracts, it is important that consideration be given to the various criticisms to which transaction cost economics has been subjected. The most important criticisms[11] would seem to be the following:

(1) The definition of transaction costs is sufficiently broad as to exclude virtually nothing and to make it difficult to distinguish transaction costs from other costs.

(2) The frequently imposed "functionalist" assumption that the contracts which exist must be efficient in transaction cost terms is quite certainly unrealistic in some circumstances. Moreover, it renders tautological explanations of the determinants of contractual choices based on transaction cost efficiency.

(3) Once the assumption of given institutions, which of course include the form of contracts, is dropped, the number and explanatory power of the available exogenous variables may be insufficient for providing viable explanations of the phenomena under consideration.

(4) Inasmuch as opportunism is usually conceived of in terms of labor shirking and malfeasance, transaction cost analysis is biased in favor of capitalists and in the defense of capitalist institutions.

---

[11]For articulate presentations of one or more of these criticisms see Akerlof (1976), Field (1981), Dow (1987), Basu, Jones and Schlicht (1987) and Kuran (1989).

(5) By relying on the operation of the "invisible hand", transaction cost analysis does not explain how the contractual choice decisions are reached.

While each of these criticisms is important and worthy of careful consideration' none of them is fatal. Likewise, while each may have some legitimacy with respect to some of the more cavalier applications of transaction cost economics, as we shall presently explain, when that analysis is properly applied, it should be possible to avoid each of them.

For example, although at present it may be difficult to operationalize transaction costs, this by no means implies that transaction costs should not and cannot be defined and measured. It should be recalled that there have been many instances in the history of social science in which the existence of operational measures of the appropriate concepts has lagged substantially behind the development of the concepts themselves.[12] The usefulness of the concepts may have to be demonstrated before the measures are developed. It should also be pointed out that highly operational measures of some components of transaction costs are already appearing,[13] and are likely to grow rapidly in number and quality in the near future.

With respect to the assumed efficiency of existing institutions, while there are indeed exceptions to the rule that what exists is efficient in transaction cost terms [Akerlof (1976), Field (1981), Basu, Jones and Schlicht (1987)], this does not mean that the rule cannot serve as a useful and potentially important working hypothesis. What it does mean is that the efficiency of existing institutions should be thoroughly examined, e.g., by probing the various parties to existing contracts in appropriate ways and by carefully examining both the benefits and costs of alternative contractual forms and the process by which decisions on contracts are actually made.

With respect to the alleged insufficiency of explanatory variables arising when institutions are endogenized, it should be realized that in any given situation there exists a hierarchy of institutions. In explaining one kind of institution, such as the form of contract among the owners of productive factors, it is both unnecessary and unrealistic to assume that *all* institutions would be determined simultaneously. Hence, it may well be appropriate in explaining the institutions which can be changed relatively quickly, such as

---

[12]Consider, for example, that national accounting methods and their refinement still lag behind the concepts articulated by Keynes and that precise measures of income distribution and poverty lagged considerably behind analyses pointing to the policy importance of these concepts.

[13]See, e.g., Alston, Datta and Nugent (1984), Datta and Nugent (1986), North and Wallis (forthcoming), and the numerous references in Williamson (1985).

the choice among contracts, to treat as given such factors as cultural rules, the fundamentals of the legal system, and other institutions of the sort that change only very slowly. In any case, the careful consideration of what is given or exogenous in any given situation is, quite naturally, a fundamental requisite of any satisfactory analysis of transaction costs.

While it may be true that some existing applications of transaction costs have given the impression of bias in favor of capitalistic firms and against workers, such a bias is certainly unnecessary and, indeed, should be avoided. To do so requires that the analyst be equally conscientious in his (her) search for the bases of opportunistic behavior in all parties to contracts.

It may be concluded that it is essential that the analysis of transaction costs be carefully and appropriately applied. In such applications the following requisites should be satisfied: (1) the analysis should be replete with operational definitions of transaction costs; (2) both the benefits and costs of all possible forms of contract should be carefully considered; and (3) attention should be paid to *all* the relevant sources of opportunistic behavior as well as to both the institutional and other circumstances within which contractual choices are made and the mechanisms or processes by which they are made. When these requisites are satisfied, however, transaction cost analysis should no longer be vulnerable to the various quite legitimate criticisms that have been raised of some applications of this form of analysis.

III. Alternative Forms of Contract and Opportunistic Behavior

As pointed out in Section I, the importance of transaction costs is likely to increase with the number of agents involved, the number and magnitude of the associated risks, the level and sophistication of technology, and the disintegration of communal, tribal, familial and cultural traditions. Nevertheless, in the face of the uneven distribution of relative factor endowments across households and groups, the need for contracting, and therefore for minimizing the transaction costs emanating from contracting, arises even in simplified settings.

As already mentioned, even in such circumstances the need for formal contractual relationships and the importance of transaction costs can be reduced considerably when both the pooling of resources takes place within households, clans, tribes and communities *and* these units are permeated with a strong sense of group solidarity and mutually agreed upon rights and responsibilities. Nevertheless, since as the size of household or community rises both the incentive for shirking and the difficulty of its detection are likely to increase, there are distinct limits on the ability of resource pooling within families, clans and so on to reduce transaction costs. What is affected by such arrangements is not the existence of transaction costs but only their locus, form, and magnitude.

Even in a simplified agrarian setting in which there are only two inputs, labor and land, the alternative arrangements boil down to one or another of three basic contracts — fixed wage, fixed rent or share contracts — or some combination thereof. An owner of land can rent the land out to an owner of labor at a fixed rent (the fixed rent contract), lease it out for a share of output (the share contract) or hold it but hire labor at a fixed wage rate (the wage contract). Naturally, he can also mix contracts by renting out part of the land, hiring labor on part of it or by compensating the worker in part by a fixed wage and in part by a share of output. Once other inputs are included and risk is brought into the picture by identifying all the relevant contingencies, the contracts can become very complex. Nevertheless, the basic sources and essential dimensions of transaction costs can be understood from a careful analysis of the forms of opportunistic behavior that would be likely to arise under each of these three simple contracts.

Since under a fixed wage contract, the worker's compensation is independent of his effort, and the cost of labor to the employer is fixed irrespective of how hard he makes the worker work, the primary forms of opportunistic behavior under wage contracts are labor-shirking on the part of the workers, and labor misuse on the part of employers.[14] Under a fixed rent contract, however, since the worker would be the residual claimant, he would not be expected to shirk in his supply of labor effort. On the other hand, and especially if the fixed rent contract were for a short period only, the incentive would be for both the landowner and especially the worker to shirk on maintenance activities and/or to over- or mis-use the land[15] so as (at the cost of less future output) to get more output in the short run than could otherwise be obtained. Hence, the primary form of opportunistic behavior in the case of fixed rent contracts is likely to be asset mismanagement.

In the case of share contracts, inasmuch as the sharecropper gets only a fraction of the marginal product of his labor, there would once again be some

---

[14]For an excellent and timely study of the perspective of the worker and an evaluation of opportunistic behavior on the part of owners and managers relative to workers see Pagano (1985).

[15]Such practices are often referred to as "mining" the land, i.e., running its value down through use. This form of opportunism has largely been ignored in the traditional literature on contractual choice. Since, as shown in Section V below, such considerations are in practice rather important, the failure to consider this form of opportunism is a major shortcoming of the traditional literature.

tendency for the worker to undersupply labor effort and for the landowner to misuse labor (though presumably not to the same extent as in the case of wage contracts). There would also be some incentive for land mismanagement under share contracts, though less so than in the case of fixed rent contracts. These problems could be eliminated or at least mitigated if sharing were applied not only to output but also to input costs. But cost-sharing could well give rise to still another form of opportunistic behavior, namely, the misreporting of inputs thereby not eliminating transaction costs but only changing their form. Under share contracts, however, another and distinctive form of opportunistic behavior would be likely to arise, namely, output-underreporting. In other words, each party to the contract would have the incentive to try to obtain a larger effective share of output by underreporting it to the other party.

While much of the literature has simply assumed that the perpetrator of the opportunistic behavior is the worker-tenant, as mentioned above in principle as well as practice, any party may have the incentive to practice opportunistic behavior at the expense of one or more other parties. Indeed, examples where the asset-owner is a perpetrator of opportunistic behavior can easily be cited. For example, under a fixed rent contract the landowner might undersupply the land, e.g., by renting a lower quality parcel of land than had been agreed upon, or by retaining some property rights over that land, e.g., by insisting that his animals be able to graze on that land, thereby lowering the agricultural output of the tenant. Likewise, under fixed wage contracts he might have a tendency to over- or mis-use the laborers to the long-term detriment of the workers but the short-term benefit of the landowner. Indeed, such considerations would seem to help explain the existence of labor-managed or labor-owned enterprises in some sectors and settings.[16]

Naturally, the incidence of these different forms of opportunistic behavior would vary considerably depending on the specific circumstances. In contrast to standard neoclassical analysis, as demonstrated in section IV below, in the transaction cost theory of contractual choice[17] considerations such as the identities of the individual asset owners, their location, their personal relations, their status, their abilities and experience, the opportunity costs of their actions, the relative strength of worker solidarity, the degree of social interaction and the size of the community are all of potential importance.

---

[16]For examples see Russell (1985) and Williamson (1985).
[17]For some examples see Epstein (1962, 1967), Landa (1981), Posner (1980) Williamson (1985), Bardhan and Rudra (1986), and Datta, O'Hara and Nugent (1986).

In industry the most important inputs are generally labor and capital instead of labor and land. Nevertheless, the alternative forms of contract would seem to be similar; (1) labor could hire capital by paying for it at a fixed interest rate; (2) capital could hire labor at a fixed wage rate, or (3) both could agree to share the output. Once again, the transaction cost explanation for the choice among such contracts would seem to revolve around the relative vulnerability of the different forms of contract to opportunistic behavior and the relative importance of each. In particular, the greater risk of labor's misuse of capital and of its inability to repay may explain why it is more common for capital to hire workers than vice versa.[18] Likewise, these considerations may explain why it is easier to rent unfurnished apartments and office space than furnished ones and why worker-owned firms (partnerships) are more common in the practice of law and certain other services where the physical assets are relatively unimportant in relation to the human capital and experience embodied in the workers. The fundamental proposition of the transaction cost approach is that, in general and in the long run, given technology, resource endowments, and preferences of the relevant agents (including those for the bearing of risk), transaction costs are sufficiently important that the relevant agent will choose among the alternative forms of contract in such a way as to minimize the total transaction costs or the "excess burden" of contracting.

In some cases, however, there may also be a tradeoff between other elements of production costs and transaction costs [Matthews (1986)]. When this is the case, situations may arise where the costs of modifying technology or even preferences may be lower than those of contract modification, suggesting that contractual choices must be made prior to, or at least simultaneous with, those with respect to product and technology [Sutinen (1975)]. Nevertheless, Williamson (1985) to the contrary, quite frequently the production cost considerations would appear to be the dominant ones, suggesting that the choice with respect to industry and technology would be made first. If so, production decisions would have to be considered given in to determining the form of contract through transaction cost minimization.[19]

While different analytical frameworks could be used for viewing such problems, including game theory, principal-agent formulations, and a variety of other general equilibrium approaches, to facilitate the use of a simple

---

[18]See especially Eswaran and Kotwal (1985c).

[19]Even if transaction cost considerations dominate over those of production costs, it would be legitimate to treat transaction costs independently if the degree of interdependence between the two were relatively small.

graphical analysis we make the following simplifying assumptions which could be relaxed at the cost of some complication without affecting the basic results:

(1) It is the worker (the owner of labor) who tries to take advantage of the landowner by practicing opportunistic behavior.

(2) The landowner tries to minimize the extent of worker opportunistic behavior by monitoring the worker's actions and imposing penalties when opportunistic behavior is detected.

(3) The monitoring costs of the landowner take monetary form, as for example when he hires supervisors or installs measuring devices.

(4) The worker knows the landowner is monitoring his actions and the land-owner both knows that the worker is likely to engage in opportunistic behavior and is able to observe the worker's reaction to his monitoring- enforcement expenditures. (As a result, the worker knows that the more he engages in opportunism, the more likely such behavior is to be detected by the landowner and the more likely he would be penalized for it. Also, the landowner knows that the more expenditures he makes the more likely he is to be able to catch the worker engaged in opportunistic behavior and impose penalties on him. By increasing the likelihood of penalties, the landowner is able to limit the extent of opportunistic behavior.)

For any given form of contract, the worker could be expected to engage in opportunistic behavior up to the point where the marginal benefit of such behavior equals its marginal cost. Likewise, the landowner would be expected to engage in monitoring-enforcement expenditures up to the point that the marginal benefits are exactly offset by the marginal costs.

Following Jensen and Meckling (1976), the total transaction cost of any contract between landowner and worker can be defined as the net sum total of: (a) the landowner's expenditure on monitoring, (b) the loss in the landowner's gross income arising from opportunism of the worker, and (c) the penalties paid by the worker when his opportunistic behavior is detected (other than those paid directly to the landowner or someone else[20]), but net of (d) the gain to the worker arising from his opportunistic behavior.

The nature of transaction cost minimization for the case of the wage contract is illustrated in Figure 2-1. The diagram translates opportunistic behavior, which in the case of wage contracts takes the form of both labor-shirking and monitoring-enforcement expenditures and which are measured on the horizontal axes, into the monetary equivalents of each of the aforementioned components of total transaction costs on the vertical axes. As men-

---

[20] A penalty paid to someone else is merely a transfer payment which would affect the distribution of income but not the allocation of resources.

tioned above, each party tries to optimize by balancing the marginal gain with
the marginal cost of his (own) action, labor-shirking in the case of the worker
and monitoring-enforcement expenditure in the case of the landowner, and
taking into consideration the (expected or observed) behavior of the other.

In the case of the worker, the marginal gross gain from shirking given by
OKL in quadrant II of the diagram could be measured either by the shadow
price of time of the worker or the wage rate, depending on whether the benefit
of shirking would take the form of extra leisure or household production on the
one hand or the wage rate earned moonlighting on the other. The marginal
cost of shirking given by OJL in the same quadrant of the diagram would be
measured in terms of the expected value of the penalty he would pay should
he be caught shirking. This would be measured in terms of the shadow price
of time or the wage rate, depending on on whether the (expected value of
the) time spent in Job-search would come at the expense of sacrificed leisure,
home production, or wage income. Naturally, the marginal-cost-of-shirking
curve OJL is for a particular level of monitoring expenditure (the expected
or observed level of such expenditure) on the part of the landowner. A lower
level of monitoring expenditure would yield a lower marginal-cost-of-shirking
curve such as that indicated by $OJ'L'$ while a higher level would shift the
curve upward to one like $OJ''L''$. In each such case the worker would choose
the amount of shirking which equates its marginal gain given by the slope
of OKL with its marginal cost for the expected level of monitoring as at
J', J or J''. Assuming that the actual level of monitoring expenditure, the
determination of which is to be explained momentarily, is the expected level,
OJL would be the relevant curve and OI would be the optimal amount of
shirking.

Meanwhile, the landowner minimizes his transaction costs as at D on the
landowner's transaction cost curve given by QDR in quadrant I. He does so
by choosing the amount of monitoring expenditure $OP = OT$ which equates
the marginal cost of monitoring, given by the slope of the monitoring cost
function OSZ (in this case 45°), with the marginal benefit of monitoring measured in terms of the lower residual loss of output from labor shirking (which
is given by the slope of the QFY curve). This latter curve is constructed from
the locus of equilibrium shirking points given by the curve $MJ'JJ''O$. The
total transaction cost of the landowner given by $OB = PD$ has two components, the monitoring cost component $OT = PS = DF$ and the residual loss
$PF = 0U$. The total transaction cost per unit of land under wage contract
is given by the distance $AB = DE$. This is computed by subtracting the net
monetary benefit of labor-shirking to the worker ($IH = IK - IJ = OC =$

Figure 2-1
Minimization of Total Transaction Costs
Per Unit of Land Under Wage Contract
by Landowner and Worker

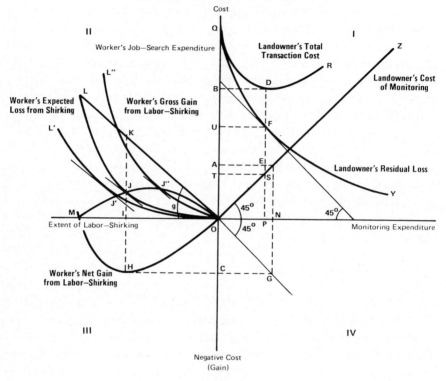

$= ON = OA$) from the total transaction cost of the landowner ($OB = PD = OT + OU$).

The graphical exposition of transaction cost minimization under rent contract would be virtually identical except that the opportunistic behavior would take the form of misuse of the land. In the case of sharecropping, because the opportunistic behavior might take any one or more of three forms, namely labor-shirking, land mismanagement and output-underreporting, the diagram would need to be modified so as to include all three forms of opportunistic behavior, each with its own separate monitoring-enforcement function. An alternative and simpler approach would be to assume that all forms of opportunistic behavior could be aggregated so as to yield single functions for net gains (or losses) and for monitoring costs and benefits.

Under the simplifying assumptions we have made, the explanations of how transaction costs would be minimized for rent and share contracts would be virtually identical to that described above for wage contracts. For each such form of contract, the worker would engage in a certain amount of opportunism but would be constrained in doing so by the monitoring activities of the landowner and the expected penalties for being caught.

It is important to realize, however, that the choice among contracts would involve the comparison of the optimal positions or minimal transaction costs of the three different contracts. Whereas transaction cost minimization *within* a given the form of contract is centered on the satisfaction of the various marginal or first- and second-order conditions derived from utility maximization of the respective agents, transaction cost minimization *between* contracts would depend primarily on the position of the relevant curves. Not unlike applied social cost-benefit analysis, therefore, the choice among contracts depends on the positions of the relevant opportunity cost curves (as opposed to the detailed characteristics of those curves) which in turn, depend on the nature of the opportunity benefits and costs pertinent to each set of circumstances. Since the position of the relevant cost and benefit curves would depend on matters such as location, size of community, degree of social interaction, and other relationships linking the relevant agents, these are all relevant considerations in determining the form of contract.

IV. The Relevance of Transaction Costs to Institutional Change.

The purpose of this section is to demonstrate the role of transaction costs in institutional change. Among the institutional changes discussed are the development of markets (for commodities and factors), property rights, firms and families. Because of the focus on institutional change, considerable attention is given to the early stages in the development of the institutions considered. As we shall see, transaction cost considerations fit more closely into what one might call the demand for institutional change, but supply considerations are also important.

One of the most important institutional changes in the history of civilizations is the rise and fall of markets. Indeed, the rise and fall of civilizations, if not actually explained by the rise and fall of markets, is at least closely intertwined with their rise and fall. The critical role of transaction costs in the rise and fall of markets is indicated by the fact that when trade routes are relatively unhindered by piracy, wars, insurrections, taxation and so on, markets tend to develop, the specialization of labor and other activities increases, incomes grow and civilizations flourish. Conversely, when trade routes are rendered increasingly risky and/or less profitable because of one or more of these sources of high transaction costs, market activities tend to decline in favor of non-market ones. This results in decreased specialization and often lower levels of development.

Naturally, transaction costs can be influenced by investments in port facilities, railroads and roads, surveillance and the enforcement of laws with respect to markets. Since such investments can be affected by the profitability of trade and exchange, the flow of causality is by no means one-way from transaction costs to market growth and trade. In any case, historical increases (reductions) in transaction costs have generally been accompanied by declines (increases) in the relative importance of markets.

In particular, as the rule of Roman law and the use of Roman roads yielded to political and military turmoil in the twilight of the Roman Empire, markets tended to decline in favor of the feudal autonomy.[21] Subsequently, however, with the greater peace and tranquility of the European renaissance, markets reemerged and feudal institutions gave way to market institutions. Of particular interest is the very beginning of the new institutions. As pointed out by Braudel (1979) in his account of the trade fairs in France's Champagne district in the 12th and 13th centuries, the first merchants in the reemerging European market economy were itinerant merchants who came to trade fairs in groups, thereby providing each other with protection. The trade fairs were at first only sporadic; by concentrating all the transactions into a short period of time, they mitigated the problems associated with "thin" markets. Gradually, as trade developed, these markets became more permanent.

The examples would seem to suggest an analogy to the well-known addage that "necessity is the mother of invention." In other words, an institution that is demanded will be supplied. Carried to the extreme, however, this theory of the primacy of demand factors in institutional change becomes tautological, the pitfall of some "functionalist" applications of transaction cost theory identified in Section II.

In fact, however, the historical record shows that, despite the probably relatively universal demand for them, the creation of permanent markets in the late Middle Ages was by no means automatic. They were created only when a mutuality of interests, including those on the supply side of institutional change, prevailed. For example, such markets and merchant laws enforced by local police appeared when not only the merchants demanded them but also the local governments and ecclesiastical authorities were will-

---

[21]The feudal economy may be interpreted as a simple "coalition economy" [Townsend (1984)]. Even in simple coalition economies, however, a considerable amount of hierarchy and supervision may be necessary in order to monitor the performance of the different agents with respect to the responsibilities with which they are charged. For evidence see Bennett (1937).

ing to supply them (so as to attract such merchants and thereby increase their revenue base). When this was not so, as for example when the ecclesiastical authorities would find such activities disadvantageous, the formation of markets could be substantially delayed.[22]

The development of factor markets has also been extremely important for economic development, in general, and the development of commodity markets and greater specialization, in particular. For example, the decline of feudalism and the rise of commodity markets in Europe beginning in the 13th century was greatly facilitated by the simultaneous development of markets for factors of production, namely, labor, land and capital. The development of factor markets, in turn, has been greatly facilitated by the existence of property rights over such factors.

One important requirement for the development of property rights and, in turn, markets for the relevant factors, is scarcity. Without scarcity and hence competition among alternative users of a particular factor of production, there would be no need for a system of property rights over that particular factor. When a particular productive factor becomes scarce, however, actual or potential conflicts with respect to its use arise, thereby inducing the development of property rights in that factor as a means of avoiding conflict and reducing transaction costs in its use.

For example, recent studies by Feeny (1982) and Lundahl (1980, 1982) have demonstrated that property rights in labor (such as slavery) have emerged in geographic and cultural settings as different as Thailand and Haiti during periods of labor scarcity. Likewise, Klein (1920) has shown that property rights in animals arose in countries like Spain after the expulsion of the Moors when land was plentiful, labor was scarce and animal husbandry was an activity which utilized lots of land per unit of labor. Similarly, property rights in land have developed in periods in which land became relatively and absolutely scarce, and as pointed out below, property rights in capital and markets for capital and finance have tended to develop when capital (in forms other than land) became a scarce factor of production. Scarcity in itself, however, is not a sufficient condition for the development of property rights. The more numerous the agents involved and the more valuable the rights to be assigned, the stronger the conflicts over their allocation are likely to be and the more important and yet also problematic collective action becomes. As shall be discussed in the next chapter, success in collective action,

---

[22]This calls attention to the relevance and importance of interest group formation, collective action and political economy in determining the relative importance of transaction cost frictions in institutional change.

requires the resolution of the often difficult-to-resolve free-rider problems[23] that typically plague such actions.

Where property rights are lacking, incomplete or ill-defined, the result can be inefficiency in the use of resources, in the extreme killing off the resources [DeVany and Sanchez (1977), Libecap (1986)]. Examples of the tragedy of the commons abound in which water, air, land, labor or other resources, whose property rights are insufficiently defined or enforced, are grossly misused.[24] On the other hand, when property rights are clearly defined, the assignment, trade and reallocation of such rights tends to become more economic. In this way, the numerous risks that attend such markets and which can be large enough to cause "market failure" can be avoided or at least mitigated. In other words, the establishment of property rights and the enforcement of laws protecting those rights may well have the effect of reducing transaction costs in the use and exchange of factors.

The completeness of markets and of the related property rights is also likely to be affected by the ability of any party to a contract to recoup any loss arising from a breach of contract. Limitations on the ability of the one party to penalize another party for breach of contract can reduce not only the efficiency of resource use but also the extent of resource accumulation. For example, if a firm cannot dismiss or otherwise discipline a worker for poor performance, it may be less likely to invest in training of that worker than would otherwise be the case. Likewise, limitations on the ability of a creditor to recoup the credit extended to a borrower (e.g. because of bankruptcy laws) might well limit his willingness to lend or induce him to insist on more collateral as part of the credit contract [Shetty (1985)]. Building on the arguments of Stiglitz and Weiss (1981) and Jaffe and Russell (1976), Braverman and Guasch (1986) argue that the special vulnerability of credit contracts to adverse selection, moral hazard and enforcement problems explains the pervasiveness of credit rationing as opposed to interest rate adjustment as a means of equilibrating supply and demand in the credit market. As noted above, Eswaran and Kotwal (1985c), in turn, argue that the presence of bankruptcy rules and other sources of limited liability are responsible for the greater

---

[23]Collective action and free-rider problems are explained in ch. 3.

[24]This should not be interpreted to imply that the substitution of private property rights for collective use and open access is necessarily desirable. Collective ownership may come with well enforced rules designed to overcome the pitfalls of misuse [Dennen (1976), Libecap (1986) and Libecap and Wiggins (1984)]. In some situations, even if desirable, the introduction of a system of private property rights and the means of enforcing these rights may be too costly for the society to bear [Runge (1986)].

propensity of capitalists to hire workers than of workers to hire capitalists.

Once again, early forms of contracts for factors are instructive. The historical work of Lopez and Raymond (1956) shows that the early contracts for capital took the form of "sea loans" to finance purchases from overseas by merchants. The goods in transit served as collateral and were accompanied by separate insurance contracts to deal with contingencies such as the shipment not arriving at the destination. When the risks were sufficiently great that no particular party was willing to absorb them in their entirety, "commendas" developed. The "commenda" was a once-and-for-all investment project in which the investors, instead of lending their funds to an entrepreneur-transporter-merchant at a fixed rate of interest, entrusted their funds or merchandise to him in return for the principal plus an agreed-upon share in the net proceeds of the project.[25] In order to attract investors to bear the risks of commenda and equity share contracts, standard accounting systems and professional auditing requirements developed. Without these and the laws to back them up, such institutional change would have been delayed or blocked entirely.

Transaction costs can also contribute very substantially to the ownership form and organizational structure of firms and the evolution thereof over time. Alchian and Demsetz (1972) explain how the very existence of firms can be attributed to the difficulties of obtaining reliable information about performance of the relevant agents. Williamson (1985), Levy (1985) and Klein, Crawford and Alchian (1978) and others have called attention to the role of transaction costs in determining the degree of vertical integration. Likewise, Forbes (1986) has suggested that the emergence of limited liability contracts may be explained by transaction cost considerations. Fama and Jensen (1983), moreover, have stressed the importance of transaction costs in determining the degree of separation between ownership and control, on the one hand, and decision management and decision control, on the other. Finally, transaction costs have been shown to be important in determining the relationships within the firm among workers, capital owners and manager-supervisors.

Notably, as pointed out by DeRoover (1948), Townsend (1984) and Williamson (1985), the first firms were partnerships of family members. This was not only because family members tend to share information about each other to a greater extent than other non-related individuals, but also because

---

[25]The commenda, therefore, involves a sharing of the risks. The investor risks his capital and the entrepreneur, his time and any resources of his own contributed [Udovitch (1970, Section VI, p. 170.)]

reports about inappropriate behavior and malfeasance both travel faster and are dealt with more seriously (in terms of earning ill-repute for the transgressing party) within families than between them. For this reason family member partners could be trusted to a greater extent than non-family member partners, thereby reducing the need for costly internal monitoring of one agent by the other. They also showed that, while credit (rental) contracts among individuals were feasible in the case of short-term credit, equity contracts in firms (including family firms) became more commonly observed when the investment funds were needed for longer periods.

Transaction costs and particularly economies of scope in supervision and coordination can help explain why both firms and families are usually hierarchical in their supervision structure [Russell (1985), Williamson (1985)] and also why they may pay wage rates above those justified by marginal productivity considerations. Williamson (1985) emphasizes the relevance of market failure considerations and firm location in explaining the appearance of company towns and paternalistic behavior on the part of firms with respect to workers in certain industries and time periods. The prominence of family farms and businesses in LDCs may be attributed to the especially high transaction costs of interhousehold transactions in such countries.[26]

Chandler (1977) and Williamson (1975, 1985) have identified changes in transaction costs and in particular improvements in communication and monitoring capabilities, and at the same time the growing importance of asset specificity as major contributors to the change in corporate form from its traditional U-form to the now dominant multi-divisional M-form. Likewise, given the absence of a consistent set of international laws, an international police force to enforce such laws and an international judicial system to settle disputes, the sizeable transaction costs with respect to international transactions help explain the rise of the multinational corporation [Teece (1976), Caves (1982) and Williamson (1985)], and the success of international joint equity ventures relative to that of common markets and other international agreements with respect to the rules governing economic transactions [Nugent (1982, 1983, 1984a, 1984b, 1986)].

The importance of families and family firms in LDCs is further strengthened by the relative importance of various kinds of risk and uncertainty in such contexts and the aforementioned asymmetries of information that may result in both adverse selection and moral hazard and hence market failure in the insurance market. Consequently, households are likely to have to re-

---

[26]See especially Ben-Porath (1980), Williamson (1985), Pollak (1985), Nugent (1985), Binswanger and Rosenzweig (1986).

sort to protecting themselves against such risks through the practice of both horizontal and vertical extension of the household. Horizontal extension, typically among brothers or sisters, may permit resource complementarity and specialization of activities within the family just like greater firm size does with respect to firms. Vertical (intergenerational) extension wherein fathers or even grandfathers live with their adult sons and grandchildren, on the other hand, may not only facilitate complementarity and specialization [Rosenzweig and Wolpin (1986)] but also reduce risks, especially those of incapacity during old age. The intergenerational extension of the household can be interpreted as an implicit insurance contract between generations wherein the younger generation agrees to take care of the older generation when and in the form needed (knowing that it, in turn, can expect to be insured in the same way by the generation).[27]

Likewise, kinship and other extrafamiliar and extrahousehold relations, such as those cemented through gift exchanges, adoption, godfathering and so on, can be understood as a further extension of the same principle in the face of risks of various kinds and the absence of satisfactory markets for capital and/or insurance (because of the inherently high transaction costs).[28]

The processes of urbanization, and geographic mobility undermine the integrity of the family unit and the social norms which make it an extremely efficient enforcer of these norms, thereby raising the transaction costs of intrafamily programs of insurance. But, it takes more than transaction costs to explain the development of the accounting and actuarial systems which increase the viability of the insurance market. Once again, it seems that collective action, the subject of the following chapter, is needed.

V. The Incidence of Different Contracts: A Review of the Evidence

The purpose of this section is to provide a brief overview of the contractual choice issues revealed in the available applied literature, especially that on the incidence of various types of contracts.

The section is divided into the following subsections: (1) agricultural contracts, (2) mining contracts, (3) fishing contracts, and (4) transportation contracts. The order of these subsections is deliberately chosen so as to start with the more familiar before going on to the unfamiliar.

---

[27]This is explained carefully in Nugent (1985) who also explains that this risk is likely to be greater for females than for males because of their greater dependence on their husbands, the greater likelihood that they will outlive their husbands and the lower probability that they will remarry after the death or the divorce of their husbands.

[28]See especially Posner (1980), Ben-Porath (1980) and Lundahl (1980, 1982).

(1) Agriculture

Agriculture is, of course, the one sector of LDC economies where form of contract, including the role of transaction costs, has received considerable attention. The dominance of owner-operated farms in most countries, and the commonality of contracting among family members (an obvious means of reducing transaction costs) serve as telling indicators of the relevance of transaction costs of various sorts in this sector. Despite the relative scarcity value of land, the property rights in land, capital and other necessary inputs, which we have seen to be crucial ingredients for the satisfactory development of various contractual arrangements and markets, are often incompletely and ambiguously defined, suggesting the possibility of institutional inefficiency.

Agricultural contracts often appear in mixed form. For example, there are plantations which rent out some land on fixed rent or share contracts and also hire labor on other parts of the plantation on wage contracts. The wage contracts may well be in both cash and kind, and some workers are hired on long term contracts and others on a daily or "casual" basis. Even if the contracts appear to be of the polar (wage and rent contract) type, they often contain some elements of cost-sharing or risk-sharing. Likewise, the elements shared and the sharing rates are by no means fixed and vary widely by crop, region, time period and the relative importance and value of the inputs contributed by the different agents [Bardhan and Rudra (1980), Robertson (1987)].

Since most contracts involve a mix of forms, the identification of contractual form necessarily involves the somewhat arbitrary delineation of the boundaries between the different contractual forms. Quite possibly, therefore, different labels might be applied by different analysts to the same institutional form, thereby limiting the comparability and hence the validity of generalizations based on observations on the incidence of different contractual forms in different settings made by different observers.

Frequently, the popular impression, at least, is that share contracts are a traditional and less efficient form of contract that has been losing ground to fixed rent and wage contracts, and which are at the current time relatively rare in DCs like the United States and Western Europe. Indeed, because of the alleged backwardness of share contracts, some countries have gone to considerable lengths to legislate them out of existence.[29] As a result, the most commonly investigated hypothesis in the literature is the inefficiency of share contracts hypothesis. As noted above, in our simple but general model of contractual choice, share contracts are necessarily inefficient *only*

---

[29]For evidence and a proposed explanation see Robertson (1987, Ch. 1).

when one ignores the monitoring costs of labor under wage contracts and the asset misuse possibilities under fixed rent contracts. The general acceptance of the inefficiency-of-sharecropping hypothesis may be attributed to the facts that the danger of asset misuse is probably less important in agriculture than in other sectors, and that even within the transaction cost literature most analysts have failed to consider the *ex post* transaction costs in which the supervision of wage labor would be important. Despite the very considerable effort that has gone into it, empirical support for the hypothesis has been weak at best.[30]

In view of the dogged adherance to the inefficiency-of-share-contracts hypothesis, the remarkable pervasiveness and resilience of share contracts [Robertson (1987)] has posed something of a paradox demanding an explanation. This is because in the traditional model of sharecropping [Bardhan and Srinivasan (1971), Bardhan (1979)] i.e., a model with neither uncertainty nor transaction costs but freedom for the tenant to choose labor and other variable inputs, labor shirking would be greater under sharecropping than under wage contracts (since the landowner chooses the input levels) or rent contracts [Cheung (1969)]. On the other hand, in the standard neoclassical framework without uncertainty and transaction costs but where the landowner also has some control over the input of labor even in sharecropping [e.g., Johnson (1950), Cheung (1969) and Reid (1976)], all contracts would be equally efficient, thus leaving theory without any predictive power. Even with production uncertainty, sharecropping is at best an unnecessary device for sharing risk between the two parties since a combination of the two polar contracts would generally be better [Stiglitz (1974), Newbery (1977), Newberry and Stiglitz (1979), Reid (1976)].

As a result, to explain sharecropping analysts have had to depart from the first-best world of no transaction costs. Institutional imperfections like indivisible inputs, nonstandard and non-marketable inputs, market power, and additional sources of risk (which add to the transaction costs of alternative

---

[30]One of the few studies with results supporting this hypothesis is that of Bell (1977) who showed that output per unit of land was higher on owned land than on land leased in under share contracts. However, this difference could well be due to adverse selection on the part of landowners with respect to the choice of land to rent out and differences in production functions on land under different contracts. See also Vyas (1970), Rudra (1982), Roumasset (1976), Truran and Fox (1979) and Otsuka and Hayami (1988, Table 2). Relatively strong agreement, however, has been reached on the fact that landowner income from land leased out under fixed rent contract is lower and the tenant's income larger than that under share contracts, implying that a riskbearing premium applies. See Otsuka and Hayami (1988, pp. 28-29).

contracts) have been relied upon to provide a rationale for sharing.[31]

Braverman and Stiglitz (1982) have argued that the indirect supervision resulting from the interlinking of share contracts and credit contracts can substantially reduce the scope for opportunistic behavior under sharecropping and thereby make share contracts economically viable. In fact, however, indirect supervision would seem to be a distinctly imperfect substitute for direct supervision. Hence, the need for direct supervision remains not only in time- rate wage contracts but also in share and fixed rent contracts, even though the extent of direct supervision per unit of labor or land may be lower in the latter cases. Alston, Datta and Nugent (1984) and Datta, O'Hara and Nugent (1986) have shown that, once transaction costs in the form of direct supervision are allowed for, the co-existence of sharecropping with other forms of contracts can be explained even in standard neoclassical models of otherwise competitive markets.

Although the above account has proceeded on the assumption of a single unified form of wage contract, namely, time rate contracts, labor contracts of other forms are also observed in agriculture. Roumasset and Uy (1981) have provided a transaction cost explanation with empirical evidence from the Philippines to explain how and when piece-rate wage contracts would be chosen over time-rate ones. Given the peaks and slacks in agricultural activities in most parts of the world, which are further reinforced by weather uncertainties, labor contracts of varying duration and degrees of attachment have been resorted to in village societies so as to hedge against uncertainties and thereby to minimize transaction costs [(Bardhan 1983b)]. Eswaran and Kotwal (1985b) have explained the presence of "permanent" workers as part of the so-called "two-tier" labor market by arguing that employers deliberately provide labor contracts of longer duration to elicit loyalty and reliability among laborers, thereby reducing the need for supervision in those activities such as maintenance which are most crucial to the long term profitability of the farm. Attempts have also been made to explain the cash and kind composition of rural wages and the interlinking of markets in terms of production and marketing risks and other types of transaction costs [Alston and Ferrie (1986), Bardhan (1980, 1983b), Datta, Nugent, Tishler and Wang (forthcoming), Kotwal (1985) and Datta, Nugent and Tishler (1985)].

As modern inputs like irrigation, credit and fertilizer come into increasing use in LDC agriculture, they increase the intensity of production and the

---

[31]See especially Binswanger and Rosenzweig (1984) for a review of such explanations. See also Jaynes (1982), Pant (1983), Datta (1983), Robertson (1970), and Feeny (1983).

importance of timing, sequence and the necessary proportions among the inputs, and hence the importance of appropriate forms of contract in order to assure their effective utilization.

With respect to empirical studies on the choice among wage, share and rent contracts, interest has focused on those areas and time periods where owner-occupied and labor-supplied farms are not dominant and yet all three forms of contract could be observed simultaneously. Examples include Europe [Ganshof and Verhulst (1966) and Jones (1966)], China [Ash (1976) Buck (1930)], Japan [Waswo (1977)] contemporary Latin America [Finkler (1980), Stuchlik (1976)], Africa [Robertson (1987)] and especially in South Asia [Bardhan and Rudra (1980), Bardhan (1983a)]. Until recently also, much of the U.S. South was this way, accounting in part for why the experience of the U.S. South has been rather extensively analyzed [Higgs (1974), Reid (1973, 1979) Alston and Higgs (1982) and Alston (1981)]. Day (1967) and Alston (1981) both noted the sharp decline in share and rent contracts and the ascendancy of wage contracts with farm mechanization of Southern agriculture after 1930. As noted above, this trend is readily explicable in transaction cost terms inasmuch as the substitution of capital for labor reduced the effort-inducing advantage of rent and share contracts relative to wage contracts and at the same time increased their asset mismanagement disadvantage.

Using data for 1911, Alston and Higgs (1982) showed that the incidence of wage and share contracts was positively, and that of fixed rent contracts negatively, related to the quality of land. This relation can also be explained in transaction cost terms since higher quality land would, on the one hand, reduce the marginal cost of labor supervision per unit of land and, on the other hand, increase the potential danger of asset mismanagement, thereby favoring wage over share (and share over fixed rent) contracts.

(2) Mining Contracts

While neither as well studied nor characterized by as much contractual diversity as agriculture, the mining sector provides another interesting field for applying the aforementioned principles of transaction costs to contractual choice. Moreover, the experience in mining would seem to be particularly relevant to LDCs not only because mining is often a relatively important sector but also because the changes that have been observed over long periods of time in DCs are likely to be collapsed into a few years in LDCs.

In general, since the 17th century the mining industry has been almost exclusively employing relatively capital intensive techniques, in large part because access to high quality mineral deposits is often extremely difficult and

costly, and the more accessible low quality deposits require deep mineshafts
and enormous amounts of crushing, purifying and refining to make them us-
able.[32] Consistent with the general model of contractual choice presented
in Section III above, in general, in those parts of the industry where capital equipment has become extremely important, wage contracts prevail and
substantial amounts of supervision are applied so as to reduce labor-shirking
to tolerable levels. Because of economies of scope in supervision, supervisors can simultaneously supervise labor, enforce mine safety regulations and
ensure the maintenance of fixed capital relatively efficiently.

Mining, however, has not always been capital-intensive and wage contracts have not always dominated. Indeed, Nef (1934) showed that prior
to the 17th century share contracts were common among European miners
and such contracts are not uncommon of in small scale mining operations
in contemporary LDCs. Moreover, thanks to the interesting and well documented studies of Umbeck (1977) and Hallagan (1978) on contractual choices
in California's historically important gold mining industry, it is possible and
instructive to explain why the earliest forms of contract in this industry did
not consist of wage contracts and then to see how and why the form of contract in this segment of the mining industry of the U.S. evolved over time in
the face of rapidly changing environmental conditions.

California was largely uninhabited until its military occupation by U.S.
forces during the war with Mexico (1846-48) and its subsequent annexation
in 1848. Upon annexation all non-privately owned land was declared the
property of the U.S. government. A few days before annexation, gold was
discovered on the American River near the present site of California's capital city, Sacramento. Even after annexation property rights remained poorly
defined inasmuch as the U.S. had no law regulating the acquisition of private
mining rights on federal land. Even if they had been clearly defined, because
of minimal government presence in the area it seems doubtful that any such
regulations could have been enforced. Miners had to provide their own protection of any mining rights they claimed. What they did was to form groups
which claimed exclusive rights over pieces of land called "mining districts."

The then-practiced technology of gold mining, known as "panning for
gold," was simple and labor intensive; water was applied to a sieve-like box
called a "cradle" and subsequently to a pan which allowed nuggets of gold
to be separated from the other materials. A small operation could be satisfactorily operated by two persons. Nevertheless, for reasons of providing
mutual security for their claimed mining rights, even in the beginning the

---

[32]See Nef (1934) and Leijonhufvud (1986).

groups ranged in size up to eight miners. The first contracts were almost invariably share contracts wherein the miners agreed to work together and then each day to share the proceeds among those working that day. The choice of share contracts was favored by two important considerations. First, since miners worked in close proximity to each other in very small groups, thereby providing mutual supervision, the underreporting of output danger of share contracts was minimized. Second, because of the primitive technology, the availability of alternative sites, the very limited tools used (all of which were owned by the miners themselves), and the small numbers of miners involved in any given day's operations, the extent of vulnerability of the share contracts to asset misuse and labor-shirking was very limited.

As more and more people were attracted to the area as a result of reports of dramatic gold discoveries, however, the competition for mining land increased and the critical number of men deemed sufficient for providing mutual protection of a claim increased. Since the incentive for labor-shirking under share contracts increases with the number of miners, Umbeck (1977) hypothesized that the increased number of miners per claim would decrease the incidence of share contracts and raise that of owner-operated individual land plots within the district. Consistent with the hypothesis, Umbeck's survey of the mining contracts revealed a distinct shift from share contracts to fixed land allotment contracts after 1850.

By 1870, however, circumstances in the gold mining region of California had changed once again. Law and order had become more firmly established and the federal government had enacted legislation formally approving the practice of land allotment of mining district claims and the sale and lease of such land. By this time also, however, the most easily accessed and richest sources had been exploited, generally requiring the new entrants to make more substantial capital investments in order to successfully mine gold. While "placer" mining could still be conducted as described above on river bed land, gold was now found either in subterranean ancient river beds, known as "drifts", which could be reached only by digging tunnels and shafts and then lifting out the rock containing the gold, or in veins of quartz ledges which had to be blasted and crushed into small pieces in crushing machines before the aforementioned "placer" techniques could be applied. In contrast to placer mining, the gold potential of drift or quartz mining claims could not be determined without making substantial investments in mine development.

Hallagan (1978) surveyed the content of 150 lease contracts on such mining claims in Placer County, California between 1870 and 1900 and found that the leases fell into two basic types, i.e., fixed rent and share contracts.

Each of these basic contractual types could be further classified, i.e., the fixed rent contracts divided according to timing of payment, either by lump sum in advance, or installment; and the share contracts into "share of the gross" and "share of the net" proceeds contracts. Hallagan found that the fixed rent contracts paid on the installment basis dominated in placer mining whereas "share of the gross" contracts dominated in drift and quartz mining.

Since the explanations provided by Hallagan for these findings are instructive in the application of transaction and information costs to contractual choice, they are repeated here although with considerable difference in emphasis. Since gold mining was still labor-intensive and labor effort sufficiently difficult to monitor, wage contracts were ruled out by their labor-shirking disadvantages. This reduced the alternatives to fixed rent and share contracts. While information about the quality of the deposit and hence its return was readily available to both parties in placer mining, it was available primarily only to the owner in drift and quartz mining. Because of the dangers of adverse selection with respect to drift and quartz claims, few non-owners would be willing to pay much for prepaid fixed rent leases on drift and quartz claims. At the same time, however, as a result of the improved law and order situation, fewer miners were needed for protection purposes, thereby reducing the magnitude of the labor-shirking disadvantage of share contracts relative to fixed rent contracts. Since such supervision would be necessary anyway in order both to avoid asset mismanagement in drift and quartz mining (given the greater importance of such assets in this type of mining) and to take advantage of the owner's knowledge and experience, because of economies of scope in supervision, the marginal costs to the owner of supplying this supervision to control the underreporting of output and labor-shirking problems of share contracts were minimal. This explains why share contracts became dominant once again in drift and quartz mining even though fixed rent contracts remained dominant in placer mining.

Risk may also have played a role. To the potential lessee, share contracts would involve less risk (since risks were shared by the owner) than fixed rent contracts, especially prepaid ones. Because of the greater risk in quartz and drift mining than in placer mining, share contracts would have a greater advantage as a risk sharing device to the potential lessee in these forms of mining than in placer mining. Of course, the payment of the fixed rent in installments might alleviate some of the risk to the lessee of fixed rent contracts. However, because of the importance of accumulated knowledge and experience to accuracy in estimating the value of such claims, share contracts possessed an additional advantage over fixed rent contracts in that they avoided the need for recontracting, something which in the case of fixed rent contracts could be avoided only by extremely complex contracts with multiple contingencies which would be very expensive to draw up and monitor.[33]

Eventually, however, as in other branches of mining, more and more asset- specific investments became necessary, implying a rise in the relative importance of the asset mismanagement disadvantages of share and fixed rent contracts. As a result, gold mining contracts came to be dominated by wage contracts.

(3) Fishing

Another sector whose experience is particulary relevant to both LDCs in general and to the application of transaction costs analysis is fishing. While the analytical literature on contractual choice in the fishing industry, consisting primarily only of Zoeteweij (1956), is less extensive than that with respect to mining, the descriptive evidence[34] concerning the incidence of different forms of contract in fishing in different parts of the world is *much more* extensive than that of mining, permitting a fairly comprehensive overview of the prevailing contractual choices in fishing.

While fixed wage, fixed rent and mixed contracts (involving elements of either wage or rent contracts) are by no means unheard of in fishing, the most distinctive feature of contractual choice in the fishing industry — worldwide — is the dominant position of share contracts. A second relatively distinctive feature of contracts in fishing is that, relative to the situation in agriculture, manufacturing and mining at least, within wage contracts there is a relatively high incidence of piece-rate wage contracts.

Given the dominance of share contracts in general, the following discussion focuses on two objectives: first, the explanation of those cases where contracts other than shares are observed and, second, explanations for the dominance of share contracts in the fishing industry.

The least common form of contract in fishing would seem to be fixed rent

---

[33]Since gold can be measured in weight and since the labor-shirking disadvantages of wage contracts could be reduced by piece rate wage contracts, one wonders why piece rate contracts might not have become more competitive with the other contracts in all types of gold mining in California after 1870. Since Hallagan's data pertain only to leases, we do not know for sure that such contracts did not appear. Further research is clearly warranted to determine whether or not piece rate contracts were used and if not why not.

[34]See, e.g., Alexander (1980), Baks and Postel-Coster (1977), Davis, Gallman and Hutchins (1985), Doeringer, Moss and Terkla (1986), Fraser (1966), McGoodwin (1980a, 1980b), Norr (1980), Platteau and Abraham (1987), International Labour Office (1952), Han (1972) and the references therein.

contracts. Fixed rent contracts are apparently observed only on the fringes of the fishing industry, primarily in sport fishing and chartering where the value of the catch is usually less important than the pleasures of competing with other fishermen, competing with fish that require skill or strength to be able to land, experiencing the beauty of the sea and perhaps visiting islands or other landmarks while fishing. Notably also, fixed rental of sport fishing boats is generally practiced in one of two situations; namely, when (1) the boat is very simple, e.g., a small rowboat without gear, or (2) the boat with gear is rented out *with* a captain and frequently other crew members as well.

Fixed rent contracts in fishing can also be observed in situations where instead of a boat, what is rented is the right to fish in a certain location. When this is done on a non-exclusive basis, this is nothing more than a license to fish. But sometimes exclusivity in the right to fish is also provided. In most such cases, the license to fish is accompanied by restrictions on the size or quantity of the fish that can be taken or on the technology used so as to mitigate the possibility of resource depletion.

Why are fixed rent contracts so rare in fishing in general and yet observed (in the aforementioned circumstances) in sport fishing and in the rental of the right to fish on a certain body of water? Since the primary disadvantage of fixed rent contracts is the greater incentive it provides for the misuse of assets, any transaction cost explanation of variations in the incidence of fixed rent contracts must focus on this problem. Indeed, the plausibility of such an explanation for the dearth of fixed rent contracts in fishing would seem to be very strong in view of the especially high risk of loss of or damage to assets in fishing which, in turn, can be attributed to (a) the distinct possibility of sudden bad weather or accident at sea, (b) the difficulty of assigning the blame for such losses (i.e., distinguishing between bad luck and carelessness) or (c) even if blame can be assigned, the difficulty of recouping the loss of assets from the guilty party (who may have drowned!) In the case of the rental of a very simple boat like a row boat very close to shore or of the right to fish on a certain body of water, the value of the assets that could be misused would be minimal. As a result, the asset misuse disadvantage of rent contracts would be small or even nonexistent relative to their effort-inducing advantage, thereby explaining the choice of fixed rent contracts in these cases.

Fixed wage (time rate) contracts, in pure form at least, are also relatively rare but are observed, perhaps increasingly so, in the more capital- and less skill-intensive ends of the industry. These same ends of the industry may be where the production and price risks are somewhat lower than in other segments of the industry. Common examples of fixed (time rate) wage contracts are fish canning boats, capital-intensive tuna fishing and canning,[35] the later vintage, more capital-intensive whaling ships [Davis et al. (1985)], and those providing bait for sport fishermen.

As mentioned above, piece rate contracts are relatively common in certain types of fishing operations, e.g., shark fishing in Mexico,[36] and salmon fishing in Bristol Bay, Alaska.[37] For example, fleet owners or canneries might well hire fishermen who would operate company owned boats on the basis of a fixed rate per fish or per unit of weight of the fish. The major advantage of piece rate wage contracts relative to fixed (time rate) wage and share contracts is that it eliminates the incentive for quantity-shirking in the supply of effort, thereby possibly eliminating the need for labor supervision. Without supervision of any kind, however, piece-rate wage contracts would be vulnerable to opportunism of the quality-shirking and asset mismanagement varieties. This explains why piece rates tend to be applied without supervision only when the boats are very simple and where the quality of the fish does not affect its value very significantly as in shark fishing, and canned as opposed to fresh or frozen fish of various kinds.

The common characteristic of those segments of the industry in which wage contracts are more commonly observed is greater capital-intensity. Several reasons may be given for this. First, any owner who can afford a large and capital-intensive fishing boat is likely to be able to more easily bear the production and price risk than the owners of smaller boats who are often fishermen themselves. Second, because of the greater capital-intensity but also the absolutely larger numbers of workers employed on such ships, the labor-shirking disadvantage of wage contracts relative to share contracts is reduced. Third, again because of their capital-intensity and large size, the danger of asset misuse, greatest under fixed rent contracts but present also under share contracts, is sufficiently large as to favor wage contracts.

Finally, we turn to the various explanations for why share contracts are so prominent in so many segments of fishing and why they have, in many cases at least, remained so over time. As mentioned above, the danger of asset mismanagement tends to rule out fixed rent contracts in most situations. Since asset mismanagement would also be problematic under share contracts, the owner needs to be able to supervise. Typically, on small boats he does so himself as the owner-captain; on larger boats, or when he has a fleet of smaller boats, he engages a captain whose loyalty can be assured by reputation or

---

[35] This is also true in fishing. See Platteau and Abraham (1987).
[36] See, e.g., McGoodwin (1980a, 1980b).
[37] This information comes from personal interviews with Alaskan fishermen.

family, ethnic group, clan or community relations (wherein the consequences of gaining ill-repute for practicing opportunistic behavior *vis-à-vis* the owner would be more serious). Economies of scope in supervision make it possible for both output-underreporting and labor-shirking to be mitigated without having to hire additional supervisors.[38]

Risk considerations also seem to be important. Several distinct types of risk are involved: production risk, price risk and, of course, risk of life. While production risk is common also to agriculture, the risks of price and life would seem to be of special importance in fishing.

The reason why price risk is important is that typically only a small portion of the catch is retained for self-consumption, implying that most fish is marketed,[39] and, because of high storage and transport costs especially in LDCs, mostly at the local level. Because of seasonality in production, the price of fish at the local level is highly volatile and variable from one market to another within relatively short distances. Therefore, access to appropriate market channels and the availability of suitable means of transport at the right time can also make a considerable difference in the determination of the value of the catch. If either party can facilitate the realization of higher values, it will be to the advantage of the other to share in these benefits. Schemes that would protect one of the parties from price risk, such as would be the case for the fisherman remunerated with piece rate wages, may actually increase overall income risk because one could expect production and price risk to offset each other to a considerable extent. As a result, both parties may prefer to share in the proceeds of the final sales. This gives both parties the incentive to work together toward the realization of the highest possible values and the ability to use price risk as a hedge against production risk.

While one can easily understand why risk-sharing may be attractive to boatowners, it is less obvious why non-owner fishermen (who are usually relatively poor) are willing to share these risks (as they necessarily do under share contracts but would not have to under wage contracts). Similarly, one might question why non-owner fishermen are as willing as they seem to

---

[38] Although piece rate wage contracts could be even more advantageous in these respects than share contracts, in view of the general importance of quality to value and the vulnerability of piece rate contracts to quality- shirking, piece rate contracts are unlikely to be viable except in the aforementioned unusual circumstances.

[39] Contributing to this result are the facts (a) that fish are a generally a high priced source of nutrition, (b) that fishermen's incomes are generally low and (c) that people everywhere seem to have a relatively low upper bound on the quantity of fish they can consume, preferring always a relatively balanced diet.

be to concede to the captain the right to exercise as much authority as they typically do. These seemingly parodoxical observations may be at least in part explained by the fact that fishermen protect themselves against production risk and risk of exploitation by maximizing their mobility and independence. For example, fishermen tend to remain single and have smaller families than men in other occupations. They also maintain the ties of ethnicity which provide networks of support in times of need [Doeringer et al. (1986), Platteau and Abraham (1987)].

Share contracts may also be useful as far as the risk of loss of life is concerned. Consider the plight of two fishermen on a rowboat that wrecks on some rocks. Their situation might be that of a prisoners' dilemma wherein in the absence of rules assuring cooperation, each fisherman would be unlikely to cooperate because not helping the other gives him a slightly better prospect for survival regardless of the action of the other, even though their joint probability of survival would be higher if they both cooperate. Only if each party can be assured about the other's cooperation would each party rationally choose to cooperate when confronted with shipwreck. The practice of share contracts backed up also by the threat of exclusion from future share contracts for lack of cooperation may have the effect of increasing each crew member's expectations of cooperation on the part of the other, and hence increase the chances of survival.[40]

The presence of large numbers of participants in the activity is apparently a less important deterent to the practice of share contracts in fishing than in other activities. There may well be several explanations for this. One such explanation would seem to be economies of scope and scale with respect to supervision, making it feasible for the captain and perhaps also a mate to supervise and coordinate large numbers of men on shipboard because of the small confines of even a relatively large ship and the especially strong authority that ship captains almost universally command. Also, because of the team nature of production in fishing, individual marginal products are undoubtedly unusually difficult to measure — even in the absence of risk.[41]

---

[40]The prisoners' dilemma problem will be discussed more completely in Chapter 3 below.

[41]Another possible advantage of share contracts is that they may permit a fuller utilization of resources — both labor and ships — than would otherwise be the case [Weitzman (1985)]. For instance, on a given day during a season in which the expected fish catch is low, boatowners quite naturally, would be unwilling to hire a fisherman and hence to use his boat if the fisherman's expected catch would be less than the fixed wage rate. On the other hand, with share contracts he would be willing to send out the boat as long as the prospects are good enough to justify his own time. Likewise, the share

(4) Transportation

In few sectors is there as much variation in form of contract as in the transport sector. Once again, a key determinant of the form of contract would seem to be the relative importance of capital equipment and its vulnerability to asset misuse.

In situations like porterage where the main input is human labor and labor shirking or misuse can be controlled, the seller of transport services generally rents out his services at fixed rates by piece or time. On the other hand, when the major input is animal or machine power, neither of which can explain to a neutral witness when and by whom it is misused, the owner of the animal or machine power is likely to hire-in labor at fixed wage rates.

Generally, capital-intensive transport services are rented out under fixed rent contracts rated by time and/or distance only when not only the equipment but also the operators and mechanics are also supplied, as for example when a tanker is chartered or a limousine is hired. One exception is the case of the cargo camels of Pakistan in areas where food and water for the camels are available at no cost [Heston, Hasnain, Hussain and Khan (1985)] in which the renter has no incentive to practice opportunistic behavior through the undersupply of maintenance. Another exception is that in which, even though the equipment is rented out without a driver, the owner may be able to keep an eye on the equipment. For example, a boat owner may rent out boats in a small lake or in the Philippines a "jeepney" owner rents out a jeepney for use on specified routes near his home base, or for short enough periods that the owner himself can supply the necessary maintenance between hires [Otsuka, Kikuchi and Hayami (1986)].

Not surprisingly, the probability of occurance of different forms of contract in transport services can also be affected by the degree to which the assets can be affected by asset misuse. Less sturdy pack and work animals like llamas and camels are less frequently rented out than bullocks. Among camels female camels are less frequently rented out than male camels because milk production (which of course they alone can produce) is more sensitive to insufficient feeding and watering than ability to transport [Heston, Hasnain, Hussain and Khan (1985)].

Because of the importance of risk of asset misuse in transport services, and the risk-pooling advantages of large numbers, the rental of equipment

---

contract fisherman would be willing to fish as long as his share of the take would exceed his reservation wage — which during the offseason may be well below the average market wage. Note, however, that this explanation does not hold up when wage rates and boat rental rates are allowed to vary with season as they seem to.

without drivers, such as in the automobile rental business of the U.S., or the taxi or rickshaw rental business of India, is typically accomplished primarily by large fleet owners who also have their own maintenance and service facilities so as to reduce transaction costs with respect to the purchase of such services [Otsuka, Kikuchi and Hayami (1986), Datta, Bhattachariya and Dey (1981)]. The difficulty of metering output and hence of detecting output-underreporting tends to make share contracts uneconomic [Turvey (1961), Otsuka and Murakami (1987)].[42]

Since the incentives for asset misuse and output-underreporting are reduced the longer is the duration of contract, and the assignment of fault is easier the fewer are the users, the renting out of sophisticated transport and other capital equipment via fixed rent and share contracts tends to be more feasible with exclusive long term contracts (leases). Special bonuses are frequently offered to induce contract renewal in contexts in which doing so can reduce transaction costs [Otsuka and Murakami (1987)].

VI. Concluding Comments

In conclusion, it must be pointed out that almost the entire discussion in this paper has focused on institutional changes and alternatives assuming that technology is given. In a broader perspective, however, technology is determined along with institutional/contractual forms through minimizing production and transaction costs. With given technology, production costs include only the costs of goods and services which physically enter into the production process. However, in a dynamic setting where technology can change, there will be transaction costs involved in gaining access to that technology and in inducing the relevant agents to adapt their routines so as to accomodate these changes. Hence, in such a setting the distinction between production and transaction costs is likely to be blurred. According to our present knowledge at least, transaction costs would seem to contribute very substantially to the determination of both institutions and technology.

Regarding the modeling of contractual choice, as we have pointed out earlier, most of the existing literature has focused almost exclusively on *ex ante* incentive mechanisms to cope with opportunistic behavior. Even within the confines of *ex ante* transaction costs, the only source of opportunistic behavior which has been given serious attention has been that of labor- shirking. Asset-misuse and output- and input-underreporting problems, which would seem to be of practical importance in all the sectors whose experience has been

---

[42]Even when there are good meters as in many taxicabs, the meters can be turned off.

reviewed above, have been largely ignored. Rarely have transaction costs, in the broader sense of including both their *ex ante* and *ex post* components, been explicitly modeled.

For a better understanding of the institutional alternatives as well as of the dynamics of institutional change, the results of this survey suggest the need for (1) a more comprehensive analysis of the possible sources of opportunistic behavior, (2) a more complete treatment of transaction costs and in particular of monitoring costs and other components of the *ex post* transaction costs, (3) better data on transaction costs, (4) a clearer picture of the variations in contractual form over time and space, and (5) greater attention to both the supply side of institutional change and the role of collective action. Only then can the modeling of transaction costs and the testing of the relative importance of different determinants proceed with any degree of confidence.

The choice among contracts is of course irrelevant in societies where the transaction costs are sufficiently high to rule out transactions between different individuals or households. Contracting is generally unnecessary also in situations where resource endowments are distributed in such a way that each individual, household or other relevant group has the resources necessary to efficiently produce its own needs with the resources it owns. As time passes, development proceeds and technology changes, however, the advantages of specialization and contracting tend to increase. Transaction costs can be reduced and institutional change facilitated by resource allocations favoring market development and security, the practice of taxes which do not discriminate against transactions, the prevalence of social norms and ideology favorable to reinforcing high standards of performance and expectations, the cohesiveness of the community, the emergence of property rights (private or collective), law and order, the adoption of uniform standards of quality, weights and measures, efficient judicial systems for adjudicating disputes, and incentive devices for avoiding, mitigating or efficiently settling such disputes.[43] As we have noted on several occasions, however, the realization of such reductions in transaction costs and efficient institutional change often has a prerequisite of successful collective action, the subject of the next chapter. As a result, the institutions which exist are not necessarily efficient and the demand for more appropriate institutions is not always sufficient to assure their creation.

---

[43]See North (1981, 1986a, 1986b) for some examples.

References

Akerlof, George, 1976, "The Economics of Caste and of the Rat Race and Other Woeful Tales," *Quarterly Journal of Economics* 90: 599-617.

Alchian, Arman and Harold Demsetz, 1972, "Production, Information Costs and Economic Organization," *American Economic Review* 62 (December): 777-795.

Alexander, Paul, 1980, "Sea Tenure in Southern Sri Lanka," in Alexander Spoehr, ed., *Maritime Adaptations.* Pittsburgh: University of Pittsburgh Press, 91-111.

Alston, Lee J., 1981, "Tenure Choice in Southern Agriculture, 1930-1960," *Explorations in Economic History* 18 (July): 211-232.

_____, Samar K. Datta, and Jeffrey B. Nugent, 1984, "Tenancy Choice in a Competitive Framework with Transaction Costs: A Theoretical and Empirical Analysis," *Journal of Political Economy* 92 (December): 1121-1133.

_____, and Joseph P. Ferrie, 1986, "Resisting the Welfare State: Southern Opposition to the Farm Security Administration," in Robert Higgs, ed., *The Emergence of the Modern Political Economy.* Greenwich: JAI Press.

_____, and Robert Higgs, 1982, "Contractual Mix in Southern Agriculture Since the Civil War: Fact, Hypotheses and Tests," *Journal of Economic History* 42 (June): 327-353.

Arrow, Kenneth J., 1974, *Limits of Organization.* New York: W.W. Norton.

Ash, Robert, 1976. *Land Tenure in Pre-Revolutionary China: Kiangsu Province in the 1920s and 1930s.* London: University of London, Contempory China Institute.

Baks, Chris and Els Postel-Coster, 1977, "Fishing Communities on the Scottish East Coast: Traditions in a Modern Setting," in *Those Who Live from the Sea.* St. Paul, NY: West Publishing Co.

Bardhan, Pranab K., 1979, "Agricultural Development and Land Tenancy in a Peasant Economy: A Theoretical and Empirical Analysis," *American Journal of Agricultural Economics* 61 (February): 48-57.

_____, 1980, "Interlocking Factor Markets and Agrarian Development: A Review of Issues," *Oxford Economic Papers* 32 (March): 82-98.

_____, 1983a, *Land, Labor and Rural Proverty.* New York: Columbia University Press.

_____, 1983b, "Labor-Tying in a Poor Agrarian Economy: A Theoretical and Empirical Analysis," *Quarterly Journal of Economics* (August): 501-514.

_____, ed. Forthcoming, *The Economic Theory of Agrarian Institutions.* New York: Oxford University Press.

_____, and Ashok Rudra, 1980, "Terms and Conditions of Sharecropping Contracts: An Analysis of Village Survey Data in India," *Journal of Development Studies* 16 (April): 287-302.

_____, and Ashok Rudra, 1986, "Labor Mobility and the Boundaries of the Village Moral Economy," *Journal of Peasant Studies* (April): 90-115.

_____, and T. N. Srinivasan, 1971, "Cropsharing Tenancy in Agriculture: A Theoretical and Empirical Analysis," *American Economic Review* 61 (March): 48-64.

Basu, Kaushik, Eric Jones and Ekkehart Schlicht, 1987, "The Growth and Decay of Custom: The Role of the New Institutional Economics in Economic History," *Explorations in Economic History* 24.

Bell, Clive, 1977, "Alternative Theories of Sharecropping: Some Tests Using Evidence Form Northeast India," *The Journal of Development Studies* 13 (July); 317-346.

Bennett, A.S., 1937, *Life on the English Manor: A Study of Peasant Conditions.* Cambridge: Cambridge University Press.

Ben-Porath, Yoram, 1980, "The F-Connection: Families, Friends and Firms and the Organization of Exchange," *Population and Development Review* 6, no. 1 (March): 1-30.

Binswanger, Hans P., and Vernon W. Ruttan, ed., 1978, *Induced Innovation: Technology, Institutions and Development.* Baltimore: Johns Hopkins University Press.

_____, and Mark R., Rosenzweig, 1984, "Contractual Arrangements, Employment and Wages in Rural Labor Markets: A Critical Review," in Binswanger and Rosenzweig, edd., *Contractual Arrangements, Employment and Wages in Rural Labor Markets in Asia.* New Haven and London: Yale University Press.

_____, 1986, "Risk, Implicit Contracts and the Family," Paper presented to the Conference on the Role of Institutions in Economic Development at Cornell University, November 1986.

Boeke, J.H., 1953, *Economics and Economic Policy of Dual Societies.* New York: Institute of Pacific Relations.

Braudel, Fernand, 1979, *The Wheels of Commerce: Civilization and Capitalism 15-18th Centuries,* vol. 2. New York: Harper and Row.

Braverman, Avishay and J. Luis Guasch, 1986, "Rural Credit Markets and Institutions in Developing Countries: Lessons for Policy Analysis from Practice and Modern Theory," San Diego: University of California, San Diego, Dept. of Economics Discussion Paper 86-6.

_____, and Joseph E. Stiglitz, 1982, "Sharecropping and the Interlinking of Agrarian Markets," *American Economic Review* 72, (September): 695-715.

Buck, J.L., 1930, *Chinese Farm Economy.* Chicago: University of Chicago Press.

Caves, Richard E., 1982, *Multinational Enterprise and Economic Analysis.* Cambridge: Cambridge University Press.

Chandler, Alfred D., Jr., 1977, *The Visible Hand: The Managerial Revolution in American Business.* Cambridge, MA: Harvard University Press.

Cheung, Steven N.S., 1969, *The Theory of Share Tenancy.* Chicago: University of Chicago Press.

_____, 1978, *The Myth of Social Cost.* London: Institute of Economic Affairs.

Datta, Samar K., 1983, "Sharecropping as 'Second-Best' Form of Tenancy in Traditional Agriculture," *Indian Economic Journal* 30, no. 4, (April-June).

_____, Arunabha Bhattachariya, and Kartick Ch. Dey, 1981, "Problems and Possibilities of Municipal Development: A Case Study of Bishnupur," Calcutta: Calcutta University.

_____, Donald O'Hara, and Jeffrey B. Nugent, 1986, "Choice of Agricultural Tenancy in the Presence of Transaction Costs," *Land Economics* 62 (May): 145-159.

_____, and Jeffrey B. Nugent, 1985, "Bahrain's Pearling Industry: How it Was, Why it Was that Way and its Implications," in J.B. Nugent and T.H. Thomas, ed., *Bahrain and the Gulf.* London: Croom Helm: 25-41.

_____, 1986, "Adversary Activities and Per Capita Income Growth," *World Development* (December): 1457-1461.

_____, and A. Tishler, 1985, "Determination of the Contractual Mix between Cash and Kind Wages for Developing Agrarian Economies," Los Angeles: University of Southern California Working Paper.

_____, and Jone-lin Wang, forthcoming, "Seasonality, Differential Access and Interlinking of Labor and Credit," *Journal of Development Studies.*

Davis, Lance E., Robert E. Gallman and Teresa Hutchins, 1985, "Technical Change, the Capital Stock and Productivity Increase: A Whale of a Tale." Pasadena: California Institute of Technology.

Day, Richard H., 1967. "The Economics of Technological Change and the Demise of the Sharecropper," *American Economic Review* 57 (June): 427-449.

DeRoover, Raymond, 1948, *Money, Banking and Credit in Medieval Bruges.* Cambridge, Mass.: Medieval Academy of America.

DeVany, Arthur and Nicolas Sanchez, 1977, "Property Rights Uncertainty, and Fertility: An Analysis of the Effect of Land Reform on Fertility in Rural Mexico," *Weltwirtschaftliches Archiv* 113:741-764.

Dennen, R. Taylor, 1976, "Cattlemen's Associations and Property Rights in Land in the American West," *Explorations in Economic History* 13: 423-436.

Doeringer, Peter B., Philip I. Moss and David G. Terkla, 1986, "Capitalism and Kinship: Do Institutions Matter in the Labor Market?" *Industrial and Labor Relations Review* 40 (October): 48-60.

Dow, Gregory K., 1987, "The Function of Authority in Transaction Cost Economics," *Journal of Economic Behavior and Organization* 8 (March): 13-38.

Epstein, T.S., 1962, *Economic Development and Social Change in South India.* Manchester: University of Manchester Press.

_____, 1967, "Productive Efficiency and Customary Systems of Rewards in Rural South India," in R. Firth, ed., *Themes in Economic Anthropology.* London: Tavistock.

Eswaran, Mukesh and Ashok Kotwal, 1985a, "A Theory of Two-Tier Labor Markets in Agrarian Economies," *American Economic Review* 75 (March): 162-177.

_____, 1985b, "A Theory of Contractual Structure in Agriculture," *American Economic Review* 75 (June): 352-367.

_____, 1985c, "Why are Capitalists the Bosses?" Vancouver: University of British Columbia.

Fama, Eugene and Michael C. Jensen, 1983, "Separation of Ownership and Control," *Journal of Law and Economics* 26 (June): 301-326.

Feeny, David, 1982, *The Political Economy of Productivity.* Vancouver: University of British Columbia Press.

_____, 1983, "The Moral or the Rational Peasant? Competing Hypotheses of Collective Action," *Journal of Asian Studies*, 42 (August): 769-789.

Field, Alexander James, 1981, "The Problem with Neoclassical Institutional Economics: A Critique with Speical Reference to the North/Thomas Model of Pre-1500 Europe," *Explorations in Economic History* 18: 174-198.

Finkler, Kaja, 1980, "Agrarian Reform and Economic Development: When is a Landlord a Client and a Sharecropper his Patron?" in P. Bartlett, ed., *Agricultural Decision Making: Anthropological Contributions to Rural Development*. New York: Academic Press.

Forbes, Kevin F., 1986, "Limited Liability and the Development of the Business Corporation," *Journal of Law, Economics and Organization* 2 (Spring): 163-177.

Fraser, Thomas M., Jr., 1966, *Fishermen of South Thailand: The Malay Villagers*. New York: Holt, Rinehard and Winston.

Ganshof, F.L. and A. Verhulst, 1966, "Medieval Agrarian Society in its Prime: France, the Low Countries and Western Germany," in M.M. Postan, ed., *The Cambridge Economic History of Europe* vol. 1: Ch. 7, 291-339.

Greenwald, Bruce C. and Robert R. Glasspiegel, 1983, "Adverse Selection in the Market for Slaves: New Orleans, 1830-1860," *Quarterly Journal of Economics* 97 (August): 479-499.

Grossman, Sanford and Oliver Hart, 1983, "An Analysis of the Principal Agent Problem," *Econometrica* 51: 7-45.

Hallagan, William S., 1978, "Share Contracting for California Gold," *Explorations in Economic History* 15: 196-210.

Han, Sang-Bok, 1972, "Socio-economic Organization and Change in Korean Fishing Villages: A Comparative Study of Three Fishing Communities," Unpublished Ph.D. Thesis, Michgan State University, Department of Anthropology.

Harris, Milton and Artur Raviv, 1978, "Some Results on Incentive Contracts with Application to Education and Employment, Health Insurance and Law Enforcement," *American Economic Review* 68: 20-30.

_____, 1979, "Optimal Incentive Contracts with Imperfect Information," *Journal of Economic Theory* 20: 231-259.

Hayami, Yujiro, 1971, "Elements of Induced Innovation: A Historical Perspective for the Green Revolution," *Explorations in Economic History* 8, 445-472.

_____, and M. Kikuchi, 1982, *Asian Village Economy at the Crossroads*. Baltimore: Johns Hopkins University Press.

_____, and Vernon W. Ruttan, 1985, *Agricultural Development: An International Perspective*. Baltimore: Johns Hopkins University Press.

Heston, Alan, H. Hasnain, S.Z. Hussain and R.N. Khan, 1985, "The Economics of Camel Transport in Pakistan," *Economic Development and Cultural Change* 34 (October): 121-141.

Higgs, John, 1974, "Patterns of Farm Rental in the Georgia Cotton Belt, 1880-1900," *Journal of Economic History* 34 (June): 468-482.

International Labour Office, 1952, *Conditions of Work in the Fishing Industry*. Geneva: International Labour Office.

Jaffe, D. and T. Russell, 1976, "Imperfect Information, Uncertainty and Credit Rationing," *Quarterly Journal of Economics* 90: 651-666.

Jaynes, Gerald David, 1982, "Production and Distribution in Agrarian Economies," *Oxford Economic Papers* 34 (July): 346-367.

Jensen, M.C. and W.H. Meckling, 1976, "Theory of the Firm: Managerial Behavior, Agency Costs and Ownership Structure," *Journal of Financial Economics* 3 (October), 305-360.

Johnson, D.G., 1950, "Resource Allocation Under Share Contracts," *Journal of Political Economy* 58 (April): 111-123.

Jones, Phillip, 1966, "Medieval Society in its Prime: Italy," in M.M. Postan, ed., *The Cambridge Economic History of Europe*, vol. 1: 340-431.

Klein, Julius, 1920, *The Mesta: A Study in Spanish Economic History 1273-1836*. Cambridge: Harvard University.

Klein, Benjamin, R.A. Crawford and Armen A. Alchian, 1978, "Vertical Integration Appropriable Rents and the Competitive Contracting Process," *Journal of Law and Economics* 21 (October): 297-326.

Kotwal, A., 1985, "The Role of Consumption Credit in Agricultural Tenancy," *Journal of Development Economics* 18 (August): 273-294.

Kuran, Timur, 1989, "The Craft Guilds of Tunis and their Amins: A Study in Institutional Atrophy." Ch. 8, this volume.

Landa, Janet T., 1981, "A Theory of the Ethnically Homogeneous Middlemen Group: An Institutional Alternative to Contract Law," *Journal of Legal Studies* 10 (June), 349-362.

Leijonhufvud, Axel, 1986, "Capitalism and the Factory System," in Richard N. Langlois, ed., *Economics as a Process: Essays in the New Institutional Economics*. Cambridge: Cambridge University Press: 203-223.

Levy, David T., 1985, "The Transaction Cost Approach to Vertical Integration," *Review of Economics and Statistics* 67 (August): 420-426.

Lewis, Tracy R., 1980, "Bonuses and Penalties in Incentive Contracting," *Bell Journal of Economics* 11: 292-301.

_____, 1984, "Reputation and Contractual Performance in Long Term Projects," Vancouver: University of British Columbia Discussion Paper #84-23.

Libecap, Gary D., 1986, "Government Policies on Property Rights to Land: U.S. Implications for Agricultural Development in Mexico," *Agricultural History*, 1986: 32-49.

_____, and Steven N. Wiggins, 1984, "Contractual Responses to the Common Pool," *American Economic Review* 74 (March):87-98.

Lopez, Robert S. and Irving W. Raymond, 1956, *Medieval Trade in the Mediterranean World*. New York: Columbia University Press.

Lucas, Robert E.B., 1979, "Sharing, Monitoring, and Incentives: Marshallian Misallocation Reassessed," *Journal of Political Economy* 87 (June): 501-521.

Lundahl, Mats, 1980, "Population Pressure and Agrarian Property Rights in Haiti," *Statsvetenskaplig Tidshrift (Swedish Journal of Political Science)* 5: 275-283.

_____, 1982, "Intergenerational Sharecropping in Haiti: A Reinterpretation of the Murray Thesis," *Journal of Economic Studies* 9, no. 1: 35-43.

Marx, Karl, 1905, *Capital*. Chicago: Modern Library Edition.

Matthews, R. C. O., 1986, "The Economics of Institutions and the Sources of Growth," *Economic Journal* 96 (December): 903-918.

McGoodwin, James R., 1980a, "Society, Economy and Shark-fishing Crews in Rural Northwest Mexico," in Alexander Spoehr, ed., *Maritime Adaptations*. Pittsburgh: University of Pittsburgh Press, 63-77.

_____, 1980b, "Pelagic Shark Fishing in Rural Mexico: A Context for Cooperative Action," in Alexander Spoehr, ed., *Maritime Adaptations*. Pittsburgh: University of Pittsburgh Press, 79-90.

Myrdal, Gunnar, 1957, *Economic Theory and Underdeveloped Regions*. London: Duckworth.

_____, 1968, *Asian Drama: An Inquiry into the Poverty of Nations*. New York: Twentieth Century Fund.

Nabli, Mustapha K. and Jeffrey B. Nugent, 1988, "Collective Action, Institutions and Development," Ch. 3, this volume.

Nalebuff, Barry J. and Joseph E. Stiglitz, 1983, "Prices and Incentives: Towards a General Theory of Compensation and Competition," *Bell Journal of Economics* 14: 21-43.

Nef, J.U., 1934, "The Progress of Technology and the Growth of Large-scale Industry in Great Britain, 1540-1640," *Economic History Review* 5(1): 3-24.

Nelson, Richard R. and Sidney G. Winter, 1982, *An Evolutionary Theory of Economic Change*. Cambridge: Harvard University Press.

Newbery, David M.G., 1974, "Cropsharing Tenancy in Agriculture: Comment," *American Economic Review* 64, no. 6 (December): 1060-1066.

_____, 1977, "Risk Sharing, Sharecropping and Uncertain Labor Markets," *Review of Economic Studies* 44, (October): 586-594.

_____, and Joseph E. Stiglitz, 1979, "Sharecropping, Risk Sharing and the Importance of Imperfect Information," in *Risk, Uncertainty and Agricultural Development*. J.A. Roumasset, J.M. Boussard and I.J. Singh, edd., SEARCH, Agricultural Development Council.

Norr, Kathleen Fordham, 1980, "The Organization of Coastal Fishing in Tamilnadu," in Alexander Spoehr, ed., *Maritime Adaptations*. Pittsburgh: University of Pittsburgh Press, 113-127.

North, Douglass C., 1981, *Structure and Change in Economic History*. New York: W.W. Norton.

_____, 1986a, "The New Institutional Economics," *Journal of Institutional and Theoretical Economics* 142 (1): 230-237.

_____, 1986b, "Institutions and Economic Growth: An Historical Introduction," paper presented to the Cornell University Conference on the Role of Institutions in Economic Development, (November 14-15, 1986).

_____, and John Wallis, forthcoming, "Measuring the Transaction Sector in the American Economy, 1870-1970," Stanley Engerman and Robert Gallman, eds., *Long-term Factors in American Economic Growth*. Chicago: University of Chicago Press.

Nugent, Jeffrey B., 1982, "The EEC as a Model for Regional Integration Among Developing Countries: Does it Fit?" *Finance and Industry*, (November): 7-20.

_____, 1984a, *Inter-Arab Joint Ventures in Western Asia: An Analysis of Their Actual and Potential Contributions to Development and Regional Cooperation.* United Nations, Economic Commission for Western Asia.

_____, 1984b, "Upheavals in International Political Relations and the Survival Capabilities of Inter Arab Joint Ventures," *Public Enterprise* 4, no. 3: 11-22.

_____, 1985, "The Old-Age Security Motive for Fertility," *Population and Development Review* 11, no. 1 (March): 75-97.

_____, 1986, "Arab Multinationals: Problems, Potential and policies," in Khushi M. Khan, ed. *Third World Multinationals: New Actors in the International Economy.* London: Frances Pinter.

Otsuka, Keijiro and Yujiro Hayami, 1986, "Theories of Share Tenancy: A Critical Survey," *Economic Development and Cultural Change* 37 (October): 31-68.

_____, Masao Kikuchi, and Yujiro Hayami, 1986, "Community and Market in Contract Choice: The Jeepney in the Philippines." *Economic Development and Cultural Change* 34 (January): 279-298.

_____, and Naoki Murakami, 1987, "Incentives, Enforcement and Contract Choice: Taxicabs in Kyoto," mimeo.

Pagano, Ugo, 1985, *Work and Leisure in Economic Theory.* Oxford and New York: Basil Blackwell.

Pant, Chandrasekhar, 1983, "Tenancy and Family Resources: A Model and Some Empirical Analysis," *Journal of Development Economics* 12 (Feb./April): 27-40.

Pauly, Mark V., 1986, "Taxation, Health Insurance and Market Failure in the Medical Economy," *Journal of Economic Literature* 24 (June) 629-675.

Platteau, Jean-Philippe and A. A. Abraham, 1987, "An Inquiry into Quasi-Credit Contracts: The Role of Reciprocal Credit and Interlinked Deals in Small-Scale Fishing Communities," *Journal of Development Studies* 23 No. 4.

Pollak, Robert A., 1985, "A Transaction Costs Approach to Families and Households," *Journal of Economic Literature* 23 (June): 581-608.

Posner, Richard A., 1980, "A Theory of Primitive Society with Special Reference to Law," *Journal of Law and Economics,* 1, (April): 1-53.

Quibria, M.G. and S. Rashid, 1984, "The Puzzle of Sharecropping: A Survey of Theories," *World Development* 12 (February): 103-114.

_____, 1986, "Sharecropping in Dual Agrarian Economies: A Synthesis," *Oxford Economic Papers.*

Reid, Joseph, 1976, "Sharecropping as an Understandable Market Response: The Post-Bellum South," *Journal of Economic History* 33: 106-130.

_____, 1976, "Sharecropping and Agricultural Uncertainty," *Economic Development and Cultural Change* 24: 549-576.

_____, 1979, "Sharecropping and Tenancy in American History," in Roumasset, Boussard and Singh, edd., *Risk, Uncertainty and Agricultural Development.* New York: Agriculture Development Council, Chapter 16.

Robertson, A.F., 1987, *The Dynamics of Productive Relationships: African Share Contracts in Comparative Perspective.* Cambridge: Cambridge University Press.

Rogerson, William P., 1983, "Repeated Moral Hazard,"

Rosenzweig, Mark R. and Kenneth I. Wolpin, 1986, "Specific Experience, Household Structure and Intergenerational Transfers: Farm Family Land

and Labor Arrangements in Developing Countries," *Quarterly Journal of Economics* 100: 961-988.

Ross, Stephen, 1973, "The Economic Theory of Agency: The Principal's Problem," *American Economic Review* 63: 134-139.

Roumasset, J., 1976, *Rice and Risk: Decision-Making Among Low Income Farmers.* The Netherlands: North-Holland, chapter 4.

_____, and Marilou Uy, 1981, "Piece Rates, Time Rates, and Teams," *Journal of Economic Behavior and Organization* 1: 343-360.

Roumasset, J. and Marilou Uy, 1984, "Specialization and Incentives in Agricultural Contracts." Mimeo.

Rudra, Ashok, 1982, *Indian Agricultural Economics: Myths and Realities.* New Delhi: Allied Publishers, Part I, Ch. 6.

Runge, Carlisle Ford, 1986, "Common Property and Collective Action in Economic Development," *World Development,* 14: 621-632.

Russell, R., 1985, "Employee Ownership and Internal Governance," *Journal of Economic Behavior and Organization* 6: 217-241.

Ruttan, Vernon W. and Yujiro Hayami, 1984 "Toward a Theory of Induced Institutional Innovation," *Journal of Development Studies* 20 (July): 203-223.

Samuelson, Paul, 1957, "Wage and Interest: A Modern Dissection of Marxian Economic Models," *American Economic Review* 47 (December): 884-912.

Sappington, David, 1983, "Limited Liability Contracts between Principal and Agent," *Journal of Economic Theory* 29: 1-21.

_____, and Joel Demski, 1983, "Single- vs. Multi-Agent Control with Private Information: A Comparison of Findings,"

Shaban, Radwan Ali, 1988, "Testing between Competing Models of Sharecropping." *Journal of Political Economy* 96:

Shetty, Sudhir, 1985, "Collateral in Loan Market Equilibrium." Durham: Duke University.

Spulber, Daniel, 1987, *Markets and Regulation.* Los Angeles: University of Southern California.

Stiglitz, Joseph, 1974, "Incentives and Risk Sharing in Sharecropping," *The Review of Economic Studies* 41 (April): 219-255.

_____, and Andrew Weiss, 1981, "Credit Rationing in Markets with Imperfect Information," *American Economic Review* :393-411.

Stuchlik, Milan, 1976, *Life on a Half Share: Mechanisms of Social Recruitment Among the Mapuche of Southern Chile.* London: Hurst.

Sundrum, R. M., 1983, *Development Economics: A Framework for Analysis and Policy.* Chichester, New York: John Wiley.

Sutinen, J.G., 1979, "Fishermen's Remuneration Systems and Implications for Fisheries Development," *Scottish Journal of Political Economy* 26 (June), 147-162.

_____, 1985, "The Rational Choice of Share Leasing and Implications for Efficiency," *American Journal of Agricultural Economics* (November): 613-621.

Teece, David, 1976, *The Multinational Corporation and the Resource Cost of International Technology Transfers.* Cambridge: Ballinger.

Townsend, Robert M., 1984, "Taking Theory to History: Explaining Financial Structure and Economic Organization," Working Paper, Carnegie-Mellon University.

Truran, James A. and Roger W. Fox, "Resource Productivity of Landowners and Sharecroppers in the Cariri Region of Ceara, Brazil," *Land Economics* 55 (February): 93-107.

Turvey, Ralph, 1961, "Some Economic Features of the London Cab Trade," *Economic Journal* 71, (March): 79-92.

Udovitch, Abraham L., 1970, *Partnership and Profit in Medieval Islam.* Princeton: Princeton University Press.

Umbeck, John, 1977, "A Theory of Contract Choice and the California Gold Rush," *Journal of Law and Economics*: 421-437.

Vyas, V.S., 1970, "Tenancy in a Dynamic Setting," *Economic and Political Weekly* 5 (June): A73-80.

Waswo, Anne, 1977, *Japanese Landlords: The Decline of a Rural Elite.* Berkeley: University of California Press.

Weitzman, Martin L., 1985, "The Simple Macroeconomics of Profit Shares," *American Economic Review* 75 (December): 937-953.

Wells, Miriam J., 1984, "The Resurgence of Sharecropping: Historical Anomaly or Political Strategy?" *American Journal of Sociology* 90, No. 1, 1-29.

Williamson, Oliver E., 1975, *Markets and Hierarchies: Analysis and Antitrust Implications.* New York: Free Press.

_____, 1981, "The Modern Corporation: Origins, Evolution, Attributes," *Journal of Economic Literature* 19 (December): 1537-1568.

_____, 1985, *The Economic Institutions of Capitalism.* New York: Free Press.

Yotopoulos, Pan A. and Jeffrey B. Nugent, 1976, *Economics of Development: Empirical Investigations.* New York: Harper and Row.

Zoeteweij, H., 1956, "Fishermen's Remuneration," in Ralph Turvey and Jack Wiseman, edd., *The Economics of Fisheries.* Rome: FAO, 18-41.

80

Chapter 3

COLLECTIVE ACTION, INSTITUTIONS
AND DEVELOPMENT*

Mustapha K. Nabli and Jeffrey B. Nugent

I. Introduction

In the previous chapter it has been argued that the theory of transaction and information costs can go a long way toward explaining choices among contracts and other institutional forms. Nevertheless, the theory is relatively silent on the mechanisms by which and conditions under which new rules and other institutional forms come into existence.

Enter the theory of collective action which attempts to explain the likelihood of success by a given set of individuals in undertaking activities, including the establishment of rules, which may benefit them collectively. The "flip" side of this theory is, of course, a theory of why and how collective action failures come about. Such failures derive primarily from the *"free-rider"* problem which stems from the public goods aspect of group action.

While there is virtually universal agreement on the desirability of distinguishing between private and public goods, the precise basis of such a distinction is nevertheless a matter of dispute. While some, e.g., Buchanan (1968), choose to make the distinction on the basis of the nature of the supplier of the good, i.e., whether the supplier is from the private or public sector, such a basis would hardly be of use in explaining why it is one or the other [Tulkens (1978)]. More satisfactory and common, therefore, are two criteria, namely *"joint consumability"* (or "jointness in supply"), on the one hand, as suggested by Samuelson (1954), and *"excludability"* which was emphasized by Musgrave (1959) and subsequently by Olson (1965). A good is "jointly consumable" if the same unit of the good can be consumed by a second, third or fourth consumer without reducing the utility that the first consumer derives from it. A good is "excludable" if for any given group its use is made available to some members of the group but can be withheld from other members.

*The authors gratefully acknowledge the useful comments of Daniel Bromley, David Feeny, Bruce Herrick, Timur Kuran, Lynne Markus, Dave Waterman and Ulrich Witt. Nabli also acknowledges support from the Université Laval, Quebec, Canada, where part of this research was carried out.

The dichotomy between public and private goods can be implemented with the first criterion by identifying jointly consumable goods as public goods and non-jointly consumable goods as private goods or with the second criterion by identifying non-excludable goods as public goods and excludable ones as private goods. Some authors, e.g. Head (1962), Chamberlin (1974) and Ostrom (1987), argue that the two criteria should be used together, i.e. a good would be public only if it were both "jointly consumable" and "non-excludable." In our opinion, however, and following Blumel, Pethig and von dem Hagen (1986), since excludability is more typically the result of exclusion technology which in turn depends very much on the institutional setup, it is less useful than joint consumability as a criterion for defining public goods and forming the basis of an analysis of institutions. Nevertheless, even if one or even both criteria may in practice not be entirely institution-free, they can be of use in distinguishing different types of problems and issues. They can, moreover, be applied either to physical goods or to intangible ones like tax reductions and subsidies.

In practice, however, no matter which criterion is used, and to which class of goods it is applied, the extent to which any particular good or service can be classified as public or private becomes a matter of degree. In the case of joint consumability, it is a matter of the degree to which crowding or congestion is likely. In the case of "excludability", it is a matter of the relative importance of the exclusion costs. Furthermore, it becomes obvious that there are in reality very few *pure* public goods from either or both perspectives. National defense, contagious disease eradication programs and general tax reductions are frequently cited (and apparently relatively rare) examples of goods satisfying both criteria since they are not subject to congestion and the costs of exluding one member of the group from the benefits are *very* high. Hamburgers, wine and clothing are of course examples of pure private goods since they are not jointly consumable and are excludable at low cost.

These two polar cases are identified in cells A1B1 and A3B3, respectively, of Figure 3-1. The remaining cells in the figure clearly demonstrate that there are many other non-polar types of goods. For example, there is cell A1B3 containing goods, such as fire protection in large cities, computer programs and old-age pension systems, which are jointly consumable without congestion but which have relatively moderate costs of exclusion. Then, there are goods like the open access natural resources such as fish in the ocean and minerals on the ocean floor which are non-jointly consumable but, because exclusion costs are very high, are placed in cell A3B1. In between the pure public goods of A1B1 and the open access natural resources of A3B1 are the common property resources of cell A2B1 which are subject to congestion. Examples of this class include grazing land, river or canal transport, the justice system, city streets, import quotas and cartel pricing. Another important class of goods are the "club goods" or "local public goods" of cell A2B3 which are jointly consumable, subject to congestion and low exclusion costs such as gymns, parking lots, swimming pools, airliners, internally distributed quotas, bridges and tunnels. Other intermediate cases are shown in Column B2.

Figure 3-1
Typology of Goods

Criterion B Excludability Criterion A Jointness in Consumption	B1 Non-Excludable (Infinite Exclusion Cost)	B2 Excludable at Moderate Cost	B3 Excludable at Negligable Cost
A1 Jointly Consumable No Congestion	Pure Public Goods National defense Contagious disease eradication General Tax reduction Tariffs with competition Farm subsidies	Public Goods with Moderate Exclusion Costs Cable TV Public demonstrations Tariffs on differentiated products	Public Goods With Exclusion Fire protection in large cities Books Computer programs Old age pension systems
A2 Jointly Consumable with Congestion	Common Property Resources Open range grazing land Large river or canal transport City streets Cartel pricing	Mixed Public and Club Goods Schools and Colleges Beaches Toll highways Street lights Farm credit system	Club Goods/Local Public Goods Gyms Parking lots Toll bridges and tunnels Swimming pools Internally distributed quotas
A3 Not Jointly Consumable (Infinite Congestion)	Open Access Natural Resources Fish in the ocean Minerals on the ocean floor	Closed Access Natural Resources Mountain spring water Irrigation canals Health clinic services	Pure Private Goods Hamburgers Wine Clothing

Because the actual character of the various goods mentioned in Figure 3-1 may vary according to environmental and institutional circumstances, the reader may quarrel with the placement of some of these goods, especially those in the A2 row in which the costs of exclusion may well vary significantly from case to case. Nevertheless, despite ambiguities in its practical application, the typology is in principle useful. Different classes of goods are subject to quite different types of problems. Most of economics, of course, deals with the pure private goods of cell A3B3. The theory of clubs developed by Buchanan (1965) and others, which was recently surveyed by Sandler and Tschirhart (1980), deals with the goods of cell A2B3 and to some extent those which spill over into cell A2B2. A literature on open access natural resources has arisen to deal with the goods of cell A3B1 and those which also spill over into cell A2B2.

The theory of collective action, which originated with Olson (1965) and was extended by G. Hardin (1968), R. Hardin (1982) and others, deals primarily with the goods of cells A1B1 and A2B1. Since these goods, whether congestible or not, share the characteristics of being jointly consumable and non- excludable, they also share the property that their existence gives rise to incentives for group members to "free-ride."

The incentive to free-ride arises with jointly consumable, non-excludable goods since, because of non-excludability, the benefits of collective action accrue even without participation in the costs of the production of the good. The more that group members are tempted to free-ride, quite naturally, the lower is the likelihood that the good will be produced or maintained, giving rise to collective action failure. At the same time, due to joint-consumability and heterogeneous preferences for public goods, selfish individuals have an incentive to deliberately reveal false preferences, thereby rendering the social benefits difficult to evaluate [Stiglitz (1986, Ch. 6), Kuran (1987a, 1987b, 1988)]. Likewise, they may deliberately under- or over-state the costs [Hirschman (1967)].

Dynamic elements can also play an important role in explaining collective action failures and institutional rigidities. Individual decisions to participate or not may not be independent of each other. Hence, concepts like bandwagon effects [Leibenstein (1950)] and critical mass [Granovetter (1978)] may be relevant, and the identities of those making early decisions to participate can influence the subsequent decisions of others [Rogers (1983)].

The purpose of this chapter is to review the rather diverse principles relevant to the analysis of collective actions, and especially to examine their usefulness in the theory and policy of economic development. However, before beginning on that task, it may be useful to reflect briefly on the relationship between the theory of collective action and that of public goods and on the impact on public economics in general.

Both the theory of public goods, recently surveyed by Blumel, Pethig and von dem Hagen (1986), and the theory of collective action address the same basic issues relating to the provision of public goods and in particular the free-rider problem. The two strands of literature have developed in parallel, but they differ in both emphasis and scope.

First, with respect to the nature of the goods considered, the theory of public goods has been primarily concerned with the physical goods mentioned in Figure 3-1 such as national defense, highways, beaches, bridges and the like. On the other hand, the theory of collective action has given consideration to the intangibles of Figure 3-1 such as tax reductions, tariffs, subsidies, cartel pricing, and import quotas.

Second, whereas the theory of public goods has been relatively abstract and axiomatic, and relied heavily on general equilibrium analysis, the theory of collective action has been practical, partial equilibrium in character and more dependent on empirical case studies and laboratory experiments.

Third, in the theory of public goods two main institutional vehicles have been considered for the production and distribution of public goods. One is the system of decentralized, independent voluntary individual actions. The other is that of a central decision maker, whose task it is to design a preference revelation mechanism for extracting preferences and the willingness to pay from the individual agents. In neither alternative approach to public goods provision is it common practice to allow for interaction among the individual agents. Even when cooperative solutions to the problem are considered, the rules for such cooperation are not explained.[1] On the other hand, in the theory of collective action center stage is devoted to the coordination of individual actions, the interactions among individuals and groups and the costs of organization are made explicit. As a result, the rules and institutions used in attaining coordination are endogeneous to the analysis. Since in the theory of collective action groups can organize themselves even in the absence of a central decision maker, collective action theory is more capable of explaining institutions than the theory of public goods.

Fourth, the theory of collective action has generated and drawn upon

---

[1] Tulkens (1978) has provided an institutional interpretation of the dynamic processes for implementing solutions to economies with public goods. These institutions, are however, exogenously designed and normative in character. Tulkens also claims that they can be given a positive interpretation. Nevertheless, inasmuch as his claim is based on the postulate of collective rationality, which is indeed very much at issue in collective action theory, the claim is not well-founded.

contributions from other disciplines (especially political science and sociology) to a greater extent than the theory of public goods.

Prior to the development of collective action theory in the early 1960s, the general presumption was that, once the common interests of a given set of individuals could be identified, individual and group rationality could be counted upon to assure that such groups would voluntarily act to attain their common objectives. Governmental policies were seen as the outcome of the interplay of many such groups in attempting to achieve their common, as well as conflicting objectives [Truman (1958)]. Presumably, success in collective action could be distinguished from failure by applying the well-developed and highly operational theory of social benefit-cost analysis. If the aggregate social benefits exceed the aggregate social costs of any public good or institutional change, it would seem to imply that, even if distributional inequities arise, the gainers should be able to compensate the losers so as to allow the public good or institutional change to be undertaken.

It was only subsequently that Mancur Olson in the first of his famous books, *The Logic of Collective Action* [Olson (1965)], and Garrett Hardin in his widely read article on the tragedy of the commons [G. Hardin (1968)] called attention to the "free rider" problem[2] which makes success in collective action so difficult to achieve. As mentioned above, preference falsification and concealment as well as interdependent expectations further compound the problem. As a result, optimism about success in collective action has quickly yielded to extreme pessimism [Ostrom (1987)]. Examples now abound in the literature of situations in which individual agents understate the benefits to avoid their share of the costs, potential compensation does not take place, detrimentally affected groups are able to resist socially beneficial collective actions, and even changes which would benefit everyone are not undertaken [Akerlof (1976), Basu, Jones and Schlicht (1987)].

Nevertheless, despite its considerable influence on public economics and indeed even other disciplines like international relations, the theory of collective action has yet to have a very substantial impact on development economics. As a result, one of our purposes in the present chapter and in all of Part III of the volume is to suggest ways in which the theory, perhaps with appropriate modifications, can be applied to LDCs and their development problems.

The remaining portion of the chapter is organized as follows: Section II introduces several examples of cooperation problems, each with its incentives

---

[2] As McMillan (1979) has shown, the origin of the free-rider problem, however, can be traced back further, at least to David Hume in 1740.

to free-ride, and then identifies different types of solutions to the problem of
free-riding. Section III deals with the most common collective action problem, namely the emergence of interest groups and organizations. Section IV
treats the relationship between interest groups and the state. Section V discusses collective action problems arising in the context of common property
resources. The relationships among collective action, institutional change
and development are treated in Section VI. The chapter is concluded with an
overall assessment of the existing theory of collective action in Section VII.

II. Cooperation and Free-riding

At the heart of collective action problems are those of coordination and
cooperation which often turn out to be more difficult to overcome than at first
might be supposed. Following the lead of Ullman-Margalit (1977), Schotter
(1981, 1986) and other researchers from various disciplines, these problems
can be characterized with some simple game-theoretic examples.

Figure 3-2
Illustration of the Coordination Problem:
Matrix of Payoffs to Two Individuals of
Driving on Different Sides of the Road

Individual A \ Individual B	Drive on Left	Drive on Right
Drive on Left	7,3	0,0
Drive on Right	0,0	2,8

We begin with the "coordination" problem which arises when for any two
players, A and B, each of whom has two available strategies, like "drive on
the left" or "drive on the right", there exists a matrix of payoffs (expressed
in some relevant unit) to A and B, respectively, like that shown in Figure
3-2. Each cell of that matrix consists of the sequence of payoffs, first that
to player A, and followed by that to B. Notice that there are two different
"equilibrium" strategies, "drive on the left" and "drive on the right." When
each player is in his preferred position, he has no incentive to change either

his own or the other player's strategy. Yet the two equilibria are inconsistent with one another. Since it yields a payoff of 7 (as opposed to one of 2), individual A would prefer the "drive on the left" equilibrium while individual B would prefer "drive on the right" since it yields a payoff of 8 (as opposed to 3). While both solutions are superior to the non-coordination solutions which yield zero benefits, neither rule is socially more efficient than the other since the sum of the payoffs to the two players of the game is the same (10) for both equilibrium solutions. Hence, while the choice between rules, such as "everyone must drive on the right" as in the U.S., much of Europe and most LDCs and "everyone must drive on the left" as in the U.K., India and until recently Sweden, is an arbitrary one, it must be made. The implementation of a coordination rule is of course rendered more difficult by the fact that neither solution may be considered "fair" to the group favoring the other inasmuch as adjustment costs will be involved and existing capital equipment may be inefficient in the wrong environment. For example, this would be the case with automobiles with steering wheels on the right side of the car in countries where one must drive on the right side of the road. With such technology, switching costs also tend to render inefficient compromise solutions such as rotating the rules from period to period. Applications of Figure 3-2 to the choice of an official language among several tribal or regional languages and that among incompatible educational, judicial, exchange rate or telecommunications systems would be equally straight-forward.

Figure 3-3
Illustration of the Prisoners' Dilemma:
Matrix of Payoffs to Prisoners A and B
With and Without Cooperation

A's Action \ B's Action	Cooperate	Not Cooperate
Cooperate	1,1	-2,2
Not Cooperate	2,-2	-1,-1

Likewise, the obstacles to cooperation identified in the "prisoners' dilemma" problem can be illustrated by Figure 3-3 which shows the payoffs for two individual prisoners, A and B, each of whom is faced with two alternative strategies, namely to cooperate (e.g., by providing the other with a suitable alibi) or not to cooperate or "free-ride" (by implicating the other). Since the two strategies are independently chosen, there are four possible outcomes, given by the four A,B sequences. If both cooperate, as indicated by the payoff 1,1 both parties have a positive payoff of 1, and when neither cooperates, they both suffer losses of 1, i.e., the payoffs are -1,-1. If A cooperates but B does not, the payoffs are -2,2 indicating that A suffers a loss of 2 and B a gain of 2, and vice-versa when B cooperates but A does not. These payoffs reveal that there is a strong disincentive to cooperate. Indeed, non-cooperation or "free-riding" is the dominant strategy for both A and B since, for each player in the game, the payoff to "not cooperate" is greater than that to "cooperate" irrespective of the strategy of the other player. Even if communciation between prisoners A and B should result in an agreement to cooperate, each has the incentive to break it. Hence, non- cooperation on the parts of both A and B is a Pareto-inferior equilibrium.

Figure 3-4
Illustration of a Collective Action Game:
Matrix of Payoffs in Dollars With and Without Cooperation

| | Group exclusive of Individual A | |
Individual A	Contribute	Not Contribute
Contribute	1,1	-0.8,0.2
Not Contribute	1.8,0.8	0,0

The game-theoretic formulation of the prisoners' dilemma problem can be made even more directly applicable to typical collective action problems by conceiving of the payoff matrix in terms of net benefits of a public good (the gross benefit minus the cost) and by replacing the entries of player B by the per capita net benefits accruing to a group (e.g., of 10 persons) as a whole less those to individual A as in Figure 3-4. Suppose that the required contribution is $1 and the gross benefit of the public good to any individual if all members contribute is \$2, implying that the net benefit to individual A and to each other member of the group is \$1. Assume also that the effect of the failure to contribute is to reduce the gross benefit of the public good proportionately. Hence, if individual A does not contribute but the other nine individuals do, the respective payoffs are 1.8 to A and 0.8 to each of the other members of the group. If everyone else does not contribute but A does, the net benefit payoffs would be -0.8 and 0.2, respectively. As Russell Hardin (1982, p. 26-28) has proved, solutions to prisoners' dilemma problems also provide solutions to collective action games, allowing the results of prisoners' dilemma analysis to be transfered to the context of collective action problems.

These simple binary choice versions of collective action problems suggest that non-cooperation tends to result from individual optimizing behavior. In the context of public goods with continuous units of quantity, such goods would be either not provided at all or under-provided. In such situations frequently it has been suggested that solutions require governments to design and enforce them. Besides posing the question of how the government itself comes into existence and gains general acceptance, this approach brings out another aspect of the free-rider problem, namely the problem of (truthful) preference revelation. In order to achieve the optimal supply of the public good the government has to establish and implement a mechanism that assures that the individual agents reveal their true preferences for the collective good. This is an integral aspect of the important task of institutional design.[3]

In the alternative approach to the free-rider problem, i.e., collective action without government intervention, solutions are generated endogenously, frequently by changing the nature of the game. For example, while in the above examples it was assumed that the individual agents faced once-and-for-all choices between one or the other of two actions, if additional alternatives are introduced or the nature of the problem is adjusted, the outcomes may be tilted in favor of cooperation. For instance, in situations where the simple games illustrated above are repeated indefinitely, period after period, and each party is able in subsequent periods to observe the action of the other in earlier periods, free-riding may no longer be optimal for the individual agent [Taylor (1976)]. In such cases, because one individual's free-riding is observable by others and behavior in subsequent periods can be adjusted accordingly, free-riding becomes costly, making cooperative outcomes to collective action problems more likely.

---

[3] For an interesting and rare example of an attempt at optimal institutional design in the context of rural credit cooperatives in LDCs see Braverman and Guasch (forthcoming).

But, of course, in practice, the relevant parties are not likely to live indefinitely or otherwise be guaranteed of the indefinite repetition of the game. Hence, the expected number of repeats is not infinite. Once the number of expected repeats is known and finite, the dominant strategy for the last period again becomes "not cooperate" or "not contribute". Once the players know in the next-to-last period that non-cooperation will prevail in the last period, non-cooperation becomes the dominant strategy in the next-to-last period and so on until non-cooperation becomes the dominant strategy for all periods.

Nevertheless, both experimental [Axelrod (1984), Marwell and Ames (1979, 1980, 1981), Oliver (1984) and Oliver, Marwell and Teixeira (1985)] and theoretical [Kreps, Milgrom, Roberts and Wilson (1982)] studies have shown that the doom of non-cooperative outcomes can be avoided in finitely repeated game situations wherein each party is uncertain about how long the game will continue and about what the other will do. Specifically, a suspicion by one party that the other may practice a "tit-for-tat" strategy induces the other to adopt the same and for both to cooperate until the other does not. The "tit-for-tat" solution is also known as "matching behavior" [Guttman (1978a)].

Another type of solution to such problems is by resort to "extra-rational" motivations wherein the coordination, cooperation or other forms of collective action can succeed without the benefits necessarily exceeding the costs of participation. If members of a collective action group accept the consequences as fair, morally right or providing self-fulfillment, even if the action does not benefit them, they may be willing to participate, thereby making it possible to achieve more collective action than would be expected on more objective and economically rational grounds. However, based on a substantial survey of what is known about the influence of such "extra-rational" considerations on collective action, R. Hardin (1982, ch. 6) concluded that there is little reason to believe that these motivations would be very effective.[4]

Especially in the context of indefinitely repeated games, the prospects for cooperative solutions can be substantially enhanced through the adoption of appropriate social norms. For example, the group of whom the individual agents are members may come to consider cooperation as the "right thing to do". In other words, cooperation becomes a social norm whose acceptance

---

[4]Note also that the conditions conducive to the relevance and importance of "extra-rational" motivation in solving such problems that are identified by Hardin overlap very considerably with those of Olson identified in section III below, implying that the possible use of extra-rational motivation does little to lighten the requirements for success in collective action.

by group members may be encouraged by the practice of social sanctions. The role of such sanctions is to affect the payoffs in such a way as to induce cooperation [Ullmann-Margalit (1977)]. In a similar vein, Brennan and Buchanan (1985) argue that an individual's uncertainty about the effects of the alternative social choices on his own position makes it easier to obtain cooperation and the adoption of rules constraining behavior in such a way as to be of informational value in making future decisions.

Another example of how social norms can help solve one collective action problem but at the same time at the cost of creating another one is the case of old-age pension and disability insurance systems. Given the vulnerability of the relevant participants in such systems to adverse selection and moral hazard reviewed in Chapter 2 above, commercial and governmental means of providing such insurance are not likely to exist, at least in rural areas of LDCs. The existence of a behavioral norm like "children should take care of their parents in their old age" is likely to enhance the likelihood and efficiency of family-based old age and disability insurance systems. The behavioral norm is itself a public good in the sense that, while it provides a solution to a collective action problem and thereby is likely to enhance the collective welfare of any community that adopts it, individual members of the group cannot be easily excluded from the benefits and they are in principle not subject to congestion. As such, both the creation and maintenance of the social norm are rendered difficult by the fact that the norm is subject to free-riding. As such, the establishment of the norm may require considerable time, experience in association and be subject to various kinds of rigidities that tend to maintain the status quo no matter how unfavorable that might be to cooperation or welfare.

The examples of the creation of social norms which help overcome the undersupply of public goods illustrate that in reality there is a hierarchy of public goods problems each involving collective action. To overcome one collective action problem, one may need a social norm which requires the solution of another collective action problem. Since some problems may be easier to overcome than others, on balance the resort to greater institutional hierarchy may facilitate solutions to social problems.

III. The Emergence of Interest Groups and Organizations

Perhaps the most common and straight-forward type of application of the theory of collective action outlined in Section II above, is to the emergence of interest groups and organizations.

While interest groups[5] and organizations are clearly distinguishable, not all interest groups having organizations and not all organizations being of interest groups, in fact (as we shall see), the two tend to go hand in hand. Once interest groups form, usually they develop organizations that are relatively permanent, hence justifying the application of collective action theory to both in the same section. The most important connection between interest groups and organizations is that organizations facilitate collective action on the part of interest groups by reducing start-up costs and/or long run average costs.

The main contributions in this field have been by Olson (1965, 1982) and his followers who have focused on the identification of *group characteristics* favorable to success in achieving collective action. While Olson (1965) has emphasized the use in his theoretical model of the non-excludability criterion in defining public goods, in fact as noted above most of his applied work has dealt with collective goods which are also jointly consumable and without much congestion. These are the goods discussed in Section I and located in cells A1B1 and A2B1 of Figure 3-1 which Olson refers to as "inclusive" goods and which are most vulnerable to free-riding.[6]

Olson's theoretical analysis deals primarily with a static game framework where non-cooperative solutions are dominant strategies. His contribution lies in the identification of restrictions on individual behavior and the interactions among group members that may lead to success in collective action despite the existence of the free-rider problem. In particular, Mancur Olson (1965, 1982) and his followers have argued that collective action is likely to be more feasible: (a) the smaller the group,[7] (b) the more homogeneous the origin of the group, (c) the longer the members of the group have been associated with one another or the group has been in existence, (d) the closer the social and

---

[5]Different authors have used different terms for interest groups such as "distributional coalitions." While in some cases, the different terms may have slightly different interpretations, in the subsequent discussion the terms interest groups, collective action groups and distributional coalitions are used interchangeably.

[6]There is some disagreement on this matter [Ostrom (1987)], however, since Olson's underlying theoretical microeconomic model would seem inconsistent with many of the illustrations of its use.

[7]Small size is alleged to be advantageous for collective action not only because communication among members is facilitated but also because the incentive for free-riding is diminished. However, as we shall see below, there are also reasons for believing that a "critical mass" of numbers or resources may be necessary in certain situations.

physical proximity among group members,[8] (e) the more differentiated (in a complementary way) the goals of different members (or subgroups) of the group,[9] (f) the greater the sensitivity of the group to a threatened loss arising from inaction, and (g) the more unequal the distribution of wealth or power among group members.[10] What makes these principles (hypotheses) relevant and potentially important is that most of them can be operationalized relatively easily. For example, characteristic (a) can be measured by membership size,[11] (b) by commonality of place or class of birth of group members, (c) by the length of time the group has been in existence, (d) by geographic or sectoral concentration, (e) by differences in stated objectives among group members, and (g) by inequality in the distribution of wealth among group members.

While, as suggested above, Olson's theoretical framework is that of a static game, his discussion of characteristics (c) and (d) as favorable to success in collective aciton can be interpreted as a recognition of the fact that, if one allows for repetitive interactions among group members, cooperative solutions are more likely to be reached.

In situations where the obstacles to collective action would otherwise seem formidable, the prospects for collective action are likely to be enhanced by the availability of *"political entrepreneurs."* As Hardin (1982, p. 35) defined them, "political entrepreneurs are people who, for their own career reasons, find it in their private interest to work to provide collective benefits to relevant groups." Political entrepreneurship can help explain why certain groups may become engaged in successful collective action even if on other bases, such as their large numbers, homogeneity of goals, geographic disper-

---

[8]Characteristics (b), (c) and (d) facilitate communication among members and make it easier for them to agree on methods and objectives. They may also lead to greater altruism among group members, increase the sense of responsibility among them and make it more difficult for individual members to refuse to go along with the wishes of the majority.

[9]Characteristic (e) makes the objectives more additive rather than competitive to one another, thereby raising the prospects for "logrolling" and other means of satisfying the different objectives of different subgroups at the same time. This raises the prospects that these subgroups will support each other and then join in a collective action benefitting all groups.

[10]This characteristic makes it likely that the critical minimum of support for the collective action can be achieved even in the event that some smaller, less wealthy and powerful members choose to free-ride.

[11]As Hardin (1982) and Ostrom (1987) have indicated, however, the measurement of size is by no means unambiguous. For example, it can mean the number of members, the amount of resources, or some combination thereof.

sion and other group characteristics, one would think that these groups would be likely to remain "latent."[12] Indeed, since large numbers and geographical dispersion may be attractive characteristics to political entrepreneurs, this can be an important offset to the Olsonian hypotheses suggested above.

Although somewhat more subjective and hence more difficult to operationalize, it may also be possible to identify certain *psychological attitudes* of group members in their particular environment which would help overcome free-rider and other problems plaguing collective action. In particular, if group members should subjectively feel a loss in status to which they have in the past become accustomed, and especially if this loss is rapid and substantial, such a group may be much more likely to engage in successful collective action to rectify the situation than another group whose current position is no worse than what it was in the past, even if the latter's position is absolutely worse. Similarly, the more essentially threatening (i.e., threatening to group members very existence and survival) is the status quo, the more likely that group is to be involved in a successful collective action.[13]

Success in collective action by a particular group, e.g., group A, may also be affected by whether or not *other groups*, such as B, C, D, etc., engage in collective action [Becker (1983)]. Specifically, group A may be deemed more likely to succeed in such action the more one of these other groups has been successful in engaging in an action which is harmful or threatening to the interests of A. By the same token, the greater the *tolerance* on the part of groups B, C, D, etc. for group A's collective action and the benefits thereof for A, the greater the likelihood that A's action will be successful. Likewise, the more that members of groups B, C, D, etc., perceive that the success of A may anticipate subsequent improvements for themselves, the more tolerant of A's actions and of the benefits accruing to it they are likely to become. This is what Hirschman calls the *"tunnel effect"* [Hirschman (1972, 1981)].[14] Of

---

[12]We use the terms "latent", "dormant," "passive" and "inactive" interchangeably to identify groups which are neither organized nor actively engaged in collective action. As shall be pointed out below, however, even latent groups can be forced to take collective action if conditions deteriorate sufficiently. Generally, however, such action is temporary in nature. After the action — successful or not — the group returns to its latent state.

[13]Strictly speaking the principle of relative deprivation is a psychological one originating at the level of the individual. It is not clear how it becomes transformed to the group level. Nevertheless, Hagen (1962) and Nelson and Winter (1982) apply this principle to explain innovative behavior in firms and Brenner (1983) and Witt (1987a) to explain other forms of innovation among groups.

[14]The basic idea is that a driver who is stuck in a traffic jam inside a tunnel

considerable importance in determining the degree of tolerance on the part of the other groups is their perception of the fairness or deservedness of the benefits to A. If these benefits are deemed to be attributable to hard work and/or skill, they are more likely to be tolerated than if they are obtained by what is perceived to be luck or unfair tactics [Hoffman and Spitzer (1985)]. Since greater tolerance and positive tunnel effects are more likely among groups with overlapping memberships, the existence of such groups may be expected to increase the likelihood of success in collective action [Olson (1965), Cummins (1987)].

The *environmental circumstances* in which group members find themselves and in particular the alternatives to collective action that are available to them may also play an important role in group actions. For example, Hirschman (1970, 1981) has focused on the likelihood of and nature of the possibilities for "exit" solutions (rather than "voice" or collective action solutions) to unfavorable circumstances. Specifically, he hypothesized that the easier it is to exit and the more attractive are the alternatives to remaining in the group, the lower is the possibility of successful collective action. For example, collective action may be less likely the easier it is to substitute private goods for public ones. On the other hand, among those who choose not to exit, those for whom exit is most attractive may well have the most influence.

Because of the importance of group perceptions, the *communication* and *organizational skills* and *knowledge* of the *technology* of collective action on the part of group members and especially those in leadership positions may also contribute to success in collective action. For example, the prospects of success may be enhanced by the ability of the proponents of the action to conceal from all parties the magnitude of the costs and to exaggerate the benefits. One way in which this might be accomplished is by suggesting an analogy between the action under consideration and previously successful, apparently similar action, even if the analogy should actually be false [Hirschman (1967)].[15] Success in collective action can be enhanced by the clarity of the logic connecting the action with its intended benefits and by the extent to which that logic is communicated to all group members [Nelson

---

with two lanes of traffic going in the same direction may feel better when the traffic in the other lane starts to move even if that in his lane doesn't. He does so because he interprets that fact as anticipating subsequent movement in traffic in his own lane. Hirschman (1968) provides an application.

[15]Naturally, this doesn't mean that deliberate deception is necessarily going to lead to success. Indeed, to be persuasive in this respect the claimant has to have credibility, something which gross misrepresentation is hardly likely to generate.

(1984)]. Organizational ability can be of considerable use. For example, the advantages of group characteristics (a) through (e) in the above list of factors favorable to collective action may be strengthened by organizing local, homogeneous groups into national (or even international) federations [Olson (1965)]. Since expectations of the ability to execute and enforce collective action may affect an individual's willingness to participate, the prestige, elite status and power of group leaders may also be highly conducive to success in collective action [Wade (1987)]. Likewise, any actual improvement in the technology of collective action which increases the expected benefits relative to the expected costs could be expected to increase the likelihood of collective action.[16]

Collective action theory can also help explain the character, size and breadth of interest groups. This is important because, as discussed in section VI, the character, size and breadth of interest groups may significantly affect economic efficiency and long term development. In particular, an important distinction drawn by Olson and his followers is that between "narrow/special-interest" and "encompassing/special-interest" groups. The first type is small in relation to the total size of the society or relevant segment of society, and tends to have homogeneous but narrowly focused objectives. On the other hand, encompassing interest groups are more heterogeneous, larger and hence more difficult to organize.

The prospects for success in collective action are also likely to be enhanced by the practice of *selective incentives*.[17] Both positive and negative incentives are likely to be useful in inducing success in collective action by an existing organization. For example, with respect to positive incentives, the prestige and honor accorded to those making especially large or well-sustained gifts as part of the organization's fund-raising appeals is often a useful tool for encouraging large and regular financial donations. Likewise, many groups find that offering rewards to their contributors and true participants in the form of special fringe benefits, such as discounts on purchases and giveaway items, is a useful means of increasing their fundraising ability. With respect

---

[16]Closely related influences are changes in social values concerning the benefits of the public goods produced by the collective action [North (1986)] and changes in knowledge about the effects [Ruttan and Hayami (1984), Ruttan (1986)].

[17]The use of selective incentives implies that the goods involved are not strictly or completely public goods of non-exclusionary character and jointness of supply. As Ostrom (1987, p. 24-25) points out, in practice public goods may conform to one of these criteria more than to the other, with possible differences in the likelihood of collective action.

to negative incentives, the ability to impose penalties in the form of fines or even physical punishment has often been found to be an effective means of reducing free-riding and accordingly increasing the prospects of success in collective action, at least in some circumstances [Olson (1965, Ch. 6), R. Hardin (1982, pp. 31-34)].[18]

A related consideration is the *by-product hypothesis* advanced by Olson according to which the group or organization may provide for private goods to members (trips, newspapers, ...) who participate in the provision of the public good. This is a way or type of selective incentive that transforms the payoffs in order to induce cooperation. However, the by-product hypothesis has been criticized on the grounds that one might suppose that there would exist private organizations which would be more efficient in providing separately for the private good, thereby undermining its usefulness as a by-product incentive.

Given the aforementioned importance of organizations in reducing the average cost of collective action, and the operational difficulty of determining the existence of organization-less interest groups, collective action theory is probably more directly applicable to the creation of interest group organizations than to the creation of the interest groups themselves.[19] In the case of broader encompassing groups, however, because they are far more difficult to organize, selective incentives would have to be emphasized. In particular, positive selective incentives may be necessary to encourage active participation and leadership and negative selective incentives to prevent members from violating group decisions.[20] Organizations may also be useful in serving the interests of political entrepreneurs [R. Hardin (1982, p. 36)] and for monitoring the activities of opposing or partner groups whose efforts may affect the results of collective action of the group.

The structure of organizations and the rules by which they function may

---

[18]An important shortcoming of the theory in this respect, however, is that it doesn't explain which selective incentives would be most conducive to success in different situations.

[19]Note that our position in this respect, though close to that of Uphoff (1986), is quite different than that of R. Hardin who states unequivocably: "The logic of collective action is not a theory about interest group organizations. Rather, it is a theory about whether there will be interest group or any kind of collective action" [R. Hardin (1982, pp. 14-15)].

[20]Indeed, the importance of selective incentives for the emergence and long-run success of encompassing groups may account for why some analysts identify the implementation of selective incentives as an important objective of the organization of interest groups [R. Hardin (1982, p. 34) and Olson (1982, pp. 38-40)].

well be determined by transaction cost considerations. Indeed, organizations would be expected to adopt governance structures designed to minimize the total long-run costs of collective action. Since selective incentives and monitoring are costly activities, formal organizations attempt to organize themselves in such a way as to reduce them as much as possible in unit cost terms. When exogenous shocks occur, well-managed organizations may institute appropriate changes in group objectives so as to avoid the start-up costs of organizing a new collective action group.

The application of the principles of collective action can be illustrated through two examples, one dealing with labor unions and the other with environmental groups. The analysis of unions by Olson (1982) concentrates on DCs where he finds considerable evidence of success in collective action. Because the kinds of activities in which unionization tends to succeed are unlikely to emerge until relatively high levels of development are achieved, except possibly in mining and other extractive industries, labor union organizations are unlikely to appear in LDCs until considerably later than in DCs. There are, however, some notable exceptions in which unions appear at a relatively early stage as a countervailing force to multinational enterprise management and ownership or when encouraged to develop for political reasons ("clientelism").

Several studies have identified homogeneity in background and origin as an important factor contributing to early success in LDC union activity. For example, historically the organizational success of the Istanbul port workers (and also their success in impeding mechanization and technological change) seems to be attributable to the fact that they were dominated by workers of closely knit ethnic minorities, namely Armenians and Greeks [Quataert (1983)]. Since mining employment is frequently concentrated in specific, relatively isolated rural areas, in which the workers are likely to be homogeneous in background, and from which the cost of "exit" from the industry is likely to be relatively high, the prospects for "voice", collective action and unionization are likely to be bright in LDC mining industries.

Because the effects of environmental deterioration are likely to be especially widely diffused over time and across the population, each person feeling only a slight and very gradual reduction in welfare, from the principles of collective action one would expect collective action in preserving the environment to be especially difficult to achieve. One would also expect that such concerns might be greater among the wealthy than among the poor who have to be concerned more with the immediate questions of satisfying basic needs. Hardin (1982) provides considerable support from within DCs for these expectations and casual empiricism would seem to suggest that environmental groups have been very slow to emerge as organized groups in LDCs. Even in DCs, the amount of funds raised by such groups is generally extremely small.

IV. Interest Groups and the State

While groups and organizations may undertake "private actions" to provide directly for their own public goods, more typically they do so indirectly by means of the state.

In fact, an important means of increasing the technical efficiency of collective action is by gaining *access to the state* and its ability not only to impose regulations but also to monitor and enforce them [R. Hardin (1982)]. Since the state can affect the degree to which groups are likely to be able to practice selective incentives, indirectly it can influence the likelihood of success in collective action. Among the means by which the state can do so are by (a) changing the level, breadth of distribution, and composition of the benefits it provides free-of-charge to the public, (b) passing judgement on the legality of imposing negative incentives upon those not participating in group activities, and (c) insisting on certain voting procedures, such as the secret ballot, which may affect the feasiblity of imposing selective incentives on those supporting or opposing collective action. Because of the state's natural interest in demonstrating its responsiveness to the desires of its constituents, the barriers to indirect collective action by way of the state may well be considerably weaker than those to direct collective action without the involvement of the state. Another important advantage of collective action by way of the state is the stamp of legitimacy that state acceptance or tacit authorization can give to such action, at least in the case of a state whose legitimacy is generally accepted [Baumol (1952, Ch. 12)].

The subsequent discussion of the relationship between interest groups and the state is organized as follows. The influence of interest groups on the policies and decisions of the state is treated in subsection A, and rent-seeking, the interest group approach to government in which the role of agents of the state in collective action is made explicit, is dealt with in subsection B. Then, in subsection C we discuss the possible effect of the character of the state on the quantity and quality of rent-seeking and finally in subsection D the processes of political exchange are identified and the role of bureaucrats within these processes articulated.

A. Interest group influence over policy

If the state plays only a mediating role in collective action, responding only passively to interest group pressures, then the principles of collective action discussed in the previous section can be directly applied to the determination of the relative influence of different interest groups over policy.

As is well known, the most characteristic feature of state policy in LDCs is the distinct tilt in such policy in favor of urban interests and against the relatively poor rural interests.[21] Especially sharp is the sizeable difference in such countries in the relative influence exerted over policy between farmers and industrialists. These biases appear in many kinds of policy, ranging from the allocation of credit and tariff rates on inputs and outputs to the provision of government services and so on.[22] In virtually all respects, farmers (excluding large plantation owners) are disadvantaged [Landsberger and Hewitt (1970), Bates (1981)] relative to industrialists.

Numerous elements of the theory of collective action identified above would seem to contribute to the explanation of these biases. Compared to farmers, industrialists are usually fewer in number, have more differentiated goals (some being more demanding of credit, others of subsidized interest rates, imports or electricity), are likely to be more highly concentrated geographically and sectorally, thereby making it easier for them to plan and execute collective action, including the monitoring of free-riding.[23] Frequently also, the industrial sector is characterized by greater inequality in the distribution of assets and size than the agricultural sector, thereby reducing the incentives for free-riding. In the early stages of industrial development, because their wage rates and hence incomes are relatively low, industrial workers are likely to spend large fractions of their disposable incomes on food, making them especially sensitive, and hence resistant, to higher food prices. By contrast, for agriculturalists, and especially for small landowners and (landless) agricultural laborers, exit in the form of migration to the cities is likely to be seen as a relatively attractive and easy alternative to the use of voice in the form of remaining in agriculture to fight for better conditions [Bates (1981)].

Another generally recognized pattern of relative influence is that the direction of the policy bias among sectors tends to be reversed in countries at higher levels of development.[24] Once again, this seeming anomaly can be

---

[21]This is what Lipton (1977) calls the "urban bias."

[22]For evidence see Balassa and Associates (1971), and Lutz and Scandizzo (1980).

[23]Naturally, the bias would be reversed when the situation is characterized by few, large, commercially oriented landholders and many small, dispersed industrial producers such as in some Latin American countries.

[24]This is demonstrated in the studies of Balassa and Associates (1971), Guttman (1978b), Krueger (1978), Binswanger and Scandizzo (1983), Anderson and Hayami (1986) and Balisacan and Roumasset (1987).

explained in terms of the theory of collective action. As development proceeds and massive rural-urban migration takes place, most of the effects described above are reversed. For instance, the industrial sector becomes larger, less geographically concentrated, more heterogeneous and thus more difficult to organize. At the same time, as agriculturalists become fewer in number, more concentrated in specific commercial crops, more dependent on the ability to market their agricultural surplus, and better endowed with capital, transport and communications, and for whom exit is a less viable possibility, both their need for collective action and their ability to bring it about are greatly enhanced. Also, because of the smaller size of the agricultural sector, the cost burden of agricultural subsidies is not likely to be as threatening to other potential coalition partners as they would have been before [Bates and Rogerson (1980) and Balisacan and Roumasset (1987)].

Another potentially fruitful application of the theory of collective action is in distinguishing success from failure in the formation, maintenance and improvement of squatter communities. For example, homogeneity of origin, the high cost of exit once their living quarters have been erected and the actual or perceived threat from the actions of opposing groups, such as the state and its instruments (the military or police), have been found to be extremely important factors in determining the strength of collective action in squatter communities [Hirschman (1984)]. The reason why the state is typically in opposition to the squatters is that most squatter communities crop up on state or community-owned land instead of on private land. Since the strength and likelihood of collective action rise with the extent of the threatened loss arising from inaction, it is easy to understand why collective action is at a peak when the threat of eviction is greatest but then, once the threat of eviction falls, even the most collectively active squatter groups almost invariably return to their original state of latency [Gilbert and Ward (1985)].

B. Rent-seeking

Even if it may now be obvious how collective action theory can explain the emergence, organization and relative influence of interest groups including that over the policies of the state, it has been increasingly recognized that the state and its agents are not neutral and passive in this process and hence that their role should be taken into consideration. In addition, since at any point in time there are many instruments for benefitting individual groups, it is by no means obvious how the specific instruments of state policy to be used by any particular group are determined.

Much of the traditional political science and public policy literature has stressed the importance of social objectives in the determination of state policy. More recently, however, public choice economists [e.g., Mueller (1979) and Brennan and Buchanan (1985)] have argued that state employees and policy-makers tend to pursue selfish objectives.[25] Enter the positive theory of *rent-seeking* or the interest group approach to government. This theory is concerned with the behavior of interest groups and their interaction in their pursuit of *"contrived rents"* as opposed to profits.[26] These rents are artificial transfers in the sense that they result from government restrictions, such as the granting of monopoly positions, protection or any other kind of regulation or rule. By contrast, *profits* arise *naturally* from the workings of dynamic competitive market processes.

The interest group theory of government attempts to explain how competing interest groups, faced with different information costs as well as different costs of devising instruments with which to deal with free-riding, interact in the political market in order to obtain regulations favorable to their interests. The analysis is usually couched in terms of wealth transfers among groups. Major contributions to the literature include those of Stigler (1971), Peltzman (1976) and McCormick and Tollison (1981). In contrast to the main thread in the theory of collective action in which the focus is virtually exclusively on the demand for collective action, the political economy of rent-seeking draws upon collective action principles to explain the supply of such transfers as well. For example, McCormick and Tollison (1981) formulate a model of both the demand for and supply of wealth transfers in which the transfers are mediated by politicians who extract them from the suppliers (whose opposition to the transfers is difficult, and hence costly, to organize). The transfers are then delivered to the demanders who are the strong and active coalitions whose support is easy, and therefore not costly, to organize.

Rent-seeking is generally portrayed as a zero- or negative-sum game [Tullock (1980)]. Hence, collective action by an interest group is usually aimed at increasing the group's share of a fixed or diminishing stock of wealth at the expense of other groups. But, why shouldn't the analysis also apply to situations which, at least in the long run, are characterized by positive-sum games? For example, one could imagine a situation in which the action promoted by group A is efficiency-increasing in the long-run, with benefits accruing both

---

[25]Although commonly stated, the hypothesis remains somewhat controversial as can be judged by the recent interchange between Quiggin (1987) and Brennan and Pincus (1987).

[26]Surveys of rent-seeking theory are provided by Tollison (1982), Hartle (1983), Colander (1984) and Tullock (1980).

to A itself and to another group B, even though in the short-run, A's net gains, might be more than offset by B's net losses. Hence, the application of rent-seeking to a positive-sum game situation might imply that, in addition to the short-run problem of competition between the two groups, there is a long-run one of cooperation.[27]

In any case, by integrating the supply and demand for transfers, the theory of rent-seeking is also capable of identifying the nature of the resources transfered. To that end it seeks to identify the efficient means of transfer, i.e., to determine what the weak group would be less able to avoid giving up that would still be of use to the relatively strong group. Naturally, the state can play a still more active role in this process by transforming what it obtains from the weak group, e.g., taxes, into the infrastructure or government services it passes on to the strong group.

While still quite simple and unsophisticated, the rent-seeking version of collective action theory can help explain how interest group action affects the structure of protection through tariffs, quotas and other non tariff barriers. In the context of the political economy of trade policies, several different theoretical models have been developed, such as those of Brock and Magee 1978), Pincus (1975), Bhagwati and Srinivasan (1980) and Mayer (1984). These models have been critically evaluated by Lavergne (1983). Given that demand and supply factors are basic to the rent-seeking approach, studies in the context of DCs usually posit the rate of protection to be the outcome of both demand factors relating to the costs and benefits of lobbying by interest groups and supply factors like the willingness on the part of the government and other relevant authorities to provide protection (which, in turn, reflects the costs and benefits to the politicians, administrators and other officials of providing such measures). As proxies for some of the relevant cost considerations might be the number of firms and the degree of concentration in the industry. Likewise among the factors affecting the expected benefits of lobbying might be variables such as labor intensity, share of value added, and industry-specific rates of growth (in relative terms). Empirical studies attempt to determine the extent to which intersectoral differences in the

---

[27]Olson's (1965, 1982) distinctions between narrow and encompassing groups would seem to reflect this range of possibilities. Whereas interactions between narrow groups might well result in the dominance of negative-sum activities and strictly competitive rent-seeking, in the case of encompassing groups the interaction might generate positive social benefits. Notably, Roumasset and La Croix (1988) attribute to rent-seeking the emergence of socially beneficial private property rights in Hawaii during the middle of the 19th century. In the same spirit Brennan and Buchanan (1985, p. 17) point out the long-term, positive-sum-game aspects of the introduction of rules and norms.

importance or relevance of the posited supply and demand factors explain
the variations in effective or nominal protection rates across sectors and/or
changes in those rates over time in DCs.[28]

Despite the availability of empirical data on protection in LDCs, attempts to explain the structure of protection in LDCs have not been readily
forthcoming. This may be because of the perceived need to make substantial
modifications in the models before applying them to LDCs. Three such modifications would seem to stand out in terms of relevance and importance. First,
as emphasized below, the models need to be designed for the "bureaucratic
authoritarian" situations which typify LDCs.[29] Second, while the motive for
protection in DCs is viewed mainly as "defensive" in nature, i.e., in order to
protect existing domestic economic interests, in LDCs the motive may well
be "offensive" in the sense that protection is designed to promote new activities, often based on infant industry arguments. More generally, national
policy goals may be important in the determination of the structure of protection in LDCs as in the so-called National Policy Model suggested for Canada
by Caves (1976). If so, economic, rather than political, considerations may
be relatively more important in the determination of protection in LDCs.[30]
Third, the state and its economic arm, the public enterprises, may be active
on the demand side for protection, thereby limiting the meaningfulness of the
distinction between the demand and the supply of protection.

The political economy of rent-seeking has also been applied with considerable success to explaining variations in income transfers to farmers from
commodity support programs from one commodity to another and over time.
Gardner (1987) shows that price support programs in the U.S. are negatively
related to the political costs of achieving collective action on the one hand
and the economic costs (deadweight losses) of such support (which are related
to the price elasticities of supply and demand) on the other hand.

C. Rent-seeking and the character of the state

---

[28]See Pincus (1975), Baldwin (1976, 1985), Finger, Hall and Nelson (1982)
and Lavergne (1983) for the United States, Caves (1976) and Helleiner (1977)
for Canada, Anderson (1980) for Australia and various other studies in Bhagwati (1982).

[29]See Findlay and Wellisz (1983) for a simple example of a model incorpo-
rating such a modification.

[30]Alikhani and Havrylyshyn (1982) have explored this issue in an empirical
study of the determinants of the structure of protection in Colombia and
South Korea, and found evidence of the importance of the economic policy
goals as opposed to the traditional pressure group influences as determinants
of the structure of protection.

A major characteristic of the applications to date of the positive theory of rent-seeking is that, like many of the other elements in the NIE, it has been analyzed mainly in the institutional framework of representative governments as in the United States.[31] As such, interest groups have been assumed to use politician-legislators as mediators in the process of producing regulations. Likewise, the relevant information about the lobbying and other activities of such groups is assumed to be open and available to all, thereby assuring that the outcome of competition among interest groups will be efficient in the sense that the given amount of income or wealth transfers is obtained in a way that minimizes the social costs of achieving them. However, since LDCs are generally characterized neither by representative governments nor by the ready availability of information on interest group activities, can the efficiency outcome still be assured? What modifications in the analysis may be required in order for the positive theory of rent-seeking to be applicable to LDCs?

Interest group interaction is likely to be less transparent and more complicated to analyze under these rather different conditions. This does not mean, however, that interest group activities wouldn't be very much present in such conditions, with some groups benefitting more than others, compared to what would be the case with open representative governments.

From the existing literature on rent-seeking it is not even clear whether there would be more or less rent-seeking under autocratic governments and dictatorships than under democratic governments.

On the one hand, one could imagine that the quantity of rent-seeking activity might be greater the freer individuals are to form and participate in interest groups and the greater is the opportunity for political entrepreneurship to assist otherwise latent groups in pressing the state for benefits. On the other hand, it is often argued [e.g., North and Thomas (1973)] that autocratic governments are especially concerned with minimizing the transaction costs of revenue collection, thereby leading them to emphasize more monopolistic restrictions and licenses from which revenue can be derived more easily than through the imposition of more broadly based taxes. As already mentioned, North (1981, 1987) also argues that autocratic governments are more prone to rent-seeking in as much as they have self-interest in keeping laws ambiguous and limiting the scope of property rights. Even in autocratic but unstable conditions, the need for self-preservation might well induce such regimes to

---

[31]This is so even though several normative rent-seeking studies have been applied to LDCs. Examples include Krueger (1974) who measured the costs for Turkey and India, and more recently Sharif and Whalley (1984) who have done so for India.

take the initiative in forming otherwise latent groups. For example, an autocratic regime might want to encourage the formation of such interest groups either (a) in order to preclude their subsequent development in ways deemed potentially threatening to the regime or (b) to communicate regime objectives to the populace. On the other hand, for reason (a) an insecure autocratic regime might alternatively act to suppress the formation and organization of interest groups.

Presumably, therefore, the net balance of whether there would be more or less rent-seeking in autocratic conditions than in open democratic ones could be determined only on the basis of empirical studies comparing the number of state-created monopolies and regulations and the magnitudes of the rents generated and degree of inefficiency under dictatorships with those under democratic regimes where presumably more competition prevails.[32] Without conducting such an exercise, Tullock (1986) speculates that there may be more rent-seeking in dictatorships.[33] However, he feels that such differences may be small and that the main difference would lie in the structural distribution of the rents, larger rents being distributed to fewer people in dictatorships that in democracies. He also follows Olson (1982) in speculating that autocratic governments would be more unstable.

In the short-run, it might be appropriate to assume (as we have heretofore assumed) that the nature of the state (representative or autocratic), its degree of instability and its goals and rules are exogenous variables which can influence, but not be influenced by, other forms of collective action and institutions. In the long-run, however, all these characteristics of the state should be considered endogenous variables that result from, rather than determine, interest group interaction. For example, dictatorships would seem most likely to arise when crisis conditions exist which demand the kinds of actions which are sufficiently inconsistent with past tradition to be unattainable with democratic governments.

---

[32]Manne (1986) and Lindenberg (1986) argue that the choice of the competitive market solution as the benchmark against which to measure the extent and costs of rent-seeking is unrealistic. Lindenberg (1986) stresses that historical antecedents, including the way in which the state emerged, which would be particular to each country and time period would greatly constrain the available choices. Manne quite correctly points out that the very substantial costs of creating and maintaining competitive markets should not be ignored.

[33]Tullock's explanation is in terms of the greater ignorance of better ways to generate revenues on the part of dictators. This explanation seems unconvincing and has received strong criticism from Manne (1986) and Lindenberg (1986).

Regardless of whether the context is a dictatorship or a representative democracy it is clear that the process of rent-seeking involves political exchange and bureaucrats. This is the subject of the next subsection.

D. Political exchange and the bureaucracy

Following on the earlier political economy tradition of Wicksell, Buchanan, Tullock and other public choice theorists view politics as merely another realm (besides that of markets) for exchange. As Buchanan puts it:

> Politics is a structure of complex exchange among individuals, a structure within which persons seek to secure collectively their own privately defined objectives that cannot be efficiently secured through simple market exchanges. In the absence of individual interest there is no interest. In the market, individuals exchange apples for oranges; in politics, individuals exchange agreed-on shares in contributions toward the costs of that which is commonly desired, from the services of the local fire station to that of the judge [Buchanan (1987, p. 1434)].

Exchange in the political realm can take many forms. One form it may take is vote-trading. Potentially, the trading of votes could be risky, thereby tending to undermine its occurrence. If legislators A and B agree to vote for each other's pet project, how can each be assured that the other will deliver? If legislative voting were by secret ballot, in legislatures of more than a few members at least, assurance about the votes of trading partners would be very difficult to determine. Not surprisingly, in order to facilitate vote-trading most legislatures use open voting. In this way, a legislator cannot misreport his (her) vote. Another assurance problem in vote-trading arises from the fact that each different bill requires a separate vote, implying that the traded votes cannot be cast simultaneously. The risks of reneging on commitments to vote-trade would seem to be exacerbated by tenure instability and high turnover among legislators. The need to reduce such risks may explain why legislators generally serve terms of fixed and relatively long duration. The various advantages of incumbents in winning elections also tend to increase the effective duration of terms of office and hence the reliability of legislators.

Most legislatures make their decisions by majority rule. While it may be easier to obtain a majority than consensus or unanimity, if every legislator were to vote his (her) private interest, the construction of majorities could still be a formidable task. Several mechanisms facilitating the construction of such majorities are, however, commonly observed. Indeed, quite possibly their usefulness in this respect may explain why such mechanisms exist.

First, there may exist politicial parties the expressed purpose of which is to mobilize winning coalitions. Such parties might well use positive and/or negative selective incentives to induce party members to tow the party line. Second, groups with overlapping interests may arise and agree to cooperate. Third, ideology in favor of some commonly held values and objectives is likely to arise, providing a higher level rationale for unified voting preferences [Kalt and Zupan (1984 and forthcoming), and Mestelman and Feeny (1988)]. Fourth, the high value that is associated with a reputation for loyalty, honesty and reliability mitigates the incentive for reneging on political commitments and promises, thereby encouraging vote-trading and the formation of voting majorities. Fifth, the committee system, which provides each committee (for issues under its jurisdiction) with a monopoly right to determine what proposals should be brought before the full legislature, assures each constituency in the legislature with *de facto* veto power over any proposal from any other group reneging on a promise to it. Sixth, the access to committee memberships is closely controlled through rules of succession and appointment. Seventh, the attainment of positions of leadership on such committees usually depends on seniority and reliability in vote-trading [Weingast and Marshall (1987)].

Much less is known about the process of political exchange in the case of autocratic governments in which legislatures, and hence the rules they adopt, are likely to be less, and bureaucracies more, important in attaining group objectives. Nevertheless, since bureaucracies are organized in ways similar to legislatures, some of the same processes may apply. Different units have prerogatives as to decisions on different issues and their implementation.

Various models of bureaucratic behavior have been developed.[34] Among the first was that of Niskanen (1971) who assumed that the bureaucrat's objective is to maximize his (her) budget. Given this objective, the counterpart to vote-trading in a legislature would occur if different ministers would agree to support each other's budgetary requests. While the tenure of a minister in any given ministry may be less secure in the case of autocratic government, cooperation among ministers may be encouraged by the adoption of the ministerial rotation pattern which seems common in such countries. Hence, at any given time he has little self-interest in cutting the budget of a ministry which he may eventually inherit. Once again, reputations for loyalty and reliability are likely to be extremely important. Another means of promoting political exchange in the bureaucratic context is by promoting linkages between the different units of the bureaucracy, such as through state enterprises attached to different ministries.

The bureaucrat is in any case not simply a passive intermediary between

---

[34] A critical survey of these models is given by Orzechowski (1977).

the supply and demand for public goods and services. Indeed, the bureaucrat is likely to be a rent-seeker who attempts to benefit personally by establishing and maintaining monopolistic control over a particular public good or service. The bureaucrat can help himself maximize his budget by deliberately overstating the benefits of the good or service he supplies and understating the cost. As such, it is in his interest to monopolize the relevant information about such matters, thereby sabotaging efforts by others to evaluate the relevant benefits and costs.

Especially in those LDCs where the bureaucrats are relatively well paid (e.g., as a result of the colonial heritage in which the bureaucrats were expatriates) and economic and political conditions relatively unstable, positions in the bureaucracy are likely to be highly cherished for their stability. Since, as Stiglitz (1986, Ch. 7) points out, mistakes are more likely to be noticed than successes, bureaucrats are likely to behave in such a way as to minimize the risks of doing anything that might turn out to be a mistake. One manifestation of this may be "red tape" and lengthy delays in decision-making that allow the blame for any resulting mistakes to be diverted to others.

V. Common Property Resources and Collective Action

As mentioned above, a well-known and socially important application of the prisoners' dilemma game is to "the tragedy of the commons" [G. Hardin (1968)]. As noted in the typology of goods given in Figure 3-1 above, the collective goods in these types of problems are characterized by considerable congestion, as well as (due for instance to some existing communal property constraint) considerable non-excludability.[35] In such situations if each party or member of the group acts independently, it is in the interest of each to overuse the commons. Applications to over-fishing of open-access fisheries, over-grazing of open-access range land and air and water pollution are straightforward. Only if each party can be assured that the other will cooperate will it be advantageous to cooperate.

The solution may involve instituting some restrictions on the use of the resource, thereby making the degree of exclusion endogenous. For example, the tragedy of the commons can be overcome by the renunciation of communal property in favor of a system of private property rights [Demsetz (1967), Alchian and Demsetz (1972, 1973)]. In terms of Figure 3-1 this amounts to shifting the good from cell A2B1 to A2B3 or even A3B3. Once the owner of a particular resource obtains exclusive and full rights of ownership, not

---

[35]Olson's analysis of exclusive groups can be considered as falling in the category since he assumes that for exclusive goods there is some degree of congestion that makes it desirable for members to restrict additional membership.

only at the present but also in the future, any higher income obtained in the short run through over-use of the resource or the pollution of the water or air around it would be offset by a cost in terms of lower property values which in a competitive market would reflect the lower future net return streams generated by the resource. Therefore, the assignment of private property rights should internalize the costs of overuse which would otherwise leak out in the form of externalities, thereby providing the incentive for non-cooperation and the tragedy of the commons.

The establishment of private property rights itself requires collective action. Indeed, because the establishment of such a system can greatly affect the distribution of wealth among individuals and groups, the transaction costs of designing and implementing such a system may be very substantial. The higher these costs, ceteris paribus, the greater the obstacles to collective action are likely to be.

Collective action may also be necessary in monitoring and enforcing the system of property rights. For example, in some situations a landowner may be able to effectively enforce his rights to that land by independent action such as building a fence around the land. In countries with considerable rainfall, like the U.K. and Ireland, this can be easily and inexpensively done by simply growing a hedge with prickly spikes. In other contexts, however, like Spain, North Africa, the Middle East, parts of the Western United States and much of Mexico, where the cost of fencing is high (for lack of local raw materials) and/or fences may be easy to break without being detected,[36] this may not be possible. In such situations, therefore, private property rights cannot be monitored and enforced without collective action, e.g., in the form of the landowners collectively hiring a police force to keep intruders off their land [Bromley (1988)].

The other commonly suggested solution to the tragedy-of-the-commons problem is external intervention by government. This approach has been enthusiastically advocated by Hardin (1968, 1978), Ehrenfeld (1972), Ophuls (1973), Heilbroner (1974), and numerous others, if not as a first-best solution, at least as a last resort. In practice, the problem with externally imposed solutions has been the excessive size of the costs of monitoring and enforcing such rules and regulations. Free-rider and hence collective action problems, moreover, are likely to crop up at every step.

Given the positive social costs of creating, monitoring and enforcing private property rights, on the one hand, and, on the other hand, in the absence of such rights, the costs of enforcing externally imposed or internally con-

---

[36]See Nugent and Sanchez (1988).

structed limitations on collective use, there is no reason to think that, in general, either private property rights or externally imposed solutions are necessarily superior to the much maligned cooperative solutions [Bromley and Chapagain (1984), Bromley (forthcoming) and Witt (1987b)]. Indeed, a surprisingly large and ever-increasing number of cases have been identified (from anthropological and other case studies) in which societies have been able to come up with imaginative ways of implementing cooperative solutions to tragedy-of-the-commons problems.[37]

Secrets to success in cooperation seem to include leadership by community elites (possibly on account of asymmetry in the distribution of income and wealth), relatively inexpensive means of monitoring and enforcing community- determined rules, barriers to entry from non-members of the community, stability in community membership and the high cost of exit from the community and its cooperative solution [Libecap (1986), Runge (1981, 1986), Ostrom (1986b), and Wade (1987)]. Cooperation and the way out of the tragedy of the commons can be made more likely by introducing "matching behavior" or "reaction rules" [Guttman (1978a, 1982), Taylor (1976), and Thompson and Faith (1981)] like the aforementioned "tit-for-tat" strategy wherein each party reacts to the behavior of the others in a matching way. For example, the adoption of an "if you stint (not overgraze), I stint, but if you don't, I won't either" rule would transform the pay-off matrices of the prisoners' dilemma, tragedy-of-the- commons problems of Figures 3-3 and 3-4 in such a way as to induce cooperation.[38]

In general, therefore, the general presumption of collective action failures and hence of the need for private property rights and/or for externally imposed solutions to cooperation problems would seem to be seriously overestimated. Cooperative solutions can be obtained and can be more efficient in transaction cost and possibly also in productive efficiency terms than private property solutions or central government dictates in certain circumstances. As a result, each system is likely to have comparative advantages and disadvantages relative to the other, implying that the choice between them is likely to be dictated by environmental and historical considerations as expressed in the transaction costs of creating and maintaining such solutions. Ostrom

---

[37]See, for example, Chopra, Kadekodi and Murty (1986), Cordell (1987), Dahlman (1980), Gilles and Jamtgaard (1981), Livingstone (1986), McKean (1987), Netting (1976, 1978), Sandford (1983) and Wade (1987).

[38]Rogers (1983) reviews a broad range of examples of the emergence of norms and identifies various characteristics of the change agent(s) which may affect the likelihood of success in that respect. For applications and evidence in the U.S. see Kalt and Zupan (1984, forthcoming).

(1985, 1986, 1987) and Blomquist and Ostrom (1985) and their colleagues at
Indiana University have recommended the undertaking and careful evaluation
of empirical case studies of situations in different countries in which tragedy-
of-the-commons problems have or have not been successfully confronted.

VI. Collective Action, Institutional Change and Development

Institutional considerations can have rather profound effects on the ability of countries to adapt to environmental shocks and to develop economically and socially. Therefore, the theory of collective action, by furthering
the understanding of society's ability to generate efficient institutions and
appropriately designed and timed policies, could be of considerable help in
allowing LDCs to achieve their development objectives at minimal cost. In
this way, collective action theory could come to play an important role in the
theory of economic and social development. Indeed, since virtually any policy or institutional change and the provision of various development-related
public goods such as infrastructure require collective action, the theory of
collective action could well provide a critically important link between institutional analysis, on the one hand, and development theory and policy, on
the other.

Until now, the emphasis in this chapter has been on the determinants of
collective action, but the institutions resulting from collective action can have
effects on the economy which may constitute an important first link between
collective action and development. The analysis has also been essentially
static in the sense that it has not addressed institutional change and the role
of collective action in facilitating or impeding such change. This constitutes
a second important link between collective action and development.

A. The effects of collective action on growth

Although the above discussion of the theory and practice of rent-seeking
makes it obvious that the nature and extent of collective action may have
important consequences for wealth distribution, there may also be some important implications for the rate of growth.

First, according to Olson (1982), in stable, secure, and nonauthoritar-
ian environments at least, once in existence, interest groups are likely to
strengthen and harden over time. There are several reasons for this. First,
as organizations mature, they can better apply selective incentives to enforce group decisions and maintain collective action. Second, the longer a
group is in existence, the more its members are likely to become more homogeneous,[39] both naturally as a result of continuous personal association and

---

[39] In view of the importance of group homogeneity for the preservation and

deliberately through the continued application of conformity-enhancing selective incentives. Third, as groups mature, they tend to grow in size and their decision-making becomes more complex and controlled by rules which make it more difficult for the group to change positions. Fourth, since among the most important selective incentives are rewards given to those in leadership positions, these leaders will find it advantageous to preserve the organization and continue its collective action even after the needs for the organization and its collective action have disappeared.[40]

Among the examples cited by Olson (1982) in support of this first hypothesis are (1) the relatively late emergence of labor unions and farm organizations even in highly developed stable countries with non-autocratic regimes, (2) the remarkably strong hold that guilds tended to have in relatively stable countries like China, India and Islamic countries prior to the 20th century and in much of Western Europe until at least the 17th century and (3) the relatively greater current strength of labor unions in stable democratic countries like Australia, New Zealand and the United Kingdom than in less stable or more autocratic countries.

A second proposition which follows quite directly from the first is that the deleterious effects of such distributional coalitions on efficiency, inequality and growth are likely to increase over time, at least as long as the aforementioned stable, secure and non-authoritarian conditions prevail. With respect to the deleterious effects on growth, Olson (1982, Ch. 4) provides an impressive amount and interesting variety of macroeconomic evidence in support of the proposition. In particular, he shows (1) that variations in growth rates of aggregate non-agricultural product across states in the United States have been negatively related to the number of years since statehood[41] (2) by and large that European growth rates in the post-World War II period are positively related to the degree of destruction during the War,[42] and (3) that

---

strengthening of interest groups over time, of considerable relevance are the examples he provides of the extreme lengths to which some organizations like the medieval guilds went in order to preserve homogeneity, including wealth equalization, equality of access to raw materials, prohibitions on extra-group marriages, the enforcement of certain codes with respect to dress and conduct and so on [Olson (1982, Ch. 6)].

[40] If the original goal of the organization or group should become redundant, the leaders of such groups are likely to search for new goals.

[41] This finding is, however, disputed by Nardinelli, Wallace and Warner (1987) who find no relationship after introducing a control for level of per capita income.

[42] See also Choi (1983), Olson (1983) and Weede (1987) but also the criticism of Pryor (1983, 1987).

lower economic growth rates have been experienced since the 1920's by stable, democratic countries like Australia, New Zealand and the United Kingdom than by those countries with greater instability.[43]

In view of the dearth of contemporary and especially historical measures of income inequality in different countries, not surprisingly the evidence presented for the correlation between maturity of interest groups and income inequality is much more anecdotal. One of the strongest pieces of evidence presented is the demonstration by Hutt (1964) that the relatively recently developed apartheid system in South Africa is attributable to the relatively late development of labor unions in that country, apartheid arising as a derivate of the efforts of white workers to limit the competition for desirable jobs in the formal sector by non-white workers. Another interesting, though admittedly more speculative, suggestion is that the inequality- preserving caste system in India may have originated in the guild system which, because of the relatively stable, secure, and non-authoritarian conditions that have prevailed in that country for many centuries (even under colonialism), had become particularly strong and fossilized. Each group might therefore view caste as a means of limiting entry into its specific occupation [Olson (1982, Ch. 6)].

Another implication is that the aforementioned effects would be less likely to be felt in new industries than in old ones. Murrell (1983) provides some evidence in support of this implication by showing that the ratio of growth rates in new industries to those of old industries in the United Kingdom (a country with a long period of stability, security and democracy) is higher than the corresponding ratio in Germany (a country with a relatively short period for which the three necessary conditions for strong interest groups have been satisfied). Another, though more casual, observation in support of this variant of the hypothesis is the fact that there is hardly any union activity in new industries like the semi-conductor industry in any country even though it is often organized in large firms and in concentrated geographic regions (like California's "Silicon Valley") which would make one think that collective action would be relatively quick to occur.

Olson (1982, especially Chapter 6) goes on to suggest how these basic propositions might be modified by varying conditions, some of which would seem to be especially relevant to LDCs. First, to the extent that stability is interrupted by war, invasion, or colonialism, the entrenched position of existing interest groups may be eliminated or at least greatly reduced, in turn increasing efficiency, decreasing inequality and raising the overall rate of growth. In this respect, Olson points to (1) the role of Japanese colonialism and wars

---

[43] Again, see Olson (1982, ch. 6).

in explaining the remarkable success of Korea in the twentieth century, (2) the role of "foreign" takeover in the case of Taiwan, and (3) the strict colonial insistence on free trade in the success of Hong Kong and Singapore. Lal (forthcoming) also cites India between 1870 and the 1920's as another example of the latter, noting the rapid growth of trade and manufacturing output that was accomplished in India before free trade was abandoned. Wartime destruction and the U.S. breakup of entrenched interest groups are given credit for some of the success of post World War II Japan in these same respects.

Likewise, Olson (1982, Ch. 5) argues that *jurisdictional integration*, such as occurred historically in the creation of nation-states out of local fiefdoms, first in England, then in Holland, and subsequently in France (especially after the French Revolution) and Germany in the late 19th century, or in the creation of regional common markets like the European Economic Community in the late 1950s, could be expected to have the effect of breaking down local interest groups and undermining their pernicious influences on efficiency, income and wealth distribution and growth. For evidence in support of this implication, Olson shows that the commercial and industrial revolutions came first to England, then to Holland and then to France, Germany, Italy and the rest of Europe. Olson also uses the opening up of frontier areas and the relative importance of immigration[44] in the United States to explain why interest groups remain relatively weaker than would be expected given that country's political stability, absence of war time destruction and democratic environment. Finally, the Meiji Restoration which broke down the feudalistic control of the local samurai, together with foreign imposition of free trade, are given credit for the rapid growth of Japan from 1870 until well into the 20th century.

Another important modification to Olson's second proposition is that those countries which encourage more encompassing (inclusive) interest groups at the expense of more narrow and exclusive ones are more likely to limit the deleterious effects of collective action. Olson (1982, Ch. 4, pp. 89-92) argues that Sweden and Norway are countries whose labor unions and employer groups are especially broad and encompassing in their memberships and then points to their relatively satisfactory growth rates — rates which are more satisfactory than would have been supposed on the basis of the relatively long period for which they have enjoyed stability, security and democracy —

---

[44]In the case of immigration, however, one could argue that it should more appropriately be looked at as an endogenous, rather than exogenous, variable. This is because an open-immigration policy is, at least in part, the result of interest group interaction in the receiving country.

as evidence in favor of this modification of this second proposition.[45]

Olson hypothesizes also that encompassing interest groups are more likely to emerge in stable, mature economies than in more unstable autocratic ones because considerably more time and effort is likely to be required to form such groups than in the case of narrow groups. Therefore relatively narrow groups can be expected to dominate in less mature and less stable environments like those of most LDCs. On the other hand, in the political arena where numbers may play an important role, either via the ballot box or through popular demonstrations, political entrepreneurs or the state itself may have an interest in forming (and also controlling) encompassing groups.[46]

B. Status Quo, conservatism and revolutions[47]

The issues addressed in the previous sections are about reaching *a* solution to the provision of public goods through collective action. From a longer term perspective, which is of course relevant to economic development, a more general problem is whether or not and how a *transition* takes place from one solution to another as circumstances change over time. From the perspective of long term development the desirability of any such transition hinges on whether or not the efficiency and accumulation-enhancing benefits of flexibility and change outweigh the cooperation and accumulation-enhancing effects of stability of expectations. As a result, change virtually inevitably presents desirability tradeoffs to individuals, groups and society as a whole.

As mentioned above, frequently the process of institutional change is extremely slow and gradual. In particular, interest groups, organizations and norms may take a long time to emerge. The reason for this is that time is required for individuals to identify group objectives and to go about realizing them. Once formed, interest groups and organizations tend to become permanent. However, not all collective action processes and interest group behavior exhibit these characteristics of continuity, progressive intensity and permanence. The observation of social phenomena reveals that in many instances interest groups are formed rapidly, often unexpectedly in or-

---

[45]Once again, however, one could read Olson as suggesting that the character of existing distributional coalitions is, in part at least, endogenous thereby making it difficult to accept this as evidence in favor of this hypothesis.

[46]For example, in those autocratic LDCs dominated by single political parties and characterized by a relatively high propensity to intervene in the formation and activities of interest groups their assistance to interest group formation might well be biased in the direction of broad, encompassing groups for purposes of mobilizing popular support.

[47]Many of the ideas in the following discussion are borrowed from Kuran (1987b, 1988).

der to achieve some specific objective, and then soon disappear. Prominent examples of such spontaneous and temporary collective action are riots of consumers against government decisions to increase the prices of basic goods (often in the context of IMF adjustment programs) and wildcat strikes by workers in a specific firm or sector. Conversely, it often occurs that institutions, rules and policies outlive their usefulness, resulting in situations where the status quo prevails and efficient institutional change does not take place.

Prior to the argument of Olson and some of the other elements of the theory of collective action mentioned in Section III above, the general expectation would seem to have been that stable democratic countries would be characterized by policy instability and perhaps cycling. Such an expectation follows from the difficulty pointed out by Arrow (1963) that individuals with differing preferences in choosing among a number of alternatives would have in reaching agreement on any specific action. Aggregations of individual rank orderings among the alternatives may be inconsistent, and majority vote (or any other) coalitions inherently unstable, suggesting that policy cycling would be likely.

As Arrow (1974) and Tullock (1981) have suggested, the remarkable stability of policy choices and institutions has posed something of a paradox begging an explanation. The substantial time requirements for organizing groups for collective action and the importance of large, encompassing interest groups with complex rules, crowded agendas and decision-making inertia may contribute in no small way to the resolution of the paradox.

Some transaction cost considerations may also help explain the paradox. First, similar to the agency problem that arises between a manager and an owner, the leader of a particular group may resist rule changes even if he knows that such changes would benefit the group as a whole inasmuch as conceding the use of faulty rule or, worse yet, responsibilty for the use of that rule might prove fatal to his chances of survival in his cherished position of group leadership. Second, in order to reduce the transaction costs in the use of group rules, the groups may introduce ideology in favor of existing rules. As a result, the ideology may have the effect of raising the cost of changing the rules, thereby contributing to the maintenance of the status quo. Indeed, along with ideology may come the application of sanctions against those making or even suggesting the possibility of rule changes. Third, following Williamson (1985), in the presence of asset specificity which otherwise could easily lead to "hold-out" behavior both within and between groups, paternalistic practices and other methods of preserving group solidarity and the status quo are likely to be introduced.

The aforementioned considerations pertain to the parties to the contract themselves. However, also having a bearing on status quo retention is the recognition by those external to the contract of the transaction costs implied by the actual or potential disruption of contractual relationships and the deleterious consequences thereof.[48] As a result, many groups not directly related to existing contractual relations may have a stake in their preservation [Goldberg (1974, 1976)]. According to Owen and Braeutigam (1978), even if they realize that the terms and conditions of such contracts are out of date, groups external to such contracts may want to see them continued so that the "rights" to their continuance can be respected. Since the status quo frequently gives rise to expectations about future continuity, and different agents make their boundedly rational decisions based on these expectations, "fairness" in many contexts implies the preservation of the status quo.[49]

Political scientists such as Frohock (1987) and Riker (1980) have argued that bounded rationality reduces the numbers and complexity of alternative proposals making it easier for majorities to form and be preserved over time. Riker (1980) and Weingast and Marshall (1987) point to the importance of the agenda setter and of the stability-enhancing way in which political institutions regulate agenda-setting in preserving the status quo. Sociologists show that individual rationality is constrained by the fact that individuals are embedded in social institutions [Wrong (1961) and Granovetter (1985)]. Frohock (1987) argues that preference orderings among political alternatives are much less unstable than might otherwise be expected inasmuch as they are conditional on reasons and principles which are not likely to be easily overturned.

Another more novel approach is that of "critical mass" models,[50] which allow for interdependencies among preferences and may also be of considerable help in explaining the unexpected stability of the status quo. The critical mass models can take several different forms, such as economies of scale and network externalities as in Arthur (1985), David (1985, 1986), and Markus

---

[48]Consider the example of divorce and the relevance of rules against divorce. While individual preferences — even among Catholics — may be for the liberty of action that freedom to divorce would provide, the church or society might well want to retain restrictions on divorce in part because of the social costs that divorce may impose on parties external to the marriage or divorce contracts.

[49]The maintenance of the status quo is likely to be deemed "fair" by parties external to the contracts not only for altruistic reasons but also according to Rawls (1971) because they might think that the costs of adjustment derived from a contractual or rule break could equally well happen to them.

[50]For a concise but informative survey of these models see Kuran (1988).

(1987), collective opinion as in Rogers (1983), tastes as in Akerlof (1976, 1980), Granovetter and Soong (1986), Schelling (1978), and Witt (1986), pressures to conform to the standards of work and behavior around one as in Jones (1984), and the formation of public expressions of preferences including preference falsification which in turn affect private preferences as in Kuran (1987a, 1987b).

Nevertheless, common to all such forms, the basic idea is that the payoff to any choice of action on the part of the individual depends on the total number of individuals choosing this option. Since the choices of others are not instantaneously available, it is the expectations of the number of others choosing such options, which, in turn, is likely to be substantially affected by past observations of the choices of others which affect current decisions. In the absence of very substantial shocks to the system, expectations are likely to be static and, being grounded on the status quo, are therefore likely to ensure that the status quo is maintained. While expectations are generally self-fulfilling, this does not mean that the status quo will always be maintained. Indeed, it may also mean that, under appropriate conditions, relatively small shocks to the system may generate bandwagon effects.

Kuran (1988, p. 29) provides the following illustration:

> ...Consider a group faced with the decision of whether to riot against the government. Each member of the group will riot only if the expected number of rioters is above his personal threshold. In the typical scenario, if sufficiently many people are expected to riot, enough do so to start a bandwagon process through which the number of rioters grows by leaps and bounds. On the other hand, if few are expected to riot, even fewer choose to join in, and, through a reverse bandwagon process, the nascent riot peters out. In sum, a major riot breaks out only if there is expected to be a "critical mass" of rioters. Groups favoring one equilibrium over the other do well in such a setting to exaggerate their support: if believed by enough decision makers, even totally false, information becomes a self-fulfilling prophecy.

A collective action will obtain only if individuals expect that a "critical mass" of individuals will engage in it. In that case, when the process is started, it feeds on itself, and other individuals increasingly join the action. Since the process is rapid, the interest group is usually neither able nor interested in developing the necessary organizational mechanisms to ensure continued existence. Even if the action is successful, therefore, the group may return to its initial state of "dormance" or "latency."

While many of these considerations which help preserve the status quo apply in autocratic as well as democratic regimes or in LDCs as well as DCs, this does not preclude the possibility that there might be some signifi-

cant differences between the two sets of conditions. Indeed, we have already
noted the implication drawn by Olson (1982) that broad, encompassing distributional coalitions would be unlikely to arise in countries with autocratic
governments.[51]

Hence, from Olson we seem to have a hypothesis that autocracy leads to
more interest groups of the small, narrow and exclusive variety which compete with each other, and make policies and institutional rules more unstable.
In other words, the flip side of the logic Olson used to explain policy regime
stability (instead of the otherwise expected policy cycling) in stable democracies would seem to lead to the expectation of policy cycling in the case of
autocratic countries.

Heiner (1983), however, suggests a possible offsetting influence. At the
level of the individual he argues that the more unstable and uncertain the environment, the more evidence contrary to the model the (boundedly) rational
individual would want to see before abandoning his model of the world, and
with it the existing set of rules designed to be consonant with it. Hence, to
the extent that the same would apply to groups as to individuals, groups in
more uncertain environments like those of LDCs might have an even greater
tendency to retain the status quo than in DCs. However, much might depend
on the character of the generated instability about which neither Olson nor
Heiner has much to say.[52]

On the other hand, since autocratic regimes are especially concerned with
security and, as argued above, are more likely to want to undertake solutions
to collective action problems by themselves, they are unlikely to remain mere
bystanders to the process of interest group interaction. For example, to the

---

[51]Several reasons for this are either explicit or implicit in his analysis. First,
autocratic regimes are more likely to find the existence of large, encompassing groups threatening. Not only are they likely to be directly threatening in
terms of numbers of people and quantity of resources that could potentially
be used in collective action against the regime, but also to the extent they
would be successful in achieving agreements on collective action among heterogeneous elements in society, this would seem to render existing autocractic
governments redundant. Second, the greater instability which would result
from the absence of encompassing groups, and hence also of the healing and
consensus-rendering benefits that they can provide, would, in turn, undermine the formation of encompassing groups. North (1981) supplements this
argument by arguing that, since autocratic governments should by Olsonian
logic be able to make decisions and change policies more quickly than democratic governments, they would be expected to have sharper and more rapid
changes in policies and hence, once again, greater instability.

[52]Heiner's hypothesis is, in fact, stated in terms of uncertainty, not instability,
but the two concepts are frequently defined so as to be fairly closely related.

extent they fear the creation of spontaneous flare-ups of anti-regime types of collective action in otherwise latent groups, autocratic regimes might themselves want to organize such groups in order to control them. In other words, the state itself might perform the task of political entrepreneurs in democractic countries. Even if autocratic regimes should not be politically active in either the mobilization or the suppression of such groups, they might be inclined to avoid the kind of sharp deterioration in the relative well-being of such groups, which, as Brenner (1983) argues, would be likely to trigger significant collective action. One might expect, therefore, autocratic regimes to be more likely than ones with democratic decision-making to cushion the impact of exogenous shocks, like rises in the import prices of basic necessities or food shortages due to harvest shortfalls, with various kinds of subsidies and/or price controls cum rationing. Even without exogenous shocks, policies of this sort might be necessary in order to overcome the necessarily negative impacts on latent groups of collective actions undertaken by the well-organized narrow, exclusive groups which from Olson's analysis would be expected to dominate in countries with autocratic governments.

Even if an autocratic regime should be unwilling or unable to do anything to overcome the sudden and severe deterioration of the economic position of the large latent groups whose action it necessarily fears, in view of the implications of the "critical mass models" reviewed above, it could be expected to undertake various kinds of actions to affect expectations in such a way as to deter collective action. In particular, once spontaneous action commences, the autocratic regime might be expected to do one or more of the following in order to avoid expectational changes favorable to participation in the collective action: (1) crush the action immediately, (2) suppress all information about the action, (3) publicize, perhaps with dramatic pictures, the dire consequences to anyone caught participating in such action, and (4) deliberately and falsely underreport the extent of such participation.[53]

An even stronger role for autocratic states in interest group formation and activity is suggested by the "corporatist" theorists.[54]

Primarily based on historical experience, corporatists argue that interest groups are likely to be formed by the state, not only for purposes of control, but also to facilitate administration and to perform certain governmental functions. When interest groups are corporatist in character, the nature of

---

[53]There may also be some situations, however, where autocratic governments may actually want to trigger such riots, as has been suggested may have been the case in Egypt, in order to rescind the IMF-sponsored abrupt removal of bread subsidies.

[54]See Schmitter (1974) and the references therein.

interest groups and the relationships between them can best be understood
in terms of the character of the state and its interests. The emphasis is then
on government influence on interest groups rather than vice versa.

A somewhat less extreme position is advocated by Bianchi (1984) who
argues that, even if interest groups are not the creations of the state, they are
very much influenced by political culture, on the one hand, and government
policies toward association, on the other. In his case study of Turkish public
enterprises, Bianchi argues that these two variables intervene in such a way
as to limit the generality and strength of the otherwise reasonable hypothesis
from sociologist Durkheim and political scientist de Tocqueville that interest
group activity should be directly related to the level of social, political and
economic development.[55]

C. Institutional change and development

Through the dynamic effects of institutional change, collective action
may be closely related to economic development. In that context let us consider some feedbacks between institutional change and development, and,
following Ruttan and Hayami (1984), let us consider them as the result of
dynamic interaction between the supply and demand for institutional change.

With respect to the demand for institutional change, as development
proceeds, among the most important and most widely observed changes are
those in the relative supplies and demands of the various factors of production,
and hence in relative factor prices. Many countries have witnessed a gradual
evolution from conditions characterized by plentiful land and scarce labor to
scarce land and plentiful labor. Feeny (1982), Hayami and Kikuchi (1982),
North and Thomas (1975) and especially Ruttan and Hayami (1984), have
all pointed to cases in which they claim that such changes have had the effect
of inducing institutional changes of the property rights type. For example,
Feeny (1982) has argued that the rise in the price of land relative to labor led
to the decline of slavery (property rights in labor) and the increase of private
property rights in land in Thailand between 1850 and 1915. Similarly, Hayami
and Kikuchi (1982) point to the role of population growth and technology –
and irrigation – induced increases in land productivity in explaining a trend
toward subtenancy in the Philippines which had the effect of increasing the
completeness of property rights in land and decreasing labor security. These
are but a few of the many examples of what has been dubbed by Ruttan and
Binswanger (1978) induced institutional change.

However, not only are some of the empirical claims offered in support

---

[55]See de Tocqueville (1974) and Durkheim (1964).

of the alleged examples of induced institutional change open to challenge on empirical grounds [e.g. by Field (1981), Runge and Bromley (1979) and Grabowski (1988)], but also the generality of these claims can be challenged on the grounds that other considerations frequently intervene in the process. As Bromley (forthcoming) and Grabowski (1988) appropriately point out, tastes, values, and attitudes also change with development and over time in such a way that once-acceptable institutions like slavery, even if they are efficient, may eventually become socially unacceptable. Similarly, ideology can change, the number of conflicting ideologies can increase [North (1984)], and the degree of social cohesion can change in ways as to either assist or impede the adoption of institutional changes induced by changes in relative scarcities.

With respect to the frequently neglected "supply" side of institutional change, Hayami and Ruttan (1985) and Ruttan (1986) point to the role that social science research and knowledge may play on the supply side of institutional change. Ruttan cites the absence of quantitative agricultural economic knowledge concerning the costs and benefits of price supports and of income payments for the delay of the shift from the more distortionary and inefficiency-inducing price support programs to income supplement programs for farmers in the United States. Likewise, Krueger (1988) points to the relevance of knowledge concerning the reaction of markets, politicians and other actors and the consequences thereof for group interests in determining the character and extent of collective action in the case of the U.S. sugar program. In the same spirit, one might argue that the detailed studies of some of the undesirable (including inequality-increasing) effects of income redistribution programs and of government regulations may have contributed to the current trend toward the dismantling of welfare programs and deregulation.[56] The character and relative influence of interest groups would subsequently be affected hence giving rise to another round of dynamic feedbacks.

Naturally, the further one goes afield from the knowledge of the benefits and costs of collective action and of the various means of controlling the free-rider problem, the more ambiguous becomes the distinction between "supply" and "demand" considerations. Nevertheless, within the same spirit of the "supply side" arguments, one might also include (1) the understanding on the part of the initiating group or the leaders thereof for the logical justification for the institutional change, (2) their ability to communicate that logic in understandable terms to other members of the group and to other groups,

---

[56]North (1986), however, feels that the importance of this influence is exaggerated.

(3) the ability of the initiators of such collective action to artfully exaggerate the benefits and underestimate the costs so as to make the net advantages appear more overwhelming than they really are, and (4) the ability of the initiator to make group members believe that the origin of the proposed action is genuinely indigenous, not an idea imposed by a foreign organization, such as the International Monetary Fund or a foreign donor, as a condition for external finance. Krueger (1984), Harberger (1984) and especially Nelson (1984) demonstrate the possibility of dynamic feedbacks involving these factors in the context of LDC stabilization programs.

For another example, consider the connection between development and the introduction of formal programs of old-age security. As development proceeds, life expectancy increases. This has several fundamental effects. One such effect is to increase the rate of return on human capital relative to physical capital, thereby encouraging families, even those in the rural areas of LDCs, to send their children to school and later on for the children to migrate to urban areas to find the kinds of jobs where education can be particularly useful. The effect is to weaken family ties and hence the expectations on the part of parents and their children that, in the absence of formal old-age security programs, children can be counted on to take care of their parents during their old age. A second such effect is to increase the number of elderly dependents in the average family, thereby increasing the need for sources of their support.

Even though from the principles of collective action the elderly as a whole are likely to be a latent group, given enough time, some subgroups such as urban-based civil servants and factory workers are likely to become sufficiently organized as to initiate collective action to obtain for themselves old-age pension and insurance systems. Development itself, moreover, increases the proportion of jobs in the well-organized sector of the economy. The introduction of such systems, of course, reduces the demand for the traditional system in which children take care of their parents while living in intergenerationally extended households.

The demonstration of success in collective action, on the one hand, coupled with the continued undermining of the viability of the traditional system, on the other, is likely to contribute to a bandwagon effect toward the general adoption of formal old-age security systems and away from the traditional intrahousehold system of intergenerational transfers. The same bandwagon effect is likely to be further enhanced by the decreased demand for children (the old-age security motive being an important component of the demand for children), thereby further increasing the family's need for external support of its elderly dependents. Still another contributing factor might be income-induced changes in tastes in favor of privacy and away from togetherness and family cohesion, leading to the breakup of extended households and thereby once again undermining the reliability of within-family intergenerational transfers as a means of dealing with the old-age security problem.[57]

VII. Taking Stock: Where to Go from Here?

As should be clear from the above exposition, the comparative static version of collective action theory developed by Mancur Olson and others is considerably more well developed than the dynamic versions which involve critical mass and bandwagon effects.

With respect to the former approach it is clear that these contributions have taken us a long way toward giving us a set of testable hypotheses that could be used in predicting the likelihood of success in collective action in different situations and in linking such theories to development and growth. Moreover, they do so with models which, although simple, contain microeconomic foundations. Nevertheless, as the following comments suggest, there is still a considerable way to go, especially as far as relevance to the conditions of the LDCs is concerned.

First, internal to the theory would seem to be some contradictions. For example, encompassing distributional coalitions are thought to be more likely to arise in stable, democratic countries and less distortionary and hence less efficiency-inhibiting than narrow ones which would be more likely to dominate in other circumstances. On the other hand, encompassing groups are more likely to have organizations which are more permanent and to be more inflexible, suggesting that the stable democratic societies with more encompassing distributional coalitions will be less able to adjust to changing circumstances. How can we know, however, which way the net balance of these considerations for growth will go? Why is it obvious, as Olson has suggested, that, overall efficiency and growth will be lower in mature, stable and democratic countries? Unless such ambiguities can be removed, the theory will remain much less operational than it otherwise might be.

Second, as a number of critics have pointed out, several of the measures and concepts suggested by Olson and the others need to be sharpened. Examples include the notion of group size (should it be measured by number of members, by budget, or by something else?), and the level of jurisdictional integration.[58]

---

[57]Rogers (1983) provides many additional examples of changes in norms induced by economic development.

[58]Lehner (1983), e.g., has pointed out that in some respects Switzerland is

Third, as suggested by Ostrom (1987) it may be that the theory would be different for different types of public goods. Similarly, Uphoff (1986) provides examples suggesting that the theory will be different depending on whether or not the collective action involves the production of public goods or only their maintenance.

Fourth, and especially with respect to Olson's theories, by focusing on individual interest groups rather than their interaction, the flavor is excessively partial equilibrium in nature. Much more relevant, though thus far leading to fewer conclusions of relevance to LDCs, are theories of rent-seeking and interest group competition.

Fifth, much more work needs to be done on rent-seeking, policy cycling and other factors in the context of bureaucracies of non-representative governments that are more characteristic of LDCs.

Sixth, with the introduction of different actors and groups and their interactions, the problem of knowledge concerning the costs and benefits of collective action and their correct evaluation by individual actors becomes critical. Also, as Kuran (1988) suggests, much of the work to date assumes that the nature of collective action or at least the list of alternative kinds of action is given, whereas in fact the inability to identify an appropriate action may be an even more fundamental problem than the decision to go ahead on a preselected form of collective action. Moreover, even when the list of alternative kinds of action, or instruments of policy, to be used is known to the relevant group, there remains the problem of explaining its choice of the most appropriate instrument for achieving its objectives.[59]

Seventh, while the analysis *does* call attention to the importance of selective incentives in achieving collective action, it *does not* provide much guidance as to which selective incentives might be more efficient than others in a particular setting.

Eighth, and rather importantly for present purposes, in general in light of the large number of factors which can induce collective action the rather extreme pessimism with respect to the prospects for successful collective action which has pervaded much of the literature on collective action would

---

very integrated but in other respects it is not. Which ones are the relevant ones?

[59]Mayer and Riezman (1988), for example, have shown that groups attempting to achieve redistribution through policy-induced factor price changes would not normally choose tariffs as the instrument for doing so, at least within the usual political economy trade models. As a result, the extent to which tariffs are in fact chosen needs to be explained perhaps in terms of enforcement and collection costs.

seem excessive. This suggests the usefulness of case studies which might help distinguish success from failure in relatively comparable circumstances.

Last, but perhaps most importantly, since it deals almost exclusively with the context of growth in DCs, it gives us little guidance as to how the hypotheses should be modified to fit the quite different conditions of the LDCs. This underscores the critical need for empirical case studies in an LDC, the subject of Part III of the volume.

With respect to the more dynamic versions of collective action theory, as promising as their applications to development would appear to be, it is clear that we are even farther from having a theory capable of yielding highly operational hypotheses. The possibilities for successful generalization would seem much more limited. For example, with respect to the aforementioned hypotheses concerning the likelihood of policy and rule cycling in LDC conditions, much would seem to depend on specific conditions, types of instability, other aspects of the social structure, the position of the state and the attitudes of its chief actors.[60] As a result, empirical case studies are likely to be necessary even for theory construction. Given all the factors that are relevant and the interdependencies in preferences, the likelihood of achieving critical mass and hence of achieving revolutions or important institutional reforms may be very difficult to predict.[61] The dynamic theories, important as they may seem, are likely to be weak in predictive power. Quite conceivably, however, they may be strengthened by taking into account potentially important interactions between transaction cost and governance and the dynamic aspects of collective action.

References

Akerlof, George, 1976, "The Economics of Caste and of the Rat Race and Other Woeful Tales," *Quarterly Journal of Economics* 90, 599-617.
——————, 1980, "A Theory of Social Custom, of which Unemployment May be One Consequence," *Quarterly Journal of Economics*, 94 (June), 749-775.
Alchian, Armen A. and Harold Demsetz, 1972, "Production, Information Costs and Economic Organization," *American Economic Review*, 62,

---

[60]This uncertain outcome about the likelihood of collective action and policy recycling is by no means inconsistent with the results of Krueger (1978, p. 37) in which it is reported that policy cycling has occured with respect to trade and exchange regimes in some autocratic LDCs but not in others.

[61]For a simple but promising attempt to draw upon static as well as dynamic collective action theory for predicting the likelihood of major policy reforms, see Nabli (1988).

777-795.

_____, 1973, "The Property Rights Paradigm," *Journal of Economic History*, 33, 16-27.

Alikhani, I. and O. Havrylyshyn, 1982, "The Political Economy of Protection in Developing Countries: A Case Study of Colombia and South Korea," Division Working Paper No. 1982-4, July, World Bank.

Anderson, K., 1980, "The Political Market for Government Assistance to Australian Manufacturing Industries," *The Economic Record*, 56 (153), pp. 132-144.

_____, and Yujiro Hayami, 1986, *The Political Economy of Agricultural Protection: East Asia in International Perspective.* Sydney: Allen and Unwin.

Arrow, Kenneth J., 1963, *Social Choice and Individual Values.* New Haven: Yale University Press, Revised Edition.

_____, 1974, *The Limits of Organization.* New York: Norton.

Arthur, W. Brian, 1985, "Competing Technologies and Lock-in by Historical Small Events: The Dynamics of Allocation under Increasing Returns." Stanford: Stanford University Center for Economic Policy Research Working Paper.

Axelrod, Robert A., 1984, *The Evolution of Cooperation.* New York: Basic Books.

Balassa, Bela and Associates, 1971, *The Structure of Protection in Developing Countries.* Baltimore: John Hopkins University Press.

Baldwin, R.E., 1976, "The Political Economy of Postwar U.S. Trade Policy," *The Bulletin No. 4*, New York University, Graduate School of Business Administration.

_____, 1985, *The Political Economy of U.S. Import Policy*, Cambridge: MIT Press.

Balisacan, Arsenio M. and James A. Roumasset, 1987, "Public Choice of Economic Policy: Growth of Agricultural Production," *Weltwirtschaftliches Archiv*, 123, Heft 2, 232-248.

Basu, Kaushik, Eric Jones and Ekkehart Schlicht, 1987, "The Growth and Decay of Custom: The Role of the New Institutional Economics in Economic History," *Explorations in Economic History* 24.

Bates, Robert M, 1981, *Markets and States in Tropical Africa: The Political Basis of Agricultural Policies.* Berkeley: University of California Press.

_____, and W.P. Rogerson, 1980, "Agriculture in Development: A Coalition Analysis," *Public Choice*, 32(5), 513-527.

Baumol, William J., 1952, *Welfare Economics and the Theory of the State.* Cambridge, Mass.: Harvard University Press.

Becker, Gary S., 1983, "Competition among Pressure Groups for Political Influence," *Quarterly Journal of Economics*, 98 (August), 371-400.

Bhagwati, J., 1982, *Import Competition and Response.* Chicago: The University of Chicago Press.

_____, and T.N. Srinivasan, 1980, "Revenue Seeking: A Generalization of the Theory of Tariffs," *Journal of Political Economy*, 88, No. 6, 1069-1087.

Bianchi: Robert, 1984, *Interest Groups and Political Development in Turkey.* Princeton: Princeton University Press.

Binswanger, Hans P. and Vernon W. Ruttan, eds., *Induced Innovation: Technology, Institutions and Development.* Baltimore: Johns Hopkins University Press.

_____, and Pasquale L. Scandizzo, 1983, *Patterns of Agricultural Protection.* World Bank, Agricultrual Research Unit, Report No. 15.

Blumel, Wolfgang, Rudiger Pethig and Oskar von dem Hagen, 1986, "The Theory of Public Goods: A Survey of Recent Issues" *Journal of Institutional and Theoretical Economics,* 142: 241-309.

Braverman, Avishay and J. Luis Guasch, forthcoming, "Institutional Analysis of Credit Cooperatives" in P. Bardhan, ed. *The Theory of Agrarian Institutions.* New York: Oxford University Press.

Brennan, Geoffrey and James Buchanan, 1985, *The Reason of Rules: Constitutional Political Economy.* Cambridge: Cambridge University Press.

_____, and Jonathan Pincus, 1987, "Rational Actor Theory in Politics: A Critical Review of John Quiggin" *The Economic Record* 63 (March), 21-32.

Brenner, Reuven, 1983, *History — the Human Gamble.* Chicago: University of Chicago Press.

Brock, William A., and Stephen P. Magee, 1978, "The Economics of Special Interest Politics: The Case of the Tariff," *American Economic Review,* 68, 246-250.

Bromley, Daniel W., 1988, "Property Relations and Economic Development: The Other Land Reform," *World Development* 16:

_____, forthcoming, *Economic Interests and Institutions: the Conceptual Foundations of Public Policy.* London: Basil Blackwell.

_____, and Devendra P. Chapagain, 1984, "The Village Against the Center: Resource Depletion in South Asia," *American Journal of Agricultural Economics* 66: 868-873.

Buchanan, James M., 1965, "An Economic Theory of Clubs," *Economica* 82 (125): 1-14.

_____, 1968, *The Demand and Supply of Public Goods.* Chicago: Rand McNally.

_____, 1987, "The Constitution of Economic Policy," *Science* 236, 1433-1436.

Caves, R.E., 1976, "Economic Models of Political Choice: Canada's Tariff Structure," *Canadian Journal of Economics,* 9(2), 278-300.

Chamberlin, John, 1974, "Provision of Collective Goods as a Function of Group Size" *American Political Science Review* 68: 707-716

Choi, Kwan, 1983, "A Statistical Test of Olson's Model," in Dennis C. Mueller, ed., *The Political Economy of Growth.* New Haven and London: Yale University Press, 57-78.

Chopra, Kanchan, Gopal K. Kadekodi and M.N. Murty, 1986, "Peoples' Participation: An Approach to the Management of Common Property Resources," Delhi: Institute of Economic Growth.

Colander, David C., ed., 1984, *Neoclassical Political Economy: The Analysis of Rent-Seeking and DUP Activities.* Cambridge, Mass: Balinger.

Cordell, John, 1987, "Sea Tenure in Bahia" in National Research Council, *Proceedings of the Conference on Common Property Research Management.* Washington, D.C.: National Research Council.

Cummins, Richard Dean, 1987, "The Influence of Industrial Pressure Groups within the People's Republic of China," Los Angeles: University of

Southern California Unpublished Ph.D Dissertation.

Dahlman, Carl, 1980, *The Open Field System and Beyond: A Property Rights Analysis of an Economic Institution.* Cambridge University Press.

David, Paul A., 1985, "Clio and the Economics of QWERTY," *American Economic Review,* 75, 332-337.

—————————, 1986, "Some New Standards for the Economics of Standardization in the Information Age," Stanford University, Technological Innovation Project Working Paper.

Demsetz, Harold, 1967, "Toward a Theory of Property Rights," *American Economic Review,* 57 (May), 347-359.

De Tocqueville, Alexis, 1974, *Democracy in America.* New York: Vintage Books.

Durkheim, Emile, 1964, *The Division of Labor in Society.* New York: The Free Press.

Ehrenfeld, David W., 1972, *Conserving Life on Earth.* New York: Oxford University Press.

Erickson-Blomquist, W.H. and Elinor Ostrom, 1984, "Institutional Capacity and the Resolution of a Commons Dilemma," Bloomington, Indiana University Workshop in Political Theory and Policy Analysis.

Feeny, David, 1982, *The Political Economy of Productivity.* Vancouver: University of British Columbia University Press.

Field, Alexander J., 1981, "The Problem with Neoclassical Economics: A Critique with Special Reference to the North-Thomas Model of Pre-1500 Europe," *Explorations in Economic History* 18 (April): 174-181.

Findlay, R. and S. Wellisz, 1983, "Some Aspects of the Political Economy of Trade Restriction," *Kyklos,* 36(3), 469-488.

Finger, I.M., H.K. Hall, and D.R. Nelson, 1982, "The Political Economy of Administered Protection," *The American Economic Review,* 72(3), 452-566.

Frohock, Fred M., 1987, *Rational Association.* Syracuse: Syracuse University Press.

Gardner, Bruce L., 1987, "Causes of U.S. Farm Commodity Programs," *Journal of Political Economy* 95 (April), 290-310.

Gilbert, Alan and Peter M. Ward, 1985, *Housing the State and the Poor.* Cambridge: Cambridge University Press.

Gilles, J.L. and K. Jamtgaard, 1981, "Overgrazing in Pastoral Areas: The Commons Reconsidered," *Sociologia Ruralis* 21, 129-141.

Goldberg, Victor P., 1974, "Institutional Change and the Quasi-invisible Hand," *Journal of Law and Economics,* 17, 461-496.

—————————, 1976, "Regulation and Administered Contracts," *Bell Journal of Economics,* 7, 426-448.

Grabowski, Richard, 1988, "The Theory of Induced Institutional Innovation: A Critique." *World Development* 16 (March): 385-394.

Granovetter, Mark, 1978, "Threshold Models of Collective Behavior," *American Journal of Scoiology,* 83, 1420-1443.

—————————, 1985, "Economic Action and Social Structure: The Problem of Embeddedness," *American Journal of Sociology* 91: 481-510.

—————————, and Roland Soong, 1986, "Threshold Models of Interpersonal Effects in Consumer Demand," *Journal of Economic Behavior and Organization* 7: 83-99.

Guttman, Joel, 1978a, "Understanding Collective Action: Matching Behavior," *American Economic Review* 68 (May), 251-255.

_____, 1978b, "Interest Groups and the Demand for Agricultural Research," *Journal of Political Economy* 86, No. 3, 467-484.

_____, 1982, "Common Property Externalities: Isolation, Assurance, and Resource Depletion in a Traditional Grazing Context: Comment," *American Journal of Agricultural Economics* (November), 781-782.

Hagen, Everett E., 1962, *On the Theory of Social Change.* Homewood, Illinois: Dorsey Press.

Harberger, Arnold C., 1984, "Economic Policy and Economic Growth," in A.C. Harberger, ed., *World Economic Growth.* San Francisco: Institute for Contemporary Studies, 427-467.

Hardin, Garett, 1968, "The Tragedy of the Commons," *Science* 162 (December): 1243-1248.

_____, 1978, "Political Requirements for Preserving our Common Heritage," in Howard P. Srokaw, ed., *Wildlife and America.* Washington, DC: Council on Environmental Quality: 310-317.

Hardin, Russell, 1982, *Collective Action.* Washington, D.C., Resources for the Future.

Hartle, D.G., 1983, "The Theory of Rent-Seeking: Some Reflections," University of To-ronto, Department of Economics Working Paper No. 8313, Toronto.

Hayami, Y., and M. Kikuchi, 1982, *Asian Village Economy at the Crossroads.* Baltimore: Johns Hopkins University Press.

_____, and Vernon W. Ruttan, 1985, *Agricultural Development: A Global Perspective.* Baltimore: Johns Hopkins Press.

Head, John G., 1962, "Public Goods and Public Policy" *Public Finance* 17: 197-219.

Heilbronner, Robert L., 1974, *An Inquiry into the Human Prospect.* New York: Norton.

Heiner, Ronald A., 1983, "The Origin of Preditable Behavior," *American Economic Review*, 83, 560-593.

Helleiner, Gerald K., 1977, "The Political Economy of Canada's Tariff Structure: An Alternative Model," *Canadian Journal of Economics*, X(2), 318-326.

Hirschman, Albert O., 1967, *Development Projects Observed.* Washington: Brookings Institution.

_____, 1968, "The Political Economy of Import-Substituting Industrialization in Latin America," *Quarterly Journal of Economics* (February), 1-32.

_____, 1970, *Exit, Voice and Loyalty: Responses to Decline in Firms, Organizations and States.* Cambridge: Harvard University Press.

_____, 1972, "The Changing Tolerance for Income Inequality in the Course of Economic Development," *Quarterly Journal of Economics*, 87 (November), 544-565.

_____, 1981, *Essays in Trespassing.* Cambridge: Cambridge University Press.

_____, 1984, *Getting Ahead Collectively: Grassroots Experiences in Latin America.* New York: Pergamon Press.

Hoffman, Elizabeth and Matthew Spitzer, 1985, "Experimental Test of the Coase Theorem with Large Bargaining Groups," *Journal of Legal Studies*, 14, 259-280.

Hutt, W.H., 1964, *The Economics of the Colour Bar*. London: Merritt and Hatcher.

Jones, Stephen, 1984, *The Economics of Conformism*. New York: Basil Blackwell.

Kalt, Joseph P. and Mark A. Zupan, 1984, "Capture and Ideology in the Economic Theory of Politics," *American Economic Review* 74 (June), 279-300.

_____, forthcoming, "The Ideological Behavior of Legislators: Rational on-the-Job Consumption or Just a Residual?"

Klein, Julius, 1920, *The Mesta 1273-1836*. Cambridge: Harvard University Press.

Kreps, David M., Paul Milgrom, John Roberts and Robert Wilson, 1982, "Rational Cooperation in the Finitely Repeated Prisoners' Dilemma," *Journal of Economic Theory* 27: 245-252.

Krueger, A.O., 1974, "The Political Economy of Rent-Seeking," *American Economic Review*, 64, 291-303.

_____, 1978, *Foreign Trade Regimes and Economic Development: Liberalization Attempts and Consequences*. Cambridge: Ballinger Publishing Co., Vol. 10, p. 37.

_____, 1984, "Problems of Liberalization," in A.C. Harberger, ed., *World Economic Growth*. San Francisco: Institute for Contemporary Studies, 403-425.

_____, 1988, "The Political Economy of Controls: American Sugar," NBER Working Paper, No 2504, February.

Kuran, Timur, 1987a, "Chameleon Voters and Public Choice" *Public Choice* 53, no. 1: 53-78.

_____, 1987b, "Preference Falsification, Policy Continuity and Collective Conservatism," *Economic Journal* 97, no. 387: 642-665.

_____, 1988, "The Tenacious Past: Theories of Personal and Collective Conservatism," *Journal of Economic Behavior and Organization* 10, no. 2: 143-171.

Lal, Deepak, forthcoming, *The Hindu Equilibrium*. Oxford: Clarendon Press.

Landsberger, Henry A. and Cynthia N. Hewitt, 1970, "Ten Sources of Weakness and Cleavage in Latin American Peasant Movements," in Rodolfo Stavenhagen, ed., *Agrarian Problems and Peasant Movements in Latin America*. New York: Doubleday.

Lavergne, Réal, 1983, *The Political Economy of U.S. Tariffs: An Empirical Analysis*. Toronto: Academic Press.

Lehner, Franz, 1983, "Pressure Politics and Economic Growth," in Dennis C. Mueller, ed., *The Political Economy of Growth*. New Haven and London: Yale University Press, 203-214.

Leibenstein, Harvey, 1950, "Bandwagon, Snob and Veblen Effects in the Theory of Consumers' Demand" *Quarterly Journal of Economics* 64 (May): 183-207.

Libecap, Gary D., 1981, "Bureaucratic Opposition to the Assignment of Property Rights: Overgrazing on the Western Range," *Journal of Economic History*, 41 (March), 152-158.

_____, 1986, "Government Policies on Property Rights to Land: U.S. Implications for Agricultural Development in Mexico," *Agricultural History*, 32-49.

Lindenberg, Siegwart, 1986, "Individual Economic Ignorance versus Social Production Functions and Precarious Enlightenment: Comment on Tullock's View of Rent Seeking in Dictatorships," *Journal of Institutional and Theoretical Economics*, 142, 20-26.

Lipton, Michael, 1977, *Why Poor People Stay Poor: A Study of Urban Bias in World Development*. London: Temple Smith.

Livingstone, Ian, 1986, "The Common Property Problem and Pastoralist Economic Behavior," *Journal of Development Studies* 23 (October),

Lutz, Ernst and Pasquale L. Scandizzo, 1980, "Price Distortions in Developing Countries: A Bias Against Agriculture," *European Review of Agricultural Economics* 7, 5-27.

Manne, Henry G., 1986, "Industrial Organization and Rent Seeking in Dictatorships: Comment," *Journal of Institutional and Theoretical Economics* 142, 16-19.

Markus, M. Lynne, 1987, "Toward A Critical Mass Theory of Interactive Media: Universal Access, Interdependence and Diffusion," *Communication Research* (October):

Marwell, Gerald and Ruth E. Ames, 1979, "Experiments on the Provision of Public Goods I: Resources, Interest Group Size and the Free Rider Problem," *American Journal of Sociology*, 84 (May): 1335-1360.

_____, 1980, "Experiments on the Provision of Public Goods II: Provision Points, States Experience and the Free Rider Problem," *American Journal of Sociology*, 85(4), 926-937.

_____, 1981, "Economists Free Ride, Does Anyone Else? Experiments on the Provision of Public Goods IV," *Journal of Public Economics*, 15, 295-310.

Mayer, Wolfgang, 1984, "Endogenous Tariff Formation," *American Economic Review*, 74, 970-985.

_____, and Raymond G. Riezman, 1988, "Endogenous Choice of Policy Instruments," *Journal of International Economics*, 23, 377-381.

McCormick, Robert E. and Robert D. Tollison, 1981, *Politicians, Legislation and the Economy: An Inquiry into the Interest Group Theory of Government*. Boston: Martinus Nijhoff.

McKean, Margaret, 1987, "Management of Traditional Commons Lands (Iriaichi) in Ja-pan" in National Research Council, *Proceedings of the Conference on Common Property Resource Management*. Washington, D.C.: National Research Council.

McMillan, John, 1979, "The Free-Rider Problem: A Survey" *The Economic Record* (June): 95-107.

Mestelman, Stuart and David Feeny, 1988, "Does Ideology Matter?: Anecdotal Experimental Evidence on the Voluntary Provision of Public Goods." *Public Choice*. 57: 281-286.

Mueller, Dennis C., 1979, *Public Choice*. Cambridge: Cambridge University Press.

Murrell, Peter, 1983, "The Comparative Structure of the Growth of West German and British Manufacturing Industry" in Dennis C. Mueller, ed., *The Political Economy of Growth*. New Haven: Yale University Press.

_____, 1984, "An Examination of the Factors Affecting the Formation of Interest Groups in OECD Countries," *Public Choice* 43, 151-171.

Musgrave, Richard A., 1959, *The Theory of Public Finance: A Study in Public Economy.* New York: McGraw-Hill.

Nabli, Mustapha K., 1988, "The Political Economy of Trade Liberalization in Developing Countries." Louvaine: Catholic University Louvaine Center for Economic Studies. International Economic Research Paper #57.

Nardinelli, Clark, Myles S. Wallace and John T. Warner, 1987, "Explaining Differences in State Growth: Catching up Versus Olson," *Public Choice* 52: 201-213.

Nelson, Joan, 1984, "The Political Economy of Stabilization: Commitment, Capacity and Public Response," *World Development*, 12(10).

Nelson, Richard R. and Sidney G. Winter, 1982, *An Evolutionary Theory of Economic Change.* Cambridge: Harvard University Press.

Netting, Robert, McC., 1976, "What Alpine Peasants Have in Common: Observations on Communal Tenure in a Swiss Village," *Human Ecology* 4: 135-146.

_____, 1978, "Of Men and Meadows: Strategies of Alpine Land Use," *Anthropological Quarterly* 45, No. 3: 132-144.

Niskanen, W.A., Jr., 1971, *Bureaucracy and Representative Government.* Chicago: Aldine-Atherton.

North, Douglass C., 1981, *Structure and Change in Economic History.* New York: Norton.

_____, 1984, "Transaction Costs, Institutions and Economic History," *Zeitschrift für die Gesamte Staatswissenschaft* 140: 7-17.

_____, 1986, "Institutions and Economic Growth: An Historical Introduction," Ithaca: Cornell University, Conference on Institutions and Development.

_____, 1987, "Institutions, Transaction Costs and Economic Growth," *Economic Inquiry* 25 (July), 419-428.

_____, and Robert Thomas, 1973, *The Rise of the Western World: A New Economic History.* Cambridge: Cambridge Univeristy Press.

Nugent, Jeffrey B. and Nicolas Sanchez, 1988, "On the Efficiency of the Mesta: A Parable." Los Angeles: University of Southern California.

Oliver, Pamela, 1980, "Rewards and Punishments as Selective Incentives for Collective Action: Theoretical Investigations," *American Journal of Sociology*, 85 (May), 1356-1375.

_____, 1984, "If You Don't Do It, Nobody Else Will: Active and Token Contributors to Local Collective Action," *American Sociologist Review*, 49 (October), 601-610.

_____, Gerald Marwell and Ruy Teixeira, 1985, "Interdependence, Group Heterogeneity and the Production of Collective Action: A Theory of Critical Mass," *American Journal of Sociology* 91 (3): 522-536.

Olson, Mancur, 1965, *The Logic of Collective Action.* Cambridge, MA: Harvard University Press.

_____, 1982, *The Rise and Decline of Nations: The Political Economy of Economic Growth, Stagflation and Social Rigidities.* New York: Yale University Press.

_____, 1983, "The Political Economy of Comparative Growth Rates," in Dennis C. Mueller, ed. *The Political Economy of Growth.* New Haven and London: Yale University Press, 1-52.

Ophuls, William, 1973, "Leviathan or Oblivion," in Herman E. Daley, ed., *Toward a Steady State Economy.* San Francisco: W.H. Freeman.

Orzechowski, William, 1977, "Economic Models of Bureaucracy: Survey, Extensions, and Evidence," in T.E. Borcherding (ed), *Budgets and Bureaucrats: The Sources of Government Growth.* Durham: Duke University Press.

Ostrom, Elinor, 1985, "Institutional Arrangements for Resolving the Commons Dilemma: Some Contending Approaches," in Ostrom and Ostrom (eds.). *Studies in Institutional Analysis and Development.*

_____, 1986a, "An Agenda for the Study of Institutions," *Public Choice,* 48, 3-25.

_____, 1986b, "Issues of Definition and Theory: Some Conclusions and Hypotheses" in National Research Council, *Proceedings of the Conference on Common Property Resource Management.* Washington, D.C. National Academy Press: 597-615.

_____, 1987, "The Implications of the Logic of Collective Inaction for Administrative Theory,"

Owen, Bruce M. and Ronald Braeutigam, 1978, *The Regulation Game.* Cambridge, MA: Ballinger.

Peltzman, Sam, 1976, "Toward a More General Theory of Regulation," *Journal of Law and Economics* 2 (August), 211-240.

Pincus, I.J., 1975, "Pressure Groups and the Pattern of Tariffs," *Journal of Political Economy,* 83(4), 757-778.

Pryor, Frederic L., 1983, "A quasi-test of Olson's Hypotheses," in Dennis C. Mueller, ed., *The Political Economy of Growth.* New Haven and London: Yale University Press, 90-105.

_____, 1987, "Testing Olson: Some Statistical Problems" *Public Choice* 52: 223-226.

Quataert, Donald, 1983, "The Port Worker Guilds and the Istanbul Quay Company," in *Social Disintegration and Popular Resistance in the Ottoman Empire,* 1881-1908. New York: New York University Press.

Quiggin, John, 1987, "Egoistic Rationality and Public Choice: A Critical Review of Theory and Evidence" *The Economic Record* 63 (March): 10-21.

Rawls, John, 1971, A Theory of Justice. Cambridge, Mass.: Harvard University Press.

Riker, William H., 1980, "Implications from the Disequilibrium of Majority Rule for the Study of Institutions," *American Political Science Review* 74 (June), 432-456.

Rogers, Everett M., 1983, *The Diffusion of Innovations.* New York: The Free Press.

Roumasset, James and Sumner J. La Croix, 1988, "The Coevolution of Property Rights and Political Order: An Illustration from Nineteenth Century Hawaii" in David Feeney, ed., *Rethinking Institutional Analysis and Development.* San Francisco: Institute for Contemporary Studies Press.

Runge, Carlisle Ford, 1981, "Common Property Externalities: Isolation Assurance and Resource Depletion in a Traditional Grazing Context," *American Journal of Agriculture of Economics* (November), 595-606.

_____, 1986, "Common Property and Collective Action in Economic Development," *World Development,* 14 (June), 623-635.

_____, and Daniel W. Bromley, 1979, "Property Rights and the First Economic Revolution: The Origins of Agriculture Reconsidered," Madison: University of Wisconsin, Center for Resource Policy Studies Working Paper No. 13.

Ruttan, Vernon W., 1986, "Institutional Innovation and Agricultural Devleopment," Itha-ca, Cornell University.

_____, and Yujiro Hayami, 1984, "Toward a Theory of Induced Institutional Innovation," *Journal of Development Studies*, 20, 203-223.

Samuelson, Paul A., 1954, "The Pure Theory of Public Expenditure," *Review of Economics and Statistics* 36: 387-389.

Sandford, Stephen, 1983, *Management of Pastoral Development in the Third World*. Chichester, N.Y.: John Wiley and Sons.

Sandler, Todd and John T. Tschirhart, 1980, "The Economic Theory of Clubs: An Evaluative Survey," *Journal of Economic Literature* 18, No. 4, 1481-1521.

Schelling, Thomas C., 1978, *Micromotives and Macrobehavior*. New York: Norton.

Schmitter, Philippe C., 1974, "Still the Century of Corporation," in *The New Corporation: Social-Political Structures in the Iberian World*. South Bend: University of Notre Dame Press.

Schotter, Andrew, 1981, *The Economic Theory of Social Institutions*. New York: Cambridge University Press.

_____, 1986, "The Evolution of Rules," in Richard N. Langlois, ed., *Economics as a Process: Essays in the New Institutional Economics*. Cambridge: Cambridge University Press: 117-133.

Sharif, Mohammed and John Whalley, 1984, "Rent-Seeking in India: Its Cost and Policy Significance," *Kyklos*, 37(3), 387-413.

Stigler, George, 1971, "The Theory of Regulation," *Bell Journal of Economics*, 2(1) (Spring), 3-21.

Stiglitz, Joseph E., 1986, *The Economics of the Public Sector*. New York: W.W. Norton.

Taylor, Michael, 1976, *Anarchy and Cooperation*. New York: John Wiley.

Thompson, Earl A. and Roger L. Faith, 1981, "A Pure Theory of Strategic Behavior and Social Institutions," *American Economic Review* 71, 366-380.

Tollison, Robert D., 1982, "Rent-Seeking: A Survey," *Kyklos*, 35(4), 575-602.

Truman, David B., 1958, *The Government Process*. New York: Alfred A. Knopf.

Tulkens, Henry, 1978, "Dynamic Processes for Public Goods: An Institution-Oriented Survey" *Journal of Public Economics* 9: 163-201.

Tullock, G., 1980, "Rent-Seeking as a Negative-Sum Game," in James Buchanan, Robert Tollison and Gordon Tullock, eds., *Toward A Theory of the Rent- Seeking Society*. College Station, TX: Texas A&M Unviersity Press, 16-36.

_____, 1981, "Why So Much Stability?" *Public Choice*, 37, 189-205.

_____, 1986, "Industrial Organizations and Rent-Seeking in Dictatorships," *Journal of Institutional and Theoretical Economics* 142, 4-15.

Ullmann-Margalit, Edna, 1978, *The Emergence of Norms*. New York: Oxford University Press.

Uphoff, Norman, 1986, *Local Institutional Development*. West Hartford: Kumarian Press.

Wade, Robert, 1987, "The Management of Common Property Resources: Finding a Cooperative Solution," *World Bank Research Observer 2*, No. 2 (July), 219-234.

Weede, Erich, 1987, "A Note on Pryor's Criticism of Olson's Rise and Decline of Nations" *Public Choice* 52: 215-222.

Weingast, Barry R. and William J. Marshall, 1987, "The Industrial Organization of Congress," *Journal of Political Economy*

Williamson, Oliver E., 1985, *The Economic Institutions of Capitalism*. New York: Free Press.

Witt, Ulrich, 1986, "Evolution and Stability of Cooperation without Enforceable Contracts," *Kyklos* 39 (Fasc. 2), 245-266.

_____, 1987a, "How Transaction Rights are Shaped to Channel Innovativeness," *Zeitschrift für die Gesamte Staatswissenschaft*, 143.

_____, 1987b, "On the Emergence of Private Property Rights," paper presented to the Public Choice Society Meetings in Tucson, Arizona, March 27-29, 1987.

Wrong, Dennis, 1961, "The Oversocialized Conception of Man in Modern Sociology," *American Sociological Review* 26: 183-193.

PART TWO

TUNISIAN CASE STUDIES APPLYING THE
THEORY OF TRANSACTION COSTS

Chapter 2 above has provided a survey of both the theory of transaction costs and its applications to contractual choice in various sectors and over time. A special attempt has been made to define transaction costs broadly, e.g., to include information costs and asymmetries, and those transaction costs associated with risk-bearing, so as to serve as a unifying framework for analyzing contractual choices. Considerable attention in the survey was given to the roles of ideology, cultural norms, and the judicial system as being potentially important in determining the magnitude of transaction costs and influencing the choice among contracts including organizational form. The purpose of Part II is to provide a number different case studies allowing a judgement on the applicability and relative importance of the different elements of transaction cost theory in explaining contractual choice in a variety of contexts. In carrying out the case studies careful attention has been given to avoiding the pitfalls and shortcomings of cavalier applications of the analysis for which, as pointed out in Chapter 2, the approach has quite appropriately been criticized.

The four different cases presented, namely, agriculture, fishing, manufacturing and tax collection, have been chosen not only to reflect a wide variety of sectors, each of which is also of obvious importance to Tunisian economic development, but also to emphasize both different aspects of transaction costs and the dominance of different types of contracts. Since all the studies draw heavily on the theory of transaction costs, the reader is advised to read Chapter 2 before taking up the chapters in this part.

Given the emphasis in the literature on the "alleged" inefficiency and demise of sharecropping, in the first of the case studies presented in Chapter 4, Matoussi and Nugent focus their attention on explaining contractual choice in a region of Tunisia, Medjez-el-bab, where there has been a discernible switch from wage and rent contracts to share contracts, in the last decade or so. Economies of scope in supervision, the proximity of owners to the farms, the emigration of supervisory labor, changing cropping patterns, and trends in relative factor prices are all found to contribute to the explanation for the switch from wage and rent contracts to share contracts.

Contractual choice in fishing in the context of Tunisia is examined in

Chapter 5 by Azabou, Bouzaïane and Nugent. The contractual forms employed in all segments of Tunisia's fishing industry are described and then analysed from the perspective of transaction costs. Exceptions to the general rule of the dominance of share contracts are explained and numerous reasons are cited for the overall dominance of share contracts. While share contracts remain dominant, the authors predict that, should the current trend toward more capital intensive fishing continue, a gradual trend toward wage contracts might be expected.

One activity in which fixed wage contracts are currently dominant in Tunisia as well as elsewhere is tax collection. Wage contracts have not always been dominant in tax collection, however, and indeed in the third case study presented in Chapter 6 Azabou and Nugent highlight the time periods in which fixed rent contracts known as tax farming were dominant in Tunisia as well as elsewhwere. They then go on to explain how and why this seemingly anachronistic form of contract continues to dominate in one specific sector, namely the taxation of Tunisia's weekly markets. The explanation hinges on the extremely high transaction costs and risk-aversion on the part of the local governments to whom the tax receipts accrue. Given the generally favorable experience with tax farming in such circumstances, the authors suggest that tax farming methods could be of use, at least in appropriate circumstances, in dealing with the tax collection problems of the increasingly important "hidden" or "underground" portion of most economies.

The fourth and last case study applying the transaction cost framework, namely that of Nabli, Nugent and Doghri presented in Chapter 7, deals with manufacturing. Instead of the contractual relationships between capital or land owners and workers, the focus in this case study is on the choice of ownership type. In contrast to some of the existing literature on such choices, which tend to emphasize the role of technological and market conditions, the authors emphasize the role of transaction costs. In doing so, however, they recognize the possible interdependencies between size and ownership type choices. Their application of the transaction cost framework to ownership form choices in Tunisian manufacturing reveals the need to consider forms of opportunistic behavior, such as tax evasion, quality- shirking, adverse selection, and regulation avoidance, other than those which have been considered in the existing applied literature. Specific transaction cost-based hypotheses of ownership form choices are derived and contrasted with the more traditional technology- and market-based hypotheses. Cross-section data on ownership form and size for 42 different manufacturing sectors in Tunisia is then used to test the relative importance of the alternative hypotheses.

Chapter 4

THE SWITCH TO SHARECROPPING IN MEDJEZ-EL-BAB*

Mohamed S. Matoussi and Jeffrey B. Nugent

I. Introduction

In many cases the infrequency of change in contractual form makes it difficult to determine whether contractual choices are better explained by transaction cost (or other efficiency) differentials, by power relations or by cultural or other differences. In order to make it easier to make such a determination, the present paper focuses on a particular region in Tunisia where a distinct shift (believed to be rather general in the country as a whole) in contractual form is known to have occured within a relatively short period of time. The area is Medjez-el-bab in Northcentral Tunisia and the period of change was the 1970's. The particular change observed was from wage and fixed rent contracts which dominated prior to 1970 to share contracts which have become much more prevalent in the region in recent years.

The purpose of the present study is to describe and explain the observed trend toward share contracts and in that context to test the relevance and validity of the various transaction cost elements of contractual choice referred to in Datta and Nugent (1988).

The presentation is divided into the following sections. The agricultural and socioeconomic characteristics of the Medjez-el-bab region along with the data collection procedures are described in Section II. This is followed in Section III with an overall explanation of the shift to share contracts based primarily on the responses of the farmers themselves. That explanation is then further elaborated in Section IV by a more detailed analysis of the incidence of sharecropping among both landowners and workers possessing different characteristics, and in particular by a logit analysis of the variation

*The authors appreciate the many useful comments offered by Lee Alston, Samar Datta, Bruce Herrick, Timur Kuran, and Mustapha Nabli on earlier versions of the paper. The assistance of Samar Datta in the preparation of the questionnaire, the support of the Ministry of Higher Education in collecting the data and the help of Khalifa Ghali in processing the data are gratefully acknowledged. An earlier version of the paper was published in Isaac M. Oferi, ed., *President Chiang Kai-Shek and Land Reform*, Taipei: China Land Reform Association: 293-308 and is published here with the Association's permission.

in that incidence across farms on the basis of the various indicators and measures deemed relevant to the transaction cost explanation of contractual choice elaborated above. Our conclusions and suggestions for future research are given in Section V.

II. Agricultural and Socioeconomic Conditions in Medjez-el-bab and Data Collection Procedures

The survey was undertaken within a portion of the Medjez-el-bab region known as El Oulja. The town of Medjez-el-bab from which the general region gets its name contains about 10,000 inhabitants and is located 5 kilometers west of El Oulja. The English translation of the Arabic word "El Oulja" is "the river bed". As its name suggests, El Oulja, is the very fertile region formed by the river bed of a former (now abandoned) course of Tunisia's principal river, the Medjerda, the meanderings of which practically surround El Oulja.

The total area sampled consists of about 4400 hectares. The largest portion of this area, specifically some 3200 hectares on the outer fringes of the region, is of lower quality and is devoted to the production of wheat and barley. Only about 20% of this land is irrigated. Only 15 households live on this land, each with an average of more than 200 hectares and none with less than 51 hectares.

The remaining 136 households all live in the inner and more productive 1200 hectares of El Oulja, 68% of which is now irrigated. Most of these farms produce two crops per year, one in the summer, usually consisting of tomatoes, peppers, or watermelons, and one in winter, generally carrots, lettuce, onions, spinach, potatoes or artichokes.

As can easily be seen from the data on the size distribution of landholding given in Table 4-1 and also the more detailed data on numbers of households, residents, emigrants and working members given in Table 4-2, the 151 households in El Oulja can be divided into three quite distinct groups. These are the 15 households living on large, generally unirrigated farms on the outskirts of El Oulja, the 54 households with less than 3 hectares of land in inner El Oulja which we call working households, and the 82 households with 3 or more hectares of land (mostly irrigated) in inner El Oulja which we refer to as landowning households.

In general, the landowning households have been residents of El Oulja for many generations, whereas the working households have moved to El Oulja rather recently, or at least during the course of the 20th century. As shown in Table 4-2, another difference is that the landowning households are typi-

Table 4-1

Distribution of Landownership by Size in El Oulja, Medjez-el-bab in 1985

Size of Landholding in hectares	Number of Households	Hectares of Land Owned	Hectares of Irrigated Land Used	Hectares of Irrigated Land Used Per Household
0	23	0	75	3.3
1-2	31	45	60	1.9
3-8	35	186	190	5.4
9-14	18	188	137	7.6
15-20	14	259	162	11.6
21-35	9	268	113	12.6
36-50	6	250	73	12.2
> 50 (Exclusively in outer El Oulja)	15	3200	645	43.0
Total 0-50 (Inner El Oulja)	136	1196	810	5.9
Total 0 - >50	151	4396	1455	9.6

cally somewhat smaller and have fewer economically active members than the working households. Moreover, in addition to being smaller, the landowning households are more likely than the working households to have one or more household members living in the town of Medjez-el-bab (20.9% versus 6.7%) or in other urban locations outside of El Oulja (19.4% versus 12.5%). In general, those living in Medjez-el-bab and elsewhere are believed to enjoy a higher standard of living, if for no other reason, because of the better social and economic infrastructure available in the towns and cities of Tunisia than in rural areas like El Oulja. Even though as indicated in Table 4-1 some of the working households have 1 or 2 hectares of land of their own and also some of them are able to operate farms with more land than they own by renting additional land from the landowning households, they remain rather dependent on the landowning households for employment as wage laborers on either a seasonal or annual ("permanent") basis.

Table 4-2

Socio-economic Characteristics of the Inhabitants of Inner El Oulja

Characteristic	Working Households (with Landholdings of Less than 3 Hectares)	Landowning Households (with 3 or More Hectares of Land)	Total
Number of Households	54	82	136
Number of Persons Considered Members of Households	401	661	1062
Household Members Resident in El Oulja	307	395	702
Household Members Resident in Medjez-el-bab	27	138	165
Household Members Resident Elsewhere	50	128	195
Number of Economically Active Persons	154	218	372
Number of Economically Active Persons Per Household	2.85	2.65	---
Number of Household Members Resident in El Oulja Per Household	5.7	4.8	---

As can be seen clearly in Table 4-3, before 1970 the dominant form of contract between the landholding class and the working class was that of wage contracts. Wage contracts accounted for over 75% of all contracts. Usually the landowner contracted for a mix of "permanent" workers, who were paid partly in cash and partly in kind by season or month, and seasonal workers who were paid in cash by the week. In second place in terms of numerical importance were fixed rent contracts. Most of these contracts were on unirrigated land and often on land owned by absentee landowners. Only 18 farms, accounting for 12.1% of the sample, used share contracts prior to 1970. Since 1970, however, an important structural change has taken place, namely a trend toward share contracts from both wage and fixed rent contracts. Indeed, the proportion of households involved in share contracts has risen dramatically from 12.1% before 1970 to 73.8% now. The rise in share contracts has come at the expense of relatively sharp declines in the incidence of wage and fixed rent contracts, i.e., from 75.2% to 22.8% and from 12.8% to 3.4%, respectively, during the same period of time.[1]

Table 4-3

Incidence of Different Types of Labor Contracts among Sampled Households before and after 1970 (not weighted by size of landholding)

Type of Contract	Before 1970		After 1970	
	Number	Percent	Number	Percent
Wage Contracts - landowners	81	54.4	28	18.8
- workers	31	20.8	6	4.0
- Total	112	75.2	34	22.8
Share Contracts	18	12.1	110	73.8
Fixed Rent Contracts	19	12.8	5	3.4
Total	149	100.0	149	100.0

[1]Since the questionnarie asked the respondents to distinguish only between wage, share and "other" contracts, we can only assume that most of the "other" contracts were fixed rent contracts.

The area was surveyed twice, once in 1981 and again in 1985. The purposes of the 1981 sample survey were primarily to describe the socioeconomic situation, the size distribution of farms, and the relative importance of irrigation, and to identify the most important forms of capital, such as beasts of burden, tractors, trucks, livestock and irrigation equipment. Of the 51 families surveyed almost all were owner- operators or wage laborers prior to 1970; after 1970, however, sharecropping became the dominant form of contract.

The 1985 survey, a copy of which is available upon request from the authors, was addressed to all households, numbering 151 in 1985, in the Medjez-el-bab region. In order to maximize the response and completion rates, the questionnaire was deliberately kept as short as possible, and confined to the main purpose of the study. In this respect, the survey focused on the form of contract, the farmer's own explanation for the choice of contracts, the exact nature of the contract, and the effects of any changes in contractual form.

---

[1]A brief revisit to the region in May, 1987 revealed that the situation in outer El Oulja was also changing as a result of increased irrigation and resulting changes in cropping patterns and contractual choice.

The data was collected with the help of two students from the region. The questions were in all cases directed to the head of household. All 151 households responded to the questionnaire. In a few cases, however, some questions were avoided or answered incompletely.

III. Explanations of the Respondents for their Switch to Share Contracts

While there are well-known problems in interpreting answers to questions concerning motivations, a reasonable place to begin would seem to be by asking those landowners who switched from wage to share contracts to explain why they did so. The 53 landowners who switched from wage to share contracts were given the six alternative explanations for the change in contractual form listed (in the order given) in Table 4-4. The respondents were asked to rank them numerically from 1 for the least important to 6 for the most important reasons for their switch. Since (a) the list is not necessarily exhaustive, (b) the responses could be biased by the order in which they were presented, (c) the alternatives are far from mutually exclusive, and (d) the factors mentioned in the alternatives may be more proximate than fundamental, the possibility that some important considerations may have been missed or that the answers may be biased in one direction or another cannot be denied. Hence, the results have to be treated with caution. Nevertheless, since few respondents seemed uncomfortable with being limited to the alternatives listed, and the list of alternatives included all those that seemed relevant to this situation and was based on a rather thorough review of existing theories of share tenancy, the results may be considered at least crudely indicative.

The results presented in Table 4-4 have been obtained by averaging the numerical rankings of the importance of the six different explanations offered. From this table it can be seen that the highest ranked explanation (with a score of 5.85) is the positive effect of share contracts on the productivity of the principal worker. This is followed at some distance by the following advantages of share contracts: reductions in supervision costs (3.53), mitigation of the effects of increased wage rates (3.04), risk-sharing advantages (with a score of 3.19), and greater ability to use family workers (2.71). Trailing in the rankings of the alternative reasons for the switch to share contracts with a score of 1.32 is "permits the utilization of the other (productive non-marketable) inputs belonging to the worker."

While the results are certainly not free from ambiguities in interpretation, the surprisingly high score for the explanation "permits increased productivity of the primary worker" would seem to be consistent with the incentive-creating or supervision cost-reducing attributes of share contracts relative to wage contracts. Most of the other alternatives can also be included in the more general concept of transaction costs. This is especially true with respect to the reduction in supervision costs and the greater use of secondary (family) workers (for whom an organized labor market may not exist) and other (not generally marketable) inputs like draught animals, implements or other forms of capital inputs belonging to the worker. For reasons given in Datta and Nugent (1988), even risk-bearing can be understood in transaction cost terms. Since virtually all the responses can be interpreted in transaction cost terms and since all such considerations would seem to be relevant for at least some of the respondents, it may be tempting to conclude that the results are strongly supportive of the transaction cost explanation of contractual choice.

At the same time, however, it should be realized that the very breadth of the concept "transaction costs" has the effect of excluding other explanations from the list of possibilities. This, in turn, implies that the results cannot be considered to reject any explanation which is not based on transaction costs. For this reason, the primary use of these results is to distinguish, at least crudely, among the various aspects of transaction costs by their relative importance in the minds of the respondents themselves.

Together with the insights provided by the interviews, our understanding of economic conditions in the region leads us to believe that the aforementioned institutional change can be attributed to four important environmental changes that have been taking place since the mid-1960s. First, real agricultural wage rates were rising quite rapidly. Second, because of the emigration of secondary workers from farm families, reliable supervisory labor was becoming particularly scarce.[2] As a result, by 1985, only a relatively small percent of landowning households possessed secondary workers who could be considered reliable supervisors. Third, the means of irrigation were becoming more readily available, making it possible to grow two different crops instead of one on any piece of land and initiating changes in cropping patterns. Indeed, by 1985 more than one-third of the households surveyed indicated that they had switched from non-irrigated to irrigated crops since 1970 and three-quarters of them had acquired some irrigation equipment. Fourth, as a result of irrigation, better transportation and better access to urban markets, the cropping pattern and technology have changed in such a way as to make know-how and supervision relatively more important.

Before 1970 wage contracts would have been advantageous on farms with ample amounts of supervisory labor and relatively low labor intensity, especially in the presence of some irrigation equipment. Likewise, rent contracts

---

[2]See, e.g., Zouari (1988).

Table 4-4

Average Ranking of the Most Important Reasons Given by the Landowning Respondents for their Substitution of Share Contracts for Wage Contracts after 1970
(6 = high, 1 = low)

Explanation	Average Ranking
Is due to the rapid growth of real wage rates	3.04
Permits increased productivity of the primary worker	5.85
Permits the use of secondary (family) workers	2.71
Alleviates the need for supervision	3.53
Lightens the burden of risk	3.19
Permits the utilization of inputs belonging to the worker	1.32
Number of Respondents	53

would have been advantageous on those farms with neither sufficient supervisory labor nor irrigation equipment, and perhaps especially so on large farms.

For landowning households using wage contracts prior to 1970, the subsequent increases in wage rates, labor intensity, and the degree of commercialization could be expected to increase the monitoring costs per unit of land under wage contracts. Since at the same time emigration was reducing the availability of supervisory labor in landowning households, the ability of such households to bear the increased monitoring costs was no doubt seriously impaired, inducing landowners, or at least those with a critical minimum of supervisory labor, to reduce the need for such monitoring by shifting to share contracts.

On the other hand, for those landowners using rent contracts prior to 1970, the increased presence of irrigation equipment provided them an incentive to move away from fixed rent contracts. Likewise, because landowners typically possess knowledge as to how to irrigate effectively, such as the best ways to provide adequate drainage and to maintain the pumps, the rise in irrigation would also make share contracts increasingly attractive to renters due to their ability to induce a greater supply of these crucial but non-marketable ingredients from landowners.

Given the heterogeneity among farms with respect to land quantity and quality, irrigation equipment, supervisory and other labor, and other inputs, even if they adopted to the changing environmental conditions instantaneously, one would not expect unanimity in contractual choice at any point in time. Costs attributable to changes in contractual form, moreover, night seriously delay such adjustments. Nevertheless, in view of the relative trength of the aforementioned environmental changes, some change in the irection of share contracts from wage and rent contracts would be expected. The connection between the environmental changes, on the one hand, and the changes in the form of contract, on the other hand, is corroborated by the inding that there were no instances of sharecropping or fixed rent on farms which practice animal husbandry — an activity which is most definitely not labor-intensive and in which the possible consequences of asset mismanagement could be very serious,[3] especially when the animals are used as inputs into agricultural production, e.g., as work stock or in producing dairy products. It is also corroborated by the fact that sharecropping is considerably more common on irrigated land and land parcels owned by households with relatively little family labor than on large extensive farms with family members available for both work and the supervision of wage laborers.

While the responses of both landowners and workers given in Table 4-4 are undoubtedly suggestive of both the relevance of and relative importance of the different transaction cost *advantages* of share contracts *vis-à-vis* wage contracts, to be convincing as an explanation for the observed change from wage and rent contracts to share contracts, one would still have to explain how the two important *disadvantages* of share contracts, namely, their susceptibility to asset mismanagement and to output underreporting, relative to wage and rent contracts are controlled in Medjez-el-bab.

The asset mismanagement danger of share (and fixed rent) contracts relative to wage contracts seem to be reduced by the following considerations. (1) Sharecropping is generally practiced in cases in which the landowner is resident on the farm and hence can directly observe the irrigation equipment or even in the case of pumps operate them himself at low cost. (2) Other than pumps operable by the owner himself, the bulk of such equipment is in the form of above-ground hoses and pipes, breaks in which are easily and

---

[3] Naturally the asset mismanagement problem of livestock under rent contracts (or share contracts) would not arise in the case in which the livestock would be owned by the worker (or sharecropper).

immediately detectable, thereby making the assignment of blame for such damage unambiguous, even in the case of share contracts. (3) In some cases, moreover, the sharecropper provides his own irrigation pump.

Again with respect to the output underreporting problem of share contracts, several considerations would seem relevant. First, even if he doesn't have enough of his own or of other reliable family members to supervise labor, given that the owner is typically resident on the farm, he may still be in an excellent position to measure output directly and to observe any attempts by the sharecropper to conceal output. Second, since the crops grown are almost entirely commercial crops like watermelons (as opposed to subsistence crops like wheat or corn) and rather bulky ones at that, they have to be taken to the market in trucks which can be easily seen, heard and inspected by resident landowners. The only form of output underreporting which might be difficult to detect by resident landowners would be the sharecropper's own consumption of output in the fields. However, in the case of the relevant truck-farm crops like watermelons and lettuce, any one of which typically constitutes only a very small fraction of the daily diet, the sharecropper is unlikely to have the stomach to take great advantage of such possibilities! Third, because of the small size of land parcels, cultivation is usually operated in such a way as to have the entire crop ripen and be harvested at precisely the same time, thereby greatly reducing the cost to the landowner of direct supervision of the harvesting and the sale of the output. Further, the fact that the sales take place right in the field at a price that is openly announced protects the sharecropper from the underreporting of price by the owner which could arise if the landowner were to undertake the marketing himself.

Relative to fixed wage contracts, share contracts would have another disadvantage as far as the working households are concerned. Instead of being paid weekly or monthly even during the pre-harvest period as under wage contracts, working households under share contracts would have to wait until after the harvest for payment. To offset this disadvantage, however, one might expect credit arrangements to arise between the landowner and worker. This conjecture is supported by the survey results in that 81% of the households involved in share contracts were also involved in credit contracts as opposed to only 51% among those involved in wage contracts.

Share contracts are, of course, not the only means of reducing the high supervision costs that are generally necessary under wage contracts. Indeed, fixed rent contracts are another and even better alternative means of reducing the supervision costs arising from the need to reduce labor-shirking. However, since the danger of asset mismanagement is especially great under fixed rent contracts, unless it is totally impossible for the owner to supervise his farm (as for example when he has emigrated abroad), or unless there is no possibility of loss from asset mismanagement,[4] share contracts could be expected to be preferred relative to fixed rent contracts.

Since the supervision cost disadvantage of wage contracts relative to share contracts and of wage and share contracts relative to fixed rent contracts can be mitigated by lengthening the time duration of wage contracts,[5] in order to keep wage contracts competitive with share contracts one might expect to see a somewhat longer duration of contract among wage than among share and rental contracts. This conjecture is supported by the fact that from the responses to questions 1 and 2 of the questionnaire it can be seen that in 1985 the incidence of "permanent" (i.e., contracts of annual or longer duration) is greater among wage contracts than among share or rent contracts.

Even if the basic factors underlying such contractual changes can be identified with some degree of confidence, this would not necessarily mean that either the timing of change in the form of contract or the particular farms to adopt the change could be satisfactorily predicted. One might ask, "Why wouldn't *all* the farms have shifted to share contracts immediately, i.e., before 1970? Or, even if one would allow for some delays due to the costs of making institutional changes, why wouldn't all the farms have adopted the change at least by 1985?" One possible answer to the latter question is provided by advocates of the behavioral theory of the firm (e.g., Nelson and Winter (1982) and Heiner (1983)) who argue that, in view of the costs of change, institutional changes of this sort would not be adopted unless the firms (in this case farm-firms) would be severely threatened, e.g., by bankruptcy and extinction. Our study provides some – though only very limited – evidence in support of this position, not from those who did change to share contracts, but from those who did not change. Specifically, 47% of the respondents to question #10 (as to why they had not changed to share contracts if they had not changed) indicated that the reason for not changing was that "things were all right the way they were." In other words, the process of diffusion of the institutional change in the region in recent years seems to have been impeded by the incomplete or insufficiently strong pressure to change on the part of some (generally large) farms which were doing relatively well with wage contracts. This was especially so, moreover, in those farms with sufficient amounts of family labor to supervise wage workers.

---

[4] This would tend to be the case when there is little or no equipment of any kind and especially on non-irrigated land.

[5] See especially Eswaran and Kotwal (1985) and Alston and Ferrie (1986).

To summarize, in this section we have provided some evidence in support of the transaction cost explanations for contractual choice in the Medjez-el-bab region of Tunisia and especially for the observed trend from wage and rent contracts to share contracts in the face of increases in agricultural wage rates, in labor-intensity and in shortages of supervisory labor in landowning households. On the other hand, because the evidence presented, which was mainly in the form of the farmer's responses to questions as to why they changed or did not change, does not allow alternative explanations to be rejected, the present analysis is primarily suggestive of the relative importance of the different components of transaction costs. The most important such component was the incentive for the principle worker to work hard and thereby to reduce supervision costs. Since however the responses given by the farmers may be biased, they cannot be used to reject the importance and relevance of non-transaction cost elements. As a result, a more detailed analysis of inter-household variations in the incidence of different forms of contract is clearly warranted.

IV. Analysis of Data

In this section we investigate the incidence of sharecropping using two different types of analysis. First, we see whether or not the incidence varies from group to group according to the transaction cost considerations discussed above. Then, we undertake a more formal logistic analysis of the inter-household variations in the incidence of share contracts.

The results of the first type of analysis are summarized in Table 4-5. The incidence of share contracts is measured both for landowning and working households with various identifiable and relevant characteristics. With respect to landowner characteristics, one would expect the work incentive advantage of share contracts relative to wage contracts, and hence the incidence of share contracts, to be greater the smaller is the available manpower in the landowning household and the better is the landowning household's access to the market. (For example, if the landowner possesses a truck or a tractor capable of taking the output to the market, as opposed to depending on the more limited numbers of buyers who come directly to the fields, the working household would be particularly anxious to have a share contract with the landowner.) Because of the overall dominance of share contracts among El Oulja landowners and workers, the variations in percentages of respondents under share contract across landowner and worker characteristics is not large. Nevertheless, with respect to landowner characteristics, all such expectations are confirmed in that the incidence of share contracts is above-average in landholding households with little manpower but considerable market access and below-average in those with the opposite characteristics.

With respect to the characteristics of working households, one would expect that the possession of complementary inputs such as tractors, trucks or hydraulic equipment and/or the presence of considerable manpower within the household would raise the benefits to the landowners, and hence the incidence, of share contracts relative to wage contracts in such households. Not only are all these expectations confirmed by the results presented in Table 4-5 but also the differences in the incidence of share contracts between working households with these characteristics and those without them are considerably greater than was the case with respect to the characteristics of landowning households.

Table 4-5

Incidence of Share Cropping in 1985 among
Households with Different Characteristics

All Landowners	70%
Landowners with little Manpower	78%
Landowners with much Manpower	62%
Landowners with a Truck	76%
Landowners with a Tractor	74%
Landowners without Means of Transport	64%
All Working Households	72%
Working Households with a Truck	75%
Working Households with Some Means of Transport	84%
Working Households without Means of Transport	51%
Working Households with Hydraulic Equipment	81%
Working Households without Hydraulic Equipment	61%
Working Households with Much Manpower	77%
Working Households with Little Manpower	63%

Next we present the results of the logit analysis. As shown in Table 4-3 and explained above, except for land owned by persons who have emigrated and thus are unable to supervise, irrigation has increased the importance of the asset-mismanagement disadvantages of fixed rent contracts to such an extent that fixed rent contracts are no longer observed with any frequency in the region. As a result, for all practical purposes the primary choice of contractual form would seem to be between fixed wage and share contracts. The incidence of share contracts is measured by the dummy variable ISHARE which assumes values of unity when share contracts are practiced on at least a part of the farm, and of zero, otherwise.[6]

Given the fact that the dependent variable is a dummy variable, the estimating equation used in testing the significance of the relevant proxies for transaction costs is of logistic form:

$$ISHARE = \alpha + B_1 ST + B_2 SI + B_3 EH + B_4 AA + B_5 CS$$
$$+ B_6 EM + B_7 MPROP + B_8 MW + B_9 CRW \qquad (1)$$

where ST represents the total endowment of land in hectares, SI the endowment of irrigated land, EH the farm's ownership of hydraulic equipment, AA, CS and EM represent three different principal occupations of the landowner, namely agriculturalist, civil servant and emigrant of any occupation, $MPROP$ and MW represent relatively large endowments of labor[7] by the landowning household and the working household, respectively, and CRW is a dummy variable for the substantial provision of credit to the working household.

Some doubts could be raised as to whether CRW can be legitimately treated as an exogenous variable in this context. This is because CRW could conceivably be thought of as being chosen simultaneously with, or even after, the choice of contractual form. For this reason we estimate equation (1) both with and without the variable CRW. In the latter case the equation can be considered as the appropriate reduced form equation of a system in which CRW would be determined simultaneously.

Because of the logistic form, the estimates of the parameters B_i, $i = 1, 2, \cdots, 9$, can be interpreted as indicating the effect of a unit change in the

---

[6]Since as shown in Table 4-3 above 7% of the households were still participating in fixed rent and other contracts for which the comparisons with share contracts would not necessarily be consistent with those hypothesized above for the choice between share and wage contracts, the analysis has also been rerun excluding those households with fixed rent contracts. The results, however, were unaffected.

[7]Relatively large endowments are defined as those with two or more principal workers in the household.

i^{th} right hand side variable (many of which are dummy variables) on the log of the odds that the household would be involved in a share contract.

Table 4-6

Logistic Regression Results for *ISHARE*

	1 Hypothesized Sign	2 Equation (1)	3 Equation (1) without CRW
Intercept		-0.475 (.429)	-0.149 (.790)
Coefficients of			
ST	-	-0.018 (.001)	-0.016 (.005)
SI	+	0.169 (.001)	0.171 (.002)
EH	+	1.213 (.024)	1.226 (.019)
AA	-	-0.445 (.450)	-0.341 (.531)
CS	?	0.908 (.507)	0.500 (.712)
EM	-	-1.271 (.318)	-1.421 (.256)
MPROP	-	-2.130 (.001)	-1.460 (.005)
MW	+	0.945 (.114)	0.544 (0.352)
CRW	+	2.844 (.001)	--- ---
Rank correlation between predicted probability and response		.723	.590

Note: Figures in parentheses indicate the significance levels of the parameters immediately above them. In other words, .01 indicates that the coefficient is significantly different than zero at the 1 percent level.

The hypothesized signs of the parameters $B_1, \cdots, B9$ which are given in column 1 of Table 4-6 can be briefly explained as follows. Because of the possibility of economies of scale in supervision, and also that farms which are large in size would be of lower quality than small farms and hence less labor intensive, the expected impact of ST would be negative. On the other hand, since irrigation increases the labor-intensity of production, for both measures of irrigation, namely SI and EH, higher values of these variables would be expected to raise the log of the odds of share contracts. If the primary occupation of the owner is agriculture, because of economies of scope in supervision one would suppose this to raise the probability of wage contracts and hence to have a negative effect on $ISHARE$. While the impact of being a civil servant could be either positive or negative, if the owner had emigrated, direct supervision would be impossible, hence (as explained above) favoring fixed rent contracts over both share and wage contracts.[8] Substantial endowments of family labor in the landowning household ($MPROP$) would reduce the need for hired labor and supervision, thereby favoring wage contracts relative to both share and rent contracts. By contrast, substantial endowments of labor in the working households (MW) would tend to favor share contracts relative to wage contracts for both landowners and workers. In the former case this would be because more work could be expected to be performed. In the latter case it would be because households with more workers would be likely to find that share contracts provide them with greater flexibility in the means of getting the work done. Finally, as has been pointed out above, one disadvantage of share contracts to the workers, which would have to be overcome in order to have workers accept share contracts, is the delay in compensation until after the crop is harvested. The provision of credit to the working household by the landowning household (CRW) could therefore be expected to have a positive influence on the odds of having share contracts.

The resulting estimates of the parameters $B_1 - B_9$ and their significance levels for equation (1) both with and without the CRW variable are given in columns 2 and 3, respectively, of Table 4-6. As can easily be seen, in most cases the hypothesized relations are confirmed. This is particularly true with respect to both the positive effects on the incidence of share contracts of irrigation (SI and EH), and of credit to the workers (CRW) and the negative effects of the size of farm (ST) and the endowment of family labor belonging to the landowner (MW). While the landowner's occupational variables have the expected signs, the parameter values are not statistically significant.[9]

---

[8] Actually, this would suggest that wage and fixed rent contracts should be distinguished. However, since there were so few fixed rent contracts, their elimination from the sample has virtually no affect on the results, except of course for the coefficient of EM.

[9] It should be reported that experiments were also conducted with respect to the inclusion of dummy variables for other equipment owned by the land

In conclusion, it can be stated that the results provide relatively strong support for the transaction-cost-based explanations for contractual choice in agriculture. Indeed, both in what the households themselves say about their motives and in the analyses of the incidence of share contracts among different groups and across different households, the common denominator seems to be the desire to find arrangements which increase the incentives to both landowning and working households to supply their complementary inputs as effectively as possbile and to reduce supervision costs. The most important complementary inputs would seem to be the land and know-how of the landlord and the labor input of the principal worker. Given that the results pertain to only a very small portion of Tunisia, however, it is not possible to say much about their generality. Further research is clearly needed before any such generalization could be made.

In the absence of such generalizations, at a minimum the present paper demonstrates the potential usefulness and applicability of transaction cost considerations in the determination of agricultural contracts. It also seems to identify supervision costs with respect to labor and other inputs and asset mismanagement as especially important components of transaction costs. Three other features of the findings should be pointed out. First, the contractual choices observed in Medjez-el-bab seem to be affected by characteristics of both landowner and working households. Second, the fact that the trend is distinctly in the direction of share contracts and that the pattern of incidence is consistent with the transaction cost and incentive-creating advantages of share contracts in situations in which the markets for some of the relevant inputs are imperfect or incomplete would seem to cast doubt on the validity of the popular view that sharecropping is an inefficient, inappropriate and outmoded form of contract.[10]

Finally, even though from the available data on the gradually rising (a) cost of regular labor, (b) scarcity of supervisory labor and (c) labor-intensity of agricultural production it is not possible to identify the precise time in which the optimal form of contract has changed from fixed rent or wage contracts to share contracts or even to be sure that it has done so, the extent of change in contractual form within a period of 15 years would seem rel-

---

owners such as tractors and trucks. In none of the revised estimating equations did these variables have a significant influence on *ISHARE*. Since their inclusion made it more difficult to avoid excessive collinearity among the various right hand side variables, the results for these variables have not been reported here.

[10] As pointed out by Wells (1984), sharecropping is also making a comeback in U.S. agriculture.

atively large, demonstrating an impressive degree of institutional flexibility. Indeed, the degree of institutional flexibility demonstrated in the agricultural contracts of Medjez-el-bab is sufficiently great relative to the notable inflexibility in other contexts as to demand some explanation for it. Although the search for such an explanation remains for future research, a crucial ingredient would seem to be the relatively few agents involved. Agricultural contracts in Medjez-el-bab involve the agreement of only the two parties directly involved, i.e., the landholder and the working household. There is no involvement of the community, or of organizations of workers or landholders. Hence, in contrast to other Tunisian institutions which have been known to be inflexible, such as the institution of the amin in the Tunis bazaar, or the role of the porter's union in the wholesale market of Tunis,[11] only a minimal amount of collective action is necessary in order to accomplish institutional change. This raises the question of why some kinds of decisions can be made at the level of individual agents whereas others involve one or more large groups.

References

Alston, Lee J. and Joseph P. Ferrie, 1986, "Resisting the Welfare State: Southern Opposition to the Farm Security Administration," in Robert Higgs (ed.). *The Emergence of the Modern Political Economy*. Greenwich: JAI Press.

Azabou, Mongi, Timur Kuran and Mustapha K. Nabli, 1988, "The Wholesale Produce Market of Tunis and Its Porters: A Tale of Market Degeneration," ch. 12, this volume.

Datta, S.K. and J.B. Nugent, 1988, "Transaction Cost Economics and Contractual Choice: Theory and Evidence," Ch. 2, this volume.

Eswaran, Mukesh and Ashok Kotwal, 1985, "A Theory of Two-Tier Labor Markets in Agrarian Economies," *American Economic Review* 75, (March): 162-177.

Heiner, Ronald A., 1983, "The Origin of Predictable Behavior," *American Economic Review* 83, No. 4 (September): 560-595.

Kuran, Timur, 1989, "The Craft Guilds of Tunis and Their Amins: A Study in Institutional Atrophy," ch. 8, this volume.

Nelson, Richard R. and Sidney G. Winter, 1982, *An Evolutionary Theory of Economic Change*, Cambridge: Harvard University Press.

Wells, Miriam J., 1984, "The Resurgence of Sharecropping: Historical Anomaly or Political Strategy?" *American Journal of Sociology* 90, No. 1: 1-29.

Zouari, Abderrazak, 1988, "Collective Action and Governance Structure in Tunisia's Labor Organization," Ch. 11, this volume.

---

[11]See Kuran (1988) and Azabou, Kuran and Nabli (1988).

Chapter 5

CONTRACTUAL CHOICE IN TUNISIAN FISHING*

Mongi Azabou, Lotfi Bouzaïane and Jeffrey B. Nugent

In Chapter 2 above Datta and Nugent have already alerted the reader to the fact that, in contrast to most other sectors in which wage contracts dominate, the fishing industry is characterized by the dominance of share contracts, at least in developed countries for which the most information is available. A distinct trend, however, toward wage contracts was also noted. In terms of the relative frequency of the different forms of contract, share contracts would seem to be followed by fixed wage (time or piece rate) contracts and by mixed wage and share contracts. Fixed rent contracts, on the other hand, are generally very rare.

The aforementioned survey of the literature provided the following list of factors tending to favor the use of share contracts in the fishing industry: (1) the work effort incentive advantage of share *vis-à-vis* wage contracts (fixed rent contracts being ruled out by their vulnerability to asset-mismanagement), (2) the relative size and importance of risk – with both a price and a production component – limiting the extent to which either the owners or the fishermen would be willing to bear the entire burden of these risks by themselves, (3) that the asset mismanagement, insufficient maintenance and output-underreporting disadvantages of share contracts *vis-à-vis* wage contracts can be mitigated by the hiring of a loyal captain who, by virtue of economies of scope in supervision, can protect the owner's interests rather effectively, (4) the relative seasonality of activity which makes it easier for share contracts to achieve a fuller degree of resource utilization than would be the case if either party had to hire the other at a prespecified factor price, (5) the team character of production which both renders the measurement of individual marginal products difficult and makes share contracts attractive because of their natural advantage in the encouragement of teamwork and cooperation, (6) the usefulness of share contracts to owners in lessening the development of adversarial relationships between owners and fishermen in

*The authors greatly appreciate their several useful discussions with and the assistance in the field research provided by Samar Datta and Ahmed Salah and the comments of Jean Philippe Platteau, Bruce Herrick, Mustapha Nabli, Abdeljabbar Bsais, and Timur Kuran.

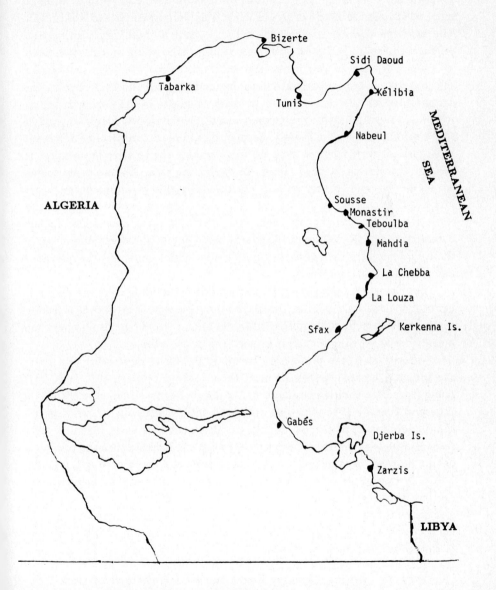

Figure 5-1
The Principal Fishing Ports of Tunisia

general and of the wage-increasing efforts of labor unions in particular, (7) the usefulness of compensation by shares in mitigating the prisoners' dilemma problem inherent in the physical risks to life and health entailed in work at sea, and (8) the usefulness of shares in eliciting unmarketable and difficult-to-contract inputs which may be both in the possession of different parties[1] and required in fishing activities from time to time, depending on circumstances.

The purposes of this paper are as follows: First, we wish to describe the contractual terrain of Tunisian fishing and in particular to determine the extent to which the pervasiveness of share contracts in the fishing industry, which was mostly based on the experience of the developed countries, applies to the fishing industry in Tunisia. Second, should share contracts be dominant in Tunisia, it would be our purpose to determine the relative importance of each of the aforementioned factors in explaining this. By the same token, we should be able to explain how the disadvantages of share contracts are minimized in specific circumstances. Third, we hope to explain any observed exceptions to the use of share contracts. Fourth, it is our aim to identify the determinants of the values of the shares belonging to the different parties to these contracts. In each of these objectives we wish to examine the relevance and role of transaction costs.

The fishing industry is an important one for investigating the determinants of contractual choice in Tunisia, not only because of the fact that fishing contracts tend to be quite different than in other sectors but also because the industry is of growing economic importance to the country.

In contrast to the production trends in fishing of most other countries, the annual fish catch in Tunisia more than doubled between 1971 and 1982, rising from 30.4 thousand tons to 62.7 thousand tons. Having reached 88.0 thousand tons by 1985 and with optimistic forecasts for the next few years, the chances for an additional doubling of production between 1982 and 1991 seem relatively safe. Indeed, government forecasts indicate that the country's fishing industry is expected to continue to grow at a rapid pace well into the 1990s. In view of the severe balance of payments constraint that Tunisia faces, the fact that, even in the decade 1976-85 for which the data are available, Tunisia's exports of fresh fish doubled in quantity and more than sextupled in value from 4.2 million dinars in 1976 to 28.0 million dinars in 1985 is indicative of the sector's strategic importance to the country's economic development.

---

[1]For example, owners may have better access to credit and to market opportunities than fishermen but the fishermen may have experience in dealing with unpredictable misfortunes arising from weather and equipment failure and may have children who may come along to help. For a careful exposition of the argument see Eswaran and Kotwal (1985).

It also explains the relatively high priority the sector has been receiving in the most recent development plans. Because of the competitive nature of the world market for fish and the growing importance that the industry is being accorded in Tunisian development, it is crucial that the factors affecting the industry's efficiency in general and the costs of transaction among its numerous different agents in particular be properly understood.

Our presentation is organized as follows: Section I describes the forms of contract which are being employed in different segments of Tunisia's fishing industry. Section II describes the nature of the share system and the way in which the shares are determined. Section III provides explanations both for the dominance of share contracts in most segments of the industry and for the exceptions in which wage and fixed rent contracts are observed. Finally, our conclusions are presented in Section IV.

I. The Forms of Contract in Different Segments of the Industry

As a result of the dearth of sources of fresh water in the country, virtually all of Tunisia's fishing industry is coastal fishing. Nevertheless, the industry is remarkably heterogeneous. Its character varies in several ways. First, it varies by port and especially by size of port, Sfax, La Goulette (the port of Tunis), Bizerte, Sousse and Gabès, being the largest and most important for large fishing vessels, but with numerous smaller ports, such as those at Tabarka, Kelibia, Monastir, Mahdia, and Ghar el Mélih, to name only a few, many of which are large enough to handle only the smallest of boats, being quite important for small boats. Second, it varies by the nature of the special product, ranging from shell fish through tuna and other edible fish to such inedible specialties as sponge and coral, the latter two products being used in household cleaning and jewelry, respectively. Finally, the industry varies by the size, capital-intensity and seaworthiness of the boats used, ranging from small coastal boats which are not always motorized and which may hold from 1-5 fishermen to relatively large motorized trawlers (chalutiers) accommodating a crew of 10-16 members. Some fishing is even done without any boats at all as in the fish farming operations off Djerba and Kerkenna islands.[2]

There are, however, some commonalities among these different dimensions of variation. In particular, sponge fishing is concentrated at Zarzis, the Kerkenna Islands and Sfax, sardine fishing is concentrated at Mehdia, Kelibia and Gabés, coral at Tabarka and Bizerte, tuna at Zarzis, Sfax, Mahdia,

---

[2]In most fish farming operations, however, small boats are used for transportation purposes.

and Sidi Daoud, shrimp at Gabés and Sfax, and general coastal fishing virtually everywhere else. The larger trawlers, i.e., the "chalutiers" and especially those with relatively large motors, are concentrated at Sfax, La Goulette and Bizerte.

Despite all the heterogeneity, by and large, share contracts are as dominant in the fishing industry of Tunisia as they are elsewhere. There are, however, a number of exceptions. The most important exception is tuna fishing where the remuneration of labor has been primarily on the basis of wage contracts, and in the past in sponge fishing for boatmen and rowers and in coral fishing (by diving) for boatmen and mate. Another exception is the fixed fishery ("pêcherie fixe") which exists on parts of the shores off Kerkenna and Djerba islands where fixed rent contracts are practiced.[3] Mixed wage and share contracts have sometimes been resorted to in sponge fishing when the owners would find it difficult to attract qualified captains ("raïs") without offering them at least a minimum wage.

On the larger trawlers, while in general share contracts dominate, those workers whose efforts less directly affect the catch, such as guards and porters on shore, are generally paid by wage contracts. The machinists on board the chalutiers are somewhere in between, typically being paid by a mix of share and wage contracts.

II. The Share System and of the Determinants of the Shares

Whereas the survey of Zoeteweij (1956) suggests that two kinds of sharing systems are common, i.e., "share of the gross" and "share of the net", in Tunisia share contracts are universally on a "share of the net" basis. In this system the shares are computed not on the gross proceeds but rather on the net proceeds obtained by subtracting from the gross proceeds (the sales value of the fish sold) certain approved costs of operations. The approved operating costs, which are deducted from gross proceeds to obtain the net proceeds (upon which the shares are computed) include the costs of fuel, lubricants, ice, repairs (such as to tools, nets, ropes), selling costs (including auction fees and municipal taxes), the fixed wage costs of landbased workers, the cost of food for the crew and the social security taxes of crew members, and sometimes on small boats, part of the costs of repair of the motor. While this list of approved deductions from the gross value of sales has been in standard practice for some time, since 1977 it has been codified in the decree (Arrête) of May 1977 of the Ministry of Agriculture [Journal Officiel de la

---

[3] For interesting technical and institutional descriptions of the various types of fishing in Tunisia as they existed some years ago see De Fages and Ponsevera (1903) and Louis (1961).

République Tunisienne du 20 Mai 1977, no. 35].

The aforementioned decree also specifies general guidelines for the distribution of shares, not only that between the owner and crew but also that among the various crew members.

First, with respect to the former, the decree states that in smaller boats the share of the owner is not to exceed 50%, the remainder going to the crew. In the larger trawlers (chalutiers) which of course have more elaborate equipment, 52% goes to the shipowner and 48% to the crew. In practice, on small boats at least, the share divisions between the owner and crew vary somewhat more widely, generally following the principle established in the literature [International Labour Office (1952), Zoeteweij (1956) and Davis, Gallman and Hutchins (1985)] that the owner's share rises in proportion to the capital-intensity of the fishing operation. As a result, the owner's share can be considerably below the 50% maximum, falling to perhaps as low as 33% for very simple boats. Naturally, the better equipped the boat, the higher is the expected productivity (both marginal and average) of the fisherman's time and effort. One can easily understand, therefore, why fishermen may well be willing to fish for lower expected shares on larger and more well equipped boats.

A specific example of how the owner's share varies in proportion to the relative importance of the equipment provided is that of coral "fishing" (by diving). Since this occurs in small boats, when the diving equipment is supplied by the owner, the owner's share is the 50% maximum for small boats. However, when the diving equipment is supplied by the diver himself, the owner's share is generally about 35% (but could be as low as 20% in the case of a diver of exceptional reputation).

Because of the increased ease of entry for small boat owners that has resulted from the increased availability of credit from banks and cooperatives for purchases of small boats, on the one hand, and rising wage rates, on the other hand, there has been some downward pressure over the last decade or so in the owner's share on small boats. For example, in sponge fishing, where much of the work is uncommonly arduous, better employment opportunities are luring experienced fishermen away from the industry and the value of the catch is also under pressure because of the increased competition from artificial sponges, the share has fallen from 40% to about 20%.

Not surprisingly, it is considerably more difficult to raise the large amounts of capital needed for large, well-equipped fishing vessels, especially in view of the various commercial as well as non commercial risks they face. Nevertheless, because of the growing importance of the abilities (a) to get to where the fish are quickly and (b) to remain at sea for long periods of time without having to incur the costs of return to port and "down time" while in port, and also because most of the important technological changes in this industry have been biased in the direction of high capital-intensity, the potential advantages of large ships in Tunisia seem to have been rising over time. In April 1986, at the insistence of the Office National de Pêche, the Ministry of Agriculture revised its 1977 decree by issuing a new decree which was similar to the 1977 decree in all other respects but provided that the owner's share could rise above 52% (up to a maximum of 70%) if the horsepower of the installed motor exceeded 500.

In traditional coastal fishing the owner's share varies also (a) from port to port (depending apparently on differences in labor market pressures), (b) with the experience and reputation of the captain (the owner reducing his own share in order to be able to recruit an especially experienced and highly qualified captain), and (c) with the nature of the relationship between owner and captain. In this latter respect, the owner's share is likely to be smaller when the captain is a relative, presumably because relatives are deemed more trustworthy, thereby inducing the owner to settle for a lower share (reflecting the lower risk premium).[4]

With respect to the distribution of the overall share of the crew among crew members, once again common rules of thumb seem to have prevailed for some time and then been codified in the aforementioned decree of May 1977. Most importantly, however, these shares are the result of a collective agreement between the captain and the other members of the crew. The owner is not directly involved in the specification of these shares.

Naturally, the collective agreement between the captain and crew is made in advance of each trip.[5] The shares are in this case expressed not as percentages but rather as portions of the crew's share of the net proceeds. While there may be room for some give and take between the captain and the individual crew member with respect to the distribution of shares, as a result of the relatively perfect mobility of fishermen to different captains and boats in a given port (though less so from one port to another), competitive pressures make the shares relatively homogeneous and, of course, known to each fisherman.

---

[4] See also Bardhan and Rudra (1986).

[5] While explicitly the duration of contract may be for as short as a single voyage, implicitly they are often for longer, since contracts are frequently renewed unless one of the parties to them is dissatisfied with the performance of one or more of the others. In the case of sardine fishing, the contracts are generally quite explicitly for an entire season.

Inasmuch as the captain has virtually complete discretion over whom to hire and the determination of the shares, and because the importance of providing special rewards as an incentive for fishermen whose loyalty and hard work have been demonstrated to the captain's satisfaction is generally appreciated, the relevant authorities, specifically, the General Commissariate for Fishing within the Ministry of Agriculture, willingly tolerate such deviations from the shares specified in the 1977 decree.

On trawlers and other large vessels the jobs in fishing are more sharply differentiated. Not surprisingly, the shares accruing to the jobs requiring more skill, experience, and responsibility, such as those of machinist, chief mate, and captain, are considerably larger than those accruing to common fishermen. Table 5-1 provides a list of the shares specified for trawlers in the 1977 decree for the different job classifications as well as an indication of the extent to which actual practice varies from the shares designated in the decree.

As can easily be seen from the table, those who are most likely to benefit from extra incentive payments are the captains and machinists. In the former case the extra incentive may come not only from his own taking of an extra share but also from the granting by the owner of extra shares from his own account. These practices are especially common in trawling (i.e., on chalutiers) and on fishing boats equipped with lanterns (pêche au feu). They are never practiced, however, in the public sector portion of the fishing industry (i.e., the "Office National de Pêche").

The main reason why the owner may grant extra shares on his own account to the captain is that in the absence of radar equipment and/or the means of aerial observation which are frequently available in the more capital-intensive ends of fishing to the fishing fleets of industrial nations, the skill of the captain is the primary means of finding the fish. Also the captain and the machinist are the members of the crew who are most vital to the protection of the owner's property. In any case, since he doesn't hire the other members of the crew, it should not be surprising that he doesn't grant them extra incentives on his own account. Nevertheless, the owner may be useful in retaining loyal, hard-working and skilled fishermen by providing them with credit, for example, during the off-season or for marriages and other special events.

On smaller boats the sharing rule among crew members is usually two shares for the captain and one share for each fisherman (usually between 1 and 4 in number). When the owner is the captain, he usually takes only one share from the crew's total, treating himself as merely equal to the other

Table 5-1
The Number of Shares Accruing to Different
Crew Members on Trawlers

	Shares of the Crew's Total		Shares to Crew Members on the Owners' Account (Practice)	Total Number of Shares (Practice)
	Legal	Practice		
Captain	3	3 to 4[1]	1 to 2	6[2]
Chief Mate	2	2.25 to 2.5	---	2.5
Machinist	2	2.5 to 3	0.5	3
Assistant Machinist	1.5	1.5	---	1.5
Net Repairmen	2	2 to 2.5	---	2.5
Experienced and Specialist Fishermen	1	1 to 1.5	---	1.5
Unskilled Fishermen	1	1	--	1

[1] Occasionally 5.
[2] In exceptional cases as high as 7.

fishermen.

It is important to realize that in addition to being able to vary the shares, every captain has at his disposal an additional incentive device, namely the allocation of the "bouillabaisse". According to the 1977 decree's specifications, the bouillabaisse is a quantity of fish reserved for the owner and crew; in particular the decree specifies that each fisherman must be given one kilogram of fish for each 24 hours at sea and the owner one half kilo of fish for every crew member. In practice, however, the owner is usually given one box of high quality fish and the crew as a whole 4 to 6 boxes of average quality. Even if the captain may be constrained by regulation in the quantitative aspects of allocating the bouillabaisse, the quality of the fish allocated to each fisherman is entirely at the discretion of the captain, and can be made to vary substantially. In contrast to the distribution of the crew's share, which is an *ex ante* contract agreed to in advance of the expedition, the bouillabaisse is an *ex post* allocation. Hence, his discretionary power over the allocation of the bouillabaisse gives the captain the ability to reward unexpectedly good performance and to penalize unexpectedly bad performance. As one might imagine, the distribution of the bouillabaisse can be a source of conflict. Indeed, the 1977 decree provides that, if the conflict is sufficiently serious, the crew can decide not to permit the distribution of the bouillabaisse.

III. Variations in Contractual Form and Other Contract Characteristics

It would seem reasonable to focus our search for explanations for the observed dominance of share contracts and exceptions thereto in Tunisian fishing on the eight factors listed above, which have been given in the literature as explanations for the dominance of share contracts in the fishing industry. To facilitate our examination of these factors, we suggest that they can be usefully classified into four general types of considerations, namely (1) risk with respect to the value of output, (2) the importance of team production and cooperation relative to that of the individual worker's productivity, (3) the relative importance of fixed assets and hence of the risk of asset mismanagement by the worker, and (4) the relative importance of skill and work effort in the value of the fish catch and the feasibility of measuring, and hence rewarding, these contributions. Naturally, the relative importance of each of these factors may be expected to vary from one segment of the industry to another.

The purpose of this section is to see to what extent these different considerations would seem to be responsible for the observed differences in the basic forms of contract and in other characteristics of the contracts from one segment of the industry to another.

As explained by Datta and Nugent (1988), where the "team" character of production is especially important, share contracts are likely to be advantageous. Likewise, when it is easy to monitor work effort, by direct supervision, or when work effort is not likely to have much of an influence on the value of the output, wage contracts are likely to be efficient. When the fixed assets are relatively unimportant, the risk of asset mismanagement is likely to be small and hence fixed rent contracts or secondarily share contracts are likely to be advantageous relative to wage contracts. As shall presently be explained, the influence of risk considerations is somewhat more complicated.

The complication arises in part from the fact that fishing is an activity which is subject to at least three different kinds of risk at the same time. First, the size of the catch is subject to abrupt changes in weather and other conditions which are beyond the control of fishermen. Hence, fishing is subject to substantial production risk. Second, since normally fish constitutes only a small portion of the daily diet even of fishermen, a relatively large portion of production is likely to be sold in the market, thereby subjecting the fisherman to price risk. Third, because of the distinct possibility of bad weather and shipwreck, both the owner's assets and the fishermen's lives are subject to risk of physical loss. While at least some of these risks are common also to agricultural and other activities, the relative importance of all three sources of risk is generally considerably greater in fishing. If it were possible to mix wage and rent contracts on a single operation as it sometimes is in agriculture, the need for share contracts as a device for sharing these risks could be reduced at least with respect to production and price risk. However, since in the case of fishing a mixing of wage and rent contracts is not feasible, at least on any single boat, the need for risk sharing can indeed be an explanation for share contracts in the case of fishing.

Normally, of course, in any fishing community the demand for fish is likely to fluctuate much less than the supply of fish, especially when most of the fish catch is marketed locally. This implies that production and price are likely to be negatively correlated. Thus price risk may normally be expected to partially offset production risk. Therefore, the magnitude of the effective risk burden implicit in any given amount of production risk is likely to be considerably greater in the absence of price risk (as might be the case when the particular fish product is subject to a fixed price regime) or when price risk exists but is independent of production risk (as, e.g., when the commodity is exported but the producer's share in the world market is very small). Although there is no sure means of protection against the risk of physical loss of assets or life, other than by purchasing insurance which, if available,[6] typically involves very high transaction costs, often these risks are somewhat lower in boats of large size and sophisticated equipment.

As mentioned in the introduction, the form of contract has a distinct effect on the allocation of the production and price risks among the parties to such contracts. The relative ability to bear such risk may therefore be an important factor in determining the choice of contract. While no form of contract can protect the shipowner from the loss of his property or the fisherman from the loss of his life or livelihood in case of shipwreck, share contracts may well be useful in this respect by helping to overcome the prisoners' dilemma problem and inducing more cooperation.

As noted above, the dominance of share contracts is more noticeable in fishing on small boats. Several factors are involved in the explanation. First, it is on small boats that the risk of physical losses from storm and

---

[6]Such insurance is in fact unlikely to be available because of the adverse selection and moral hazard problems that are inherent to most such schemes. These difficulties make the transaction costs for such schemes very high.

shipwreck is greatest. Second, because of the small number of individuals involved on small boats, the effectiveness in reducing these risks that the extra cooperation and teamwork induced by the practice of share contracts is likely to be greater on small boats than on larger ones. Third, in the absence of ship mobility and sophisticated equipment, the skills and effort supply of individual fishermen and the captain are likely to be more important than on large boats, thereby underscoring the effort-enhancing advantages of rent and share contracts *vis-à-vis* wage contracts. Fourth, cooperation and flexibility in work assignments are likely to be especially important for success in fishing on small boats, thereby favoring the use of share contracts. Fifth, because of the comparative ease of entry to ownership of small boats, owners of small boats are not likely to be very different from fishermen on such boats in their willingness and ability to absorb risk.[7] Sixth, because the use of other inputs like fuel, food, and repair on any single expedition of a small fishing vessel is likely to be quite limited and easy to observe, the cost of monitoring their use as is implicit in "share of the net" contracts would be relatively low on small boats.[8]

At the present time the only exception to the use of share contracts on small boats is the payment of fixed wages to boatmen and mates (as opposed to the divers) on coral fishing by diving. Because of the importance of diving to the success of such operations, and the diver's ability to supervise the boatman and mate, the boatman and mate are generally hired directly by the diver. Except for ability to follow the directions of the diver, absolutely no skill or extra effort and cooperation on the part of boatman and mate are needed. At the relevant margin, neither the boatman's effort nor that of his mate has much effect on the quantity or value of production. Being unskilled, the boatman is generally very poor and thus unwilling and unable to accept the burden of risk in production. On the other hand, with a relatively high share in the value of output, the diver is likely to be sufficiently well off to bear the risk relatively well, hence making him willing to pay the boatman a fixed wage.

Until recently there were two other notable exceptions to the use of share contracts on small boats, namely the public sector segment of coral fishing

---

[7] In many situations, moreover, there is considerable mobility between boatowner and fisherman occupations, boatowners being fishermen who have managed to save enough to own their boats and fishermen sometimes being former boatowners who have not been able to pay off their debts.

[8] This advantage would not arise if the shares were computed in terms of share of the gross proceeds. For an explanation for the use of share of the net as opposed to share of the gross proceeds see Datta and Nugent (1988).

by the cross method[9] and the boatmen and rowers in sponge fishing. In the former case, as mentioned above, this activity has now been prohibited and in the latter case share contracts have recently been substituted for fixed wage contracts. Nevertheless, the two cases did represent exceptions and hence also warrant explanations.

In the case of sponge fishing on the island of Kerkenna, in the earlier days, i.e., before the greater ease of entry to the industry, the income differences between boatowner and boatman were quite substantial, in our opinion contributing in a substantial way to the choice of wage contracts. It also seems likely that in the vicinity of the Kerkenna Islands, and especially prior to the existence of rapid means of transportation to Sfax and its labor market, the boatman-laborer presumably had little in the way of other viable means of satisfying his minimal consumption requirements. In this situation, therefore, one would expect the boatowners to be considerably more willing and able to bear the risk of insufficient production than the boatmen. Moreover, since sponges are primarily exported, their price movements are largely independent of variations in local production, implying that price risk cannot be counted on as a partial hedge against production risk in this segment of the industry. Consistent with this explanation is the observation that the wage rates of boatmen were especially low in these activities, in part reflecting the transfer of the reward for accepting production risk from the boatman to the boatowners and captains (raïses).

The other earlier exception to the dominance of share contracts on small fishing vessels was the use of wage contracts in that portion of coral fishing by the cross method which took place on boats owned and operated by the public sector (i.e., the "Office National de Pêche"). The explanation for the use of wage contracts in this segment of the industry would seem to parallel that in sponge fishing; neither skill nor cooperation and teamwork were very important. While production was subject to very considerable production risk, risk in production was largely independent of the effort of the boatmen. As with sponge fishing, the activity was concentrated in a port (Tabarka in the north-western part of the country) where wage rates were especially low and alternative sources of employment limited. In such conditions one might assume that the boatmen would be especially unwilling to accept the comparatively high production risk. Because the boats were small, however, one would not expect private sector boatowners to be much more willing to

---

[9]Coral fishing by the cross method consists of trawling with a wooden cross which, when dragging the ocean floor, picks up branches of coral. Because of the damage which this method inflects on the fauna of the sea floor in general and coral in particular, this kind of coral fishing has recently been banned.

bear this risk than the boatmen. Moreover, because there are some effort-inducing advantages of share contracts in separating the coral from seaweed, one would normally not expect to find wage contracts in this segment of the industry. Consistent with this expectation, in the private sector component of this segment of the industry, at least, share contracts did dominate. In that portion of the industry owned and operated by the public sector, however, the boatowner (the Office National de Pêche) would be much more willing to bear the risk not only because of its size and ease of access to capital but also because of the breadth of its portfolio of fishing boats which are located in many different ports and engaged in many different activities.[10]

The single most important segment of Tunisian fishing in which wage contracts are observed either in pure form or as part of a mix with share contracts is tuna fishing. One important characteristic of this industry that would seem to favor wage contracts is that tuna is a migratory species, the catch of which is subject to exceptionally great production risk. Since the price of tuna is fixed in advance of the season,[11] there is of course no price offset to production risk. Because of the especially high production risk involved, in the absence of a price risk offset, fishermen in tuna fishing would not be expected to be attracted to share contracts since these would have the effect of forcing them to accept much of the relatively high production risk. Another consequence of the fixed price regime is that the quality of the fish has little effect on the value of the catch. Since it is the quality of the fish that can be most affected by extra effort in the care and handling of the fish, it is normally because of quality considerations that the effort-enhancing advantages of share contracts would normally come into their own and tip the choice in favor of share contracts. Therefore, the fact that the fixed price regime drastically limits the importance of product quality in the remuneration of tuna fishing activities greatly mitigates the effort-inducing advantage of share contracts in this industry.[12] Likewise, since considerations like skill

---

[10] It also might feel less pressure than private firms to be efficient in the choice of contracts because of both the small size of these activities relative to the overall operation and the expectation that any overall financial losses might be passed on to the central government.

[11] In fact, it is only a minimum price which is fixed in advance. The agreement between the shipowners and the fish canneries allows the industrialists to pay higher prices if the prices of tuna in the wholesale market rise above the preset minimum as they sometimes do.

[12] The lack of importance of quality in the value of the catch in this segment of fishing also has an impact on the form of the incentive payments that are typically mixed with the fixed wage in tuna fishing. Instead of the incentive payments being determined in terms of the value of production, they are

and the willingness and ability to cooperate, the presence of which tend to favor share contracts over wage contracts, are not particularly important in tuna fishing, but since the disadvantage of share contracts relative to wage contracts with respect to vulnerability to asset mismanagement is especially great (because of the relative importance of capital assets on such boats), share contracts would presumably be considerably less advantageous in the case of tuna than in other segments of the industry.

In other segments of fishing where the trawlers are large but employ less equipment than in tuna fishing, and hence where the boatowner's assets are not likely to be tied up to such an extent in a single boat, the asset mismanagement disadvantage of share contracts *vis-à-vis* wage contracts would tend to be weaker and controllable by hiring a loyal captain. As noted above, the loyalty of a captain can be purchased, by hiring either a relative or a nonrelative with an especially good reputation for reliability. The owner can further protect himself against the possibility of asset misuse under share contracts by providing the captain and other members of the crew whose efforts most directly affect the value of the owner's assets, namely, the machinist and sometimes the assistant machinist, with incentive payments. Given the importance of these incentive payments to the captain and the relevance of his reputation for skill, efficiency and loyalty to the owner to his future earnings, the captain has every incentive to hire the best and most cooperative crew members he can find and to closely supervise all their activities but especially those most directly affecting the owner's assets. Another way in which the possibility of asset misuse under share contracts is mitigated is that the share contracts, which as mentioned above are in fact "share of the net" proceeds contracts, allow for deductions for necessary repairs, replacement and delays brought about by the need to repair or replace broken nets, tools and other equipment. As a result, every crew member – not just the captain – has the incentive to use the nets, equipment and tools carefully so as to avoid the need for otherwise unnecessary repairs. In this way, the need for direct supervision by the captain is somewhat reduced. As noted in the previous section, by his powers (1) to set the terms of employment with the individual fisherman before the latter signs on to any fishing expedition and (2) to allocate the bouillabaisse, the captain has the instruments for rewarding both the *ex ante* and the *ex post* efficiency of his fellow fishermen. He also can influence the owner's decision as to whether to provide consumption loans to the fishermen.

Likewise, because of economies of scope in supervision, the possibilities

---

stated strictly in terms of quantities, i.e., as a payment per ton of catch.

for output-underreporting on the part of individual crew members can be limited to tolerable levels by the captain's supervision. Moreover, the captain has the ability to dismiss fishermen who either don't work sufficiently hard or who attempt to underreport output to their private advantage at virtually a moment's notice. Also, in some cases the captain may be able to impose additional penalties for opportunistic behavior. Hence, normally the captain is likely to be in a good position to supervise and control the behavior of the fishermen to reduce all forms of opportunistic behavior on the part of the fishermen to tolerable levels. At the same time, because of the crew member's mobility and ability to affect the reputation of the captain, and by virtue of his ability to observe opportunistic behavior on the part of the captain, the crew member is able, at least partially, to protect himself against opportunism on the part of the captain.

In all other respects, namely, the incentives for (a) teamwork and cooperation, including that which is useful in reducing the possibility of loss of life, (b) the fuller utilization of assets, (c) the work effort on the part of crew members and the diligent application of their skills, and (d) the care and attention needed in order to attain quality capable of obtaining the highest possible price for the fish, share contracts are likely to be superior, i.e., imply lower transaction costs. Hence, it would seem that on all except the largest and most capital-intensive and public sector-dominated segments of the fishing industry in Tunisia, share contracts are likely to remain efficient in the transaction cost sense for some time to come.

The one other segment of the fishing industry whose contractual choice should be explained is the fixed fishery or fish farming operations which as mentioned above are largely confined to the shores of Djerba and Kerkenna Islands. In this segment of the industry fixed rent contracts prevail. Specifically, private fishermen-entrepreneurs buy the rights to fish in designated waters by paying a fixed rent to the municipality to whom these waters belong. Frequently, these rights are sold to the highest bidder in competitive auctions. Fixed rent contracts, which would normally be vulnerable to asset misuse on the part of the tenant fisherman, are invulnerable in this specific case because in many cases there are, in fact, no assets. The fisherman rents only the fishing grounds, everything else – nets, equipment, etc. – he has to supply himself. Two additional factors contributing to the choice of fixed rent contracts should be mentioned. First, the fact that the dangers of physical loss to life and property are much reduced as a result of all operations being immediately offshore has the effect of decreasing the relevance of the share contract advantage in this respect. Second, because these contracts are typically for a year's duration instead of for the customary single fishing expedition, production risk is considerably lower, in relative terms, at least, inasmuch as production varies considerably less from year to year than it does from day to day or week to week. Although production risk is not especially high, it is certainly non-negligible. Since (1) the municipalities involved have relatively fixed expenditures for the services they provide, (2) the income from these fixed fisheries is risky and typically a relatively important part of their total revenues, and (3) these public authorities are not in a position to borrow, the municipalities prefer fixed rent contracts because the entire burden of production risk is shifted to the tenant.

In those fixed fisheries in which fixed assets are relatively important such as in the "madrugues" for tuna which exist at Sidi Daoud in the northeastern part of Tunisia and on Kuriat Island in the east-central part of the country, the owner-operator which is the public sector "Office National de Pêche" hires the fishermen-workers under a mix of wage and share contracts. The use of wage contracts is attributable to (a) economies of scale and scope in the operation and supervision of workers, (b) the relative importance of avoiding asset misuse and (c) the relative willingness and ability of the Office National de Pêche to bear risk.

IV. Other Considerations and Conclusions

While the explanations given in the preceding section by no means narrow the explanation for the observed variation in contracts across segments of the Tunisian fishing industry to a single factor, they do help in distinguishing the more important from the less important factors of the factors (1) – (8) identified in our introduction. More or less in order of importance, the most important considerations would seem to be differences in (2), i.e., the relative importance of production risk and of differences between owner and fisherman in the ability to bear such risks, (3), the relative importance of susceptability of the owner's assets to misuse, and (1) and (5), the relative importance of fisherman effort and skill, on the one hand, and teamwork and cooperation, on the other.

By and large, fixed rent contracts are ruled out because in most segments of the industry the owner's assets are relatively important and rent contracts are especially vulnerable to opportunistic behavior of the asset misuse variety. The single exception to this rule is the case of fixed fisheries where for the most part there are no assets involved. Wage contracts are common only on the capital-intensive tuna fishing-boats, and in the fixed fishery madrugues for tuna where (a) the owner's assets are sufficiently important that even relatively well supervised share contracts insufficiently protect the owner's interests against the risk of asset mismanagement by the crew and (b) the effort, skill and cooperation of the fishermen are generally less important than in other segments of the fishing industry. This is not to deny that crew members on other fishing boats also frequently call for wage contracts in order to reduce their vulnerability to production risk. The failure of such calls for change is indicative of the fact that this disadvantage of share contracts to the fishermen is not sufficient to offset the other advantages.

In virtually all other segments of the industry, the exceptions being where factor (3) on the list of 8 given in the introduction is especially important, the owner's ability to hire a loyal captain and the captain's several instruments for rewarding efficient and cooperative behavior on the part of crew members, and the relative ease of supervision by the captain attributable to the close quarters that work on a ship entail are sufficient to reduce the dangers of asset misuse under share contracts. As long as the asset mismanagement danger of share contracts is not too high, the advantages of share contracts with respect to factor (2) are likely to be telling, and share contracts are likely to prevail.

Since in general one would expect fishermen like most others to be risk-averse,[13] it is important to explain why it is that relatively poor fishermen are willing to accept part of the burden of the production and price risk by accepting share contracts. The need for such an explanation is rendered even more important by virtue of the fact that work at sea is generally considerably rougher, more risky, unhealthy, inconvenient and irregular than land-based sources of employment.

An important part of the explanation is that the expected values of the fishermen's share of wage rates are considerably higher than those they could expect to make on land-based jobs of equal skill requirements. For example, even in tuna fishing where the catch is largely independent of labor effort and skill, the fixed wage rate is fifty percent higher than the legal minimum wage. In those segments of the industry where the skill requirements are more important and the fisherman is entitled to a risk premium for bearing a portion of the risk by accepting payment in share contracts, the income advantage of the fisherman can be considerably greater.

In other words, the average fisherman is not in such a bad position to accept risk as one might imagine. On the other hand, the fishermen themselves recognize the effort-enhancing advantages of share contracts relative to wage contracts and hence recognize that it is worthwhile to accept a share of the risk. In emergencies, moreover, they may be able to count on loans

---

[13]Note, however, that Gordon (1954) cited fishermen as examples of people who are risk-lovers.

from family members and even from owners. Fishermen also typically live in communities characterized by stronger interhousehold reciprocal assistance relations than do non-fishermen.

Another consideration which deserves some additional attention is the possibility of an effect of contractual choice on investment. In his survey, Zoeteweij (1956) gave considerable attention to the possibility that the practice of share contracts could have a strong negative effect on investment and innovation, at least relative to what would be expected under wage contracts where the owner is the only residual claimant. He argued that the owner of a boat under share contract would have less incentive to invest because any profits would be shared with the members of the crew. On the other hand, since the downside risks are also shared, share contracts could reduce the risk of investment to the owner and hence encourage investment. So, too, as noted above, the practice of share contracts would tend to increase the utilization of the shipowner's assets, thereby increasing the stimulus for investment relative to what it would otherwise be.

In Tunisia, at least, share contracts do not seem to have discouraged investment. Our interviews brought to our attention many boat owners who, although starting with a single boat, within a few years were able to accumulate two, three or more boats. Indeed, the ability to manage risk by accumulating a portfolio of different ships can act as another incentive to investment. The barriers to investment are more attributable to capital market imperfections than to the prevalence of share contracts.

References

Bardhan, Pranab K. and Ashok Rudra, 1986, "Labor Mobility and the Boundaries of the Village Moral Economy," *Journal of Peasant Studies* (April): 90-115.

Datta, Samar K. and Jeffrey B. Nugent, 1988, "Transaction Cost Economics and Contractual Choice: Theory and Evidence," Ch. 2, this volume.

Davis, Lance E., Robert E. Gallman and Teresa Hutchins, 1985, "Technical Change, the Capital Stock and Productivity Increase: A Whale of a Tale." Pasadena: California Institute of Technology, mimeo.

De Fages E., et C. Ponzevera, 1903, *Les Pêches Maritimes de la Tunisie* (réimprimé). Tunis: Mis-à-jour M. Bourje (1908) Editions Bouslama, 1977.

Eswaran, Mukesh and Ashok Kotwal, 1985, "A Theory of Contractual Structure in Agriculture," *American Economic Review* 75 (June): 352-367.

Gordon, Howard Scott, 1954, "The Economic Theory of a Common-Property Resource: The Fishery," *Journal of Political Economy* 62 (April): 122-142.

International Labour Office, 1952, *Conditions of Work in the Fishing Industry*. Geneva: International Labour Office.

Louis, Andre, 1961, *Les Iles Kerkena (Tunisia)*. Tunis: Institut des Belles Lettres Arabes, Etudes d'Ethnografie Tunisienne de Géografie Humaine. V. 1.

Platteau, Jean Philippe, forthcoming, "The Penetration of Capitalism into Small-scale Third World Fisheries: An Investigation of Historical Processes and Organizational Forms." *Development and Change*.

——————————, and A. Abraham, 1985, "An Inquiry into Quasi-credit Contracts: The Role of Reciprocal Credit and Interlinked Deals in Small Scale Fishing Communities," *Journal of Development Studies* 23, No. 4.

Zoeteweij, H., 1956, "Fishermen's Remuneration," in Ralph Turvey and Jack Wiseman, eds., *The Economics of Fisheries*. Rome: FAO.

Chapter 6

TAX FARMING: ANACHRONISM
OR OPTIMAL CONTRACT?*

(An Illustration with Respect to Tunisia's Weekly Markets)

Mongi Azabou and Jeffrey B. Nugent

Tax evasion is certainly a sufficiently pervasive phenomenon to merit serious investigation of alternative incentive devices and other mechanisms for collecting more of the taxes stipulated by law. In principle, taxes can be collected with three quite different forms of contract between the tax collecting authority and the tax collector: wage, share and fixed rent contracts. Wage contracts occur when the government hires on fixed wages tax collection agents who agree to turn over to the government all the taxes they collect; share contracts occur when in lieu of a wage payment the agent holds onto a prespecified share of the taxes collected; finally, fixed rent contracts are those in which the tax collector (farmer) agrees to pay a prespecified fixed sum to the government in return for the right to all the proceeds of the taxes he collects. At present, however, wage contracts are so dominant in tax collection activities around the world that their use is frequently taken for granted. In order to examine the experience with these alternative contractual forms in tax collection activities, therefore, one must turn to history.

The purpose of the present paper is to examine both some historical experience with, and one contemporary example of, the use of rent contracts in tax collection activities. The rent contract approach to tax collection has generally been referred to as "tax farming". While the historical experience with tax farming is rich, emphasis is placed on the experience in North Africa and the Middle East where tax farming was especially prominent.[1] The contemporary example featured in the paper is the taxation of transactions in

*We wish to thank Khalifa Ghali, Mahmoud Chtourou, Director, Ministry of the Interior and Khalifa Chaouch, Faculté de Lettres de Tunis for their help in obtaining the information used in this study. We also thank Timur Kuran, Mohamed Bechri and Bruce Herrick for suggestions and comments. Portions of this paper in revised form appeared as "Contractual Choice in Tax Collection Activities: Some Implications of the Experience with Tax Farming" in *Journal of Theoretical and Institutional Economics*, V. 144 (1988), 684-705. Permission to draw upon that paper is gratefully acknowledged.

[1]See especially İnalcık (1973).

the periodic (mostly weekly) markets of Tunisia where tax farming remains dominant.

The presentation of this paper is divided into the following sections. Section I selectively reviews the historical experience for clues as to factors responsible for the waxing and waning of tax farming in different settings. Section II describes the origin of tax farming in Tunisia and in particular also the model of tax farming in the context of the country's weekly markets. Section III attempts to explain the variations in the incidence of tax farming over time in Tunisia and in the world as a whole in terms of transaction costs. Finally, Section IV provides some conclusions and suggestions for policy and future research.

I. Some Historical Experience

Latouche (1961) points out that tax farming was the dominant form of tax collection with respect to agriculture in the Roman Empire. He also provides some interesting clues as to the factors leading to its decline and replacement by wage contracts. In particular, he notes that tax farming seemed to disappear mainly as a result of default on the part of tax farmers. This was especially common in the later phases of the Roman Empire when as law and order declined, the agricultural workers, who were increasingly subject to the invasions of others, started to leave the land and/or to invest less in their land, leading to decreased output. With the rent payments of the tax farmers set by historical experience, the tax farmers found their tax farms increasingly unprofitable, inducing them to abandon them voluntarily.[2]

Another factor may have been that, as the tax farmers became more permanent, the desire to maximize their own revenues may have induced them to gradually exercise more and more control over farming operations, thereby increasing their own political power base relative to the Roman state and decreasing the ability of the state to extract revenues from them.

Hicks (1969) attributes the rebirth of tax farming in Europe in the late Middle Ages to the rising need for finance and credit on the part of states. Not only could the right to collect taxes be rented out in return for a fixed rent payable in advance but, if the need for revenue were sufficiently great, the right to collect taxes indefinitely into the future could even be sold. Even if the right to collect the taxes was only rented out, the tax farmer was usually in a

---

[2]This problem would not arise if the fixed payments were flexible downwards. In situtations where the contracts were only renewed rather infrequently and governments were strapped with fixed expenditures, however, one could well imagine that tax farm rents would be insufficiently flexible in the downward direction.

good position to raise loans which could in turn be forwarded to the state. It should be considered that until relatively recently states were relatively weak and lacked the power to borrow on their own since it had generally proved difficult for creditors to make sovereigns pay. As Fryde (1958) points out, even for tax farmers, the provision of credit to the state could get tax farmers into trouble when the states were unwilling, unable or very slow in repaying its debts. Sometimes, all the merchants formed a tightly knit syndicate of tax farmers for the expressed purpose of redeeming through tax collecting the delinquent loans they had made to the state. Gradually, however, the power of the states increased *vis-à-vis* the tax farmers. Indeed, states found competitive public auctions of tax farms a convenient vehicle for extracting maximal revenues from the tax farmers and at the same time undermining the cartelization of merchant-tax farmers.

By the 16th century, tax farming seemed to be the dominant form of tax collection in Europe. As a result of the proliferation of various kinds of indirect taxes on transactions, one could well imagine that intimate knowledge of each industry, of product prices and of the way in which transactions take place would all be important ingredients of success in collecting taxes. The state might well find it difficult and/or expensive to hire people with such knowledge on a wage contract basis. Nevertheless, because of their considerable experience in and knowledge of all such matters and perhaps because of economies of scope in supervision, one might suppose that merchants would be willing and able to serve as tax farmers. This expectation is strongly supported by the assertions of Jeannin (1972) that the tax farmers were usually the leading merchants in the line of activity relevant to the item whose transactions were being taxed.

The competitive auction process and the need to pay in advance, of course, frequently caused the tax farmer to go into debt from which he was not always able to extricate himself. Indeed, many a tax farmer fell victim to his creditors. The threat of bankruptcy and his absolutely small size often put the individual tax farmer in a weak position to collect the taxes from his creditors who were frequently other merchants in the same line of activity. Such weakness made it even more difficult for the tax farmer to succeed in making profits on his tax farm and accentuated his vulnerability to financial failure. Bankrupt or financially weak tax farmers were of course also not in the interest of the state since they could hardly be of much use in raising credit for the state.

To avoid these problems and to take advantage of risk-pooling, by the 17th century "great" or "general" tax farms were much in evidence especially in England [Newton (1918)] and France [Mathews (1958)]. In these new types of tax farms the right to collect the taxes was often for a longer period of time than for a single year (which had been the common practice earlier). Also, the scope of activity of an individual tax farmer was often much broader than had previously been the case. Naturally, however, the magnitude of the fixed payments involved greatly reduced the number of potential bidders. As a result, the competitive auction gave way in such circumstances to bilateral bargaining with the incumbent tax farmer. The incumbent tax farmer could sometimes be pushed into paying some bills of the tax receiver to maintain favor. The greater the power of the tax farmer, the greater was the likelihood of abuses on the part of the tax farmers in collecting more than the legally specified taxes from the transacting agents. Overzealous large, monopolistic tax farmers, driven by the incentive to collect as much in the way of taxes as possible, in the course of time tended to give tax farming a bad reputation and gave rise to complaints on the part of the taxpayers. This led to demands for more monitoring on the part of the state of the tax farmers' practices.

Another problem was that, despite their greater size, even large tax farmers were not always able to satisfy the ever-increasing demand for revenues on the part of the state. Bankruptcies were still common among tax farmers, and even those tax farmers who were not strictly bankrupt were sometimes unwilling to renew their contracts with the state. Tax farming was, therefore, somewhat unreliable. As a result, governments were sometimes confronted with the need to collect their own taxes on very short notice.

Naturally, if the state was compelled to hire monitors of the activities of tax farmers or at least a small corps of employee tax collectors to be used in case of emergency, the extra cost to the state of simply doing its own tax collecting was considerably reduced. The rising power of the state may also have contributed to making it easier for the state itself to collect the taxes owed to it. Although tax evasion remained a serious problem under wage contracts, tracts, by the 19th century wage contracts became the dominant form of tax collection. As Hicks (1969) points out, the trend toward wage contracts in tax collection was also greatly facilitated by the spread of accounting and the publication of such accounts which had the effect of lowering the transaction costs of tax collecting, making intimate knowledge of each specific type of transaction less necessary, and reducing the cost of monitoring the tax collectors.

Elvin (1973) and Ho (1959) trace the somewhat parallel checkered history of tax farming in China. Especially in China, where the state was relatively weak and tax codes relatively complicated, the vulnerability of the system to illegal tax gouging on the part of overzealous tax farmers was a recurring problem. Although tax farming continued to be practiced in China until relatively recently, the occupation of tax farmer was throughout much of Chinese history the occupation which was most despised by the general populace.[3]

Despite its importance in Europe, China and elsewhere for substantial periods of time and in many activities, it was apparently the Ottoman Empire which made the greatest use of tax farming and for the longest period of time. Even in those lands at the fringes of the empire which were only indirectly influenced by the Ottoman Empire, such as India under the Moghul kings in the 16th and 17th century, tax farming seems to have been the dominant form of tax collection [Habib (1963, 1967)]. Nevertheless, even within the Ottoman Empire, there were periods in which tax farming was much less dominant and took somewhat different form. Indeed, the form it took in the Ottoman Empire seemed to depend very much on the changing needs of the state [İnalcık (1973), Baer (1968), Lewis (1979), Shaw (1968), and Shaw and Shaw (1977)].[4]

Given the importance of the cavalry to the rise and early expansion of the Ottoman state in the 14th and 15th centuries, and the relative abundance of land accruing to the Ottoman state in the form of conquered territories, at first the right to collect taxes on the newly acquired lands were simply given in the form of "timar" land in lieu of wage payment to cavalrymen ("sipahi") in return for their loyal service in time of need [İnalcık (1973), Shaw (1968)]. Once the zenith of the Ottoman Empire's territorial expansion had been reached, and hence as land became scarcer, and also as the importance of permanent salaried infantrymen and janissaries and of purchasable firearms and gunpowder in warfare increased relative to the cavalry, however, the state found that its need for taxes in the form of cash to have increased and its ability to provide land to tax farmers to have decreased. It, therefore, switched from the timar-sipahi form of tax farming to direct collection of taxes by salaried agents, typically minorities and foreigners. One reason for the use of minority members as salaried state tax collectors may have been that they could be expected to be less able to establish a local political base and to be more loyal to the Ottoman government than military men, Muslem bureaucrats, or the members of the populations indigenous to the various provinces of the Ottoman Empire.[5] Nevertheless, despite the political weakness and the extreme dependence of such people on the state, the Ottoman

---

[3]See especially Elvin (1973).
[4]See also Donohue (1984), Jwaideh (1984) and Rafeq (1984).
[5]For such a suggestion see Issawi (1982).

state gradually came to realize the vulnerability of tax collection via wage contract to the undersupply of effort on the part of the tax collectors. Hence, by the 16th century when Tunisia had come under the control of the Ottoman Empire, the Ottoman government was forced to return to the more orthodox system of tax collection, namely tax farming.

The practice of tax farming throughout the territorial domain of the Ottoman Empire was facilitated by the fact that the tax laws were for the most part both familiar to all and widely accepted as fair. This was in large part because the taxes had been articulated in Islamic Law, known by all Muslems and by all those non-Muslems living in regions ruled by Muslems. Many of these taxes were relatively easy to measure, consisting of specified flat tax rates like one-tenth, one-fourth, etc. depending on the item taxed.

While the tax farmers did not own the land, their incentive to collect as much tax as possible, subject to the constraint of the tax rates established by law which could not easily be violated because of their religious origin, induced them to exercise a considerable amount of control over the activities of the farmers and agricultural workers. Indeed, in the course of time, the control exercised by the tax farmer over the agriculturalists became sufficiently strong that the agriculturalists were often unable to choose what crop to produce without in advance obtaining the approval of the tax farmer. As in Europe, the duration of tax farm contracts tended to get longer so as to be for several years at a time, and were in some cases even inherited.

Over time as the central power of the state gradually diminished, and the monopolistic powers of the tax farmer increased, the system became increasingly subject to abuses on the part of overzealous tax farmers. Competitive auctions became increasingly difficult to simulate and there were fewer and fewer Ottoman authorities who were willing and able to monitor the activities of the farmers. Since modern forms of enterprise became prominent much later in North Africa and the Middle East than elsewhere where, the introduction and spread of formal accounting systems much delayed, thereby raising the transaction costs to the state of tax collection through wage contracts. The economic viability of tax farming has also been facilitated by the fact that most urban activities were organized into craft-specific guilds, each with a leader, in Tunisia called the "amin", who could be called upon to collect the taxes of guild members for the government. As a result, tax farming techniques have tended to remain competitive *vis-à-vis* wage contracts in tax collecting activities, at least until much more recently, than has been the case in Europe and North America.

Eventually, however, under the influence of colonial regimes, virtually all

of which had already adopted wage contracts in their tax collection activities,
wage contracts have come to dominate even in North Africa and the Middle
East. Once wage contracts have become the established form of contract
in tax collection activities, moreover, the existence of a rather aggressive
and highly organized group of salaried civil servants in defense of their own
interests has undermined any possible effort to return to share or fixed rent
"tax farm"forms of contract in tax collection.

II. Tax Farming in Tunisia

It is now time to turn our attention more specifically to Tunisia. Between
the last half of the 16th century and the last half of the 19th century Tunisia
was under the control (sometimes only nominal) of the Ottoman Empire. Not
surprisingly, therefore, during this period tax farming was widely practiced
in Tunisia.

Prior to that, however, during the latter part of the Middle Ages under
the Hafsides, tax farming was practiced only rarely. These relatively rare instances of tax farming occurred in collecting customs duties and taxes on wine
and even in these cases the tax farming rights were assigned not to members
of the Muslem majority but to members of the Christian minority [Brun-
schvig (1947)]. Before that, it was probably not practiced at all subsequent
to Tunisia's conversion to Islam in the 7th century A.D. This supposition is
based on the fact that Islam implicitly condemned tax farming as a means
of collecting taxes [Benaïssa (1982)]. Moreover, there is ample evidence that
from the time of the first caliphs of Islam the tax collectors were invariably
permanent employees paid out of the state budget. The tax collectors were
to be chosen from among the "preachers of the faith" so that their honesty
and integrity would be sure to be beyond reproach [Ibn Khaldun (1978)].

In the course of time and especially with the expansion of Islamic ter-
ritory, provincial governors ("wali" or "āmil") became responsible for the
collection of taxes which was carried out with the help of a specialized corps
of salaried tax collectors. The governors became authorized to withhold from
the tax revenues collected the amounts necessary to cover their own needs
as well as those of the civilian and military personnel placed under their
authority. But as Brunschvig (1947) emphasizes, as functionaries and representatives of the central authority of the state, the governors could not be
considered tax farmers.

Despite considerable evidence of abuses in the system, wage contracts
continued to dominate in tax collection activities until the eve of the coming
of the Ottoman Empire. In particular, the governors (then called "caïds"),
as one might have expected and as has been subsequently confirmed by the

numerous recorded complaints to the central authority [Dachraoui (1981)], tended, on the one hand, to impose more than the legally determined taxes and, on the other hand, to underreport the amounts collected.

During the Ottoman period beginning in the latter half of the 16th century tax farming was introduced not only in the collection of taxes per se such as the customs and the tax on chechias (the felt hats Tunisia exported through Africa and the Middle East), but also on various markets of distributing vegetable oil, grains, wood and soap, and the wholesale market of Tunis and the operation of state monopolies, such as those of tobacco, salt, the dressing of hides and skins. The local rulers (beys), moreover, used tax farming as the means of utilizing their own agricultural lands.

In all these activities, the farms (lizma) were conceded to relatively trustworthy rich individuals and to non-Muslems (Christians and Jews). The concession to collect standard (income and wealth) taxes as well as other special taxes in the case of the sedentary population was assigned to the local governors (caïds). In the case of the tribal and nomadic population areas, however, these taxes were collected directly by the military commanders in these areas.[6]

Although in the 17th century the rights to tax farm in certain provinces were assigned to the caïds on the basis of relatively public auctions [Chérif (1986)], this practice was not very general until the reign of Hammuda Pasha at the end of the 18th century.[7] Even before that, by the end of the 17th century these caïds-lazzam (caïds-farmers) began to form a stable and immensely important group. They were organized in a hierarchial manner with a chief caïd ("caïd-el-quwwad") at the top. Many of these caïds amassed sizeable fortunes and, together with other farmers, formed virtual dynasties of money and power and became the true pillars of the beylical regime. When needed, they could be counted upon to make large financial sacrifices to help satisfy the needs of public finance in difficult years and to help the beys arm their troops and resist attacks from abroad such as that from Algeria in 1807 [Chérif (1986)].

Given the fact that the caïds-lazzam were the provincial governors, i.e., the representatives in the provinces of the central administration, and hence had at their disposal the entire military and police personnel stationed in the

---

[6] In those areas less under central control these taxes were usually collected once a year by troops sent from Tunis specifically for this purpose and commanded by the heir to the throne (whose loyality could be trusted) [Hénia (1980), Chérif (1986)].

[7] Hénia (1980) cites the well known 19th century writer Bīn Diyaf (1964) for evidence on this point.

region, it is not surprising that numerous and almost indescribable abuses by the caïd-lazzam of the local populace took place. Chérif (1986), for example, cites anecdotes in which the non-fulfilment of one's tax obligation being penalized by having to spend a night in the hands of the caïd-lazzam was regarded "as a fate worse than death."

In the middle of the 19th century under the reformer Khereddine, the functions of the caïd and tax farmer were separated and tax collection again began to be administered through regular salaried agents who were to surrender all the taxes collected to the authorities. At the same time, the use of the army to collect taxes in the tribal areas was prohibited [Smida (1970)]. This marked the beginning of the decline of tax farming and of the switch back to wage contracts in tax collection activities. This trend continued and became further accentuated during the period of the French occupation, to the point that wage contracts came to dominate in all forms of tax collection activities in both rural and urban areas.

After independence, the desire on the part of government leaders to practice patronage through government employment and the government's adherence (albeit increasingly timidly and nominally) to socialist principles have helped to keep wage contracts the dominant form of tax collection throughout Tunisia.

The one area of tax collection activity in which tax farming remains the dominant, though by no means exclusive, form of contract is with respect to Tunisia's periodic (i.e., non-permanent) markets.[8] Whereas daily markets are generally taxed directly by salaried agents who in many cases have to do nothing more than collect a rental for the use of a stall in the market of a certain size and location, periodic markets, most of which are rural, are generally taxed by a tax farmer who wins the right to collect as much tax revenue as he can (subject to the constraint of the tax rates set by law) by being the highest bidder in a public auction organized by the municipality in which the market is located. Indeed, according to a 1919 beylical decree the municipalities were given the right to collect the taxes in the periodic and daily markets within their confines. More recently (in 1963) the markets outside the municipal centers were decreed to come under the jurisdiction of the Council of the Governorate in which they appeared. No matter whether the relevant government is the municipality or the Council of the governorate, three different forms of management and taxation of the periodic markets are

---

[8] Tax farming is also used in collecting taxes on municipal land – usually undeveloped – when the land is used for private purposes, e.g., by cafes, restaurants, fairs and other activities. For an excellent anthropological account of Tunisia's periodic markets see Michalak (1983).

provided for: (a) "regie directe" wherein a government salaried employee is responsible for the management and taxation of such markets, (b) "regie interessée" or "indirecte" wherein an agent is given these tasks and responsibilities in return for the right to retain a specified share of the tax receipts, and (c) tax farming, wherein the right to collect taxes at the rates established by national law is auctioned off (generally to the highest bidder) in a public auction.

In practice, however, the use of "regie directe" is limited to the market for carpets and the "regie interessée" is not applied at the present time. Hence, tax farming remains the dominant contractual form for collecting taxes from periodic markets.

The conditions of contract and the rules for the award of such contracts to the tax farmer through public auction are codified by the Ministry of the Interior. As a result, they are the same for all municipalities in the country. Quite likely, the codifications introduced by the Ministry of Interior merely formalize what had been common practice. There is no indication of any deliberate attempt at institutional change. In view of the importance of the effectiveness of public auctions to the usefulness of tax farming to the state, and its relevance to our objective of trying to understand why Tunisian institutions are the way they are, we deem it important to briefly describe the rules of the auction and the procedure for selecting the winning bid.

First, the date and place of the public auction must be announced in advance in the *Journal Officiel* of the Republic. Even more importantly, several of the municipalities also advertise the time and place of their auction in local newspapers, and public places in different parts of the country. These means of communication, plus the fact that there are no residential restrictions, such as to be from the same municipality or governorate in which the market is located, make it clear that the competition is intended to be a *national* one with as few restrictions as possible. The only exclusions are for (a) those who had defaulted on any previous tax farm contracts in which they may have been involved, (b) those who had been taken to court and convicted for previous infractions of the laws relative to periodic markets (such as forcing the merchants to pay more than would be justified in the tax laws pertaining to these markets) and (c) those excluded for reasons of "morality" (a rather vague restriction which seems not to have played a measurable role).

Any bidder must make a deposit equal to 10 percent of the previous year's price of the tax farm. The winning (highest) bidder is also required to deposit within twenty-four hours of his selection a guarantee payment of one-quarter of his winning bid. The guarantee payment is refundable only at the end of the year and only when all the tax farmer's obligations to the city or governorate have been met. These requirements are obviously designed to screen candidates for minimum financial viability and to protect the municipality against the risk of default. Should the winning bidder not be able to make the guarantee payment within twenty-four hours, the municipality has two options, namely, to accept another bidder or to call for a new auction. If in a new auction the price should be below that of the original one, the defaulting winning bidder of the first auction is required to make up the difference between the two winning bids. This rule would seem to have the effects of discouraging deliberate attempts to bring the price down by strategic behavior on the part of the bidders and of protecting the municipality against any demonstration effect of financial default on the part of a winning bidder on other subsequent bids. Once again, the option of calling a new public auction can be interpreted as encouraging the greatest possible competition in each year's auctions.

The tax farmer is required to pay the full price of the tax farm in equal monthly installments payable at the beginning of each month. The fact that the payments are as frequent as once a month greatly reduces the financial requirements of the tax farmer and hence once again has the effect of encouraging more entries into the auctions of tax farms.[9] While there are also requirements that the tax farmer provide a monthly accounting of taxes collected through a system of numbered receipts and seek the municipality's consent to his choice of personnel to be employed in carrying out the tax collection operations, in general, such requirements on the mode of operation of the tax farmers are not enforced. Most importantly, in taxing the market the tax farmer must impose taxes at the tax rates specified for the whole country by presidential decree.[10] The fact that the tax rates are set by presidential decree and have not been changed for many years reduces the possibility that by virtue of their ignorance of the legal rates, the merchants could be made to pay the tax farmer more than the law requires them to pay. This is not meant to imply that the tax farmer would not be able to extort excessive payments from the merchants in other ways and, indeed, there is in some municipalities evidence of relatively frequent complaints by the merchants of the imposition of excessive charges by the tax farmer.

Our description of the way that tax farming works in the case of Tunisia's

---

[9] Moreover, in practice, regularity of payments is not strictly enforced.

[10] While the presidential decree merely sets maximum tax rates, leaving it up to the municipalities to set their own rates, virtually without exception the municipal decrees set the rates at the nationally prescribed maximum levels.

periodic markets would not be complete without an account of the methods used by the tax farmers in carrying out their responsibilities. Usually the personnel they hire are engaged on the basis of wage contracts of relatively short duration but with the promise of contract renewal on the basis of satisfactory performance. The system of receipts helps protect the farmer against underreporting on the part of his workers. Frequently two different wage workers are able to check on the honesty of the other. To guard against undercharging of the merchants by friendly tax collectors, many of the employees are from outside the region and are chosen on the basis of their agressive behavior and their loyalty to the employer. Although subcontracting is prohibited by law, in practice it is fairly common for the tax farmer to (sub)contract out portions of the tax farm on a short term basis to his own employees.[11]

Despite the deliberate efforts of the local authorities and the national legislation to encourage competitive bidding for the right to collect the taxes on periodic markets and thereby to assure the municipalities of as much revenue as possible, because of the risk of financial loss that inevitably would accrue to an inexperienced tax farmer and new bidders, especially in view of the asymmetries of information which are biased in favor of existing holders of tax farming rights, the bidding process tends to be incompletely competitive, with infrequent turnover among the holders of tax farms. Even where turnover exists, moreover, the change is frequently from one member to another within a particular coalition or cartel of tax farmers who are allied with one another frequently on a national scale.[12] Not only are the conditions prevailing in such auctions precisely those in which market failure is likely to take place[13] but also the members of the cartel or coalition have every incentive to keep it that way and hence to deliberately misinform other competing bidders by erratic bidding. One of our interviewees mentioned a case in which the holder of the tax farm kept other bidders from entering the site of the auction by physical force. In the long run these factors have the effect of raising the effective risk to potential entrants, thereby reducing the average price of winning bids. The existence of such cartels or coalitions can no doubt also be explained in large part by the risk- and information-sharing benefits provided by participation in such coalitions or cartels.

---

[11]See especially Chaouch (1975).

[12]Such cartels are prohibited by law [Chaouch (1975].

[13]Unlike markets for second-hand cars and other forms of property, the holder of the tax farm does not have the right to sell his right, thereby implying that this potential vehicle for limiting market failure [Feinstein, Block and Nold (1985)] would not be present in this case.

III. Explaining Variations in the Incidence of Tax Farming over Time and Space

Given the vulnerability of tax sharing and wage contracts to output-underreporting and the undersupply of effort in tax collection, and the inevitable incentive for evasion on the part of taxpayers, the supervision cost advantages of fixed rent or tax-farming techniques in tax collection are easy to see.

Naturally, the relative importance of these supervision cost advantages of tax farming could be expected to vary from one situation to another. For example, the collection of some taxes under wage contracts might be easier to supervise than others. For example, once virtually all imports began to arrive in large ships which can be unloaded only in those seaports with deep and protected harbors, it became much easier to monitor the efforts of wage contract tax collectors in collecting import duties. Since this occured relatively early in history, it undoubtedly explains why the taxation of the customs duties was one of the first in which tax farming was replaced by state tax collectors on wage contracts. Likewise, the importance of not easily observable qualitative factors and the relative importance of weather in the determination of agricultural output undoubtedly explains why tax farming has been rather common in the taxation of agricultural output throughout history.

The lack of familiarity with markets and with intricacies of the modes of industrial production and of the costs thereof and the lack of access to other relevant information would also be factors favoring the use of tax farming. With greater experience and information availability in the hands of government officials, it would be easier for them to collect taxes on markets and manufacturing industries by employing their own agents on wage contracts. This undoubtedly explains why tax farming was more common in industry and commerce in their early stages than at present. Note also that tax farming was practiced in the wholesale produce market of Tunis in the years immediately after its inception but was later replaced by salaried tax collectors once it was possible to get a better idea of the value of space occupied by each commissioner and the expected volume of market transactions.[14]

The aforementioned change in tax laws from payment in kind to payment in cash in the Ottoman Empire could be expected to reduce the transaction costs of tax collection considerably. Not surprisingly, therefore, soon after this change occured, land taxes began to be collected by salaried agents rather than exclusively by tax farmers [Shaw (1968)]. Additional evidence in support

---

[14]See especially Azabou, Kuran and Nabli (1988).

of this expectation is provided by Baer (1968) who showed that in Egypt the tax farming role of the market shayks or amins in allocating the tax quota among guild members was abolished in favor of fixed wage employees of the state who began to collect the taxes directly soon after the tax laws on guild-merchants were changed by Mohammed Ali so as to require payment in cash in the 1840s. The decreasing disadvantage of tax collection by salaried tax collectors *vis-à-vis* that by (fixed rent) tax farming attributable to the growing importance of economies of scale and of scope in supervision could be offset to some extent by expanding the scale and the scope of tax farms from specific local ones to general national ones as in the general tax farms of France [Matthews (1958)]. However, as noted above, no such change could be accomplished without deleteriously affecting the degree of competition for the right of being the tax farmer.

Another development no doubt contributing to the secular drift toward wage contracts in tax collection in most societies has been the accounting revolution and the expansion of formal double entry accounting procedures, especially in the formal or modern sectors. Once formal accounting procedures become widespread, and payroll deduction methods are in place, it becomes considerably easier for governments to collect their sales, wage and income taxes. This no doubt explains why tax farming is presently virtually unheard of in the modern sector of economies where modern accounting methods are in use.

In other circumstances, however, where taxes are likely to be difficult to collect (i.e., the transaction costs of their collection are relatively high), the advantages of tax farming or fixed rent methods of collecting the taxes may be rather substantial. Moreover, the advantages of tax farming need not be limited to those arising from a narrow definition of the transaction costs directly arising in the process of tax collection. For example, in agriculture when the tax farmer has to pay a fixed amount to government but is free to (and hence has the incentive to) collect as much in the way of taxes as he can, the tax farmer would have every incentive to assure that the most profitable crops were produced and in the most efficient way possible. Not surprisingly, therefore, in situations where markets are sufficiently imperfect to induce the agriculturalists themselves to be efficient, tax farmers have often come to exercise considerable control over the farmers, industrial producers, and merchants from whom they have the right to collect the legally set taxes. As markets become more complete and more competitive, and hence the opportunities for further increases in allocative or technical efficiency decline, this extra advantage of tax farming is likely to diminish in importance.

Still another factor favoring the replacement of tax farming by salaried tax collectors is the growing monopoly of police power in the hands of the state. Considering the importance of physical threat to the successful collection of taxes, in the early days of the guilds when the power of the state in Tunisia and elsewhere within the Ottoman Empire was relatively weak, and arms dispersed among the populace, it was efficient for the well-armed leaders of the guilds to collect the taxes. More recently, however, as the preponderance of arms has become more and more concentrated in the hands of the military, (as has been the case in many developing countries), it has become more efficient for government agents to collect the taxes directly rather than indirectly.[15]

Now we come to the main focus of the paper. Why does tax farming remain dominant in the periodic markets of Tunisia? Many of the aforementioned considerations would seem relevant. First, these markets are very informal; formal accounts are seldom kept. Second, because of the infrequency and irregularity of their operations, it is certainly difficult for any agent who would be engaged only part time in assessing taxes in such a market to be able to properly assess the value of items transacted. Third, the distance of such periodic markets, at least relative to other markets and most other taxable activities, from municipal centers makes it costly for salaried tax agents whose other work is in the municipal center to get to and monitor such markets. Such difficulties are compounded by the fact that the activities in such markets are relatively widely dispersed both with respect to physical space and with respect to time of day. Fourth, because each individual transaction is generally bargained separately and the information about realized prices and quantities is usually maintained as private information, even everpresent monitors have considerable difficulty in making assessments, thereby accentuating the importance of the transaction cost advantages of tax farming. Fifth, the fact that the tax rates are specific to each commodity and often are specified in specific as opposed to *ad valorem* terms also raises the transaction costs of collecting the taxes in such markets. This is not to say that certain economies of scale and of scope in monitoring and tax collection cannot be reaped but these can be captured through the use of "general" tax farms instead of necessarily by a common salaried tax collector. No-

---

[15]The reliability and loyalty of the salaried tax collector to the ruler was maximized through the selection of foreigners and minority members as tax collectors [Shaw (1968)]. Shaw also points out, however, that as law and order declined and hence the transaction costs of tax collection increased once again in the 17th century, the role of tax farmers in collecting agricultural taxes in Egypt increased again.

tably, it is the right to tax all taxable activities in a given periodic market that is auctioned off, not the right to tax only chickens, to tax grain, to tax handicrafts, toys, medicines and so on.[16] This means that the advantages of tax farming can be reaped without giving up the economies of scope in supervision which generally accrue primarily to centralized tax collection by wage contracts. Moreover, since the auctions of different markets are held on different days and there are no restrictions on entry by those from outside the municipality or holding tax farms in other communities, it is relatively easy for a tax farmer to be in possession of the tax farms on several different periodic markets in a given region at the same time.

For another important part of the explanation for the use of the tax farming in Tunisia's periodic markets we have to consider the perspective of the municipality. While a detailed discussion of public finance in Tunisia's municipalities is beyond the scope of this paper,[17] several important characteristics should be pointed out. First, most of the expenditure requirements of the municipalities are fixed in the form of the fixed salaries of those employees who are needed to provide a basic minimum of public services. Second, the alternative forms of tax revenue available to the municipalities are extremely limited. While grants from the central government have been rising in importance, the use of such funds is tied to specific projects and programs which often also require additional expenditures by the municipalities themselves. While a loan program for municipalities in financial distress exists, administrative difficulties have thus far prevented the program from being of practical use. Third, one must appreciate that the levels of activity in the periodic markets of any one municipality are highly volatile, varying quite sharply from week to week, season to season, and year to year depending on weather, economic conditions and so on. In view of the fixity of their expenditures, the limited and often uncertain amounts of alternative revenue sources, and the volatility of the tax base of the periodic markets, one can easily understand the reluctance of municipal governments to bear the risks that would be involved in direct collection of these taxes through salaried tax collectors. Tax farming, therefore, is attractive because it passes these risks along to the tax farmers. The tax farmers, on the other hand, are in a rela-

---

[16]In some cases, however, the periodic markets are specialized, thereby somewhat reducing the economies of scope in supervision which tend to make tax farming advantageous. Indeed, it is notable that the one exception to the practice of tax farming occurs in one specialized market, namely that for carpets.

[17]For a relatively complete discussion of the sources of finance of municipalities as a whole see Derycke (1983) and Nellis (1985).

tively good position to bear these risks both because their employees are hired
on very short-term contracts which can thereby be relatively easily adjusted
in proportion to expected revenues and because they generally participate in
coalitions with other tax farmers to help spread the risks. The same coalitions, moreover, by limiting the degree of competition in the auctions of tax
farms and thereby keeping the profitability of the tax farms relatively high,
have the effect of compensating the tax farmers for their ability to bear risk.[18]

Another factor tending to preserve the viability of tax farming in periodic markets – most of which are rural – is the lesser degree of monopoly of
power and omnipresence on the part of the state in these environments. By
contrast, a relatively well-heeled tax farmer, especially one who is assisted by
large sized and aggressive agents, can exert a lot more pressure on a recalci-
trant merchant to pay the legal tax than would be the case with a timid civil
servant without a police force or army to back him up. When such powers
are in the hands of tax farmers, however, one could certainly imagine that
substantial abuses of power in the form of imposing more than the legal tax
rates on the merchants might take place.[19] In practice, however, in the case
of Tunisia's periodic markets at least, such behavior seems to be sufficiently
constrained as to limit these abuses to more or less tolerable levels, except
perhaps in some situations. One such constraint on overtaxation by the tax
farmers is that the tax rates are uniform throughout the entire nation and
have been constant over time, thereby making it easy for all the relevant parties to be well informed as to the legal rates. Another such constraint in that
the tax farmer has to consider that the abused merchants can have recourse to
a judicial system for redress of such abuses presumably at his expense. While
(as in most countries) the transaction costs to relatively poor individuals for
using the judicial system for such purposes are relatively high, at least the
opportunity is there. More importantly, a lower cost alternative is available,
namely that the abused or anyone else can register a complaint with the municipal authorities. Since the municipal authorities want to be spared the
unpleasantness and loss of time of having to hear and investigate such complaints, they are unlikely to re-award tax farms to tax farmers whose actions
have given rise to numerous complaints. As noted above, this nonrenewal

---

[18]Another advantage of the municipalities of tax farming is that they can
thereby avoid payment of the social security and other fringe benefits which
they would be required to provide for their salaried government workers. Tax
farmers do not pay such benefits.

[19]Riordan and Sappington (1985) point out in a somewhat different context
that toleration of at least a certain amount of abuse in this respect may be
necessary incentives for obtaining satisfactorily high bids.

to holders of tax farms who have been charged with immoral or unethical behavior is even codified in law. Not surprisingly, several of the municipal authorities interviewed felt that the threat of potential loss of the tax farm arising from frequent complaints is a more significant constraint on the abuse of merchants by tax farmers than the availability of a judicial system.

The municipalities may recognize that a certain amount of coalition- formation among tax farmers may be necessary in order to allow the tax farmers to bear the risks of uncertain revenues which the municipalities themselves are unwilling to bear. Naturally, however, they have to be concerned that it could also lead to collusion in the bidding process which, in turn, could have the effect of lowering the price of winning bids to unacceptable levels (i.e., to levels which yield the tax farmers profits above and beyond those justified by the risk premium). As mentioned in Section II above, the municipalities are at least somewhat protected in this respect by (1) the insistence on widespread announcement of the auctions, (2) the fact that the competition is to be conducted on a national (as opposed to only a local) basis, (3) the fact that the tax farmer's payments are limited to a relatively modest advance payment and then relatively small installment payments thereby lowering the fixed costs of winning entries, (4) that, under certain conditions at least, the municipalities retain the right to call new auctions if they don't like the price of the winning bid, (5) that the municipalities always have the option to collect the taxes themselves if they think that such an action would be warranted, and (6) the information-enhancing and hence cost-reducing effect that public disclosure of all winning bids may have, especially for new entrants into the bidding process.

IV. Conclusions and Implications for the Future of Tax Farming

The preceding analysis has identified the factors that explain the gradual replacement of fixed rent (tax farming) approaches to tax collection by wage contract methods. Among the most important of these influences have been (1) the change in the form of tax payment from kind to cash, (2) the development and expansion of accounting procedures and dissemination of such accounts to government and the public, (3) the growing concentration of power in the hands of the state, (4) the high and perhaps even rising importance of the central government *vis-à-vis* local government,[20] (5) the growing

---

[20] All governments have several goals, only one of which is to maximize their ability to collect the legally determined tax rates, and one of which is likely to include public popularity, the attainment of which is likely to be negatively affected by the strict enforcement of the tax laws. Since there is likely to be more at stake in the loss of power for a central government than for a local

relative ability of the state and even of local governments to bear the risk
of insufficient revenue generation and (6) the accumulation of knowledge and
experience concerning the technology of and the economic forces affecting the
item taxed and the diffusion of that knowledge.

Even in situations where the conditions remain favorable to tax farming, however, the historical experience has shown that the efficient practice of
tax farming can be marred by either one or both of the following degeneracy
problems. First, competitive auctions may degenerate into those in which the
bidders collude with one another in order to keep the winning bid artificially
low. Second, the rental or sale to the tax farmer of the right to collect the
taxes and to keep any proceeds collected above and beyond the fixed amount
owed to the government can induce the tax farmer to practice unscrupulous
behavior in extracting excessive amounts of tax from the parties taxed. Experience has shown that the latter degeneracy problem is most likely to arise
when (1) there are insufficient constraints on the behavior of the tax farmer,
(2) knowledge of the tax laws is imperfect and incomplete, and (3) the tax
laws are ambiguous.

Both of these degeneracy problems have arisen from time to time in the
case of the tax farming of Tunisia's periodic markets. However, in general
and by the mechanisms detailed above the Tunisian authorities have been
relatively successful in encouraging a sufficient amount of competition in the
auction process and in keeping the practice of "mafia"-type exploitative behavior down to tolerable limits in most parts of the country.

The Tunisian experience with tax farming of periodic markets underscores the importance of constant vigilance for the appearance of the degeneracy problems mentioned above. It also demonstrates, however, that
tax farming can constitute a low transaction cost, relatively efficient means
of collecting taxes in conditions which make for high transaction costs and
hence for great difficulty in collecting the taxes via wage or share contracts.
Indeed, the experience seems to have been sufficiently positive to suggest that
serious consideration by governments should be given to the possible use of
tax farming contracts in collecting their taxes in other high transaction cost
situations. Since a little imagination can lead one to identify many such situations, it could be that tax farming techniques could have a relatively bright
future.

For example, even in those highly developed countries where most con-

government, and the flexibility to adjust to revenue shortfalls is likely to be
greater, central governments are less likely to attach as high a priority to
efficiency in tax collection as local governments.

ditions are such as to make tax collection by wage contract advantageous (i.e., accounting methods are well developed and their use widely diffused, the experience with the technology and economy of the items taxed has been accumulated and disseminated rather widely, and the power of the state is strong relative to that of its citizens) more and more potential revenues are being lost by the government by virtue of the eclipse and erosion of the formal sector and its tax base in favor of the "underground" economy. Estimates of the relative importance of the "underground" economy or "informal" sector in aggregate economic activity of such countries range from 5 percent to almost 50 percent depending on the country and method of estimation.[21] Moreover, it is generally agreed that the share is growing rapidly. The growing importance of the underground economy has to be viewed with concern from the perspective of public finance since the ability of governments to collect taxes from this sphere of economic activity is almost nonexistent. This is by no means surprising in view of the fact that this sector deliberately eschews the use of formal accounting principles, thereby making it extremely easy for its participants to underreport output, sales, wages and incomes for purposes of computing tax payments.

The transaction costs of trying to detect and prove tax evasion on the part of tax collectors paid by wage contract tax are undoubtedly prohibitively high. Too many layers of supervision would be necessary, thereby explaining why governments seldom invest much in the way of resources in trying to accomplish it. On the other hand, one might expect that, by providing the incentive for private firms knowledgeable about these activities and thus able to calculate the tax base and collect the taxes relatively easily, much more in the way of legitimate government revenue could be obtained from this growing sector of economic activity than is generally the case at present. Moreover, once private firms and individuals would come to recognize that, through the practice of tax farming techniques, the underground economy would be forced to pay its fair share of taxes, there would no longer be tax-evasion incentive to withdraw from the formal sector of the economy and hence to eschew the otherwise advantageous use of formal accounting procedures.[22]

References

Azabou, Mongi, Timur Kuran and Mustapha K. Nabli, 1988, "The Wholesale

---

[21]See, e.g., Feige (1979), Tanzi (1982) and Simon and Witte (1982).
[22]Such a recommendation would complement those for self-assessment by Shoup (1983) and Strassman (1982).

Produce Market of Tunis and Its Porters: A Tale of Market Degeneration." ch. 12, this volume.

Baer, Gabriel, 1968, "Social Change in Egypt: 1800-1914," in P.M. Holt, ed. *Political and Social Change in Modern Eygpt*. London: Oxford University Press: 135-161.

Benaïssa, Said, 1982, *Introduction aux Finances Publiques. Etude Comparative des Systèmes Financiers Islamique, Liberal et Socialiste*. Algiers.

Bin Diyaf, Ahmed, 1964, *Ithâf Ahl al-Zamân... The Chronicles of the Tunisian Beys*. (Reprint of 19th century manuscript), Tunis: Publications de Secretariat d'Etat aux Affairs Culturelles. (8 Volumes).

Brunschvig, Robert, 1947, *La Berberie Orientale sous les Hafsides. Des Origines à la Fin du XVe Siècle*. Paris: Librairie d'Amérique et d'Orient.

Chaouch, Khalifa, 1975, *Moknine et son Souk (Etude Geographique)*. Unpublished thesis, doctorat 3^{me}cycle, Université de Paris VII; Tunis, CERES.

Chefif, Mohamed-Hedi, 1986, *Le Pouvoir et Societé dans la Tunisie de Húsayn Bin'Ali (1705-1740)*. Tunis: Publications de l'Université de Tunis, Faculté des Lettres, (2 Volumes).

Dachraoui, Farhat, 1981, *Le Califat Fatimide au Maghreb. Histoire Politique et Institutions*. Tunis: Société Tunisienne de Diffusion.

Derycke, Pierre-Henri, 1983, "Le Systéme Financier Local de Deux Villes Africaines: Tunis et Abidjan. Une Etude Exploratoire." C.E.R.E.V.E, Université de Paris X - Nanterre.

Donohue, John S.J., 1984, "Land Tenure in Hilal al-Sabi's al-Wuzarā" in Tarif Khalidi, ed. *Land Tenure and Social Transformation in the Middle East*. Beirut: American University of Beirut, 121-130.

Elvin, Mark, 1973, *The Pattern of the Chinese Past*. Stanford: Stanford University Press.

Feige, Edgar L., 1979, "How Big is the Irregular Economy?" *Challenge* (November-December): 5-13.

Feinstein, Jonathan S., Michael K. Block and Frederick C. Nold, 1985, "Asymmetric Information and Collusive Behavior in Auction Markets," *American Economic Review* 75 (June): 441-460.

Fryde, E.B., 1958, "The English Farmers of the Customs 1343-51," *Transaction of the Royal Historical Society* 9, Fifth Series: 1-17.

Habib, Irfan, 1963, *Agrarian Systems of Moghul India*. Bombay.

―――――――――, 1967, "Aspects of Agrarian Relations and Economy in a Region of Uttar Pradesh during the 16th Century." *Indian Economic and Social History Review* 4 (No. 3): 205-232

Hénia, Abdelhamid, 1980, *Le Grid. Ses Rapports avec le Beylik de Tunis (1676-1840)*. Tunis: Publications de l'Université de Tunis.

Hicks, John, 1969, *A Theory of Economic History*. London, New York: Oxford University Press, Ch. 6.

Ho, Ping-ti, 1959, *Studies on the Population of China, 1368-1953*.

Ibn Khaldoun, Abderrahman, 1978, *Discours sur l'Histoire Universelle - Al Muqaddima*. (in 14th century in Arabic). Translated into French by Monteil, Vincent). Paris: Sindbad.

İnalcık, Halil, 1973, *The Ottoman Empire: The Classical Age 1300-1600*. New York: Praeger Publishers.

Issawi, Charles, 1982, *An Economic History of the Middle East and North Africa*. New York: Columbia Univesity Press.

Jeannin, Pierre, 1972, *Merchants of the Sixteenth Century.* (translated from French by Paul Fittingoff) New York: Harper and Row.

Jwaideh, Albertine, 1984, "Aspects of Land Tenure and Social Change in Lower Iraq" in Tarif Khalidi, ed., *Land Tenure and Social Transformation in the Middle East.* Beirut: American University of Beirut, 333-356.

Latouche, Robert, 1961, *The Birth of Western Economy.* London: Methuen (English Translation).

Lewis, Bernard, 1979, "Ottoman Land Tenure and Taxation in Syria," *Studia Islamica* 50: 109-124.

Mathews, George, 1958, *The Royal General Farms in Eighteenth Century France.* New York: Columbia University Press.

Michalak, Lawrence Otis, 1983, *The Changing Weekly Markets of Tunisia.* Ph.D. dissertation, Department of Anthropology, University of California, Berkeley.

Nellis, John R., 1985, "Decentralization and Local Public Finance in Tunisia," *Public Administration and Development* 5 (May): 187-204.

Newton, Arthur Percival, 1918, "The Establishment of the Great Farm of the English Customs," *Transactions of the Royal Historical Society,* Series 4, vol. 1: 129-155.

Rafeq, Abdul-Karim, 1984, "Land Tenure Problems and their Social Impact in Syria around the Middle of the Nineteenth Century" in Tarif Khalidi, ed., *Land Tenure and Social Transformation in the Middle East.* Beirut: American University of Beirut, 371-396.

Riordan, Michael H. and David E.M. Sappington, 1985, "Awarding Monopoly Franchises," *American Economic Review* 77: 375-387.

Shaw, Stanford, 1968, "Landholding and Land-tax Revenues in Ottoman Egypt," in P.M. Holt, ed., *Political and Social Change in Modern Egypt.* London: Oxford University Press: 156-170.

_____, and Ezel Shaw, 1977, *History of the Ottoman Empire and Modern Turkey.* Cambridge: Cambridge University Press.

Shoup, Donald C., 1983, "Intervention through Property Taxation and Public Ownership," in Harold B. Dunkerley, ed., *Urban Land Policy: Issues and Opportunities.* New York: Oxford University Press: 132-152.

Simon, Carl P. and Ann D. Witte, 1982, *Beating the System: The Underground Economy.* Boston: Auburn Publishing Company.

Smida, Mongi, 1970, *Khéreddine. Ministre Réformateur 1873-1877.* Tunis: Maison Tunisienne de l'Edition.

Strassman, W. Paul, 1982, *The Transformation of Urban Housing.* Baltimore: Johns Hopkins University Press.

Tanzi, Vito, ed., 1982, *The Underground Economy in the U.S. and Other Countries.* Lexington, Mass: D.C. Heath.

Chapter 7

THE SIZE DISTRIBUTION AND OWNERSHIP TYPE OF FIRMS IN TUNISIAN MANUFACTURING*

Mustapha K. Nabli, Jeffrey B. Nugent and Lamine Doghri

I. Introduction: Technology, Market Size and Transaction Costs as Determinants of Firm Size and Ownership Type

Traditionally, it has been assumed that the various characteristics of firms - such as their size, form of organization, and ownership type - are determined primarily by technological and market conditions, in particular the degree of economies of scale, and the relative factor-intensity of technology, on the one hand, and the size and riskiness of the their domestic and/or foreign markets as well as barriers to entry,[1] on the other hand.

The existence of a non-degenerate distribution, i.e. the coexistence of large and small sized plants, can also be explained by the presence of transportation and distribution costs with firms catering to regional markets, as well as product differentiation. The cost disadvantage of small relative to large plants is a determinant of the extent and significance of these factors in determining the size distribution. Therefore, market size variables may be used to help explain the truncation of the upper tail of the distribution. The smaller the size of the market relative to the minimum efficient size, the fewer firms of large size are to be found.

These effects are to be distinguished from those that tend to extend the lower tail of the distribution, and can be considered as leading to suboptimal scales of operation. Non-competitive market structures and concentration allowing firms to price above costs and to deter entry may lead to less than optimal scale. Two other factors have received particular attention mostly in the context of analyses of Canadian manufacturing. First, foreign ownership, which through the "miniature replica effect" (Canadian industry being a

---

*The authors express their gratitude to Bruce Herrick, Timur Kuran, Carl Liedholm, Donald Mead, Mario Tello and numerous seminar participants in Paris, USC and Calcutta for useful comments, references and suggestions, and to the Institut National de la Statistique for supplying unpublished data used in this study.

[1] See, for example, Bain (1966), Arrow (1964), Scherer (1973, 1980), Teitel (1975), Ijiro and Simon (1981) and Kirkpatrick, Lee and Nixson (1984). For a recent survey of issues and empirical findings, especially with respect to concentration see Curry and George (1983).

smaller version of U.S. industry with most of the leading U.S. firms present), leads to inefficient scale. Second, according to the so-called Eastman- Stykolt hypothesis (Stykolt and Eastman (1960)), a higher degree of trade protection, combined with collusive behavior in the domestic industry, leads to higher prices and profits, thereby leading to a phenomenon of "excessive entry" and the proliferation of small, inefficient producers. Various empirical tests of these hypotheses have been made, in particular by Baldwin and Gorecki (1985, 1987) who have found support for them.

Only quite recently has the role of transaction cost considerations been acknowledged.[2] Virtually all applications of transaction costs in this context, moreover, have been limited to enterprises in developed countries. As such, these applications have implicitly assumed the kinds of institutional and environmental conditions which prevail in such countries, such as the extensive use of modern accounting methods, the availability of such accounts on individual enterprises to governments, consumers, and shareholders and the existence of well developed markets for equity capital, credit, managers and skilled technicians, but, at the same time also, the weakness of family, ethnic, clan and community bonds and cultural norms.

Since LDC conditions differ widely in these respects from those which have been assumed in the previous applications of technological and market conditions or transaction cost determinants of firm size, organizational form and ownership type choices, it is only appropriate that doubts be raised as to

---

[2]For example, Chandler (1962, 1977) and North (1981) have pointed out the extent to which transaction costs have tended to act as an offset to economies of scale in determining firm size. Chandler (1977) and Williamson (1975, 1981, 1985) have identified changes in transaction costs and in particular improvements in communications and monitoring capabilities, and at the same time the growing importance of asset specificity as major contributors to the change in corporate form from its traditional U-form to the now dominant multi-divisional M-form. Williamson (1985) and Klein, Crawford and Alchian (1978) among others have called attention to the role of transaction costs in determining the degree of vertical integration. Likewise, Forbes (1986) has suggested that the emergence of limited liability may be better, and more fundamentally, explained by transaction cost considerations than by changes either in preferences for risk-aversion or in objective assessments of risk. Fama and Jensen (1983), moreover, have stressed the importance of transaction costs in determining the degree of separation between ownership and control, on the one hand, and decision management and decision control, on the other. Finally, transaction costs have also been shown to be important in determining the relationships within the firm among workers, capital owners and manager- supervisors [Alchian and Demsetz (1972), Berle and Means (1932), Coase (1937, 1972), Demsetz (1983), Fama (1980), and Jensen and Meckling (1976)].

the transferability to LDCs of either the existing hypotheses or their policy and other implications. Indeed, applications of either the traditional approach or the transaction cost approach to similar issues and problems in LDCs may well require significant modifications. Such modifications quite possibly could have the effect of enriching and broadening either kind of analysis and extending its applicability. This would seem especially true with respect to the economics of transaction costs.

One of the consequences of assuming the aforementioned conditions prevailing in DCs with respect to the application of transaction cost economics to firm size and ownership type issues is that the forms of opportunistic behavior considered have been limited to those internal to the firm, such as between workers and managers or between managers and shareholders. Thereby, such studies have failed to consider those forms which occur between one or more agents within a particular firm, such as owner-managers, and others external to that firm, such as governments or consumers.

Another such consequence is that the sources, nature and magnitude of the relevant transaction costs may be very different in LDCs than in DCs. For example, the absence of a market for managers or technicians may make it more difficult for the owner to learn about the experience, reliability and effectiveness of a manager in an LDC than would be the case in a DC where such characteristics are generally communicated by a market-determined salary. It would also tend to decrease the mobility of managers and technicians and to increase the asset-specificity of their human capital investments, once again (for the reasons so persuasively argued by Williamson (1985), Klein (1983) and others) increasing the possibilities for opportunistic behavior on the part of managers and hence also the importance of careful monitoring by the owner.[3] Likewise, the absence of equity capital markets in LDCs should be expected to greatly reduce the mobility of the risk-bearing owners of capital, thereby raising their need for monitoring managers, technicians and workers and for thoroughly investigating and controlling the environment of their investment, thereby raising the importance of transaction costs.[4]

Still another consequence of the difference in conditions between DCs and LDCs is the effect of the greater importance of family, clan, ethnic and

---

[3]The absence of markets for managers and technicians would also increase the concern on their part for opportunistic or exploitative behavior on the part of the owner, again increasing their need for information, search and the monitoring of owners.

[4]By the same token, the dearth of such markets would also increase the need for managers to supervise owners, once again having the effect of increasing transaction costs.

community ties and cultural norms on the need for monitoring. For example, if the manager and owner should belong to the same family as is commonly the case in LDCs, the importance attached to reputation among members of the same family and the speed with which the practice of opportunistic behavior translates lates into ill-repute may act as a significant deterrent to opportunistic behavior on the part of either party, thereby reducing the need for monitoring, possibly very significantly.[5] Whereas the relative lack of availability of markets for managers, technicians and equity capital tends to increase the concerns of owners and managers alike for opportunistic behavior on the part of the other party, the relative importance of family, clan and community relations and also of reputations for honesty and performance within such groups tends to reduce the need for monitoring. Therefore, while the net direction of these different effects for transaction costs may be difficult to determine *a priori*, it should be very clear that the relevant source and channels of information are likely to be very different in the two types of countries.

The purpose of the present paper is to examine the applicability of transaction cost economics to the determination of size of establishment and ownership type in Tunisian manufacturing. In view of the objective of an application to a developing country, it would seem appropriate to consider opportunistic behavior on the part of the different agents within the firm, not only as is usual with respect to each other, but also with respect to parties external to the firm. In a sense this focus can be thought of as providing a link between the economics of transaction costs and that of rent-seeking.

In focusing on transaction cost considerations, it is by no means our intent to deny the relevance of the more traditional technological and market-condition determinants of firm size and form of ownership. Indeed, quite to the contrary, we shall pay special attention to possible interdependencies between technology, market size and risk, on the one hand, and the various sorts of opportunism (which give rise to transaction costs), on the other. Specifically, we wish to consider the possibility that the effects of technology, market size and other traditional concerns may be attenuated, enhanced, or otherwise distorted by the interaction of these influences with those of the different environmental and institutional constraints within which LDC agents must operate.

To motivate the reader's attention to this possibility consider the data

---

[5] See, e.g., Dubetsky (1976) on the role of community of origin in reducing transaction costs in Turkish manufacturing industries. The same factors may explain the importance of economic groups in LDC manufacturing [Leff (1976, 1978)].

on the size distribution of firms in the wearing apparel, hosiery and footwear sectors of Tunisian manufacturing which are given in Table 7-1. The interesting feature of this table is that it affords a comparison between those firms producing for the domestic and/or international market which are subject to the normal legal and institutional regime prevailing in the country and those producing exclusively for export which are subject to the special provisions of the industrial promotion legislation of April 1972. Since the firms subject to this latter legislation are in large part exempted from the several institutional and other constraints (which will be described in detail in Section III below) to which most Tunisian firms producing for the domestic and foreign markets are subject, the table affords a comparison of the size distributions of Tunisian manufacturing firms between those subject to, and those exempt from, the prevailing institutional constraints.

The striking result which emerges from such a comparison is the following. On the one hand, those firms subject to the normal institutional regime (that for firms producing for the "domestic" market) are generally small, the vast majority in all three sectors having less than 50 (permanent) employees; in no case does the percentage of firms with 100 or more employees exceed 17 percent. On the other hand, however, those "export" firms which are largely exempted from the normal institutional constraints are generally rather large, with at least 60% and as much as 83% of the firms having 100 or more workers. Since (1) the technology of the two types of firms is rather similar, (2) a significant percentage of products produced by "domestic" firms is in fact exported (13% of sales are exported in apparel, 9% in knitting and 2% in footwear in 1981), and (3) the number of firms (even among those producing largely for the domestic market) is large, differences in firm size between the two sets of firms cannot be attributed to either technology or market size. In a very real sense, the purpose of this paper is to identify the institutional and other determinants of such differences in size and ownership type across a broad range of Tunisian manufacturing industries.

II. The Ownership and Size Distribution of Tunisian Firms

Prior to independence in 1956 Tunisia had been experiencing a relative decline of its manufacturing sector, at least since the early part of the 19th century.[6] This decline is usually attributed to a number of factors. One

---

[6]See, especially Mahjoub (1983). For the most part these influences were common throughout the Middle East between 1800 and the early post-World War II period. See, e.g., Issawi (1982).

Table 7-1
Size Distribution of Export and Domestic Regime Firms (1981)

Sector	Number of Establishments	Structure by Size			
		10-19	20-49	50-99	100+
Wearing Apparel					
Export	109	1.8	8.2	24.8	65.1
Domestic Regime	109	26.6	45.0	18.3	10.1
Hosiery					
Export	6	0	0	16.7	83.3
Domestic Regime	47	17.0	44.7	21.3	17.0
Footwear					
Export	10	0	20.0	20.0	60.0
Domestic Regime	33	21.2	39.4	24.2	15.1

Source: Computations based on data supplied by the Institut National de la Statistique -- based on the 1981 Recensement des Activités Industrielles. See footnote 11 for definition of size.

such factor was the failure of Tunisian industries (one of which, namely, the shashiya industry, had dominated in world markets) to innovate and adapt to changing tastes and techniques in the face of increasing competition from Europe. Another was the existence of policies which were oriented to protecting the interests of urban consumers relative to primarily rural producers, i.e., the "urban bias." Still another factor was the imposition of free trade policies and special preferences to foreigners, especially during the protectorate period 1881-1956.

While the two world wars interrupted the inflow of French and other imported manufactures to Tunisia, the effect was primarily that of providing a temporary reprieve for the old artisan sector.[7] Hence, serious development of Tunisian industry awaited independence in 1956. In the 1960's Tunisia became a rather extreme practitioner of import substituting industrialization.[8] As in other LDCs, in Tunisia the public sector came to play a substantial role in the development of manufacturing industries, especially in those activities based on local raw materials, such as basic chemicals, petroleum refining and canning. Nevertheless, as a result of the post-independence exodus of the vast majority of French and other members of the foreign business community, private industry continued to remain underdeveloped.

Only in the 1970's did the indigenous private sector start to develop. The

---

[7]See especially Tlili, (1977).
[8]For a brief description and evaluation of the policy see Nabli (1981).

rapid growth in number of firms is demonstrated by the figures given in Table
7-2. These data pertain to those firms of the private manufacturing sector
that come under the domestic regime and are covered by the Annual Industrial Survey.[9] This survey covers practically all of the larger firms (those with
20 employees or more). Its coverage of the smaller firms is less comprehensive,
and in recent years it has completely excluded enterprises with less than 10
employees. Hence, the data used below probably understate the importance
of the smaller size classes and the growth in total number of firms.[10] Despite these limitations, the figures show that the number of firms more than
doubled between 1972 and 1981.

The remaining columns of Table 7-2 present data on the distribution of
domestic regime private firms according to size as measured by number of
permanent employees, and to type of ownership for the years 1972 and 1981.
The table also distinguishes three ownership forms which account for the vast
preponderance of firms; they are individually owned enterprises (IP), partnerships (société anonyme à responsabilité limitée (SARL)) and corporations
(société anonyme (SA)).

The SARL form is a partnership between two or more persons but which
cannot solicit equity capital from the public. Its initial capital need be no
more than 1000 Tunisian dinars, which in 1986 was equivalent to about 1300
U.S. dollars, all of which must be provided by the partners themselves, and
must be paid in full upon creation of the firm. There are two further characteristics which distinguish the SARL form from other forms. First, a partner's
share in the capital cannot be sold or transfered to an outsider without the
approval of all other partners. Second, the liability of each partner is limited
to his contribution to the capital of the firm. A SARL is run by a "manager"
who is usually one of the partners and who exercises relatively complete control over the enterprise. All of these characteristics make the SARL a form

---

[9] Recensement des Activités Industrielles of the Institut National de la Statistique (INS). The INS publishes aggregated sectoral data annually. The data
used in this study for the years 1972 and 1981 are taken from the more detailed computer files of INS. For a more complete evaluation of such data and
an analysis of results see Doghri (1984).

[10] For some studies showing that the resulting underenumeration could be
quite significant, see Liedholm and Mead (1986) and United States, Small
Business Administration (1985). Anderson (1982) surveys the evidence on
the importance of small-scale industry in LDC's, and particularly that of
household establishments across countries and over time. However, for the
most part such firms are individually owned and operated for reasons easily understood. Moreover, if one makes the assumption of proportionality
between the 0-9 and 10-49 class, the results reported below for the size distribution equations would not be affected.

Table 7-2
Size and Ownership Type Characteristics
in the Private Domestic Regime
Sector of Tunisian Manufacturing, 1972 and 1981

Ownership Type	Number of Establishments	Share in Total	Average size	Percentage by Class Size			
				10-19	20-49	50-99	100+
Individual Property (IP)							
1972	141	22	31	57	28	9	6
1981	375	28	23	73	21	4	2
SARL							
1972	285	45	49	30	41	19	10
1981	579	44	41	34	45	14	7
SA							
1972	140	22	104	16	26	24	34
1981	285	21	90	13	32	27	28
Other							
1972	74	11	53	26	47	12	15
1981	90	7	37	48	33	10	9
Total							
1972	640	100.0	57	32	36	17	15
1981	1329	100.0	46	41	35	14	11

Source: See text and footnote 11.

of business that is relatively close to the IP form. It is commonly used for family owned enterprises.

The SA or corporate form is one with a minimum of seven shareholders. Only one-fourth of the capital has to be fully paid immediately upon creation of the firm, but the remaining three-fourths must be paid within five years. Control of SAs tends to be considerably more difficult since there are three levels of responsibility and decision-making. At the lowest level there is the general assembly of shareholders which elects and controls the activity of the Administrative Council or Board of Directors. The latter elects a chairman, the "president directeur général or P.D.G." who is responsible for the management. Finally, there is the P.D.G. and his staff who run the day to day operations of the firm. The P.D.G. does not have to be a shareholder. Although public and mixed capital firms are not included in Table 7-2 and the subsequent analysis, it is worth noting that all such firms have to be set up in the form of an SA.

As can be seen from Table 7-2, the SARL form is the most common one among private firms in Tunisian manufacturing. The SA form was as prevalent as the IP form in 1972, but by 1981 it was significantly less numerically important than the IP form. Other types of firms include cooperatives and various other types of partnerships which are of only marginal importance at the present time and hence which are ignored in the subsequent analysis.

With respect to the size distribution of firms,[11] from the "total" row at the bottom of the table, one can see that in terms of numbers of establishments at least, small enterprises dominate. Specifically, 68% of such establishments had less than 50 permanent workers in 1972 and by 1981 that percentage had increased to 76%. Note also that the mode of the distribution was the 20-49 size class in 1972 whereas in 1981 it was the 10-19 size class.

Table 7-2 also shows evidence of a strong linkage between ownership type and size of firm. The average size of establishment is twice as large for SARL as for IP, and that for SA is more than twice as large as that of SARL. The distributions by size class for different types of ownership give additional evidence on this correlation. Individually owned firms are mostly (60 to 70%) in the lowest class size, whereas almost half of SARL firms are in the medium sized class, 20-49. On the other hand, more than half of SA firms are in the two upper classes, i.e., those having 50 and more employees.

During the decade 1972-1981 the ownership and size distribution of private firms in Tunisian manufacturing evolved in such a way that the IP share expanded relatively sharply, primarily at the expense of "other" forms of ownership, mainly cooperatives. This shift can no doubt be attributed to the decline of the cooperative movement during this decade after the lavish support - both financial and legal - given to it by the authorities during the 1960s. Even though the average size of SARL, SA and "other" forms all decreased, at least modestly, between 1972 and 1981, the major contributors to the overall decline in size from 57 permanent employees per establishment in 1972 to 46 in 1981 were (1) the sharp increase in the relative importance of IP firms whose size was even in 1972 on average only slightly above half the overall average, and (2) the especially sharp decline in average size of IP firms which was in turn attributable to the sharp rise in the relative importance of IP firms in the lowest size class (10-19 permanent workers).

Whereas the data in Table 7-2 characterize private domestic regime Tunisian manufacturing establishments as a whole with respect to ownership type and size, there is considerable variation among activities in this

---

[11]Size is measured by the number of permanent employees, where a permanent employee is defined by INS as a person who is normally employed throughout the year, thereby excluding seasonal workers.

respect. This paper deals with the effects of institutional constraints on size and ownership through their differential effects among economic activities. The industrial survey data disaggregated by sector to the 3-digit level are used for that purpose. The manufacturing sector is disaggregated, according to this classification, into 65 different activities that have in most cases relatively homogeneous products. For the analysis in this paper these activities are aggregated into 44 sectors for two reasons. The first is to put together activities that are not sufficiently differentiated by the original classification and which include similar product lines. The second is to make as close as possible the correspondence between these sectors and those designated in the classification codes of the international standard industrial classification (ISIC), the Tunisian input-output (I-O) table and the industrial classification used in the United States (US-SIC), all of which will be used in the work reported below. The correspondence among these classifications and the detailed definition of activities included in these 44 sectors are given in Appendix Table A.4 (available upon request). Two of the 44 sectors are excluded because they consist exclusively of public enterprises, leaving us with 42 sectors to be used in the subsequent analysis. Data on these 42 activities concerning size and ownership distributions are available on request in Appendix Tables A.1, A.2 and A.3, respectively.

Specifically, Table A.2 parallels Table 7-2 in that it shows the distribution of private domestic regime firms according to ownership type and related information on average size and distribution by size. Limiting our attention to the 1981 information, it shows that the SARL form is predominant in most activities. Its share varies from 17% to 92% but for 32 of the 42 included sectors its share is between 30% and 68% . The average size varies across such activities from 16 to 100 but mostly in the range of 20-49 permanent employees.

The relative importance of the IP and SA forms is, however, much more variable. The IP form's share in the total number of firms varies from 0 to 66%. It is relatively predominant (one-third or more) in a few activities, such as bakeries (5), biscuits (6), sawmills, wood manufactures and cork (18), wood furniture and fixtures (19), printing and publishing (21), construction materials (29), engines (38) and motor vehicle parts and repairs (40). By contrast, for quite a few activities the IP form is hardly used (10% or less). In this group can be found many traditional manufacturing activities, such as dairy products (1), canning and preserving of fruits and vegetables (2), grain milling (4), sugar and confectionary products (7), cereal preparations

(8), vegetable oils and fats (9)[12] , other foods (10), spinning, weaving and textiles (14), knitting (15) and footwear (16). But, we also find new and modern industries such as rubber products (24), chemicals (25), paints and varnishes (26), glassware (30), ceramics (31), metallic products (33), other machinery (35), motor vehicles and motorcycles (39), plastics (41) and other manufactures (42). The IP share is highest for bakeries, where 66% of the firms are of IP form and all have fewer than 50 employees. On the other hand, closely related activities like grain milling and cereal preparation do not have any firms of IP form.

The SA share in the total number of firms also varies widely, specifically from 0 to 75%. Among the many activities where the IP form is not important and the SA form is predominant are dairy products, grain milling, vegetable oils, paper and paperboard, rubber products, chemicals, paints, ceramics, metallic products, household appliances, electrical apparatus, motor vehicles and plastics. However, for most activities this share is smaller than 40%.

Additional evidence concerning the relationship between ownership form and establishment size can be seen by comparing the average size of establishment of the three forms of ownership. Whereas there is considerable variation in average size from sector to sector for each form, with the exception of five sectors (2, 3, 6, 25 and 31), the average size of enterprise of the SA form exceeds that of both the IP and SARL forms, in most cases by a considerable margin. In no sector is the average size of IP establishments greater than 100 and in only two (knitting (15) and electrical apparatus (36)) is it greater than 50. Also, in only one sector (ceramics (31)) is the average size of SARL establishments greater than 100 permanent workers. For six activities it is greater than 50 and for most it is between 25 and 50. On the other hand, among SA establishments the average size of establishment is less than 50 permanent workers in only five sectors, namely, canning (2, 3), cereal preparation (8), ceramics (31) and other manufactures (42), but is greater than 100 in 12 activities.

The third column of each head in Table A.2, shows that the percentage of firms with less than 50 permanent employees is generally rather high for both the IP and SARL forms but is relatively low for establishments of the SA form. Indeed, for 20 of the 30 sectors for which there are IP firms in 1972 and for 19 of the 30 of them in 1981, *all* IP firms had fewer than 50 employees.

---

[12]For vegetable oils and soaps under-representation of firms in the survey seems likely and may be responsible for this result. Only 15 firms were covered by the survey whereas the total number of enterprises engaged in olive oil activities is much larger, many of them being small and probably individually owned.

The dominance of small-sized firms is also apparent for the SARL form. In most cases less than 30% of these firms are of a size greater than 50 employees. On the other hand, the SA form is more frequently associated with large firms: about two-thirds of the firms in the SA category have a size greater than 50 employees.

Table A.1 (again available on request) shows the distribution by size of employment for the 42 activities. As could be inferred from the distribution of ownership type and its correlation with size, the distribution of firms by size varies widely from sector to sector. However, a few additional remarks can be made. The modal class for the distribution in 1981 is the 20-49 size class for 23 activities and the 10-19 class for 15 activities. Most activities are dominated by firms with fewer than 50 workers. Only four activities have a mode in the upper two classes, namely, dairy products (1), grain milling (4), ceramics (31) and other machinery (35).

Since a large proportion of the firms are small, even aside from those firms with less than 10 permanent workers which are excluded from the table, it may be deemed relevant and important to supplement the preceeding analysis with one in which the distribution across the different size classes is measured not in terms of number of firms but in terms of the number of permanent employees. Data on total employment, average size and the shares of total employment attributable to each of the same four different size classes are presented in Table A.3 (available on request).

In contrast to the shares measured in terms of the number of enterprises presented in Table A.1 in which the small size classes dominated and the top size class had shares below 20 percent, the corresponding entries in Table A.3 show that in terms of employment, the two smallest size classes together contributed only 28 percent of total employment in 1972 and 35 percent in 1981. Meanwhile, the top size class (100 or more "permanent" employees) accounted for more than one-half of manufacturing employment in 1972 and 44% in 1981.[13] In general, therefore, the results underscore that the numerical preponderance of small enterprises does *not* translate into dominance in terms of employment. Quite to the contrary, at least in most sectors, establishments with more than 100 "permanent" employees dominate as far as employment is concerned.

There are, however, some notable exceptions. Among these are canning of fruits, vegetables and fish (2, 3), bakeries (5) sugar, confectionary (7), other

---

[13] These statements have, of course, to be qualified due to omission of what is probably a large number of firms in both the 0-9 and the 10-19 size classes by the industrial survey. The total employment impact of this "informal sector" may be significant.

foods (10), animal feed (11) and printing and publishing (21), perfumes (28), engines (38) and motor vehicle parts and repairs (40) where the employment shares of the two smallest size classes are relatively large (greater than 50%) and that of the largest size class, namely the "100+ permanent employee" size class, is relatively low.

Even in terms of the distribution of employment, however, in contrast to an expected increase in the relative importance of the large size classes, by comparing the corresponding entries in the "total" rows of 1972 and 1981, Table A.3 shows that between 1972 and 1981 there were significant increases in the shares in total employment of the two smallest size classes (i.e., those with 10-19 and 20-49 permanent employees) and a corresponding decrease in the employment share of the largest size class. The employment share belonging to the 10-19 permanent employee class rose between 1972 and 1981 in 20 of the 38 individual sectors (for which comparisons can be made) and at least doubled in quite a few of them, namely, sectors 5, 6, 12, 16, 18, 23, 29, 35, 37, 38, 40, 41, and 42. Correspondingly, the employment share of firms with more than 50 permanent employees decreased in 21 sectors, namely, in sectors 5, 6, 12, 13, 14, 15, 16, 18, 20, 22, 23, 25, 29, 30, 31, 34, 35, 38, 40, 41 and 42.

III. The Institutional and Economic Environment for Size and Organizational Form Choices of Tunisian Industrial Enterprises

Before proceeding to the analysis of the variations in the size distribution of private firms in Tunisian manufacturing described in the previous section, it is important to review the most important of these constraints,[14] laws and institutions and particularly those developed in recent years as part of the strategy of encouraging industrial development and in particular the private sector's role in that development.

The first and perhaps most basic constraint within which Tunisian firms operate is that with respect to the incompleteness and imperfection of the capital market. As in many developing and also developed countries, Tunisia pegs interest rates below the rates at which equilibrium would occur and then resorts to credit rationing in order to allocate the limited credit available among those demanding it. Once any individual borrower reaches his credit ceiling from these inexpensive institutional sources, he has to fall back

---

[14]Schmitz (1982) provides a critical review of the constraints on the growth of small scale manufacturing in LDCs. Although he provides no underlying theoretical framework, he identifies some specific constraints, such as access to credit, and managerial ability, which are considered below.

on more costly sources of finance for his remaining credit needs. Hence, the effective rate of interest facing the individual borrower tends to rise, albeit discretely, with the amount borrowed. At the same time, however, since relatively large and well endowed individuals and firms receive priority attention in credit rationing, the effective cost of capital is likely to be lowest for those individuals and firms with the largest endowments of capital, land, and other resources and to be highest for those with the poorest resource endowments. Ceteris paribus, these conditions tend to perpetuate dualism wherein large, well financed firms are able to get bigger, but small, poorly financed ones are unable to do so.

Naturally, this raises the question as to why capital markets are so imperfect and why the market for institutional credit is characterized by below-equilibrium interest rates and credit rationing. Given the substantial effect of default risk on the creditor's need for information about the borrower and the diseconomies of small scale in obtaining such information, the dualistic character of the market can be understood in transaction cost terms. The weakness of the market for debt and equity capital is also a relevant consideration. While a market for bonds and equity capital, namely the Tunis Stock Exchange, has existed since 1969, it remains thin and underdeveloped. Many factors would seem to contribute to the weakness of this market. One such factor is that the incentive to brokers for selling stock may be insufficient inasmuch as the brokers are in fact banks which may regard equity capital as competitive with their interest in dispensing bank credit. Another is the thinness of the market which makes it difficult at any given time for a seller to find a buyer without having to lower the offer price excessively. Another is the high rate of taxation, namely, 25% on dividends and taxes at progressive rates on capital gains on all shares sold within five years of purchase. Still another is that small and minority stockholders have no means of protecting themselves from being disadvantaged by the decisions of the large and majority stockholders. Both in terms of the transparency of the stock market and in recourse to the legal system for protection, small and minority stockholders are at a disadvantage. For instance, the stock market authorities have little power or incentive to make sure that the published accounts of the firm are adequate and the declared profits are correct. This insufficient protection for minority shareholders tends to limit the viability of the market for equity capital and its importance as a source of finance.

Whereas the minority rights of equity capital holders may be difficult to protect even in the best of circumstances, in a market as small and insufficiently developed as that in Tunisia, they have much less protection than elsewhere. Likewise, given the danger of loss of control implied by reliance on equity finance, a small firm is likely to be deterred from expanding beyond a size it can achieve from the personal resources of its owner supplemented by what it can borrow on favorable terms in the institutional credit market.

Another important constraint within which Tunisian firms operate is the scarcity of managerial and skilled labor. One might expect such expertise to be more essential in large and complex enterprises (such as those of the corporate (SA) form) than in those of the IP and/or SARL forms. At the same time, the risk-pooling advantages of large corporate firms might give such firms a distinct advantage in the recruitment of such personnel.

Also among the overall national-level institutional constraints are those arising from legislation enacted in Tunisia during the last decade or two. One of the relevant laws is the Labor Code of 1966 which is a revised and more elaborate version of an earlier law (Law 60-31 of 1960). According to article 157 of the 1966 Labor Code, any firm with 20 or more employees must have a system for electing delegates. More importantly, and more specifically, any firm with 50 or more employees must have a "council" or union where workers are represented. As explained in Zouari (1988), since union rules and wage bargaining in Tunisia have been rather incompatible with incentives for hard work, productive efficiency and cooperative teamwork, these regulations in the labor code undoubtedly exercise a definite bias in the direction of small size. This bias is further accentuated by article 153 of the same Labor Code which requires any firm with 40 or more employees to have its own medical service.

Since the most costly of these labor code provisions begin when there are 40 or 50 "permanent" employees, but apprentices and part-time employees do not figure in the count, one would expect a clustering of firms in the second size class of 20-49 permanent employees. Evidence in support of this implication is contained in Table 7-2 and Appendix Table A.1, which indeed show the 20-49 size class to be the modal size class overall, in the most popular SARL form and in most individual sectors. One would also expect to find relatively greater use of apprentices in small firms than in large ones. This expectation is supported by the following statistics on the percentages of apprentices in the labor force by size class: 9.5% and 8.0% for the 10-19 and 20-49 size classes as opposed to 6.1% and 4.1% for the 50-99 and 100+ size classes, respectively.

A second set of institutional constraints is more sector-specific and introduces differentials among economic activities. One very important institutional influence on size and organizational form choices of Tunisian firms over the last several decades has been the system of price controls. As a result of the evolution of policy with respect to price, by 1981 the following five different price regimes could be identified, each applying to a specific and distinct set of commodities and sectors:

(1) The "Fixed Price" Regime. Under this regime prices are fixed by the government with variations in the differences between these official prices and foreign or domestic opportunity cost prices representing implicit tax or subsidy rates. This regime applies to basic foodstuffs, energy, transportation and medical services (as might be expected), but also to construction materials and TV sets.

(2) The "Authorized Price (Homologation)" Regime. This regime, which especially before 1982 was the most common one for manufactured goods, is one of fixed administered prices. Firms are able to change existing fixed prices only by presenting the relevant cost data to the relevant governmental authorities and receiving prior approval by these authorities for the requested changes. In practice, the process of obtaining the necessary permission for such changes in the fixed prices involves long delays, indeed sometimes several years.

(3) The "Self-authorized Price (Auto-homologation)" Regime. This system is the same as the "authorized price" regime except that prior approval by the authorities to compensate for documented cost changes is not required. Prior to 1982 this regime was primarily limited to the distribution sector; after 1982, however, it has begun to be applied to an increasing number of manufactured products previously under the "authorized price" regime.

(4) The "Controlled Free Price" Regime. This regime allows firms to change their prices at will without submitting cost accounts by simply informing the authorities of such changes. The authorities reserve the right to later rescind the changes should they subsequently deem such action appropriate.

(5) The "Free Price" Regime. This regime which applies only to the prices of some agricultural and fish products allows prices to be determined entirely by market forces.

The authorities responsible for the setting of prices are those of the Ministry of Commerce. Prices are fixed for a given commodity and apply to all firms, usually with no allowance for quality differences.

Since four of the five regimes are essentially variants on fixed prices,[15] it is clear that the influence of the pricing system hinges on the effect that fixed

---

[15] Although in a legal sense the controls on prices only establish price ceilings, because the officially determined margins are low and the tax authorities often use the price ceilings as the basis for sales and other taxes, the individual firms have no incentive to operate below the legally set ceilings.

prices could be expected to exert on size and organizational form choices. First, with fixed prices firms are less capable of increasing their market share than they would be were they able to undercut their rivals by selling at lower prices. Second, because prices are set at fixed markups above costs, firms have little incentive to achieve cost reductions as can sometimes be achieved with larger scale and greater specialization. Third, the system provides incentives for the overreporting of costs and the underreporting of sales. However, since these forms of opportunistic behavior are less feasible for large firms with external auditors and whose accounts would be more likely to be carefully monitored by government agencies and shareholders, the possibility of practicing such forms of opportunistic behavior would naturally be considerably greater for smaller, individually owned firms than for large, corporate ones. Moreover, in industries dominated by small firms, the government would find it considerably more difficult to monitor and penalize such behavior than in industries in which there are but a small number of large producers.

On the other hand, in systems like the "self-authorized price" and "authorized price" regimes one might expect large firms to be in a better position than small firms in documenting cost increases, preparing the necessary paper work and monitoring the progress of such requests through the relevant bureaucracies. In general, however, one might hypothesize that, other things (such as technology) being equal, the relative importance of small firms would vary with the degree of rigidity of fixed prices.

Another imperfection that affects the allocation of real capital and which could exert a distinct bias on the size distribution of firms is the practice of investment licensing. Virtually all industrial investments require authorization. Because of the fiscal and other incentives that apply to such investments, the screening of proposals to receive such benefits is understandable. Since 1974 the primary role for administering controls over industrial investment has been assigned to the Agence de Promotion des Investissements (Agency for the Promotion of Investment) known as API. Previously, the role had been distributed among various ministries according to the type of investment. While the creation of API has done much to centralize, homogenize and perhaps streamline investment authorization decisions, the procedure involves several levels of approval,[16] each quite possibly involving considerable delays

---

[16]The levels of approval or steps in the procedure are as follows: First API itself must grant approval, this approval necessarily coming from a relatively cumbersome committee on which several ministries and the Central Bank are represented. Second, bank approval must be obtained for any required finance. Third, a license to import any necessary imports must be obtained from the office within the Ministry of National Economy which is responsible

and each fraught with uncertainties of outcome. The process is somewhat less cumbersome for enterprises requesting investments of less than 200,000 Tunisian dinars than it is for larger investments. Those requesting investments of less than 20,000 Tunisian dinars in certain traditional industries have the option of by-passing API in favor of the Small Enterprise Division of the Ministry of National Economy. Since the latter alternative is simpler and provides highly subsidized loan opportunities[17] and tax benefits, this can be a substantial advantage for very small firms.

Another policy or institutional influence on size and organizational form choices is the system of protecting domestic producers from foreign imports and the inherent bias of import-substituting policies against exports. The bias against exports naturally implies that firms are generally constrained by the small size of the domestic market. Together with the aforementioned rules which enforce the dominance of mark-up pricing, this tends to induce firms to choose small size and to avoid the SA form. On the other hand, one might expect industries with a small number of large firms to be more successful in achieving collective action and hence to achieve more protection from foreign competition. Large firms would also be expected to be in a more favorable position to obtain the necessary licenses to import needed raw materials and equipment. Another way in which tariff protection is likely to be biased against small firms is that the items they use as capital equipment such as small motors, bicycles, refrigerators, etc., are generally classified as consumer durables and subject to very high tariffs whereas larger firms use forms of capital goods to which very low tariff rates apply [Haggblade, Liedholm and Mead (1986)].

As noted above, since many of the aforementioned constraints, such as the capital constraint, the market size constraint, the skilled management and labor constraints, and the advantages of small size for opportunistic behavior, would not apply to public enterprises, in our empirical tests we concentrate on the size and ownership form choices of private sector enterprises. Moreover, since public enterprises are required to be of the SA form, the issue of

---

for trade licenses. Fourth, approval from the Central Bank must be obtained for any foreign exchange requirements.

[17]Beginning in 1981 these credits have been made available through Fonds National de Promotion de L'Artisanat et des Petits Metiers (FONAPRAM). More than two-thirds of the loans extended have been 11 year loans with a grace period of 7 years made to firms making investments amounting to less than TD 10,000 for which there is no interest charge on 36 percent of the loan and the remainder has an interest rate of 6.75 percent per annum. The investor can put up as little as 4 percent of the total investment.

ownership form does not even arise in this case.[18]

IV. Transaction Costs in Ownership Type and Size Choices: Hypothesis Generation

It should be recalled from Section II that three features with respect to ownership form and size stand out. One such feature is the sharp difference (reflected in Table 7-1) in the size distribution of such firms among those which are subject to the normal institutional constraints pertaining to the "domestic regime" on the one hand and those largely exempt from these constraints by being subject to the "export regime," on the other hand. A second feature is the relatively high correlation reflected in Tables 7-2 and A.2 between ownership type and size of firm, the IP form being associated with very small firms (especially those with fewer than 20 permanent workers), the SARL form with medium-sized firms (i.e., those with 20-49 permanent employees), and the SA form with relatively large firms, i.e., those with 50 or more permanent workers. The third feature is the relative dominance of the SARL form, this form alone accounting for almost half of all private manufacturing firms in the country in both 1972 and 1981.

The purpose of this section is to suggest ways in which transaction cost economics may help explain not only these features but also more generally the variation in ownership form and size of firm from one sector to another in the private sector of Tunisian manufacturing.

Let us begin with the observed dominance of the SARL form. The dominance of this form in most sectors of manufacturing activity would seem to be attributable to the fact that, in the context of a society in which reputations for honesty and reliability among members of the same family are much revered and easily and reliably communicated, the formation of partnerships among family members can constitute an efficient means of avoiding the disadvantage of extremely small size without paying the otherwise relatively high price in terms of transaction costs of larger size and more complex form. The reason why these transaction costs rise with size and complexity of the firm arises from the simultaneous needs of shareholders to protect themselves against exploitation by opportunistic managers and of managers to protect themselves from opportunistic shareholders through costly investments in information, monitoring, and systems of conflict resolution. The fact that the SARL form also provides limited liability has the effect of lowering both the risk of losses to potential partners and the need for expensive monitoring of

---

[18]See Grissa (1988) for an institutional analysis of the public enterprise sector in Tunisia.

one partner relative to another. In other words, in the absence of well developed markets for managers, equity capital, insurance and technical expertise, the confinement of such contractual arrangements to members of tightly knit families, clans, ethnic groups or communities has the effect of lowering the transaction costs required for achieving both limited liability and the size necessary in order to avoid the diseconomies of very small scale, especially relative to what these costs would otherwise be.

Both the observed correlation between ownership form and size and the theoretical grounds for such a relationship are sufficiently strong as to lead us to postulate from the beginning that departures from the intermediate SARL form either in the direction of smaller size and simpler form, i.e., the IP form, or in that of the larger and more complex SA form, revolve on a hypothesized tradeoff between the advantages of scale and access to scarce inputs for which the markets are imperfect and incomplete, on the one hand, and those of control and low transaction costs on the other hand. Or to put it otherwise, entrepreneurs are seen to minimize total costs which are the sum of production costs and transaction costs. In those sectors in which the advantages of large scale and access to the scarce inputs whose markets are incomplete and imperfect are especially important, one would expect to find a relatively large portion of the firms with SA form and relatively large size. On the other hand, where the possibilities of opportunistic behavior on the part of agents within firms relative to government and other agents outside the firm are especially great, one might expect firms to favor greater control over better access to inputs and hence to choose the IP form and smaller size.

By making explicit the relationship between desired firm size on the one hand and ownership form on the other hand, we avoid the criticism of the Fama and Jensen (1983) (transaction cost-based) analysis of enterprise form raised by Klein (1983) and others. In that analysis the size of firm is completely exogenous to organizational form choices, something which would seem unrealistic. In our analysis, we make firm size and organizational form jointly determined endogenous variables. In order to operationalize this relationship in the context of explaining ownership form (OF) and firm size (FS), we postulate a model of the form shown in Figure 7-1. Variations in OF are measured by the percentages of enterprises in the industry (activity) in each of the three most important ownership forms, IP, SARL and SA (defined in Section II). Likewise, variations in firm size are measured in terms of the percentage of private firms having 50 or more permanent employees (SIZL), where SIZL is obtained by adding the percentages of firms in the last two columns of Table A.1 (available on request).

According to the model depicted in Figure 7-1, we hypothesize (1) that SIZL varies across activities according to both exogenous factors, like the technological and market size characteristics of these activities and recent growth considerations (reflecting for example changes in the age structure of firms and/or the degree to which actual firm size is adjusting to desired firm size), and the jointly determined ownership form (OF) measured by IP, SARL and SA, and (2) that the percentages of firms of the IP, SARL and SA forms vary across activities according to the jointly determined variations in SIZL and the exogenously given differences in institutional rules and circumstances (including various sources of opportunistic behavior) and variations in their relative importance.

Figure 7-1
Model of Ownership Form and Firm Size

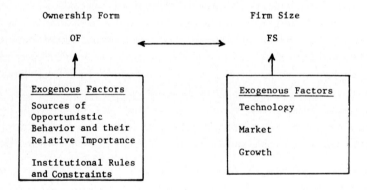

Firms vs. Establishments

In the previous discussion we have used interchangeably the concepts of firm and establishment. However, on both theoretical and empirical grounds the two concepts should be distinguished.

From the point of view of the analysis of ownership form, the relevant unit of analysis would be the firm, irrespective of the number of establishments possessed by the firm. This is because the firm is the center of decision and control that is relevant in terms of opportunistic behavior and transaction cost minimization. On the other hand, it is the establishment, or the industrial unit, that is the relevant unit of analysis for investigating the technological determinants of size.

It is clear that the two units of analysis and measurement are highly interdependent; a given firm may choose an organizational structure with many establishments integrated vertically or horizontally. To the extent that technological considerations permit it, diversification by way of multiple establishments may provide a solution to the control problems associated with large size. It would, therefore, be appropriate to introduce this aspect of diversification into our analysis.

In the empirical part of our analysis, however, we ignore this problem for two reasons. The first is that an adequate treatment of both ownership form and organizational structure simultaneously would further complicate the analysis and severely limit the possibilities for identifying the relevant empirical equations. The second is that in our case study there is a virtually a one-to-one relationship between firms and establisments. In almost all cases a firm in Tunisia corresponds to a single establishment. When it comes time to expanding their activities, Tunisian entrepreneurs seem to prefer the creation of new firms over the creation of additional plants within existing firms. Therefore, we will continue to use the terms firm and establishment interchangeably.

Technological and Market Size Characteristics and Their Expected Effects on Firm Size

As a measure of a technological characteristic deemed relevant to choices with respect to size of firm, we use the capital-labor ratio measured for the corresponding manufacturing activities in the United States. Specifically, we use the gross book value of depreciable assets[19] divided by the number of employees (KLUS) as taken from the data presented in U.S. Department of Commerce (1981), according to the correspondence of classification systems shown in Table A.4. The U.S. data are used in this context, not only because they are readily available and widely used, but also because they are unlikely to be affected by the institutional constraints and considerations which are under investigation.

The direction of the effect of KLUS on SIZL, however, is ambiguous. This is because there are at least two different effects. First, with SIZL measured strictly in terms of number of employees, a higher capital-labor ratio might allow firms to achieve any given target volume of output with a smaller number of employees, i.e., a lower value of SIZL, due to capital-

---

[19]This measure is a simple average of the values at the beginning and end of the year 1977.

labor substitution. On the other hand, however, because of the well-known association of greater capital-intensity with both greater technical efficiency and scale economies, one might expect that KLUS would have a positive effect on SIZL.

An increase in the size of the market would be expected to increase firm size and hence to have a positive effect on SIZL. Likewise, better access to export markets would presumably have the effect of increasing the effective size of the market. For this reason and for the several other reasons identified by the United Nations ECLAC (1985), a positive relationship between the percentage of exports in total sales (EXP) and SIZL would be expected.

Since SIZL is measured at a particular period of time, namely the year 1981, it may be affected not only by the aforementioned long-term considerations like technology and market size but also by shorter term considerations such as the sector-specific idiosyncracies of recent dynamics with respect to the number of firms and employment which would affect the age structure of firms. For this reason we include in the specifications of the SIZL equation also measures for growth both in the number of firms (GN) and in the number of employees (GE) in the industry during the period 1972-1981. These measures represent the effect of licensing decisions, market growth, and changes in the age structure of firms, which could be assumed to be exogenous to firm size and organizational form choices in 1981. Naturally, GN and GE would be expected to have negative and positive effects, respectively, on SIZL.

Institutional Characteristics and Their Expected Effects on Ownership Form

Unfortunately, we have not found it possible to obtain satisfactory measures for all the institutional factors whose relevance to firm size and ownership form choices was mentioned above. A major impediment to measurement in this context is that many of these factors vary not so much across sectors as across countries. In such cases, even the best of measures cannot be useful in explaining variations in ownership form across sectors within a given country. Among the institutional considerations which have had to be ignored because of our focus on a single country are (a) the incompleteness of markets for insurance, (b) the incompleteness of markets for equity capital, and (c) to a large extent at least, also the effects of social legislation.

Nevertheless, several of the other aforementioned institutional factors vary across sectors and, even in the case of some of those which don't, their relative importance may be expected to vary across sectors. This makes it possible to introduce a number of these institutional factors, albeit somewhat incompletely and imperfectly, into our intranational, cross-sectional analysis.

In all cases it is our purpose to stress the transaction cost explanation of their role. We begin with the more familiar institutional factors and then go on to some of the more neglected ones and to those which may be relatively special to Tunisia.

Although the degree of completeness of the credit market varies only slightly within the Tunisian manufacturing sector, the relative importance of credit varies considerably from sector to sector. To the suppliers of credit, namely the commercial banks, whose interest rates and overall credit availability are tightly controlled by government regulation and decisions of the Central Bank, default risk considerations and hence the cost of monitoring would seem to be of primary importance in determining the allocation of credit. The cost of monitoring, however, would seem likely to vary considerably by organizational form. One would suppose the SA form to be especially advantageous because it requires an external audit and the distribution of the externally audited accounts to shareholders. At the other extreme, because of its closed nature, the accounts of an IP firm would be especially difficult to obtain and verify. The SARL form would seem to be intermediate in this respect. As a measure of the importance of bank credit to the sector we use the share of financial charges in the year 1981 in total cost for SARL and SA firms (FCSS). This measure varies considerably across the activities included in the analysis from a minimum of 1.32 percent in bakeries (5) to a maximum of 20.45 percent in sawmills and wood manufacturing (18). The more important is bank credit to the sector, as represented by FCSS, the more the balance of advantages of the more complex SA form relative to those of the simpler IP form would tip in favor of the SA form. Therefore, we would expect the effect of FCSS on SA to be positive, that on IP to be negative, and that on SARL to be somewhere in between.

Similarly, with respect to management and skilled labor (like engineers), even though the degree of completeness of the market for managers and engineers may vary little across manufacturing sectors within the country, the importance of management and engineering may well vary considerably from sector to sector. Since the importance of management and engineering would also vary by size, large firms being more complex but also being better able to take advantage of economies of scale in the use of managers and engineers than small firms, in constructing our measure of the relative importance of managers and engineers, we deem it important to hold size constant. Therefore, for our measure of the relative importance of management and engineering we use the percentage of managers and engineers in the employed labor force of firms in the 50-99 size category (MAN50).

Given the absence in Tunisia of well-functioning and developed markets for managers and engineers, their mobility tends to be much more limited than in developed country settings. In such situations, from the point of view of the manager searching for a position, his interest is to minimize the probability of falling victim to exploitative opportunistic behavior on the part of the owner(s) and/or of bankruptcy of the firm which would force him to reenter the market under unfavorable circumstances, i.e., as a "used" manager who (just like a used car) may be suspected of being a "lemon". The more open the firm, the easier it is for the manager or engineer to obtain relevant information and hence to lower the risk of having to reenter the market under unfavorable conditions. Hence, we hypothesize that the higher the index of the need for managers and engineers in the sector (MAN50), the greater would be the disadvantage of IP form and the advantage of SA, and perhaps also SARL, form.

As mentioned above, all Tunisian manufacturing firms are subject to the same social legislation and hence the same aforementioned costs of firms with more permanent workers, including the mandatory organization of the firms' workers into unions, the provision of medical services, and the imposition of social security taxes. Nevertheless, the ability to substitute apprentice and temporary workers (who do not count as permanent workers) for permanent workers may well vary considerably from sector to sector depending again on the nature of the activity, thereby affecting the ability to avoid the costs of the social legislation. Once again, since the use of apprentices might also vary with size of firm, for our measure of the ability to substitute apprentices for permanent workers we hold size constant by concentrating on a single size class (that which is most intensive in the use of apprentices, namely the 20-49 size class). Specifically, we use the share of apprentices in the labor force among all private firms engaged in that activity in the 20-49 size class (APR20). We hypothesize that the easier it is to substitute apprentices for permanent workers, the more likely firms would choose the IP form and possibly also the SARL form for their control and opportunistic behavior advantages over the SA form.

Since the effects of tariff protection on X efficiency and managerial shirking have received considerable attention in the development literature [Leibenstein (1978) and Bergsman (1974)], we also include the nominal rate of protection (NRP) in our analysis.[20] Higher rates of NRP would make it possible

---

[20]The use of effective protection rates as opposed to nominal rates does not modify the results in any significant way. The data on trade protection are from Nabli and Bousselmi (1985), and relate to 1980. The correspondence

for managers to achieve sufficiently high profits with less work on their part. The higher the NRP, therefore, the greater would be the incentive for owners to want to closely monitor the managers and to exercise control. Likewise, the higher the NRP, the more firms might worry about their excess profits being scrutinized by government, and the more convenient they would find the more closed IP form for concealing their profits. Therefore, the higher the NRP, the more the IP, and to a lesser extent SARL, forms could be expected to be chosen over the SA form.

This is consistent with the Eastman-Stykolt hypothesis discussed above, which would be relevant in the context of Tunisian manufacturing. Higher protection, combined with the more easily achievable collusive behavior, leads to excessive entry and a higher number of smaller sized firms. What our analysis suggests is that collusive behavior is rendered easier through individual ownership in the presence of protection, thereby strengthening the Eastman-Stykolt effect.

As noted above, under the authorized and fixed price regimes practiced in Tunisia, the firms are barred from using price reductions as a means of increasing market share and have less incentive to compete by way of efficiency, style and other adjustments which would raise profits by way of increasing their market share and sales volume. Rather, the most attractive means of making and retaining more profits is by practicing opportunistic behavior *vis-à-vis* other agents, e.g., the government and workers. Since, as mentioned in Section III, the self-authorized price regime did not become operative in Tunisian manufacturing until after 1981 (the year for which the data used in this empirical test is available) and the difference between the controlled free price and free price regimes was minimal, there were for all practical purposes only three different price regimes. Since the application of price regimes varies from sector to sector, we have introduced dummy variables for two of the regimes, namely for the authorized price regime (DA) and for the fixed price regime (DF). One would expect that the existence of DA and DF in a given sector would raise the likelihood that firms in that sector would choose the IP form over the SA form. The explanation is simply that the less freedom and ability the firms in the industry have to utilize other instruments for affecting after-tax profits, such as price competition, the more these firms would seek to satisfy their retained profit objectives by way of profit, and perhaps also quality, concealment which can best be accomplished by tight control in closed firms of the IP form and in which rapid exit (and subsequent

---

with the I - O Table classification used in the protection study is given in Table A.4 of the Appendix (available on request).

reentry) is more feasible.

V. Results and Conclusions

Now that all the hypotheses have been generated and explained and the measures of the relevant variables identified, we proceed directly to the empirical estimation of the model depicted in Figure 7-1. The model, composed of one equation for size (SIZL) and two for different forms of ownership, namely IP and SA, each of the latter with the same specification of right hand side variables, is estimated both with Ordinary Least Squares (OLS)[21] and with two stage least squares (2SLS) on the basis of the cross-sectional data on the 42 manufacturing activities listed in Tables A.1 and A.2 (available on request). The results are presented in Table 7-3. Several important conclusions emerge from these results.

First, it can be noticed that there is strong evidence to support the hypothesized two-way interdependence between firm size and ownership form. Both the coefficients of SIZL in the IP and SA equations, and conversely those of IP and SA in the SIZL equation, are of the expected signs. With OLS estimation, all these coefficients are highly significant. The level of significance is somewhat reduced, however, when 2SLS estimation is used, especially in the case of the SA and SIZL equations. The statistical differences in estimation between OLS and 2SLS point to the importance of taking into consideration the simultaneity in the determination of ownership form and size of firm. Except for the variation in significance levels between estimation procedures, the magnitudes of the parameters remain grossly similar and the signs unchanged.

Second, with respect to explanatory power, note that the ability to explain the proportions of firms of IP and SA forms and those of large size is quite high. Particularly strong is the explanation of the IP form of ownership.

Third, and perhaps of greatest relevance to the theme of this paper is the relatively strong support for the various transaction cost based institutional determinants of ownership form developed above. As hypothesized, the greater the importance of bank credit to the sector (FCSS), the more that sector is likely to favor the SA form and to avoid the IP form. Again as hypothesized, the greater the importance of managers and engineers (for whom the labor market is poorly developed) in a sector, i.e., the higher is

---

[21]The error term in the equations for IP and SA may be correlated. But for this case of the seemingly unrelated system of equations, there is no gain in efficiency by generalized least squares estimation since the explanatory variables are the same in both equations.

Table 7-3
Ownership Form and Firm Size Regression Results

(1) Ownership form Equations

Estimation Method	Dependent Variable	C	Explanatory Variables								$\bar{R}^2$	S.E.E.	Mean
			SIZL	FCSS	MAN50	APR20	NRP	DA	DF			
OLS	IP	18.766** (2.16)	-0.446*** (4.73)	-0.581 (1.48)	-0.600 (0.54)	1.315*** (4.55)	0.093 (1.19)	7.983* (1.87)	22.163*** (3.81)	0.60	10.80	16.59
2SLS	IP	15.790 (1.54)	-0.355* (1.92)	-0.615 (1.53)	-0.577 (0.51)	1.321*** (4.51)	0.105 (1.27)	8.485* (1.93)	21.594*** (3.61)	-	10.95	16.59
OLS	SA	10.126 (0.84)	0.549*** (4.23)	0.297 (0.55)	2.551 (1.66)	-0.135 (0.34)	-0.203* (1.87)	0.021 (0.00)	-8.586 (1.07)	0.38	14.89	29.07
2SLS	SA	21.680 (1.41)	0.199 (0.71)	0.431 (0.72)	2.464 (1.46)	-0.159 (0.36)	-0.248** (2.01)	-1.926 (0.29)	-6.382 (0.71)	-	16.41	29.07

(2) Size Equation

Estimation Method	Dependent Variable	C	IP	SA	KLUS	EXP	GN	GE	$\bar{R}^2$	S.E.E.	Mean
OLS	SIZL	32.216*** (5.16)	-0.380*** (2.71)	0.448*** (3.51)	-0.175 (1.441)	-0.591*** (3.32)	-0.020*** (3.02)	0.003* (1.69)	0.55	12.64	29.50
2SLS	SIZL	28.132** (2.41)	-0.227 (0.99)	0.477 (1.44)	-0.155 (1.13)	-0.559*** (2.99)	-0.020*** (2.94)	0.003* (1.67)	-	12.87	29.50

Notes: For definition of variables see text.
Figures in parentheses represent t-values.
*; ** and *** indicate that the associated coefficient is significant at the 10, 5 and 1 percent level, respectively. (For 2SLS the tests are based on the asymptotically valid normal distribution).

MAN50, the lower is the incidence of the IP form and the higher is the incidence of the SA form.[22]

With respect to the relevance of social legislation, note that the coefficient of APR20 in the IP equation is positive and significant while that in the SA equation is negative but insignificant. This result is consistent with the view that Tunisian social legislation, which imposes costs primarily on large firms, is perceived by the firms to be a relatively important constraint on firm size and organizational complexity. While this perception may not vary across industries, the ability to get around this constraint by substituting apprentices - who are exempted from the provisions of the legislation - for permanent employees does appear to vary considerably from sector to sector. The result shows that, ceteris paribus, those sectors in which forms of 20-49 permanent employees are able to use a larger percentage of apprentices in their work force than other sectors are likely to have a larger percentage of firms of IP form and smaller percentages of firms of SA form than in other sectors.

Evidence is also provided for the hypothesized incentives for opportunistic behavior created by protection (NRP) and the application of the more tightly controlled price regimes (DA and DF). Specifically, the effect of NRP on IP is positive and that on SA negative and significant. Likewise, the effects of the authorized price regime (DA) and the fixed price regime (DF) on IP are positive and significant while those on SA are negative but not significant.

In general, therefore, the empirical support for our transaction cost-based explanations for intersectoral variations in ownership form is surprisingly strong. While in some cases the ways in which the variables are measured or the relationships specified could bias the results in favor of the stated hypotheses, in other cases the results stand up despite possible methodological biases against the hypotheses. While motives are, of course, difficult to prove, the results are certainly consistent with the desire on the part of owner and managers within firms to practice opportunistic behavior *vis-à-vis* government, workers and consumers being an important determinant of the ownership form and size choices of firms. While certainly not definitive, the results would seem to suggest that such considerations should be given more attention in both the theory of the NIE and industrial organization and industrial policy.

The effects of the transactions cost considerations on size distribution are

---

[22]In this particular case, however, one cannot reject the possibility that the causality may be the other way around, i.e., ceteris paribus, firms with SA form may want to employ more managers and engineers than those of IP form. If so, the results could be biased in favor of the hypothesis.

accounted for through the ownership form variables. As to the technological and market size effects on size, they turn out to be surprisingly weak and even contrary to expectations. The capital-labor ratio has a negative sign, opposite to the usually advanced hypothesis, but is not significant. Likewise, the effect on size of the relative importance of exports in total sales seems to be negative, again contrary to the expected relationship. On the other hand, the growth variables, i.e., the growth in number of firms and in number of employees, turn out to be important variables in the explanation of size and have the expected signs. Dynamic adjustments are to be taken account of in the explanation of the size distribution at a given point in time.

Our analysis has several important limitations which could be, and hopefully will be, overcome by further research. With respect to theory, the analysis has abstracted from another determinant of the size of firm, namely, the degree of vertical integration. The issue of vertical integration has been deliberately avoided since trying to combine this issue with those investigated here would greatly complicate the analysis. There is, however, considerable overlap and interdependence among the choices with regard to vertical integration, size and ownership form, and judging from the relevant literature,[23] transaction cost economics would seem to play an important role in vertical integration as well. This suggests that a more comprehensive framework which would include vertical integration would be highly desirable.

Another limitation is that the analysis is excessively static. In the course of time, however, firms change size and in some cases also their organizational or ownership form. Organizational form may be more closely related to expected future firm size than current firm size as was assumed in our empirical analysis. An interesting hypothesis suggested by the review of Tunisian institutions and regulations given in Section III is that the incentives may be such that an existing firm may decide against enlargement but in favor of splintering and proliferation, i.e., creating new firms and establishments of small size. An analysis of such choices would require a more dynamic perspective than has been employed here. Another issue deserving of more detailed investigation is to corroborate and explain the surprising finding that the relative importance of exports was negatively related to size in the industries studied. To do justice to these issues the empirical data would have to be of the panel variety, data which was not available to us.[24]

The empirical analysis of the institutional constraints applying to Tuni-

---

[23]See especially Williamson (1985) and Klein, Crawford and Alchian (1978).
[24]For a pioneering study in which such data were available and used see Wedervang (1965).

sian manufacturing firms has also been limited by the fact that the study
was limited to a cross-section of Tunisian manufacturing sectors. This is an
important limitation because many of the relevant institutional factors do
not vary across sectors but only across countries, suggesting that it would be
useful to extend the analysis to international cross-section data.

References

Alchian, Armen A. and Harold Demsetz, 1972, "Production, Information
  Costs and Economic Organization," *American Economic Review* 62, no.
  5, 777-795.
Anderson, Dennis, 1982, "Small Industry in Developing Countries: A Discus-
  sion of Issues," *World Development* 10, no. 11, 913-948.
Arrow, Kenneth J., 1964, "The Role of Securities in the Optimal Allocation
  of Risk Bearing," *Review of Economic Studies* 31 (April), 91-96.
Bain, Joe S., 1966, *International Differences in Industrial Structure.* New
  Haven: Yale University Press.
Baldwin, J.R. and P.K. Gorecki, 1985, "The Determinants of Small Plant
  Market Share in Canadian Manufacturing Industries in the 1970's," *Re-
  view of Eocnomics and Statistics*, 156-161.
_____, 1987, "The Impact of High Tariffs and Imperfect Market
  Structure on Plant Scale Inefficiency in Canadian Manufacturing Indus-
  tries in the 1970's," *Recherces Economiques de Louvain 53*, no. 1, 51-73.
Bergsman, J., 1974, "Commercial Policy, Allocative Efficiency and X-Effici-
  ency," *Quarterly Journal of Economics* (August): 409-433.
Berle, Adolf A. and Gardiner C. Means, 1932, *The Modern Corporation and
  Private Property.* New York: Macmillan.
Chandler, A.D., Jr., 1962, *Strategy and Structure.* Cambridge, MA: MIT
  Press.
_____, 1977, *The Visible Hand: The Managerial Revolution in
  American Business.* Cambridge, MA: Harvard University Press.
Coase, R.H., 1937, "The Nature of the Firm," *Economica* (New Series) 4:
  386-405.
_____, 1972, "Industrial Organization: A Proposal For Research,"
  in V. Fuchs, ed., *Policy Issues and Research Opportunities in Industrial
  Organization.* New York: National Bureau of Economic Research: 59-73.
Curry, B. and K.D. George, 1983, "Industrial Concentration: A Survey,"
  Journal of Industrial Economics, 31, no. 3, 203-255.
Demsetz, Harold, 1983, "The Structure of Ownership and the Theory of the
  Firm," *Journal of Law and Economics* 26 (June), 375-390.
Doghri, Lamine, 1984, "*Dimension et Comportement des Entreprises: Essai
  d'application au Secteur Industriel Tunisien,*" Tunis: Faculté de Droit
  et de Sciences Politiques et Economiques de Tunis, Thèse de Doctorat
  d'Etat.
Dubetsky, Alan, 1976, "Kinship, Primordial Ties and Factory Organization
  in Turkey: An Anthropological View," *International Journal of Middle
  East Studies* 7: 433-451.

Fama, Eugene F., 1980, "Agency Problems and the Theory of The Firm," *Journal of Political Economy* 88 (April): 288-307.

_____ and Michael C. Jensen, 1983, "Separation of Ownership and Control," *Journal of Law and Economics* 26 (June): 301-326.

Forbes, Kevin F., 1986, "Limited Liability and the Development of the Business Corporation," *Journal of Law, Economics and Organization* 2, no. 1 (Spring): 163-177.

Grissa, Abdessatar, 1988, "An Interest Group Analysis of Tunisia's State Enterprises," ch. 14, this volume.

Haggblade, Steve, Carl Liedholm and Donald C. Mead, 1986, "The Effect of Policy and Policy Reforms on Non-Agricultural Enterprises and Employment in Developing Countries: A Review of Past Exprience." East Lansing: Michigan State University, International Development Papers, Working Paper No. 27.

Ijiri, Y. and Herbert Simon, 1981, *The Size Distribution of Firms.* Amsterdam: North-Holland.

Issawi, Charles, 1982, *An Economic History of the Middle East and North Africa.* Columbia University Press: New York, especailly Ch. 1, 2, 5 and 8.

Jensen, Michael C. and William H. Meckling, 1976, "Theory of the Firm: Managerial Behavior, Agency Costs and Ownership Structure," *Journal of Financial Economics* 3, no. 4 (October): 305-360.

Kirkpatrick, C.H., N. Lee and F.I. Nixson, 1984, *Industrial Structure and Policy in Less Developed Countries.* London: George Allen and Unwin.

Klein, Benjamin, 1983, "Contracting Costs and Residual Claims: The Separation of Ownership and Control," *The Journal of Law and Economics* 26 (June): 367-374.

_____, R.A. Crawford and A.A. Alchian, 1978, "Vertical Integration, Appropriable Rents and the Competitive Contracting Process," *Journal of Law and Economics* 21 (October): 297-326.

Leff, Nathaniel H., 1976, "Capital Markets in LDCs: the Group Principle," R.I. Mckinnon, ed., *Money and Finance in Economic Growth and Development.* N.Y., Basel: Marcel Dekker.

_____, 1978, "Industrial Organization and Entrepreneurship in the Developing Countries: The Economic Groups," *Economic Development and Cultural Change* 26: 661.

Leibenstein, Harvey, 1978, *General X-Efficiency Theory and Economic Development.* New York: Oxford University Press.

Liedholm, Carl and Donald Mead, 1986, "Small Scale Enterprises in Developing Countries: A Review of the State of the Art." Michigan State University, mimeo.

Mahjoub, Azzam, 1983, *Industrie et Accumulation du Capital en Tunisie: Première Partie: de la Fin du XVIII Siecle jusqu'à la Seconde Guerre Mondiale.* Tunis: Bibliothèque de Droit de Sciences Politiques et Economiques. C.E.R.P.

Nabli, Mustapha K., 1981, "Alternative Trade Policies and Employment in Tunisia," in Anne O. Krueger, Hal B. Lary, Terry Monson and Narongchai Akrasanee (eds.) *Trade and Employment in Developing Countries: Individual Studies.* Chicago: University of Chicago Press.

_____, and Nejib Bousselmi, 1985, *Evolution de la Protection et des Incitations Effectives des Activitès Economiques en 1977, 1980, et*

1983 Synthèse et Annexes. Tunis: Institut d'Economie Quantitative.

North, Douglass, 1981, *Structure and Change in Economic History.* New York: W.W. Norton.

Scherer, F.M., 1973, "The Determinants of Industrial Plant Sizes in the Six Nations," *The Review of Economics and Statistics* 55, 135-145.

_____, 1980, *Industrial Market Structure and Economic Performance, Second Edition.* Boston: Houghton Mifflin.

Schmitz, Hubert, 1982, "Growth Constraints on Small-scale Manufacturing in Developing Countries: A Critical Review," *World Development,* 10, no. 6, 429-450.

Stykolt, S. and H. Eastman, 1960, "A Model for the Study of Protected Oligopolies," *Economic Jurnal* 70, 336-347.

Teitel, Simón, 1975, "Economies of Scale and Size of Plants: The Evidence and the Implications for Developing Countries," *Journal of Common Market Studies* 13: 92-115.

Tlili, Ridha, 1977, *Préliminaires à l'étude du Syndicalisme Patronal en Tunisie.* Paris: Université de Paris VII; Thèse Doctorat du Troisi'eme Cycle.

United Nations, ECLAC, 1985, *Market Structure, Firm Size and Brazilian Exports.* United Nations: IPEA, Brasilia.

United States Department of Commerce, 1981, *1977 Census of Manufactures Volume 1.* Washington, D.C.: U.S. Department of Commerce, September.

United States Small Business Administration, 1985, *The State of Small Business: A Report of The President Transmitted to the Congress.* Washington, D.C.: Small Business Administration.

Wedervang, Froystein, 1965, *Development of a Population of Industrial Firms.* Oslo: Bergen Universitetsforlaget.

Williamson, Oliver E., 1975, *Markets and Hierarchies: Analysis and Antitrust Implications.* New York: Free Press.

_____, 1981, "The Modern Corporation: Origins, Evolution, Attributes," *Journal of Economic Literature* 19 (December): 1537-1568.

_____, 1985, *The Economic Institutions of Capitalism.* New York: Free Press.

Zouari, Abderrazak, 1988, "Collective Action and Governance Structure in Tunisia's Labor Organization," ch. 11, this volume.

PART THREE

TUNISIAN CASE STUDIES APPLYING
THE THEORY OF COLLECTIVE ACTION

The theory of collective action and its applications to a variety of problems were surveyed in Chapter 3. The general need for empirical work was emphasized, especially in order to evaluate the relative strength of the different factors in collective action in determining success or failure, to evaluate the alternative hypotheses that have been proposed, and to assess the social effects of such collective action. It was also pointed out that, with the major exception of that relating to common property resources, most existing studies, especially those of an empirical nature, have dealt with DCs. This leaves open to question the usefulness and applicability of the various hypotheses to LDCs. Of particular interest in the LDC context is the role of the state in collective action and the determinants of state behavior, especially since LDC governments tend to be more autocratic than those in the DCs which have been more carefully and thoroughly studied.

The case studies in Part III of this volume are presented from this dual perspective of empirical work on collective action theory and its application to LDCs. Most of the case studies focus on one of the major themes discussed in Chapter 3, namely the formation of interest groups and organizations and their relative strength and importance. Another theme that is treated in the case studies is the dynamics of institutional change and the explanation of how institutions can outlive their usefulness. Other themes in Chapter 3, which are not treated in case studies are the emergence of norms, and collective action with respect to common property resources. The former is not treated in as much as norms change only very slowly and require lengthy periods of time to complete, thereby posing major methodological difficulties for a study such as this which concentrates primarily on the latter half of the 20th century. The latter is not explicity dealt with in the case studies because these problems have already received a great deal of attention in the LDC context.

The case studies in Part III have been deliberately chosen so as to deal with both an interesting variety of sectors and a number of different interest groups and organizations. Among the latter are their formation, the determination of their relative strength, the mechanisms they choose for achieving their objectives, the character of the state and its activities and institutional rigidities.

The first two studies in Part Three have a relatively long term perspective and address the issue of institutional rigidity. Both case studies illustrate situations in which the institutional changes required to respond effectively to the various shocks and environmental changes did not take place. In Chapter 8, Kuran analyses the case of the amins in the craft guilds of Tunis and provides an explanation for their decline during the period leading up to the middle of the 20th Century. In his explanation Kuran draws upon several strands in the collective action literature reviewed in Chapter 3, including those of Olson, Hirschman and the "critical mass" models. In Chapter 9, Bsaies takes up the problem of the failure of Tunisia to introduce modern secular education until well into the 20th Century. His analysis is couched in terms of the supply and demand for institutional change, and he points to critical role of the powerful religious establishment known as the Ulama in impeding institutional change. Both studies show that groups with vested interests in existing institutions succeed in maintaining them, while those desirous of change were unsuccessful in organizing themselves so as to achieve their objectives.

The next four studies are more closely related to Olson's theories of interest groups and organizations. The studies in Chapters 10 and 11 deal with the wide-ranging producer and labor organizations of Tunisia. In Chapter 10, Nugent uses Olson's approach to collective action to explain not only the relatively late appearance and overall weakness of producer organizations in Tunisia, but also the observed variations in their relative strength from one group to another over time. He also treats the strategy of the Tunisian government in influencing this process and assesses its consequences. In the case study of Chapter 11 Zouari deals with Tunisia's labor union which is an "encompassing" organization in the sense of Olson. An original feature of the study is that Zouari draws on both Williamson's transaction cost-based analysis of governance structure and the theory of collective action in explaining not only the motive for, but also the dynamics of, the evolution of wage bargaining in Tunisia in the post-independence period. He points out the strong linkage that exists between the internal governance structure of the labor organization and the nature of the bargaining process.

The studies in chapters 12 and 13 have a narrower scope in that they deal with two specific markets. In Chapter 12 Azabou, Kuran and Nabli consider a remarkable case of success in collective action, namely, that of the porters of the wholesale market for produce in Tunis. The relative strength of the porters' union *vis-à-vis* the other relevant groups and the union's choice of instruments for collective action are explained. Finally, these authors consider the effects on the functioning of this important market and the implications thereof for the static and dynamic efficiency of the Tunisian economy and the distribution of income. In Chapter 13, Bechri draws upon Olson's interest group theory to explain the determinants of both the level and the structure of interest rates in Tunisia. He traces the evolution of the relative strength of the relevant groups on both the supply and demand sides of the credit market over time, and emphasizes their role in explaining the observed inertia in interest rates in the 1960's and 1970's. He also explains the substantial reforms of 1981 and 1987 and considers the prospects for the future.

Finally in Chapter 14, Grissa uses the theory of collective action to explain the evolution and performance of Tunisia's state enterprises. This case study differs from the preceding ones in that the major "interest groups" involved, and particularly the bureaucracy which plays a central role in his analysis, are not formally organized. It is an interesting case of a group that is neither latent nor explicitly organized but is able to act in such a way as to further its interests. However, in the context of an autocratic regime, bureaucrats to a greater extent than workers are able to use public enterprises to their advantage, thereby affecting negatively the truly "latent" groups such as consumers, taxpayers and future generations. The consequences for the stability, growth and equity of the Tunisian economy are also considered.

Chapter 8

THE CRAFT GUILDS OF TUNIS AND THEIR AMINS:
A STUDY IN INSTITUTIONAL ATROPHY*

Timur Kuran

I. Introduction

Roughly at the center of Tunis, as in all the great cities where Islamic civilization flourished, can be found a cluster of *suqs*, or specialized markets. For many centuries every suq was home to a separate craft guild. At the head of each guild was an *amin*, a guildmaster selected to play a variety of roles, some of which were contradictory. As protector of the guild's interests, the amin tried to promote cooperation among the membership on a variety of matters such as the maintenance of customary oligopolistic prices. At the same time, he was expected to serve as an administrative link between the guild and the state; his duties in this capacity often included the enforcement of price ceilings.

Until the European economic penetration, and in some cases even until the early twentieth century, the amins of Tunis were important and respected officials. Today they have all but disappeared. A few remain but, with one exception, only as figureheads. Their historical functions having passed to other agents, they have no important duties and wield little authority. They continue to be admired by many, but this tends to be a romantic admiration, much like the reverence one feels toward the once-commanding walls of old Tunis.

What explains the fate of the amins? There are several reasons, apart from historical curiosity, why the question might be of interest.

For one thing, prominent orientalists attribute the decline of Islamic civilization to the conservatism of the Islamic guilds.[1] This is a far-reaching

---

*The bulk of the research embodied in this paper was carried out during visits to Tunis in 1983, 1984, and 1986. In the course of my visits I benefited from discussions with Mohamed Talbi, Taoufik Bachrouch, and Ahmed Boubaker, and my field work was facilitated by Mohamed Matoussi, Jamel Chichti, Mongi Azabou, and Mustapha Nabli. Both Reuven Brenner and Jeffrey Nugent read the first draft of the paper and made valuable suggestions that resulted in substantive and stylistic improvements. At a later stage, I received helpful comments from Yassine Essid and Bruce Herrick, as well as from participants in a University of Tunis workshop where the paper was discussed.

[1] These include Gibb and Bowen (1950).

claim, but it has not been substantiated through systematic argument. An exploration of the amins' role in the urban economy would constitute a step in evaluating the suggested link.

Second, and on the theoretical side, the experiences of the Tunisian guilds and of their amins can provide a test of the thesis, supported by a variety of theories, that institutions may outlive their purpose.[2] A major implication of this thesis is that the institutional evolution that accompanies economic development comes about through the replacement of old organizations by new ones. Existing organizations, the argument goes, adapt to changes in environmental conditions more slowly than entrepreneurs can develop new organizations, which means that new organizations are able to establish footholds in the economy and over time gain in importance relative to old ones. If the thesis were wrong, then the institutional evolution of an economy would be the result of deliberate variations by existing organizations in response to environmental changes. It would reflect successful adaptation by existing organizations, not the rise of new organizations and the decline of old ones.[3]

There is, finally, a practical reason for taking up this subject. The mode of industrial organization that was prevalent when Muslim states held their own against Europe is currently being idealized by various groups throughout the Islamic world — not just Islamic traditionalists but also secular intellectuals repulsed by Western individualism. It is believed in such circles that the underdevelopment of the Islamic world stems principally from the abandonment of traditional economic practices in favor of "corrupt" Western ones. As far as markets are concerned, the solution envisaged is the reestablishment of the non-competitive, fraternal, relatively egalitarian order of the old guilds, whose members, it is believed, were typically fair and honest. In the Tunisian case at least, this proposal has received support even from some Western students of the guilds.[4] And as of this writing, the Tunisian government is attempting seriously to resuscitate the office of the amin. Assessment of this revivalism can be advanced by exploring whether the conditions that once made the amin an effective functionary continue to exist in the modern world.

The objective of the paper is not to furnish detailed historical descriptions, but rather to provide an explanation for the decline of the Tunisian

---

[2] Among these theories are those of Olson (1982), Hirschman (1970), and Kuran (1987b). For a critical survey, see Kuran (1988).

[3] For more on this implication, see Hannan and Freeman (1984).

[4] See, for instance, Atger (1909), especially p. 124, and Payre (1940), pp. 21-24.

guilds, and in particular, for the amins' role in this decline. While descriptive accounts are given throughout the paper to back up arguments, the level of detail is kept to a minimum. Not that the descriptive literature on the Tunisian guilds is satisfactory; it consists of a few, mostly rudimentary, accounts by scholars and some impressionistic writings by European travellers.[5] My justification is that more and more facts, however well supported by historical sources, will only become a burden on the memory, until one has a framework into which these will somehow fit. With a conceptual framework, attention to finer details can lead to greater understanding of the past and provide valuable lessons for public action; without one, it will merely raise more questions and generate greater confusion.

The paper is organized as follows. The stage for the analysis is set in Section II, which examines the guilds' relationship with the state during the period running roughly from the mid-sixteenth century to the mid-nineteenth. Section III then explores the amins' functions during this period, the golden age of the Tunisian guilds. The subsequent section turns to the period of rapid decline precipitated by the European economic intrusions into the country. Special attention is given to the guilds' resistance to modern economic practices, and to the amins' responses to the colossal shocks of the era. The amins' experiences in the modern era are addressed in Section V. The final section contains conclusions pertaining to the above-mentioned issues and controversies.

II. The Guilds and the State

In many ways, the Islamic guilds resembled those of medieval Europe. Always confined to a single town, they were craft or trade associations that tried to serve their members' economic and social interests. As in Europe, the state regarded the guilds as potential sources of opposition and therefore kept a close eye on them, regulating some of their activities. By and large, however, the guilds were self-governing bodies. Their economic and political powers varied, of course, depending on the towns in which they existed, particularities of their crafts, and historical circumstances they faced.

There is a longstanding controversy among orientalists concerning the

---

[5]The most important scholarly accounts of the Tunisian guilds are those of Atger (1909), Payre (1940), Pennec (1964), and Valensi (1969). Also relevant are accounts by Lewis (1937) and Lapidus (1967) on the Islamic guilds in general. The richest studies of particular Islamic guilds are of those in Turkey and Egypt. On the Turkish guilds, see Mantran (1962), Baer (1970a, 1970b, 1982), İnalcık (1969), and Gerber (1976); and on the Egyptian guilds, Baer (1964) and Raymond (1974).

origins of the Islamic guilds. Some writers argue that unlike the European guilds, which were created by the craftsmen and traders themselves, the Islamic guilds were organized by the state. Others maintain that the guilds were brought to life by producers acting on their own. Proponents of the latter thesis rest their case on evidence which suggests that from the very beginning the guildsmen maintained a hostile attitude toward the state and that public authorities always distrusted the guilds.[6] Of course, neither side is on firm ground here, since the available information is scant. At any rate, the two theses are not necessarily inconsistent. It is possible for the state first to have tried in vain to break up through repression the rudimentary ties that had sprung up among practitioners of a craft, and then later to have assisted in their formalization. Even without the government's stewardship, these ties would have become stronger over time, but at a slower pace. Economic and sociological research suggests that there tends to be a lag between the emergence of an occupation and the time its members succeed in organizing to further their common interests.[7]

This lag was undoubtedly present in the medieval Islamic world. It must have been the case that, following the introduction of a craft to a town through conquest or migration of populations, its practitioners came only gradually to cooperate on professional matters. The public authorities, suspicious as they always were of autonomous organizations, would have tried to obstruct the development of the bourgeoning organizations into elaborate guilds capable of forming nuclei of political opposition. Hence, the hostile sentiments between the public authorities and guildsmen, detected by a number of historians. The authorities possessed, however, an alternative course of action: to encourage the craftsmen to organize formally, but in a manner that allowed the state to control certain key activities. There is a bit of evidence that in Tunisia and the rest of the Maghreb the cooperative course of action took hold rather quickly: in contrast to their counterparts in Turkey and the Arab Middle East, the Maghrebi guildsmen seem not to have developed strong anti-establishment feelings.[8]

Organizational assistance by the state took various forms. The state participated in the formalization, and then in the enforcement, of a series of entry barriers, which we shall discuss presently. It helped settle disputes over the boundaries between professions, which facilitated the determination

---

[6] For the former argument, see Lapidus (1967), pp. 95-105; and for the latter, Lewis (1937).

[7] See Olson (1982), pp. 38-41.

[8] See Zghal and Stambouli (1974), p. 232.

of whom to include in each guild. Most important, it constructed the suqs, enabling the geographic centralization of each non-itinerant profession. The suqs of Tunis, naturally illuminated, vaulted passages, were built and rebuilt over nearly a millennium. Some of those that exist today, like the suq for perfumes *(Suq al-Attarin)*, date from the fourteenth century or before. The suq for *shashiyas*, the distinctive brimless hats which for three centuries constituted Tunisia's principal export product, was built in the seventeenth century, as this profession grew enormously following the Andalousian immigrations of the preceding century. Later years saw the construction of, among others, the suq of Turks *(Suq el-Trouk)* for Turkish-style garments.[9]

The state's participation in the development of the guilds was prompted, as mentioned, by a fear of their turning into centers of opposition. Left to themselves, it was believed, the guilds would pose a threat to the established order. Properly conscribed, they could be a bedrock of stability. The requisite limitations included, in the eyes of the authorities, precise specifications of each guild's economic domain.[10] Thus, the makers of woollen clothes were not allowed to sell cottons, and the silk weavers were barred from creating a door to the adjoining suq.[11] Such restrictions were designed to prevent any one group of craftsmen from becoming a source of social tension by directly and overtly encroaching upon the market of another; they could not, of course, prevent secular shifts in the guilds' relative fortunes.

Like their counterparts elsewhere, the Tunisian authorities were especially anxious to forestall commodity crises, which in the pre-modern world were often the harbingers of riots and even coups. With large segments of the population living close to subsistence, wild price fluctuations or shortages in markets for food, clothing, and other basic products could lead to extensive despair, impairing the rulers' legitimacy. The state felt it necessary, there-

---

[9] On the suqs' construction histories, see Brunschvig (1934) and Pennec (1964), pp. 19-32. According to these accounts, some suqs changed functions over time. For instance, the suq for the sale of black slaves *(Suq al Birka)* was taken over by jewelers after slavery was abolished in the mid-nineteenth century. Oddly, the suq's original name has been retained.

[10] These limitations applied not only to the craft guilds but also to the mercantile guilds. For most professions, they precluded connections between the guilds of different towns. The economic principles involved are discussed by İnalcık (1969), who notes that these have prevailed from antiquity right up to the modern era throughout the Middle East and North Africa.

[11] See Atger (1909), pp. 100-104, for regulations along these lines, which were promulgated by the nineteenth-century statesman Khayr al-Din. In earlier centuries such specifications seem to have been embodied in customs, not written rules.

fore, to regulate these markets in order to ensure the adequacy of supplies and to moderate disappointments of price expectations. The market laws of the Islamic *hisba* doctrine, which, like the Christian doctrine of the just price, aimed at preventing economic injustices, were undoubtedly developed as a moral rationale for the authorities' widespread interferences in market processes.[12] The implementation of the hisba laws was helped by the guilds, organized as they were in separate suqs. For one thing, it was easier to supervise prices, quantities, and quality when all sellers of a given product were tightly organized in one location than when they were disorganized and dispersed. Secondly, forcing all exchanges to occur in one place enhanced the flow of price information and promoted the convergence of people's expectations.

Yet another reason why the state supported the guild system is that this facilitated taxation. Tunisian rulers, like other autocratic rulers of the pre-modern era, tried to maximize their revenues as a means of fortifying their power.[13] To this end they taxed the income and wealth that was most easily collected.[14] While agriculture bore the brunt of taxation, the urban crafts were not spared. Primarily two types of taxes were imposed on the guilds: taxes on inputs such as wool and precious metals, and export taxes. Both taxes were collected at the city gates.[15] Significantly, finished products sold locally were not taxed, presumably because the costs of administering an excise tax were prohibitive. Inputs were easily taxed, because for reasons to be explored, each guild procured its members' inputs through a centralized process. In addition to these regular taxes, a lump-sum charge was imposed on each guild whenever a new ruler acceded to power.

Although the state took a keen interest in the guilds' affairs, it did not manage them directly. It engaged in price and quality controls, and saw to it that supplies were not interrupted, but ordinarily it meddled neither in production nor in the guilds' administration. Only in times of crisis, or if a guild became too unpopular, did the authorities broaden their supervision into these other spheres. This does not mean, however, that the guilds constituted essentially independent bodies, even in so far as production and

---

[12]On the hisba, see Cahen and Talbi (1971) and Essid (1988), part 2, ch. 2. The Christian doctrine is examined by Roover (1958).

[13]For a detailed argument, see North (1981), especially ch. 3. İnalcık (1969) presents the same view with regard to Middle Eastern states in particular.

[14]See Brown (1974), pp. 134-137, for evidence from the early nineteenth century.

[15]See Pennec (1964), p. 464, n. 1.

administration were concerned, for in their internal decisions the guilds took care not to stray too far from the authorities' wishes. The amins played a key role in this self-regulation.

III. The Amins in the Golden Age of the Guilds

The amin of a guild was officially selected by the state from among the guildsmen who enjoyed the greatest respect. While the government had a right to appoint anyone it pleased, even an outsider, it took care in practice to honor the sentiments of the guild members.[16] Appointing someone unpopular would go against the government's general policy of avoiding friction with significant groups. Moreover, an amin who was not liked and trusted would have difficulty discharging his administrative duties. The extent to which the state took the guild members' desires into account depended, as one would expect, on the guild's economic importance and political clout. Thus, the most powerful of all the guilds, the shashiya guild, determined its own choice by a formal vote.[17] Other guilds, it seems, transmitted their feelings to the government through less formal means.

Nominations were made for an indefinite period, and in practice, a guildsman, once appointed amin, retained the position for life. There is a remarkable difference in this regard between the Islamic guilds and their medieval European counterparts. In Europe the guild leader was replaced periodically — in general at least once a year — to prevent the creation of "magisterial dynasties which might perpetuate themselves at will."[18] Thus, for all their egalitarianism in other respects, the Islamic guilds were relatively undemocratic organizations. This suggests that at least in the Middle Ages, the guildsmen and the state were confident that the amin would remain impartial throughout his life, and that in any case, he could be prevented, through the threat of dismissal, from abusing his powers. Presumably, moreover, the state valued the resulting low turnover of amins, because this enhanced the stability of the economic system. But whatever the origins of the setup, it had far-reaching consequences at a later stage in the guilds' existence. We shall take these up in Section V.

Among the primary functions of the amin was to control prices. He served the state by preventing prices from rising unexpectedly. At the same time, however, he served his fellow guildsmen by controlling competitive price-

---

[16] Le Tourneau (1957), pp. 35-36, and Pennec (1964), pp. 41-43. Baer (1982), pp. 204-205, notes that the selection criteria were much the same in most cities of the Ottoman Empire.

[17] Atger (1909), pp. 48-49.

[18] Renard (1918), p. 30.

cutting. In each of these instances the amin played the crucial role in protecting the guildsmen from themselves — in solving, that is, a free-rider problem.[19] In a guild comprising anywhere from 25 to 500 masters, no one master could precipitate state intervention by charging unexpectedly high prices; nor could he, given the limits on his allotment of inputs (see below), appreciably injure the guild by charging uncustomarily low prices. But if all masters acted upon this reasoning, the guild would surely suffer. It was essential, therefore, for the guildsmen to constrain themselves by empowering the amin with the right to control prices. Any losses the individual guildsman may have incurred from limitations on his own pricing decisions must have been far outweighed by his gains from parallel limitations on his fellows' choices.

The amin's guidance notwithstanding, the guild did not operate as a tight cartel. For most products, exchanges could take place at diverse prices, which helped maintain the appearance of competition among the guildsmen. What the amin did was to keep prices within acceptable bounds, generally through moral suasion, but occasionally through social sanctions and even corporal punishment.[20] The amin routinely monitored the market for information on realized prices. His task was easiest when deals were consummated through public auctions where all transaction prices instantly became public knowledge. Greater skills were involved when deals were settled through bargaining between buyers and sellers, as they generally were with finished products.[21] The physical layout of the suq, which allowed guild members to observe each other's activities, was a help in this regard. So, too, was the fact that consumers could call on the amin if they felt that they were being exploited. The amin then arbitrated, not infrequently deciding in favor of the consumer.

Further problems the amin helped resolve arose from the fact that no two hand-produced goods are ever exactly alike. Oligopoly theory suggests that product heterogeneity complicates the task of price coordination by increasing the dimensions of competition. Further, it raises the risk of conflict both between the sellers themselves and between sellers and buyers.[22] One solution to the problem is to encourage standardization of inputs, production

---

[19] The classic analysis of the free-rider problem lies in the work of Olson (1965).

[20] Payre (1940), p. 6, speaks of one amin who had people bastinadoed in public.

[21] See Pennec (1964), pp. 454-467.

[22] See Scherer (1980), pp. 200-205.

methods, and product specifications. This solution was in fact pursued by
the Tunisian guilds through the offices of the amin.[23] The state's interest in
social harmony prompted it to support these efforts. There seems to be no
evidence, however, except after the mid-nineteenth century when the guilds
had begun to disintegrate, that the state officially set standards.[24] During
the heyday of the guilds, it influenced standards more subtly, usually by a
simple appeal to the amin.

The amin's production controls were aimed not only at standardization
but also at the prevention of fraud. To keep consumers content, and thereby
forestall government intervention, the guild needed to cultivate a reputation
of honesty. This required the guildsmen to provide accurate information to
consumers regarding the nature of inputs and quality of workmanship. Once
again, however, the individual guildsman's incentives in this regard differed
from those of the guild at large.[25] To make these incentives congruent, the
amin regularly inspected the goods produced and checked into consumers'
complaints. He also made his expertise available to shoppers who doubted
a guildsman's quality claims. In the case, for instance, where a prospective
buyer of a wool blanket was suspicious about its declared characteristics, he
could call on the amin, who in his role of a trustworthy intermediary, would
then carefully inspect the workmanship and set fire to a strand of fibers to
determine, from the smell, the quality of the wool used.

The literal meaning of the term amin is, in fact, trustworthy. It is not
clear when that term came into use in Tunisia to designate guild leaders,
although we know that at one time the term el arif (literally, knowledgeable)
was used instead.[26] The interesting point here is that the guild leaders first
developed the reputation for being trustworthy and then acquired the title
amin.

What explains the trustworthiness of the amins? It is common in the
literature on Islamic guilds to ascribe it simply to the Islamic injunction,
associated with the hisba, to promote good and restrain evil, which in this
context is understood to entail protection of the consumer.[27] But this hardly
constitutes an explanation. Some of the amin's activities, for instance his
role in preventing competitive price-cutting and in protecting his guild's entry barriers, violate the free-trade provisions of Islamic dogma and hurt the

---

[23]See Pennec (1964), pp. 45-49, and Atger (1909), pp. 97-102.
[24]Atger (1909), pp. 25-26.
[25]For a general theoretical argument, see Akerlof (1970).
[26]Atger (1909), p. 8.
[27]See, for instance, Payre (1940), pp. 3-4, and Lapidus (1967), p. 98.

An ambiguous position vis-à-vis the consumer

consumer. The popular explanation is incomplete, then, since it elucidates neither why Islam was only partially followed, nor why the consumer was protected through some measures but exploited through others. One must also confront the fact that non-Islamic guilds, in Europe and elsewhere, were also led by respected and trusted people.[28]

It would appear that the explanation has more to do with the nature of medieval urban society than with religion in general, or Islam in particular. Just as the economic specialization of the suq and the lack of privacy within it allowed the amin to monitor the activities of his fellow guildsmen relatively easily, so too did these same conditions allow the guildsmen to monitor the amin. An amin who abused his powers by violating accepted standards of justice would rapidly lose his reputation for trustworthiness and risk being ousted in disgrace. If this argument is correct, the hisba merely provided moral justification for the office of the amin; it neither gave rise to the position, nor defined the functions it involved. It is worth pointing out that in societies far more primitive than pre-modern urban society, where people have virtually no privacy, trustworthiness is valued to an even greater extent and is observed to be more pervasive.[29] At the other extreme, in contemporary industrialized societies where people enjoy a great deal of privacy, trustworthiness is considered to be a relatively uncommon character trait, as implied by lamentations about the so-called moral crisis engendered by modern civilization.

Since the establishment of trust between buyer and seller was an important issue, one might expect trademarking to have been common. It seems, however, that until fairly recently trademarks were employed in very few of the guilds. The medieval European guilds, in contrast, are known to have relied on them extensively.[30] The reasons why the Tunisian and other Islamic guilds did not are lost in history. But one clue to the difference is the fact that the European guild leaders served for very short terms, whereas their Islamic counterparts tended to hold lifetime appointments. This stability meant that an amin could perform the cheating-deterrence function that in Europe had to be performed by trademarks.

Consider a person who purchases a blanket in the expectation, clearly reinforced by the seller, that it will last for life. A mere five years later, the blanket falls apart. Realizing that he has been taken, the man heads back

---

[28]See Renard (1918), pp. 30-31.
[29]For similar arguments in other contexts, see Posner (1980) and Brenner (1983), especially ch. 3.
[30]See Renard (1918), pp. 32-35.

to the suq to confront the blanket maker who sold him the shoddy blanket;
but alas, he is unable to pick him out from among the hundred-odd blanket
makers who now somehow look identical. Added to our indignant buyer's
injury is the fact that he is not even able to prevent his family members from
patronizing the same unscrupulous blanket maker.

Now suppose the blanket had been trademarked. Even many years after
the purchase, the buyer would have little trouble finding the seller — unless,
of course, the seller had died or retired from the business. He could appeal for
a replacement, and in any event, he could get even with the blanket maker by
advising his family and acquaintances to withhold their business from him.
Knowing that the buyer had the means of imposing such costs on him, the
blanket maker would probably have refrained from cheating in the first place.
We see that a trademark deters dishonesty because it is a long-lasting asset
whose value is depreciated with each instance of cheating.

An alternative mechanism to prevent cheating is to have some continuing
party with a vital stake in avoiding dishonest practices monitor the production
process.[31] The Tunisian amin, who was seldom removed from office except by
death, and who was held responsible by the authorities for the performance
of his guild, had a clear interest in preventing dishonesty. Since he had the
power to punish offenders, he was ideally suited to serve as a quality-control
agent.

Interestingly, one of the few guilds that used trademarks was the shashiya
guild,[32] which in the 1750s had over 300 masters.[33] The guild felt, presumably, that its size made it impossible for the amin to control quality ade-
quately. It chose, therefore, to utilize an additional quality-control device.[34]
A complementary explanation is that the bulk of the shashiyas were exported.
Trademarks would be expected to serve a relatively more important function
with exports because foreign buyers have greater difficulty determining the
maker of a particular item. Without trademarking, any poor quality item

---

[31]For more on the theory involved, see Klein, Crawford, and Alchian (1978),
pp. 302-307 and especially n. 17.

[32]Atger (1909), pp. 71-72.

[33]Valensi (1969), p. 381.

[34]Since trademarking reduces the need for monitoring by a continuing third
party, one might expect the amin for shashiyas to have been replaced more
frequently than the amins for other guilds. There is no evidence, however, to
this effect. It would be interesting to explore whether this is related to the ease
with which non-Tunisian shashiya makers could imitate the trademarks of the
Tunisians. If they could do so with impunity, shashiya trademarks would not
have played a significant role in deterring cheating, and a continuing third
party would still have been necessary.

would tarnish the reputation of the entire guild with which it was associated; with trademaking, the damage would fall primarily on the maker of the item.

We have seen how the amin tried on several fronts to protect the guild's independence by struggling to minimize conflicts. Another area where the amin played this role was in ensuring the guild's apprentices and non-indentured laborers a minimum standard of living. While in principle guild-masters were free to pay their workers no more than market rates, when necessary, the amin pressured them into being more generous.[35] In this role, as in several others, the amin appeared to serve as an agent of the state. In fact, he was also serving the interests of his fellow guildsmen, however much they resented individual acts of interference, because they themselves were among the principal beneficiaries of a stable order.

The amin of a guild was not alone in exercising his duties. In grave circumstances, and especially in matters involving more than one guild, he was assisted by a Commercial Council consisting of ten amins. The president of this council was always the amin of the shashiya guild, a reflection no doubt of the supreme importance of this guild in the economic life of Tunisia.[36] While little is known about how the other members of the Council were selected, it is possible that seats were also reserved for the amins of other important guilds. Above the Commercial Council stood the *shaykh al-madina*, who performed many of the duties of a modern mayor. The shaykh al-madina had supervisory powers over all the amins; for this he was called "amin of the amins".[37] But in accordance with the principle of giving the guilds as much freedom as possible, he seldom interfered overtly in the amins' decisions. Quiet persuasion seems to have been the order of the day.

In his capacity as administrative link between the government and his guild, the amin also served as a transmitter of opinions. He petitioned the government on behalf of the guild and carried the authorities' views to the guildsmen. The amin was ideally suited to the purpose, given his reputation for being goodhearted and scrupulously honest.

Up to this point we have taken the guild's membership as given, when in fact, it was always changing, as a result of deaths and of promotions to mastership. The amin of the guild played a role in deciding who would be

---

[35]The evidence on such pressure is scant, because it never assumed a written form, although Atger (1909), p. 42, indicates that it was routinely exercised. Regarding the guilds of Egypt, Baer (1964), pp. 103-104, and Raymond (1974), p. 566, also argue in the absence of solid evidence that the amin must have had a say in wage matters.

[36]Atger (1909), p. 36.

[37]Brown (1974), pp. 190-191.

admitted. He made his decisions after consulting his fellow guildsmen and the Commercial Council. But the state had the final say, and on occasion it would veto an amin's decision.[38]

Among the criteria that in principle affected the amin's choice, foremost were honesty, generosity, and openness to cooperation. Unwelcome was the shamelessly selfish and opportunistic individual, who, like the textbook description of *homo economicus*, would be willing to crush his neighbor to make a few more sales. The ideal, spelled out in the *futuwwa* principles, was for the guildsmen to content themselves with a "fair" share of the guild's business and with limited profits. It thus required them to refrain from promoting their wares.[39] Exactly the same ideal, though under different names, guided members of the medieval European guilds.[40] But it retained its appeal much longer in the Islamic world than in Europe. As late as the early twentieth century, Western visitors to Tunisia expressed bewilderment at the suqs' uncompetitive atmosphere and at the modesty of the guildsmen.[41]

In trying to do away with competition within his guild, the amin relied, however, on more than just limiting admission to people of "good character". He strived, in addition, to make all guildsmen use the same raw materials. Equally important, he tried to ensure an equitable division of the available supplies of inputs.[42] Workers, when scarce, were also apportioned among the guildsmen in a manner perceived to be equitable. There is no indication that equity was interpreted in the sense of equality. Rather, it was perceived as implying the protection of the status quo. So while poor members of the guild were guaranteed a continuing share of the business, their more prosperous brethren were, in return, protected from losing their dominant positions.

As already indicated, the Tunisian guilds exhibited a hierarchical structure. Below the masters stood the journeymen, and below them the apprentices. In some guilds non-indentured workers were also brought in from time to time. The amin had some say regarding all promotions. Interestingly, and in contrast to Turkey and Western Europe, the number of masters was not strictly set. This suggests that the Tunisian amin had somewhat greater

---

[38]See Atger (1909), pp. 44-46.

[39]See Taeschner (1965) and İnalcık (1969), especially pp. 97-108.

[40]See Renard (1918), pp. 40-44 and Landes (1983), ch. 13.

[41]See, for instance, Sladen (1906), p. 372.

[42]See Macgill (1811), p. 157, Atger (1909), pp. 54-55, Pennec (1964), p. 127, and Valensi (1969), p. 385. This practice is easily explained in terms of oligopoly theory. If all practitioners of a craft use the same inputs, their marginal costs are the same. As a result, a major source of conflict over pricing choices is eliminated. See Scherer (1980), pp. 156-160.

latitude over promotions than his counterparts elsewhere. He apparently had the right to block the promotion of an apprentice; at the same time, the apprentice could not be fired without his consent.[43] But if the lack of evidence of labor conflicts is any indication, the amins seem to have been judicious in their use of these powers.

Toward potential competitors from outside the guild, the amin always reacted without pity. Jealously guarding the guild's customary domain, he categorically opposed the opening of any rival shop outside the suq.[44] This same protectionist vigor extended to the guild's input supplies as well. The amin often mobilized the authorities to prevent another guild from threatening the availability of his guild's raw materials.

An additional duty of the amin was to apportion the lump-sum tax imposed on the guild by a new ruler.[45] In at least some guilds the amin had still another function: managing the guild's common fund. The shashiya guild, for instance, had a fund built up through production levies, initiation fees on new masters, and voluntary donations. The proceeds were used primarily to improve the suq and the guild's joint production facilities. They also served insurance purposes: the amin could use them to provide advances to needy guildsmen and charitable help to dependents of deceased members.[46]

For all their services, what were the amins paid? Not much information has survived on this issue, although it is clear that great differences existed among guilds.[47] In principle, each amin received a small periodic fee known as *aada*, or "habit". Beyond the aada, some, like the amins of the goldsmiths and silversmiths, received commissions on transactions for which they served as intermediary.[48] In most guilds, the amin was himself a practicing craftsmen, so he was not totally dependent on such fees. All considered, there is nothing to suggest that the amins became substantially richer than the guildsmen they served. There must, however, have existed major differences from guild to guild: the amin of a properous guild was in all likelihood better off than that of a guild fighting for its survival.[49] At any rate, the amin also received

---

[43]See Atger (1909), especially pp. 27-28, 37-47, and 87-96, and Pennec (1964), especially pp. 33-39.

[44]See Atger (1909), p. 97.

[45]Le Tourneau (1957), pp. 51-52.

[46]Atger (1909), pp. 52-54. See also Pennec (1964), pp. 140-141.

[47]See Payre (1940), pp. 12-13.

[48]Lallemand (1893), p. 99.

[49]Raymond (1974), pp. 551-559, documents that this was the case in Egypt. Although I know of no direct evidence regarding Tunis, it is significant that the richest and most influential Tunisians tended to place their sons in par-

non-monetary rewards for his efforts: he was admired, honored, and treated with great respect. In a society where people relied on each other for personal favors to a far greater extent than they do in the modern world, such prestige must have translated into substantial tangible benefits.

IV. The Decline of the Guilds

The Tunisian guilds, like those in the rest of the Islamic world, were rocked in the nineteenth century by an invasion of cheap European goods. These fruits of the mechanized new industrial order in Europe profoundly altered the world in which the guilds had been accustomed to operating. Some guilds, including two of the three involved in the production of firearms, succumbed to the competition before the century was out.[50] The majority survived, although they lost market share, and their profits shrank substantially. Many of the textile guilds were among the losers.[51] Even the venerable shashiya guild suffered, as mass-produced French, Italian, and Austrian imitations, priced 60 to 90 percent lower than the cheapest of the hand-made Tunisians,[52] penetrated not only Tunisia's export markets, but the country's heartland as well.[53] Although the European shashiyas were not nearly as fine or durable as the ones made in Tunis through traditional, labor-intensive methods, their low prices made them popular throughout the Mediterranean and beyond.

Meanwhile, the guilds were also shaken by changes in the political arena: the country's administration came increasingly under European influence, a development which was to culminate in 1881 in the establishment of a French protectorate. From our standpoint here, the interesting issue concerns how the guilds reacted to these momentous environmental changes. Of particular interest is the role the amins played in charting the course of the guilds. What measures did they advocate and why?

The guilds' immediate response to the inflow of European goods was to appeal for protection. With some success in the beginning, they tried to block the entry of foreign goods, or at the very least to subject them to stiff tariffs. There is nothing at all surprising about this response. It is exactly how they had guarded their monopolies throughout their long history. The fact

---

ticular guilds. In the nineteenth century, according to Lallemand (1893), p. 99, the most popular guilds were those of the shashiya makers, saddlers, perfumers, and weavers.
[50]Lallemand (1893), pp. 119-120.
[51]See Pelissier (1843), p. 365, and Lallemand (1893), pp. 109-115.
[52]See Lallemand (1893), p. 118, and Valensi (1969), pp. 399-400.
[53]See Macgill (1811), p. 124, and Atger (1909), pp. 79-85.

that this latest instance of competition was a tidal wave fed by revolutionary production methods did not seem to call for an entirely new type of response. As far as the guilds were concerned, this merely increased the urgency of the matter and the severity of the protection required.

Yet the economy around them would not stand still. Enterprising Tunisians saw an opportunity to introduce the more efficient European production methods into the country. Significantly, the initial successes in this regard generally came from European immigrants and their protégés, who were exempt from the hisba and could thereby escape the authority of the amin. Thus, a group of Jews enjoying French protection established in 1855 the first tanneries outside the suqs, where they employed the nascent European tanning technology.[54] Another Jew became in 1912 the first Tunisian to organize the mechanized production of cloth.[55] Such developments spelled immense trouble for the old guilds. The new establishments undercut the guilds' prices, often below their costs, and introduced new styles. The processes that had already sealed the fate of the European guilds were thus put into motion in Tunisia.

Another blow to the guilds came from the Westernization of tastes that accompanied the European penetration. With the rise in Tunisia's European population from 20,000 in 1881 to 150,000 in 1911, a huge, prosperous clientele emerged for European-style goods.[56] Native townspeople of means, the Arabs generally more cautiously than the Jews, emulated the new lifestyles and consumption patterns. They switched, for instance, from coarsely made, traditional Arab shoes, like the *belgha* and the *kountra,* to the European-style shoes sold by the rising new merchants and industrialists.[57] New industries and trade establishments outside the traditional suqs, freed from the heavy baggage of regulations accumulated by the guilds, became the prime movers of the economy.[58] Although still a center for handicrafts, the suqs began to fade in importance. With these changes, the guilds started to lose some of their ablest apprentices and journeymen. Even some masters joined the exodus, leaving the suqs to open shops in the city's newer districts, or to become workers in the nascent factory system.[59]

---

[54]Chater (1978), p. 107.
[55]Sebag (1951), pp. 97, and 131-134.
[56]Sebag (1951), pp. 124-126, and Pennec (1964), p. 245.
[57]Pennec (1964), p. 340.
[58]See İnalcık (1969), especially p. 98, for a general argument along these lines, applying to Islamic society as a whole.
[59]Lallemand (1893), p. 120, Sebag (1951), p. 131, Pennec (1964), p. 403,

The amins tried to stem the tide, only to find their authority on the wane. They could not prevent the desertions, because too many guildsmen were leaving, and because their new establishments also had clout. Nor could they prevent the quality decline that afflicted their guilds. Stuck with ancient production techniques, the artisans were finding that they could match the lower prices of their mass-producing rivals only by cutting the quality of their raw materials, or their workmanship, or both. As quality diminished, however, demand for the guilds' products fell even further.[60] To stem this quality decline, the amins advocated the strengthening of their powers to enforce the guilds' time-tested regulations.[61] It was not necessary, they evidently felt, to launch a new beginning, with a new mode of organization and a new technology. In accordance with this stand, they appear to have conducted no serious investigations of European technology and organizational structures, which, whether they liked it or not, were finding a place in Tunisian society.

The amins took their case to the government, which did not always give them what they wanted. Concerning imports, the state was not free to erect all the barriers requested, if only because the European powers on which it depended financially preferred to keep Tunisia open. But it encouraged the amins to consolidate the guilds' old rules. To this end, the statesman Khayr al-Din undertook in the 1870s the legal codification of many of the guilds' rules pertaining to production and internal management – rules that until then had rested primarily on custom.[62] Evidently Khayr al-Din attributed the crisis to indiscipline resulting from the imprecision of customary law, and not to the guilds' monopolistic privileges, their mode of internal governance, or their production methods.[63] It has been said of Khayr al-Din's so-called reform that it killed whatever chances there were of the traditional suqs reversing their decline.[64]

But whatever the actual effects of Khayr al-Din's regulations, no major reforms were undertaken in the decades that followed. Writing in 1893, one commentator observed that some production processes of the guilds could be traced to the Phoenicians. The tanners, he pointed out, employed ancient

---

and Brown (1974), p. 360.

[60]See Pennec (1964), pp. 282-289.

[61]Atger (1909), pp. 106-107.

[62]See Pennec (1964), pp. 55-59, and Atger (1909), pp. 100-104.

[63]For a detailed commentary on Khayr al-Din's socio-economic views, see Tlili (1974), ch. 8.

[64]Among those who have taken this position is Louis Massignon. See Pennec (1964), p. 55.

Obstacle to modernization.

techniques that made little use of post-medieval developments in chemistry.[65] A decade later, another visitor remarked that the shashiya makers' shops "are destitute of interesting machinery, for everything is done by hand with the simplest appliances".[66] Subsequent decades saw the institution of additional obstacles to modernization. In 1922 the government issued a decree banning the mechanization of shashiya production, and in 1937 it prohibited the mechanized production of silk.[67]

The foregoing description of the Tunisian guilds' encounter with modern capitalism has purposefully been kept brief. But the relevant point has been made: the guilds, under the leadership of their amins and with the state's support, sought to solve their colossal problems within the old order. To be sure, not all of the guilds reacted exactly alike. Some did make adaptations, however minor; in the late nineteenth century, for instance, a few silk weavers began to produce untraditionally large pieces of cloth, which they marketed in Europe as curtain material.[68] Moreover, within each guild there were disagreements as to the most appropriate response: some guildsmen raised their voices in favor of the rationalization of production and of adapting to consumers' changing tastes. On the whole, however, the guilds responded very conservatively. Why so? Was it by historical accident that the guild system failed to evolve and develop in a way that would preserve its preeminence in the economy? Or rather, was it already in a state of sclerosis when the first shock waves of the industrial revolution hit the Tunisian shores?

There are several interrelated reasons for believing that the guilds were intrinsically unprepared to adapt. As we saw earlier, they were designed to protect urban craftsmen from the vicissitudes of the marketplace and to enhance social stability. They formed a stagnant system, exhibiting tight boundaries between the professions and an anti-competitive code of conduct. Their rules precluded organizational, technological, and financial innovations as well as cooperative ventures between guilds. They imparted to their members neither the motivation nor the skills necessary to succeed in a dynamic capitalist economy.

The amins who played such an important role in running the guilds were devoid of economic initiative. Not that they were expected to be enterprising leaders. On the contrary, they were appointed to uphold the prevailing customs of their guilds, and to protect the status quo. Experienced as they

---

[65]Lallemand (1893), pp. 111 and 116.
[66]Sladen (1906), p. 389.
[67]Sebag (1951), p. 128.
[68]Lallemand (1893), p. 111.

Modernizers within the guilds are facing a collective-action / organizing problem

were in resolving conflicts between guild and state, between guildsman and customer, and between master and subordinate, they were bound to be ineffectual in dealing with the onslaught of capitalism. In an earlier age when the guilds were secure in their monopolies, the amins' conservatism might have been a boon. With the guilds' very survival now in question, it had turned into a major handicap.

Or so it seems in retrospect. We cannot know how many guildsmen recognized the dangers of failing to reform the guild system, or in particular, of failing to overhaul the amins' functions. What we do know is that the responses charted by the amins were not unanimously approved. It seems, though, that only a minority of the disconcerted guildsmen voiced their feelings, mindful of the strong social pressures, backed by religious and patriotic sentiments, to support the guilds' longstanding traditions. Some reform-minded guildsmen must have silently watched the guild system seal its own fate, unaware that more than a few of their fellows were similarly falsifying their unorthodox preferences and opinions. Had all these reformists publicized their opposition to the guilds' conservative policies, they may have discovered that they constituted a potentially significant force, which could have led to the formation of a counter-lobby. This is not to say that a policy of silent passivism was irrational from the standpoint of the individual guildsman. It certainly was not, given the traditionalists' power. At any rate, the effect of these individual policies of silence must have been to lower the chances that the guilds would be modernized.[69]

One reason is that preference and opinion falsification on the part of guildsmen favoring reform would have kept their traditionalist fellows from having to reflect on possible alternatives to the old guild system. These other guildsmen were, like the amins, obstacles to change. They knew only the customary arrangements, because it had never seemed necessary to consider any others. Their ranks might have diminished had the proponents of reform been forthcoming about their true desires and thoughts. A bandwagon might have developed, with each new participant in the reform movement inducing still more to join in. To get started, however, bandwagons typically require a critical mass.[70] Two factors prevented this from forming.

First, the guildsmen possessed, as we have seen, an alternative to reforming the old system: leaving the guild to launch a new career outside the traditional suqs. To use Albert Hirschman's celebrated terminology, they

---

[69] For the theoretical basis of this argument, see Kuran (1987a).
[70] See Kuran (1987a, 1987b).

Exit, not voice.

could, instead of choosing to *voice* their frustrations, simply *exit*.[71] The exit option was never easy to use, of course, because the amin, with the backing of the public authorities, tried to block desertions. Yet exit became increasingly possible as the guild system weakened and the Tunisian authorities fell under European influence. At the same time, it became increasingly attractive as consumer tastes shifted away from traditional handicrafts. Its use undoubtedly sapped the guilds of their most reform-oriented members, reducing in the process the chances of forming the critical mass needed to start a self-sustaining reform movement.

A second factor was that there existed as many ways of the reforming the guilds as there were proponents of reform. Even in retrospect it appears that multiple options were available; in the mid-nineteenth century, when world capitalism was still in its formative period, a bewildering array of options must have presented itself. Thus, one guild member may have pinned his hopes on large-scale production, another on aggressive marketing, still another on scientific education. Such divisions in the ranks of the would-be reformers would have reduced the chances of a critical mass forming in favor of any one reform program. The opponents of reform were in comparison highly united; any differences that existed among them as to the nature of the traditional system were relatively minor.

There were other obstacles to reform as well. Any social reform hurts many parties, and arranging compensation for them is notoriously difficult, if only because determining the amount to be paid by each poses a complex collective problem. Among those who would reasonably have expected to lose from a reform were the amins, who might have been forced to relinquish some of their traditional functions and privileges, and aging artisans, for whom adaptation to a new order might have been especially painful. The prospect of receiving appropriate compensation would have seemed dim, and so they would have fought reformist ideas passionately.[72]

Another obstacle to reform was that public opinion did not coalesce to support it. The Husaynid dynasty, which ruled from 1710 to 1881, the waning years of the guilds, came to recognize the necessity of borrowing technology and social institutions from Europe, and even undertook reforms in a few areas; but it does not seem to have appreciated the significance of

---

[71]See Hirschman (1970).

[72]Students of other pre-industrial guilds have also found that the most privileged and the oldest members took the lead in fighting innovations. See, for instance, Landes (1983), pp. 300-302 and 321-328.

the crisis afflicting the guilds.[73] The religious establishment was for the most part downright hostile to reformist efforts, which it perceived as a threat to the existing social hierarchy.[74] And the general public, suspicious as it was of foreign intrusions, was hardly in a mood to encourage experimentation with European economic institutions.[75] It would not be an exaggeration to say that the amins who struggled to preserve the traditional structure of the guilds did so with the consent of the Tunisian people.

V. The Twilight of the Amins

In the absence of significant reform, the guilds of Tunis continued to lose ground to modern industry and gradually disappeared into obscurity. The extent of the decline is hidden, perhaps, by the fact that the traditional suqs are still alive with business. A telling indication of the decline is that the share of the population of Tunis employed in the suqs, or in nearby workshops serving the suqs, has fallen from over 20 percent in 1881 to about one percent today.[76] Another is that the remaining artisans suffer from high disguised unemployment.[77]

As the twentieth century draws to a close, the suqs serve primarily two clienteles. The first consists of tradition-bound urbanites and peasants who are not yet fully integrated into the modern economy. Commodities such as shashiyas, silk shawls *(safsaris)* and traditional Arab shoes are bought exclusively by them. The other major clientele consists of tourists to whom scores of shops now offer a wide range of products, from cheap imitations of traditional metalwork to expensive rugs. The tourist-oriented shops are spread over a number of different suqs, in violation, of course, of the traditional principle of separation among the professions.

This mixing of the professions is only one manifestation of the dras-

---

[73]See Brown (1974), especially chs. 6-10.

[74]See Green (1978).

[75]It is instructive that in an earlier age large segments of the European public had been similarly hostile to modern industrialism. When Turgot, Prime Minister of France in the late eighteenth century, sponsored the abolition of the guilds, people rose against him. He was dismissed, and the guilds were reestablished. See Clune (1943), p. 226.

[76]According to a survey conducted in 1962 by the Société Centrale d'Equipement du Territoire, the total work force stood at 8,000; in the same year, the population of Tunis and its suburbs was around 800,000. Pennec (1964), pp. 292-308, provides an extensive account of numbers in earlier times. His sources reveal that in 1881, when greater Tunis had a population around 100,000, the workforce numbered about 20,000.

[77]Pennec (1964), p. 508.

amins' traditional roles have died out.

tic changes that have befallen the suqs over the last century or so. The anti-competitive spirit has subsided even among the traditional shopkeepers. Merchants catering to tourists are not under its influence at all: they openly advertise and compete for customers. Competition, as one would expect, seems to have intensified inequalities in store sizes: side by side with traditional holes-in-the-wall are huge establishments carrying, like modern stores elsewhere in the city, a wide selection of products and styles. In some of the traditional suqs a division of labor has arisen: certain masters specialize in production, others in sales.[78] And in some suqs production has ceased almost completely. Mirroring this sharp decline in production is the fact that apprentices have all but disappeared.

These changes, which constitute adaptations to the new realities of a partially market-oriented, semi-industrial Tunisian economy, signal the eclipse of the amins' traditional functions. Indeed, in most professions where an amin still exists, the title-holder performs few special duties. The amin of the clothiers, an aged man known for his probity and magnanimity, tries to foster a fraternal atmosphere among the merchants and to settle their disputes with customers — tasks made difficult by the dispersion of the clothiers. From discussions with other merchants, one gathers the impression that although his efforts in these areas are appreciated, he wields little authority in regulating prices or in setting quality standards. The perfumers have an amin who appears to do nothing whatsoever that would justify the title. Revealingly, some of the younger perfumers do not even know that their profession has an amin. The burnous merchants have an unusually young amin, who recently inherited the title from this father. His competitors say that he exploits his position, telling customers that he earned his title because his products are consistently of exceptional quality. The sellers of traditional shoes do not even have an amin, the last one having died several years ago; they do not seem eager to elect another one. The shashiya merchants are also without an amin at present, but they intend to elect one eventually.

One amin who still plays an important role is the amin of the jewelers. As the officially recognized appraiser of jewelry, his shop bustles with activity throughout the day. Because he receives a four percent commission on all sales effected through his office, he is apparently quite rich. The benefits of the position are evident from the fact that it is coveted by other jewelers. The runner-up in the election that followed the death, many years ago, of the previous amin still resents his loss. Claiming that the present amin was chosen because the position had long been in his family, he maintains that

---

[78]For examples, see Pennec (1964), pp. 450-453.

Today, the state solves informational problems (qual./price control)

customers are ill-served by the current arrangement.

The position of the amin has in fact become hereditary in most of the professions where it still exists. Even the well-respected amin of the clothiers effectively inherited the position from his father. In the guilds' days of glory dynasties had been the exception, not the rule. Even before the European intrusions, however, positions of both amin and master were becoming increasingly bestowable: many masters were being barred from becoming amin simply on account of birth, and apprentices who were not a son or an in-law were having a hard time acquiring a mastership.[79] These developments are not at all surprising: many organizations develop a proclivity toward nepotism as they mature. Their members, once they achieve security and learn the ropes, succeed in gaining favors for their kin. The precedents they set lead gradually to a degeneration of the organization. The emergence of hereditary power, which created a sharp division in the ranks of the working class, is regarded as one of the principal causes of the death of the European guilds.[80] It is possible that this same factor would eventually have destroyed the Tunisian guilds as well, had the blows of European capitalism not accomplished the task sooner.

As the guild system weakened and the amins lost control of events, the state repeatedly iterated its belief in the importance and special status of the guilds. It gave credence to these reaffirmations when, as noted earlier, it put the guilds' production regulations into law, and blocked mechanization. As years went by, however, the state could not but notice that the guilds, and with them the city's traditional economy, was dying. It set out to prevent this, partly because handicrafts constitute a symbol of national identity, and partly because the traditional suqs help attract tourists. Recognizing, however, that by themselves the guilds were unlikely to revitalize the suqs, and that the amins had lost their authority, the state chose to take over many of the amins' responsibilities. Thus, an office of handicrafts was created in 1959 to set standards, control quality, and encourage craftsmen to apply traditional motifs to modern objects. A specialized agency now checks weights and measures, and in the investigation of fraud, the police and the civil courts overshadow the amins. Meanwhile, taxes are collected directly by the Ministry of Finance, and serious labor disagreements are arbitrated by the Ministry of Labor.

A couple of facets of the amins' descent into obscurity deserve to be highlighted. First, this did not take place overnight. It happened gradually over

---

[79]See Lallemand (1893), p. 116, and Valensi (1969), p. 388.
[80]See Renard (1918), ch. 7, and Landes (1983), p. 211.

more than a century, first as the amins became increasingly unable to perform their duties, and then as the state officially took over one responsibility
after another. A second fact, seldom appreciated, is that while the amins'
role was diminishing, their title remained exactly the same. This exemplifies
a widespread tendency in the process of institutional atrophy: rarely will the
loss in an institution's economic importance be matched by changes in its
name. This is so because the task of changing a title represents a gargantuan
collective action problem, and also because keeping a title intact serves to
dampen its bearer's sense of loss.

VI. Conclusions

It was suggested in the introduction that the paper would shed light on
three controversies. We are prepared now to take these up directly.

The discussion gives credence to the charge that the guilds' conservatism
played an important role in the decline of Islamic civilization. It does so not
simply by listing restrictive practices that impeded technological change and
organizational adaptations, but by offering, in addition, some reasons as to
why these restrictive practices were maintained for so long.

The analysis also lends support to the thesis that institutions can outlive
the conditions that gave rise to them. The Tunisian guilds' web of customary
rules developed in an era when they seemed to have a secure future, and
when the state was more concerned with stabilizing an almost closed economy
than with maintaining Tunisian competitiveness in a dynamic international
marketplace. But the state did not really alter its policies toward the guild
system until long after it became concerned with the guilds' failure to hold
their own against the nascent industries of Europe. For their part, the guilds
were extremely slow in throwing off their baggage of ancient customs. Under
the leadership of their amins, and with the state's support, they continued
to fight for the old order, even as they lost ground to foreign and domestic
agents of industrialism.

Through their conservatism, the guilds helped delay the technological
and institutional modernization of the Tunisian economy. In the end, however, they were unsuccessful in preventing the economy's adaptation to new
conditions. Modern establishments were created outside the suqs and became
increasingly free to ignore the guilds' age-old restrictions. These establishments prospered, as the guilds continued to lose their glitter. They, and not
the old guilds, became the instruments of Tunisia's struggle to redesign its
economy. This is not to say that the guilds made no adaptations at all. But
these adaptations were too small and came too slowly in relation to the size of
the shocks of the industrial revolution and the speed at which these arrived.

What led, then, to the guilds' decline into obscurity was not their failure to respond. It was, rather, the faintness and slowness of their responses, coupled with the internal competition provided by the new establishments that were better able to take advantage of the emerging economic opportunities.

We come, finally, to the controversy over efforts to bring back the market practices that prevailed during the guilds' golden age, and in particular, to reestablish the amins' authority. It would seem that the revivalist agenda rests on profound misunderstandings about honesty, the perception of fairness, and non-competition.

The impression that traders displayed less dishonesty during the heyday of the guilds than they do now is probably valid. The reason for this difference is not to be found, however, in the relaxation of moral standards. Rather, by the nineteenth century an enforcement mechanism appropriate to Tunis' essentially closed economy was well established, whereas mechanisms suitable to the city's incomparably more complex economy are not yet entirely in place. Among these mechanisms are brand names, warranties, and consumer reports. As the use of such mechanisms spreads, consumer confidence in merchants' honesty will undoubtedly rise. Under current circumstances it is sheer romanticism to expect that the amins would be effective in enforcing honesty.

Fairness is a matter of subjective judgment. No one has ever succeeded in developing a set of universally valid criteria of fairness, and in practice what passes as fair is simply what is customary. It is not surprising that market transactions would have seemed more fair in the old Tunisian economy than in the modern. In pre-modern times, the range of commodities changed very slowly and for most goods demand conditions were rather stable. For these reasons, and because of the guild regulations, prices often remained constant for long periods. Over time, the established prices came to be regarded as fair.

As for non-competition, its damage to the economy is likely to outweigh the presumed benefits associated with the atmosphere of fraternal coexistence that it helps create. On the other side of the balance sheet are a variety of losses: to consumers from higher prices; to workers from the resulting fall in employment; and most important of all, to the economy as a whole from the induced technological and institutional stagnation. The most telling evidence of the long-run harm done by policies that restrict economic competition is given by the Tunisian guilds' inability to withstand the European penetration into their markets. Looked at in this light, the guilds' non-competitive ethic does not appear appropriate to today's Tunisian economy, struggling as it is to learn how to compete in the international marketplace.

As mentioned in the introduction, the government is currently trying to resuscitate the office of the amin, as part of a campaign to reinvigorate the country's traditional handicrafts. According to the government's proposal (most components of which have already been signed into law), each craft is to have an amin appointed by the government itself from among the craftsmen who have good professional and moral reputations.[81] As a knowledgeable agent of the state, the amin is to enforce quality standards and help his fellow craftsmen perfect their art. Interestingly, the government intends to dismiss most of the current amins and replace them with craftsmen who are able to follow written orders and file written reports. Since this will facilitate the government's involvement with the suqs, it seems that the government plans to take a more active interest in the production and distribution of handicrafts than it has in the recent past.

The government seems especially anxious to ensure that handicrafts be practiced solely by artisans steeped in traditional Tunisian craftsmanship. To this end, it has decreed that from now on working in the suqs will be subject to certification, and that licensed craftsmen will have to abide by the aesthetic guidelines set by the amin and other experts. On the other hand, and in sharp departure from the old order of the guilds, craftsmen will not be constrained as to production methods, which means that they will be free to use machines. Moreover, they will be on their own in procuring inputs. Very reasonably, the government will allow the craftsmen to compete with one another, at least along the cost dimension. At the same time, it wishes to recreate, through the offices of the amin, the non-competitive, fraternal atmosphere of the old guilds, in the hope that this would help raise the quality of handicrafts. However, the opposite is entirely possible, since fraternity facilitates collusion, which in turn suppresses the drive to perfect.

The government also expects the amin to help restore consumer confidence by eliminating deceit and exploitation. The argument presented suggests that this expectation will probably be frustrated, given the complexity, dynamism, and openness of the modern Tunisian economy. At any rate, no details are given as to how the amin will address this task. It remains to be seen how tomorrow's amin will differ from his legendary ancestor.

---

[81] The most important law that has been passed in connection with the current campaign to save traditional handicrafts is Law No. 83-106 (December 3, 1983). As of July 1986, a second law, dealing specifically with the amin, was pending. In the intervening years, three ministries, namely Tourism and Handicrafts, the National Economy, and Social Affairs, have issued various decrees pertaining to details.

References

Akerlof, George, 1970. "The Market for 'Lemons': Quality Uncertainty and the Market Mechanism." *Quarterly Journal of Economics*, Vol. 84, No. 3, August, pp. 488-500.

Atger, Arthur, 1909. *Les Corporations Tunisiennes*. Paris: Arthur Rousseau.

Baer, Gabriel, 1964. *Egyptian Guilds in Modern Times*. Jerusalem: Israel Oriental Society.

_____, 1970a. "Administrative, Economic and Social Functions of Turkish Guilds." *International Journal of Middle East Studies*, Vol. 1, No. 1, January, pp. 1-23.

_____, 1970b. "Monopolies and Restrictive Practices of Turkish Guilds." *Journal of the Economic and Social History of the Orient*, Vol. 13, Part 2, April, pp. 145-165.

_____, 1982. "The Structure of Turkish Guilds and its Significance for Ottoman Social History." In his *Fellah and Townsman in the Middle East*, pp. 193-211. London: Cass.

Brenner, Reuven, 1983. *History — The Human Gamble*. Chicago: University of Chicago Press.

Brown, L. Carl, 1974. *The Tunisia of Ahmad Bey, 1837-1855*. Princeton: Princeton University Press.

Brunschvig, Robert, 1934. "Tunis." In *Encyclopedia of Islam*, Vol. 4, pp. 837-844.

Cahen, Claude and Mohamed Talbi, 1971. "Hisba." In *Encyclopedia of Islam*, 2nd ed., Vol. 3, pp. 485-489.

Chater, Khélifa, 1978. "La Ville Tunisienne au XIXè Siècle: Théorie et Réalités." *Les Cahiers de Tunisie*, Vol. 26, No. 103-104, pp. 85-108.

Clune, George, 1943. *The Medieval Gild System*. Dublin: Browne and Nolan.

Essid, Yassine, 1988. *Les Ecrivains Grecs et la Genèse de la Pensée Economique: Les Developpements Médiévaux Chez les Auteurs Arabes*, 2 vols. Thèse de doctorat d'état, Université de Paris I, Sorbonne.

Gerber, Haim, 1976. "Guilds in Seventeenth-Century Anatolian Bursa." *Asian and African Studies*, Vol. 11, No. 1, Summer, pp. 59-86.

Gibb, Hamilton A.R. and Harold Bowen, 1950. *Islamic Society and the West*, Vol. 1. Oxford: Oxford University Press.

Green, Arnold H., 1978. *The Tunisian Ulama, 1873-1915*. Leiden: E.J. Brill.

Hannan, Michael T. and John Freeman, 1984. "Structural Inertia and Organizational Change." *American Sociological Review*, Vol. 49, No. 2, April, pp. 149-164.

Hirschman, Albert O., 1970. *Exit, Voice, and Loyalty*. Cambridge: Harvard University Press.

İnalcık, Halil, 1969. "Capital Formation in the Ottoman Empire." *Journal of Economic History*, Vol. 19, No. 1, pp. 97-140.

Klein, Benjamin, Robert G. Crawford and Armen A. Alchian, 1978. "Vertical Integration, Appropriable Rents, and the Competitive Contracting Process." *Journal of Law and Economics*, Vol. 21, No. 2, October, pp. 297-326.

Kuran, Timur, 1987a. "Chameleon Voters and Public Choice." *Public Choice*, Vol. 53, No. 1, pp. 53-78.

_____, 1987b. "Preference Falsification, Policy Continuity and Collective Conservatism." *Economic Journal,* Vol. 97, No. 387, pp. 642-665.

_____, 1988. "The Tenacious Past: Theories of Personal and Collective Conservatism." *Journal of Economic Behavior and Organization,* Vol. 10, No. 2, pp. 143-171.

Lallemand, Charles, 1893. *Tunis et Ses Environs.* Algiers: Gervais Courtellemont.

Landes, David S., 1983. *Revolution in Time.* Cambridge: Harvard University Press.

Lapidus, Ira Marvin, 1967. *Muslim Cities in the Later Middle Ages.* Cambridge: Harvard University Press.

Le Tourneau, Roger, 1957. *Les Villes Musulmanes de l'Afrique du Nord.* Algiers: La Maison des Livres.

Lewis, Bernard, 1937. "The Islamic Guilds." *Economic History Review,* Vol. 8, No. 1, November, pp. 20-37.

Macgill, Thomas, 1811. *An Account of Tunis: Of its Government, Manners, Customs, and Antiquities; Especially of its Productions, Manufactures, and Commerce.* Glasgow: Longman, Hurst, Rees, Orme, and Brown.

Mantran, Robert, 1962. *Istanbul Dans la Seconde Moitié du XVIIe Siècle.* Paris: Librairie Adrien Maisonneuve.

North, Douglass C., 1981. *Structure and Change in Economic History.* New York: Norton.

Olson, Mancur, 1965. *The Logic of Collective Action.* Cambridge: Harvard University Press.

_____, 1982. *The Rise and Decline of Nations.* New Haven: Yale University Press.

Payre, Gabriel, 1940. *Les Amines en Tunisie.* Paris: Comité de l'Afrique Française.

Pellissier, E., 1843. *Exploration Scientifique de l'Algérie pendant les Années 1840, 1841, 1842.* Paris: Imprimerie Impériale.

Pennec, Pierre, 1964. *Les Transformations des Corps de Métiers de Tunis.* Tunis: Institut des Sciences Économiques Appliquées – Afrique du Nord, March (mimeographed).

Posner, Richard A., 1980. "A Theory of Primitive Society with Special Reference to Law." *Journal of Law and Economics,* Vol. 23, No. 1, April, pp. 1-53.

Raymond, André, 1974. *Artisans et Commercants au Caire au XVIIIe Siècle,* 2 vols. Damascus: Institut Français de Damas.

Renard, Georges, 1918. *Guilds in the Middle Ages.* London: G. Bell and Sons.

Roover, Raymond de, 1958. "The Concept of the Just Price: Theory and Economic Policy." *Journal of Economic History,* Vol. 18, No. 4, December, pp. 418-438.

Scherer, F.M., 1980. *Industrial Market Structure and Economic Performance,* 2nd ed. Boston: Houghton Mifflin.

Sebag, Paul, 1951. *La Tunisie.* Paris: Editions Sociales.

Sladen, Douglas, 1906. *Carthage and Tunis.* London: Hutchinson.

Société Centrale d'Equipement du Territoire, 1963. *L'Artisanat Tunisien,* 2 vols. Tunis: Secrétariat au Plan et aux Finances.

264 T. Kuran

Taeschner, Franz, 1965. "Futuwwa." In *Encyclopedia of Islam*, 2nd ed., Vol. 2, pp. 961-969.
Tlili, Béchir, 1974. *Etudes d'Histoire Sociale Tunisienne du XIXe Siècle.* Tunis: l'Université de Tunis.
Valensi, Lucette, 1969. "Islam et Capitalisme: Production et Commerce des Chéchias en Tunisie et en France aux XVIIIe et XIXe Siècles." *Revue d'Histoire Moderne et Contemporaine*, Vol. 16, pp. 376-400.
Zghal, Abdelkader and Fredj Stambouli, 1974. "La Vie Urbaine dans le Maghreb Precolonial." *Revue Tunisienne des Sciences Sociales*, Vol. 11, No. 36-39, pp. 221-242.

Chapter 9

EDUCATIONAL CHANGE AND THE ULAMA
IN THE 19TH AND EARLY 20TH CENTURIES*

Abdeljabbar Bsaies

I. Introduction

In 1867, in his essay entitled *Aqwam Al Massalik*[1] the great Tunisian reformer Khayr-al-Din sought to prove that the success of Europe in all fields was due to the proper functioning of institutions appropriately adapted to suit their time. Drawing attention to the need to do the same in Tunisia, in his essay he invited Tunisian officialdom to accept the reforms inspired by the European model.

Among the various reforms advocated by Khayr-al-Din, those related to education had a prominent place in his program. He, together with others, realized that Tunisia's educational institutions, at least as they functioned at the time, would not allow the country which was then in a process of relatively pronounced economic decay and decline to adapt successfully to the pressures exerted by Europe. Khayr-al-Din's efforts at persuasion were focused on the country's intellectual elite, the *Ulama*, who because of their great influence within Tunisian society, had to be favorable, or at least neutral, to the proposed reforms for them to have any chance of being implemented [Green (1978, p. 107)]. Given the decayed state of its social structure, and the degree to which it was being shaken by European penetration, Khayr-al-Din's initiative, which he would attempt to put into practice once in power in 1873, was long overdue.

This was the case because the country had not yet made the necessary adjustments to the changes to which the economy had been subjected since the first third of the 19th century. More specifically, concerning the system

---

*I would like to express my gratitude to Yassine Essid, Jeffrey Nugent and Mustapha Nabli for their comments, suggestions and encouragement during the preparation of this paper. I am also grateful to M. Azabou, L. Bouzaiane and L. Doghri who read an earlier version and offered useful comments.

[1] Khayr-al-Din was born in 1820 of Circassian origin. He arrived in Tunisia in 1940 after a stay in Turkey. Among his writings *Akwam Al Massalik* is the best contribution, written in Arabic and published in 1867. The introduction to this work was published by Brown (1967).

of education in general and the al-Zitouna[2] in particular, very little had been done to adapt its content to the requirements of modern education. The need for the latter had been felt ever since the country's first experience with mechanized industry in the 1840's, whose setting up and functioning had necessitated recourse to foreign manpower. The existing educational system was so solidly embedded in the overall social system that it was practically impossible to consider substantial modifications in either content or method.

Even later when it became increasingly obvious that things could no longer remain as they were, those responsible for the educational system, the Ulama maintained their opposition to any reform. While it could be argued that until the first third of the 19th century there was a correspondence between the educational system and the needs of Tunisian society, by the second half of the century and increasingly thereafter, that correspondence became weaker and weaker. While the usefulness of the Ulama in preserving the system could be acknowledged as long as that correspondence prevailed, such a position could no longer be justified once that correspondence broke down. As early as 1840, signs of change were discernible and some Tunisian reformers set about proposing reforms. Scorning the proposed changes, the Ulama-dominated institution of higher education, the al-Zitouna, persisted in maintaining tradition in both content and method of instruction.

While these general features of recent Tunisian history are well known, there has been little analysis of the reasons for the observed lack of change and institutional rigidity. The aim of the present paper, therefore, is to explain the intransigence of Tunisian educational institutions by applying the principles of collective action. The analysis centers on the important role played by one particular interest group, the Ulama, in the resistance to change. Section II, which follows, describes the prevailing educational system and the Ulama and assesses the success of this particular group in collective action in terms of group characteristics. Section III describes the educational and institutional equilibrium prevailing in Tunisia prior to the mid-19th century and analyses the demand for and supply of institutional change in the form of the educational system from the mid-19th century to the early 20th century. Section IV deals with the demand for change and its relative weakness. Section V focuses on the role of the Ulama in blocking institutional change and maintaining the status quo. Some conclusions are given in Section VI.

---

[2] Al-Zitouna is the name of the largest Mosque in the Center of Tunis. It was also the site of higher education.

II. The Educational System and the Ulama in the Early 19th Century

In order to explain the role of the Ulama in the early 19th century (and even much earlier) and the sense in which it can be considered an interest group, we first present some important characteristics of Tunisia's educational, social and productive systems. Until the establishment of the Protectorate in 1881, Tunisian education, all of which was in Arabic, was divided into three levels: elementary, intermediate and higher. Elementary education which took place in the *Kouttab* or Quranic Schools consisted primarily of learning the Quran, and in that process of course, the basics of reading, writing and arithmetic [Ben Mustapha (1908)]. Intermediate education was open to those who had been able to memorize a certain number of chapters (surats) of the Quran. The bulk of such education was related to Islam and was transmitted either in the *medersas* (religious high schools) or in mosques and their annexes.

Finally, higher education took place in the great Mosque of al-Zitouna, which carried the rank of a university. At this level many courses were given almost all of which were related to religious sciences [Kraïem (1973) and Zaouche (1932)]. Among these courses were those related to jurisprudence (*fikh*), the Quran, commentaries and explanation (*tafsir*), studies of the Oneness of God (*tawhid*), and the origin and basis of Islamic laws (*Oussou*). Others, like grammar and morphology, could be considered tools for engaging in the former. The university issued two types of diplomas: the *Tatwi*, roughly equivalent to a bachelor's degree, and the *al-alimiya* or professorate.

The system had functioned in this way for centuries and had undergone very few changes. Its continuity was ensured by the leading role of those called the *Ulama*, Ulama being the plural of *Alim*. An *Alim*, as Green (1978, ch. 1) puts it, is "one who is versed in the religious." Since this definition is fairly general, for practical purposes it is easier to identify an *alim* by the religious functions he exercises [Green (1978, ch. 1)].[3] Specifically, an *alim* may serve as a *cadhi* (judge), *mufti* or *bash mufti* (jurisconsult-interpreter and major interpreter of law), *sheikh-al-Islam*, *mudariss* (professor), *imam* (prayer leader), *adl* (notary), or *wakil* (lawyer-agent, trustee-lawyer). The several functions [Green (1978, ch. 1)] can be grouped into three rather distinct categories of activities: justice or *sharia*, education, and worship, each designed to satisfy the needs of the population in a particular field.

For example, justice was the task of *cadhis, muftis* and *bashmuftis*. In

---

[3]Green (1978) is a main source on the Ulama despite the fact that he covered only a part of the period under consideration in this paper.

Tunis each of these professions was divided into two according to membership in the main rites practiced in Tunisia, namely, the Malikite and the Hanefite.[4] Each sect had its own president, vice-president, *cadhi*, *muftis*, clerics and a council or *mijliss*, a kind of supreme authority which played a consultative role to the political leaders, the Beys[5] or rulers of that period. In the provinces, the same structure was found in the larger towns, but in the villages, there were only *cadhis* to dispense justice.

For its personnel the educational system relied on the *mutawiin*, i.e., the holders of the *tatwii*, and on the *mudarissun*, of the first and second class and, later on also, of the third class. The *mutawiin* gave courses on grammar and the *hadith* (the Prophet's Words). Their status was close to that of adjunct professors. The *mudarissun* assumed responsibility for the more essential courses and had regular faculty status and remuneration.

Finally, the functions related to religious services such as the celebration of the five daily prayers were performed at either simple mosques or sermon mosques (jemaâ).[6] In practice, only the Imams of the great mosques could be considered members of the Ulama. Although some members of the Ulama functioned as notaries or *adl*, the exercise of which was made possible only as a result of the acknowledged acquisition of religious erudition, a monopoly of the al-Zitouna, most of the Ulama were involved in the exercise of the three more basic religious functions.

For centuries, the Ulama coalesced and strengthened until they came to be recognized as a distinct social group. What was the basic feature or characteristic of the Ulama as a group? According to Green (1978, ch. 2) they constituted neither a class in the ordinary sociological sense nor, given their social mobility,[7] a caste [Green (1978, p. 43)] nor even a distinct occupational group. Nevertheless, they exercised considerable influence and, given Tunisia's social structure, it can be asserted that the Ulama represented an elite situated near the top of the social hierachy.

----

[4] Within the Sunni tradition of Islam, there are four rites, each based on the codification of a major theologian, and carry his name, i.e., Maliki, Hanefi, Chaffai, Hanbali. In Tunisia the dominant rite is the Maliki, but the Hanefi one is also present.

[5] The Beys belonged to the Husseinite Dynasty whose rule began in 1705 with Hussein Bey. The last Bey was deposed in 1957 shortly after Tunisia became a Republic.

[6] In Islam, a collective prayer is held on Friday in a mosque, and is preceded by a sermon (khotba) by the prayer leader.

[7] This aspect of mobility will be discussed later and its limits shown. Green (1978, p. 91) suggests that it was lateral.

That status can be justified by applying certain criteria believed to form the basis for social stratification, namely: family origin, erudition, piety, official responsibility and wealth. In all these respects, the members of the Ulama were generally highly respected in society. They were the learned; they occupied the positions of highest responsability (other than political) in the society, such as professors, judges and imams. Likewise, their ancestry made them eminent aristocrats (*ayan*). Finally, most of them were wealthy.

From the perspective of collective action theory, this homogeneity of background should make them successful in organizing and executing collective action. In addition, they shared many of the other characteristics identified by Olson (1965, 1982) and Hardin (1982) as being favorable to success in collective action, such as relatively small size, long duration of association, proximity and concentration, each such characteristic facilitating communication among group members.

Brown (1974) provides valuable information on those characteristics of the Ulama. While precise numbers are not available, he cites an estimate of 143 for the Ulama who died between 1814 and 1872.[8] He also says that the number of permanent staff members at al-Zitouna was 40 and the total number of teachers there was 102. As a result, one might speculate that relatively strictly defined, at any time the membership of the Ulama would have numbered not much more than one hundred. This made for a relatively small group most of whom should have been able to know each other rather well. From a sample of 105 for whom the information was available, 59 were born in Tunis, and 74 spent all or most of their careers there. In addition, of the 59 Ulama born in Tunis, 49 had fathers who were also Ulama, and of a total of 96 Ulama there were 71 whose fathers were from the religious establishment. These figures clearly indicate the relative homogeneity of background, the long-term association and geographic concentration of the group. While persons from outside of Tunis were permitted entry to the Ulama, the length of the educational process assured their smooth assimilation into the group.

In order to reinforce their homgeneity over time the Ulama came to adopt a number of behavioral rules and norms of conduct. The rules and norms allow for the application of selective incentives when necessary. Indeed, with respect to appearance, the Ulama had their own way to dress [Green (1978, p. 50), Brown (1974, p. 161)] which distinguished them from the rest of the population. There was a proper way of conversing and behaving to force respect and thereby to maintain their monopolistic position with respect to status and the ability to perform the most important functions in society.

---

[8] The data are based on biographies by Bin Diyaf (1964).

According to Brown (1974, p. 161):

> The 'ulama prized strict observance of traditionally established behavior patterns. An 'alim was expected to live an exemplary life in conformity with the precepts of Islam, free of scandal. He should affect a certain gravity, avoid the popular cafes, and not let himself be seen in public laughing, speaking in a loud voice, or eating. In his speech he was expected not only to avoid the trivial and the evanescent in favor of weightier matters but also to adopt a more formal, classical Arabic than that used by the man in the street. The ideal 'alim adorned his discussion with appropriate citations from the Quran, hadith, and principal religious authorities. The ability to turn a phrase was highly valued, and the 'alim who could write poetry and was familiar with the secular Arabic literature earned additional esteem. An elaborate code of *politesse* governed his daily contact with others and with his fellow 'ulama.

Moreover, they were distinguished from the rest of the population by some important privileges. For example, in addition to their relatively high remuneration, they received substantial grants and exemptions from levies and taxes. They married, *noblesse oblige*, into the wealthiest families of the country. Lastly, only rarely were the Ulama not also landlords.[9] They were landowners not only through direct inheritance but also through marriage, land purchases, and/or grants from the Beys. These sources of income and wealth allowed them a life of luxury complete with sumptuous residences in the city of Tunis or its suburbs, servants and means of transport. From the social point of view, their status and its various manifestations were considered appropriate considering both the esteem professed for the erudite and particularly for the religious among them and their own *esprit de corps*. In fact, the members of the Ulama were conscious of the role they played in society and expressed their intention to continue in it. One of them quoted by Green (1978, p. 51) stated that "it is the Ulama who personify the religion of Islam in Tunisia". Another member asserted that "one of the goals of Islamic education is that of producing leaders who should be lights to rightly guide the *Umma* (i.e., the Islamic community)" [Green (1978, p. 51)]. Hence, it is clear that the members of the Ulama expected to play leadership roles.

Ulama members also considered themselves to be the protectors and guardians of the holy laws from the attacks of both foreigners and internal heretics.[10] The best means for ensuring this defense was to perpetuate tradition through, among other things, the education dispensed. In this respect,

---

[9]See Green (1978, p. 50) and Berque (1972).

[10]Among the latter were the moatazilites who were rethinking the principles of Islam on a rationalist basis.

the membership perpetuated itself and secured its dominance. It became the only source of knowledge, and until 1875 the entire educational system was within its domain. Moreover, the authority of the Ulama was such that all intellectual activity was either their own achievement or emanated from them. Therefore, they had such a quasi-monopoly on intellectual production that reform initiatives could not even be contemplated if they would not conform to existing values and rules. This was the case in particular of the aforementioned great reformer Khayr-al-Din.

Although unlike guild members the Ulama had neither a formal organization nor formal rules strictly enforced and acknowledged by all members, they did undertake certain practices which allowed them to perpetuate group cohesion. Cohesion and continuity were assured essentially in two ways: the static content of education and the practice of dynastic clientelism. In the former respect, only ancient books were utilized as reference books and textbooks and memorization was the primary intellectual faculty used [Kraiem (1971, vol. II, p. 166-167)]. Examinations, for example, were based entirely on the command over or the reproduction of knowledge, a process which naturally excluded critical inquiry and the consideration or investigation of unorthodox ideas. As a result, any teacher who dared to put forth doctrines which were not part of the acknowledged line would likely be ostracised by his peers and his career would be likely to suffer [Zaouche (1932, p. 18)].

With respect to dynastic clientelism, the members of the Ulama assured the cohesion and continuity of the group through self-reproduction, Ulama members being the sole possessors of knowledge and beneficiaries of privileged positions. Even though the corps was, as we noted earlier, characterized by a certain degree of social mobility, in fact from early times there is evidence of the dynastic transference of posts in quasi-hereditary ways.[11]. Such was the case of families such as: Bayram, Bin-el-Kouja, Ennaifar, Mohsen, and Baroudi [Green (1978, ch. 3, p. 77), Abdelmoula (1971, p. 57)]. On the other hand, for people not belonging to those families, the access to a somewhat important post, such as "mudariss" or "cadhi", could be obtained only either indirectly through patronage[12] from a dignitary of the regime who was in

---

[11]Particularly for the 1st class professorships, of which the provincials (or Afaki) were practically excluded, see Green (1978), ch. 3

[12]Green (1978, p. 90) writes: "Such a relationship was particularly important for *Afaki* (provincials) who regularly became the protegés of influential kinsmen or countrymen in the capital or of sympathetic Tunisi (from Tunis) dignitaries. Indeed, virtually every provincial Sheikh, who succeeded in penetrating into the capital's Ulama corps, had a patron who was partly responsible for his success."

good terms with the Ulama, or directly from a member the Ulama. Although considerations of personal merit were not excluded, in this way the Ulama managed to master the crucial problem of recruitment and renewal.

Finally, another means of consolidation for the Ulama was their relationship with the political leaders. Although remunerated by the government, owing to their high status and positions held, the Ulama had been able to preserve their autonomy. Moreover, being aware of the extent the country was attached to values of Islam, they were able to exert pressure on the leadership to such an extent that the latter was obliged to seek the favor of the Ulama if it wanted to exercise efficient control over its subjects. Thus, the different Beys, often themselves being very religious [Ben Youssef (1900), Bin Diyaf (1964)], had reinforced the Ulama's importance within the social body in different ways. First, they attended to the construction of religious buildings (mosques, mesjeds, medersas) in order to prove their religious zeal. Second, they listened to the advice of the Ulama and consulted them either individually or by summoning the Council of Justice (Sharia Mijliss) before taking important decisions [Green (1978), p. 56]. In return, the Ulama assured the Beys of their support either in domestic crises, such as in the case of the 1864 revolt,[13] or foreign ones such as in Ahmed Bey's relations with Europe and Turkey [Tlili (1974, p. 486)]. These relations with the Beys provided the Ulama with positions of preeminence within the ruling system itself and reinforced their social status.

III. The Old Equilibrium

The status of the Ulama was also maintained through the support of various other economic groups and especially the craft guilds. This can be explained by examining the state of the Tunisian economy in general in the early 19th century, and the status of the bazaar in particular.

Most historians admit that Tunisia was at the time a backward country economically. Agriculture was archaic [Kraïem (1971, vol. II, p. 20)]. Even over long periods of time, it experienced very few innovations either in cultivation processes or in the techniques of production. In the existing conditions "the art of agriculture was acquired through observation and heredity" [Kraïem (1971, vol. II, p. 25)].

Handicrafts, although better organized, were characterized by production techniques which had progressed remarkably little. While the division of labor in most of the crafts (*chechias, belgha,* weaving, jewelry, metal work,

---

[13]This revolt followed an increase in taxes that became too heavy for the countryside. It was led by Ali Ben Ghdahem. See Tlili (1976, pp. 541-548).

etc.) was relatively advanced, it was not sufficient to generate the factory system. The productive, commercial and social activities and the internal and external relations of each guild were highly regulated by an *amin* [Kuran (1988)] who was selected by a court consisting of guild members. Guild members were distinguished by a professional hierarchy, consisting of master artisans at the top, followed by the companions, semi-companions, workers and finally the apprentices. Given the fact that promotion was strictly internal, this structure implied that training took place on the job. That system was sufficiently satisfactory considering that the prevailing technical processes were so rudimentary that one had only to see them to learn them. Training thus had a traditional nature, and practically all crafts required only that form which met their needs.

As for the government, its needs for trained personnel were limited since it was poorly administered and for centuries many of its vital revenue-raising activities had been rented out to private tax farmers [Azabou and Nugent (1988)]. Outside of government, the level and living was sufficiently low that, as backward as it was, the crafts sector was capable of satisfying most of the needs of the various social groups and classes. Indeed, there was a rural-urban equilibrium which had assured both relative prosperity and a favorable trade balance until the first third of the 19th century. Some wealth was accumulated by merchants, merchant-producers and producers themselves, especially among the few families who were able to become well-established in the various crafts and to become notables (*Beldi*). Nevertheless these leading bourgeois families acquiesced to the values and life style promoted by the Ulama and, indeed, were closely allied to them both materially and spiritually. It is interesting to note, for example, that many marriages occured between members of the Ulama and families of master craftsmen in the leading guilds (*chaouchis*, perfume-merchants, silk merchants, jewellers, and *belgagis*) [Green (1978, Appendix I)]. The close relationship between the Ulama and the bazaar also stemmed from their common perceptions of society including the importance of stability. The primary means of implementing these objectives was by demonstrating the kind of exemplary behavior fitting to their status as an elite and *Beldi*.[14] In all aspects of social life, including the belief in Islam, tradition and custom (*el aouyed*), and the maintenance of norms concerning the way of life, the bazaar's leaders joined with the Ulama in playing a leading role in the defense of traditional values. The result was

---

[14] *Beldi* means literally someone from the city, and is opposite to *Afaki*, someone from "far away". In practice, *Beldi* came to mean the urban bourgeois. As for *Ayan* it designated the aristocratic or upper-class urban.

a sort of symbiosis between the Ulama and the bazaar in the reproduction of society and consequently of themselves.

That alliance was further reinforced by the need to confront the effects of European penetration and to protest against "the foreigner". On the one hand, fearing the loss of their monopolisitc positions in the supply of education, the Ulama saw the reforms, the most important of which were Western-inspired, as a means whereby the acquired values of Islam would be undermined. On the other hand, the bazaar, unable to compete effectively with European products, vowed an outspoken hostility to the "foreigner". Neither group knew how, or wanted, to adapt to the new situation in which the country found itself in the mid-19th century. In the face of those changes, the handicrafts sector was powerless to respond to the economic pressures and the al-Zitouna openly resisted any educational reforms.

IV. New Pressures, Challenges and the Demand for Institutional Change

By the mid-19th century, however, the economic, social, and military pressures from abroad were increasingly serious. The guilds were declining [Kuran (1988)] and many of the traditional activities were losing their competitive advantages. New methods of production and distribution were being introduced, in large part through the burgeoning foreign communities (Maltese, Italian, French and English). Quite naturally, the foreigners brought with them new life styles in terms of dress, architecture and culture. The foreign powers demonstrated increasing arrogance and willingness to interfere in the affairs of the country. With the French occupation of Algeria in 1830 the western borders were threatened. With the reestablishment of direct Ottoman control over Libya, the eastern borders were also rendered insecure. Increased competition, on one hand, among the European powers, and, on the other hand, between Europe and the Ottoman Empire left Tunisia in a very awkward and fragile position.

These new pressures posed a number of challenges to the country and to its rulers. It was obvious to many that the country had to adapt in a number of ways in order to be able to cope with the problems posed. This would have to translate into a demand for institutional change in different fields, including of course education. Following Ruttan and Hayami (1984), these pressures would seem to constitute a demand for institutional change. In the case of education, the new needs of the socio-economic system for trained people became the driving force behind the demand for educational reform.

The movement for reform started with the accession to power of Ahmed Bey who ruled from 1837 to 1855. Much impressed by the success of Europe

[Ganiage (1968, p. 98-99), Brown (1974)], and following the lead of Muhamed Ali in Egypt, Ahmed Bey undertook to modernize the country. Preoccupied primarily by political and military problems, Ahmed Bey started with the army, providing it with the necessary equipment produced locally. He created modern manufactures[15] for which he had to import the needed machinery and specialized manpower, including engineers, technicians and skilled workers [Ganiage (1968, p. 157), Mahjoub (1983, p. 95-96)]. Also, in order to realize his program he recruited foreign officers to reorganize the army and run the Military School or Polytechnic of Bardo that was created in 1838. Its curriculum included mathematics, languages, history, geography, topography and military arts, all of which were taught by foreigners. Nationals were entrusted only with teaching Arabic and Arab literature.

The introduction for the first time of modern manufactures in the country was a major innovation. Despite their eventual failure and abandonment, the experience called the attention of reformers such as Bin Diyaf[16] to this new type of production system. The creation of the Military School of Bardo was also a genuine innovation in that it constituted the first formal education in the country produced outside of the religious establishment and containing a modern curriculum [Smida (1970, p. 292-293)].

While the school's creation had the appearance of achieving a very specific objective, the training of military personnel, in fact, Ahmed Bey intended it as a stepping stone with which to renovate the whole educational system including the reorganization of al-Zitouna. Indeed, the *moallaqa* reforms of 1842 attempted to reorganize al-Zitouna so as to make it capable of training the skilled personnel for the new and expanding needs of the Bey's administration [Smida (1970, p. 29)]. In practice, the reforms were limited to renovating the administrative structure of al-Zitouna[17] since Ahmad Bey could not go so far as a complete restructuring of its educational programs. No matter how much of a reformist he might be, he had to take into account the social realities around him. Hence, he could not openly call into question an institution which was so deeply rooted in society, especially considering his dependence on the support of the Ulama in his opposition to the Sublime

---

[15] Among these were manufactures of military cloth, leather, grain milling, oil extraction and foundries for cannon powder. [Mahjoub (1983, pp. 95-99)].

[16] See Bin Biyaf (1964), a contemporary of these 19th Century events.

[17] According to the *Moallaqa*, the al-Zitouna would be controlled by a higher administrative and pedagogical council, the number of teachers, their salaries and recruitment being subject to regulations. See Tlili (1974, p. 440) and Smida (1970, pp. 294-295)

Porte which was pressing him to adopt the Tanzimats[18] or reforms of 1839 that were applied in Turkey [Tlili (1974, pp. 487, 489 and 494)].

That reform was considered as the beginning of a reformist movement which would intensify in the future. Despite its limited scope, the reform was well received by a good number of intellectuals who were sensitive to the aspirations of some segments of society and saw change as a necessity for Arab and Muslim countries. Various reform movements were active in different Arab countries during this period, e.g., those promoted by al-Afghani and Tahtaoui in Egypt and the Tanzimats in Turkey, Syria and Lebanon. All these movements, generally designated by Nahdha, were a response to the European challenge. Tunisia was no exception in this regard and reformist ideas were making headway, although with less vigor than in the Middle East. This desire for reform was based on the reformers' belief that the traditional mechanism of social regulation had broken down, requiring the creation of a new order.

The creation of the Military School of Bardo and the reforms of 1842 were clear indications that a genuine reformist movement existed in Tunisia. In this connection Tlili (1974, p. 496) wrote (our translation):

> Thus the reform of the Zaitounian educational system, the efforts deployed by Sheikh Ibrahim al-Riahi for renewing traditional teaching methods, the encouragements by Ahmed Bey or other Tunisian dignitaries to educational institutions, traditional and modern, the frequent visits to al-Zitouna and the Polytechnic of Bardo by Ahmed Bey and his ministers, among other facts, were preparing the mutation of Tunisian society and consequently the creation of a new social group in favor of the adaptation of the traditional social system to the new requirements of change.

This movement was composed of two groups favorable to reform. The first included persons close to Ahmed Bey, and who were reinforced by new trainees of the School of Bardo [Tlili (1974), p. 450]. Some of this group's illustrous members were Ahmed Bin Diyaf, Mustapha Sahib al-Taba, Hassouna al-Murali and Mustapha Agha. The second group came from al-Zitouna and included those who were convinced of the necessity of change. The most famous of these, on account of his rank and piety, was Sheikh Ibrahim al-

---

[18] The Sublime Porte refers to the center of power, i.e., the locus of government of the Ottoman Empire situated in Istanbul. The Tanzimats were a kind of Organic Charter for reorganizing the political and judicial institutions of the Empire. The reforms were based on a liberal ideology and a modernist approach. The Charter distinguished between the religious and judiciary, the political and spiritual, and recognized the equality of all subjects with respect to the law and liberties. The Tanzimats were followed by judicial, penal, civil, commercial and maritime codes [Tlili (1974, pp. 377-388].

Riahi. Another important member was Sheikh Qabadou whose influence on Khayr-al-Din, a student of his at the School of Bardo, was crucial. Other modernists included Mohamad Bayrem, Ahmed Belkhodja, Salem Bouhajib and Mohamed Senoussi [Smida (1970), p. 296]. There was a perfect symbiosis between the two groups who shared the common conviction of the necessity of modernization but at the same time also the importance of preserving its Islamic foundation. They considered that what came from the West, and was not contrary to the precepts of Islam, could be used in order to reinforce the potentialities of the country in all fields. The reformers were particularly interested in the adoption of some foreign institutions in the fields of government organization, and the introduction of the sciences and modern methods of education. In that respect, and in addition to the creation of the School of Bardo and the reforms of 1842, the activities of the foreign religious missionaries were welcomed. The missionaries provided a modern type of education on the European model[19] for both Europeans and Tunisians; by 1852 there were about 15 such schools [Tlili (1974), p. 446]. Ahmad Bey encouraged them by awarding subsidies.

In terms of the demand for institutional change, these attempts at reform call for a number of remarks. First, there seems to have been no meaningful action from the organized private sector in favor of reform. As shown by Kuran (1988), the guilds themselves had failed to adapt and to become demanders for new skills to be trained by the educational system. As shown below, they even became allied with the Ulama who, as the monopolistic suppliers of traditional education, managed to block all reforms. Those new private sector activities needing trained people did not organize to push for reforms for many reasons. These demanders were probably quite dispersed geographically, consisting of both foreigners and Tunisian nationals, making them heterogeneous in background. Moreover, they could "exit" by calling upon foreign technicians and personnel much more easily than to exercise "voice" and collective action for reform. In any case, the sector did not develop sufficiently to allow for any successful collective action. This may be contrasted with the case of the mountains of Lebanon where according to Huxley (1984) the mechanization of silk was already sufficiently strong by the middle of the 19th century to generate demands for the reform of education.

Second, the dominant source of demand for change was the public sector. Indeed, it was the needs for modernizing the army and the administration

---

[19]The first European educational establishment was created in 1845 by Abbe Bourgade. Other schools were created by missionaries, later on mainly by Italians.

which most stimulated the interest of the rulers in changing the educational system. As a result, there were no other groups or coalitions pressuring the rulers to implement reforms and helping to neutralize the opposition of the Ulama to institutional change. Even in such an autocratic system and even though the government itself was a party to the supply of modern education, it could not ignore the interests of the powerful and influential Ulama.

V. The Ulama, Resistance to Change and the Fossilization of the Educational Institutions

In his 1867 essay analyzing the causes of Tunisian decadence Khayr-al-Din first noted the lack of change and adaptation to the new conditions of the century. He first blamed the Ulama "whose great ignorance is one of the causes of decline" and then added:

> Most of our Ulama who are entrusted with the twofold mission of safeguarding the spiritual and material interests of our theocratic law and of developing the successive applications of the latter with an intelligent interpretation suitable to the needs of the time, prove not anxious to understand the domestic affairs of their country and, ignoring completely what is taking place in others, they consequently find it impossible to fulfil their temporal mission adequately.[20]

Commenting on this passage Smida (1970, p. 64) writes: "Thus those whose duty is to stimulate, to urge progress and the development of civilization, themselves constitute the first obstacle to any development." This calls attention to the negative role played by the Ulama and al-Zitouna in the evolution of Tunisian society during the 19th century and early 20th century.

In the face of the modernization efforts, particularly those in education, the resistance of the traditionalists was not slow in developing. In that context Tlili (1974, p. 442) argues that the progress of modern education and western influence "met with obstacles of all sorts and in particular from the religious ideology of the traditional society which was the dominant ideology" (our translation).

Strong evidence of this opposition can be found from the experience of Sheikh Mohamed Qabadu who was trained at al-Zitouna, but who became convinced of the necessity of Nahdha or the renaissance of the Arab-Islamic world. He thought and defended the idea that such a renaissance necessitated the Muslim reappropriation of the modern sciences which were then in exclusively European hands. For that purpose, he himself undertook the task of translating into Arabic several treatises in the fields of military art, physics, etc.. He even attempted to introduce the teaching of mathematics

---

[20]Quoted by Smida (1970, p. 64), our translation from French.

and sciences in one Medersa [Berque (1962) quoted by Sayadi (1974, p. 37)].
Apparently, however, his actions aroused violent opposition on the part of the
Ulama as can be seen in the poems[21] he wrote in response to their attacks.
The arguments of the traditionalists, addressed to Qabadou in particular,
were twofold. First, they objected that the teaching of science was profane.
Second, they argued that any overture to the West constituted infidelity to
Islamic tradition, undermining its foundation and thereby leading to its de-
struction [Tlili (1974), pp. 523-525]. These arguments were to be tirelessly
repeated by the traditionalists throughout the remainder of the 19th and
early 20th centuries.

Concerning political, judicial and administrative institutions, the reformers pushed for their modernization, and urged the adoption of the Tanzimats.
However, despite pressures from Istanbul, Ahmed Bey refused to adopt them
in Tunisia in fear of Turkish intervention in the affairs of the country. For an
ally in resisting Turkish pressures he had to depend on the Ulama in order
to consolidate his position. Since the reforms would have reduced the role of
the Ulama and their position particularly in the judiciary, quite naturally the
Ulama were opposed to the Tanzimats.

Despite these obstacles the reformers continued to press for reforms in
all directions. They obtained some success during the regime of Mohamed
Bey, 1855-1859, and the early part of that of Mohamed Essadok Bey. As
a matter of fact, a well-organized group of reformers, led by Khayr-al-Din,
lobbied Mohamed Bey to introduce reforms of an institutional nature which,
according to them, would be a necessary step for the modernization of the
country. In this context was born, in 1857, the *Pacte Fondamental*[22] a sort
of liberal charter which would secure, among other things, several guarantees
to nationals and foreigners [Tlili (1974, pp. 529-530)].

The reformers knew well that this movement for institutional renewal
and reform would run into resistance particularly from the Ulama. As Tlili
(1974, p. 530) puts it (our translation):

> However, this process of renewal of traditional institutions and
> innovation could not develop without great difficulties and obstacles

---

[21]El Khidr (1971) describes the institution of al-Zitouna, and presents a bi-
ography of some of its main figures such as Qabadou (p. 82-88). He describes
Qabadou's problems with his peers, and the poems he wrote in response to
their attacks.

[22]In Arabic Ahd-al-Aman or Charter. It proclaimed 11 principles, inspired by
the Turkish Imperial decrees of 1839 and 1856, such as civil liberty, religious
freedom, equality in taxation, freedom of trade, a system of commercial law,
courts, etc.

raised naturally by both the conservatives and some of the foreign powers.[23]

The Ulama's opposition to reforms became clear when the principles of the *Pacte* were debated by the committee formed for that purpose and in which the Ulama were invited to participate. The Ulama first expressed only some reservations, but later on they refused to participate even in the meetings of the committee. The Ulama were to take the same attitude when the first Tunisian constitution was proclaimed in 1861, again giving evidence of their firm opposition to change. The reason for this was that the constitution took over some of the principles in the "Pacte Fondamental" and introduced profound changes in the constitutional, legal and administrative system of the country. Its main innovation was the creation of a "Great Council" including many members of the elite which had the effect of transforming the Tunisian regime into a constitutional monarchy. Here again the Ulama, as expected, opposed the project and declined to be part of the "Great Council" in which they were to have participated *de jure* [Tlili (1974, p. 535)]. The Ulama were criticized for their action, not only by the reformers, but also by a large portion of the more or less enlightened population. Such criticism, however, was not sufficient to shake the Ulama's determination. It was a real confrontation between the traditionalists, who were gathered behind the Ulama and those militating for change [Tlili (1974, p. 535)]. Because of its strong impact on public opinion, the Ulama had to resort to religious objections according to which, since the reforms were drawn from a western system of government, which was admitted to by the reformers, were contrary to Islamic precepts. The Ulama chose to ignore the fact that in Turkey subsequent to the Tanzimats (1839), some eminent Turkish Ulama had defended the compatability of those western-inspired reforms with Islam [Tlili (1974, p. 389 and 495)].

Such a point of view was accepted by the Tunisian Ulama when they finally approved the *Pacte Fondamental* before its promulgation [Tlili (1974, p. 531)] and admitted that it was in conformity with religious precepts [Bin Diyaf (1964) vol. IV, pp. 246-247)]. But, once the reforms were to be put into practice with the introduction of the Constitution of 1861, the Ulama withdrew their approval, clearly demonstrating the depth of their anti-reform spirit.[24] With reference to this, Green (1978, pp. 104-105) notes: "that the

---

[23] Aiming to detach Tunisia from the Ottoman Empire in order to have greater influence over it, France was therefore hostile to Turkish inspired reforms. Other powers interested in Tunisia were Italy and England.

[24] Promulgated in January 1861, the constitution was put into effect in April 1861 and suspended three years later in April 1864.

pre-1873 Ulama generally manifested an anti-reform attitude" and "...the generally negative attitude of the Tunisian Ulama toward these early reforms..." It was for that negative attitude in particular that they were reproached by Khayr-al-Din in his 1867 essay. To him, it was the Ulama's duty as the protector of learning and the intellectual elite of the country to adjust their science and adapt it to the realities of modern times especially by a personal effort of interpretation or *ijtihad*. But the Ulama refused to accept any such responsability by arguing that their duties were incompatible with what they called "the matters of this world."

Khayr-al-Din did not hesitate to criticize them for this, especially after the reforms undertaken by Emir Abdelakader in Algeria during the first half of the 19th century. The pious Algerian Emir had been aware of the necessities of the times and had not hesitated to engage in building a modern society in Algeria while respecting the precepts of Islam [Tlili (1974, pp. 396-400)]. This attempt, well known to the Tunisian Ulama, proved how misleading were their religious arguments.

One can also mention the reforms taken in Lebanon in the middle of the 19th century by the Maronite clergy [Huxley (1984)]. In this multiconfessional country, the clergy knew how to organize the Christian community by instituting reforms of its own internal structures and in particular by developing education. Faced with the economic transformation stimulated by the mechanization of silk production introduced by Europeans, the clergy as well as the Muslim community, promoted the introduction of modern methods of education (American, French and Russian missions) to train the native population to take positions in manufacturing [Huxley (1984, p. 14)].

These examples are sufficient to show that the arguments of the Tunisian Ulama were nothing but alibis put forward to reject any kind of reform which would run against their own interests. This appears even more clearly in the case of the reforms of the al-Zitouna itself in the 1870s.

These reforms were initiated by Khayr-al-Din who came to office in 1870 as prime minister when the country was in the middle of a financial crisis. Quickly, he started reorganizing the country taking the reforms prepared in advance of his access to power. The main aim of his work[25] was to "adapt Muslim society to the modern way of life" [Tlili (1974, p. 557)]. In attempting to put these reforms into practice, Khayr-al-Din expected to face, if not the Ulama's hostility, at least their resistance. He tried to neutralize this resistance by attempting to get the Ulama involved in his action. Despite his efforts Khayr-al-Din failed to disarm the opposition of the ma-

---

[25]More details on Khayr-al-Din's reforms are given by Smida (1970).

jority of the Ulama represented by the Malikites of Tunis. In fact, only the provincial Malikites and a few Hanefites, including some famous ones like Bayram V, supported the reforms. As Green (1974, p. 124) puts it: "Led by the urban Maliki families but not restricted to them, those Ulama having a vested socio-economic interest in the status-quo, consequently did their best to obstruct the reforms of Khayr-al-Din." This opposition was strengthened by the alliance between the Ulama and the Bazaar to obstruct the reforms [Green (1974, p. 123)]. The Ulama's opposition, was surprising considering the lengths to which Khayr-al-Din went so as to avoid alienating this group.

Khayr-al-Din became fully aware of the need to extend modern teaching methods in Tunisia by the increasing activities of the foreign missions. Accordingly, in 1875 he established the *Collège Sadiki* with the objective of creating an institution capable of providing Muslims with a mixed education balancing European technical training with Arab cultural attainments.[26] In that way he took into account the apprehensions of the al-Zitouna people who would never tolerate the introduction of scientific branches. While the creation of the *Collège Sadiki* was well received by those favourable to the introduction of modern education, only a small minority of the Ulama agreed to participate in its teaching program and to allow their children to attend.

With respect to al-Zitouna, Khayr-al-Din started with a partial reform limited to teaching methods and not interfering with the educational content [Smida (1970, p. 327) Green (1978, p. 114), Abdelmoula (1971, p. 85)]. Nevertheless, this reform was greeted with the hostile opposition of the Ulama, a reaction which was understandable for a number of reasons. To begin with, the reform incorporated the great Mosque, hitherto independent, into the new Ministry of Public Education,[27] thereby implying its submission to administrative as well as to educational regulations. A panel consisting of Sheikh-inspectors was to provide the higher authority with reports about the monthly activities of the institution. Another control was for a civil servant to prepare a monthly report [Tlili (1974, p. 609)]. On the pedagogical level, the reform essentially condemned the prevailing methods of teaching.[28] It recommended the introduction of new methods which rely more on intellect than memory,[29] and for which the Ulama were obviously not well trained. Finally, the reform codified the status of the teachers, the *Mudarissun*, which was

---

[26]See also Smida (1970) on the organization of Collège Sadiki.

[27]It was nominally under the Bey's control.

[28]Particular criticism was addressed to the method of "Superposed Glosses", which "on the basis of a very concise text consisted in contracting chains of commentaries, often voluminous and without interest" [Tlili (1974), p. 611].

[29]See Tlili (1974, p. 609-610) for details.

seen as a real threat to the long-standing dominance of the leading families of the city in the recruitment and promotion of the teachers. That was usually done, as explained earlier, on a hereditary basis and by giving preference to children of the upper classes to the detriment of those from the country's interior, the *afakis* [Green (1978, p. 91), Abdelmoula (1971, p. 84 and 138), Berque (1972, p. 104)]. These considerations explain the Ulama's hostility to the reform which, moreover, was never put into practice since Khayr-al-Din was forced to resign from power in 1878.

In analysing the reasons behind the Ulama's attitude and especially their opposition to Khayr-al-Din's reforms, Green (1974, ch. IV) poses the issue as one of self-interest on the part of the privileged Ulama, and particularly those of the Malikite families of Tunis. This elite had for a long time enjoyed socio-economic positions that were very high in relation to those born from unknown families such as *afakis* of lower position. Any change could jeopardize positions of privilege. Those of lower position had nothing to lose and, thereby, were more favourable to reforms, seeing such changes as a means of achieving the kind of social change and promotion not attainable in a system controlled by the great families [Green (1978, ch. IV), Abdelmoula (1971, p. 136)]. Thus the resistance of the Ulama to change, although not excluding the role of theology, unquestionably had a socio-economic basis.

Resistance of the Ulama was to continue after Khayr-al-Din's attempts at reform, again using the secular and profane character of the modern sciences as the alleged justification for their opposition. Nevertheless, education in the sciences was increasingly demanded by various proponents, especially by the group of reformers associated with the newspaper *El-Hadhira*. This group included reformers of different opinions and in particular Sadiki alumni. They offered to carry on Khayr-al-Din's work with greater intensity. In 1894 they expressed their demands, again aiming at the modernization of the country as a whole, including the expansion of the teaching of modern sciences. Once again, however, the traditional cultural and religious *milieu* of the al-Zitouna showed their hostility and their resolve to remain closed to the modern sciences [Tlili (1978, pp. 34-37)].

Subsequently, the reformers tried to by-pass al-Zitouna, and decided to strengthen modern education by creating a complementary institution, the "al-Khaldunia." In doing so, the modernist elites tried to "take the reform program in hand and to remove it from the traditionalists of the al-Zitouna" [Sayadi (1974, p. 36)]. Among these reformers were those belonging to Khayr-al-Din's group, the Sadiki alumni and a few from within the al-Zitouna. Among the latter were sheikhs Tahar Ben Achour, Bouhajeb, al-Makki, and al-Nakhli, who were under the influence of the modernist ideas of Sheikh Mohammad Abdu[30] from the University of al-Azhar in Cairo.

Though modernists, the reformers were respectful of al-Zitouna and, because of this respect, planned to create al-Khaldunia as a complementary institution for teaching the modern sciences to the students of al-Zitouna who otherwise had no opportunity to study them [Zaouche 1932, ch. III)]. Before the opening of al-Khaldunia, the reformers tried to dissipate the Ulama's fears by referring to the authority of a respected Alim (Sheikh Bouhajeb) who suggested that the proposed teaching was compatible with the spirit of Islamic law. But, despite all the precautions taken (teaching in a building outside al-Zitouna, and demonstrating compatibility with Islam), the traditionalists opposed the project with great vigor. In this case, it is obvious that the opposition of the conservative Ulama could be explained only by its fear of losing control of the educational system and the privileges connected with it. On this subject, Sayadi (1974) wrote (our translation):

> On the whole, the conservatives feared that the project of al-Khaldounia would lead in the future to the neglect of religious sciences and could put in jeopardy the very teaching they provided in al-Zitouna. Moreover, they discovered that they lost control of the process of reforms, which rested with the leadership of al-Khaldounia. There results their opposition and their negativist attitude...nothing could calm the fear of those for whom any modernization was seen as a threat.

However, by their resistance the Ulama succeeded in preventing al-Zitouna students from having access to modern sciences at al-Khaldounia.

Later, on the occasion of discussions concerning a reform project suggested for the al-Zitouna in 1898 by the French Director of Public Education M. Machuel, a committee was established in which participated reformers, such as B. Sfar, who again suggested that the responsibility for the teaching of science be given to al-Khaldounia [Green (1978. p. 180)]. Once again, the Ulama united in opposition, causing Green to write: "when al-Bashir Sfar suggested that Zitouna students take their modern courses at the Khaldounia, the Sheikh al-Islam made it clear that he opposed any plan which made secular education obligatory for Zitouna students..." Finally, a compromise was reached between the Tunisian reformers and French liberals on the one side, and the traditionalists on the other, in which it was decided that al-Zitouna itself would offer elective courses in arithmetic, history and

---

[30]Mohamed Abdu was a great Egyptian thinker and reformer who visited Tunisia on two occasions, the first of which was in December 1884 - January 1885.

geography. By agreeing to that, the Ulama knew that few students would volunteer for these optional courses. This solution was described by Green (1978, p. 182) as a victory of the conservative Ulama: "The outcome of the 1898 Zitouna reform commission thus represented a victory for the conservative Ulama in their confrontation with the alliance of French liberals and Tunisian 'evoluès'." The Ulama's anticipations were correct for in 1900 only 5 students were attending arithmetic courses, while 700 were attending the normal classes of al-Zitouna. However, the Ulama compromise demonstrated that these sciences were not so profane as they had earlier claimed them to be. Their objection was indeed nothing but an excuse intended to oppose any change deemed harmful to their interests. This was also Green's opinion (1978, pp. 182-183) when he stated, that "In this regard the Sheikhs undoubtedly preferred to have the new courses taught at al-Zitouna itself rather than at al-Khaldounia in order to maintain their control over the situation."

Again and on another occasion, this defense was facilitated when the French authorities, worried about the demands of the reformers of the new-born *Jeunes Tunisiens* movement, tried to move closer to the conservative group of the al-Zitouna. As a matter of fact, after 1907 the alliance of French liberals and Tunisian reformers was shaken by the reaction of the *Colons Français* party which questioned the principle of joint sovereignty accepted up to that date. Therefore, the Tunisians hardened their attitude and gathered around the *Jeunes Tunisiens* movement which was questioning the French occupation of Tunisia. This drew the French authorities closer to the conservative Ulama who were also in conflict with the *Jeunes Tunisiens* group [Green (1978, pp. 208-211)]. This could be seen clearly when there were strikes of al-Zitouna students in 1910 demanding modernization of both the content of the curriculum and the teaching methods of the grand Mosque. The Ulama's opposition to these demands shouldn't be surprising, except that it was to profit from the discreet support of the protectorate administration as pointed out by Green (1978, p. 219): "The French were apparently sabotoging the reform efforts in order to cultivate the friendship of the religious leaders." This support was revealed again in 1920, and then around 1930, when the reform projects for al-Zitouna were under consideration [Zaouche (1932, ch. III)]. The introduction of modern science in al-Zitouna and the improvement of teaching methods were still the main issues. In both cases, the French side dragged their feet on the reforms, again allowing the Ulama to maintain the status-quo. This implicit alliance between the French authorities and the Ulama put the latter under suspicion by reformists, now nationalists, of collaboration with the French occupation. This explains why, when the country recovered its sovereignty, the nationalists in power put an end to al-Zitouna as an educational institution.[31]

Hence, on the supply side of institutional change, it appears that the Ulama have played a critical blocking role. Their opposition made it costly for the rulers and authorities to introduce the necessary changes in the educational system. Despite the advantages the rulers could expect from a reformed system in terms of a modernized administrative structure and army, they were unable to overcome the opposition of a strong and active interest group with a vested interest in the status-quo. The rulers were fearful that the Ulama would oppose them, jeopardizing their power. While there were political entrepreneurs who like Khayr-al-Din, based their careers on institutional changes and reforms, they failed in the face of a stronger opponent. Because of its small numbers, length of association, concentration in Tunis and the high cost of "exit", the Ulama were successful in blocking institutional reform. Had they lost the struggle, they would also have lost their privileges and status. On the other hand, by deliberately hiding the social benefits of institutional change [Hirschman (1967)] and exaggerating the costs in ideological-religious terms, they managed to sell their point of view to other less committed groups.

VI. Conclusions

Until the early part of the 20th Century the Tunisian educational system had remained practically unchanged. It had undergone little institutional change despite occasional pressures and various attempts to transform it. However, our study has shown that the demand for institutional change was fairly weak. The main movement for reform rested with an elite which was linked to an autocratic, bureaucratic government, which initiated reforms from the "top" [Brown (1974, conclusion)]. There were no significant pressures for educational change and reform from "below". It was a story of a demand failure for institutional change.

This analysis of the demand for institutional change leads to the wider problem of the failure of modernization in 19th and early 20th Century Tunisia, a time in which as a result of foreign penetration the system was subjected to considerable pressures to modernize. The educational system was but one of many that was subjected to pressures for modernization. The economic structure failed to evolve and adapt to the new pressures and conditions. The failure of the guilds to respond appropriately to European pene-

---

[31]There was created a modern university college: *Faculté Théologie*, of lesser importance than al-Zitouna.

tration and to transform its production and distribution methods translated into an absence of demand for educational change. This institutional analysis in terms of collective action on behalf of educational change may be useful in the study of the other aspects of modernization, and help improve our understanding of demand side failure. This analysis may be applied to the guilds and manufactures, the provision of infrastructure, the reform of the judicial system, trade policy and so on.

Nevertheless, the supply side of institutional change seems deserving of more attention. Indeed, in the case of education we have seen that the resistance of a powerful interest group on the supply side, the Ulama, was critical to the maintenance of the status quo and the continued dominance of al- Zitouna. While this collective action by the Ulama was successful in the short run since it allowed them to maintain their privileges and to avoid the costs of change, it also damaged their long run interests. After the early part of the 20th Century the pressures became increasingly strong, and the solution to the modernization of education was to evolve outside and parallel to the traditional system. The example of Collège Sadiki was to be followed, and later on the protectorate established a modern public educational system capable of responding to the needs of the changing society. The effect was to progressively weaken the traditional educational system and the power of the Ulama. Increasing numbers of people were educated in Europe, and France in particular, constituting a new elite, the leadership of the nationalist movement, that would challenge the power of al-Zitouna in many areas. Once independence was achieved in 1956, the new leadership completely did away with al-Zitouna and its traditional Ulama establishment and replaced it with a modern public educational system.

References

Abdelmoula, Mahmoud, 1971, *L'Université Zaytounienne et la Societé Tunisienne*, Tunis: Thèse de Doctorat de 3e Cycle en sociologie.

Azabou, Mongi and Jeffrey B. Nugent, 1988, "Tax Farming: Anachronism or Optimal Contract?," Ch. 6, this volume.

Ben Mustapha, Khairallah, 1910, *L'Enseignement Primaire des Indigènes en Tunisie - Rapport Présenté au Congrès de l'Afrique du Nord en 1908*. Tunis: Société Anonyme de l'Imprimerie Rapide de Tunis.

Ben Youssef, Mohamed Seghir, 1900, *Mechra El Melki, Chronique Tunisienne (1705-1771)*. Tunis: Imprimerie Rapide.

Berque, Jacques, 1972, Ulemas Tunisois de Jadis et de Naguère, Notes de Lecture sur les Musamarat al-Zarif, *Les Cahiers de Tunisie*, Tome XX, No. 77-78.

Bin Diyaf, Ahmed, 1964, *Ithâf Ahl al-Zamân*, Tunis: Publications du Secrétariat d'Etat aux Affaires Culturelles.

Brown, Leon Carl, 1967, *The Surest Path: The Political Treatise of a Nineteenth-Century Muslim Statesman,* Cambridge: Harvard Middle Eastern Monograph Series, XVI.

El Khidr, Mohamed Hossein, 1971, *Tounis Wa Djama'Ezzitouna,* Damascus: L'Imprimerie Mutuelle.

Ganiage, Jean, 1968, *Les Origines du Protectorat Français en Tunisie (1861-1881).* Tunis: Maison Tunisienne de l'Edition.

Green, Arnold H., 1978, *The Tunisian Ulama 1873-1915 Social Structure and Response to Ideological Currents,* Leiden: E.J. Brill.

Hardin, Garrett, 1968, "The Tragedy of the Commons," *Science* 162 (December), pp. 1243-1248.

Hardin, Russell, 1982, *Collective Action,* Washington D.C., Resources for the Future.

Hirschman, Albert O., 1967, *Development Projects Observed,* Washington: The Brookings Institution.

_____, 1980, *Exit, Voice and Loyalty: Response to Decline in Firms, Organizations and States,* Cambridge: Harvard University Press.

Huxley, Frederick C. 1984. "Formal and Informal Polity in Lebanese History," Department of Anthropology, University of California, Davis.

Khayr-al-Din, 1867, *Akwam Al Messalik,* Dar Ettalia', Beyrouth.

Kraïem, Mustapha, 1971, *La Tunisie Précoloniale,* 2 vol., Tunis: Société Tunisienne de Diffusion.

Kuran, Timur, 1988, "The Craft Guilds of Tunis and their Amins: A Study in Institutional Atrophy," Ch. 8 this volume.

Mahjoub, Azzam, 1983, *Industrie et Accumulation du Capital en Tunisie: De la Fin du XVIIIe Siècle jusqu'à la Seconde Guerre Mondiale,* Tunis: Imprimerie Oficielle de la République Tunisienne.

Olson, Mancur, 1965, *The Logic of Collective Action,* Cambridge: Harvard University Press.

_____, 1982, *The Rise and Decline of Nations: Economic Growth, Stagflation and Social Rigidities,* New Haven: Yale University Press.

Ruttan, Vernon and Yujiro Hayami, 1984, "Toward a Theory of Induced Institutional Innovation," *The Journal of Development Studies,* vol. 20 (July), 203-223.

Sayadi, Mongi, 1974, *Al Jam'iyya al Khalduniyya: 1896-1958,* Tunis: Maison Tunisienne de l'Edition.

Smida, Mongi, 1970, *Khéreddine Ministre Réformateur,* Tunis: Maison Tunisienne de l'Edition.

Tlili, Béchir, 1974, *Les Rapports Culturels et Idéologiques entre l'Orient et l'Occident en Tunisie, au XIXe Siecle (1830-1880),* Tunis: Publications de l'Université de Tunis.

_____, 1978. *Crises et Mutations dans le Monde Islamo-méditerranéen Contemporain, 1907-1918,* vol. 1, *Fondements et Positions des Réformistes,* Tunis: Publications de l'Université de Tunis.

Zaouche, Abdeljelil, 1932, *L'Enseignement Arabe en Tunisie,* Paris: Société d'Editions Géographiques, Maritimes et Coloniales.

Chapter 10

COLLECTIVE ACTION IN TUNISIA'S PRODUCER ORGANIZATIONS: SOME VARIATIONS ON THE OLSONIAN THEME*

Jeffrey B. Nugent

I. Introduction

Despite the enormous legacy of Mancur Olson (1965, 1982), Hirschman (1970) and others reviewed in Chapter 3 above and the large number of descriptive analyses of interest groups,[1] analytical studies have been relatively rare. Most of these, moreover, have focused on political issues such as the political channels through which the groups operate, the extent to which they challenge existing regimes, the socio-economic backgrounds of the political leaders, the policy of the state toward such groups, and the influence of political structure. A surprisingly large portion of the studies on economic aspects of interest group behavior have been either strictly theoretical or experimental.[2] The relatively few empirical studies oriented to economic issues have generally been limited to international cross-section regressions focusing on a single indicator of interest group activity,[3] or a single measure of group success.[4] Unfortunately, among these the more quantitatively rigorous the

---

*The author gratefully acknowledges the help of Moncef BenSlama and Mustapha Nabli in arranging interviews with the various producer organizations, Massaoud Boudhiaf, Abderazak Zouari, Abdelhai Chouikha and Daphne Nugent in conducting the interviews, of Mustapha Nabli in obtaining statistical data and of Mohamed Bechri, Dean Cummins, Timur Kuran, and especially Mustapha Nabli for their comments and criticism on earlier versions of the paper.

[1] See, for example, Ehrmann (1958), Korpi (1981), Timberg (1969), Bianchi (1984) and Kochanek (1983).

[2] Examples include Marwell and Ames (1979, 1980, 1981), Oliver (1980, 1984) and Oliver, Marwell and Teixeira (1985), Hoffman and Spitzer (1985), Plott (1986) and Smith (1986).

[3] For example, Murrell (1984) used the number of associations as the measure of interest group activity.

[4] For example, Cohen (1974) measured success in terms of the time required in order to respond in terms of political pressure to a given signal; Pennock (1962) measured it by number of members or alternatively by staff size, Huntington (1961), Ziegler (1964) and Levitan and Cooper (1984) by the influence exerted and Stigler (1971) by regulation.

study, the narrower has been its focus, scope and importance.[5] Rigourous or
not, very few of the analytic studies pertain to LDCs, exceptions being Cohen
(1974), Bates 1981), Bianchi (1984) and Cummins (1987). Finally, even in
these latter studies the focus of the analysis has been on factors which may
be considered given exogenously and hence useless for policy. In order to at
least partially overcome these shortcomings, the present paper applies the
principles of collective action to explain the origin and variation in the relative strength of various Tunisian producer organizations both across sectors
and over time. It does so at both an aggregate level and so as to be of use
in evaluating alternative producer organization strategies at a more disaggre-
gate level. The analysis relies on a combination of quantitive and qualitative
indicators of success in collective action and draws upon both the responses
to a questionaire addressed to a sample of Tunisian producer organizations
and press reports[6] concerning the activities of such organizations.

The presentation is organized as follows: Section II documents the relative weakness of producer groups in North Africa and the Middle East as
a whole. Section III describes the origin and evolution of Tunisia's producer
organizations. Section IV presents some indicators for measuring variations
in the strength of Tunisia's producer organizations across sectors and examines the extent to which the theory of collective action explains the observed
variations in such indicators. In order to be more useful for policy, in Section V we present a comparative analysis of the different approaches taken
to common problems by different producer groups. Finally, some conclusions
are given in Section VI.

II. The Relative Weakness of Producer Organizations in North Africa and the Middle East

The modern history of nation-states and their approach to economic
policy is such that policies are generally biased in favor of the interests of
producers, especially those of manufactures, and against consumers. For
example, in commenting on the mercantile policies practiced by the nation-
states of his time Adam Smith said:

> It cannot be very difficult to determine who have been the con-
> trivers of this whole mercantile system; not the consumers, whose
> interests have been entirely neglected, but the producers, whose in-

---

[5]Of the empirical studies two of the most rigorous would seem to be the
study of Dutch firms in the shipbuilding industry by Braam (1981) and the
aforementioned international cross-section study of Murrell (1984).

[6]Especially useful in the industrial context were those contained in *Flash-
UTICA*, a weekly publication of the Union Tunisienne de l'Industrie du Commerce et de l'Artisanat (UTICA).

terests have been so carefully attended to; and among this latter class our merchants and manufacturers have been by far the principal architects [Smith (1937, p. 626)].

According to standard textbooks [e.g., Ethier (1983, Chapter 6)], the pattern observed in Smith's day would seem to hold *a fortiori* at present.

At least until very recently, North Africa and the Middle East have constituted a rather remarkable exception. As Issawi (1982) has shown, in this region the strong groups have been workers, consumers and suppliers of government services (including the military) and the weak groups the producers of agricultural and manufactured products; as a result, government policies were biased in favor of consumers and against producers. Some temporary exceptions in which were practiced alternative political-economic policies include Egypt during the early 19th century when Mohammad Ali invested heavily in agriculture and industry, Turkey in the 1840's [Clark (1974)] and Tunisia in the 1850's when Ahmed Bey provided monopolistic protection for the domestic production of military goods [Brown (1974)]. Even in these cases, however, support was generally limited to public enterprises.

According to Mustafa (1968), El Sayed (1968), Issawi (1982) and others, this unusual situation in North Africa and the Middle East resulted from a coalition of three otherwise very different groups, namely the Islamic intelligentsia known as the ulama, the military, and the working class, against the economically productive classes.[7]

Lacking any substantial military or economic power of their own, the ulama played up to the working classes and used the threat of popular uprisings as a way of defending their own interests *vis-à-vis* those of the military. Likewise, the military, neither understanding nor trusting the merchant and business classes, felt it in their interest to keep the merchant and business classes weak. As a result, most parts of the Ottoman Empire were characterized by a political economy which favored urban workers by keeping the prices of consumption goods low through the taxation of exports and free entry for imports. While certainly there are other plausible explanations, e.g., Kuran (1988), for why industrialization, capital formation and the preceding rise in agricultural productivity (which have been identified with the take off into self-sustained economic development by Rostow and other economic historians) did not occur in the Middle East and North Africa until considerably

---

[7]This is not meant to deny that there were warm personal relationships and marriages consumated between the ulama and leaders of the bazaar sector [Bsaies (1988)].

later than they had occurred in Europe,[8] the dominance of this remarkably anti-producer economic policy regime is one possible explanation.

Economic development, in general, and agricultural and industrial development, in particular, remain high on the list of stated priorities in Tunisia and other countries of the region. In some recent research based on the historical experience of 23 DCs and LDCs between 1850 and 1914, Morris and Adelman (1987) and Adelman, Lohmöller and Morris (1987) demonstrate that the relatively balanced development of agricultural and industrial production capabilities by indigenous actors (rather than dependency on traditional exports and foreign expertise) is highly conducive to the achievement of such goals. In view of Tunisia's heretofore limited success in achieving its goals, therefore, serious attention should be given to the extent of the continuing weakness of Tunisia's producer organizations, the reasons for this, and the prospects for change.

III. The Origin and Evolution of Tunisia's Producer Organizations

The organization of employers into producer groups for collective action is a surprisingly recent phenomenon in Tunisia. Before this, Tunisian employers and workers were usually organized along "corporate" lines. That is, agricultural landowners and workers were related along neo-feudalist and/or communal lines, and industrial and commercial workers and owners were integrated into guilds or *corporations*.[9] Any collective action *vis-à-vis* the state or any other group was undertaken by the corporation or community as a whole, not separately by worker or producer groups.

Significantly, the first initiatives to break out of this mold were motivated by strong external pressures and by severe relative deprivation in particular. For example, the earliest example of collective action on the part of workers in Tunisia occured in the late 19th and early 20th century among Italian, French and other foreign workers. According to Tlili (1977), what prompted these workers, who at the time constituted the bulk of Tunisia's modern sector work force, to organize was their desire to be remunerated on a par with their compatriots back home. Since these workers were relatively new to the country, rather than comparing themselves with their considerably worse off Tunisian counterparts, they compared themselves with their counterparts and

---

[8] See, for example, Ashtor (1978) and El Sayed (1968).

[9] *Corporation* is the French word for guild. For studies of guilds in North Africa and the Middle East see especially Lewis (1937), Pennec (1964), Baer (1964, 1970) and Kuran (1988). For more general discussion of the corporatist approach see Schmitter (1974).

friends back in their countries of origin. Because workers in Europe were at the time highly successful in gaining higher wages, this made those Europeans working in Tunisia feel relatively worse off, inducing them to undertake collective action to redress their sense of relative deprivation.[10] Similarly, since by World War I some of the largest and most productive farms were concentrated in French hands, the first producer organization to emerge in Tunisia's agricultural sector was an organization of French farmers.

The first serious attempts on the part of indigenous Tunisian workers and producers to undertake collective action outside of the corporatist mold occured shortly after World War I. By cutting off the flow of competing imported manufactures into Tunisia, the war had brought prosperity back to Tunisia's artisan and merchant classes. However, once the war was over, the reentry of imports eliminated this prosperity in import-competing sectors. Likewise, the world depression of the 1930s had a devastating effect on Tunisia's exports. Indeed, it was the mid-1930s before collective action on the part of Tunisian workers and producers began to gather momentum. The organization of producer groups in the 1930's probably was nudged along by the prior unionization of Tunisian workers [Zouari (1988)] who managed to obtain, albeit aided by similar occurences in metropolitan France, governmental regulation of working hours and conditions.

Not surprisingly, when prosperity returned to the artisan sector as a result of the cutoff of competing imported products during World War II, the employer organizations that had been formed at that time, namely the *Union des Syndicats Patronaux Tunisiens* and the *Fédération Générale des Syndicats du Commerce et de l'Industrie de Tunisie*, each of which at its peak had a dozen or so member unions, died out rather abruptly.

After the European phase of the war was concluded, however, Tunisian artisans once again found themselves caught in a squeeze; imported manufactures again competed favorably with Tunisian production. At the same time, the raw material shortages arising from continuing controls on imports of the necessary raw materials made it necessary to purchase them on the black market at inflated prices. The resulting profit squeeze led to a resurgence in collective action by artisans and merchant groups immediately after World War II. First, in March 1945 the *Fédération des Artisans et Petits Commerçants de Tunisie*, consisting of more than one hundred individual unions of artisans and small merchants, was formed with leadership from the Commu-

---

[10]Notably, the strike action of foreign workers during these years was not joined by Tunisian workers who, because of their limited contact with Europe, would not have felt relatively deprived in these circumstances.

nist Party of Tunisia.[11] This group was successful in securing a share in the import quotas of the necessary raw materials for small artisan and importer groups. Fearing communist control, in January, 1947 the nationalist Neo-Destour Party initiated a competing central union, the *Union des Syndicats des Artisans et Petits Commercants de Tunisie* (USAPCT) with 157 sectoral and 11 regional unions. Since the latter organization's leadership was elected, whereas the former's was not, the claims of the latter were considered more credible. Moreover, since USAPCT was also supported by the Neo-Destour-backed workers' union (UGTT), it soon became the dominant organization of artisans and merchants. The number of its member unions increased to 280 by 1948.

In 1948 USAPCT members were informed that the neo-Destour Party desired a change of name to the *Union Tunisienne de l'Artisanat et du Commerce* (UTAC) and the inclusion of the previously excluded larger merchants. While only reluctantly did the membership accept these changes, UTAC remained a nationalist organization from which French firms were excluded. In exchange, however, it received official status as the sole representative of Tunisian producers.

Since the large French firms were also deleteriously affected in the immediate postwar period by the combined pressure on the prices of finished products and inflated prices of raw material inputs, they, too, were induced to organize. They formed the *Confédération Générale du Commerce et des l'Industrie* (CGCI) which established relations with its counterpart organization in France [Timoumi (1983)].

Both UTAC and the workers union, *Union Générale des Travailleurs Tunisiens* (UGTT), were increasingly critical of the colonial authorities in Tunis for what they perceived to be unsympathetic reactions to their various requests. UTAC (1) opposed the various new taxes that were imposed on transport, firms and sales, (2) called for reductions in the numbers of government officials, and (3) urged the replacement of French ones by Tunisian ones. By 1955 both UTAC and UGTT were firmly behind the independence movement and demanded the release of its detained leaders and the repatriation of exiled ones [Tlili (1977)]. After independence UTAC used its "proven loyalty to the new government" in appealing to it for help in the form of protectionist legislation and access to credit on favorable terms.

In the immediate post-independence period, however, the state's primary objective was to consolidate its power and to weaken any possible threats to

---

[11]The relevance of political initiative in the early formation of Tunisia's producer unions suggests the relevance of "political entrepreneurship."

its dominance [Moore (1965)]. From then until at least the late 1960's, and only to a somewhat lesser degree until the present, Tunisian labor unions and producer organizations alike were seen primarily as instruments of governmental control. Leaders who threatened the regime were regularly replaced by leaders deemed to be more loyal to it. In this way, neither producer nor worker organizations were able to exercise their independence.

One sign of weakness of producer organizations in the immediate post-independence period was the gradual imposition of a "top-down" cooperative system on most producing sectors. At first, the cooperatives were imposed primarily only on nationalized foreign land and enterprises. Later, however, the system was expanded to include communally and privately held land and enterprises. Cooperativization was supported by urban workers who saw it as a vehicle for barring monopolies and lowering the prices of basic consumption goods. Indeed, the initiator of and the driving force behind the cooperative movement was the former leader of the UGTT, Ahmed Ben Salah, who in the 1960's was elevated to a position of national leadership, a "super minister" and, in practical terms at least, the number two man in the Tunisian government (behind President Habib Bourguiba) [Gunn (1987)]. Naturally, cooperativization of private property would not have been possible if producer organizations had been strong.

One of the strategies that the Tunisian state has rather consistently used with respect to producer groups is their amalgamation into overall umbrella organizations,or in Olson's terminology "encompassing" groups. For example, in the immediate post-independence period the producers' organization UTAC was broadened to include the members of the French-dominated enterprises (CGCI). Then, in the mid-1960s, while the cooperative movement was still being extended into agriculture, fishing, industry and commerce, UTAC was broadened to include all service sectors. UTAC was reconstituted in April, 1966 as *l'Union Tunisienne de l'Industrie, du Commerce et de l'Artisanat* (UTICA). Membership in UTICA was made automatic (i.e., compulsory) for all employers outside of agriculture. In the mid-1970's the financing of UTICA was assured by the imposition of a mandatory tax of 0.8% on the wage bill of all employers.[12] While the purpose of UTICA remains to

---

[12]There is little evidence that the imposition of the mandatory tax on the wage bill was the result of any grassroots movement. Rather, it would seem to have resulted from the leadership of the bureaucratic leaders of the organization itself who would naturally have a stake in assuring the source of their salaries and positions and the few relatively large enterprises who were already contributing and who would therefore want to avoid free-riding on the part of the others.

defend the interests of its members, the mechanisms it provides for doing this are primarily those of embedding and connecting UTICA leaders and staff into the national planning and decision-making process.

Similarly, the *Union Nationale des Agriculteurs Tunisiens* (UNAT) is a broadly based organization which includes all farmers and fishermen. In practice, however, since no system of taxation has yet been devised for financing UNAT, only a small fraction of the eligible membership actually pay their dues. This is, moreover, in spite of the fact that the dues are low (1.2 Tunisian dinars or less than 2 US dollars per year). Although in the case of UTICA its financial base makes it possible to hire its own staff to an increasing extent, UTICA and especially UNAT remain heavily dependent on staff loaned to these organizations by the relevant ministries (the Ministry of Agriculture in the case of UNAT and various other ministries in the case of UTICA). Moreover, even when their leadership is selected by popular election, since influence over powerful decision makers is an important criterion for leadership, the rank and file of these organizations frequently choose leaders acceptable, and personally or otherwise related, to those in power.

As a result, both UNAT and UTICA are strongly influenced by government and embedded in the official decision-making process. We do not mean to imply that producers are weak because of UNAT and UTICA; indeed, other things remaining the same, without these organizations Tunisian producers undoubtedly would have considerably less means of having their grievances heard and addressed than they do at present. Nevertheless, in personal interviews the leaders of some of the stronger and more independent unions within these umbrella organizations expressed considerable criticism of the leadership of UNAT and UTICA for being insufficiently independent of the bureaucracy and insufficiently aggressive in pursuing the interests of their members.

Since UNAT and UTICA are only umbrella organizations, i.e., unions of individual employers' unions, there is nothing inherent in these organizations to prevent independent collective action by individual member unions. In practice, however, since UNAT and UTICA provide considerable assistance in the formation and activities of the individual unions and have to approve their statutes, the individual unions are strongly influenced by these umbrella organizations and the bureaucracy.[13] It should also be noted that neither UNAT nor UTICA prohibits individual enterprises from joining more than

---

[13]From the perspective of the umbrella organizations themselves, however, the failure of individual unions to exercise independence and to achieve effective collective action is more frequently attributed to the indifference and/or incompetence of the leadership of the individual unions.

one union or federation.

Given the breadth of scope of the umbrella organizations UNAT and UTICA, quite naturally conflicts among member unions frequently arise. For example, within a well developed sector like textiles there are separate unions for producers of different kinds of textiles, such as wool, artificial fibres, etc., for producers in the different stages of production, such as spinners, weavers and producers of finished clothing, and also for importers, exporters, merchants and artisans. The interests of these different subgroups, of course, diverge substantially. Since one of UTICA's functions is to resolve these conflicts, UTICA has attempted to merge these different and potentially conflicting unions into *federations* of unions. Hence, all the aforementioned individual unions representing different segments of the textile industry are brought together in the Federation of Textiles.

Since priority in the allocation of UTICA's resources seems to have gone to the creation and assistance of such federations, it is important to consider the effects of this strategy on collective action. On the one hand, the federation strategy would seem to have contributed to heterogeneity of background of producer groups and thereby, inadvertantly at least, to greater difficulty in achieving collective action.[14] On the other hand, it has also contributed to heterogeneity of goals, size asymmetry, improved communication among members and better access to government officials, all of which facilitate collective action. The direction of the net balance of these diverging effects of Tunisian government policy on the likelihood of collective action is, therefore, by no means obvious.

IV. Variations in the Relative Strength of Tunisian Producer Interest Groups and their Explanation

Of course, the late start and general weakness of producer organizations in Tunisia do not imply that all producer unions in the country are forever doomed to weakness and collective action failure. To the contrary, as we shall soon see, some individual producer organizations are already relatively strong and well organized and others apparently on the way to becoming so. Even now, there exists considerable variation in relative success from sector to sector. Our purpose in this section is to describe and explain such differences. Naturally, our ability to do so is highly dependent on the ability to measure success in collective action. While it may be possible to measure interest group strength and success in collective action in many different ways, in our

---

[14]It should also be noted that the leaders of UNAT and UTICA have been primarily political leaders with relatively close ties to the top layers of government.

application to Tunisian producer organizations we use a combination of measures and allow for the fact that the relevant considerations quite naturally vary from sector to sector and also over time.

Table 10-1

Absolute and Relative Ratios of Total Bank Credit to Gross Domestic Product at Factor Cost in Tunisia by Sector and Year, 1965-1986

Sector	Item	Year 1965	1972	1980	1984	1986
Agriculture and	a	.077	.114	.261	.311	.348
Fishing	b	.278	.373	.474	.439	.444
Mining	a	.107	.846	1.085	1.156	1.885
	b	.386	2.773	1.969	1.632	2.404
Petroleum and gas	a	.870	.045	.012	.027	.052
	b	3.140	.148	.022	.039	.066
Electricity and	a	.014	.001	.303	.406	.354
	b	.050	.003	.549	.573	.452
Food industries	a	.697	.357	1.120	1.373	1.330
	b	2.516	1.170	2.032	1.939	1.696
Construction materials	a	1.234	.981	1.412	1.768	1.944
	b	4.455	3.216	2.562	2.497	2.480
Mechanical and	a	1.349	1.212	2.605	3.226	3.334
electrical industries	b	4.870	3.973	4.728	4.556	4.253
Chemicals	a	.361	.272	1.329	4.917	7.961
	b	1.303	.891	2.412	6.945	10.154
Textiles, clothing	a	1.798	1.170	.954	.944	.526
and leather	b	6.490	3.836	1.731	1.333	.671
Wood, paper and	a	1.260	.962	1.109	1.222	1.207
miscellaneous	b	4.549	3.154	2.012	1.725	1.539
Construction	a	.385	.486	.387	.514	.619
	b	1.390	1.593	.702	.726	.790
Transport and	a	.115	.119	.321	.415	.319
communications	b	.415	.390	.583	.586	.407
Tourism	a	1.539	1.246	.771	1.178	1.622
	b	5.556	4.085	1.399	1.664	2.068
Commerce and	a	.208	.231	.299	.322	.669
other services	b	.751	.758	.543	.454	.853
Total	a	.277	.305	.551	.708	.784

Source: Computed from data in Banque Centrale de Tunisie, Statistiques Financières, Sept. 1974 and Sept. 1986, 1987.

Note: Row "a" is in absolute terms, Row "b" in relative terms and is defined as the row "a" entry relative to the row "a" Total entry. (Further explanation in text).

During most of Tunisia's post-independence period credit from institutional sources has been rationed and offered at interest rates well below those in world markets, indeed often at negative real rates of interest [Bechri (1988)]. Since at such rates and in such circumstances access to credit is a virtual *sine qua non* for becoming wealthy, we use it as one indicator of group influence. More specifically, in rows "a" of Table 10-1 we present for each sector and for various years between 1965 and 1986 the credit to product ratio. This ratio is obtained by dividing for each sector and year the sum of the end-of-year short term and long term credit stocks by its corresponding value added from data obtained from the Central Bank of Tunisia. In the "total" row we also present the same ratio for the economy as a whole. Given the increased degree of monetization and increased importance of capital formation (which generally requires credit) from 1965 to 1986, not surprisingly the credit-product ratio for the economy as a whole has grown substantially over the period under consideration. Indeed, the ratio almost tripled, going from .277 in 1965 to .784 in 1986 (the last date for which comparable data was available at the time of writing).

As a measure of each sector's *relative* success in gaining access to the rationed credit at any given point in time, in row "b" of the table we present the sectoral entry of row "a" divided by the corresponding "total" entry. For construction, the credit-product ratios were generally relatively close to the national averages. However, in the construction materials, chemicals (except for 1972), mining (except for 1965), mechanical and electrical industries, food industries, textiles, clothing and leather (except for 1986), wood, paper and miscellaneous industries and tourism sectors, these ratios have been consistently above the national averages. By contrast, in agriculture and fishing, electricity and water, petroleum and gas (except for 1965), transport and communications, and commerce and other services they have been consistently below the national averages.

Among the sectors with consistently below-average credit-product ratios, the cases of electricity and water and petroleum and gas can be explained rather easily. This is because each of these sectors or components thereof consists of a single large and powerful public enterprise capable of issuing its own government-guaranteed bonds. Hence, these sectors do not have to depend on financing from the banking system. That leaves agriculture-fishing, transport-communications and commerce-other services as three sectors with conspicuously poor access to credit. Indeed, given the comparatively high labor-intensity of the agriculture-fishing and commerce-other services sectors, the below-average allocations of credit received by these sectors would be even more striking if they were measured on a per employee basis.

As shown in row "b" of the table, there has been a gradual increase in the relative allocation of credit to agriculture and fishing over time from 27.9% of the national average in 1965 to 44.4% of the (considerably higher) national average in 1984 and 1986. A somewhat less dramatic improvement in relative position was registered by the transport and communications sector. On the other hand, the already disadvantaged position of commerce and other services has deteriorated relatively sharply, i.e., its credit-product ratio declining from 75.1% in 1965 to 45.6% of the national average in 1984. As a result, in 1984 it was only marginally above the agriculture and fishing sector at the bottom of the list as far as relative credit allocation is concerned, though rebounding significantly by 1986.

On the other hand, at the high end of the scale, in 1965 textiles and tourism ranked first and second with credit-product ratios well over 5 times the national average. By 1986 both of these sectors had fallen considerably in the rankings.[15] In the case of tourism, however, it continues to receive credit-product allocations well above the national average, and the downward trend was rather sharply reversed between 1980 and 1986. As of 1986 the sectors with the highest credit-product ratios were chemicals, mechanical and electrical industries and construction materials.

As a second measure of the relative strength of interest group activity in defense of producer interests across sectors and over time, in Table 10-2 we present various estimates of *effective* rates of protection by sector for 1980. Each such rate represents the tariff rate per unit of domestic value added in the industry. In contrast to *nominal* tariff rates, *effective* rates of protection consider the tariff rates that apply to both the inputs and outputs of each sector and the structure of inputs. Unfortunately, as is well known to applied trade theorists, the measurement of effective protection is beset with a number of problems. Among these are the treatment of non-traded inputs, taxes and subsidies other than tariffs, and non-tariff barriers. As a result, a number of different formulas have been proposed for calculating effective rates of protection. The so-called Balassa method [Balassa and Schydlowsky (1968) and Balassa et al. (1971, 1982)] treats non-traded inputs as traded inputs with zero tariff rates. The Corden [Corden (1971)] method, however, includes the primary input content in non-traded inputs with the value added of the protected activity. Both measures can be applied to tariffs alone or

---

[15]The secular decline in the credit-product ratios in these sectors is understandable since these sectors have had increasing access to foreign equity finance. Hence, these declines may not be indicative of declining strength of collective action.

more comprehensively to tariffs, taxes and subsidies as a whole. Experience has shown that the calculations of effective rates can be rather sensitive to the various differences in measurement and coverage.

Table 10-2

Effective Rates of Protection in Tunisia by Sector 1980

Sector	Exclusive of Subsidies and other Incentives	Inclusive of Subsidies and other Incentives	
	Balassa Method	Balassa Method	Corden Method
Agriculture	.14	.22	.20
Fishing	.08	.28	.18
Food Industries	.30	.78	.29
Textiles, Clothing and Leather	-.01	.00	.00
Wood, Paper and Miscellaneous Manufactures	1.66	2.06	.94
Chemicals	.10	.27	.21
Mechanical and Electrical Industries	.46	.52	.36
Construction Materials and Glass	1.50	2.19	.96
Mining	.13	.40	.24
Petroleum and Gas	-.54	-.53	-.51
Transport	.02	.06	.04
Tourism	-.20	-.10	-.08

Source: Nabli, M. K. and N. Bousselmi, Evolution de la Protection et des Incitations Effectives des Activités Economiques en 1977, 1980 et 1983, Tables Annexes. Tunis: Institute d'Economie Quantitative, 1985.

In Table 10-2, therefore, we present for 1980 the following measures of effective rates of protection by sector: (a) the Balassa method applied to tariffs alone, (b) the Balassa method applied to tariffs inclusive of subsidies and other incentives and (c) the Corden method applied to tariffs inclusive of subsidies and other incentives. Even at the high level of sectoral aggregation used, the table reveals considerable variation in the effective rates of protection across sectors. In particular, the effective rates of protection are negative for the petroleum and gas and tourism sectors, approximately zero for textiles, clothing and leather, 25% or less for agriculture, fishing, chemicals, mining and transport, 25%-100% for food industries, and mechanical and electrical industries and probably more than 100% for wood, paper and miscellaneous manufactures and construction materials and glass.

Not surprisingly, the export sectors — agriculture, fishing, textiles, chemicals, mining, petroleum and tourism — have low or negative rates of protection and the import-substituting industries, such as wood, paper and miscellaneous manufactures and construction materials and glass, have the highest rates. Indeed, export-intensity seems to be an important determinant of intrasectoral differences in effective rates of protection. For example, although subsectoral data on effective rates of protection are not given in the tables (but are available upon request from the author), within agriculture export-oriented subsectors like fresh fruit have low rates but import-substituting ones like poultry and eggs have high ones. Similarly, within manufactures of food and beverages, export-oriented subsectors like olive oil and fish canning have low or negative rates whereas import-competing ones like fruit and vegetable canning, beer and soft drinks have especially high rates.

Table 10-3
Shares of Individual Sectors in Total Commodity
Exports of Tunisia* 1966-1984 (in percent)

Petroleum	47.2
Textiles, Leather	17.5
Chemicals	13.6
Food Processing	9.2
Mining	6.4
Agriculture	2.5
Fishing	1.3
Other	2.3
Total	100.0

Note: *If invisible exports were included, tourism would also constitute a major export sector.

Source: Banque Centrale de Tunisie, Statistiques Financières, Feb. 1985.

Hence, one has both to be careful in using effective rates of protection as an indicator of strength in collective action, and in particular to consider the relative importance of exports. For the reader's convenience, the shares of different sectors in exports for the years 1966-1984 are presented in Table 10-3. The producers of an exportable may be well-organized and successful in collective action but, because protection would be harmful to their ability to export, would seek subsidies of various kinds instead of protection.

Therefore, as the measure of overall success in collective action we use the combination of the two measures, credit-product ratios and effective protection rates, and suggest the following criteria in applying them. If a particular sector were low on both measures, this would be a good indication of genuine weakness in collective action. Conversely, if it were relatively high on both measures, this would be a good indication of strength. If an export-oriented sector, such as one at the top of the list in Table 10-3, were to have a low effective rate of protection but an above-average credit allocation, this would also be grounds for classifying it as a relatively strong sector from the point of view of collective action. Less clear would be a sector with below-average credit and export shares but a relatively high rate of effective protection. Those sectors with below-average credit-product ratios, but dominated by public enterprises with the ability to raise funds in the bond and stock market, need not be considered weak.

Table 10-4
Classification of Sectors by Strength of Collective Action in Early 1980s

Sectors Strong in Collective Action

A. Sectors with High Credit-Product Ratios and High Effective Protection.
 Construction Materials
 Mechanical and Electrical Industries
 Wood and Paper (Miscellaneous Industries)
 Food Industries

B. Sectors with High Credit-Product Ratios and Low Effective Protection Rates but High Export Shares.
 Textiles, Clothing and Leather
 Chemicals
 Tourism
 Mining

Sector Intermediate in Collective Action
 Construction

Sectors Weak in Collective Action
 Sectors with Low Credit-Product Ratios and Low Effective Protection.
 Agriculture
 Fishing

 Sectors with Low Credit-Product Ratio.
 Commerce
 Transport and Communications

The sectoral entries of Tables 10-1, 10-2 and 10-3 can now be used in order to apply these criteria to distinguish sectors according to the effectiveness of collective action. After excluding the electricity-water and petroleum-gas sectors in which collective action is irrelevant because these sectors consist of single large public enterprises, the results for the remaining sectors are shown in Table 10-4. Because of below-average credit-product ratios in Table 10-1 and below-average export shares and effective protection rates in

Tables 10-2 and 10-3, respectively, agriculture, fishing, commerce, and transport and communications would seem to be relatively weak sectors. On the other hand, because of high credit-product ratios and high rates of effective protection, the construction materials, mechanical and electrical industries, food industries and wood, paper and miscellaneous manufactures would seem to be relatively strong. Because of high credit-product ratios and high export shares (despite relatively low rates of effective protection), mining, textiles, clothing and leather, chemicals and tourism would also seem to be relatively strong sectors. The construction sector whose credit-product ratio has generally been about average is classified as being intermediate in strength of collective action.

In Table 10-5 we present several indicators of group characteristics considered relevant for explaining the observed variations in the indicators of collective action across the sectors presented in Table 10-4. In column 1 is a simple measure of group size, the number of establishments. The number of establishments ranges from one or two hundred in the case of mining and tourism to an estimated 400,000 in the case of agriculture and fishing. In column 2 we present a measure of size asymmetry, the percentage of employment in firms with more than 100 permanent workers. These estimates range from less than 1% in agriculture and fishing to over 90% in mining. An index of geographic concentration, namely, the percentage of sectoral employment in Tunis is given in column 3. These percentages range from a low of 2.1% in agriculture and fishing to 57.7% in the mechanical and electrical industries. Estimates of the percentage of employment in public enterprise, ranging from a low of less than 1% in agriculture and fishing and commerce and other services to 50+% in mining, are presented in column 4.[16] Finally, in column 5 as a proxy for the cost of "exit" we present estimates of value added per employee, ranging from .6 in agriculture and fishing to 8 in tourism. According to the hypotheses identified in Chapter 3 above, we would expect the strength of collective action to be inversely related to group size in column 1, and positively related to the size concentration of employment in column 2, the geographic concentration of activity in Tunis in column 3, the relative importance of public enterprise in column 4 and the cost of exit in column 5.

The aforementioned observed intersectoral variations in the relative strength of producer group collective action in contemporary Tunisia would seem to be consistent with several of the determinants of collective action measured in Table 10-5. In particular, the weak sectors have many members,

---

[16]For an explanation of the usefulness of public enterprise in collective action in Tunisia see Grissa (1988).

are unlikely to have employment concentrated in establishments of large size, are relatively dispersed in location, have relatively attractive opportunities for exit, and are likely to be privately owned. At the same time, the relatively strong sectors have smaller numbers, are more concentrated in establishments of large size and the capital city, more dominated by the state sector, because of the greater importance of "sunk costs" are less likely to view "exit" as a viable alternative and hence are more likely to be inclined to use "voice", and frequently at least are engaged in international competition which makes collective action more imperative.

Table 10-5
Group Characteristics and Other Variables

	1	2	3	4	5
	Number of Enterprises in 1981	Percentage of Employment in Firms of More Than 100 Workers	Percentage Concentration of Employment in Tunis 1980	Percentage Share of Public Enterprise in 1981	Value Added Per Worker in Thousands Tunisian Dinars 1980
Agric. & Fishing	approx. 400,000	< 1	2.1	< 1	.6
Mining	approx. 100	> 90	11.1	50+	2.8
Food Industrie	362	46.2	44.9	5.1	2.6
Construction Materials	232	74.1	28.4	6.7	3.3
Mech. & Elect. Ind.	236	74.0	57.7	3.5	2.1
Chemical	145	70.4	55.1	44.0	3.7
Textiles, Clothing Leather	433	74.1	66.7	6.1	1.6
Wood, Paper and Miscellaneous	174	66.8	57.2	13.2	1.9
Construction	several thousand	83.4	17.6	low	1.4
Transport. & Comm.	several thousand	low	37.8	low	3.8
Tourism	more than 100	high	33.5	< 10	8.0
Commerce & Other Services	several thousand	low	33.6	< 1	1.0

Source: Institut National de la Statistique, Recensement des Activités Industrielles, 1980, 1981; Enquête Population – Emploi 1980, and unpublished data.

The same principles also would seem to go quite far in explaining changes in the effectiveness of collective action over time. For example, the agricultural sector has clearly been changing in such a way[17] as to explain the secular rise in its credit-product ratios and rates of effective protection. Likewise, the increasing deficits of public enterprises and the growing diversity and capital-intensity in the mining sector all contribute to the explanation for the rising credit-product ratios and effective rates of protection in this sector. On the other hand, greater numbers and decreased homogeneity of background would seem to have contributed to the declining trends in credit-product ratios and effective rates of protection for textiles and tourism.

Since as mentioned above data on effective protection are available on a more disaggregated level, in the event that more disaggregated credit allocation data would also become available, the same principles could undoubtedly be used to explain the observed variations in the indicators of success in collective action across subsectors but within sectors. For example, it is generally understood that one of the most substantially protected sectors is poultry and eggs and that much of the credit allocated to agriculture has actually gone to the poultry and eggs subsector, implying that this subsector has been one of the most successful in collective action. Since this sector is dominated by larger farms located near urban areas and requiring relatively large investments in capital, this outcome is very consistent with the aforementioned principles of collective action.

One can certainly conclude that the results support several Olsonian hypotheses concerning the relevance of group characteristics. Nevertheless, without Hirschman's hypothesis concerning the relative cost of exit, one would not be able to explain the comparative strength of producer organizations in textiles and hotels and to a lesser extent also electricity and petroleum.

However, considering the small number of available observations (due to the highly aggregative nature of the data) and that the results are consistent with several of the aforementioned hypothesized determinants of collective action at the same time, unfortunately they shed little light on the relative strength of these various determinants.

V. Differing Approaches to Common Problems of Producer Organizations: A Comparative Analysis

The results of the previous sections show that several elements in the the-

---

[17]The more commercially oriented and agro-industry ends of the industry dominated by large urban-based farmers have been growing in importance relative to those parts of the industry dominated by the smaller subsistence farmers. Also, capital and other modern inputs have been of growing importance.

ory of collective action articulated in Chapter 3 above can help explain the origin and relative strength of different producer groups in Tunisia. Nevertheless, since virtually all the factors investigated, such as group characteristics and environmental considerations, may be considered exogenously given to any group at any particular point in time, one might suppose these collective action principles to be rather useless for policy purposes. As we shall soon see, however, for some Tunisian producers at least, this does not seem to have been the case.

To investigate the possibility that the principles of collective action might be applicable to strategic policy decisions of individual producer groups, in this section we provide a comparative analysis of the approaches that different producer organizations have taken to common problems. The problems considered are: (1) free-riding, (2) free entry, (3) price competition and (4) quality control and the need for other services.

Before drawing conclusions from the comparative experience of different producer organizations, it is important to bear in mind both the overall relative weakness of producer organizations in Tunisia and the diverse circumstances of the different sectors. Because of the first consideration, one should not expect great success among Tunisia's producer organizations in dealing with any of the problems facing them; because of the second, one should be extremely cautious in drawing general conclusions inasmuch as in this case the conceptually useful *ceteris paribus* conditions clearly do not hold across sectors.

A. Approaches to the Control of Free-Riding

As noted above, the most basic obstacle to success in collective action is free-riding. Free-riding can take many different forms. For example, in the context of business organizations, free-riding can take the form of non-payment of dues, non-participation in meetings and other activities of the organization, and non-adherence to group decisions.

Free-riding in the form of non-payment of dues appears to be very common in Tunisian producer organizations. Moreover, variations in the avoidance of paying dues across sectors would seem to be consistent with the principles of collective action. In particular, the non-payment of dues is much more common among the many and diversely located members of UNAT than among industrialists, hotel owners, stock brokers, and banks which are much fewer in number, more concentrated in location and more capital-intensive. Moreover, the high delinquency rate in paying membership dues observed among farmers occurs in spite of the fact that their dues are low (less than

$2 US per annum)[18] and the absence of delinquency in such payments among stock brokers occurs despite the high dues (more than $4000 per annum) in this sector. Nevertheless, there would still seem to be room for the influence of deliberate policies and strategies in explaining differential success in limiting free-riding.

The non-payment of dues was a big problem for UTICA before 1975. As mentioned above, however, in 1976 the payment of UTICA dues at a rate of 0.8% of gross sales was made automatic as part of the social security payments for all industrial enterprises. Since the payments do not go directly to UTICA but rather to a more general government-controlled fund to which UTICA has to appeal for support, and still, once obtained, UTICA's funds go primarily only to its sectoral federations but *not* to its individual producer organizations, non-payment of dues remains an important problem for the individual unions.

Some of the devices used by individual producer unions to reduce delinquency in the payment of dues are: (1) to link such payment to voting rights (as in the hotel organization),[19] (2) to make the dues seem fair by varying them by size of firm (as for hotels and architects)[20] and (3) to link the payment of dues to services rendered. Some organizations have also found that the circulation of a list of members delinquent in their payment of dues has been a useful device in inducing payment of dues. While it is generally recognized that in principle the withdrawal of benefits to non-paying members is the best solution, in practice, since many services of producer organizations are of a public good type, quite frequently this solution is infeasible.

Naturally, in a relatively heterogeneous producer union the value of any service rendered by the union producer varies considerably from one member to another according to their size, location and other circumstances. Since the provision of highly valued services can be an important incentive for dues payment, producer organizations frequently find it desirable to offer a

---

[18] In our interviews, many producer organizations stated that it is currently imperative to keep the dues at low levels in view of (a) the limited experience to date in paying dues, (b) the limited ability of dues payers to see the benefits thereof and (c) the lack of experience with cooperative solutions (as evidenced by the dominance of family businesses in most sectors of the economy). Then, once group solidarity develops, members come to appreciate the potential benefits of collective action, and non-payment of dues can be eliminated, they expect that dues may be raised without lowering dues payment rates.

[19] The hotel organization is a federation, *Fédération Tunisienne de l'Hôtellerie*, as opposed to a union (syndicate) because it consists of five regional unions.

[20] The architects union is known as the *Ordre des Architectes de Tunisie*.

very diverse set of services. While the provision of large numbers of services may be facilitated by economies of *scope* in the provision of such services, economies of *scale* in the provision of individual services tend to limit the number of services which producer organizations can afford to supply. As a result, another strategy followed by some of Tunisia's producer organizations is to preserve sectoral homogeneity, (as in the case of customs clearers) by defining the sector of activity relatively narrowly and in some cases (as in the case of lawyers) by keeping firms homogeneously small[21] or as in the case of taxis and hotels by restricting membership to a certain city or town.

The Tunisian experience shows that, when free-riding with respect to the payment of dues is low, as in the aforementioned case of UTICA as a whole, free-riding may be pervasive in other forms, such as non-participation in union meetings and non-adherance to group decisions. Active participation in group activities is likely to be especially costly in the early stages in which most Tunisian producer organizations still find themselves. This is because all such organizations and activities require substantial start-up costs, the benefits of which are likely to be attainable only after a considerable period of time. Given the relatively young profile of Tunisian firms, the costs of active participation in terms of both time (which for firm managers is invariably in scarce supply) and money are likely to be sufficiently high to seriously discourage active participation, thereby contributing to the overall weakness of Tunisia's producer organizations.

In the interviews several leaders of individual producer unions indicated that positive selective incentives had been very useful in encouraging their participation. For example, since many of Tunisia's producer organizations are affiliated with counterpart international organizations, in a country with relatively strong exchange controls, the right to participate in international meetings with expenses paid by the organization, which is frequently given to the top officers of such organizations, can be an attractive incentive. Another important selective incentive for active participation is that one's access (for private purposes) to high officials in government is likely to be enhanced when one goes as the officer or representative of a producer union or federation. The awareness of the need for such selective incentives in encouraging participation by the leaders of individual unions in the sectoral federations, perhaps explains why, at present at least, the only non-bank, non-government members of the board of governors of the Central Bank of Tunisia, which plays such an important role in the rationing of bank credit among sectors, happen to be the presidents of two of the more active federations associated with

---

[21]The rule making this possible is discussed below under "control of entry."

UTICA (those of hotels and exporters).[22] Both UTICA and UNAT also acknowledge that they try to lighten the cost of active participation in unions and federations by sharing in the costs of their activities.

Another strategy that some group leaders have found useful for overcoming free-riding is to join several different producer unions. Quite naturally, the practice of multiple memberships leads to overlapping memberships, a characteristic which seems to facilitate collective action. For example, several informants cited examples in which subgroups of firms, frustrated by their inability to obtain collective action within relatively large producer groups, without withdrawing from these groups have formed new, smaller and more homogeneous groups which have succeeded in undertaking the desired collective action. The practice of membership in multiple and overlapping producer groups not only allows for more collective action than might otherwise be the case,[23] but also has the effect of introducing some competition for membership among different group leaders. Hence, it gives group leaders an incentive to undertake collective action conducive to the interests of group members.

When as in the Tunisian context multiple memberships are possible, large members with good contacts with government officials are likely to be in an especially advantageous position to achieve desired collective action. For example, a resourceful manager of a large and important member of a particular producer organization may be able to exercise considerable clout over other members in achieving collective action by threatening to exit that group in favor of another if the other group members refuse to go along.

Another important means of overcoming the free-rider problem is by practicing the lessons of Hirschman's "tunnel effect," wherein the quasi-collective good can first be provided to those for whom its provision is seen as most deserving or badly needed on the understanding that the turn of others will come, thereby encouraging their active participation in the meantime.

An interesting example of the successful application of such a strategy is the taxi federation, a federation that includes three distinct taxi unions, the unions of popular taxis, collective taxis (mostly used for taking groups of passengers from one city to another) and tourist taxis (used for long distance

---

[22]The exporter organization known as the *Fédération Tunisienne des Exportateurs* is the most recently created federation.

[23]Specifically, in cases in which group homogeneity is more essential to success in collective action than economies of scale and of scope in the production of the public good, membership in a small group may be useful for collective action. On the other hand, in cases in which the latter are more important than the former, membership in larger, more heterogeneous groups may be beneficial.

travel and excursions for individuals or small groups). The taxi federation realized that a commom problem facing all taxis but in different degrees of urgency was the high rate of taxation on imported or domestically produced automobiles. In the absence of exemptions from such taxes, the taxi owners would have been unable to replace their depreciated automobiles with new ones, with unfavorable effects on operating costs in the long run. Early in the federation's existence, the need for replacement was deemed to be most severe for the popular taxis since they consisted of the smallest and cheapest automobiles which were generally in the poorest condition. Strategically, therefore, the taxi federation pressed for tax exemptions on replacement automobiles for the popular taxis only (and on a time schedule such that the revenue loss to government in any given year would not be particularly severe). Moreover, since the tax rates were lower for small vehicles than for large ones, and yet more users would benefit from newer, better functioning popular taxis, the benefits relative to costs of such exemptions were especially high.

The other taxi unions remained active in pressing the relevant government officials to accept the federation's proposal for tax exemptions on replacement popular taxis, anticipating that, once the principle was established, it could be subsequently applied to them. Since in their case the tax rates were higher, but the initial state of their vehicles generally better, the wait for these exemptions could be well worthwhile. Interestingly enough, the government has recently accorded the tax concessions on replacement to collective taxis, thereby both validating and reinforcing the tunnel effect as far as the tourist taxis are concerned.

B. Approaches to Control of Entry

The fear of excessive competition from other producers — domestic or foreign — is of course a basic concern for producers in any sector, regardless of whether they pay dues, attend meetings and abide by group rules. Not surprisingly, therefore, all but the weakest sectors, like agriculture, fishing and commerce, have succeeded in imposing important barriers to entry. In some cases the barriers to entry are primarily directed against foreign competitors. This is especially true, of course, where foreign competitors have important advantages over domestic producers in terms of access to technology, skilled labor, marketing techniques or lower cost sources of labor or raw materials. Indeed, it is the general relevance and importance of foreign competition that accounts for our use in the previous section of effective rates of protection as an important indicator of success in collective action.

Nevertheless, since the creation of a tariff is a public good in which the benefits to local producers apply to *all* such producers regardless of their participation in the collective action responsible for their imposition, collective action to impose protective tariffs is vulnerable to free-riding incentives. Of course, import quotas can be designed in such a way as to have the same effect on consumer and producer welfare and balance of payments as tariffs. Moreover, several of Tunisia's producer unions have realized that the imposition of quotas can have important advantages over tariffs in terms of collective action. In particular, since quotas generate rents for those able to obtain import licenses, the producer organization may be able to reward participation in collective action by influencing the allocation of quotas in the direction of active participants. Indeed, as noted above, almost from their very inception, several Tunisian producer groups have been successful in obtaining protection against imports through the imposition of restrictive import quotas and at the same time securing allocations of profitable import licenses for activist local producers.

In some sectors, however, neither tariff nor quota protection is practicable and, even if it were, protection from "excessive" competition from domestic suppliers may be more relevant. Naturally, protection from domestic competitors becomes relatively more important once, for whatever reasons, foreign competition is excluded. Some attempts to limit entry of domestic producers are quite direct, as in the case of taxis, most industries, hotels and banks, where licensing is practiced. In most of these cases, the producer groups tend to pressure the authorities to limit the number of new licenses issued.[24] In the case of large industrial investments, by law, approvals at many levels of authority must be obtained and the views of existing producers must be heard before the new investments can be made.[25] In the case of hotels it takes the form of negotiations on the number of new beds authorized in the tourism component of the five year development plans.

---

[24] In the case of collective taxis, the official political party seems to have played a role in restricting entry and allocating licenses inasmuch as party members, and especially those who were active in the pre-independence period, are reported to be disproportionately prominent among the owners of such licenses.

[25] Because of complaints about the multiplicity of permissions needed in order to obtain an investment license, in the 1970's the *Agence de Promotion des Investissements* (API) was created to "coordinate" and facilitate the process. In practice, however, it has meant still another level for denying entry. Not surprisingly, API has on occasion been charged with corruption and with favoritism in protecting well-established firms. Its official rule, however, is to deny all applications in sectors for which resulting capacity would exceed the existing size of the domestic market by 20% or more.

In some cases, however, the barriers to entry that producer groups erect are more indirect. For example, after Tunisian independence, foreigners who previously had dominated the legal profession were effectively excluded by changing the official language of the legal system from French to Arabic [Quentin (1971)]. Several producer organizations have limitations in the form of minimum age (e.g., stock brokers), years of experience (apartment building and shopping center developers) and proficiency tests (customs clearers). Still others deter entry by requiring financial deposits with the relevant authorities (e.g., the Stock Exchange in the case of stock brokers) or in-kind deposits in the case of popular taxis since taxi owners must prove ownership of the automobile before becoming eligible for a license). In other cases, as in the case of apartment and shopping center developers and lawyers where membership in the sectoral organization is a condition for entry, members can exercise their control over entry by voting upon new members.

Another means of limiting competition is by control of size. Individual lawyers are protected by the restriction that individual lawyers may participate in only one association of lawyers with a maximum of three members in any such association.[26] In industry, licensing procedures generally apply to expansions of existing plants as well as to new ones. Several of Tunisia's industrial incentives are greater for small firms than for large ones and licenses are easier to obtain for small investments than for large ones.

In still other cases, barriers to entry take the form of quality control. For example, the hotel federation has instituted stiff requirements for quality for anyone wanting to open a hotel.[27] Taxis have to satisfy certain safety and other requirements in a physical inspection. Architects have to have their credentials approved. Freight forwarders have to pass an exam.[28]

Even the best of these formal restrictions are unlikely to be effective if they cannot be effectively enforced. For example, even though architects have been able to create formal barriers to entry, since many building permits are granted to uncertified architects (including mechanical engineers), they remain a relatively weak group. Licensed taxis face competition from unlicensed taxis. Licensed and hence taxed commercial enterprises receive competition from unlicensed and often untaxed street vendors. While many

---

[26]Naturally, such restrictions may undermine the prospects for successful collective action by increasing the size of the group and reducing size asymmetry.

[27]Nevertheless, the image of the quality of Tunisian hotels abroad is reported to be fairly low.

[28]None of these testing procedures is anywhere near as restrictive as in the case of lawyers in Japan or movie directors in the U.S. where only tiny fractions of the eligible test takers manage to pass.

of the officers of producer organizations speak of the need for laws with sanctions against illegal competitors, clearly laws may not be sufficient. In such circumstances, therefore, success in collective action may require not only laws but also their effective enforcement. Naturally, however, success with any one particular type of regulation may generate rents inducing the competition for these rents and hence the need for new kinds of restrictions in order to preserve them.

C. Approaches to the Control of Price Competition

Since (as we have seen) restrictions on entry are generally much less than perfect, firms frequently try to protect their ability to make profits by limiting the amount of price competition. Until recently (as noted in ch. 7 above), three different price regimes have prevailed: fixed prices (which apply to basic foodstuffs, energy, transportation, medical services, construction materials and TV sets), authorized prices (prices approved on the basis of authorized margins based on presubmitted cost schedules which apply to most manufactured goods) and free prices (which apply only to agricultural and fish products and to hotels). Since changes in authorized prices typically require considerable documentation and delays (not infrequently several years), for all practical purposes authorized prices are prices fixed by a markup rule. Nevertheless, inasmuch as the fixed price regime is generally applied in order to protect consumer interests whereas under the authorized price regime the relatively high margins (generally about 20%) virtually guarantee producer profitability, from the perspective of producers there is a tremendous difference between these two price regimes. Only with the accelerated inflationary forces of the late 1970's and early 1980's did producers begin to campaign for a relaxation of the authorized price regime which applied to most non-agricultural sectors. Indeed, UTICA played a major role in this process by getting the authorities to allow the firms in a particular sector to change their authorized prices without prior approval as long as they would submit the evidence on industry costs justifying the need for higher prices. By and large, this "self-authorized price" regime has been satisfactory to producers since its fixed markup rule guarantees profitability and discourages price competition by other firms.

Quite naturally, many producer organizations have sought to increase the allowable margins, usually arguing that the existing allowable costs don't account for some real costs. For example, the fruit and vegetable canners charge that their margins should be increased to compensate for spoilage and losses in transport from farm to factory for which cost allowances are not made. The apartment and shopping center developers argue that the delays caused by the complex and time-consuming approval process required by the authorities impose costs not allowed for in the official cost calculations and which therefore justify compensation in the form of higher margins.

In the case of the service sector where product homogeneity is conspicuously lacking, fixed price regimes are understandably more difficult to enforce. Nevertheless, our interviews indicated that, even in the service sectors, the producer organizations were frequently in the process of trying to get certain fixed margins argeed to and codified in law, but with only varying degrees of success.[29] The stock brokers have been successful in getting prespecified (and relatively high) commissions varying (by the type of stock traded) from 4% to 8%. Architects have succeeded in obtaining 4.5% commissions on the total cost of any *government* project in which they are involved.[30]

In the case of sectors where prices are set too low to guarantee profits, producers have chosen one or the other of two strategies. Relatively strong groups like the butchers, who were increasingly caught in a cost squeeze by virtue of the sharply increasing costs of their raw materials but fixed prices of their finished products, have managed to change to free price regimes. An alternative strategy, pursued by other relatively strong groups like the large, commercial farmers and some food processors, has been to get the government to establish a floor to prices by agreeing to buy their output at pre-specified floor prices. Relatively weak producer and export groups, on the other hand, have put their emphasis on removing taxes from, and in some cases obtaining subsidies on, inputs. Examples of the latter include subsidized credit for farmers and exporters, subsidized fuel in the case of taxis and farmers, and exemptions from import duties and other taxes on new and replacement capital in the case of taxis, hotels and some manufacturing sectors.

One desirable consequence of the emphasis, in the case of products for the domestic market, on fixed margins and limitations on the scope and incentive of increasing market shares, and, in the case of those products aimed at foreign markets, on price flexibility, is that most producer organizations put considerable emphasis on promotional activities that would increase the overall size of the market. Especially prominent in this respect is the promotional emphasis of the stock broker organization. This organization's efforts are

---

[29]Notably, most of the failures are in those segments of the service sector with characteristics not particularly favorable to success in collective action.
[30]In the case of private sector projects, however, the prevailing rate is more like 3% and, even at that lower rate, the vast majority of such projects is completed without the use of licensed architects.

largely aimed at regulatory reforms which would have the effect of increasing
the size and vitality of the market.

D. Efforts to Control Quality and to Provide Other Services to Members

A requisite to the promotion of any sector's product is of course quality
control. While product quality is relatively easy to determine prior to purchase in the case of agricultural and fishing products, it is considerably more
difficult to determine and hence to assure for manufactures and services.[31] As
Kuran (1988) has shown, traditionally many producer organizations in the
suq of Tunis managed to control quality through the institution of the *amin*.
The amin was at the same time (a) an intermediary between the state and
the producers, (b) a respected producer, (c) an honest arbitor of disputes between producers and consumers, and (d) an enforcer of quality norms among
the various producers. Over time, however, the guilds were unable to compete with foreign manufactures, resulting in (among other things) the loss
of market, the eventual disappearance of the amin and decreased product
quality.

Our interviews and the available press reports have shown that, in recent
years especially, Tunisia's producer organizations have been devoting considerable attention to product quality. Many of them have undertaken training
activities wherein they demonstrate to member firms both the importance
and the means of producing products of uniformly high quality. Several such
organizations also undertake public relations campaigns to inform the relevant
consuming public about the allegedly high quality of the sector's products.

Several such producer groups have gone further by trying to introduce
tests for the quality of key professionals in member firms as in the case of
architects, customs clearers, taxis, doctors and so on, or to establish industry norms for product standardization and quality control as in the case of
several industrial producer organizations. As pointed out by Kindleberger
(1983), standards serve several useful purposes as far as producing firms are
concerned. Their existence may reduce transaction costs and also capital requirements since, without quality assurance, firms might have to sell their
goods on consignment, thereby tieing up working capital. Product standardization can also serve as a barrier to entry by new firms. Several industrial
unions and the hotel federation have hired consultants to advise member
firms on how to improve product quality. Finally, several professional organi-

---

[31]Eastwood (1985) distinguishes in this respect between products one can
determine prior to purchase, immediately after purchase, long after purchase
and not at all.

zations have attempted (but without much success) to get their members to abide by a code of conduct which would reduce the scope for "unscrupulous entrepreneurial" activities (which might involve price and quality-cutting).

Other activities, not directly related to the control of free-riding, entry, price competition or quality, but which producer organizations have found useful to their members are: (1) intervention on behalf of their members with the relevant governmental authorities, especially in trying to reduce the customary long delays to member requests, (2) providing members with up-to-date information on the relevant laws, foreign market opportunities and technological developments, (3) developing and circulating to members lists of customers who have in the past proved themselves unreliable in paying their bills or of suppliers who have failed to deliver on schedule or at the expected quality (as in the case of customs clearers and apartment and shopping center developers), (4) coordinating their activities with those of related producer organizations (such as travel agents in the case of hotels), and (5) simplifying and unifying accounting procedures and regulations so as to reduce administrative costs (as in the case of hotels).

One strategy implicit in several of the aforementioned examples of relative success of Tunisian producer organizations in approaching several of their common problems and which has not yet been given much attention in the literature on collective action is what might be called the "foot-in-the-door" strategy. This is a dynamic strategy wherein long run success in collective action can be furthered by deliberately concentrating in an initial stage on obtaining a "token" amount of rents from government intervention on behalf of the group. By limiting the amount of rents sought to a small level or for a temporary period, the opposition to such action can be undermined and the subject focus and the timing of the action chosen in such a way as to maximize the probability of government acceptance. Later on, once this token amount of intervention is obtained, the precedent of such intervention can allow more substantial rents to be generated by broadening and deepening the previously accepted intervention.[32]

V. Concluding Remarks

The preceding sections have demonstrated that, by and large, Tunisian producers started late in their efforts to organize and remain weak relative to bureaucrats, workers and their counterparts in other countries. Nevertheless, eventually producer organizations in almost all sectors have emerged and gradually gained in strength.

---

[32]Such a principle would seem implicit in Higgs (1987).

One important conclusion on the relative importance of Olsonian and other principles of collective action in explaining the emergence and subsequently the relative strength of individual producer groups in Tunisia is that the relative importance of the different determinants varies considerably from one form of collective action to another.

For example, feelings of relative deprivation by the relevant groups and political entrepreneurship in the pre-independence period would seem to have been paramount in explaining the origin of Tunisia's producer organizations. Since independence, however, the influence of the Tunisian state or bureaucracy on the subsequent development and character of Tunisia's producer organizations has been very substantial. The bureaucracy has molded the producer organizations into federations and overall umbrella organizations in which bureaucratic control is substantial. The encompassing character of such organizations has exerted mixed effects on the effectiveness of these organizations. Only very gradually are some producer unions becoming stronger and more independent of the government.

Generally speaking, the relative strength of individual producer unions relative to the overall average and changes therein over time would seem to be enhanced, at least in part, by favorable Olsonian group characteristics, such as small size, size asymmetry, duration, geographic concentration, homogeneity of background and heterogeneity of goals. The more dynamic Hirschmanian concepts of "exit", "voice", and "tunnel effects" also seem relevant in this respect.

Finally, the experience of the different producer organizations in dealing with common problems reveals that there is considerable room for leadership, individual initiative and strategic behavior on the part of union leaders. Indeed, since clever and resourceful leaders have been able to use some of the principles of collective action to become more successful, this experience provides still another reason for paying attention to the applicability of such principles in the LDC context. Especially prominent in this respect has been the "foot-in-the-door" dynamic strategy wherein producer unions first concentrate on government policies limited in such a way as to assure acceptance and then, later on, the precedence of these policies can be used as a basis for their subsequent expansion in both scope and duration. But "tunnel effects," the threat of exit, the practice of multiple and overlapping memberships and above all selective incentives have also been useful to individual producer unions in stimulating collective action.

Hence, besides revealing empirical support for variations in both the Olsonian and non-Olsonian principles of collective action, the present results demonstrate that collective action theory can be of practical use to group leaders and policy makers. In other words, while some of these more structural elements are obviously exogenous, limiting at least partially the room to maneuver, innovate and lead on the part of leaders of producer organizations, others are subject to manipulation by group leaders.

Again with respect to the efficiency and growth effects of producer organization activities, a mixed picture emerges. On the one hand, the activities of those groups dependent on healthy markets have been very favorable to efficiency and growth by undertaking actions designed to allow these markets to flourish. On the other hand, many producer group collective actions are of the more typical rent-seeking type which generate barriers to entry that benefit the group but at the cost of inefficiency and slower long run growth in the economy as a whole.

References

Adelman, Irma, Jan Bernd Lohmöller and Cynthia Taft Morris, 1987, "A Latent Variable Regression Model of Nineteenth Century Economic Development," Berkeley: University of California, Department of Agricultural and Resource Economics.

Ashtor, E., 1978, "Underdevelopment in the Pre-Industrial Era," *Journal of European Economic History* 7.

Baer, Gabriel, 1964, *Egyptian Guilds in Modern Times*. Jerusalem: Israel Oriental Society.

_____, 1970, "Monopolies and Restrictive Practices of Turkish Guilds," *Journal of the Economic and Social History of the Orient* 13, Part II (April): 145-165.

Balassa, Bela and Daniel M. Schydlowsky, 1968, "Effective Tariffs, Domestic Cost of Foreign Exchange and the Equilibrium Exchange Rate," *Journal of Political Economy* 76 (May/June): 348-360.

_____, et al., 1971, *The Structure of Protection in Developing Countries*, Baltimore: Johns Hopkins University Press.

_____, 1982, *Development Strategies in Semi-industrial Economies*, Baltimore: Johns Hopkins University Press.

Bates, Robert H., 1981, *Market and States in Tropical Africa*. Berkeley: University of California Press.

Bechri, Mohamed Z., 1988, "The Political Economy of Interest Rate Determination in Tunisia," ch. 13, this volume.

Bianchi, Robert, 1984, *Interest Groups and Political Development in Turkey*. Princeton: Princeton University Press.

Braam, Geert P.A., 1981, *The Influence of Business Firms on the Government*. The Hague, Paris, New York: Mouton.

Brown, L. Carl, 1974, *The Tunisia of Ahmad Bey, 1837-1855*, Princeton: Princeton University Press.

Bsaies, Abdejabbar, 1988, "Educational Change and the Ulama in the 19th and Early 20th Centuries," ch. 9, this volume.

Chichti, Jameleddine, 1981, *Strategie Totale et Restructuration de la Bourse des Valeurs Mobilières de Tunisie.* Paris: Université de Paris IX Dauphine.

Clark, Edward C., 1974, "The Ottoman Industrial Revolution," *International Journal of Middle East Studies* 5: 65-76.

Cohen, Michael A., 1974, *Urban Policy and Political Conflict in Africa.* Chicago: University of Chicago Press.

Corden, W. Max, 1971, *The Theory of Protection*, London: Oxford University Press, esp. ch. 7.

Cummins, Dean, 1987, "The Influence of Industrial Pressure Groups within the People's Republic of China," Los Angeles: University of Southern California, Unpublished Ph.D. dissertation.

Eastwood, David, 1985, *Economics of Consumer Behavior*, Boston: Allyn and Bacon.

Ehrmann, Henry W., ed., 1958, *Interest Groups on Four Continents.* Pittsburgh: University of Pittsburgh Press.

El Sayed, Afaf Loutfi, 1968, "The Role of the Ulama in Egypt during the Early Nineteenth Century," in P.M. Holt, ed., *Political and Social Change in Modern Egypt.* London: Oxford University Press.

Ethier, Wilfred, 1983, *Modern International Economics.* New York: W.W. Norton.

Grissa, Abdessatar, 1988, "An Interest Group Analysis of Tunisia's State Enterprises," ch. 14, this volume.

Gunn, Leslie JoAnn, 1987, *The Socialist Experiment in Tunisia 1961-1969*, Los Angeles, University of Southern California, Unpublished Ph.D. Dissertation.

Higgs, Robert, 1987, *Crisis and Leviathan*, New York: Oxford University Press.

Hirschman, Albert O., 1970, *Exit, Voice and Loyalty: Responses to Decline in Organizations and States.* Cambridge: Harvard University Press.

Hoffman, Elizabeth and Mathew Spitzer, 1985, "Experimental Test of the Coase Theorem with Large Bargaining Groups," *Journal of Legal Studies* 14, 259-280.

Huntington, Samuel, 1961, *The Common Defense, Strategic Programmes in National Defence.* New York: Columbia University Press.

Issawi, Charles, 1982, *An Economic History of the Middle East and North Africa*, New York: Columbia University Press.

Kindleberger, Charles P., 1983, "Standards as Public Collective and Private Goals," *Kyklos* 36 Fasc 3: 377-396.

Kochanek, Stanley A., 1983, *Interest Groups and Development: Business and Politics in Pakistan.* Delhi: Oxford University Press.

Korpi, Walter, 1981, "Sweden: Conflict, Power and Politics in Industrial Relations" in P. Doeringer, ed. *Industrial Relations in International Perspective.*

Kuran, Timur, 1988, "The Craft Guilds of Tunis and Their Amins: A Study in Institutional Atrophy," ch. 8, this volume.

Levitan, Sar A. and Martha R. Cooper, 1984, *Business Lobbies, The Public Good and the Bottom Line.* Baltimore: Johns Hopkins University Press.

Lewis, Bernard, 1937, "The Islamic Guilds," *Economic History Review* 8 (November): 20-37.

Marwell, Gerald and Ruth E. Ames, 1979, "Experiments on the Provision of Public Goods I: Resources, Interest Group Size and the Free Rider Problem," *American Journal of Sociology* 84 (May): 1335-1360.

_____, 1980, "Experiments on the Provision of Public Goods II: Provision Points, States Experience and the Free Rider Problem," *American Journal of Sociology* 85 No. 4: 926-937.

_____, 1981, "Economists Free Ride, Does Anyone Else? Experiments on the Provision of Public Goods IV," *Journal of Public Economics* 15: 295-310.

Moore, Clement Henry, 1965, *Tunisia Since Independence: The Dynamics of One-Party Government*, Berkeley and Los Angeles: University of California Press.

Morris, Cynthia Taft and Irma Adelman, 1987, *Comparative Patterns of Economic Growth, 1850-1914*, Baltimore: Johns Hopkins University Press.

Murrell, Peter, 1984, "An Examination of the Factors Affecting the Formation of Interest Groups in OECD Countries," *Public Choice* 43: 151-171.

Mustafa, Ahmed Abdel-Rahim, 1968, "The Breakdown of the Monopoly System in Egypt after 1840," in P.M. Holt, ed., *Political and Social Change in Modern Egypt*. London: Oxford University Press.

Oliver, Pamela, 1980, "Rewards and Punishments as Selective Incentives for Collective Action: Theoretical Investigations," *American Journal of Sociology* 85 (May): 1356-1375.

_____, 1984, "If You Don't Do It, Nobody Else Will: Active and Token Contributors to Local Collective Action," *American Sociologist Review* 49 (October): 601-610.

_____, Gerald Marwell and Ruy Teixeira, 1985, "Interdependence, Group Heterogeneity and the Production of Collective Action: A Theory of Critical Mass," *American Journal of Sociology* 91 (3): 522-556.

Olson, Mancur, 1965, *The Logic of Collective Action*. Cambridge, Mass.: Harvard University Press.

_____, 1982, *The Rise and Decline of Nations: The Political Economy of Economic Growth, Stagflation and Social Rigidities*. New Haven: Yale University Press.

Pennec, Pierre, 1964, *Les Transformations des Corps de Métiers de Tunis*. Tunis: Institut des Sciences Economiques Appliquées.

Pennock, J. Roland, 1962, "Responsible Government, Separated Powers and Special Interests: Agricultural Subsidies in Britain and America," *American Political Science Review*.

Plott, Charles, 1986, "Laboratory Experiments in Economics: The Implications of Posted Price Institutions." *Science* 232 (9 May): 732-738.

Quentin, J., 1971, "Quelques Réflexions sur le Statut de la Profession d'Avocat en Tunisie," Tunis: Ecole Nationale d' Administration, Centre de Recherches et d'Etudes Administrations No. 7.

Schmitter, Philippe C., 1974, "Still the Century of Corporations?" in Fredrich Pike and Thomas Stoitch, edd. *The New Corporation: Social-Political Structures in the Iberian World*. Notre Dame: University of Notre Dame Press: 85-131.

Smith, Adam, 1937, *The Wealth of Nations*. New York: Modern Library.

Smith, Vernon, L., 1986, "Experimental Methods in the Political Economy of Exchange." *Science* 234 (10 October): 167-173.

Stigler, George, 1971, "The Theory of Economic Regulation," *Bell Journal of Economics* 2 No. 1 (Spring): 3-21.

Timberg, Thomas A., 1969, "Industrial Entrepreneurship Among the Trading Communities of India."

Timoumi, Hedi, 1983, *Organisations Patronales Tunisiennes 1932-1955*. Sfax, Tunisia: Editions Mohamed Ali El Hammi.

Tlili, Ridha, 1977, *Préliminaires à l'Etude du Syndicalisme Patronal en Tunisie*. Paris: Université de Paris VII, Thèse de Doctorat du Troisième Cycle.

Ziegler, Harmon, 1964. *Interest Groups in American Society*. Englewood Cliffs, NJ: Prentice Hall.

Zouari, Abderrazak, 1988, "Collective Action and Governance Structure in Tunisia's Labor Organization," ch. 11, this volume.

Chapter 11

COLLECTIVE ACTION AND GOVERNANCE
STRUCTURE IN TUNISIA'S LABOR ORGANIZATION*

Abderrazak Zouari

I. Introduction

In the standard (neo-classical) theory of wage determination, which is incorporated even in non-neoclassical theories like that of Phillips curves, wage rates are determined exclusively by the interaction of supply and demand.[1] If they appear at all in such analyses, institutions such as unions and minimum wage legislation appear as exogenous monopolistic factors affecting supply. By contrast, the new institutional economics (NIE) insists that such institutions can be and should be explained by recognizing the two different roles that such institutions play.

First, wage fixing often occurs, in contemporary economies, through collective bargaining where unions play the role of groups performing collective action whose logic and implications have been analysed, in particular, by Olson (1965, 1982) and Hardin (1982). In most studies related to wage formation, the union is perceived as a monopoly whose aim is to raise wages by controlling the supply of labor [Freeman and Medoff (1979)]. But, by so doing, unions provide a public good[2] since that rise in wage rates benefits all workers, not just union workers. This means that free-riding is likely and hence suggests the relevance of Olson's (1965, 1982) hypotheses as to the determinants of success in such collective action.[3] Although some authors, e.g., Asselain and Morisson (1983), have suggested that Olson's theory may be fruitful for analysing issues in LDCs, thus far the theories have been tested primarily in developed countries [Pryor (1983), and Choi (1983)].

---

*I would like to express my gratitude to J.B. Nugent and M.K. Nabli for their encouragement, advice, suggestions and comments during the preparation of this study.
[1]See for example Nugent and Glezakos (1982).
[2]Hardin (1982, p. 19) has noted that "it is the higher wage rate sought by the union that might be seen as a public good, if, once the rate is established, it benefits all the relevant workers so that one worker's receipt of the higher rate does not reduce the rate available to others."
[3]These hypotheses are summarized in Nabli and Nugent (1988).

Second, the transaction cost approach developed mostly by Williamson (1975, 1985) emphasises the importance of the governance structures in which labor is organized and the role of continuity in the employment relation. This continuity depends on the skill level of the workers. If this level is high, continuity in the employment relation is sought, which encourages these workers to organize. Otherwise, continuity in the employment relation is not sought and, as a result, unskilled workers[4] groups find it hard to organize. In fact, the transactions cost approach allows us to distinguish between two types of unions.

In the first type of union, unions of workers of specific skill types or "craft" unions, continuity of the employment relation is important and serves efficiency considerations. Among these, the union's role is to perform "agency functions" while being a source of information about worker preferences and having an assistance function for the workers [Williamson 1985, Williamson, Wachter and Harris (1975)]. In this case it is in the interest of all workers, whatever their specificity, that the union be able to perform these functions [Freeman and Medoff (1979)]. This type of union tends to arise in small groups of workers with homogeneous objectives. The chances of success of this type of union will depend on the relative importance of two characteristics: small size which tends to favor success by limiting free-riding, and homogeneity of objectives which may be an obstacle to it.

In the second type of union, unions of workers of heterogeneous skills or "class" unions, the unions are typically large, therefore having heterogeneous objectives. This type of union will generally be unable to aggregate the preferences of its members. It will then find it hard to play an effective "agency" role. The chances of success of this type of union will also depend, among other things, on the relative importance of the same two factors. In this case, however, because the characteristics are the opposite of those in the first type of union, success depends on whether or not the positive heterogeneity of objectives effect sufficiently counterbalances the collective action-inhibiting effect of large size. Heterogeneity is likely to induce the union to centralize itself in order to limit intergroup differences, which would also give rise to a leadership oligarchy. In fact, there can be no large institutions without power being delegated to a small number of people responsible at the top of the hierarchy [Lipset (1962)], who may act in such a way as to pursue their own interests.[5] A union that is heterogeneous, centralized, hierarchical in

---

[4]See Williamson (1985, p. 243).
[5]This aspect has been developed by Hardin (1982) and in the public choice literature.

structure and headed by an oligarchy is likely to appear as a class union that defends the interests of all workers as a group [Freeman (1986)]. Its action implies a political struggle using dialogue, persuasion and organization. The functioning of such a union is threatened by the tendency to free-ride, i.e., "to contribute little or nothing toward the cost of the good, while enjoying its benefits as fully as any other member of the group."[6] This tendency arises from several factors related to the functioning of the union. First, in a large group, the incentive not to contribute is very strong. Second, the inability of the large group to perform its agency functions may induce "exit", in the sense of Hirschman (1970), by the subgroups which consider that they are hurt, thereby inducing them to substitute individually arranged contracts for the public good provided by the union. Finally, if the leadership oligarchy, pursuing its own interests, is not able to convince the rank and file that its leadership is effective, these adherents will have a tendency to free-ride[7] or exit.

The character of collective bargaining will clearly be different in the two types of union. In unions of the first type, collective negotiation will occur at the level of the firm and will therefore be closer to the interests of the workers involved. In those of the second type, collective negotiation will occur in a centralized way. Its objective will be not only to provide the public good (to increase the wage rates) but also to limit free-riding, and to obtain the necessary resources with which to reward the union's leadership with benefits. Consequently, there is an interaction between collective action and governance structures. The nature of the collective action is determined by the internal structure of the union. On the other hand, the results of the collective action may affect the internal structure of the union.

The purpose of this paper is to analyse Tunisia's labor organization from this dual or interactive perspective. In Section II we describe and analyze in static terms the nature of the organization and the relationship between its governance structure and the collective bargaining process in Tunisia. Both collective action theory and transaction costs are shown to be highly relevant. In Section III we develop the hypothesis that the post-independence evolution of Tunisia's labor relations can be explained by a dynamic cycle of interaction between the governance structure of the labor organization and collective action. Some concluding remarks are presented in Section IV.

---

[6]See Kim and Walker (1984, p. 8).
[7]See R. Hardin (1982, p. 108).

II. Tunisia's Labor Organization: The UGTT

The present day Tunisian labor organization, *l'Union Générale des Travailleurs de Tunisie* (UGTT), was created in January 1946 and has existed ever since. In view of the preceding distinction it is a class union since it presents itself as a very large group of workers which builds its action on labor solidarity, regardless of the members' profession and skill level. This aspect of UGTT results from its historical origin and evolution. Prior to the founding of the UGTT, there had been two attempts to create a Tunisian labor union, one in 1924 and one in 1937.[8] Both attempts had clear nationalistic undertones, which induced the authorities of the protectorate to ban unions. Therefore, the union struggle became identified with the struggle of all social classes for national independence.

The new UGTT created in 1946 regrouped fifty so-called autonomous unions. As a result, the UGTT was from its inception a coalition of autonomous craft unions, speaking on behalf of its members but wanting to be the protector of all Tunisians' national interests facing the colonial system. Thus, the creation and evolution of the UGTT were closely related to the struggle for independence,[9] thereby giving the union movement a political character.[10] This political role has been maintained by the UGTT which, from then on, has been a force struggling not only for the interests of workers

---

[8] At first, the protectorate authorities and also the French union leaders were opposed to the creation of a Tunisian union. The French workers' union founded in 1894 was the first union organization in Tunisia. Afterwards, within the *Confédération Générale des Travailleurs* (CGT) created in 1920, the Tunisian workers tried to defend their interests. But very quickly, contradictions between the French and Tunisian workers' interests emerged. In 1924, the first purely Tunisian organization was born: the *Confédération Générale Tunisienne du Travail* (CGTT) that had nationalistic undertones. Strikes commenced and very quickly the colonial authorities banned the union and condemned their leaders [Kraïem (1976), Ben Hamida (1979) and Mzid (1985)]. Subsequently, under the more favorable circumstances resulting from the rise to power of the Popular Front government in France in 1936, the CGTT was recreated in 1937. This new CGTT was characterized by a new heterogeneity (workers and employers). Very quickly an internal conflict emerged between the respective advocates of two different conceptions of the Union, one in which it is an instrument of the struggle against colonialism, and another stressing its autonomy in relation to political action. Later on, the CGT and CGTT entered into conflict, prompting the colonial authorities to take advantage of the situation by banning them both in 1938 [Liauzu (1978), Mzid (1985)].

[9] The UGTT did not hesitate to call strikes for both material and political objectives.

[10] According to Farhat Hached, the founder of the UGTT assassinated in 1952 by colonialists, "if we can afford to ignore politics, politics itself does

but of all employees irrespective of occupation, skill or sector of employment.

The UGTT is a large and heterogeneous union. The number of members claimed by the UGTT in December 1984 was 284,000[11] or about 27% of the wage-earning population of 1,077,000. Despite the absence of accurate data, it is generally agreed that the union is best rooted in the public sector where the skill level of workers is somewhat greater. In contrast, it is not well established in the informal sector or in sectors with few skilled wage-earners. Table 1 reveals the high concentration of skilled workers in large state enterprises and the relatively low percentage of skilled labor in small private enterprises like those of construction and textiles, clothing and leather. Worker concentration is much greater in the public sector (an average size of 773 workers per firm) than in the private sector (70 workers per firm). Not surprisingly, therefore, trade unionism is well established in the public sector where large firms employ a large share of the wage earners, such as energy, transportation, mining, and some manufacturing industries (chemical, mechanical and electrical industries), but weak in the sectors with low concentrations of wage-earners such as construction, textiles, food industries and agriculture.

For farm workers just as for unskilled workers in construction, textiles and clothing, the "governance structure is needed and direct market contracting will characterize transactions of that kind."[12] Therefore, we should expect considerable resistance to unionism from both employers and workers in these sectors. Not surprisingly, therefore, in Tunisia the union has focused its efforts on urban areas. As a result, agricultural unions have been unable to induce the employers to negotiate, hence making for a large gap between farm workers and other workers with respect to both wage rates and employment security.

The members of the UGTT are of three different types.[13] A first group consists of workers, low-level employees, and petty clerks whose objective is essentially the basic public good provided by the union, namely higher wage rates and job security. A second group is composed of medium- level employees, including teachers, whose objectives are basically higher wage rates and for some, the possibility of access to leadership positions in the hierarchy of

---

not ignore us. In his struggle for liberation and social progress, the Tunisian worker comes up against political obstacles which he must overcome, and he can overcome them only by placing himself on the same ground" [quoted by Saussois (1971, p. 75)].

[11]This is according to the newspaper *Es-Chaab* of December 22, 1984.

[12]See Williamson (1985, p. 272).

[13]See Toumi (1982, pp. 308-309).

Table 11-1
Employee Characteristics by Sector

	Average number of permanent workers per firm		Employment in the public sector in relation to total employment	share of skilled in total labor
	Public sector	Private[a] sector	(%)	(%)
Energy	4299	-	100.0	60.9
Mining	3566	356	98.0	20.0
Transportation	1630	45	97.9	36.4
Construction Materials and glass	441	62	59.4	19.5
Chemicals	544	45	59.0	30.6
Food and beverages	416	49	49.3	23.0
Mechanical and electrical	575	90	47.9	20.1
Textiles, clothing and leather	1594	96	29.1	14.1
Misc. manufactures	324	64	26.3	26.4
Construction	153	89	16.0	12.5

Notes: [a]Excludes all individually owned firms, which are of even lower size.

Source: Our calculations from data of institut d'Economie Quantitative (unpublished Tales) based on Survey by the Institut National de la Statistique (Recensement des Activités Industrielles, 1983).

the UGTT. The third group is made up of high-level employees and professionals whose objectives are the purchasing power of their wages and bonuses. Members of this group are also prompted by extra-rational motivations such as the desire "for self-development through participation."[14]

The heterogeneity of the union has important implications for its char-

---

[14]See Hardin (1982, p. 102).

acter, role and effectiveness. As a class union, the UGTT is hierarchical in structure and has an oligarchy at the top which possesses far-reaching powers. The base union constitutes the primary cell of the organization, and groups together all the workers of a single firm regardless of skill level. The overall heterogeneity is therefore encountered even at the level of the base union. The latter has limited autonomy, for its functions are largely limited to implementing the directives from above. The base unions are then grouped into both sectoral and regional organizations. First, they are attached to a vast sectoral "federation" that encompasses all the branches of a sector.[15] The grouping together of differing occupational and skill groups aims at creating a strong and united front. The labor solidarity is based on large numbers but not the community of interests that might arise from a single occupation or skill group. Therefore, within the UGTT , we find a certain number of large sectoral federations, such as those of transport, food and beverages, petrochemicals, textiles and clothing, construction and public works, and financial institutions. The base unions are also grouped into regional federations. In each "governorate" or district, there exists a "regional union" encompassing all base unions located in the region. Its role is to coordinate the activities of the base unions, to take up with regional authorities the conflicts that cannot be settled directly with the employer at the firm level, and to centralize the proposals and requests presented to the central union. The sectoral federations and the regional unions are thus characterized to an even greater extent by the heterogeneity noticed at the level of the base unions. Finally, the federations and regional unions are grouped into a central organization at the national level which is, of course, even more heterogeneous in composition.

This centralized and hierarchical structure of the UGTT brings forth the existence of a number of union militants at the head of the federations and the regional unions. This allows an oligarchy[16] to exist within the UGTT, thereby leading to the conclusion that "we cannot have large institutions... without turning over effective power to the few who are at the summit of these institutions" [Lipset (1962, p. 15)]. The role of this oligarchy is to synthesize the various claims of the union's members (wages, job security, health, education...) and to speak on behalf of the entire working class. Besides, the union's leadership takes part in the collective bargaining and participates in resolving collective and individual conflicts. However, the

---

[15]For instance, the food and beverage federation includes many different sectors: canning, dairy products, beverages, bakeries, sweets, flour mills, hotels, restaurants... This is also the case with respect to the federation of petrochemicals which includes leather, paint, petroleum and plastics.

[16]"Who says organization says oligarchy" [Michels (1962 p. 365)].

"leadership of unions, like the leadership of other large institutions, is thus often in a position to entrench itself and/or pursue its interests" [Williamson (1985) p. 264]. The militancy of these officials is encouraged and facilitated by the existence of selective incentives inducing some members of the union to such positions of leadership and responsibility within the union. Among these incentives is the system of "detachment" wherein union officials may be placed at the union's disposal as permanent staff but, at the same time, may continue to get paid by their employers. This system is applied mostly among public sector employees and allows the UGTT to have a well-staffed administration estimated at the end of the 1970s to be about 300 persons. With their salaries paid by their employers, union permanent staff may also receive bonuses and various other in-kind advantages granted by the union. Moreover, union officials use their status so as to advance various requests for themselves or for their clients to different organizations and to the government for housing, cars, plots of land and loans. The existence of these incentives encourages collective action and allows the union to have an oligarchy that is willing to spend the time required to bring its actions to successful outcomes. These successful outcomes do not necessarily coincide with the objectives of the organization or most of its members.

To finance its activities, the UGTT relies first on members' contributions. For the public sector, since 1958 these contributions have been collected automatically and obligatorily by the state to the benefit of the union. The member pays his contribution automatically, once he accepts membership in the union, by allowing the employer to withhold 1% of his wage earnings.[17] This system allowed the UGTT to minimize free-riding with respect to dues payment by public sector employees. However, in the private sector there has always been a system of direct payment of contributions.[18] The union also owns various assets including a hotel, a printing press, an insurance company, a fishing cooperative, a tiling company, and finally several plots of land.[19] All these assets, income and staff support allow the union to have a large administration and distribute a variety of benefits to union officials.

In sum, the heterogeneity of UGTT membership, its class character and

---

[17]This source contributed about 80% of total revenue. This system was discontinued in September 1985 when the government and the UGTT were in the midst of a conflict which posed serious problems for the union.

[18]The dues are collected by the delegates in the firm level, who then transfer them to the central union through the regional organizations. The federations do not receive direct contributions and have to depend on the central union for finance.

[19]See *Réalités*, October 25, 1985.

finally its self-interested oligarchy imply a high degree of centralization. This centralization has to be carried out at either the national or sectoral levels.

The centralization of the UGTT and its oligarchy at the top permit only global negotiations which hinder the ability of the UGTT to play an "agency" role. The centralized collective negotiation has to, on the one hand, defend the interests of the numerically important low-income workers and, on the other hand, obtain benefits for other groups in order to minimize free-riding.

Collective bargaining is carried out differently in each of three types of settings: government, public enterprises and the private sector. For the first group, the institutional framework is the "statute of state employees." There is no collective bargaining proper for this group, but unions are associated in matters of working conditions, promotions and disciplinary actions through their representatives in various committees. For the second group, there is a law organizing social relations within the public enterprises. Then, individual enterprises may have a particular "statute" defining wage rates and structure, working condiitons and so on. For the third group, collective bargaining on the national level has led to two major overall collective agreements, a *Convention Collective Cadre* in 1973 and a "Social Pact" in 1977, in both cases negotiated by the government, the UGTT and the business and producer umbrella organizations, UNAT and UTICA [Nugent (1988)].

While the bargaining regime and the issues are different in the case of the government itself, they are very similar and interlinked for the public and private enterprises. For instance, it is only since 1973, the date of the first global collective agreement in the private sector, that the practice of individual statutes for public enterprises has been generalized. Such agreements have been achieved for 80 public enterprises out of a total of more than 200 to 400 enterprises (depending on the definition adopted). In fact, public enterprises that do not have a special statute are subject to the collective sectoral agreements which are, as explained below, negotiated for the private sector. However, a public enterprise in a given sector may have a statute different from that of the corresponding sectoral collective convention. But in general, collective conventions for the private sector and statues of public enterprises obey very similar bargaining processes. Due to absence of data on the former, we concentrate our attention on the private sector.

The first agreement or *Convention Collective Cadre* was signed on March 20, 1973; its objective was to organize social relations on sound and rational bases so as to promote social peace and avoid collective conflicts. The result of the global convention has been to reinforce the authority of the two central labor and business organizations as the only permanent and structured

representatives of the workers and employers [Tarchouna (1986, p. 238)].
The global collective convention was presented as a model for subsequent
sectoral collective conventions. It includes 52 articles which are compulsory
for sectoral agreements. Each sectoral convention is required to define its
own objectives, field of application, duration, denunciation and revision procedures, means of coming into effect, and employee representation system. It
has to guarantee the free exercise of union rights, establish the conditions for
firing and hiring, the professional classification table, the wage grid, overtime
rates, the conditions and wage rates applying to night work, apprenticeship
and professional training, working hours, weekly holidays, annual leaves and
holidays, hygiene and security conditions, the retirement system and production norms. Therefore, the global collective convention signed on a national
level requires that sectoral collective conventions be of similar content.

At the sectoral level, between 1974 and 1977, 39 collective agreements
or "conventions" were signed between employers and labor union federations.
The negotiating unit was, in each case, that of the sector or activity, regardless of the character of the individual or skill level of the workers. Each union
federation leads the negotiations for the several activities that are in its domain. Thus, the food federation has led the negotiations in no fewer than
13 collective conventions, the petrochemicals federation in 9 conventions and
that of textiles in 3 conventions. The collective conventions of such varied activities as the mechanical, electrical, wood and printing sectors have all been
signed by the same federation. This means that even if, in a given branch,
the union is weak, it receives the support of a strong federation representing
a large number of activities. It is through this means that the union tries to
obtain the maximum of benefits even for branches which do not have high
union participation rates and for unskilled workers for whom the continuity
of the employment relationship is not important. The collective convention
serves as a general and complete charter for the sector. It organizes *all* working relationships, and applies authoritatively to *all* enterprises in the sector
and branch and, within these enterprises to *all* workers. The collective convention at the firm level has to be fully compatible with the branch collective
convention, and its function must be to apply the branch convention to the
firm's specific conditions. But it cannot provide less favorable conditions
to the workers in the specific firm than to others in the branch. This means
that not a single firm's collective convention, nor a single work contract freely
signed can give the employee more favorable conditions than those given by
the branch collective convention. The latter applies uniformly to all firms
whatever their peculiar chacteristics may be, and to all workers regardless of

their job or their socio-professional category. Since the collective convention applies to all workers, it is difficult to know whether or not the workers are regular members of the union, and whether or not they pay their dues.

Collective conventions fix wages by socio-professional category based on the unskilled worker minimum wage rate (*Salaire Minimum Interprofession- nel Garanté* or "SMIG") set by the government.[20] The conventions establish movements in the hierarchical wage grid and determine the base wage pro- gressions within each category through automatic seniority-based promotions.

According to the collective conventions, unions were not allowed to seek revisions in wage and salary rates for at least three years. Since there was no indexing, the benefits obtained were generally rapidly neutralized by price inflation. Conflicts and strikes soon reappeared which led again to a central- ization of the bargaining process.

This resulted in the second major collective agreement, or Social Pact reached in January 1977 among the government, the UGTT and producers organizations (UTICA and UNAT). This agreement, in effect between 1977 and 1981, introduced the indexation of wage rates to the cost of living in return for the union's committment to guarantee social peace. Wages were to be adjusted, at least annually, after global-level negotiations.

From Table 11-2, it can be seen that the collective conventions resulted in a relatively homogeneous wage structure both in 1977, when they were first introduced, and again when they were reintroduced in revised form in 1983. Especially for blue collar workers and supervisory personnel, about 30 out of the 37 conventions have set the wage rates of all workers within narrow limits of a common average. The conventions with wages inferior to the average are those for construction, textiles, food industries, hotels, cafés and restaurants, all branches in which the informal sector is quite important. In contrast, the conventions that pay above-average wage rates are in sectors in which the public sector is important, such as banks, petroleum and salt. This appears to

---

[20]The decree of March 25, 1973 states that the wages fixed in the collective conventions are based on the SMIG. The global collective convention also refers to SMIG as a basis for the wages fixed by the collective conventions. The SMIG is fixed by the government on the basis of proposals suggested by a SMIG National Committee instituted by the decree of April 20, 1974. This is an organism for study, consultation, and advice that has no decision-making power. In practice, the SMIG tends to be subject to non-institutionalized negotiations between the government and the union. Therefore, it is in the very center of wage bargaining. The union exerts great pressure to obtain a SMIG rate close to its preferences. The global convention of 1973 stated that the SMIG is set on the basis of the cost of living but no pegging mechanism was established.

be the consequence of the fact that the strongest union federations are those which represent the sectors with large public sector representation (energy, mining, transport, petroleum, banks, chemicals), and the weakest are those with predominantly small, non-structured firms (construction, textiles...).

Table 11-2
Distribution of Conventions by Monthly Salary Class
and by Skill Level in 1977 and 1983.

	Blue Collar Workers		Supervisory Personnel		Engineers and Management	
	Salary class (dinars/ month)	Number of conventions[a]	Salary class (dinars/ month)	number of conventions	Salary class (dinars/ month)	Number of conventions[b]
1977	< 30	5	< 80	4	< 180	7
	30-40	29	80-100	32	180-220	13
	> 40	3	> 100	1	> 220	3
1983	< 60	1	< 115	4	< 220	7
	60-70	32	115-135	26	220-260	13
	> 70	4	> 135	7	> 260	3

Notes: (a) The data are for 37 conventions out of a total of 39. For two conventions either data are not available (Printing), or there was no wage grid (docks workers).

          (b) The number of conventions for the Engineers and Management is only 23 out of 37.

Source: Collective Conventions, from Institut d'Economie Quantitative (1984).

Despite these differences, the government's fixing of the SMIG to which all wages are linked, and the homogeneous content of the sectoral conventions imposed by the overall collective convention implies considerable similarity in wage rates and other conditions among workers in different firms and sectors. This is attributable to the global level of bargaining. Centralization allows the UGTT to homogenize the branches irrespective of variations in union strength across branches, and reinforces the central organization's role as the unique and permanent representative of all workers. The ensuing abandonment of the agency role results in both free-riding and exit of the groups that do not feel satisfied by the union's activities and thereby the weakening of the union. On the other hand, however, the UGTT tries to mitigate this phenomena through centralized negotiation. The evolution of the UGTT role is seen as the resultant of the dynamic interaction between these two important tendencies.

III. The Dynamic Evolution of Tunisia's Labor Relations: Interactions Between Hierarchical Structure and Collective Action

As demonstrated in the preceding section, there exist strong interactions between the union's "collective action" and "governance structures." In our view, the analysis of such interactions can be very fruitful in understanding the dynamic evolution of the union.[21] On the one hand, the nature of collective action is determined by the union's internal structure. On the other hand, the results of collective action operate ceaselessly on the union's internal structure. It should be recalled that as a result of the UGTT's historical evolution, its governance structure is exogenous to the collective bargaining process. It is highly centralized and has not been modified in any significant way since its inception. Given its general governance structure, the interaction occurs between its hierarchy and collective action, that is between the internal power relationships in the union and collective action. It is this interaction which explains both the cyclical nature of the union's strength and the juxtaposition between collective wage bargaining and its absence.

In the absence of collective bargaining, the union does not even succeed in providing its principal collective good and, as a result, real wages decrease. This general fall in real wage rates induces the different disaffected groups within the UGTT to strengthen the UGTT bargaining power. To achieve this objective, these groups sacrifice their own particular objectives for the common good. The strength acquired by the union, particularly if associated with a period of democratic opening, allows for collective bargaining as the means of fixing wage rates. In accordance with the character of the UGTT, this negotiation has to be highly centralized. As such, the process allows the union to provide the collective good but at the same time, plants the seeds of discontent of exit, free-riding and internal conflicts that eventually lead to its weakening, the questioning of the union's hierarchical structure, crisis and the downfall of collective bargaining.

Before 1936 in Tunisia, wages were fixed through individual negotia-

---

[21]R. Hardin (1982, p. 12) notes that "Most of the discussion of collective action is static... social life is sometimes, but not always, captured in static analyses."

tions by contracts between employers and wage-earners. Hence, only since 1936 has collective wage bargaining been adopted.[22] Its emergence was the consequence of adopting the collective contractual law in organizing working relationships which arose as a result of the coming to power of the *Front Popular* government in France. This did not last long, however, inasmuch as after the Second World War, the regime of wage-fixing exclusively by the state was established and pursued until the early 1970s. It is only in 1973, as seen above, that the principle of negotiating wages through collective conventions with the participation of union organizations has been re-established. Collective bargaining was temporarily interrupted during the years 1978-80 but was resumed between 1980 and 1985.

Since 1985, collective bargaining has once again been suspended. Therefore, we can distinguish, from 1960 until the present time, three periods with no collective bargaining: 1960-72, 1978-80 and from 1985 to present; and two periods of collective bargaining: from 1972 to 1978 and from 1980 to 1985.

In our analysis of this evolution we should forget neither the importance of economic growth and of political factors [Olson (1982)], such as democratic opening or "getting tough" on the part of the regime for real wages and union strength, nor the role played by the public sector's skilled workers who represent the important actors in the UGTT's evolution. During the 1960-1972 period, wages were fixed in a statutory way, that is directly by the government. Within this policy, the UGTT had only an advisory role that it expressed within the wage commissions. This policy allowed the government to adapt wage-fixing to varying regional and sectoral conditions on the one hand, and government objectives on the other hand, implying the absence of a connection between minimum and average wages per category and the marginal character of bonuses. The UGTT was induced to relegate to the background the defense of the narrow interests of wage-earners and to emphasize the "participation in the national effort for development." One can say that the union was not able to provide the collective good expected by its members, i.e., higher wage rates. In fact, Table 11-3 shows that both the minimum industrial real wage rate and the average real wage rate fell between 1960 and 1970 and that the rise recorded between 1970 and 1972 was not sufficient to reach the 1963 level. Furthermore, the wage structure during this period displayed the following characteristics [Nabli (1981b)]: (1) skill differences accounting for a significant portion of the observed wage differences especially in the non-monopolistic private sector, (2) wage rates for unskilled workers in the public sector greatly exceeding those in the private

---

[22]The decree of August 4, 1936 introduced collective bargaining in Tunisia.

sector, (3) monopolistic private sector wage rates exceeding those in the non-monopolistic and informal private sector, and (4) wage rates increasing with enterprise size.

These elements show that the negatively affected groups of workers are the skilled workers of the public sector and the unskilled workers of the private sector, both of whom would tend to exit. The absence of collective bargaining does not allow the union to mitigate this phenomenon which, although general, is most evident in these two groups. As indicated above, the fact that union dues in the public sector are withheld at the source has allowed the union to limit the free-riding phenomenon in this sector.

Table 11-3
Evolution of Minimum and Average Real Wage Rates 1960-1972
(Indexes, 1966 = 100)

	Real minimum wage		Average real industrial wage
	Industry	Agriculture	
1960	102	92	-
1963	105	105	103
1963	97	97	100
1967	90	128	99
1972	103	130	101

Source: Nabli (1981a) p. 445.

The weakness of the union can also be seen in its role at the level of the enterprise. The labor code of 1966 provides for the existence of "enterprise committees" for enterprises having 50 or more employees and "personnel delegates" for those with 20 or more.[23] The enterprise committees are only of an advisory nature, which explains why until 1977 at least they did not have the expected success. Only 188 were created, and these almost exclusively in the large public enterprises; only 38 were able to function more or less regularly.[24] In addition, the governing political party created professional cells

---

[23]See Nabli, Nugent and Doghri (1988).
[24]Ministére des Affaires Sociales (1976).

within the enterprise which competed with the union for supporters.[25] Hence,
the unionists were distrustful of these cells.[26] The union's activity was at least
partially curtailed by these cells, thereby helping to explain the fall in the real
wage rate during this period. It also explains why work conflicts were scarce
if not nonexistant in the 1960's. For instance, over the year 1968, there was
only one labor conflict [International Labor Office (1980)].

The main economic characteristic of the following decade was the rise in
the rate of economic growth. Thus the real GNP growth rate went up from
4.1% for the period 1966-69 to 10.1% for the period 1970-75. This rise in the
growth rate to a large extent was due to agriculture since the growth rate
of industrial production grew only from 7.8% to 9.6% per annum. Likewise,
the growth rate of GNP per capita increased from 1.7% to 7.6%. Finally,
real GNP per capita increased by 80% from 1961 to 1975 to reach 194 dinars
(460 $ US) in 1975 [Nabli (1981a)]. Moreover, the industrialization policy
conducted since the 1960's has favored the concentration of workers in the
urban areas. This new situation allowed the UGTT to attract increasing
numbers of workers who, regardless of their occupation or skill level, were
dissatisfied with the wage rates. This movement first occurred in the early
1970's at the level of the base unions, taking the form of wildcat strikes
affecting the public sector in particular and especially mining and transport.[27]
The number of conflicts rose from 1 conflict involving 350 workers with a loss
of 88 working days in 1968 to 49 involving 18,473 workers and a loss of
49,653 working days in 1973 [International Labor Office (1980)]. As a result,
authoritarian wage-fixing could no longer be maintained, and in 1973, wage
bargaining through collective conventions was introduced.

One of the reasons for this change was the government's new acceptance
of social diversity. Olson (1982) develops the idea that in a stable society, the
number of organizations increases as time passes, depending on the degree
of democracy, the socio-economic level and the degree of social diversity, unless it is blocked by institutional constraints such as totalitarian government.
Political liberalization, however, does not necessarily increase the number of
organizations. For example, it has been shown by Murrell (1984, p. 166)
that the variables measuring the characteristics of the political system "can

---

[25]The "professional cells" at the firm level are part of the structure of the
Parti Socialiste Destourien, the governing and unique political party until the
1980's. The cell can take two types of action: one political (workers' political
training), the other socio-economic seeking to attain the highest productivity
[See Mzid (1985)].

[26]See the newspaper *Es-Chaab* May 27, 1977 and September 14, 1984.

[27]*Annuaire de l'Afrique du Nord* (1982).

be rejected because no test results support them." This is explained by the existence of significant transaction costs in creating new organizations on the one hand, and the possibilities for increased collective action within existing organizations on the other hand.

In Tunisia, with the acceptance of greater social and political liberalization, existing organizations acquire an autonomy of action that allows them to affect the bargaining process. The latter is seen as the only means capable of reconciling divergences among the interests of the different classes of workers. Thereafter, the role of the UGTT became one of defending its supporters' interests through the collective convention bargaining, but within the limits of the overall policy to which it is expected to adhere. The quality of the UGTT as a partner is recognized only to the extent it makes use of its role in order to organize, supervise and orient its members' activities according to the fixed policy and in order to ensure social peace.

Increased income levels and the acceptance of a certain diversity of society have raised the UGTT's role to that of a social partner to UTICA. However, it should be pointed out that this system of negotiations does not necessarily result in either efficiency or equity. Olson (1982) has suggested that some groups such as consumers, taxpayers and the unemployed cannot organize themselves to perform collective actions. Therefore, they will be unable to block the measures that run counter to their interests. In Tunisia, such groups include farmworkers, temporary workers and wage earners of the informal sector. Collective bargaining affects ultimately only the minority of workers who are defended by UGTT. In 1980, out of an active population of 1,577,000 workers, only public administration workers (192,000), the employees of public enterprises (194,800) and the employees of the structured private productive sector (269,400), altogether a total of 656,200 or 41.6% of the total, are defended by UGTT.

Even if it can apply to only part of the labor force, between 1973 and 1978 collective bargaining became very important for the UGTT. In addition to the increase in wage rates, it has provided UGTT officials with various selective incentives, thereby mitigating the free-riding problem.

Of course, wage negotiations did not become completely free since the state continued to interfere. Such interference occurs, in part, because the state constitutes the principal employer in Tunisia. In 1980, the public sector employed 41% of all wage-earners. Also, in its role of preserving social stability, the state interferes directly in fixing the minimum wage (SMIG), which in turn, forms the basis of the wage rates set in the collective conventions. Therefore, wage policy follows the following scenario: the government fixes

the basic minimum wage, then the collective conventions and public enterprise statutes set up the different minimum wage rates and other benefits
for each socio-professional category. A similar linkage affects the government
employees. This new policy allowed a remarkable rise in wage rates. The
average wage increased during the period 1972-81 by 10.5% a year, which
represented a rise in the average real wage rate of 4.6% a year. During the
same period the minimum real wage rate increased by 5.2% a year. The
public sector firms saw their average real wage increase by 5.8% while that
of the private firms increased only by 3.1% a year during the period 1972-81
[Institut d' Economie Quantitative (1982b, 1983a)].

The increase in the real minimum wage and its impact on other wage
rates has been such that it is the minimum wage earners who have gained
the most from the new system in which the UGTT has played a more active
role in collective bargaining. The most important increase took place in 1977
when the nominal minimum wage rose by 33% and the other wage rates
increasing by an absolute amount corresponding to the 33% increase in the
minimum wage. These increases were uniform for all activities. Whereas
the minimum wage level was 37.6% of the average wage in 1970, it reached
61.8% of it in 1983. In addition to base wage rates, the collective conventions
have introduced various workers bonuses. The most important of these is
the *prime de rendement* or productivity bonus. This bonus applies to most
activities and to all permanent personnel in each enterprise.[28] It is granted
according to a grade given the worker which in turn depends on production,
profession, attendance and behaviour at work. For lack of objective criteria for
evaluating the individual wage earner's productivity, however, this bonus does
not discriminate among workers and constitutes a disguised wage increase.

Since the productivity bonus is specified as a percentage of the regular
wage (from 0 to 150%), it amplifies the wage gap between blue collar workers, supervisory personnel and engineers and managers. There are also other
bonuses paid at the end of the year like the year-end gratuities, the encouragement bonus, the balance-sheet bonus, and the "thirteenth" month. Notably,
these bonuses do not apply to all sectors. Not surprising, they apply primarily
to those sectors dominated by public enterprises such as banks and insurance
companies, petroleum, explosives and newspaper printing. Other bonuses are
granted to compensate for risk, stress, and level of responsibility which apply

---

[28]Some activities have a so-called *prime de productivité* (pharmacies, trade
services, salt, explosives, foundries) but no *prime de rendement*. But the two
bonuses are very similar and can be considered of the same type. Only two
conventions have both bonuses (grain milling, cereal foods), but the "productivity" bonus is negligible.

primarily to high level staff. Finally, different bonuses are allocated either to encourage attendance or to signify significant family or personal events. All these bonuses have allowed for some differentiation among different types of workers. According to one study by the Ministére des Affaires Sociales (1978), the bonus portion in the total wage was on average 28.6%. This portion was 27.3% for the blue collar workers, 33.8% for the supervisory personnel and 40.5% for engineers and managers. At the sectoral level, the bonus portion in the average remuneration was 22.4% in construction, 26.8% in textiles and 27.4% in bank and insurance companies.

Despite the fact that the bonuses constitute an element of differentiation between various skill levels and sectors, the main result of collective bargaining in Tunisia was a significant reduction in wage differentiation. This phenomenon is in accord with the hypothesis of Williamson (1985, p. 250) that "according to the voice view of unionism, income inequality — within a firm or within an industry — is reduced among organized workers." Also, Olson (1982) developed the same idea by showing that the "distributional coalitions once big enough to succeed are exclusive, and seek to limit the diversity of incomes and values of their membership." The contraction of the wage gap aims at ensuring greater cohesion among heterogeneous members.

The data in Table 11-4 show clearly that the wage gap decreased significantly and for all skill levels between 1975 and 1977 during the first period of collective bargaining. This is particularly noticeable for skilled workers and engineers and managers, while it is less extreme for the intermediate groups. The general movement in the wage structure is therefore in conformity with our hypothesis that centralized bargaining would have to be at the expense of wage differentials, and in favor of greater homogeneity.

Collective bargaining also allowed the UGTT to obtain selective incentive benefits for union officials. The overall collective convention consolidates the role of the union in the firm since it forces the employer to receive union delegates at least once a month on their request. Therefore, they assume the function of representing collective and individual complaints and requests. The centralized and hierarchical structure of the UGTT, however, induces the occupants of the tops ranks in this structure to interfere in and control the internal actions of the local delegates. The union's permanent officials external to the firm, therefore, just like the local union delegates themselves, have the ability to negotiate the moral and material interests of the firm's personnel. The local union delegates are to organize and animate the movement inside the firm. They also ensure the articulation between the firm and the overall union movement. To play this role successfully, the UGTT has

Table 11-4
Index of Wage Differentials among Salaried Workers according to Skill Level (Index relative to unskilled workers)

Professional category	1975	1977	1980	1985
Unskilled workers	100	100	100	100
Workers (with some skill)	140	124	138	132
Employers	201	199	196	175
Supervisory personnel	285	277	248	219
Engineers and managers	581	515	502	408

Source: Data from Institut d'Economie Quantitative based on survey by Ministère des Affaires Sociales.

used the collective conventions to obtain incentives to offer selectively to its delegates. These benefits are not enjoyed equally in all sectors. For instance, the collective conventions for petroleum, insurance and banks are the only ones that grant the union delegates one hour of work time for their union activities. The overall collective convention grants absence permissions to union delegates to attend union meetings but only the newspaper convention considers these absences as regular work hours. As indicated above, the overall collective convention also allows a union delegate to be at the service of the union administration while receiving from his original employer his entire pay, half of it or none of it. The rest of the pay would have to be provided by the union itself. However, some sectoral collective conventions require full pay to be automatically provided by enterprises with 100 or more employees (flour mills, insurance, canned foods...). Even while detached, the employee keeps his status at the firm with all its benefits, and at the end of detachment has the right to return to his original post. Since any sanction, even if it is justified, can be interpreted as anti-union, this gives *de facto* protection to union delegates against lay-offs and disciplinary sanctions. Furthermore, delegates are frequently paid at rates well above those for which they would normally qualify, are granted fictitious extra work hours, and receive rapid promotions.

Since collective conventions can only be signed by the leaders of the unions, this gives the UGTT a *de facto* monopoly of worker representation and results in a closed shop system. The contractual policy has also introduced new institutions inside the firm. The overall collective convention of 1973 provided for the establishment of "parity or advisory committees"[29] whose role is to examine conflicts created by applying the collective conventions as well as questions pertaining to promotion and the assignment of bonuses. These commissions have been generalized to all firms with 20 employees or more. The reason for this lies in the fact that these commissions allow unions to play more important roles in firm hiring, promotion, firing decisions, and in the implementation of collective conventions.

The application of collective conventions to all firms has produced an exit phenomenon on the part of the employers who are unable or refuse to apply them. The employers of the small firms have difficulties in applying the obligatory content of the law and the collective conventions. This results in the devlopment of the informal sector, that is a sector made up of small firms employing only a few workers. Because of the alternative of being unemployed, the latter are obliged to accept working conditions and wages less favorable than those imposed by the regulations [Nabli, Nugent and Doghri (1988)]. The development of the informal sector constitutes an element undermining the strength of the union. The success of the union depends not only on the actions of its supporters but also on the reactions of employers who, by joining the informal sector and maintaining firms of very small size, can undermine its success. As Freeman (1986) has suggested, "the decision to unionize is dependent on management as well as workers."

We conclude by asserting that collective bargaining in Tunisia has had the following results: (1) it has made far greater homogeneity between branches and between firms of each branch, (2) it has tightened the wage gap, and (3) it has provided the UGTT with the means of giving selective incentives to its leaders and to all those willing to devote time to union activities.

These results comprise in themselves the germs of the weakening of the UGTT. In fact, the distribution of benefits obtained through bargaining does not appear equitable to all union members. This gives rise to discontent among those who are disappointed by the results of bargaining, which finds expression in the multiplication of work conflicts, the strengthening of the

---

[29]The advisory or Parity Committees are called *Commission Paritaire* or "equal representation committees" and are composed of 3 representatives of the employer and 3 representatives of labor. It plays the role of a disciplinary committee, and is called on to study the problems of training, retirement, social work, hygiene and security. It also sets up a personnel promotion table, gives its opinion about the granting of the productivity bonus, and appropriate responses to workers. Finally, it makes sure that the collective convention is applied [Tarchouna (1986)].

intermediate-level leaders relative to the higher-level ones, exit and free-riding. In fact, while the UGTT was actively involved in the centralized collective bargaining process in 1976, a renewed outbreak of strikes was observed in different sectors (railways, teachers). The union's leadership, which was apparently in disagreement with some of these strikes, did not want to lose control of the situation and, while declaring the legitimacy of worker demands, declared the strikes illegal,[30] which surely created dissension inside the union. But then, subsequently and under heavy pressure, the same leadership reversed itself and supported the strikes decided upon by the base unions and federations. In fact, the centralized leadership of UGTT began to lose control of the process which was resulting in more and more excesses. The attempt in January 1977 to recentralize bargaining in the form of the Social Pact, whose purpose was to guarantee social peace, did not succeed. Indeed, in that year, the number of conflicts was 452 involving 88,535 workers, causing a loss of 140,200 work-days [International Labor Office (1980)]. There appeared a conflict between the higher-level leaders of the UGTT who, by signing the Social Pact, committed themselves to guarantee social peace, and the lower and intermediate-level leaders who questioned the desirability of this Pact.[31] Despite having signed the Social Pact, the higher-level leaders were forced to support the strike movement so as to avoid aggravating the internal conflicts and thus losing their control over the union.

The multiplication of labor conflicts during periods of successful collective bargaining may seem paradoxical, especially when compared with their scarcity during periods of administrative wage-fixing such as in the 1960's. From our analysis this paradoxical occurance was the result of the homogenization inherent in centralized collective bargaining.[32] The absence of an agency role of the union leads to conflicts when particular groups realize that their preferences and requests are neither represented nor pursued. Skilled white-collar employees felt in particular that their interests had been neglected. In 1982-83 for instance this category of employees at the national

---

[30]Karoui and Messaoudi (1982).

[31]As early as February-March 1977, hundreds of unionists rejected the Social Pact and strikes broke out. A petition was signed in this sense by 600 unionists. See newspaper *Le Mode* of the March 31, 1977.

[32]For instance, when a wage increase is granted to one particular occupation, workers of similar occupations ask for a similar treatment, such as in the cases of the strike of the high school teachers in 1981, who based their claims on equality with those in other occupations with the same university diplomas. In this way, whenever there is a wage increase for one group, other groups who believe themselves to have the same skill level go on strike.

airline (Tunis Air) created an autonomous union. Such actions led inevitably to increased internal conflicts. This situation is further aggravated by employer attempts to avoid application of those agreements deemed constraining.

The conflicts of 1976-77 between the UGTT and the government led to an open conflict in January 1978 which resulted in the bloody repression of the union by the authorities. The latter undertook to control the UGTT again, a process which was facilitated by dissension and conflict within the UGTT. A new leadership, more servile to the wishes of the regime, was installed and the old one jailed. During the years 1978-80, the UGTT went through a period of retrogression in collective action. Negotiations were blocked, and real wages fell; between 1978 and 1980, the annual real wage in the public sector fell by 0.3% (from 1,943 dinars to 1,937), in the private sector by 5.6% (from 1,243 to 1,174 dinars), while the real SMIG rate declined by 9.5% [Institut d'Economie Quantitative (1982a)]. Despite the fall in real wage rates during these years, the number of labor conflicts also decreased from 452 during the year 1977 to 240 in 1979 [International Labor Office (1980)]. The absence of collective bargaining at the top made it possible to opt for greater decentralization, thereby allowing the base unions to regain their power, and union activities to become more closely alligned to the real aspirations of the workers. The data in Table 11-4 show that the inter-occupational wage differentials between skilled and unskilled workers have, in contrast to the preceding period, narrowed from 1977 to 1980 and practically stabilized for other groups. In addition, the generalized fall in real wage rates induced the different members of the skill classes to set aside their own individual interests and to devote themselves to strengthening the union as a whole so as to make it capable of defending their combined interests. Therefore, there followed a significant movement to consolidate the UGTT, resulting in the absence of internal conflicts and an emphasis on the common objective of regaining control of the union. In the absence of collective bargaining, the union develops the seeds which eventually allow it to become strong and once again to be an indispensible partner in wage bargaining.

In 1980-81 and again associated with a period of political liberalization, the UGTT again managed to regain its autonomy and strength. The preceding period of consolidation and opposition to the leadership imposed by the regime allowed the UGTT to minimize its internal conflicts and present a unified position. The UGTT again reenforced its centralized structure and approach to collective bargaining, but thereby exposing itself to the same problems as in the years 1976-77. To avoid these problems, the UGTT did not want to commit itself for a long period; as a result wage increases were announced once a year in 1981, 1982 and 1983. The SMIG rose by 36% in 1982 and 11% in 1983, while the average annual wage rate increased by 23.5% and 16.2%, respectively. As a result, the rise in wage rates exceeded that of the cost of living index. For instance, while the cost of living index increased by 34% between 1980 and 1983, the SMIG increased by 75% and the average annual wage rate by 58% [Institut d'Economie Quantitative (1983b)].

Furthermore, while the collective conventions were being revised in 1983, the rise in base wage rates was uniform for all sectors and all skills. The base wage increase was between 30 and 40 dinars per month for nearly all the conventions for both white and blue collar workers. For the engineers and managers, most of the conventions recorded increases of 40 to 50 dinars. The results are similar to those of the period 1973-78, namely a real wage increase and reduced skill differentials. Again, as shown in Table 11-4, the wage gap was significantly reduced for all professional categories between 1980 and 1985. The reduction was most striking for the higher skilled categories who lost between 10% and 20% of their differential with respect to unskilled workers. As this reduction in the gap occured, it became harder to repress the demands of the workers in the individual professional groups. As had been the case in 1977, their dissatifaction grew and as a result the agreements negotiated at the top were increasingly questioned by the professional federations, sowing the seeds for internal conflicts.[33] The idea of a Social Pact necessary for maintaining UGTT homogeneity and providing selective incentive benefits was increasingly challenged by the lower echelons of the UGTT. Thus, in spite of the rise of wage rates, strikes increased, thereby putting the leadership of UGTT in the untenable position of being unable to insure social peace, a prerequisite for obtaining further benefits. Among the latter demands, we find on the one hand a generalization to all firms of the withholding of membership dues at the source, and on the other hand the automatic detachment without any preliminary agreement from the employer.

With a leadership unable to obtain further concessions from employers and federations refusing to keep social peace, the UGTT was again plunged into internal conflicts. A dissident group within the UGTT joined forces with all discontented members, essentially those who were not elected and who were, as a result, in danger of losing their place in the union, to create in 1984 a new union, the Union Nationale des Travailleurs de Tunisie (UNTT).[34] This

---

[33] According to the President of the UGTT, no fewer than 12 political currents coexist within the union (See the Magazine *Le Maghreb*, May 1, 1982).

[34] Seven members of the executive board of the UGTT published a petition

example of exit threatens the power of the leaders and forces them to be more agressive in their demands in order to prevent their members from joining the UNTT. At the same time, the country entered a period of recession in economic activity. While real wages were increasing in 1981-83, productivity declined by 0.9% [Institut d'Economie Quantitative (1987)].

With declining productivity, the government began to find it increasingly difficult to reconcile union demands for higher wages with employers' need to reduce labor costs. It tried to mitigate the problem by limiting the rise in consumer prices, thereby reducing the need to increase wage rates and allowing an increase in producer prices. This resulted in a massive growth of subsidies which, of course, posed serious problems for the country's budget. The expenditures on subsidies, which were only 0.7% of GNP before 1974, rose to 3.0% during the years 1975-1981 [Institut d'Economie Quantitative (1982a)]. This increase in expenditures was seemingly expected by Olson (1982, p. 71) who noted that "lobbying obviously also adds in another way to the scope of govenment when it leads to government expenditures and programs to serve special interest groups."

The economic difficulties, together with employers' pressures, since 1984, has led to open conflict with the government. The latter was no longer willing to grant wage increases, and the wage bargaining process was blocked. At the same time the UGTT was in a weakened position due to internal conflicts, exit and the creation of the competing union (UNTT). What has happened since then is reminiscent of 1978-1980, the conflict with the government becoming more threatening to the UGTT. Besides impeding wage rate increases, the government has significantly tightened the squeeze on the union. In 1985, it cancelled the privilege accorded to UGTT in terms of the state's collection of membership dues, and the system of detachment. As a result, the leadership was once again replaced by a new one acceptable to the regime, but in this case without street violence. The labor organization was reunited by the reintegration of the UNTT into the UGTT.[35] The UGTT was clearly once again in a weak phase, more decentralized but less divided by internal conflicts.

---

protesting against financial mismanagement within the union, and the authoritative behaviour and personal power of the president (See Newspaper *Le Temps*, November 29, 1983). These members have been excluded from the UGTT. Once a few autonomous unions were formed, they announced the constitution of the UNTT. The number of its members was about 50,000 against 284,130 in the UGTT.

[35]The leader of UNTT becomes head of the whole reunified UGTT organization.

V. Conclusions

This paper has emphasized the strong relationship that exists between the collective action undertaken by an organization, in particular Tunisia's UGTT, and its governance structure. In addition, we have shown how this interaction can help explain the dynamic evolution of Tunisian labor relations over three decades.

The analysis allows us to make two remarks on some propositions in the NIE. The first is that the case of Tunisia's labor organization is not consistent with Olson's hypothesis that "encompassing organizations which represent a large proportion of the income earning capacity of a country... have some incentive to make society more prosperous and an incentive to redistribute income to their members with as little excess burden as possible and to cease such redistribution unless the amount redistributed is substantial in relation to the social cost of the redistribution" [Olson (1982, p. 53)]. Indeed, our analysis has shown that an encompassing organization such as the UGTT has to be primarily concerned with problems of distribution regardless of the social cost of such redistribution. Olson's error, in our opinion, comes from transposing the analysis from the level of the firm to the national level. It is true that at the firm level we may expect an encompassing organization to seek the firm's prosperity, for only by seeking this prosperity can the workers realize substantial gains. But transposed to the national level, the centralized encompassing union need not be concerned with the increase in the country's wealth but only with the share it may gain for its members. Moreover, and in opposition to Olson's statement that "no amount of bargaining power can force a firm in a desperate financial situation to raise wages" [Olson (1982, p. 49)], the Tunisian firms, whatever their financial situation and the efficiency and social losses involved, are obliged to pay the wage fixed by the collective convention. This is due to the fact that the negotiation is centralized and does not take into account the characteristics of individual firms.

Second, our case study has revealed substantial interdependence between the extent of collective action and the political environment. A labor union becomes stronger and more active during periods of political liberalization. Contrary to the prediction by Olson, a democratic opening is not associated with an increase in the number of organizations. On the contrary, in the Tunisian case such an opening has led to increased centralization in the wage bargaining process. This fact may not be unrelated to the autocratic nature of the political system, quite unlike that envisioned by Olson in deriving his propositions.

What are the implications for the future of collective bargaining in

Tunisia and for Tunisia's labor organization? The recent trend of economic policy has been towards a more liberal, outward-looking economy. This would seem to imply a gradual reduction and privatization of the public sector. Even if the union should remain centralized, negotiations would be expected to become more responsive to both skill-class type demands and the environment of individual firms. Collective bargaining would become more decentralized, the union playing a greater agency role. However, in the near future, this tendency should be at least partly neutralized by the declining real wage rates and rising unemployment rates resulting from the macroeconomic adjustments that are in progress. These factors encourage the greater centralization of bargaining aimed at increasing wages, reducing intra-union conflicts and creating greater homogeneity. But in the long run, the structural changes in the economy should dominate, hence reversing this short-term movement.

A number of issues are raised by the study and suggest directions for future research. One issue relates to the explanation of the persistence over such a long period of time of the UGTT as a centralized "encompassing organization." In our analysis we have attributed this characteristic to its historical origins, but why did it remain so and why has there not developed a decentralized alternative means of wage bargaining? The answer may be, as suggested above, linked to the autocratic nature of the regime. A second issue is the need for a more explicit and detailed study of the internal structure and working of the UGTT. This would require more information than was available at the time the present study was undertaken. A third issue concerns the interaction of labor and employer organizations in the bargaining process. In this study it would seem that the employers are relatively passive and the UGTT is the more active player. This is confirmed by the Nugent (1988) assessment of the overall weakness of business organizations. As is implicit in our finding of some differentiation in the results of bargaining across activities, interaction between the two organizations remains and may be significant for various sectors and activities.

References

Asselain, Jean-Charles and Christian Marisson, 1983, "Economic Growth and Interest Groups: The French Experience" *The Political Economy of Growth*, Dennis C. Mueller, ed. New Haven and London: Yale University Press.

Benhamida, Abdessalam, 1982, "Le syndicalisme Tunisien et la Question de l'autonomie Syndicale de 1944 à 1956," *Annuaire de l'Afrique du Nord*. Paris: CNRS.

Bowles, Samuel and John Eatwell, 1983, "Between Two Worlds: Interest

Groups, Class Structure and Capitalist Growth," *The Political Economy of Growth*, D.C. Mueller, ed., New Haven and London: Yale University Press.

Buchanan, James M., Robert D. Tollison and Gordon Tullock, eds., 1980, *Toward a Theory of Rent Seeking Society*. College Station: Texas A& M University Press.

Choi, Kwang, 1983, "Statistical Test of Olson's Model," *The Political Economy of Growth*, Dennis C. Meuller, ed. New Haven and London: Yale University Press.

Freeman, Richard B., 1986, "The Effect of the Union Wage Differential on Management Opposition and Union Organizing Success," *American Economic Review, Papers and Proceedings*, Vol. 76, No. 2.

_____, and James L. Medoff, 1979, "The Two Faces of Unionism," *Public Interest* (Fall), p. 69-93.

Hardin, Russell, 1982, *Collective Action*. Baltimore and London: Johns Hopkins University Press.

Hennart, Jean-Francois, 1983, "The Political Economy of Comparative Growth Rates: The Case of France," *The Political Economy of Growth*, D.C. Mueller, ed. New Haven and London: Yale University Press.

Hirschman, Albert O., 1970, *Exit, Voice and Loyalty*. Cambridge, MA: Harvard University Press.

Horvat, Branko, 1982, *The Political Economy of Socialism*. New York: M.E. Sharpe.

Institut d'Economie Quantitative, 1982a, *Document de Travail: Données sur les Revenus, No AM/821021*, Tunis.

_____, 1982b, *Document de Travail: Données sur les Revenus, No AM/821021*, Tunis.

_____, 1983a, *Revenus et Productivité*, No HG/830516, Tunis.

_____, 1983b, *Les Salaires en 1983, No HG/831014*, Tunis.

_____, 1984, *Document de Travail Rassemblant les Conventions Collectives Nationales*, (grille des salaires, avantages et indemnités), No 840627, Tunis.

_____, 1987, *Evolution de la Productivité*, No MBC/870511, Tunis.

International Labor Office, 1980, *Labor Statistics Yearbook*.

Karoui, Hachemi and Malidi Messaoudi, 1982, "Le discours syndical en Tunisie á la Veille du 26 Janvier 1978: l'élan Suspendu," *Annuaire de l'Afrique du Nord*, Paris: CNRS.

Kim, Oliver and Mark Walker, 1984, "The Free-Rider Problem: Experimental Evidence," *Public Choice*, 43, p. 3-24.

Kraïem, Mustapha, 1976, *Nationalisme et Syndicalisme en Tunisie, (1918-1929)*. Tunis: Imprimerie de l'UGTT.

Liauzu, Claude, 1978, "Salariat et Mouvement Ouvrier en Tunisie, Crises et Mutations (1938-1939)," *Cahiers du CRESM No. 9*.

Lipset, Seymour M., 1962, *"Introduction" in Michels (1962)*

Michels, R., 1962, *Political Parties*. Glencoe: Free Press.

Ministére des Affaires Sociales, 1976, *Pour un Dialogue Social dans l'entreprise*, Tunis.

_____, 1978, *Enquête sur les Salaires dans les Branches non Agricoles de l'économie Tunisienne*, Tunis.

Murrell, Peter, 1984, "An Examining of the Factors Affecting the Formation of Interest Groups in OECD Countries," *Public Choice* 43, 151-171.

Mzid, Nacem, 1985, *Le Syndicat dans l'entreprise en Tunisie*, Thèse de Doctorat, Paris.

Nabli, Mustapha K., 1981a, "Alternative Trade Policies and Employment in Tunisia," in A.O. Krueger, H.B. Lary, T. Monson and N. Akrasane, eds., *Trade and Employment in Developing Countries: Individual Studies*, National Bureau of Economic Research, University of Chicago Press.

_____, 1981b, "Inter-Industry Wage Differentials and Distortion in Developing Countries: The Case of Tunisia," *Tijdschrift voor Economie en Management*, Vol. XXVI, No. 2.

_____ and Jeffrey B. Nugent, 1988, "Collective Action, Institutions and Development," Ch. 3, this volume.

_____, and Lamine Doghri, 1988, "The Size Distribution and Ownership Type of Firms in Tunisian Manufacturing," Ch. 7, this volume.

Nugent, Jeffrey B., 1988, "Collective Action in Tunisia's Producer Organizations: Some Variations on the Olsonian Theme," Ch. 10, this volume.

_____, and Constantine Glezakos, 1982, "Phillips Curves in Developing Countries: The Latin American Case," *Economic Development and Cultural Change*, 30(2), 321-34.

Olson, Mancur, 1965, *The Logic of Collective Action*. Cambridge, MA: Harvard University Press.

_____, 1982, *The Rise and Decline of Nations: Economic Growth, Stagflation and Social Rigidities*. New Haven and London: Yale University Press.

Pryor, Frederic L., 1983, "A Quasi Test of Olson's Hypotheses," *The Political Economy of Growth*, D.C. Mueller, ed. New Haven and London: Yale University Press.

Saussois, Jean-Marie, 1971, *Problèmes du Travail et de la Direction des Entreprises dans l'industrialisation de la Tunisie*. Thèse Doctorat, Paris.

Tarchouna, Mongi, 1986, *La Négociation Collective en Tunisie*, Thèse en Droit, Paris.

Toumi, Mohsen, 1982, "Le Discours 'Ouvrier' en Tunisie: Usages Syndicaux et Usages Politiques," *Annuaire de l'Afrique du Nord*, XXI, Paris: CNRS.

Williamson, Oliver E., 1975, *Markets and Hierarchies: Analysis and Antitrust Implications*. New York: Free Press.

_____, *The Economic Institutions of Capitalism*. New York: The Free Press.

_____, Michael L. Wachter, and Jeffrey E. Harris, 1975, "Understanding the Employment Relation: The Analysis of Idiosyncratic Exchange," *Bell Journal of Economics*, 6 (Spring) p. 250-80.

Chapter 12

THE WHOLESALE PRODUCE MARKET OF TUNIS
AND ITS PORTERS:
A TALE OF MARKET DEGENERATION*

Mongi Azabou, Timur Kuran and Mustapha K. Nabli

I. Introduction

For more than half a century, Tunis' wholesale produce market has played a prominent role in both the city's and the country's economy. Over time, however, the market's importance has diminished substantially: whereas in 1957-59 it handled 33.5 percent of the fruits (in terms of weight) and 28.2 percent of the vegetables produced in Tunisia, only 13.1 percent of the fruits and 12.1 percent of the vegetables passed through it in 1980-82. For certain commodities the drop has been even more pronounced. The share of potatoes, for instance, fell from 52.6 percent to 16.7 percent. Further details may be found in Table 12-1, which also shows that other Tunisian markets have declined in importance as well. But the decline in Tunis appears especially significant, since the capital's share in the country's population rose from around 16 percent in 1957-59 to 20 percent in 1981-82. Some related information is presented in Table 12-2, which indicates that since the late 1950s the volume of fruits and vegetables handled by the wholesale market of Tunis has grown at less than half the rate of production.

Why might the market have failed to grow in proportion to production? One answer involves physical constraints. Situated as it was in a bustling business district, the market was not free to expand its floor area. This problem lasted until late 1984, when the wholesale market moved to more spacious and modern quarters at Bir-Kassaa, on the outskirts of the city.

A complementary explanation for the observed decline in the wholesale market's share of business is that the cost of transacting through it has risen more appreciably than the cost of transacting through alternative channels. To the extent that this were true, traders would choose to bypass the wholesale market and use other channels instead. In the period under considera-

---

*For their invaluable help in obtaining information, we are grateful to Kacem Ouassim, the former director of the municipal markets of Tunis, as well as to Jilani Daoussi and Hamza Boumedienne. We are also grateful to Jeffrey Nugent and Bruce Herrick, who both read an earlier version of the paper and offered useful suggestions.

Table 12-1
Proportion of the Tonnage of Output Handled by the Wholesale Market of Tunis and Other Wholesale Markets

(A) Tunis							
	1957-59	1960-62	1963-65	1966-70	1971-75	1976-80	1981-82
Melons, watermelons	13.9	12.3	20.2	20.7	13.1	10.9	6.7
Oranges*	19.8	25.5	21.3	25.9	26.8	17.2	17.9
ALL FRUITS	33.5	29.8	29.8	33.4	31.3	16.2	13.1
Tomatoes	27.5	20.9	11.7	10.9	7.0	5.7	5.7
Potatoes	52.6	49.3	39.3	36.3	28.4	21.8	16.7
Peppers	16.4	15.0	13.6	10.5	10.0	8.8	13.9
ALL VEGETABLES	28.2	25.5	20.8	17.9	14.2	13.0	12.1

(B) Other Wholesale Markets**					
	1964-65	1966-70	1971-75	1976-80	1981-82
Melons, watermelons	23.6	14.6	14.8	10.9	7.8
Oranges*	19.5	28.4	23.4	16.2	18.9
ALL FRUITS	16.8	11.3	17.4	11.6	8.3
Tomatoes	15.3	9.4	6.1	5.2	4.0
Potatoes	19.5	20.5	23.5	22.5	15.3
Peppers	26.0	12.8	15.3	12.2	9.5
ALL VEGETABLES	19.6	14.1	13.3	10.8	7.8

*Other than Malta oranges.
**Those of Béja, Bizerte, Gafsa, Gabès, Jendouba, Kairouan, Kasserine, Le Kef, Medenine, Nabeul, Sfax and Sousse.

Source. Various issues of Annuaire Statistique de la Tunisie, published by the Institut National de la Statistique.

Table 12-2
Tunisia's Total Production and Transactions in the Wholesale Market of Tunis: Annual Averages in Thousands of Tons

	1957-59	1980-82	Average annual growth rate*
FRUITS			
Total production	131.2	430.2	5.3%
Transactions	43.9	53.8	1.0%
VEGETABLES			
Total production	277.3	1,169.0	6.5%
Transactions	76.7	147.9	2.9%

*For 1958-1981

Source. Various issues of Annuaire Statistique de la Tunisie, published by the Institut National de la Statistique.

tion, the officially sanctioned cost of transacting through the market rose to
13.3 percent of transaction value for sellers and 3 percent for buyers, for a
total of 16.3 percent.[1] Both sellers and buyers also incurred various hidden
and officially unrecognized costs, which also rose greatly during the period.
A major component in all the increases was the cost of portage, whose rise
followed the establishment in 1960 of a porters' cooperative, the Coopérative
de Manutentionnaires du Marché de Gros, commonly known by its acronym,
COOPMAG.[2]

Our objective is to explore how COOPMAG has raised the cost of portage,
and how it has managed to maintain a monopoly over portage services despite
widespread dissatisfaction with its performance. The paper is organized as
follows. The next two sections describe the market's operation in the pre-
1960 and 1960-84 periods, respectively. Section IV examines COOPMAG
itself, focusing on its internal operation and on the methods it uses to suppress outside competition. The distributional and efficiency implications of
COOPMAG's policies are taken up in Section V. We then turn, in Section
VI, to the question of why opposition to COOPMAG has been weak. The
final section puts the arguments into perspective.

II. The Way It Was

Tunis' wholesale market for fruits and vegetables was recognized offici-
cally in 1884, and in 1919 the authority for running it was accorded to the
municipality. At first, the municipality chose to have private parties adminis-
ter the market under a tax-farming arrangement. But in 1926 it took over the
task itself and did not relinquish this until 1984. A team of functionaries was
appointed, who became responsible for maintenance of the market's physical facilities. This team also had supervisory duties, involving monitoring of
transactions, prevention of tax evasion, and enforcement of government price
ceilings.[3]

Of course, the official motive for running the market was not to pro-

---

[1] In the mid-1970s, the charges to a seller consisted of 4 percent for the commissioner, and 3 percent for COOPMAG, in addition to a 2 percent municipal
tax and various state taxes totalling 4.3 percent. A buyer payed a 3 percent
commission to COOPMAG. See District de Tunis (1978), p. 42.

[2] Transaction costs, especially those related to portage, also registered dramatic increases in other Tunisian wholesale markets, including Sfax and
Sousse. Information provided by Berbèche (1986) suggests that in each case
the explanation resembles that which we develop here for Tunis.

[3] For details of the regime instituted in 1926, see the *Journal Officiel Tunisien*
of July 10, 1926. Further information can be found in District de Tunis (1978),
pp. 3-5.

vide new employment opportunities for municipal employees. Rather, it was to facilitate the flow of produce from farmers and their agents to various wholesale buyers from Tunis and elsewhere, including grocers and collectivities such as schools, hospitals, prisons, and military units. To the extent that the market worked efficiently, buyers would be spared the inconvenience of having to make separate arrangements with farmers located in different places; they would make their purchases in one spot, with substantial savings in transportation and transaction costs.

These savings did not come free, for the market could not function without intermediaries. Most crucial among them were the so-called commissioners *(habbata)*, whose primary duty was to set prices in accordance, to the extent permitted by government controls, with market conditions. Each commissioner rented a small area containing one or more scales for weighing produce. The scale was the focal point of transactions, where sellers came in contact with buyers. On all transactions he effectuated, the commissioner took a 4 percent cut, out of which he payed various small taxes.[4] An important consequence of the standardization of commissions was suppression of price competition among the commissioners.[5]

On the eve of COOPMAG's establishment in 1960, there were about 50 commissioners. There were also 90 or so associate commissioners, who performed the same tasks as the commissioners, and also received 4 percent commissions. The difference was that the associate paid a large share of his commission (usually a quarter) to some commissioner in return for operating under his name. In the mid-1960s, the heyday of the cooperative movement, a commissioners' cooperative was formed. At first, its 58 members consisted mostly of associates, although some commissioners subsequently joined in. With the movement's collapse at the end of the decade, the associates formed a new organization, the Société Tunisienne des Vendeurs du Marché de Gros (STVMG), which eventually succeeded in raising the status of all associates to that of commissioner. Not surprisingly, those who had enjoyed commissioner status all along stayed out of STVMG.[6] The most interesting point here is that the commissioners did not form a tight-knit pressure group.

Each commissioner or associate commissioner hired one or more secre-

---

[4]See District de Tunis (1978), pp. 30-31. In principle, the commissioner was supposed to levy an additional 1 percent as a floor tax to be passed on directly to the municipality. But many commissioners balked at playing the role of tax collector, exhorting the municipality to do the job itself.

[5]Before 1945, which is when the "4 percent commission" was instituted, commissioners' fees were not standardized.

[6]Municipalité de Tunis (1968), vol. 4, p. 15.

taries *(katib)* to assist him in the tasks of weighing merchandise, recording transactions, arranging payments, and most importantly, collecting commissions. For these services, the secretaries received from their commissioners a share of the commissions, usually 1 percent of transactions.

The physical task of transporting merchandise from producers' trucks to the scales, and then from there to the vehicles of retailers, belonged to another class of intermediaries, the porters. Recruited by the commissioners in teams of up to ten members, of which one was recognized as leader, they were paid by the piece. Thus, the individual porter's pay varied in direct proportion to the loads he carried. The porters were also expected to protect merchandise and containers against theft. While they did not receive regular pay for this service, they undoubtedly received tips from market participants for successful interventions.

By 1960 there were some 820 regular porters *(hammal garneb)* who enjoyed job security and who generally carried only boxed merchandise. There were also 400 or so "fortune porters" *(hammal koffa)*, who generally performed the least desirable tasks, in particular, the portage of produce sold in bulk, which at the time included lettuce, carrots, and melons. The fortune porters' employment opportunities were tied closely to market fluctuations.[7]

Whatever their status, the porters performed onerous tasks: working the early hours of the day, they carried loads averaging 50 to 60 kilos on their backs.[8] For this, they earned pitiful incomes and lived in abject poverty. A municipal survey conducted in the mid-1960s shows that the typical porter earned an annual income around DT200-250, which put him in the city's bottom fifth in terms of income.[9] A striking indication of the porters' poverty is that to the question "If you received an additional DT5, on what would you spend it?" over half responded "food".[10] As one might have expected, the porters came from the least skilled ranks of society. The same survey shows that 77 percent of the porters had received no schooling whatsoever, and that of the rest, most had attended Koranic schools, as opposed to secular public schools.[11]

The porters did not become formally organized until 1960, which is not surprising given their large numbers and low levels of education.[12] They did,

---

[7]Municipalité de Tunis (1968), vol. 3, p. 8.

[8]Municipalité de Tunis (1968), vol. 3, p. 39.

[9]DT stands for the Tunisian Dinar. It was worth US $1.92 in 1965, $2.48 in 1975, and $1.29 in 1984.

[10]Municipalité de Tunis (1968), vol. 3, pp. 21-37.

[11]Municipalité de Tunis (1968), vol. 3, pp. 14-15.

[12]For an argument as to why it takes time for a large group to organize itself,

of course, finally establish a cooperative, but not without considerable help and guidance, over a long period, from outsiders. In the 1920s, the local branch of France's communist Confédération Générale des Travailleurs (CGT) tried to organize them. Another such attempt was made by the nationalist Union Générale des Travailleurs Tunisiens (UGTT) soon after its formation in the 1940s.[13] Perhaps the main reason why the porters received attention is that the wholesale market served as a daily meeting place for thousands of people from all corners of the country, which meant that it could play an important role in the dissemination of information and in the transit of arms. With the beginning of armed resistance in 1952, the anti-colonial movement did in fact benefit from some porters' cooperation.[14] The Neo-Destour Party that led this movement did not lose interest in the porters even after independence. As we shall see later, it has since kept a close eye on their activities.

III. What It Became

Under the leadership of UGTT and the Neo-Destour Party, in 1960 the porters finally established their own cooperative, COOPMAG. The cooperative's stated objective was to defend its members' economic interests. High on its agenda were the enhancement of job security and the provision of old-age pensions. Initially, its members included only the regular porters.

Throughout the 1960s, COOPMAG campaigned for a new system of remuneration that would eliminate the commissioners' role in determining the porters' income. Victory came in 1968 when the customary portage fee was abolished, and in its place the cooperative was granted a 5 percent *ad valorem* cut on all market transactions.[15] The significant aspect of this change was that it made COOPMAG's income independent not only of the commissioners' whims but also of the porters' work effort. From then on, COOPMAG's income was to depend chiefly on the volume of market transactions.

The municipality played a prominent role in the imposition of an *ad valorem* portage fee. It did so for its own reasons, namely to replace the existing municipal tax with an easier-to-collect *ad valorem* tax. Under the old

---

see Olson (1965).

[13]There exists little written evidence on these attempts, although Hermassi (1966), pp. 83 and 150, reports that the porters were involved in the union movement of the 1920s. Our information is based essentially on recollections of a contemporary witness, Ahmed Ben Miled, who has just published a treatise on one of the leading syndicalists of the 1920s, M'hamed Ali.

[14]Based on eyewitness accounts, communicated to us orally.

[15]Although officially approved in 1968, the new regime did not take effect until 1969.

system, sellers entering the market paid quantity-based taxes to municipal agents. The system led to large scale evasion: according to a municipal estimate sellers were paying only half their legal obligations. Like COOPMAG, therefore, the municipality was keenly interested in reform. It so happened that the producers were not entirely happy with the existing system either. Even though it allowed tax evasion, it had the undesirable feature that when prices were sufficiently low their taxes plus fees would exceed their revenues.

It is not surprising, then, that the imposition of an *ad valorem* portage fee coincided with the imposition of an *ad valorem* municipal tax. The new municipal tax was set at 2 percent of transactions, ostensibly to yield the same amount of revenue that would have been collected under the old regime in the absence of evasion. The municipality hoped that under the new system, where *all* levies were *ad valorem*, tax evasion would be minimal. With considerable justification, it reasoned that both the commissioners and COOPMAG would have little to gain and much to lose from underreporting the produce they handled.

As COOPMAG succeeded in obtaining benefits for its members, it came under increasing pressure from the fortune porters, who sought membership. The regular porters were against this, fearing that it would result in less income per member. The issue was finally resolved, with the help of the municipality, in 1972. COOPMAG granted the fortune porters membership, and in return, the municipality ratified a rise in COOPMAG's *ad valorem* cut from 5 percent to 6 percent. The cooperative's membership thus rose to 1200.

The rise of COOPMAG has affected the commissioners' role, in that they no longer control the porters. In the pre-COOPMAG period, they themselves selected the porters they would work with. Under the new regime, in contrast, COOPMAG allocates its members among the commissioners as it sees fit. Each morning porters check in at the COOPMAG office and are given their assignments of the day.

The team leader's role has also changed in accordance with the shift in control. Whereas he previously represented the interests of the commissioner, he now works for COOPMAG. Moreover, his duties have increased: while he continues to coordinate his team's work, he also keeps an eye on the commissioner's accounts to ensure that COOPMAG receives its proper share. Given the demands of being an effective watchman, he no longer has time to participate in his team's physical work.[16]

---

[16]In and of itself, this has a negative effect on the quantity of portage. Other changes have occurred, however, whose effects have been just the opposite.

As coordinator of his team's work, the team leader is in a position to enrich himself by selling favors. It is in fact the case that, for a fee in cash or in kind, a team leader will give priority at the scale to a producer or retailer who is in a hurry. Again for a fee, he will provide preferred floor space to a producer wishing to display his merchandise prominently. He will even arrange deliveries to a retailer unable to attend the market himself. A few team leaders, emulating some bold commissioners, have gone so far as to buy and sell for personal profit, although this is strictly illegal. While in principle a team leader gets paid little more than the porters he supervises, it is obvious that he enjoys substantial side benefits.

The porters also receive side benefits, which get added, of course, to their share of COOPMAG's revenues, about which more will be said later. Since they no longer need to provide swift and conscientious service to keep their jobs — as they did in the pre-COOPMAG period, when their income was tied directly to work performed — a producer or retailer must tip them to get merchandise moved. Frequently, according to widespread reports, he must also endure in silence the pilferage of his merchandise by COOPMAG members, sometimes the very porters he has tipped generously. Many a transactor thus pays three times: a substantial official fee, plus a tip, plus a portion of his merchandise. Despite the additional benefits they receive, absenteeism among porters is endemic. On an average day only 500-600 COOPMAG members show up to work, including the team leaders; the rest of the 1200 members are to be found resting, doing personal chores, or perhaps most commonly, moonlighting.

This absenteeism, coupled with the rise in the cost of portage services, would undoubtedly have led to a sharp absolute decline in the size of the market, but for the appearance on the floor of a group of mostly very young "unofficial" porters. On any given day, at least 150 unofficial porters, out of a pool of 300, can be found working. They are paid directly by transactors who turn to them in frustration when they are unable to get proper service from the official porters. And although none of its members has lifted a finger, COOPMAG still collects its 6 percent fee.

Given that COOPMAG gets paid anyway, one would expect it to encourage the unofficial porters to work. Indeed, it lends them carts, and even pays them a small daily salary.[17] Of course, COOPMAG does not allow unlimited entry into its market. Through its control over carts, which its members have

---

For instance, the porters now use carts, which greatly facilitates and speeds up their work.

[17] As of 1984, DT2 a day (about US $2.58).

been using since 1969, it strictly limits the number of unofficial porters.

This arrangement serves several complementary purposes. For one thing, it enables more COOPMAG members to skip work and allows those who do show up to shirk their duties in comfort. Secondly, entry pressures are somewhat alleviated, and the portage profession appears less protected than it really is. Finally, a market collapse — which would probably lead to government regulation of the portage business — is averted. For a modest price, therefore, COOPMAG manages to keep alive the goose that lays golden eggs. It is very possible that in determining the number of outsiders to allow onto its turf, COOPMAG is influenced by such considerations. The cooperative is probably also influenced by a fear that the lower the ratio of official to unofficial porters on the floor, the less control it will have over market activities.

While the number of COOPMAG members stays fixed, there is turnover. Members drop out for a variety of reasons, including old age and death. Their places are then filled by a person of their choice, who is usually a family member. It is alleged that turnover also takes place through the sale of membership rights, as in the taxicab business in cities all over the world. In the early 1980s, figures ranging from DT2,000 to 3,000 were being cited as the price of one position.[18] As we shall see presently, such a sum constitutes around two years of income.

As far as COOPMAG is concerned, the market's operation has hardly changed since the move to Bir-Kassaa. COOPMAG still collects a 6 percent commission on all merchandise that passes through the market, whether or not its members help move it. Transactors must still tip the official porters to obtain their services. And a substantial share of the portage work is still undertaken by unofficial porters. The commissioners, on the other hand, have been affected directly and significantly. While their commissions have remained at 4 percent, each day they now pay DT0.1 per square meter of floor space to the Société Tunisienne des Marchés de Gros (SOTUMAG), which runs the market.[19]

IV. COOPMAG's Internal Affairs

We have discussed how the porters have succeeded in raising their revenues in spite of a vast deterioration of their services. This would scarcely have been possible had COOPMAG not been a highly united organization.

---

[18]For the sake of comparison, the *annual* rent that accrues to the owner of a Tunis taxi medallion ranges from DT600 to 1,200. Owners of inter-city taxi medallions earn considerably more, anywhere from DT2,400 to 4,200.

[19]The market's new regime is outlined in the *Journal Officiel de la République Tunisienne* of April 16, 1985.

It is of interest, therefore, to inquire into the factors that underlie COOP-MAG's solidarity. Three such factors stand out: the ethnic composition of COOPMAG's membership, its discouragement of internal competition, and its suppression of dissent.

Until the 1960s, almost all the porters belonged to the Nefzaoua tribe *(arsh* or *kabileh)* of southern Tunisia. Like other North African tribes, the Nefzaoua is made up of many factions *(béni* or *ouled)*, which are distinguished from one another by real or imagined kinship ties. Since the early twentieth century, when the Nefzaoua became sedentary, geographical ties have gained in importance, and the clan, which incorporates all the factions (or subfactions) living in a given area, has for many purposes become the tribe's basic unit. According to the municipal survey of the mid-1960s, more than half of COOPMAG's 820 members belonged to two clans, one based in the town of Douiret, the other in Guermassa. There were about 320 Douiri and 240 Guermassi.[20] At one level, then, COOPMAG's membership was ethnically rather homogeneous: a large majority belonged to the Nefzaoua tribe. At another level, it was quite heterogeneous, divided as it was into subgroups.

One would expect the members' tribal bonds to have enhanced its unity, and hence, its ability to implement its goals.[21] There is some evidence to this effect. Like other tribes, the Nefzaoua has an ethical code requiring its members to cooperate with and exhibit generosity toward one another, and to refrain from partnerships with outsiders. Enforced by mental and social sanctions, this code has undoubtedly facilitated COOPMAG's task of maintaining its members' loyalty, while also thwarting opponents' efforts to divide it.[22]

On the other hand, elements of heterogeneity within COOPMAG have undermined its unity. Most noticeably, there is a strong rivalry between the Douiri and Guermassi, which even gives rise to physical fights.[23] A perpetual source of friction is the fact that during most of COOPMAG's history, its chief administrator has been a Douiri. In the 1970s, another source of heterogeneity arose when the fortune porters, the great majority of whom were from northwestern Tunisia (mostly from around Béja), joined COOPMAG

---

[20]Municipalité de Tunis (1968), vol. 3, pp. 9-13.

[21]For a detailed argument as to why ethnic homogeneity raises a group's level of solidarity, see Landa (1981).

[22]On North African tribes in general, see Berque (1974), pp. 22-34. On the Nefzaoua in particular, see Moreau (1947).

[23]On the Douiri-Guermassi rivalry in COOPMAG's early years, see Municipalité de Tunis (1968), vol. 3, p. 13. The rest of the information is based on our own inquiries.

en masse. Currently the northwesterners in COOPMAG number about 300, which suggests that they form a sizeable swing group that can play the Douiri against the Guermassi.

We shall discuss shortly how COOPMAG deals with frictions generated by the heterogeneity of its membership. But first let us turn to a more serious cause of disunity: competition among porters for income. As mentioned earlier, the porters have three sources of income: tips, COOPMAG-designated salaries and amenities, and outside earnings. While each of these could be the object of fierce competition, COOPMAG has so far had remarkable success in keeping all forms of competition among porters within tight bounds.

Competition for tips is deterred by having each team leader pool the tips received by his team and then distribute the total among members equally. This procedure not only reduces a porter's personal gain from seeking tips for himself, but also raises substantially his gain from teammates' tips. It does not, of course, eliminate the problem altogether, for the porters might underreport their tips. It appears, however, that this problem is not serious, perhaps because the teams are composed of at most ten members, all of whom tend to know each other intimately. This no doubt improves the possibility of mutual surveillance, and also attenuates the porters' desire to cheat.

An important side effect of suppressing competition for tips ought to be mentioned in passing. Since one manifestation of such competition is greater effort, its suppression most certainly has lowered the quality of portage services.

The primary object of the porters' competition with one another is the disbursement of COOPMAG's income. As of 1984, annual income from commissions was around DT2,900,000.[24] If divided equally among the 1200 members, this sum, which excludes COOPMAG's investment income, would provide DT2,417 per member. In reality, the individual porter derives nowhere near this income from the cooperative. Our investigations indicate that in the same year a porter who worked everyday of the year the market was open, or roughly 310 days, would have received from COOPMAG DT1,600. But only about 600 porters worked on any given day, which is to say that the representative porter worked 155 days, earning only DT800 from COOPMAG. Thus, COOPMAG's salary disbursement must have been DT960,000, which corresponds to 33.1 percent of its income from commissions.[25]

Evidently, there is a huge gap between what the porters would receive

---

[24]This is 6 percent of the volume of recorded transactions, as given in unpublished documents provided by the Municipality of Tunis.

[25]DT1,600 x 600 = DT800 x 1200 = DT960,000.

if COOPMAG's revenues were fully distributed, and what they actually receive. Where does the surplus go? Another major category of expenditure is social security: COOPMAG is required by law to deposit into Tunisia's social security fund a sum equivalent to 26 percent of its total salary disbursement. If COOPMAG does in fact pay the 26 percent in full (which we have not been able to verify), its social security expenditure would account for an additional 8.6 percent of its income from commissions.[26] Operational expenses appear to be small, their most important component being the DT93,000 per annum payed to the unofficial porters, which corresponds to 3.2 percent of its income from commissions.[27] Even if we assume that the cooperative's other operational expenses add up to 5 percent of its income from commissions, over half its income would remain unaccounted for.[28]

Two other categories of expenditure can be distinguished: investments and managerial compensation. COOPMAG invested in a beverage distribution company in 1973, and more recently it bought three buses. It also has been operating a cart repair shop and an infirmary.[29] Regarding managerial compensation, a tight lid is kept on relevant information, which constitutes circumstantial evidence that managers pay themselves handsomely. This suggestion is supported by the fact that charges of management corruption have been heard routinely, ever since the cooperative was founded.

As one might expect, there is agitation among the membership for a greater share of COOPMAG's revenues. And as one might also expect, this agitation is aimed partly at gains that would affect members differentially — for instance, larger family allowances, which would benefit disproportionately members with families. Some members manage to secure special favors exempting them from the rule that salaries are proportional to days actually worked. They get payed for days they were on the floor but worked little or not at all, or for days they spent moonlighting.

There are, then, numerous causes for disharmony within COOPMAG's ranks, and the membership has ample reason for being displeased with the cooperative's management. Wary of losing power, management discourages those who oppose its policies from speaking out. To this end, it withholds favors from its vocal opponents, and it also resorts to punitive measures. In one incident in 1962, over 20 porters who openly criticized management

---

[26] (DT960,000 x 0.26)/DT2,900,000 = 0.086.

[27] DT2 x 150 x 310 = DT93,000, which is 3.2 percent of DT2,900,000. The first two multiplicands come from Section 3.

[28] 100 percent - (33.1 + 8.6 + 3.2 + 5.0) percent = 51.1 percent.

[29] See District de Tunis (1978), p. 37.

were expelled from the cooperative, and hence barred from working.[30] Since then, according to oral reports we have received, numerous other critics and opponents have been expelled, or otherwise punished, mostly in the wake of leadership struggles. One effect of these measures has probably been to keep individual porters ignorant about the extent of the opposition. Indeed, if most porters who disapprove of management refrain from publicizing their opposition, the individual opponent will perceive that he belongs to a small minority. With many opponents believing likewise, a movement aimed, say, at reducing management's share of COOPMAG's income will fail to gain momentum, even if a substantial majority of the members would be happy to see such a reduction.[31] On the other hand, even if most porters know that opposition is widespread, an opposition movement may fail to get organized simply because nobody wants to be among the first to step forward.

V. Distributional and Efficiency Implications

All these grievances notwithstanding, the average porter of the wholesale market is clearly better off, as can be seen in Table 12-3, than he would have been in the absence of the restrictions enforced by COOPMAG. Under free competition, entry would undoubtedly have driven the returns from portage way down, since it requires no special skills, and since the city of Tunis features high unemployment and underemployment. Yet, from his COOP-MAG salary alone, the representative porter working full-time now makes considerably more than an industrial worker earning the minimum wage. The comparison would look substantially more unequal if we took into account that, unlike the typical industrial worker, the porter receives a second income in the form of tips and pilfered merchandise.

Greater beneficiaries of COOPMAG are its managers and, to a lesser extent, the team leaders. Certain members of the political establishment are probably also compensated handsomely for tolerating COOPMAG's policies. But as is so often the case with such transfers, it would be extremely difficult to find hard evidence of kickbacks. One can only suspect their existence, based on the observation that ties between COOPMAG's managers and the establishment are cordial.

These gains to various parties imply losses for producers of fruits and vegetables as well as for final consumers. To see systematically what these losses entail, let us first turn to Figure 12-1, in which the curve D represents

---

[30]Municipalité de Tunis (1968), vol. 3, pp. 51-2.
[31]On the theory of why policies disapproved by a majority may nonetheless be retained, see Kuran (1987).

a hypothetical demand function of the final consumers, drawn under the assumption that the transaction costs borne by them are nil.

Table 12-3
Evolution of the Representative
COOPMAG Member's Annual Salary

		1968	1984	Real increase*
(1)	Representative member's full-time salary	DT240	DT1,600	137%
(2)	Annual income at the minimum industral wage	DT210	DT1,140	93%

*The consumer price index rose from 100 in 1968 to 281.2 in 1984. See Ministry of Planning, Principaux Agrégats, Série Rétrospective, June 1985, Table VII-1.

(1) The derivation of the 1984 figure is explained in Section 4. The 1968 figure is based on information provided in Municipalité de Tunis (1968), vol. 3, p. 21, and on the assumption that the member worked 310 days.

(2) The minimum wage was DT0.084 per hour in 1968 and DT0.457 per hour in 1984. The figures presented are for a person who worked 8 hours a day for 312 days.

In reality, of course, the consumers do incur some transaction costs. It takes time, for instance, to shop for groceries. From the standpoint of this analysis, however, the crucial transaction costs to consider are those incurred by retailers at the wholesale market and then *passed on* to final consumers. The retailers use up time at the wholesale market; they pay portage fees; they incur spoilage costs; and they spend resources to operate their stores or stalls. For this analysis let us consider all these costs as being borne ultimately by the consumers. This means that for the consumers these costs play the role of a consumption tax, which must shift their demand curve inward.

The curve D' in the figure represents another hypothetical demand curve, which is based on the assumption that the consumers bear all of the transaction costs they actually incur now, except that their portage costs are as low as they could possibly be. Attaining the lowest possible cost of portage would require a measure of competition among porters, some form of coordination of their work, and some possibility of entry.

The curves S and S' are the supply-side counterparts of D and D', respectively. Thus, the former is drawn under the assumption that the producers' transaction costs are nil; the latter under the assumption that they

Figure 12-1
Price and Quantity Effects of Transaction Costs

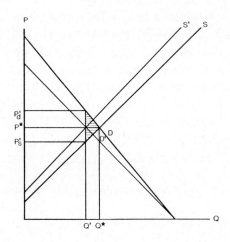

Figure 12-2
Price and Quantity Effects of Excess Portage Costs

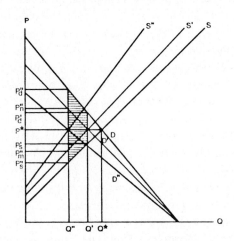

bear all the transaction costs they incur now, except that their portage costs are minimal. The producers' other transaction costs include the resources they and their agents spend in getting their merchandise to the market and in negotiating sales, as well as various taxes and commissions.

The shape and position of D' and S' reflect the assumption that the transaction costs borne by the consumers and producers all take the form of *ad valorem* charges. Although some of the costs involved are better characterized as lump sum, this is a reasonable representation for the task at hand, since most of those with which we are directly concerned happen to be *ad valorem*.

The figure shows that if neither the consumers nor the producers incurred transaction costs, they would trade Q^* units of produce at the price P^* per unit — assuming, as is reasonable, that the market for produce is competitive. With transaction costs, P^* could rise, stay constant, or fall, depending on who bears how much. For simplicity, we have portrayed the case where the demand and supply curves shift in such a way as to leave price unaffected. Yet, quantity transacted falls to Q'. Another significant change is that P^* now represents neither the consumers' total cost nor the producers' net revenue. The former magnitude is $P'_d > P^*$, and the latter $P'_s < P^*$.

The figure allows one to distinguish between two types of losses due to transaction costs. First, there is $(P'_d - P'_s)Q'$, which is a loss shared by the producers and consumers. Part of this magnitude is captured by the retailers, porters, commissioners, and other agents who perform transactional services; and part of it, for instance the portion due to consumers' time devoted to shopping, is a deadweight loss, in the sense that it does not accrue to anyone. The second type of loss in the figure is represented by the shaded area, all of which constitutes a deadweight loss.

Now let us turn to Figure 12-2, in which the curves D'' and S'' represent the *actual* demand and supply curves. They lie to the left of D' and S', respectively, because the actual cost of portage is higher than it would be under conditions that are ideal for the producers and final consumers. Wholesale buyers and sellers each pay COOPMAG a fee equal to 3 percent of the transaction price, which adds up to the already discussed 6 percent fee. They each also incur various other losses, in such forms as tips, spoiled or stolen produce, and idle time on the floor of the market. For simplicity, we have assumed again that the shifts leave the transaction price unaffected.

These new shifts reduce the quantity transacted even further to Q''. Also, the consumers' total cost per unit rises to P''_d, while the producers' net revenue per unit falls to P''_s. The excess cost incurred by consumers is $(P''_d - P'_d)Q''$, and that incurred by producers $(P'_s - P''_s)Q''$. However, COOPMAG's excess profit differs from the sum of these two: it is $(1-\epsilon)(P_n'' - P_m'')Q''$, where $\epsilon < 1$ is the share of produce wasted due to inefficient portage. Note that the entire shaded area represents an additional deadweight loss due to lower trade.

The main point of the preceding discussion is that COOPMAG's gains come at the expense of relatively greater losses to producers and consumers. If COOPMAG ceased to exist, though, the consumers' and producers' transaction costs would not disappear. They would only get smaller, assuming that if the porters' market were competitive, the porters would have a stronger incentive to work, and the price of portage would be lower.

Most of COOPMAG's gains can be regarded as a rent created by the various privileges it enjoys. Following the theory of rent-seeking behavior, one would expect resources to be spent in the pursuit of this rent.[32] Thus, individual porters might undertake efforts geared at obtaining or retaining a management position within COOPMAG. Outsiders, meanwhile, might focus their energies on reaching a position within the political establishment, which would give them access to this rent, or alternatively, on entering COOPMAG. Although such rent-seeking activities may be very rewarding for some of those who engage in them — as was the case for the northwesterners who in the early 1970s succeeded in their efforts to attain COOPMAG membership — they are harmful to society, coming as they do at the expense of socially productive work.

There are two other classes of agents, besides the producers and the final consumers, who are directly influenced by COOPMAG's policies: the commissioners and the retailers. As already discussed, the commissioners no longer have control over their porters. Since this has led to a deterioration of portage services, and as we shall see shortly, adversely affected the volume of transactions, one would expect it to have hurt the commissioners as a group. It does not follow, though, that individual commissioners have suffered appreciably, because the volume of transactions per commissioner also depends on the *number* of commissioners, which has remained about the same. Moreover, the commissioners' income still takes the form of a fixed percentage of transactions.

A similar argument applies to the retailers. Their markups are fixed by the government, usually at 20 percent of wholesale cost, where this cost is defined to include all recorded charges. This means, perversely, that the higher the cost of portage, the higher the individual retailer's profit on any

---

[32]The classic theoretical and empirical articles on rent seeking have been compiled in a volume by Buchanan, Tollison, and Tullock (1980). For a survey of recent developments, see Tollison (1982).

given item. On the other hand, the retailer cannot *legally* pass on to the consumer tips he has payed to the porters. Nor can he pass on his losses from spoilage, or the opportunity cost of the extra time he spends at the market. The greater these losses of the individual retailer, the lower his quality of service is likely to be, and the more likely he is to cheat, by misrepresenting, for instance, the grade of a crate of peaches.

The new regime, whereby the commissioners and COOPMAG both receive fixed *ad valorem* cuts on merchandise passing through the market, has harmonized their incentives in at least one crucial respect: they now both prefer to handle merchandise of high value per weight. Accordingly, they habitually cooperate in giving priority to expensive off-season fruits, such as hothouse-grown strawberries. Relatively cheap and bulky commodities, such as potatoes and watermelons, get shorter shrift.[33] This means that the market favors rich consumers at the expense of the poor. It does not mean, however, that the rich gain absolutely, because the commissioners and COOPMAG have a common stake in supporting higher prices for *all* fruits and vegetables.

It is frequently alleged, in fact, that a commissioner-porter conspiracy is responsible for keeping wholesale prices high. The government itself makes this allegation to justify its extensive price controls. Given the politically explosive nature of food prices — witness the 1984 bread riots — it seems impossible to determine with confidence whether the commissioners and porters are actually successful at raising prices. If they are, however, agricultural producers must benefit, and their losses from higher transaction costs must be at least partially offset.

To the extent that the cost of using the wholesale market is high, one would expect transactors to look for substitute channels. In fact, and as mentioned in the introduction, the share of produce handled by this market has declined markedly over the past few decades. Evidently, a large proportion of the agricultural producers are choosing to bypass the market altogether, as are a good many buyers. Some of these transactors have created their own networks for selling or buying. But most are relying on a new breed of intermediaries: independent transporter-traders, who buy produce directly from the farm, transport it to the city in their own pickup trucks, and sell either to retailers or directly to consumers. That these transporter-traders have created a booming business is observable to the naked eye: throughout the country, highways are dotted by their distinctive trucks.

If hordes of producers, retailers, and consumers have turned to the transporter-traders, a major reason is that COOPMAG's policies have led

---

[33]This claim is borne out by the figures presented in Table 12-1.

to the wholesale market's degeneration. The increase in the effective cost of portage, through higher commissions and tips as well as deterioration of service, has made the market less attractive to buyers and sellers alike. This is not to say that if COOPMAG had never been formed the market would have retained its importance. There are undoubtedly other reasons, both technological and transactional, as to why the transporter-traders' share of the business has skyrocketed. One is downtown traffic congestion.[34] Another, no doubt more important, is that by using alternative channels, transactors have been able to avoid paying the 2 percent municipal tax and other taxes. Still, it probably is not an exaggeration to say that the porters bear a major responsibility for the market's decline. The transactors themselves commonly attribute their decision not to use the wholesale market to the high cost and scandalously low quality of portage services. Significantly, one of the major features of the transporter-traders' mode of operation is that it reduces the number of loadings and unloadings.

By no means is this the first time that a porters' organization has seriously impaired a market. A notable instance occurred in turn-of-the-century Istanbul, where for close to two decades the port worker guilds successfully blocked the use of quays already built to accommodate large steam vessels. They forced ships to moor to buoys away from shore, which, by complicating the task of unloading, increased the amount of portage work. In the process, they diminished the efficiency of the Istanbul port, damaged the profitability of trade, and most certainly contributed to the relative decline of Istanbul as a commercial center in the Eastern Mediterranean.[35]

VI. Opposition to COOPMAG

Since COOPMAG's policies affect vast numbers of Tunisian consumers, as well as scores of agricultural producers, and since a large portion of those affected are affected negatively, one might expect to see an active opposition to COOPMAG. The cooperative does indeed have its critics, but until now it has had no organized opposition to speak of. Some losers have muted their opposition because they benefit from certain aspects of current arrangements. Others have responded, but simply by withdrawing from the market, rather than organizing to change things. Still others, by far the majority, have remained essentially ignorant about consequences of the market's particular-

---

[34]Now that the market has moved to the outskirts of Tunis, traffic congestion is no longer a problem. In a few years, therefore, it should be possible to quantify the relative importance of this factor in the wholesale market's decline.

[35]See Quataert (1983), ch. 5.

ities; for them, forming an opposition to COOPMAG has not even become an issue.

As already discussed, the commissioners' income has not been affected substantially by the market's COOPMAG-dominated regime. This is probably a major reason why, even though COOPMAG has made it difficult for them to intermediate properly between buyers and sellers, the commissioners have not formed a vocal opposition. Another factor could be the fear that a reform movement aimed at eliminating COOPMAG's abuses might threaten their own privileges, too. Still another reason for the absence of open conflict is that many commissioners come from the same region as most porters: one out of every two commissioners is either a Douiri or a Guermassi.[36] Coupled with the fact that some commissioners were themselves porters at one time, these regional ties no doubt dampen the commissioners' desire to launch a campaign against the porters' cooperative. This does not mean that they have no grievances against the porters, only that they are reticent to go public. One does not sense these grievances in talking to the commissioners themselves. Those we interviewed all maintained that they are very happy with current market arrangements. Reminded about their loss of control over market activities, they tended to respond by saying that this does not bother them, since it has alleviated their responsibilities.

The agricultural producers and the various wholesale buyers have plenty of reasons to oppose the current regime, even though the former benefit to a degree from a rise in agricultural prices, and the latter are able to pass the commissions they are charged at least partly onto consumers. Both groups incur heavy losses in terms of tips, stolen and damaged merchandise, and lost time. Yet, their never-ending complaints have not generated a concerted opposition movement. In the case of the producers, the main reason is probably that they form a very large, geographically dispersed, ethnically heterogeneous group, which therefore is difficult to organize for collective action. The wholesale buyers, too, are numerous and dispersed.

At any rate, the emergence of transporter-traders has given the producers and wholesale buyers, as well as the final consumers, the option of responding to COOPMAG's harmful activities by exiting from the market, as opposed to voicing their frustrations.[37] Since many members of these groups have chosen the exit option, the number of COOPMAG's critics is much smaller than it would have been had this option been closed. Meanwhile, those remaining in the market have probably become less inclined to devote time and other

---

[36]See Municipalité de Tunis (1968), vol. 4, p. 18.
[37]On the exit-voice dilemma, see Hirschman (1970).

resources to an opposition movement, since their expected marginal returns from anti-COOPMAG activity is lowered by the knowledge that they will exit if the cost of using the wholesale market passes a certain threshold.

Those final consumers for whom the exit option is unattractive clearly bear the brunt of the costs from degeneration of the wholesale market. Still, they remain totally unorganized, which is understandable given that the largest relevant group tends to be the last to get organized.[38] Significantly, the typical consumer knows nothing about the inefficiencies that plague the wholesale market, let alone their sources. And the exceptional consumer who has some awareness tends not to ascribe any blame to the porters. All too often, his image of them is that of an impoverished, exploited band of un-educated migrants, rather than of a tight-knit cooperative that effectively runs the market. One should not be amazed by this. Given that a person's cognitive abilities are severly limited, he will choose to reserve his attention to matters he might be able to influence, and to remain ignorant about mat-ters over which he has no control.[39] Accordingly, the representative consumer chooses not to invest in any information on the wholesale market, because he correctly senses that he himself, the atomistic player that he is in city-wide issues, could not in any case perceptibly influence the market's structure.

Two organizations that are anything but powerless *vis-à-vis* COOPMAG are the Neo-Destour Party and UGTT. Constituting major links in the coun-try's establishment, these organizations could, if they so desired, provide leadership to an anti-COOPMAG movement. Instead, however, they have effectively chosen to shield the cooperative from its adversaries. This policy is in line with the establishment's general strategy of trying to coopt groups that might pose a threat to political stability. Being heavily concentrated in a strategic part of the capital, the porters are naturally seen as a poten-tial source of trouble. Accordingly, both the Neo-Destour Party and UGTT have made concerted efforts to direct the porters' political passions, and in particular, to prevent COOPMAG from falling under the influence of desta-bilizing movements.[40] It appears that, in return for COOPMAG's allegiance, the establishment has tacitly agreed not to challenge the wholesale market's mode of operation. As already argued, some officials have probably also had personal incentives, in the form of kickbacks from COOPMAG, for actively

---

[38]See Olson (1965).

[39]For a detailed argument, see Downs (1957), chs. 11-14.

[40]This possibility turned to reality in 1983 when COOPMAG shifted its allegiance from UGTT to the Union Nationale des Travailleurs de Tunisie (UNTT), formed in 1981 by a UGTT faction. As of 1986, UNTT and COOP-MAG are back in the fold.

supporting the COOPMAG-preferred mode.

VII. Concluding Remarks

The mode of operation that took shape in the wholesale market of Tunis with the establishment of COOPMAG has seriously impaired the market's viability as a clearinghouse, as evidenced by the fact that by 1985 most agricultural producers and retailers were avoiding it. A major consequence of this degeneration is that fruits and vegetables cost more at the retail level than they otherwise might. A portion of the consumers' losses are recouped by those members of the cooperative who personally perform onerous physical work. But the big gainers are COOPMAG's managers, over whom the membership exercises little control, and who effectively have been running the show for more than two decades.

It is almost certain that society as a whole is worse off than if the wholesale market were run efficiently. Time, effort, and produce are wasted because of the slow and careless manner in which portage services are rendered. Additional productive resources are used up in personal efforts to capture rents accruing to COOPMAG. A further effect — which, though difficult to quantify, is possibly the most important of all — involves society's perception of the relative rewards from rent seeking. To the extent that it seems possible to attain great wealth and prestige through rent seeking, productive activity loses its appeal.

References

Berbèche, M., 1986. "Les Marchés de Gros des Fruits et Légumes." *Conjoncture*, No. 113, June/July.

Berque, Jacques, 1974. *Maghreb: Histoire et Sociétés.* Algiers: Editions J. du Duculot, S.N.E.D.

Buchanan, James M., Robert D. Tollison, and Gordon Tullock, eds., 1980. *Toward a Theory of the Rent-Seeking Society.* College Station: Texas A&M University Press.

District de Tunis, 1978. *Nouveau Marché de Gros de Tunis*, Vol. 1. March.

Downs, Anthony, 1957. *An Economic Theory of Democracy.* New York: Harper.

Hermassi, Abdelbaki, 1966. *Mouvement Ouvrier en Société Coloniale: La Tunisie entre les Deux Guerres.* Paris: Ecole Pratique des Hautes Etudes, Thèse de Doctorat de Troisième Cycle.

Hirschman, Albert O., 1970, *Exit, Voice, and Loyalty.* Cambridge, Mass.: Harvard University Press.

Kuran, Timur, 1987. "Chameleon Voters and Public Choice." *Public Choice*, Vol. 53, No. 1, pp. 53-78.

Landa, Janet T., 1981. "A Theory of the Ethnically Homogeneous Middleman Group: An Institutional Alternative to Contract Law." *Journal of Legal*

Studies, Vol. 10, June, pp. 349-362.

Moreau, P., 1947. "Des Lacs de Sel aux Chaos de Sable: Le Pays des Nefza-ouas." *IBLA*, 1st trimester, pp. 19-47.

Municipalité de Tunis, 1968. *Étude sur la Commercialisation des Fruits et Légumes*, 4 vols. January.

Olson, Mancur, 1965. *The Logic of Collective Action*. Cambridge: Harvard University Press.

Quataert, Donald, 1983. *Social Disintegration and Popular Resistance in the Ottoman Empire, 1881-1908*. New York: New York University Press.

Tollison, Robert D., 1982. "Rent Seeking: A Survey." *Kyklos*, Vol. 35, pp. 575-602.

Chapter 13

THE POLITICAL ECONOMY OF
INTEREST RATE DETERMINATION IN TUNISIA*

Mohamed Z. Bechri

Disequilibrium interest rates have been and remain common phenomena in less developed countries (LDCs). Usually the explanations given are macroeconomic in nature, focusing on the allegedly beneficial effects of low interest rates on investment, and hence on growth and the rate of inflation. Nevertheless, since the mid-1960s the negative effects of such policies have been increasingly realized and various reforms, starting with that of Korea in 1965, encouraged.

The continuing pervasiveness and persistence of such policies more than twenty years after the lessons of this experience had been learned make it increasingly doubtful that their continued existence can be attributed to the fact that the policy makers are misguided.

What are the factors lying behind the apparent inertia to policy change and reform with respect to interest rates and credit policy? Are the groups which benefit from low interest rates sufficiently strong so as to maintain the status quo at the expense of economic efficiency on the national level? Why are the potential beneficiaries of reform unable to mobilize corrective actions? Is it because of negative religious attitudes toward interest and usury? What has been the precise role of the banking system? Have the banks been content with the prevailing situation, or have they been trying to change it? If the latter should be the case, why have their efforts gone to no avail?

In order to provide answers to these questions, our analysis proceeds by investigating both the demand and supply sides of the credit market. Our basic finding is that the pressures against an upward adjustment of interest rates on the part of demanders of credit have not been strong enough. On the other hand, the central government and relatively weak groups such as exporters and farmers have benefited from these low rates. The more powerful interest groups, namely industrialists and public enterprises, have also

*I would like to thank all the executives I interviewed in different banks and associations whose actions are analyzed here. I am also grateful to Mustapha Nabli, Jeffrey Nugent and Timur Kuran of USC for their helpful comments which led to substantial improvements. Nugent's help in translating the French version of the paper into English is also gratefully appreciated.

benefited from cheap credit though not on especially favorable terms. They have accepted these not particularly favorable terms because they have been able to succeed in accomplishing their objectives more effectively and directly through other means, such as through regulated prices in the case of the former group, and favorable credit allocations and subsidies in the case of the latter group. On the other hand, those groups which would be expected to demand interest rate increases, such as those unable to receive bank credit at the disequilibrium interest rates, like household savers, and the suppliers of credit, namely the banking institutions themselves, have either been unsuccessful in collective action or have adapted to the prevailing situation.

For different sub-periods we focus on the institutional changes affecting interest rate conditions. In the process, we demonstrate the applicability of some concepts of the NIE in explaining both the level and structure of interest rates in Tunisia and their evolution over time. We also use this analysis to speculate about future developments.

The study is organized as follows: Section I deals with the rationale behind the policy of low interest rates in LDCs and the relevance of the institutional approach in explaining this phenomena. In Sections II, III and IV changes in the relative strength and effectiveness of different interest groups are used in explaining the level and structure of Tunisian interest rates in each of the three different periods, namely the period of repressed inflation (1960-75), the period of accelerating inflation but constant interest rates (1975-1985), and finally the period beginning in April 1985. The conclusions are presented in Section V.

I. The Rationale for Below-equilibrium Interest Rates

After World War II, LDC governments began to intervene in their economies on a rather massive scale, in part to compensate for an apparent lack of private initiative. An important vehicle for implementing this interventionist policy was the practice of making credit available on "easy" terms, but only to preferred customers and industries. Such bank credit was typically rationed according to criteria fixed by government planners and articulated by the Central Bank. In the next section we will see how the relative strengths of influence of different groups affected the allocation of credit. In any case, it was the practice of disequilibrium rates which enabled credit to be allocated according to politically imposed criteria.

Beginning in the early 1960s, it was observed that interest rates were typically higher in LDCs than in the developed countries (DCs) [Wai (1980)]. For example, as shown in Table 13-1, during the years 1960-65 the Central Bank discount rate was on average 4.2% in India, 8.8% in Brazil, and 13.8%

Table 13-1
Discount Rates of the Central Bank (R), Rates of Inflation (P) and Real Interest Rates (R-P) in Selected Countries, 1960-1980

	1960-65			1966-70			1971-75			1976-80		
	R	Ṗ	(R-Ṗ)	R	Ṗ	(R-Ṗ)	R	Ṗ	(R-Ṗ)	R	Ṗ	(R-Ṗ)
India	4.2	7.0	-2.8	5.4	5.6	-0.2	7.4	13.7	-6.3	9.0	7.1	1.9
Korea	13.8	17.1	-3.3	24.0	12.6	11.4	12.6	15.7	-3.1	14.8	17.7	-2.9
Brazil	8.8	9.2	-0.4	19.2	24.3	-5.1	18.8	21.2	-2.4	32.8	53.5	-20.7
Ivory Cost	3.5	0.3	3.2	3.5	5.3	-1.8	5.2	9.8	-4.6	8.5	17.7	-9.2
Morocco	3.5	4.5	-1.0	3.5	0.9	2.6	3.9	7.8	-3.9	4.5	10.0	-5.5
Tunisia	3.6	2.3	1.3	5.0	2.6	2.4	5.0	5.0	0.0	5.6	7.6	-2.0
France	3.6	4.0	-0.4	5.6	4.8	0.8	9.2	9.7	-0.5	9.7	10.6	-0.9
United States	3.5	1.3	2.2	5.2	4.5	0.7	6.0	7.3	-1.3	9.1	9.6	-0.5

Source: International Financial Statistics, various issues.

in South Korea, compared to an average of 3.5% in France and the USA. This was only the case in nominal terms, however, since, as also shown in Table 13-1, because of higher rates of inflation, the real rates of interest were lower in most LDCs than in DCs. In other words, LDC interest rates did not reflect the presumed greater scarcity value of capital in those countries [Chandavarkar (1971)]. In the case of India, for example, the "dual" rate of interest was estimated to be betweeen 8% and 12%, i.e., roughly double the official market rate [Chakravarty (1964)]. Likewise, interest rates in the well developed unorganized credit markets of Asian countries were estimated to be generally higher than 20% [Wai (1957)].

Different arguments were advanced to explain and to justify these "low" rates of interest in countries in the early stages of development. One such argument was that expansionary monetary policies were needed to allow for the necessary monetization of their growing economies, low interest rates being the consequence of rapidly increasing money supplies [Khatkhate (1977)]. Such ideas are sometimes characterized as implying that the supply of finance can lead to economic development [Patrick (1966)]. A second explanation was that low interest rates were required; otherwise, the rates of return on investment, especially on those in infant industries, agriculture and infrastructure, would be sufficiently low to render the investments unprofitable, thereby undermining the inducement for additional capital formation. A third argument was that low interest rates were justified so as to avoid the harmful consequences of the artificially high levels that would result from the oligopolistic nature of the banking system of these countries. Fourth, low interest rates were deemed necessary to reduce inflation, working capital being an important ingredient of total cost. Finally, higher interest rates would force debtor governments into larger budget deficits, triggering monetary expansion and inflation.

Naturally, to the extent that LDC policy-makers maintain these views concerning the beneficial effects of low interest rates, this could explain their reluctance to accept significant upward adjustments. Aside from those countries which were forced by external pressures to adopt stabilization programs, of which interest rate increases were one element (e.g., Korea in 1965, Portugal in 1978 and Turkey in 1980), despite rising interest rates in DCs, interest rates in LDCs remained negative in real terms. Note also the low frequency of changes in the discount rates despite variations in and the acceleration of the rate of inflation over time.[1] For example, in neither Morocco nor Tunisia was

---

[1]As mentioned in Table 13-1, for purposes of data comparability the price index used is the consumer price index (CPI). Its growth rate obviously un-

there any significant change in nominal rates between 1960 and 1975 despite accelerating rates of inflation.

Despite the above arguments in favor of low interest rates and expansionary monetary policies, by the early 1970s numerous academic studies demonstrating the negative effects of such policies were beginning to appear. "Financial repression", i.e., the maintenance of interest rates below inflation rates, was shown to negatively affect the growth of the financial sector, to impede the mobilization of domestic resources, and to lead to inefficiency in the allocation of investment.[2] The pioneering experience of Korea in 1965 was used by the IMF and other international organizations to support the implementation of interest rate reforms in other countries. What is somewhat surprising is that even in the late 1980's financial repression remains rather general in LDCs despite the fact that concerns about its ill effects have been repeatedly brought to the attention of the monetary authorities. In Tunisia, for example, the Central Bank has for some time admitted to the following three important negative effects of this policy:[3] lower savings, less financial intermediation, and excessive international borrowing.

These worries led the Central Bank to adopt changes in interest rates in 1977, 1981, April 1985 and January 1987. As shown in Table 13-2, the changes in 1977 and 1981 were, however, of minor importance despite accelerating inflation and increasing world interest rates.[4]

Again, the same question has to be raised: How can these rigidities be explained even though the ill-effects of these policies were widely appreciated? Why did Tunisia and other LDCs continue to practice these artificially low interest rates long after the introduction of important reforms in fiscal, trade and other policies?

Indeed, the failure to adjust to changing circumstances is particularly surprising in view of the fact that one would have expected the authorities to go along with the financial reforms (including high interest rates) advocated by the International Monetary Fund and other international organizations because of the decisive and increasing roles these organizations were playing in providing credit to countries in balance of payments difficulties.

---

derestimates the effective inflation rate in any country with price controls and subsidies. In subsequent sections dealing with the Tunisian case, however, the rate of inflation is measured by the GDP deflator.

[2] The basic models were developed by McKinnon (1973) and Shaw (1973). Empirical tests for a sample of Asian countries were attempted by Fry (1978).

[3] See the annual reports of the Central Bank of Tunisia for the years 1977 and 1981.

[4] An analysis of these reforms is presented in Sections III and IV below.

Table 13-2
Bank Loan Rate (Lr), the Corresponding Central Bank
Rediscount Rate (Rr) and the Margin (m = Lr-Rr) in Tunisia
(in percent)

	1974			1977			1981			1985		
	Lr	Rr	m	Lr	Rr	m	Lr	Rr	m	Lr	Rr	m
Export prefinancing	--	4	--	5.75	4.25	1.5	6.25	4.75	1.5	6	4	2
Medium term financing · Agriculture equipment	--	4.25	--	7	4	3	6.25	3.5	2.75	7	5.5	1.5
· Investment in export industries	--	4.25	--	7	4	3	8	5	3	8	6.5	1.5
Long term credit to agriculture	--	--	--	--	--	--	10.5	7.25	3.25	12	10.5	1.5

Source: Central Bank of Tunisia: <u>Statistiques Financières</u>, various issues.

Because Tunisia and other LDCs lack the financial markets wherein interest rates could be determined by the continuous interaction of demand and supply forces, we argue that Central Bank determination of interest rates is the result of a lengthy bargaining process. In the following sections, we show that the Central Bank of Tunisia's decisions have been the resultant of various pressures in different directions by different groups, and even the small increase decided on in 1977 (of an average 1/4 point) took more than one year of negotiations to accomplish.

The present study focuses primarily on the distributional effects of Tunisian interest rates in the post-colonial period: How are the different groups affected? Under what conditions can we expect effective collective action? How and why can a particular group succeed in attaining its objectives? How does the structure of Tunisian pressure groups influence interest rates over time? Even with reference to the relatively short post-colonial era, it can be seen that considerable change has taken place in interest group structure. Indeed, by the mid-1980s certain groups, which were practically non-existent, or at best passive, in the early 1960s, were generally recognized to be among the most influential and active. Throughout the paper we emphasize the role of institutional considerations in general and interest group competition in particular in explaining both the historically observed rigidities in interest rates and the recent changes therein.

II. Tunisian Interest Groups and their Relative Influence
Under Repressed Inflation (1960-1973)

If groups tend to act in their own self interest, one would expect them to participate in collective action to change interest rates only when, and to the extent, their profitability and viability are seen to be threatened by continuation of the status quo. One would expect this principle to apply to the relevant groups on both sides of the credit market, namely the public enterprises, industrialists, farmers, municipalities, central government and households on the demand side and the household savers and financial intermediaries on the supply side.

A greater degree of power and political influence on the part of any group, however, does not automatically translate into a greater role in interest rate determination. The reason for this lies in the fact that, when the interested party has attractive alternative means of attaining its objectives, it may be expected to concentrate its efforts and influence on those measures that allow it to reach its objectives in the least costly way. Hence, rather than fighting for lower interest rates which in any case may be only a second-or third-best instrument for achieving these objectives, the group may choose to concentrate on other policy options like tariff rates, non-tariff protection and credit availability. Consequently, for each group, one should identify the alternatives available to it so as to be able to judge the influence which that group would be likely to exert over any single policy option like interest rates.

Given (or holding constant) the policy alternatives, however, we argue that the extent of influence should be related to the power of the group and to its potential for success in collective action. In what follows, we draw on the principles of collective action summarized in Nabli and Nugent (1988) for purposes of assessing the influences on interest rates exerted by different interest groups.

In the wake of independence in the mid-1950s, Tunisia was a predominantly agricultural economy. Most Tunisian agriculturalists were essentially subsistence farmers and were distributed throughout the country without either realistic possibilities for success in or the motivation for collective action. The attractiveness of the "exit" solution, moreover, contributed greatly to the weak influence of this group. In the case of small farmers and landless workers this took the form of migration to wage jobs in urban areas; in the case of large or wealthy landowners it frequently took the form of investments in more profitable activities, such as commerce and industry. Furthermore, the homogeneity of their goals contributed to the development of a free-rider mentality wherein small farmers could expect to rely on their larger urban-based counterparts for leadership in accomplishing their objectives. Not surprisingly, therefore, the strength of their association — *Union Nationale des Agriculteurs Tunisiens* (UNAT) — is largely confined to the big cities where its main source of support is the minority of large agro-industrial farmers living in or near urban areas. The extent of contact between this minority of urban-based farmers and those in rural areas is likely to be rather sporadic and for individual purposes. Not surprisingly, therefore, in many rural areas even the most basic UNAT activities, such as the mere calling of meetings, are virtually unknown.[5]

To the worsening situation of agriculture corresponds a shift to industry. Between 1965 and 1970 production in manufacturing increased by 48.7% whereas that in agriculture increased by only 23.8%. The growing importance of public enterprises had a lot to do with the shift in favor of industry inasmuch as public enterprises played a pioneering role in launching new economic activities in this sector. The ability of public enterprises to succeed in collective action has been enhanced by both complementarity in goals and the fact that any such enterprise needs the approval or support of only the one or two particular ministries with which it is affiliated. Since each such enterprise has to deal individually with its corresponding authority and there are no general rules or formulas for determining the level or form of privileges granted to public enterprises, the problem of free-riding hardly arises.

Since in the 1960's industrialization was mainly in the hands of the public sector, private industrialists were but a small elite incipient group which had previously succeeded in other more traditional activities, such as agriculture, commerce and administration. Their potential for success in collective action was enhanced, however, by their small number and by their concentration in a few urban areas.

Several other groups may have been expected to affect interest rates but, in practice, their action could be expected to be rather limited for different reasons. Households might be expected to favor high (equilibrium) interest rates since such rates would help them obtain credit. Some subgroups, however, such as the urban elite (government officials and bureaucrats, members of powerful groups such as doctors, attorneys, etc.) may be expected to push for lower interest rates given their capacity to obtain credit. On the other hand, households in general would be inhibited in their collective action efforts by their large number, heterogeneity of background, lack of concentration and homogeneity of goals.

Asymmetrically, groups that favor low interest rates on the demand side might also have the incentive to push for higher interest rates on the supply side if they have excess liquidity, but here the free-rider problem would come into its own. It should also be mentioned that, as suppliers of finance, house-

---

[5]On this see also Nugent (1988) who discusses the relative influence and role of UNAT.

hold savers would be expected to face the same limitations in their attempts at collective action that they face when they act as borrowers.

The remaining important group on the supply side of the credit market is composed of financial intermediaries. Their influence in an LDC is dependent on their role in the development process which is in turn related to the level of development. At Tunisia's stage of development in the 60's and 70's, commercial banks were the primary source of external finance for firms. Its banking system was well developed, and for an LDC it had an unusually high degree of monetization.[6] What was lacking, however, was a meaningful degree of competition. This derives both from the relatively small number of banks and from the fact that the sector was dominated by public enterprises. As a result, the system operated under the close supervision of the public authorities, either monetary or non-monetary. On the formal level, the monetary authorities have implemented a set of regulations to guarantee direct control of banks.

During the 1960s and the early 1970s this control primarily took the form of rediscount quotas and the requirement that banks had to use 10% and 30% of their total bank deposits for medium and long term loans to the private and public sectors, respectively. In addition, the banks were constantly under pressure from both central and local authorities to make loans to especially favored firms and especially to specific public enterprises. During the period of relative stability prior to 1974, however, the Tunisian banking system managed to survive these constraints, benefiting in part from the existence of refinancing facilities. During this period the rediscount rate was maintained at a level below the bank loan rate, thereby virtually guaranteeing a minimum return. In addition, commissions were earned for the management of specific funds of either national or foreign origin.

Banks as a group could be expected to be successful in their collective action because of their limited number, geographic concentration and homogeneity of background. The one source of weakness was homogeneity of goals, 11 of 14 banks in the early 1970's being publicly owned deposit banks operating in similar environments and having to follow the same rules with respect to their financing and the use of their resources.[7]

The 1960s and early 1970s were a period of relative macroeconomic sta-

---

[6]For example, using the ratio of M_2 to GNP, since the early 1970s this ratio has been greater than 40% in Tunisia. This is rather high compared to the LDC average.

[7]This is especially true for some specialized institutions such as the *Banque Nationale de Tunisie* (BNT) for agriculture and the *Banque du Sud* (BS) for development of the southern region.

bility for the Tunisian economy. The inflation rate was, on the average, 4% per annum from 1961 to 1973. But interest rates were even lower, the rate on time deposits, for example, being 3% until 1966 when it was raised to 4%. Although in 1971 it was raised to 5.5%, it was still low in comparison with the rate of inflation which by 1974 had reached 19%. Negative real rates of interest prevailed for the Central Bank's rediscount rate and most loan rates.

How does one explain the prevailing "low" level of interest rates? To answer this fundamental question we have to analyze the expected roles *vis-à-vis* interest rates of different groups on both the demand and the supply sides of the credit market. One has to recognize, however, that any group's attitudes towards interest rates are likely to be highly dependent on both that group's degree of access to credit and the nature of credit rationing in Tunisia.

Stiglitz and Weiss (1981) have argued that, even when interest rates are competitively determined, credit rationing would be likely to occur. The reason is that, at higher interest rates, riskier borrowers would be accepted, leading to a decrease in the net return of the banks relative to that which would be expected if credit were rationed to a small number of less risky borrowers. In this situation, of course, credit would be supply-determined. At the given "optimal" interest rate for banks, there would be an excess demand for credit. The volume of credit realized would correspond to the level of supply, and banks would be able to choose among the potential borrowers, i.e., to determine the allocation of credit.

In LDCs, however, environmental conditions differ significantly from those assumed by Stiglitz and Weiss. First, the given interest rate is not competitively set, and its level need not be optimal for the banks. Indeed, credit rationing occurs in the presence (or even because) of interest rates which are perceived, even by banks and other agents on the demand side, to be "artificially low." Second, LDC central banks often impose on the banks allocation ratios or at least guidelines as to how credit should be allocated, and government officials may also intervene individually in directing the available credit to specific uses and users. Third, the below-equilibrium interest rates which are associated with credit rationing are quite frequently far from homogeneous and vary in ways that are unrelated to comparative costs and/or the profit maximization objectives of the banks. Quite naturally, borrowers generally want to borrow at the lowest possible rates; hence those in any given sector may seek preferentially low rates. If all rates were below the rates which would equilibrate the demand for and supply of credit, however, the demanders of credit would generally be more interested in obtaining larger quantities of credit than they can obtain with the preferential rates.

The choice between more credit at the "normal" loan rate and less credit at a preferential rate of interest is obviously a quantitative matter which would depend on the rate of return and the alternative credit and interest rate levels. Suppose that there are two specific options: to get 60% of the available credit at a rate of 9%, or to get the remaining 40% of the available credit at a preferential loan rate of 6%. It can easily be seen that the former choice will be preferable as long as the rate of return is at least 15 percent.

Whereas we have seen that interest rate changes clearly require success in collective action, since in Tunisia there are no formal regulations on credit, credit can generally be obtained by individual firms by their own (individual) actions and according to their relative power and position. Furthermore, this explains why the loan-quantity rationing wherein some borrowers get nothing and others get all they want is more common than loan-size rationing.

In measuring relative success of a given group in access to credit we follow Virmani (1982) in using the ratio of the group's share in bank credit to its share in GDP. Since industry is more capital intensive than services and agriculture, one would expect industry's ratio of credit to GDP share to be somewhat larger than those of the other sectors. In Table 13-3 we present the shares of the different sectors in bank credit and GDP for various periods from 1966 to 1984.

For those borrower groups with access to bank credit, the prevailing situation could be ideal. As Benoit (1985) explained: the "policy of interest rates at an artificially low level is popular not only for politicians who consider subsidized loans as an easy way to obtain political support, but also for a large public which benefits from such loans, such as farmers, small entrepreneurs, etc."

We have mentioned that in disequilibrium interest rate situations the availability of credit is more likely to be important to borrowers than the interest rate itself since preferential interest rates could be either an indicator of power or the lack of it depending on the perceived importance of lower interest rates relative to that of other means of obtaining group goals. For each group, we have to analyze the importance of interest rates to the satisfaction of group objectives.

The three specific groups which were benefiting most continuously and directly from subsidized loans were exporters, farmers and the government. Since during this period of time export activities were mainly in the hands of public enterprises, one would not have expected much of a collective response by private exporters.

Table 13-3
Sectoral Shares in Bank Credit
and GDP (in percentages) 1966-69 to 1982-84

	1966-69		1970-73		1974-77		1978-81		1982-84	
	Credit	GDP	Credit	GDP	Credit	GDP	Credit	GDP	Credit	GDP
1. Agriculture	11	18.7	10.8	21.9	7.9	20.1	8.5	16.1	8.1	14.8
2. Industry of which:	45	24.8	39.2	25.0	43.9	31.2	47.0	35.0	51.2	35.1
- Textiles & Leather	7.7	1.5	8.2	1.9	8.2	2.4	6.7	3.3	5.1	3.3
3. Services of which:	43.7	56.5	49.8	53.1	48.1	48.7	42.5	48.9	40.6	50.1
- Tourism	13.2	2.0	17.7	3.1	10.9	4.0	7.5	4.5	6.6	4.2
- Commerce	19.6	12.3	19.9	13.2	19.7	n.a	15.5	n.a	14.4	n.a

Source: Central Bank of Tunisia, Statistiques Financières, various issues.

Agriculture was the sector benefiting from the lowest interest rates among borrowers. But this was hardly an indicator of agriculture's strength in collective action. During the 1960s and early 1970s, the weakness of agriculture is demonstrated by the fact that as shown in Table 13-3 its share in credit was only 11% whereas its share in GDP was almost 20%. Also, the sector remained subject to deleterious price controls and its overall position tended to deteriorate.

The factors contributing to the weakness of collective action among farmers have already been identified. Furthermore, claims for price increases of agricultural products were strongly resisted by other groups on social and political grounds. The sector's exceptionally small share in the credit to be rationed is also attributable to the fact that banks are not encouraged to finance this sector. The reason for this is that farm loans, even when discounted, are less profitable for commercial banks than loans to other sectors.[8] Consequently, agriculture was financed primarily by means of certain external credit sources which were tied to and controlled by rather specific programs, of ministries, local authorities, UNAT, and other organizations.

In fact, it seems that the strategy of preferentially low interest rates could be an optimal strategy for UNAT. Since it is dominated by large and

---

[8] See the intervention of S. Zidi of the La Banque du Sud in the meeting organized by the UNAT on "Prospects of Agriculture Financing," Tounes El Khadra, May, 1983. Von Pischke (1981) gave the following explanation: "low formal interest rates on the types of loans most useful to rural people tend paradoxically to restrict their access to formal sector financial services. Rural customers at low levels of financing activity are a costly market to serve. They tend to deal in small transactions which are relatively costly for formal financial institutions to process."

urban-based farmers who are virtually the only farmers to receive institutional credit, by pushing for discriminatory interest rate concessions, UNAT benefits its most influential members more significantly and exclusively than it could by other measures.

In sum, it appears that the ability of farmers to obtain credit at preferentially low rates of interest is hardly the result of successful collective action on the part of farmers in general. Rather, it is the result of the relative strength of the privileged minority of farmers who are able to obtain access to the little credit available to the sector on extremely favorable terms.

The attitude of the central government *vis-à-vis* interest rates needs more clarification. In the aggregate, low interest rates, with their negative impact on economic growth, could be expected to lead to a loss of tax revenue for the government [North (1981)]. However, this would not be true in the case of most LDCs, even in a relatively stable country like Tunisia. Inasmuch as short run success is generally an absolutely essential condition for the government's ability to remain in power, at any given time, short run considerations may be expected to dominate over long run ones. Indeed, the diversity of the government's interests and that of the groups which it represents help explain the preference for policies which produce distortions and inefficiencies. Indeed, despite their negative long run effects for society and government alike, low interest rates make it possible for banks on behalf of the government to finance the budget deficit at low cost.

Engaged as it is in expensive development activities, the government has had to finance its deficit, at least in part, by borrowing from the banking system. However, the share of commercial banks in deficit financing was generally low (14.5% in the years 1961-1965, 3.4% in the years 1966-1970, and 14.1% in 1970-1973). This indicates that the largest part of the budget deficit had to be financed by other sources.

The main borrowers, industrialists and public enterprises, however, do not benefit from preferential interest rates. This is despite the fact that both groups are very influential. In what follows we explain this apparent paradox and point out the real nature of their action on interest rates.

For industrialists, high prices of finished goods, protection from foreign competition, the avoidance of taxes, and the availability of credit, all of which they seem to be benefiting from, would seem to be more important in the satisfaction of their objectives than still lower rates of interest.[9]

---

[9] For example, even though the rates of effective protection vary from one industrial activity to another, industry as a whole is well protected, especially compared to agriculture. For prices, see the example given in footnote 11.

As a result, as shown in Table 13-3, industrialists were able to obtain 42% of the bank credit while their share of GDP was only 25%. Those shares, of course, included both private and public enterprises. While unfortunately we have no precise information about the share of public enterprises in the credit allocations during this period, the general consensus is that public enterprises accounted for a large part of the credit allocated to the industrial and service sectors. This is not surprising inasmuch as these enterprises are the chief beneficiaries of official intervention.

For public enterprises, the first priority for a manager is to ensure the survival of the unit. Since public enterprises are generally underfinanced to begin with and then quite frequently continue to run deficits in their operating budgets, obtaining credit is their top priority. Hence, preferential interest rates are of only secondary importance to public enterprises.

Indeed, since both industrialists and public enterprises have generally been able to succeed with respect to other more fundamental objectives, their lack of success in obtaining preferentially low interest rates is indicative of the fact that their demand for such rates has not been strong. If they had concentrated on such demands, undoubtedly they would have succeeded. Hence, only farmers have exerted pressures for preferential rates.

Since the social costs of "financial repression" deriving from low levels of interest rates on both saving deposits and non-subsidized loans in a country like Tunisia are now widely appreciated, the above analysis of the demand for credit gives no direct explanation for the general prevalence of low interest rates. If, for example, there were no mechanisms to allow for sizable discrepancies between rates of interest, then the action of farmers would be of considerable importance in explaining the overall low level of interest rates. However, in the Tunisian context of the 1960's and early 1970's, the practice of subsidized interest rates and the availability of Central Bank rediscounting at low interest rates made it possible to have low interest rates for some borrowing sectors without necessarily having low deposit rates. Therefore, what explains the persistence of financial repression?

We should first bear in mind the historical context in which financial repression has occurred. The low or negative real interest rates prevailing in Tunisia and most LDCs are not so much the result of decreases in nominal rates as the result of insufficient increases in nominal rates to offset accelerating rates of inflation. The explanation for the virtual failure of interest rates to adjust lies in the comparative failure in collective action either on the part of any of the groups excluded from receiving credit or by those groups supplying credit, namely household depositors and banks.

The most important groups excluded from institutional credit (at any interest rate) were small farmers, small manufacturers and households. Since all three of these groups (except for elite subgroups of households) would be expected to be weak because of their large numbers, their lack of geographic concentration, the heterogeneity in their backgrounds and the homogeneity of their goals, their failure either to obtain credit at disequilibrium (low) rates or to raise interest rates in order to be in a better position to obtain credit is hardly surprising. Weakness of collective action of households also explains their failure to obtain higher rates for the deposits which they would otherwise have supplied. An Islamic-based aversion to usury does not seem to be an important part of the explanation since usurious interest rates are in fact commonly practiced even in Islamic countries.[10] Rather, the prevalence of low deposit rates induces "exit," in this case a flight from potential financial deposits into durable goods consumption and the acquisition of real estate, in both cases undermining the viability of financial intermediation.

The impetus for collective action on the part of banks — the one group with expected potential for success in collective action — to raise interest rates in order to mobilize deposits has been diffused by (1) their homogeneity in goals and (2) the availability of (a) interest rate subsidies by the government, (b) rediscounting by the Central Bank of Tunisia at especially low interest rates, and (c) special management fees for handling the "special funds" of budgetary and foreign origin (which have accounted for as much as 20% of total credit), all of which have helped to guarantee the banks an acceptable rate of profit. Moreover, with time deposits of enterprises and households at commercial banks growing (in nominal terms) at an average rate of 23% per annum between 1964 and 1973, as a result of relatively rapid income growth and urbanization and little competition for mobilizing savings, the banks did not feel the need to increase deposit rates. With respect to the absence of competition, it should be noted that ten of the eleven deposit banks in existence during this period were state-owned, and hence not expected to operate exclusively for profits.

III. Inflationary Pressures and Inertia in Interest Rate Adjustments (1974-1985)

After 1973 like many other economies the Tunisian economy began to face increased inflationary pressures. As shall be explained presently (again

---

[10]See Kuran (1986). On the other hand, collective action on the part of the Islamic communities in some countries, such as Saudi Arabia and Kuwait, have tended to deflect such demands toward the creation of recent Islamic banks.

in terms of the theory of collective action), even the 19% inflation rate of 1974 did not succeed in prompting corrective action.

A. Institutional Changes

On the demand side for credit, the most important changes (relative to the earlier period) were the rising power of industrialists, the emergence of a new, homogeneous and well-mobilized group of exporters, and the greater reliance of government on commercial bank financing. On the supply side of the market, the most important changes were the improved organization of banks and decreased homogeneity in goals, both contributing to greater success in collective action.

Industrialists became increasingly concentrated in the urban areas, but also more diversified by sector, and hence more heterogeneous with respect to goals. Even if within the individual sectors homogeneity of goals could be expected to lead to free-riding, increased homogeneity of background, and greater ease of communication within their economy-wide association the *Union Tunisienne de l'Industrie du Commerce et de l'Artisanat* (UTICA) tended to place them in a much better position than before for affecting policies in such a way as to help them realize their main objectives.[11]

Although in the 1960s export activities were dominated by public enterprises, beginning in the early 1970s, an increasing number of private industrialists began to sell abroad. Their greater ability to organize collective action is due both to their increased geographic concentration in Tunis and to the larger expected gains of participation. Even though an entrepreneur dealing with the local market could probably do without UTICA, for an exporter the existence of specialized institutions is crucial for obtaining the information and foreign currency needed to investigate foreign markets. Furthermore, the fact that the new exporters are mainly an elite of dynamic businessmen who have succeeded in getting around the constraints imposed by the small size of the local market is undoubtedly helping them to improve their position within UTICA and other organizations.

Indeed, the success of exporters since the early 1970s in the realization of different objectives is quite remarkable. In 1973 a specialized government-financed center the *Centre de Promotion des Exportations* (CEPEX) was created. As the link between Tunisian exporters and foreign markets, CEPEX is supposed to identify potential markets abroad, to organize promotional activities in those markets, and to participate in trade fairs and exhibitions.

---

[11]For example, UTICA has played an important role in determining prices and limiting competition in the textile industry. See also Nugent (1988).

On the basis of its analysis of the deficiencies of the actual system and the recommendations of the exporters themselves from round tables and seminars organized with representatives of the relevant ministries, the banking system and other institutions, CEPEX was called upon to play a significant role in the implementation of a coherent foreign trade strategy. Among other achievements of exporters in recent years are a system of credit insurance for exports, specialized export companies, the "Export Promotion Fund" for financing export activities and the creation of an "exporters' club" as an additional channel to help mobilize exporters for collective action.

Despite the increasing power of the private sector and the recent shift in policy in favor of privatization, public enterprises continue to play a crucial role in the Tunisian economy and can be expected to continue to play a major role in employment and regional development.[12] The political allocation of resources which has given rise to their creation has generated a category of rent-seekers who, on the regional level at least, serve as a strong force in preserving the status quo.

On the other hand, for farmers the deteriorating trend has accelerated since the early 1970s. As a result, the "exit" solution has become ever more attractive, especially in the light of the new opportunities offered to the private sector in new activities, including small scale industries.

On the supply side, an important change is that Tunisian banks have become grouped since the early 1970s under a new and relatively strong association, the *Assocation Professionelle de Banques* (APB). The APB's objective was to negotiate collectively with respect to regulations imposed by the Central Bank. An undeclared objective was also to prevent competition among members and to counter the initiatives of the trade union organization. For example, as explained in Zouari (1988), the banking convention signed with the union in 1974 constrained all members to pay the same wage rate for all employees in the same category. Thus, not only did the creation of the APB reflect the relatively strong position of commercial banks in the early 1970s, but also its creation has served to consolidate and accentuate this capacity.

Another important change in the position of the banks is the creation since 1980 of five new development banks for financing large scale projects. One-half the capital of those banks is subscribed by the Tunisian government,

---

[12]The will to benefit from infrastructure and proximity to the government and imported inputs makes the capital city of Tunis an ideal location for most private investments. The location of public enterprises, however, is decided primarily according to political criteria, even at the price of considerably higher costs in certain cases.

and the other half by foreign parties, mainly Gulf country governments, agencies and private investors. The fact that these development banks have to rely on the international financial market for finance makes it important for them that their loan rates be aligned with those in the international market. This is especially true since the development banks, unlike the commercial banks, have no access to the highly subsidized rediscount window of the Central Bank. The entrance of these new institutions, therefore, would seem to have strengthened greatly the position of banks with respect to collective action to raise loan rates unless divisions between commercial banks and development banks might have arisen in such a way as to weaken their collective resolve. Given the small number of banks involved, and the aforementioned creation of the APB integrating *all* banks, no such divisions have appeared.

B. Group Action and Interest Rate Inertia

For the reasons mentioned above, industrialists and public enterprises could still be expected to accommodate to higher interest rates because of their favorable treatment in the allocation of credit and other considerations. As shown in Table 13-3, the increasingly powerful group of industrialists was able to improve its share in bank credit from 40% in the early 1970s to 51% in more recent years. Industrialists have also continued to benefit in a variety of other ways such as protection and taxation. Similarly, and despite the lack of detailed statistics, according to recent estimates, public enterprises now seem to count for at least one-third of total bank credit.[13] In recent years, moreover, not only have industrialists refrained from any significant collective action on behalf of preferential rates, but also they have come to accept credit from the new development banks at rates about 2% above those on credit from the commercial banks, a practice which is formally allowed by the Central Bank.

For farmers, however, the combination of increased inflation rates and controls on agricultural prices has had the effect of worsening the terms of trade between agriculture and the other sectors and decreasing the profitability of farming.[14] As shown in Table 13-3 the share of agriculture in credit decreased from 11% in the earlier period to about 8% in the years 1974-1984 and was always well below that of its share in GDP. This is particularly striking since this sector has come to receive priority in all the important official policy declarations since 1980, including the Sixth Development Plan (1982-

---

[13]See World Bank (1984) and Grissa (1988).
[14]See the document presented by UNAT: "At the margin of the negotiations between the social partners," in Arabic, *El-Oumma* February 7, 1982.

1986). With bank credit continuing to be concentrated on the elite 20-25% of all farmers [World Bank (1984)] and the continuing constraints on the upward adjustment of agricultural prices, our conclusions for the previous period remain valid, thereby explaining how the privileged minority of farmers have been able to obtain credit at preferential interest rates.

Now let us consider the preferences for interest rates among the increasingly important group of exporters. Deprived of various types of subsidies, exporters often find themselves at a disadvantage in this respect relative to the international competition. In addition, exporters have not been able to obtain the credit needed. Indeed, Central Bank of Tunisia (1981) shows that the portion of exports financed by bank loans decreased from 7.4% in 1977 to 4.9% in 1980 and even further thereafter despite increasing recognition of the importance of credit for export growth and of export growth for overall economic growth. This decrease in the share of exporters in credit can also be seen in Table 13-3 from the decrease in the share of some specific branches such as textiles and tourism which are known as export-oriented industries in the overall allocation of credit. A conventional rule of thumb is that the prefinancing of exports should cover the cost of primary inputs which most exporters consider to be more than 30% of total costs [CEPEX (1980)]. In fact, however, the proportion of export values eligible for prefinancing was for many years limited to 10% before being raised to 20% in 1985. Moreover, while credit is now mobilized without any need for the Central Bank's "prior authorization" or "rediscount agreement" at the time export operations commence, the time duration of this credit, though recently raised from 90 to 180 days, is still shorter than what is observed in other countries. Not surprisingly, since the terms of the credit contract are crucial for exporters, the demands of exporters have concentrated on obtaining the credit at preferentially low interest rates. In the absence of such, as a result of administrative formalities, exporters were being forced to obtain bank overdrafts at much higher interest rates.[15]

Since the mid-1970s the government has emerged as an important borrower from the commercial banks. As mentioned above, this credit is made compulsory by the banking regulations. Consequently, commercial bank finance of the budget deficit increased from 5.2% in the years 1974-1975 to 34.9% in 1976 and 50.3% in 1979. In such circumstances any rise in the interest rate would have led to a corresponding rise in interest payments by the government and hence would have been a cause for governmental concern.

---

[15]Note also that the overdraft interest rate is on average 30% above the preferential rate for exports.

In general, therefore, the most important changes on the demand side of the credit market since the 1970s would seem to have been the greater pressures for preferential interest rates exerted by farmers, exporters (a new group) and the government (the latter becoming an important borrower from banks). On the supply side, because of greater heterogeneity of goals and decreased security and profitability, collective action on the part of banks for higher interest rates would be expected to be more successful than in the past. Indeed, it is the delay in such action until 1985 which deserves explanation.

On the formal level, banks have been the only group participating directly in negotiations with the Central Bank over interest rate reform. Through the APB, such meetings are organized regularly each quarter and involve the president of the APB, the presidents of the banks and the governor of the Central Bank. The discussions have dealt primarily with different aspects of existing regulations.

It was primarily the high rate of inflation observed since 1974 that has instigated the discussion on interest rate reform and the creation of an *ad hoc* committee for that purpose in 1976. In fact, however, in all interest rate negotiations since 1976 there has been conflict between two positions. The official position of the monetary authorities was to maintain a fixed margin for banks (defined as the spread between the loan rate of the banks and the rediscount rate of the Central Bank). Any rise in interest rates would, therefore, be designed to benefit savers exclusively, but to leave fixed the spread between the interest rates on loans and deposits. On the other hand, the position of the banks as represented by the APB was that a rise in their margins was necessary in order to compensate for the deterioration in their situation resulting from inflation.[16]

Until 1980, except for one development bank, all other commerical banks continued to operate in similar environments and to follow the same rules with regard both to financing from the Central Bank and their use of the funds at their disposal.[17] Naturally, the banks also faced the same interest rates on both deposits and loans. As a result, one would expect a certain degree of similarity in changes in profitability among the different banks.

---

[16]This was decided in a meeting of the APB on April 22, 1977.

[17]Specifically, since 1975 the banks have been required to use (a) 20% of their deposits to subscribe to state issued bills at an interest rate of 5.5%, (b) 5% of deposits to subscribe to the "National Fund for Housing Savings" and (c) 18% of deposits to provide credit to small and medium-sized private enterprises. Moreover, since the aforementioned subscription rates are automatic and violations of the credit allocation rule are subject to penalties taking the form of mandatory non-interest-bearing deposits at the Central Bank of Tunisia, compliance with these regulations is virtually complete.

In Table 13-4 we present some data that can be used in assessing the degree to which this expectation has been realized. Within a generalized system of administered interest rates, and for a given economic environment, variations in costs (other than deposit rates) would be the main factors affecting the profitability of banks. Since the factors affecting costs (rental rates, wage rates and the prices of goods and services) are generally highly correlated with the rate of inflation, in general bank profitability should be negatively related to the rate of inflation. The measure of profitability used in the table is the ratio of profits to total assets for different commercial banks. While there are some significant differences in this ratio among the banks listed, e.g., for the year 1982, ranging from .63% for the largest "national" bank (STB) to .23% for the smallest private one (CFCT), notice that, in general, the ratios of all banks tend to vary together over time inversely to the rate of inflation. For example, note the improvement in bank profitability with the lower rates of inflation observed in 1975-76, followed by the decline in bank profitability with accelerated inflation until 1978. Note also that the return of the Tunisian economy to double-digit inflation in the year 1980 led to further deterioration in bank profitability, which was further aggravated by the substantial governmentally conceded wage increases of 1982.

Table 13-4
The Ratio of Profits to Total Assets of Leading Banks
1974 - 1982 (in %)

Banks[a]	1974	1975	1976	1977	1978	1979	1980	1981	1982
STB	0.55	0.88	0.88	0.88	0.85	0.82	0.81	0.68	0.63
BNT	0.59	0.67	0.73	0.62	0.59	0.56	0.55	0.49	0.48
UBCI	0.54	0.48	0.58	0.55	0.53	0.48	0.46	0.26	0.25
BT	0.55	0.52	0.55	0.51	0.53	0.52	0.48	0.46	0.48
UIB	0.87	0.90	0.98	0.59	0.49	0.51	0.58	0.51	0.53
BS	0.71	0.67	0.55	0.57	0.56	0.38	0.54	0.55	0.57
CFCT			0.82	0.51	0.49	0.58	0.59	0.20	0.23
BIAT	--	--	--	--	--	0.59	0.45	0.42	0.43
Inflation Rate[b]	19.1	4.3	2.0	7.7	5.3	5.2	12.9	11.4	16.0

[a]The abbreviations are defined as follows: STB — La Societé Tunisienne de Banque, BNT — La Banque Nationale de Tunisie, UBCI — Union Bancaire du Commerce et de L'Industrie, BT — Banque de Tunisie, UIB — Union Internationale des Banques, BS — La Banque du Sud, CFCT — Le Comptoir Financier et Commercial de Tunisie, and BIAT — La Banque International Arabe de Tunisie.

[b]It is the annual growth rate of GDP deflator. Source: M.K. Nabli (1980), "L'inflation en Tunisie" Tunis: CERP, Faculté de Droit et Sciences Politiques et Economiques, for 1974-79; and Budget Economique 1987, Ministère du Plan.

It should be pointed out, however, that rising inflation would not necessarily justify increases in interest rate margins as long as both bank deposits and loans would be inelastic with respect to interest rates. If with prices rising at say 15% per annum, interest rate inelasticity would imply that deposits, loans, bank margins, operating costs and profits would all increase at the rate of inflation, all such variables would remain constant in real terms. An adjustment of interest rates to the rate of inflation would become necessary, however, if (as would seem realistic) the demand for bank deposits (in real terms) with respect to the real rate of interest were not zero and/or some costs would rise at rates higher than the overall rate of inflation.

As shown in Table 13-5, the data on time deposits at Tunisia's commercial banks reveal a clear deceleration in the growth rate in years of particularly high inflation. Furthermore, in real terms, time deposits decreased during the two years with the highest rates of inflation during the entire period, namely 1974 and 1982.

Moreover, even if the negative effect of inflation on bank deposits were not as important as it seems to have been, bank profitability would still be expected to suffer from operating costs rising faster than the general price level and total bank assets. An international comparison among LDCs shows that the ratio of operating costs to total assets tends to be high in years of rapid inflation. This ratio averaged 1.5% in Tunisia in the years 1981-1982. It reached 8.8% in Turkey in 1980, 12.2% in Brazil in 1981 and 13.5% in Argentina in 1986 [Hanson and Rocha (1986)]. The rise in this ratio with greater inflation and the resulting decrease in bank profitability are due to (a) the negative impact of inflation on deposits (and thus on loans and other bank assets, especially those forms of capital which are not reevaluated with price increases), (b) the positive effect of inflation on the degree of uncertainty and hence on contracts of shorter duration requiring increased administrative costs[18] and (c) with nominal interest rates fixed, the effect of increased pressures to attract deposits (in order to compensate for the negative real returns to customers) by providing better services and opening more branches.

Consequently, in times of high or rising inflation in highly regulated economies like Tunisia, one would expect banking institutions to press for upward adjustments of interest rates, margins or both so as to avert decreases in deposits, profitability or both.

Even if from a macroeconomic perspective an upward adjustment of interest rate levels would be preferable to one of interest rate margins (because of the previously explained insufficient incentives on the part of the banks for mobilizing savings), banks would not necessarily adopt this position since

---

[18]See also Fisher and Modigliani (1978).

Table 13-5
Commercial Bank Conditions (1974-1984)

	1974	1975	1976	1977	1978	1979	1980	1981	1982	1983	1984
Time Deposits(a)											
• Value in millions of dinars	141.9	192.4	258.4	300.3	361.5	433.6	292.7	609.4	671.5	775.9	949.9
• Annual growth rate (%)	6.6	35.5	34.3	16.2	20.3	19.9	14.0	23.1	10.1	15.5	22.4
Banks Total Assets(b)	664.8	780.4	865.9	1017.6	1172.9	1489.2	1776.1	2232.1	2673.6	n.a.	n.a.
• Annual growth rate (%)	--	17.3	10.9	17.5	15.2	19.2	19.2	25.6	19.7	n.a.	n.a.
NBP											
• Value in millions of dinars	18.7	21.6	24.8	27.3	29.9	39.0	46.1	61.2	82.3	n.a.	n.a.
• Annual growth (%)	--	15.5	14.8	10.0	9.5		11.8	32.7	34.4		
• Real growth rate (%)	--	11.2	12.8	2.3	4.2			21.7	18.6		
NBP (%) Total Assets	2.81	2.76	2.86	2.68	2.54	2.61	2.59	2.74	3.07	n.a.	n.a.
Net Profit(b)											
• Value in millions of dinars	4.534	5.853	6.617	6.895	7.644	9.465	11.200	11.856	13.677	18.200	
• Growth rate (%)	--	29.1	13.0	4.2	10.8		18.5	5.8	15.4	33.0	
• Real growth rate (%)	--	24.8	11.0	-3.5	5.5		5.6	-5.6	-0.6	23.7	
Inflation rate(c) (%)	19.1	4.3	2.0	7.7	5.3	5.2	12.9	11.4	16.0	9.3	7.4

(a)Source: Central Bank of Tunisia: Statistiques Financières, different issues.

(b)Source: Accounts of the commercial banks annual reports of the "Association Professionnelle des Banques". Since 1979, data on two additional banks BFT and BIAT were added.

(c)Source: see Table 4.

increases in the level of interest rates might generate stiffer opposition from borrower groups than increased margins.

The mid-1970s through the early 1980s was a period of failure in collective action by the banks. Neither a significant increase in margins nor an upward adjustment of interest rates was obtained. Consequently, the profitability of banks deteriorated. As shown in Table 13-5, net profits in real terms fell in 1977, 1981 and 1982. This failure in collective action can be attributed to several factors, but especially to free-riding on the part of the smaller banks and the fact that the larger banks were doing relatively well without taking any action.[19]

IV. The Rationale for the Interest Rate Reforms of April, 1985 and January, 1987

Only on April 15, 1985 and again in January 1987 did substantial reforms take place. In the first of these reforms domestic loan rates were raised to international levels and the rate on time deposits was raised so as to make the real rate positive for the first time in a long while. Although the timing of the action indicates its link to World Bank recommendations following upon a 1984 special experts' report on the Tunisian financial system, it is rather the changing interest group alignments subsequent to 1981 which seems to provide the underlying explanation for this reform.

The only opposition to upward adjustments in loan rates was from those groups already benefiting from preferential rates. These groups were weak, however, and in any case could be appeased by retaining differential margins even if at higher interest rates. While this might indicate that the opposition to higher rates was weak at this time, it doesn't explain the source of the initiative for higher rates.

Several factors would seem to have been responsible for the pressure of banks for higher rates of interest. First, having learned from their previous failure in collective action, all banks had come to appreciate the importance of group solidarity for success in collective action. Second, the experience with the minor interest rate changes of 1977 and 1981 convinced the banks that further attempts to increase the margins were not likely to be successful. 1981, a crisis year for the banks, stimulated a demand for stronger reaction. Double-digit inflation returned, forcing accelerated wage increases and turning real profits downward. Moreover, in contrast to earlier years, in 1982 credit funds coming from "special sources" accounted for only 12% of the credit extended. This provided a signal, especially to the two largest banks (the STB and BNT), that the ability of banks to extend credit would from

---

[19]See also Fisher and Modigliani (1978).

then on be much more closely linked to their own ability to mobilize deposits and that an increase in deposit rates would be necessary for this to happen. Meanwhile, the pressure within the APB to raise interest rates on loans emanated primarily from the new development banks which, because of their external source of funds, were conscious indeed of the opportunity cost of their funds. The interests of the commercial banks and the development banks were therefore similar; the commercial banks wanted higher interest rates in order to allow them to offer higher rates to depositors and the development banks insisted on higher rates in order to cover the unprecedentedly high rates of interest in the international market.

Hence, on April 15, 1985 interest rates were raised by about 2 percentage points. The new structure of deposit rates is shown in Table 13-6. As can easily be seen, with a nominal rate of 10.5%, the real rate on deposits became positive. Furthermore, we should also mention that, according to our analysis, the increased pressure from the weaker borrowing groups, who were the strongest elements in the resistance to higher interest rates, is what caused the widening of the interest rate differentials in favor of farmers and exporters shown in Table 13-7.

This reform was "completed" by a further liberalization of interest rates on January 2, 1987 in which: (a) on the lending side, banks were given the freedom to set the interest rate as long as the rate was no more than 3% above the money market rate; (b) the only exceptions were loans to exporters, farmers and small and medium-sized enterprises; and (c) interest rates on deposits were freely determined except for those on "savings accounts" where the interest rates were to be continuously adjusted to the money market rate minus a constant spread of 2%.

The immediate reaction of banks was collusion to fix interest rates and reduce competition: margins were agreed on for debit and credit rates. This was followed by the emergence of fierce competition in attracting savers. This took the form of not only higher deposit rates but also, for the first time in Tunisia, financial innovations and marketing campaigns.[20]

What additional effects of the 1985-1987 reforms may be expected to emerge over the next few years? First, as a result of the substantial rise in the overdraft rate, public enterprises especially can be expected to face increasing pressure from rising financial costs. Second, the banks themselves may be expected to face higher costs of borrowing from the Central Bank. Moreover, since 1982, banking regulations have been changed so as to fix a ceiling of 17.5% of deposits as the maximum amount that any individual bank

---

[20]See "Banques: A L'heure du Produit Spécifique," *La Presse*, June 5, 1987.

Table 13-6
The Structure of Interest Rates on
Deposits in Tunisia (in %)[a]

	1963	1967	1974	1977	1982	1985	1987
Demand Deposit	1.95	1.15	1	2	2	2	Free
Time Deposit							
3-6 months	2.5	3	2	2.5	4.5	5.5	Indexed
6-12 months	3	3.5	2.75	4	6	7	on
12-18 months	3.5	4	3.5	5.25	7	8	money
18-24 months	3.5	4	4.25	6.50	8	9	market
24-30 months	3.5	4	5	7.50	9	10	rate
30-60 months	3.5	4	5.5	7.50	9	10.5	
Inflation rate[b]	6.5	4.8	19.1	7.7	16.0	4.7	n.a.
Real interest rate on time deposit (more than 30 months)	-3.0	-0.8	-13.6	-0.2	-7.0	+5.8	n.a.

[a]Source: Central Bank of Tunisia: <u>Statistiques Financiéres</u>, various issues.

[b]Source: see Table 4.

Table 13-7
Loan Rates of Interest (in %)

	1977	1978	1981	1985	1987
- Overdraft Rate	8.75	8.75	10.50	12.625	n.a.
- Base Rate of Interest	5.75	5.75	7	9.25	n.a.
Preferential rates:					
- Export pre-Fanancing	5.75	5.75	6.25	6.25	6
- Investment in Agriculture (Medium term)	7	6.25	6.25	7	7
- Investment in Export industry	7	7	8	8	8
- Long term farm loans	x	x	10.5	12	n.a.

Source: Central Bank of Tunisia: <u>Statistiques Financières</u>, various issues

Note: n.a. indicates not available.

can obtain from both the rediscount window and the money market, and loans corresponding to the range 15-17.5% of deposits must be paid at the overdraft interest rate instead of the money market rate. Furthermore, the banks are expected to face higher opportunity costs in terms of foregone earning arising from Central Bank regulations requiring them to hold 20% of their deposits in the form of government bonds earning a fixed interest rate of 5.5%. Third, as a result of the increased interest rate differentials, the credit market is becoming more segmented. Fourth, under these conditions, subsidized borrowers like farmers and exporters are likely to find it increasingly difficult to obtain credit. Against these increasingly problematic effects have to be matched the macroeconomic benefits arising from both the increased ability of the banking system to attract deposits and thereby perform its intermediation role and the decreased incentives to substitute scarce but underpriced capital for plentiful but overpriced labor.

V. Conclusion

Based on the Tunisian experience reported here, it is our contention that the institutional approach can be rather useful for understanding the inertia that has characterized monetary policy, in general, and interest rates, in particular. In Tunisia only the relatively less powerful groups such as farmers and exporters who lack the ability to achieve their goals with other more advantageous policy instruments are benefiting from the system of preferential rates of interest. The insights of collective action theory are crucial in shedding light on the prospects for interest rate reforms. According to our analysis, the inertia in interest rate adjustment (to changes in the rate of inflation, international interest rates, etc.) was due mainly to the lack of effective action on the part of banks. The greater recent success of banks in collective action, which can be expected to increase the responsiveness of interest rates to various exogenous shocks, is attributable to decreased homogeneity in goals, and the higher opportunity cost of their funds.

Future adjustments in the structure of interest rates on loans will depend (as in the past) on the nature of relative political influences, in particular the position of exporters and farmers relative to others. If these groups could get enough power to achieve their goals through more effective instruments, there would be less reason for them to oppose a rise in their loan rates. We could anticipate the abolition of preferential rates to farmers and exporters only if (as seems unlikely) these groups could benefit from the same advantages as industrialists in terms of prices, effective protection, etc. Otherwise, the maintenance of preferential rates for farmers and possibly other weak groups is likely to continue. Further interest rate reforms, therefore, are likely to result in greater segmentation of the credit market.

References

Association Professionelle des Banques, *Rapport Annuel*, different issues.

Bénoit, J.V.P., 1985, "Taux d'intérêts Administrés et Taux d'intérêt du Marché," in D. Kessler and P.A. Ullmo ed., *Epargne et Développement*, Paris.

Central Bank of Tunisia, 1977, *Etude Préliminaire sur le Taux d'Intérêt en Tunisie.*

—————————, 1981, *Note sur L'impact des Taux d'intérêt sur le Commerce Extérieur et la Consommation,* March.

—————————, *Rapport Annuel,* different issues.

—————————, *Statistiques Financières,* different issues.

CEPEX, 1980, *Financement de Exportations,* meeting of November 17 at CEPEX headquarters, Tunis.

—————————, 1984, *Seminaire sur le Financement des Exportations,* May 26.

Chakravarty, S., 1964, "The Use of Shadow Prices in Program Evaluation," in *Capital Formation and Economic Development,* Rosenstein-Rodan ed., Cambridge: MIT Press: 48-67.

Chandavarkar, A.G., 1971, "Some Aspects of Interest Rate Policies in Less Developed Economics," *IMF Staff Papers,* March: 48-112.

Fisher, S. and F. Modigliani, 1978, "Towards an Understanding of the Real Effects and Costs of Inflation," *Weltwirtschaftliches Archiv.* Vol. 114, pp. 810-833.

Fry, M.J., 1978, "Money and Capital or Financial Deepening in Economic Development", *Journal of Money, Credit and Banking,* Vol. 10, pp. 464-75.

Grissa, Abdessatar, 1988, "An Interest Group Analysis of State Enterprises in Tunisia," ch. 14, this volume.

Hanson, J.A. and R. Derezende Rocha, 1986, "High Interest Rates, Spreads and the Costs of Intermediation," *World Bank Industry and Finance Series,* 18.

International Monetary Fund, "Interest Rates Policy in Developing Countries," *Occasional Papers,* No. 22.

Khatkhate, D.R., 1977, "Analytic Basis of the Working of Monetary Policy in Less Developed Countries," *IMF Staff Papers,* November, pp. 533-577.

Kuran, T., 1986, "The Economic System in Contemporary Islamic Thought: Interpretation and Assessment," *Int. J. Middle East Studies* 18: 135-64.

McKinnon, R.I., 1973, *Money and Capital in Economic Development,* Brookings: Washington.

Nabli, Mustapha T. and Jeffrey B. Nugent, 1988, "Collective Action, Institutions and Development," ch. 3, this volume.

North, D., 1981, *Structure and Change in Economic History,* New York: W.W. Norton.

Nugent, J.B., 1988, "Collective Action in Tunisia's Producer Organizations: Some Variations on the Olsonian Theme," ch. 10, this volume.

Patrick, H., 1966, "Financial Development and Economic Growth in Underdeveloped Countries," *Economic Development and Cultural Change* 14, pp. 174- 183.

Shaw, E., 1973, *Financial Deepening in Economic Development,* Oxford: Oxford University Press.

Stiglitz, J.E. and A. Weiss, 1981, "Credit Rationing in Markets with Imperfect Information," *American Economic Review* 71(3): 393-410.

UNAT, 1983, "Prospects of Agriculture Financing," in Arabic, *Tounes el Khadra,* (May).

Wai, U. Tun., 1957, "Interest Rates Outside the Organized Money Markets of Underdeveloped Countries," *IMF Staff Papers,* Vol. 6, pp. 80-83.

_____, 1980, *Economic Essays on Developing Countries*, Sijhoff & Nordoff.

Virmani, A., 1982, "The Nature of Credit Markets in Developing Countries: A Framework for Policy Analysis," *World Bank Staff Working Paper* No. 524.

von Pischke, J.D., 1981, "The Political Economy of Specific Farm Credit Institutions in Low Income Countries," *World Bank Staff Working Paper* No. 446.

World Bank, 1984, *Le Système Financier Tunisien*, Washington, D..C.

Zouari, A., 1988, "Collective Action and Governance Structure in Tunisia's Labor Organization," ch. 11, this volume.

Chapter 14

AN INTEREST GROUP ANALYSIS OF TUNISIA'S
STATE ENTERPRISES

Abdessatar Grissa

The purpose of this chapter is to study the effects of competing interest groups on the growth and performance of the Tunisian state enterprise sector from the perspective of the theory of collective action. The paper focuses on the following issues: (a) the institutional environment in which the expansion of the state enterprise sector has taken place, (b) the role of competing interest groups in the management and exploitation of the resources put at the disposal of state enterprises, (c) the effect of conflicts among benefitting groups on the performance and viability of state enterprises, (d) the consequences of the (excessive) exploitation of these group benefits for the rest of the economy, (e) the reaction of these competing groups to the eventual exhaustion of the exploitable benefits arising from both the production activities of these enterprises and the resources put at their disposal by government subsidies, and (f) the reaction of latent groups to the resulting deterioration in their situation and the economic and social consequences thereof.

In applying collective action theory to the state enterprises of Tunisia, consideration has to be given to the political and social realities of the country, such as the autocratic nature of the regime, and its attempts to diversify its support base among different organized interest groups.[1] In this environment the state is compelled to satisfy in so far as possible the conflicting interests of the different interest groups, and to do so in accordance with the objectives of the central authority, and in particular its vital need for survival. Since the central authority identifies its own survival with that of the country's independence, all other political, economic and social objectives become subservient to its need for survival which, in turn, becomes a determining factor in the use, operation, and performance of Tunisia's state enterprises.

---

[1] The attempts of the regime to diversify its support base are essentially motivated by an inherent desire to legitimize itself through popularity. Consequently, both official communiques and the press constantly repeat the theme that the regime owes its existence to the popular will of all social groups. This popularity, it is stressed, is due to the regime's achievements as reflected both in the country's independence and everything that has been achieved since independence.

The paper begins in Section I with a review of the circumstances leading to the growth of Tunisia's state enterprise sector. This is followed in Section II with an analysis of the various groups benefiting from the expansion of this sector and their conflicts of interest. Section III analyzes the effect of group competition on the performance both of the state enterprises and the rest of the economy. Some conclusions are presented in Section IV.

I. Background

Prior to Tunisia's independence in March, 1956, its "state enterprise" sector included no more than the telephone and postal system, forest land, and a number of hospitals and similar institutions. Since these were, (and still are) integral components of the administrative departments of the government, they were (and still are) covered by its budgetary regulations. The only state enterprises operating independently from such regulations were the port, salt, tobacco, and alcohol monopolies whose objectives were to facilitate the collection of taxes, not to promote economic and social development.

Before 1956, there was also very limited industrial activity in Tunisia. The country's openness to French exports restricted the domestic employment and production opportunities to sectors with which imports could not compete effectively such as agriculture, mining, construction, commerce, and other essential services. An economic survey conducted in February 1956 (one month before the declaration of independence) revealed that there were only 290 industrial enterprises in the country employing 50 persons or more. Of these enterprises only 6, in textiles and clothing, faced competition from imports. Moreover, 257 of these enterprises were owned by European nationals who also constituted 40 per cent of the total work force and occupied virtually all the managerial and technical positions in these enterprises.

However, once (even prior to independence) the European settlers began their mass exodus from the country, the productive capacities under their control were allowed to deteriorate. This was reflected in the decline in the share of gross capital formation in GDP from 15.1% in 1955 to 9.7% in 1957. Moreover, despite a precipitous fall in property values during this period, only a limited proportion of the relatively smaller properties could find local buyers. This prompted government intervention to take over those enterprises remaining in foreign hands.

There were, however, three other important purposes of this intervention by the government of the newly independent Tunisian state, namely, (a) to assert, in the eyes of the local population, its newly won authority, (b) to protect the inherited economic base as the foundation upon which to launch future development efforts, and (c) to satisfy the demands of certain interest groups, particularly the labor movement, for greater participation in management of the economy and the distribution of benefits.

The assertion of authority was considered vital to the state's survival,[2] not only because its authority was being contested by various opposing groups, but also to demonstrate the country's ability to manage its own affairs, something which the ex-colonial power (France) had repeatedly denied.

The expansion of state enterprises[3] in the period 1956-1961, was reflected in the growth of investment in such enterprises relative to GNP from practically nil in 1956 to 1.8% in 1960 and 6.0 % in 1961; and in the growth of the share of state enterprise investment in aggregate gross domestic investment from 11.5% in 1960 to 31.9% in 1961. This growth in the investment of the state sector was the result of both the creation of new firms and the restoration and expansion of the productive capacity of the pre-existing nationalized enterprises. During the 1956-61 period, therefore, the Tunisification of the administration, the establishment of a monetary system independent of the French franc, and the strengthening of the infrastructural bases of the new state were the primary objectives of the growing government intervention.

The 1956-61 period was followed by one of "collectivization" which lasted from 1962 to September, 1969. During these years virtually all facets of the economy were integrated into government-controlled "cooperatives". The implementation of the cooperative system began with the formation in 1962 of a few cooperative enterprises on government-owned agricultural land into which were also incorporated adjacent small private plots. This cooperative experiment was rapidly extended, particularly after the remaining European-owned farms and other business properties were nationalized in May, 1964.[4] By 1968-69 it engulfed virtually every imaginable economic activity, including shoeshine boys and street peddlers.

As a result, the share of investment in state enterprises in GNP rose further from 6% in 1961 to 11.2% in 1965 but declined temporarily to 6.0% in 1969 as a result of economic crisis and the decline in the share of capital formation in the country's GNP (from 24.4% in 1965 to 20.1% in 1969).

---

[2]President Bourguiba, who also presided as Prime Minister over the first national government, very often insisted in his numerous speeches on the need to safeguard the authority of the state and to preserve national unity.

[3]By state enterprises we refer only to those operating outside of the regular government budget and the regulations pertaining thereto. For an early study of Tunisia's state enterprises see Zidi (1973).

[4]Significantly, it was in this year that the name of the ruling (and effectively unique) political party was changed from the "New Constitutional" to the "Socialist Constitutional" Party.

After the dissolution of the cooperative movement in September, 1969 the state enterprise sector was left considerably enlarged as a result of the following quite distinct changes: (a) the return of the previously nationalized European business enterprises and farms to the state sector, (b) the creation of new state enterprises to serve as poles for the promotion of industrial development, particularly in the interior of the country, and (c) the transformation of indivisible and service cooperatives into state enterprises even though the state's share in their capital rarely exceeded 20%.

The 1970-73 period was one of relative liberalization of the economy, during which time investment in state enterprises, though remaining rather constant in relation to GNP, declined in relation to gross domestic investment to 28.8% in 1973. But this was only a temporary pause. After the rise of petroleum prices in 1973, improvements in the balance of payments and government revenues permitted the government to embark on a new expansion of the state enterprise sector. This expansion involved both the enlargement of existing enterprises and the creation of new ones. These new units were concentrated in banking and relatively capital-intensive manufacturing industries, such as chemicals and cement. Consequently, by 1977 the investment realized by the state enterprises rose to 14.1% of GNP, and to 47.0% of gross capital formation. Despite the fact that the ratio of gross capital formation to GNP remained quite stable at around 30% from 1977 to 1982, by 1982 the shares of state enterprise investment in GNP and gross domestic capital formation had declined slightly to 13.4% and 40.8%, respectively.

Although the assertion of state sovereignty and the need to fill the vacuum created by the massive exodus of European settlers were certainly important factors leading to Tunisian government takeover of foreign-owned enterprises in the *immediate* post-independence period, organized interest groups played an increasingly important role in the *subsequent* expansion of the state sector. The most important group to press for the early development of the state enterprise sector was the labor union organization, the Union Générale des Travailleurs Tunisiens (UGTT).[5] Its influence was particularly pronounced from 1961 to 1969 under the leadership of Ahmed Ben Salah who, after losing his post as head of UGTT in the late 1950's, made a spectacular entry to the government, and eventually became a "super minister," i.e., the Minister of Economics, Finance, Agriculture, and Planning.[6] It was during this period that the state sector (inclusive of cooperatives)

---

[5] See Zouari (1988), for an analysis of this organization.

[6] He was also given, in addition to these responsibilities, the Ministry of Education in 1968.

experienced its most rapid expansion.

Currently, there are about 400 active state enterprises in the country, which during the period 1971-80 contributed 24.5% of the country's GDP, 39.2% of its gross fixed capital formation, 26% of its non-agricultural wage bill and 77.5% of its merchandise exports, thereby underscoring the importance of state enterprises to the Tunisian economy. Further details, including their growing importance over time, are given in Table 14-1 below.

II. Interest Group Conflicts and the Evolution of State Enterprises

The groups benefiting most directly from the expansion, both in number and size, of the state enterprises are their employees, sometimes their immediate customers and the country's governmental bureaucracy.

In the case of the employees of state enterprises, the benefits consist of greater and more secure employment and higher salaries and fringe benefits, including retirement benefits, sick pay, and payments in kind; in the case of their customers, the benefits typically take the form of assured supplies of goods and services at prices lower than those expected to be charged by private producers; finally, in the case of the bureaucracy, the benefits take the form of the potential for patronage and control over the allocation of, and access to, managerial posts in the enterprises concerned.

It is evident, however, that these groups have conflicting interests which can often be satisfied only at the expense either of each other or the rest of society. If the rest of society were able to resist paying the bill for these benefits, the three aforementioned interest groups could collectively succeed in satisfying their short-term objectives only at the cost of a steady decline in the real flow of their future social benefits.

Quite naturally, there is considerable competition among the different groups [Becker (1983)], each attempting to squeeze from the system the highest possible benefits for itself and endeavoring to divert the corresponding costs to other groups, either at present or in the future. However, since according to Olson (1965), the employees of the state enterprises should be better able to engage in collective action than the more widely scattered consumers and taxpayers, this explains why, on the whole at least, the employees have been more successful in temporarily increasing their benefits relative to their incurred costs. Moreover, since the benefits obtained by those working for the state enterprises might be expected to spread to those working in the private sector, thereby constituting an example of the Hirschmanian "tunnel effect" [Hirschman (1981) and Nabli and Nugent (1988)], the employees of private enterprises should find it in their interest to push for wage increases in the state enterprise sector. Further, as explained by Zouari (1988) since the UGTT is dominated by the employees of the state enterprises and wage negotiations are global in nature, especially with respect to adjustments in the minimum wage rates of industry and agriculture, a wage increase in one sector tends to spread rapidly to the rest of the economy. Since the state enterprises have less reason to resist labor's demands, given the nature of their funds and the treasury support they enjoy, they are invariably the first candidates for attack by organized labor.

The questions that arise in this context are: (1) To what extent and how long will consumers and/or the rest of society allow this process to continue by bearing the cost of the wage increases? (2) What will be the role of the state itself in this process?

Olson (1982) suggested that in effective democracies one might expect the emergence of both (a) large, encompassing groups which would mitigate the distortionary effects of interest group activities and (b), under the pressure of political competition, political entrepreneurs capable of organizing large, difficult-to-organize groups like consumers, retirees, etc., who might otherwise be latent.[7] In both cases, the result might be decreased tolerance for improvements in the position of state enterprise employees. If our contention (again based on Olson's arguments) is correct, in autocratic settings like that of contemporary Tunisia, small, narrow and exclusive groups would be expected to dominate. At the same time, being especially fearful of spontaneous collective action by large groups which might threaten its position of security, the central authority would be likely to intervene by cushioning the blow to consumers of the distortionary consequences of the collective action of the small, well organized groups by subsidizing production. While such subsidies conceal the costs of concessions to small well-organized groups like the employees of state enterprises, eventually they have to be paid for by society at large, through either inflation or taxes, neither of which is likely to make the central authority popular. Therefore, the state has to carefully assess both the benefits and costs of allowing such groups to have their way.

In general, for lack of political entrepreneurs, in autocratic countries, large, weak and dispersed groups, such as the aged, unemployed, peasants and consumers, are likely to remain latent and have their interests sacrificed in favor of small, narrow groups. This is because, being well-organized and politically conscious, the latter groups pose a more immediate danger to the security of the regime than the former. This helps account for the greater

---

[7]The importance of this factor can be seen in the relative success of retired workers and other senior citizens in the exercise of influence over policy in most countries of North America and Western Europe in recent years.

degree of dualism, especially urban-rural dualism, which exists in countries like Tunisia than in more highly developed and democratic countries.[8]

Consequently, in an autocratic context like that of Tunisia, the more organized and active is a group, the more that group becomes both useful and (yet also) costly to the regime. Whether such groups should be courted or suppressed depends, therefore, on the effective cost of such action relative to the overall objective to be attained, i.e., the long-term survival of the regime. While it may be useful and rewarding to court a particular group at one point in time, the cost of this courtship may rise over time relative to the group's usefulness to the regime. If so, the regime may eventually switch from support to suppression of the group. In any case, the regime itself is unlikely to remain an independent bystander to interest group activity and interaction. Not only is an autocratic government likely to limit freedom of speech and political choice, but also it is likely to prevent the emergence of genuinely independent consumer and other associations. In countries with autocratic regimes, therefore, associations are likely to be tolerated primarily in order to facilitate their manipulation in the corporatist tradition [Schmitter (1974)] and thereby to futher the regime's economic, political or other objectives. Consequently, once these associations start to act independently, and to deviate from the tasks for which they are accepted, they are likely to be suppressed.

It is interesting to compare this situation with that described by Alexis de Tocqueville (1964) with regard to the pre-revolutionary French regime:

> The least independent group being formed without its assistance frightens it; the smallest free association, whatever its objective, is considered to be troublesome; it allows to subsist only what it has arbitrarily created and over which it presides (p.136).

Labor

The employees of state enterprises tend to benefit from the establishment of such entities to a much greater extent than the more anonymous and geographically diffused consumers of their products. Under the relatively autocratic conditions of Tunisia, consumers are able to exercise very limited political influence in defense of their interests.[9] Consequently, what they avoid

---

[8]Note, for example, that the average income of the Tunisian agricultural population is less than 40% of that of the non-agricultural population whereas in many West European countries the corresponding figure is more like 70% or 80%. Note also that the overwhelming portion of government expenditures and services, such as those of education, health, and housing, is concentrated on urban residents.

[9]Any genuine attempt to defend the interest of consumers against those of the

paying for in terms of higher prices, they pay for in terms of lower quality or higher taxes. In fact, given the pervasiveness of monopolized production activities,[10] the prices Tunisian consumers are forced to pay are generally high in relation to the quality they receive. This is evident in the dirty, dilapidated and crowded conditions of the buses and trains operated by their respective state enterprises, their frequent breakdowns, the slow pace and arrogant attitudes displayed by their employees, and above all the substantial discount at which domestically produced state sector commodities sell in relation to their imported counterparts. Moreover, on average over 75% of the government tax revenue in Tunisia comes from indirect taxes, which are on the whole rather regressive, and tend, therefore, to negate any possible income distribution benefits of tax-financed subsidies to state enterprises.

Thus, although the consumers may not be aware of it, it is they who in effect subsidize the state enterprises by paying higher direct and indirect taxes, and by accepting products of inferior quality. Therefore, what appears to them to be bought at subsidized prices is in large part paid for by higher prices elsewhere, resulting in distortions in the allocation of resources, lower welfare, and a lower rate of economic growth.[11] Even these latent groups can, when pushed hard enough, engage in spontaneous (though temporary) collective action, which because of their large numbers can be threatening to the regime. Therefore, in order to cushion and diffuse the inevitably detrimental effects of these subsidies on the current welfare of the latent groups, the Tunisian authorities had, at least partially, to finance these subsidies by

---

licensed monopolies can not be tolerated because this would be considered a rejection of the authority of a regime that is supposed to know better than the broader public what is in the national interest. While this has been the declared objective of almost every autocratic regime, in practice the sacrifice of the former to achieve a small gain in terms of the latter has often been astonishingly high.

[10]The main officially claimed justification for the establishment of these monopolies is the narrowness of the domestic market which is bound to become even narrower through the exploitation of monopolistic power. In the case of the state enterprises, which lack the counterbalancing power of shareholders, the benefits of this exploitation tend to accrue to the bureaucracy and organized labor. These characteristics seem to be shared by state enterprises in other LDCs [Jones (1982) and Wålstedt (1980)].

[11]This rising cost of subsidization is due, on the one hand, to the increased volume of consumption of subsidized goods and services and, on the other hand, to the higher unit cost of producing these goods and services. The main purpose of this subsidization is to prevent the rise in production costs from being transmitted to the final consumers of the products concerned, and thereby to avoid reducing the quantity consumed.

external borrowing. Between 1974 and 1984 the external debt relative to GNP at current market prices from rose 32.5% to 50% and the debt servicing requirements in relation to the country's exports of goods and services increased from 9% to 24.4%. However, the rapidly rising servicing cost of this indebtedness became progressively more difficult to sustain in the face of the higher world interest rates and the decreased foreign exchange earning (resulting from lower oil prices), in the early 1980s. Finally the authorities were forced to restrict the growth of aggregate demand. The result was a marked increase in open unemployment and a decline in the annual growth rate of GNP from 7.5% per annum in 1974-78 to 2.9% per annum in 1982-86.

A persistent increase, therefore, in the cost of subsidization is sooner or later likely to backfire and lead to lower employment and poorer working conditions.[12] Moreover, there is always a point beyond which the burden of supporting further increases in the real wage relative to the productivity of labor is likely to begin to fall more heavily on the state enterprise employees themselves. By the end of the 1970's this situation began to be faced by Tunisia's UGTT. As worker demands could no longer be met with the same facility and impunity, as in the past, a growing dissatisfaction with UGTT leadership began to arise among its rank and file, eventually forcing its leadership to sever its traditionally close ties with the ruling political party.[13]

UGTT influence is strong primarily in the state sector, where, because of the relatively large size and monopolistic position of the state enterprises, and their opportunities for patronage on the part of the ruling political party, the conditions for success in collective action are satisfied, thereby making organized labor a major supporting force. Notably, the secretary general of the UGTT has been, except for the periods 1977-79 and 1982-86, a permanent member of the ruling party's Politburo, and regional trade union officials have almost invariably formed an integral part of the party's regional organizations.

However, since this collaboration between organized labor and the official party is based on a mutual exchange of benefits, it can be assured of enduring only as long as the benefits outweigh the costs for both partners. In the case of organized labor, these costs arise from its loss of autonomy and its

---

[12]In addition to the trade union organization, the governing party controls the Union of Tunisian Employers (UTICA), the Union of Tunisian Farmers (UNAT), the Union of Tunisan Women, the various sports associations and up to the early 1970's, the Union of Tunisian Students. The refusal, subsequent to this date, of the majority of students to be patronized by the party led to the dissolution of their union. At present, there is no legally recognized unified student organization.

[13]Again see Zouari (1988) for more details.

support for an autocratic party whose popularity seems to have waned with the duration of its rule; in the case of the party, these costs arise from its responsibility for the hardships imposed on the economy as a result of real wages rising faster than labor productivity, and the growing cost of implicit employment subsidies. The party leadership's responsibilities to consumers and other interest groups limits the extent to which it can continue to satisfy labor's demands.

There are, therefore, trade-offs, not only on the side of the political leadership, between the benefits of UGTT support and the dissatisfaction of other groups, but also on the side of organized labor, between its loss of autonomy and initiative and the pecuniary gains it obtains in exchange for towing the party line. Consequently, neither can the country's political leadership be expected to continue to sacrifice the interests of other groups for the sake of organized labor when the costs of doing so increase, nor can organized labor be expected to maintain its traditional support for this leadership when the benefits it receives in exchange are progressively eroded. This erosion is forced by the growing losses of the state enterprises and their increasing need for government subsidization. In other words, as the financial burden imposed by the increased subsidies rises in relation to the capacity of the rest of the economy to pay for it, eventually it is bound to rupture the established relationship between organized labor and the ruling party as was the case in 1978 and again in 1985-86.

The UGTT has, therefore, lost some of its political importance, and with it some of its bargaining power for raising, or even preserving, its share of the national pie. The party, on the other hand, has other sources of support, such as the bureaucracy itself, whose interests do not necessarily coincide with those of the UGTT.

The Bureaucracy

The Tunisian bureaucracy, which includes that of the ruling political party, is an even greater beneficiary from the expansion of the state enterprise sector. Since there is no distinction in the Tunisian environment between the party and the state, all those working for the party are employees of the state or of its enterprises but put at the disposal of the party organization.[14] Moreover, since working for the party is associated with greater privileges,

---

[14]This same practice is used with the trade union organization, which not only puts it at the mercy of the government, but also induces its leadership to spend lavishly, and thus to increase its dependence on government- authorized subsidies. Such extravagance can subsequently be exposed and used as one excuse for prosecuting deposed leaders.

better possibilities of promotion, and more direct access to other sources of private gain, there is considerable competition, especially through the use of personal connections, to accede to the party bureaucracy. Ability, therefore, is not the overriding criterion in the choice of such personnel, as was reaffirmed by the Tunisian President in June, 1986, when he directed that the naming of people to posts of responsibility should be undertaken first and foremost on the basis of their party loyalty.

However, the gains of the bureaucracy from the expansion of the state enterprise sector are not limited to the direct economic advantages resulting from the assumption of managerial positions but rather stem indirectly from the political and patronage power which these institutions offer. Moreover, the managers of state enterprises are frequently more powerful, and, therefore, more feared than even the ministers by whom they are supposed to be controlled. Furthermore, managerial positions in state enterprises are often used as stepping stones to ministerial posts. Over 70% of the ministers in office in September, 1986, including the Prime Minister, were at one time or another heads of state enterprises. On the other hand, despite the relatively long duration of the occupation of ministerial posts in Tunisia, which in some cases exceeds twenty years, those promoted to ministerial posts frequently try to keep their old nests in the state enterprises feathered so that they may revert to them when the need arises. Insurance of this type is likely to be highly valued and hence not easily relinquished, even by a minister.[15]

However, since the power exercised by these people is due not to their administrative or managerial ability but rather to their political connections, they are generally untouchable as long as the protective network of relationships woven around them remains strong. In this framework, the survival of any member of the group is strongly related to the survival of the others. Protection and patronage are mutually exchanged and the stronger and more extended the network of this protection, the greater becomes the influence of the group and consequently its chances of survival. While the group may from time to time sacrifice an embarrassing member, whose incompetence, misappropriation of public funds, and corrupt activities become too obvious to deny, only rarely are such cases allowed to reach the courts for fear that the names of other members would be cited. Even when this happens, the persons involved are mere scapegoats who help to camouflage major political errors, such as Tunisia's costly experiment with cooperatives, and to divert

---

[15]Without mentioning names, suffice it to say that, in the case of Tunisia, there are numerous examples of ministers who, along with their ministerial functions, hold important posts in the state enterprises.

attention from mismanagement and the illegal use of funds.

In the autocratic system of Tunisia, the power of the bureaucracy is rather absolute. Apart from its own internal checks, its decisions are exempt from all other means of supervision and control. Even the members of parliament are generally appointed by the central political authority, mostly from the bureaucratic ranks of the party, government and the UGTT, to single lists which are elected without opposition. Moreover, here too, there is considerable mobility between the managers of the state enterprises and the members of parliament, the former being much more valued than the latter due to their greater material advantages.

Tunisian legislators, therefore, constitute merely another integral part of the bureaucracy, and as instruments in its hands, their manipulation gives the appearance of legality to its decisions. Even the Court of Accounts, whose mission is to supervise the legality of the financial operations and the validity of the administrative and management decisions of the bureaucracy, is attached to the office of the Prime Minister. Its power is weak in comparison with that exercised by those it is supposed to control. The personnel of this court are, therefore, watchdogs muzzled in such a way that they can neither bite nor bark.

Despite the fact that the bureaucracy is in control of the processes of decision making, and should be expected to resist any reduction in its acquired privileges, the extent of the central authority's emphasis on survival may lead it to reduce the privileges and benefits of its bureaucracy in order to assuage the increasingly keen and outspoken dissatisfaction of other interest groups. This may take place both through the sacrifice of scapegoats and, although this may be more apparent than real, through changes in policy. Scapegoats are needed, not only in order to bear the blame for previous failures, but also in order to reassert the will of the central authority; changes in policy are necessary from time to time in order to create a general expectation of better things to come. This approach has been applied in Tunisia on three major occasions: 1969-70, 1980-81, and 1985-86.

The benefits enjoyed by the bureaucracy, which are large relative to the country's economic means, are, in part at least, necessary in order to compensate them for the considerable risks associated with their functions. Since posts in government enterprises are remunerative, they provide an important source of such benefits. However, their high salaries contribute to the deficit of such enterprises, ways have to be found to guarantee their continuance, typically through continued access to subsidized bank credit and subsidies from the central government. However, given that sooner or later any loyal bureaucrat or legislator can count on having some time in such a position, it is not in the interest of any member of the group to "blow the whistle."[16] Only the growing burden of these transfers and the understandable clamor of other interest groups for some benefits of their own can induce the central authority, perhaps under pressure from international financiers, to purge the system from time to time and prevent its complete disintegration.

III. Effects of Interest Group Competition on the Performance of State Enterprises

From the indicators of relative importance given at the end of section I and in more detail in Table 14-1 below, it should be noted that Tunisia's state enterprises employ technology which is capital-intensive relative to that used in the rest of the economy, and have rather high ratios of labor cost to value added. The main explanations for these characteristics are as follows: (a) investment is subsidized through budgetary transfers, low or even negative real rates of interest, and the importation of capital equipment at the official overvalued exchange rate; (b) in order to render the projects more acceptable within the competitive process of the bureaucratic system, the effective economic and financial costs are systematically underestimated and the productivity of the undertaken projects overestimated;[17] (c) the protection and monopolization of production have favored the development of excess capacity; (d) the choice of projects is based much more on employment creation and hence their potential for patronage than on economic efficiency criteria.

These four reasons are, of course, closely interrelated, the first, third, and fourth being highly dependent on the second. As the bureaucratization of investment decisions has the effect of underestimating effective costs, investment levels exceed those which can be justified on efficiency grounds.[18] The consequences of this are further aggravated by the rent-seeking competition among bureaucrats for realizable projects. The following correlary of Olson's logic would seem to be at work. In particular, since each competitive faction realizes that it must bear at most only a fraction of the total cost of the benefits of collective action, the result is a level of public sector investment activity that is far beyond the country's ability to finance it from domestic savings. The need for foreign borrowing, therefore, tends to increase, on the

---

[16]This may be interpreted as a specific manifestation of Hirschman's tunnel effect [Nabli and Nugent (1988), and Hirschman (1981)].

[17]This is reminiscent of Hirschman's (1967) principle of the "hiding hand". This is explained in Nabli and Nugent (1988).

[18]All of this seems to be consistent with the budget-maximizing-bureaucrat model of Niskanen (1971) and McCormack and Tollison (1984).

one hand, with the intensity of this competition and, on the other hand, with the laxity of the central authority's control over it. The competition for patronage on investment projects and the ability of foreign borrowing to defer cost into the future make foreign borrowing especially attractive as a means of allowing this process to continue longer than it otherwise might.[19]

Because of the inherently low productivity of public sector investments, the projects undertaken generally cannot pay the real rate of interest applicable to the externally borrowed funds.[20] This explains the need of state enterprises for subsidies both direct, in the form of budgetary transfers, and indirect, in the form of nominal interest rates set below the rate of domestic inflation, or the rate of change in the real exchange rate plus the foreign nominal rate of interest.[21] Because those who make the investment decisions are themselves the guarantors of the subsequent financial needs of the enterprises, profitability is a relatively unimportant investment criterion. However, the facility with which funds flow between the government budget and these enterprises renders superfluous any distinction between them and the administrative departments. Since the budgetary constraint is the main factor limiting both the investment and the production levels of such enterprises, every financial problem affecting this budget is bound to have repercussions throughout the state sector, and hence the rest of the economy. In the case of Tunisia, such financial problems began to arise in the early 1980's with the fall

---

[19]This was undoubtedly a major cause of the sharp increase in external indebtedness of most developing countries in the years 1973-1984.

[20]This rate should in fact be the effective marginal cost of capital to the borrowing country, and it is this rate which should be used in the calculation of the profitability of the proposed investment project. The inherently low productivity of the public sector investment is more eloquently expressed by the managing director of Fiat Auto on their purchase of the state-owned Alfa Romeo: "As a state company, Alfa's priority has been employment and production volumes. They were not so much interested in profits. We have to reconcile employment, profits and volumes for the sake of the company. We are not a charity." (*Financial Times*, December 2, 1986, p. 18).

[21]That is $(i+de/e)$, where i is the foreign nominal borrowing rate of interest, and de/e is the rate of change in the real exchange rate, measured in units of the national currency. Normally, however, we should expect the rate of change in the real exchange rate to be given by $de/e = dp/p - dp^*x/ p^*x$, with p and p^* being respectively the domestic and foreign price indices. Any intervention, therefore, that has the effect of preventing the exchange rate from adjusting to a more rapid increase in domestic relative to foreign prices, or of preventing domestic prices from rising with the rise of production costs, is bound to lead to greater recourse to external borrowing due, on the one hand, to the widening of the investment-saving gap, and, on the other hand, to the lower effective costs of this borrowing.

of petroleum prices and the limitations on the country's external borrowing possibilities.

In order to minimize the need for subsidization and external borrowing, state enterprises are granted protection against competition, both internal and external. This permits the protected enterprises not only to raise their prices, but also to reduce their costs by lowering product quality.

From Tunisian press reports, political speeches, and development plans, the most frequently cited criterion in the choice of investment projects is the number of jobs created. Matters such as the opportunity costs of investment and economic viability are generally ignored. Moreover, in order to justify the proposed projects, the number of jobs to be created tends to be grossly exaggerated, as indicated by the persistent differences between planned and realized employment. The importance of labor and its use in the choice and allocation of investment is also evident in the high ratios of salary payments to gross value added of these enterprises.

Therefore, it can be said that organized labor and the bureaucracy use each other in order to promote their respective ends. This is reflected, on the side of labor, as shown in Tables 14-1 and 14-2 in its relatively high and rising share in value added, and on the side of the bureaucracy, in the extension of its political power and the corresponding pecuniary advantages. Since an important part of the remuneration to labor in state enterprises accrues to the managers, managers can hardly be expected to offer much resistance to salary increases. As already mentioned, the relatively high share of these enterprises in total salary payments can be largely attributed to the relatively high capital and skill intensities of the industries in which they are engaged.

In order to avoid a rise in the labor cost per unit of output, real wages and salaries would have to rise no faster than labor productivity. Should this condition not be fulfilled, the result would be a rise in the ratio of salary payments to value added, and either higher prices of the goods and services produced and/or a decline in enterprise profitability (and hence also either a decline in effective employment or increasing subsidization).

This is precisely what has occured in Tunisian state enterprises. As can be seen from Table 14-1, while their shares in wage and salaried non-agricultural employment and GDP remained almost unchanged between 1969-72 and 1977-80, their share in total wage and salary payments, and the ratio of their labor cost to value added increased by 47% and 26%, respectively. This was despite the fact that productivity increases have been negligible. The available data on individual enterprises given in Table 14-2 show that the ratio of labor cost to sales revenue rose markedly between 1978-79 and

1982-84 for all the listed state enterprises, but declined in the case of three out of the four listed private enterprises (and rose in the other private firm by less than in any state enterprise). As shown below, these increases in the relative cost of labor have had a detrimental effect on the profitability of Tunisia's state enterprises.

Table 14-1
Percentage Shares of State Enterprises

Share of State Enterprises	1969-72	1977-80
In Nonagricultural Employment	21.0	22.5
In GDP	25.0	25.5
In Total Wage and Salary Payments	20.0	29.5
The Ratio of Their Wage and Salary Payment to Their Value Added	39.3	49.5

Source: Commission de Synthèse du VIe Plan "Réforme des Enterprises Publiques," Government of Tunisia, February, 1982.

Table 14-2
Evolution of Labor Cost Relative to Sales Revenue of Selected Public and Private Enterprises (in percent)

Enterprise	1974-76	1978-79	1982-84
A. Public Sector			
Confort (household appliances)	10.0	15.2	23.3
STIL[1] (milk conditioning and distribution)	7.7	9.3	10.8
Tunis Air (air transport)	--	23.5	26.5
STIA[2] (automobile assembly)	7.8	6.9	8.0
STM[3] (trucking)	30.7	32.0	39.2
S.T. Liège[4] (cork)	33.1	42.3	53.9
C.T.N.[5] (maritime transportation)	23.1	14.0	16.7
SIAPE[6] (chemical fertilizer)	10.8	11.4	14.2
C. Ph. Gafsa[7] (phosphate mining)	27.1	35.0	44.2
Skanès Meubles (furniture)	36.7	42.2	46.0
S.T. de Sucre (sugar)	6.0	9.3	14.1
B. Private Sector			
Bata (shoes)	28.8	29.4	25.5
Esso Standard Tunisia (oil)	n.a.	3.3	2.5
SFB[8] Tunis (brewery)	n.a.	14.8	15.5
STOA[9] (oxygen)	n.a.	23.1	15.8

Source: Annual reports of the firms concerned. These are the main non-banking public and private firms listed on the permanent side of the Tunisian stock exchange.

Notes: [1]Société Tunisienne d'Industrie Laitière, [2]Société Tunisienne d'Industrie Automobile, [3]Société de Transport de Marchandises, [4]Société Tunisienne de Liège, [5]Compagnie Tunisienne de Navigation, [6]Société Industrielle d'Acide Phosphorique et d'Engrais, [7]Compagnie de Phosphotes de Gafsa, [8]Société Frigorifique et Brasserie de Tunis, [9]Société Tunisienne d'Oxygène et d'Acétylene.

Government transfers are a major source of investment finance for Tunisian state enterprises. These transfers, which do not include current subsidies, averaged 43.5% of the investment realized by these enterprises during the period 1972-83.[22] The fact that this percentage remained rather stable, especially between 1973 and 1983, does not imply that the government has made these transfers on the basis of rational choice and motivated by the higher productivity of the investment undertaken by these enterprises. On the contrary, these transfers constitute an expenditure imposed on the government by the inability of the state-supported enterprises to mobilize on their own the necessary funds to finance the investment programs elaborated for them by the bureaucracy. In fact, given the relative importance of the state sector, especially in industry, transportation, mining, and agriculture, the investment programs of these enterprises constitute the backbone of the country's overall development plans. These plans constitute, in fact, the main instrument through which the bureaucracy is able to manipulate its power and intervene in the name of promoting the country's economic development and growth. The tasks alloted to these enterprises, and the way they are managed and treated by the controlling authorities, their employees, and in some cases their customers, inhibit their performance and increase their financial dependence on government transfers and financial guarantees. However, since the government is not in a position to generate sufficient budgetary savings for financing these transfers, it has been forced to borrow heavily in order to continue providing them.

The amounts borrowed by the government from both domestic and foreign sources during the period 1972-83 accounted for 97.1% of the capital transfers to the state enterprises over the same period.[23] What the government borrowed with one hand, it handed over with the other. Moreover, 37.7% of this borrowing came from foreign sources and accounted for 45% of the country's total net external borrowing during the same period. On the other hand, between 1972 and 1983 government capital transfers to the state enterprises averaged 4.9% of GNP and the country's total external borrowing averaged 3.8% of GNP.

Furthermore, the assistance provided by the government to the state enterprises has not been limited to these current and capital subsidies. Other methods of assistance have included: exoneration from taxes, subsidized interest rates, priority in credit allocation, protection from competition, the granting of special import and commercial licences, priority in the execu-

---

[22] Figures from Annual Reports of the Central Bank of Tunisia.
[23] Figures are from Annual Reports of the Central Bank of Tunisia.

tion of projects, the transfer of land and other assets at symbolic prices, and debt guarantees. These other sources of assistance are made inevitable by the constant intervention of the government in the investment, employment, production, and commercial policies of these enterprises. Moreover, without this guarantee of their debts, state enterprises would not have been able to borrow as much as they have been able to over the last decade and to survive. Naturally, by its subsidies and transfers, the government both reduces the extent to which such debts need to accumulate and absorbs an important share of their interest cost, two measures without which many Tunisian state enterprises would have been unable to remain in operation.

Table 14-3
Outstanding Debt Relative to Capital and Reserves
of Selected Public and Private Enterprises, 1983 (in percent)

Enterprise[1]	Total Debt	Financial Debt
A. Public Sector		
- Confort	313	90
- STIL	848	178
- Tunis Air	475	101
- STIA	895	244
- STM	212	74
- S.T. Liège	316	57
- C.T.N.	305	53
- SIAPE	247	75
- C.Ph. Gafsa	404	107
- Skanès Meubles	371	200
B. Private Sector		
- Bata	43	15
- Esso Standard Tunisia	62	---
- SFBT	159	40
- STOA	109	31

Source: Annual reports of the firms concerned.

Notes: See the notes of Table 2 for the complete names of enterprises and the nature of their activities.

Despite all these subsidies, the relative indebtedness of many state enterprises has become excessive, especially in comparison with private enterprises. As shown in Table 14-3 in contrast to the private sector the financial debts of such enterprises often greatly exceed their capital and reserves and remain year after year without much hope of ever being paid off.

Although the cost of this indebtedness is not indicated in the published accounts of the individual enterprises, according to the 1985 Economic Budget of the government, in the case of the Phosphate Company of Gafsa it amounted to 10.7% of its sales revenue for 1983, or 42.7% of its labor costs.[24] This relatively high cost of debt, which would be expected to be even higher for enterprises having higher debt ratios, would not be tolerated in an environment giving greater attention to efficiency and profitability. The debt situation handicaps management with respect to inventories of spare parts and other inputs, the maintenance and replacement of equipment, and the expansion of its productive capacity, all of which are seen as deferable luxuries under these circumstances.

An unpublished statistical document relating to 1983, the only known source of data on the profitability of Tunisia's state enterprises,[25] and which was distributed to members of Parliament, shows that out of 170 reporting state enterprises, excluding banks, two oil companies, and administrative institutions, 83 made losses equal to 133 million dinars, and 87 made profits amounting to 33.5 million. However, 55 per cent of the losses occurred in two sectors: transport and mining; and 52 per cent of the profits were made by five enterprises, four of which are monopolies, namely, electricity, water, ports, and the import of certain products like sugar, coffee and tea and the fifth a petroleum distribution company. Although these losses seem to have risen since 1983, the relative importance of government transfers for 1983 may be considered indicative of the persistency of deficits.

It should also be noted that the management of the state enterprises is often accused of inflating their declared profits, and of deflating their declared losses, at the expense of their depreciation allowances. But though this may not have a significant effect on the total assistance required of the government, it reduces the need for current subsidies and increases the need for capital

---

[24]The country's railway company received in the form of government transfers 42.2 million dinars in 1984, of which 10.8 million was for the servicing of its debt, 13.1 million for covering other current obligations, and 18.3 million to help it realize its investment projects.

[25]Much more work of this sort has been done on the relative inefficiency of the state enterprises in the United Kingdom. See for example Kay, Mayer, and Thompson, eds. (1986).

transfers, thereby putting the current accounts of the enterprises concerned in an artificially favourable light. Consequently, though profits are rarely distributed, this distribution is generally made with great fanfare and without revealing that in many cases their production is declining and their equipment depreciating rapidly. Both the bureaucracy and the management of these enterprises find themseleves in need of such publicity from time to time, generally at the expense of lower efficiency in the long run.

This sacrificed efficiency of the state enterprises[26] is in effect an inevitable consequence of their use by the governing bureaucracy in the promotion of its particular ends. As mentioned above, in the Tunisian case there would seem little possibility that the bureaucracy can resist the temptation to make use of the state enterprises for its own rent-seeking purposes. In a democracy, parliamentary control of the purse[27] may make it possible to limit the bureaucracy's ability to do so. In the absence of such checks, however, it is in the nature of autocracy to misuse its power, at least for the sake of preserving it, and the state enterprises, with their important employment and patronage benefits for workers and bureaucrats, offer great possibilities for the extension and the manipulation of this power.[28]

---

[26] The form of such inefficiency may not necessarily be technical in nature. Indeed, Svejnar and Hariga (1987) provide evidence that technical efficiency or total factor productivity does not vary between private and public sector enterprise but also suggests that allocative efficiency is likely to be somewhat lower in Tunisian state enterprises than in private ones.

[27] The Financial Times wrote in a comment on the Italian party wrangling over the nomination of presidents to the 76 state controlled banks: "The moment of decision has arrived because the five parties which make up the Italian coalition government have made what is for them a superhuman effort to redistribute the spoils of power within the banking sector." Party rivalries have "illustrated how (they) feed on patronage offered by an extensive public sector without creating real confidence that appointments are based on merit." (November 24, 1986)

[28] Gordon Tullock (1986) pointed out that, though it may be more rewarding for the regime to hire competent managers so as to be able to draw upon the higher profits of state enterprises to compensate any incompetent loyal supporters that must be retained, the explanation he advances for its failure to do so is the "ignorance" of its leadership. This explanation overlooks two facts, however: (a) that these people must justify what they get by at least appearing to be working for it; and (b) competent managers may not be disposed to tolerate the use of the enterprises under their direction for purposes other than those determined by their business efficiency. Moreover, given the social and political objectives assigned to these enterprises, it would be difficult to attribute the losses they make to inherent incompetence on the part of their management. The case of Renault in France has become a classic example of this since it accumulated about 3.5 billion dollars of losses in 1983-

The intensity of competition among the benefiting groups over the spoils to be obtained from the control of, working for, and being clients to, the state enterprises results, not only in the confusion of objectives and the growing number of bureaucratic manipulators, but also in the rapid exhaustion of the benefits realizable from the over-exploitation of the system. The exhaustion of the exploitable possibilities has resulted in two temporary, but strong and potentially threatening, examples of collective action by otherwise latent groups, namely, the workers rebellion of January, 1978, and the consumers revolt of January, 1984.

This resort to street violence can be attributed mainly to the absence of effective alternative means for the masses to express their desires to the decision makers. The subsidization of food, public transport, rents, and the construction of low cost housing can be interpreted as the price paid in order to keep the masses quiet while the bureaucracy actively extends its power and the sources of its pecuniary benefits. This price tends to rise, however, not only with the increasing demands of the masses (whose appetite tends to grow with the feeding), but also with the expansion of the benefits obtained by the bureaucracy. In other words, the bureaucracy has to expand these subsidies in order to be able to continue expanding its own power base in a seemingly contented society. What counts is not reality, but appearance. This requires, above all, that provocations of popular discontent, which would be contrary to the well-cultivated popularity myth, be avoided. What has kept this process going is, therefore the growing subsidization, financed, first, by petroleum windfalls and, subsequently, by foreign borrowing.

Recent developments would seem to suggest that this process is finally being forced to come to an end by the decline in petroleum revenues and by the country's increasing difficulty in obtaining external credit. With the termination of the bonanza days, the competition among the different interest groups is transformed into a competition for avoiding the consequences of the resulting austerity. For example, labor and other groups argue that the mess in which the country finds itself is the creation of the bureaucracy, and that it is the bureaucracy which should therefore bear the full consequences. But, with the bureaucracy firmly entrenched in its position, it would seem to be labor and the rest of the population who in the end must accept most of the burden of austerity. Here too, somebody must pay; but the ones who eventually pay are not those benefited by the collective action they have

---

86 even though it had George Besse, one of the best managers in the country, at its head. Indeed it appears that Besse was assassinated as a result of his efforts to reduce these losses by reducing the company's work force.

brought about. Rather, those who pay are the weaker groups who benefit less in periods of prosperity, and suffer more in the subsequent periods of austerity than the bureaucracy. It is through its ability to manipulate power that the bureaucracy can avoid serious losses in periods of declining economic activity.

In the absence of an effective parliamentary democracy, the bureaucracy becomes the supreme beneficiary in the country and the sole arbiter of conflicts of interests. While some are prone to defend what they consider to be "enlightened bureaucracies," in our opinion such a defense is dangerous in the face of the tendency of unchecked autocracies to become corrupted in their use of power. Consequently, the succession of coups and governments in the non-democratic countries may bring sighs of relief from this arbitrary and corrupt use of power, but invariably the process resumes again, often with more avidity and violence, to the extent that the public may come to regret the demise of a deposed autocratic system. The new may come with its own rallying cry, but it rapidly discovers that it cannot rule without having to rely heavily on the established bureaucracy, of which it subsequently becomes the instrument and the prisoner. Under these circumstances, governments may come and go, but the bureaucracy, which has tremendous resilience and capacity to adapt, is likely to remain the effective ruling power. Moreover, as long as it retains this power, it tends to prohibit the rise of effective democratic controls, the primary aim of which should be to check the arbitrary and corrupt use of bureaucratic authority.

IV. Conclusions

The creation, proliferation and growth of Tunisia's state enterprises constitute a rather remarkable example of success in collective action. Quite naturally, and as suggested by Krueger (1974), Buchanan and Tullock (1980), Tollison (1982) there has arisen considerable competiton among the different groups for the rents generated by such enterprises. Each group attempts to maximize the benefits for itself while diverting the costs to others. However, since workers in public enterprises are in a better position to engage in collective action than consumers, being fewer in number, more concentrated and with poorer opportunities for "exit", not surprisingly the employees of public enterprises are more successful in securing their higher wages without sacrificing employment than are the consumers in resisting paying the higher prices or the taxes to subsidize the enterprises. Conceivably, the employees of private enterprises might be expected to resent the improvement in the relative position of employees of state enterprises. However, since the generally better working conditions of the state enterprises might be expected to spread to the private sector, thereby constituting an example of the Hirschmanian "tunnel effect" mentioned in Chapter 3 above, in fact they welcome wage increases or pressures to provide such wage increases in the state enterprise sector. Moreover, as explained by Zouari (1988), the fact that employees of state enterprises dominate the principal labor union (UGTT) and the fact that all wage negotiations are global in nature further impedes the development of any such opposition from within labor union ranks.

Only recently after the sharp fall in the value of the country's petroleum exports and the growing burden of its external debt in late 1986 has the cost of subsidizing these enterprises become so large in relation to the government's capacity to finance them, as to finally force the authorities to come out openly for privatization. This sudden change of attitude from a policy of state involvement in the country's production activities to one of divestiture is not due to a fundamental ideological transformation. Rather, it is forced by an increasing inability to pay the costs arising from state enterprises for whom productive efficiency is not one of its basic aims. The principal objective of this intended privatization is to disentangle the government budget from a financial burden which has become increasingly difficult to support, and a serious threat to its capacity to meet other more urgent obligations. In other words, it is the rising opportunity cost of the required subsidization of the state enterprises which has induced the government to resort to privatization.

It is our contention that this remarkable transformation in policy should not be interpreted as being solely attributable to unfavorable macroeconomic developments but rather in large part to the interest group dynamics which have been featured in Section II above. Indeed, it is important to point out that the resort to privatization of state enterprises was announced only after the increasingly independent labor union leaders were deposed, the union being (as noted above) an early and consistent supporter of Tunisia's state enterprise sector. As a result of the effects of interest group pressures, especially those of the bureaucracy and organized labor, on the nation's debt, an incumbent autocratic regime may feel its survival threatened. In such cases it may be induced to crush one or more of these groups, and the extent of the sacrifices would be greater the more serious the threats to the regime are perceived to be.

References

Becker, Gary S., 1983. "Competition Among Pressure Groups for Political

Influence," *Quarterly Journal of Economics* 98, (August).

Buchanan, James, Robert D. Tollison, and Gordon Tullock, eds., 1980. *Toward a Theory of Rent-Seeking Society*. College Station: Texas A&M University Press.

Grissa, Abdessatar, 1987. "Les Conditions Nécessaires à la Réussite d'un Programme de Privatization en Tunisie," paper presented to the Seminar on Privatization, Tunis, April 22-25.

Hirschman, Albert O. 1967. *Development Projects Observed*. Washington, D.C.: Brookings Institution.

———, 1981. *Essays in Trespassing*. Cambridge: Cambridge University Press.

Jones, Leroy, ed., 1982. *Public Enterprises in Less-Developed Countries*. Cambridge: Cambridge University Press.

Kay, John, Colin Mayer and David Thompson, eds., 1986. *Privatisation and Regulation: The U.K. Experience*. Oxford: Clarendon Press.

Krueger, Anne, O., 1974. "The Political Economy of Rent-Seeking Society," *American Economic Review* 64 (June), 291-303.

McCormack, Robert E. and Robert D. Tollison, 1981. *Politicians, Legislation and the Economy: An Inquiry into the Interest Group Theory of Government*, Boston: Martinus Nijhoff.

Nabli, Mustapha K. and Jeffrey B. Nugent, 1988. "Collective Action, Institutions and Development," ch. 3, this volume.

Niskanen, William A. Jr., 1971. *Bureaucracy and Representative Government*. Chicago: Aldine-Atherton.

Olson, Mancur, 1965. *The Logic of Collective Action*. Cambridge: Harvard University Press.

———, 1982. *The Rise and Decline of Nations*. New Haven: Yale University Press.

Schmitter, Philippe C., 1974. "Still the Century of Corporation" in *The New Corporation: Social-Political Structures in the Iberian World*. South Bend: University of Notre Dame Press.

Svejnar, Jan and Moncer Hariga, 1987. "Public vs. Private Ownership, Export Orientation and Enterprise Productivity in a Developing Economy: Evidence from Tunisia," Pittsburgh: University of Pittsburgh, Dept. of Economics Working Paper 217.

de Tocqueville, Alexis, 1964. *L'Ancien Régime et la Revolution*. Paris: Edition Idées.

Tollison, Robert D., 1982. "Rent-Seeking, A Survey," *Kyklos* 34(4): 575-602.

Weber, Max, 1922. *Wirtschaft und Gesellschaft*. Tübingen, Part III, ch. 6, 650-678, translation by M.M. Gerth and C. Wright Mills, ed. from Max Weber, *Essays in Sociology*. New York: Oxford University Press, 1946.

Wålstedt, Bertil, 1980. *State Manufacturing Enterprise in a Mixed Economy: The Turkish Case*. Baltimore: Johns Hopkins University Press.

Zidi, Makki, 1973. *Rapport sur les Entreprises Publiques*. Tunis: République Tunisienne.

Zouari, Abderrazzak, 1988. "Collective Action and Governance Structure in Tunisia's Labor Organization," ch 11, this volume.

428

PART FOUR

CONCLUDING PERSPECTIVES

The fourth and last part of the book is very brief. It consists of two short chapters designed to put the NIE and the applications thereof to Tunisian development in perspective.

The first of these, Chapter 15 by Herrick, puts the NIE in the perspective of the history of ideas and the choice among paradigms for explaining development. Herrick calls attention to the potential contributions that may come from applications of NIE in broadening the scope of the field. While Herrick suggests that the applicability of NIE to development may be rather general, he also points out a number of loose ends and unresolved issues which will have to be cleared up before the new approach can be applied with much confidence.

Finally, Chapter 16 pulls together some of the more striking substantive results from the case studies on the application of both transaction cost economics and the theory of collective action. More importantly, it emphasizes some of the interactions between the two approaches, identifies shortcomings and makes suggestions for future research.

Chapter 15

A NEW PARADIGM FOR THE STUDY
OF ECONOMIC DEVELOPMENT

Bruce Herrick

I. Old Institutionalism and New

As a school of thought in economics, institutionalism gained a critical mass in the late nineteeth century. Preceded by the historical school and by Marx's theory of stages of development, institutional economics arose in the sweaty confusion of America's definitive conversion to an industrial nation. While Thorstein Veblen's economic anthropology seemed unbounded by time or location in its appetite for inquiry, it was as often focused on the behavior of American industrialists as on primitive tribes. Methodologically, it relied on "proof by example," using the suggestive anecdote or the familiar vignette to gain its persuasive effect. His writings produced their arresting insights in an era before quantitative empiricism had been incorporated in mainstream economics.

At American institutionalism's birth, a Marshallian reliance on deductive logic clearly predominated in economics. Despite Marshall's evident knowledge of and concern for social and economic institutions, his epistemology coupled with an expository style that neglected events in the world of affairs. Only occasionally was casual empiricism used to cite results conveniently consistent with those of purely logical deduction. In short, the centuries-old intellectual traditions of the cloister and the academy, detached as they had been from continuous demands of congruence to the real world, remained firmly established.

In that world institutionalism was born, attracted attention, and later faded during the 1930's, in the face of applied mathematical techniques in pure theory and applied statistics in empirical studies. A world in depression might have called into question the economic methods that had gone before. Yet we see the Marshallian deductive tradition guiding Hicks's *Value and Capital* and *Theory of Wages*, which treatises in turn gave the mathematical appendices of Marshall's *Principles* a second wind. Even Keynes, Marshall's most prominent student, followed his mentor's methodological precepts. And on the empirical side, the birth of econometrics in its contemporary form sought scope and generalization that frequently rejected as economically uninteresting or statistically unscientific the "old" institutionalism's detailed studies of

individuals and their fascinating variations in cultures, values, social movements, and industrial sectors. The original institutionalism of Veblen, J. M.
Clark, Mitchell, and Commons was effectively elbowed aside in the ongoing
competition among economic paradigms.

It seems easiest to characterize the "new" institutionalism as the application of post-World-War-II developments in microeconomics to human
behavior. Let me list first some examples and then go on to generalize. The
aggressive expansion of the scope of modern microeconomics is familiar to
every reader. No active economist remains unconscious of contemporary consideration and incorporation into economic theory of studies in information
costs, transactions costs, bounded rationality, satisficing behavior, property
rights, the economics of contracts, collective action, rent-seeking behavior,
human capital, the economics of marriage and family, the economics of dis-
crimination, law-and-economics, and a host of other topics.

Given the diversity of these applications and their interdisciplinary nature, one might ask, what's "economic" about the new institutional economics? The answer can be succinctly expressed and it encompasses the
research described in this volume. The new institutional economics is choice
theoretic and posits maximizing behavior under constraints in ways familiar
to every professionally prepared economist. To be sure, it deals with many
topics not covered by conventional approaches. But when reduced to its simplest terms, these common characteristics involving individual choice in the
service of a set of maximands renders the approach "economic" in ways that
should not be painful to any objective observer.

Colleagues in neighboring social sciences feel keenly that their intellectual
turf has been invaded. Accordingly, they have been quick to lodge charges
of intellectual imperialism against the variety of new subjects covered by the
old economics. For understandable reasons, these colleagues would feel more
comfortable if modern economics could be burlesqued as a simplistic ode to
material greed and quickly dismissed. Economists, however, have not been
happy to oblige. Indeed the most enthusiastic of today's microeconomists
stand accused of intellectual hubris. Nevertheless, bold ventures such as the
expanded scope of economics — an expansion that has continued since the late
1930's and has accelerated during the last two decades — stir the imagination,
much as Veblen did originally on other grounds, and thus merit the close
attention of every serious intellectual.

These topics are economic in nature, in the sense that most use the
individual as a starting point and assume systematic rather than random
behavior. At the same time, hypotheses about group behavior and conclusions

about society as a whole follow readily from them. In that way, economics takes on a life of its own and pushes energetically to encompass areas hitherto thought beyond its scope.

II. A New Paradigm for Development Economics?

In particular, the possible application of the new institutional economics (NIE) to the understanding of low-income countries is a worthy goal. In the fullness of time the NIE may or may not prove qualified to be a new "paradigm." But terminological quibbles are not the point here. If the NIE "works" in countries where poverty is majoritarian rather than exceptional, that is, if it provides a basis for greater understanding, then economists sufficiently innovative to transpose it from its applications in developed countries will have made a considerable advance.

The intellectual transfer process may be inhibited by the breadth of the notion of an "institution". The introductory chapter to this anthology reminds us that institutions could include any of the following, or a combination of all of them: (1) organizations, (2) markets, (3) contracts, and (4) cultural rules. The size of the set to be called "institutions" is thus prospectively dismaying. For some economists, consideration of the NIE may be prematurely suffocated by an inspection of that list. Another and more positive interpretation, however, asserts that the robustness of the NIE is shown precisely by its capability to provide insight into all of these variants — insight both intellectually intriguing and practically implementable. In fact, the contents of the present anthology taken as a whole provide considerable evidence about the power of the NIE.

Suppose one sought to defend the proposition that the NIE formed the core of a new paradigm in economics. To appreciate some of the ways in which the NIE is an extension of standard economic principles, it may be helpful to reflect on the microeconomic approach that centers on an individual's utility maximization within constraints. The customary constraints are those of relative prices of the items found in the objective function, together with the individual's income. Besides being unnecessarily static, the constraints are too narrowly defined in such a conventional approach. The institutions of contract and cultural rules provide constraints (or alternatively, modify the simple objective function) in ways that are implicit at best and ignored by theory at worst.

For example, in affluent and low-income countries alike, most people choose not to steal, although the bundle of goods available for their consumption would increase if they did so. They are deterred from theft by one or more of the following institutional constraints: (1) the awareness of society's norms against stealing and fear of the penalties associated with violating the norms, (2) psychological conditioning that regards stealing as undesirable behavior, even if enforcement were nonexistent (that is, even if the individual could "get away with it"), (3) regard for the disdain that other individuals feel toward thieves, even if the individual's personal moral code regarded stealing as acceptable behavior. Other examples are plentiful, as the foregoing chapters have made clear.

Thus the NIE expands the constraints in the classic Benthamite utility-maximimization framework. Equally important, it recognizes the possibility of their alteration over time. Just as changes in relative prices would change the composition of the optimal consumption package, so too a change in other constraints would have a similar effect. To return to the example of theft, more effective enforcement of the sanctions against stealing, a greater individual distaste for stolen goods, or a heightened regard for the disdain that others have of thieves — any of these changes would affect the consumption bundle acquired by the individual seeking an optimal state of personal utility. In this sense, the NIE acts as a heuristically simple extension of familiar constrained maximum problems.

III. Applications of the NIE Extend far beyond Tunisia

The detailed contents of the present anthology lead readily to the conclusion that the NIE can be successfully applied by a group of knowledgeable and hard-working scholars to the institutions that characterize Tunisian life and economy. The conclusion, in turn, suggests a question of considerably broader scope: Can the framework of the expanded microeconomics encapsulated by the NIE be used with equal effectiveness in other low-income countries? One swallow doesn't make a summer, after all. A Yiddish proverb reminds us that "'For instance' isn't proof." Yet these results, scrupulously examined within a Tunisian cultural and historical context, seem so far-reaching as to indicate great promise for applications of this approach far beyond Tunisia.

A couple of examples of broad application may suffice. Both examples focus on cultural values. Consider first, the internationally comparative sociological research of Inkeles and Smith (1974) into the set of attitudes that characterize "modernization" and thus promote economic development. The attitudes are themselves "institutions" in at least one of the senses cited earlier. At the center of the development economist's concerns could be a differentiation between (a) traditional attitudes that postpone or prevent development and (b) modern attitudes and beliefs that augment the possibilities for development. Summarizing the latter, Inkeles and Smith note that

The modern man's character, as it emerges from our study, may be summed up under four major headings. He is an informed participant citizen; he has a marked sense of personal efficacy; he is highly independent and autonomous in his relations to traditional sources of influence, especially when he is making basic decisions about how to conduct his personal affairs; and he is ready for new experiences and ideas, that is, he is relatively open-minded and cognitively flexible.

As an informed participant citizen, the modern man identifies with the newer, larger entities of region and state, takes an interest in public affairs, national and international as well as local, joins organizations, keeps himself informed about major events in the news, and votes or otherwise takes some part in the political process. The modern man's sense of efficacy is reflected in his belief that, either alone or in concert with others, he may take actions which can affect the course of his life and that of his community; in his active efforts to improve his own condition and that of his family; and his rejection of passivity, resignation, and fatalism toward the course of life's events. His independence of traditional sources of authority is manifested in public issues by his following the advice of public officials or trade-union leaders rather than priests and village elders, and in personal matters by his choosing the job and the bride he prefers even if his parents prefer some other position or other person. The modern man's openness to new experience is reflected in his interest in technical innovation, his support of scientific exploration of hiterto sacred or taboo subjects, his readiness to meet strangers, and his willingness to allow women to take advantage of opportunities outside the confines of the household. [pp. 290-291].

In the NIE, attitude formation and subsequent modification become grist for the economist's mill. Development economists have written persuasively about the economic rationality of peasants' conservatism in the face of limited information, high transactions costs, lack of access to financial or physical capital, and low income coupled with uncertainties of weather and prices. An attitude of fatalism in such circumstances reflects sensitivity to the economic environment rather than the primacy of so-called non-economic (or "irrational") motives. These attitudes no longer are regarded as falling outside the scope of the development economist's interest and area of expertise. Instead they can now be examined for their economic content. The possibilities of fomenting development-oriented changes in attitudes within a traditional setting constitute an obvious normative application of this line of reasoning and one which clearly extends to societies beyond Tunisia.

Continuing with the notion that institutions include not only organizations, laws, and contracts, but also cultural values, consider a position as stimulating as it is controversial, taken by Peter Bauer (1972). In his first collection of essays, *Dissent on Development*, he noted:

Examples of significant attitudes, beliefs, and modes of conduct unfavourable to material progress include lack of interest in material advance, combined with resignation in the face of poverty; lack of initiative, self-reliance and a sense of personal responsibility for the economic fortune of oneself and one's family; high leisure preference, together with a lassitude often found in tropical climates; relatively high prestige of passive or contemplative life compared to active life; the prestige of mysticism and of renunciation of the world compared to acquisition and achievement; acceptance of the idea of a preordained, unchanging and unchangeable universe; emphasis on performance of duties and acceptance of obligations, rather than on achievement of results, or assertion or even a recognition of personal rights; lack of sustained curiosity, experimentation and interest in change; belief in the efficacy of supernatural and occult forces and of their influence over one's destiny; insistence on the unity of the organic universe, and on the need to live with nature rather than conquer it or harness it to man's needs, an attitude of which reluctance to take animal life is a corollary; belief in perpetual reincarnation, which reduces the significance of effort in the course of the present life; recognized status of beggary, together with a lack of stigma in the acceptance of charity; opposition of women's work outside the household [pp. 78-79].

While Bauer's position is considerably more pointed and controversial than that of Inkeles and Smith, the passage provides another good example of the development economist's concerns, formerly considered non-economic and now incorporated within the scope of the NIE. I've already commented on the economic rationality of fatalism or passivity in the context of mass poverty.

The quotation from Bauer contains other highlights, however. Consider, for example, the reference to "high leisure preference" often coupled with "lassitude" (a euphemism for laziness) found in the tropics. The knowledgeable institutional economist notes that this "attitude" — this set of "tastes" for leisure — has a high and positive correlation with the incidence of parasitic infestation. What may look like lassitude to the external observer turns out to be a rational, indeed an imperative, physiological response to internal conditions. Similarly, an "insistence on the unity of the organic universe, and on the need to live with nature" is increasingly considered in the affluent countries an economically rational response to detrimental externalities (external diseconomies) created by industrial activity.

In short, I conclude that the *new* institutionalist point of view, representing the use of economic principles to respond to a vastly amplified set of questions, has application far beyond those of the Tunisian case studies explored in this anthology.

IV. Loose Ends in the New Institutional Economics

While it's easy to be optimistic about further applications of the NIE to situations in the low-income countries, it's hardly surprising that some unresolved problems prospectively remain. First, institutions, in all their varied forms, do not always evolve toward efficient configurations. The point is worth emphasizing, if only because conventional economists strive with such forceful bias to find efficiency-seeking change. Their empirical research is much more likely to highlight a newly efficient land-title scheme, for example, than one that fulfills other societal values. It is hard to believe, however, that institutional change moves monotonically toward greater efficiency. To state only the most obvious counter-example, to the extent that a trade-off between efficiency and equality exists, institutional evolution is as likely to move toward greater equality as it is to approach optimal efficiency.

But if institutions don't evolve reliably toward a single and simply described economic outcome, then the theoretical base on which institutionalism is constructed has less intellectual appeal. To speak more formally, as social scientists we appear to seek unified and unitary teleological conclusions and to denigrate non-monolithic approaches. This is not a new problem. The "old" institutional economics failed to win universal acceptance not because it ignored property rights or information costs or contract enforcement. Its problems lay precisely in its eclectic character, a character which it uncomfortably shares with its younger sibling.

In much the same vein, the NIE is not yet capable of generating a unified set of hypotheses concerning institutional change. This follows from the previous remarks. A theory in which anything is possible is a theory in which outcomes can't be predicted. And such a theory, by definition or convention, is not yet a full-fledged "theory". In this context, the principle of parsimony in the elaboration of scientific theories should be recalled. While the producer of theories seeks singular descriptions of the world that are economical, frugal, parsimonious in their explanatory elements, he or she must also avoid carefully the hazards of reductionism. In general, the theories that are most nearly unified or unitary have had the greatest heuristic appeal.

Finally, as indicated by most of the articles in this anthology, the NIE typically presents only qualitative evidence. Cardinal quantification of many of the variables interesting to researchers still eludes our capability. In a sense, we find ourselves conditioned by the epistemology of modern econometric training to regard quantitative demonstrations more persuasive than qualitative ones.

V. Theories of Development: Complements, Supplements, Substitutes

A final question: How does the NIE add insights to other contemporary theories of development? Does it supplement them or compete with them? The answers vary with the theory under scrutiny and reveal as much about the NIE as they do about the state of theorizing in development economics.

Consider first neoclassical theories of economic development. The limitations of this antecedent and narrower neoclassical analysis are sharply revealed by the NIE. The memorialization of the narrow microeconomic analysis in standard textbooks, coupled with an inevitable cultural lag, means that traditional microeconomics won't disappear instantly, but the NIE, while adopting many of its postulates and assumed maximands, goes far beyond it. One might confidently expect that information and transactions costs, collective action and free-riders, and public choice more broadly conceived will quickly find their way into conventional analysis used by development economists.

Because the other paradigms used commonly in development economics have less in common methodologically with the NIE, it is more difficult to anticipate the NIE's influence on them. For example, they do not, in general, postulate choice theoretic or maximizing individuals as elementary units of analysis.

Radical and Marxist economics, to be sure, begin from a careful study of the evolution of economic and social relations — much as does any valid institutional economic analysis. But in Marxist economics' fixation on the centrality of a class struggle, historical inevitability, and revolution, the distance between radical and Marxist economics on the one hand and the NIE on the other is clearly manifested. At the same time, the contrast can be overstated. The evolution and entrenchment of vested interests are as much the target of analyses using the NIE as they are for Marxist analysis. The circumstances under which interest groups ("rent-seeking coalitions") might potentially be weakened or even dislodged are also of common concern.

Equally compelling is the contrast between the normative emphasis of radical and Marxist economics and the positive slant of the NIE. Both are potentially valuable approaches. For all these reasons, the two schools appear to complement one another in useful ways.

A stronger distinction can be drawn between structural and disequilibrium approaches to economic development and those of the NIE. To review briefly, the macromodels of structuralism ignore the events of economic history at the same time that they rely on (historical) data from which structural coefficients are derived. The historical data, of course, come from a real world in which the postulates of *ceteris paribus* and marginal change are ignored. Everything changes at once in history — technology, institutions, economic structure itself. Thus the challenge to economic analysis in general and to structural analysis in particular lies in the formulation of the critical experiment. It must seek to distinguish between the effects on the economy of the multitude of simultaneous changes.

To the extent that structuralist theories and the models that flow from them are policy oriented, they focus on the exigencies of the short term. Again, while long-term data have led to the derivation of quantified parameters, most structural models seek to provide economic guidance during a period so short, in fact, that parameters describing the structural behavior of the economy are constant. Thus structuralism in the analysis of development, while useful, has stood against an approach convinced of the value of historical studies, of relative prices, and of a period of time sufficiently long for basic institutional change to occur.

Research Program

A new paradigm (I drift self-consciously to that terminology in the Kuhnian sense) is recognized as such in part when it generates a research program. To flourish, it must stimulate the imagination of scientists discontent with existing approaches and lead them to seek to apply new theories. The first test of the potential validity of the NIE in development economics will come as concentrated research efforts such as the one presented in this collection deal with countries other than contemporary Tunisia. I join the other authors here when I regard that prospect as an inviting one.

References

Bauer, P.T., 1972, *Dissent on Development — Studies and Debates in Development Economics.* Cambridge, MA: Harvard University Press.

Hicks, J.R., 1932, *The Theory of Wages.* London: Macmillan, [first edition].

_____, 1946, *Value and Capital — An Inquiry into some Fundamental Principles of Economic Theory.* Oxford: Oxford University Press, second edition.

Inkeles, Alex and David H. Smith, 1974, *Becoming Modern —Individual Change in Six Developing Countries.* London: Heineman.

Marshall, Alfred, 1920, *Principles of Economics.* New York: Macmillian, 1948 [4th edition].

Meier, Gerald M. and Dudley Seers, eds., 1984, *Pioneers in Development.* New York: Oxford University Press.

_____, ed., 1987, *Pioneers in Development — Second Series.* New York: Oxford University Press.

Chapter 16

THE NEW INSTITUTIONAL ECONOMICS AND DEVELOPMENT: CONCLUDING REMARKS

Mustapha K. Nabli and Jeffrey B. Nugent

The purpose of this chapter is not to repeat or summarize the particular conclusions arrived at in the individual case studies applying the NIE to Tunisia that were presented in Parts II and III above but rather to draw some general conclusions from them and to assess their implications for theory.

Following the order of the preceding presentation, in Section I we make this assessment with respect to the applications of the economics of transaction and information costs. Then, in Section II we do so with respect to the applications of the theory of collective action. The chapter is concluded in Section III with some remarks on the interactions between the two approaches, their common shortcomings and suggestions for future research.

I. The Economics of Transaction and Information Costs

As suggested in Chapter 2 above, when transaction costs are defined sufficiently broadly to include the costs of information, negotiation, monitoring and enforcement with respect to all the relevant inputs in the production and distribution processes, including the bearing of the relevant risks, the transaction cost framework can serve as a unifying one for analyzing contractual choices. As such, this framework offers the potential for explaining the choices among different types of contracts and organizational forms and formulating empirical tests of the relative importance of the various factors relevant to and underlying these choices.

Indeed, the transaction cost framework would seem capable of identifying the factors responsible for the switch from wage and rent contracts in the agricultural sector of Tunisia's Medjez-el-Bab region. These include the outmigration of family supervisors, the increase in irrigation (and hence in labor intensity) and the rise in the relative cost of labor (and hence the relative cost of labor-shirking). Variations in contractual choices across sample households seem to be explained, as the theory would suggest, by variations in both working household and landowning household characteristics.

It also seems capable of identifying not only the many factors which contribute to the overall dominance of share contracts in Tunisian fishing but also the particular factors which account for the special exceptions in which wage and fixed rent contracts can be observed. Again in the case of the taxation of weekly markets, the transaction cost framework identifies many factors contributing to the dominance of tax farming or fixed rent contracts.

Although it also provided empirical support for the relevance of some of the more traditional determinants, the study of size distribution and ownership type in Tunisian manufacturing provides surprisingly strong evidence for the relevance of transaction cost considerations such as the relative importance of bank credit, inputs like those of managers and engineers for whom the labor market is poorly developed, the ability of firms to avoid the impact of social legislation (e.g., through the use of apprentices) and the type of price regime to which the industry is subject.

While an overall judgement is left to the reader, taken together, the empirical findings of the four case studies in Part II would seem to provide rather impressive support for the relevance of many of the different elements in our generalized version of transaction costs in explaining contractual choices in Tunisia. The results, however, also underscore the dangers of mechanical application of the standard (Williamson) framework to LDCs like Tunisia. Both the framework and its applications have to be modified to better suit LDCs. In terms of their importance three specific shortcomings in this respect stand out.

The first is that, since the overwhelming portion of the applied literature on contractual choices, especially that with respect to contractual choices in LDCs, has been concentrated on agriculture in general and sharecropping in particular, some of the implications for modelling as well as for policy that have been suggested in that literature may be incomplete or even misleading in applications to other sectors. In particular, since agricultural land is not as vulnerable to opportunism of the asset-misuse variety as assets in other sectors, insufficient attention has been given to this form of opportunism in the analytical literature. Since from the more general perspective in which opportunism of the asset-misuse type is included the relative advantages of the various contracts are very different from those taken from a perspective in which labor-shirking is the only form of opportunistic behavior, the consequences of this neglect can be serious.

The second shortcoming is that, whereas the opportunistic behavior that is treated in the transaction cost framework is generally that practiced by one of the parties to the contract relative to another party to the contract, the case studies have demonstrated that the opportunistic behavior is frequently at the expense of parties external to the contract. In the case of fishing, fishermen may be willing to work for a captain or owner who under-reports output to them but at the same time is able to help them get a larger output (catch of fish) by getting around the existing conservation and other regulations. In the case of contracts between the tax collector and the government, it takes the form of opportunistic behavior practiced by the tax farmer *vis-à-vis* the merchants or the public. Finally, in the case of the organizational form of private enterprise, it takes the form of opportunistic behavior by the owners and/or managers of the firm *vis-à-vis* the government or consumers.

The third shortcoming is that the problem of bonding seems to have received insufficient attention. Since the costs of information, search, negotiation and performance risk can be lowered significantly by contract renewal among the same parties to the contract, bonding in the form of the promise of contract renewal as a reward for good performance can be attractive to the various contracting parties and at the same time can be a useful incentive device. Both in fishing and agriculture there is evidence that, should they wish to do so, employers can offer their better employees sufficient incentives to renew contracts at the expiration of old ones. The prospect of renewal must be neither too large nor too small. For example, if it is too large and the contracting parties feel that contract renewal is guaranteed, there may be little incentive to perform effectively, and at least one of the parties is likely to feel harmed by being locked into an undesirable long term relationship. On the other hand, if the prospect of renewal seems too slight, the incentive to perform may be insufficient, and at least one of the parties may be stuck with the risk of not finding satisfactory contractual partners and terms of contract in the future. As Crawford (1988) puts the issue: When is a single long-term contract better than a series of renewable short-term ones?

Naturally, the optimal degree of contractual security (prospect of renewal) may vary from one situation to another according to the relative magnitudes of the costs of search and monitoring, the extent to which past performance can be communicated among the relevant agents and the degree of development of the relevant markets. In the case of relatively unskilled workers, such as agricultural workers and fishermen, in local markets within which reputations can easily be communicated among the relevant agents relatively short-term contracts seem optimal. By limiting the contracts to the short-run, such workers can avoid the problems of being locked into undesirable, or what (as pointed out in Chapters 1 and 2) are sometimes called "exploitative" situations by their employers. Indeed, mobility is a desired means of obtaining security against "exploitation" by an overly demanding or unreliable employer. On the other hand, in cases where more technical skills and teamwork are involved, it may be optimal to have a high likelihood

of contract renewal or to have contracts of long term duration. This would
be especially true when asset-specificity is relatively important, and the market for such labor types is not only "thin" in terms of numbers, but also,
because of asymmetries in information, subject to market failure. (E.g., in
the case of an experienced worker who upon reentering the market, becomes
a natural suspect for being a "lemon". As a result, the promise of mobility
is considerably less suitable as a means of assuring against exploitation). In
such cases, actual or implicit long term contracts may be useful, at least when
they are supplemented with monitoring and incentives for good performance.
For this reason and as suggested by Williamson (1985), skilled and managerial workers may prefer to work for more bureaucratic corporations which are
more permanent and hierarchical in structure than for individually owned
enterprises which are more inclined to short-term contracts and flexibility of
function.

Finally, four other issues in the context of contractual choice deserve
consideration. First, it may be quite useful and appropriate in such analyses
to take social conventions and societal norms as given. Our case studies
have repeatedly shown that the existence of social norms, such as the relative
strength of the family and the importance of loyalty among family members,
can have very significant influences on the choice among contracts. Since in
the process of development certain social norms are virtually certain to erode
and to be replaced by others, one can predict that expected changes in norms
will have the effect of inducing substantial changes in contractual form. For
example, as Tunisia continues to develop economically and socially, one can
expect family loyalty to decline and the quality of the market as an instrument
for communicating information of various sorts to improve, thereby leading
to the choice of more formal and longer term contractual arrangements in
the future than in the past. In the long run, these changes in norms need
to be explained. As suggested below, both transaction cost considerations
and collective action theory would seem to contribute to the explanation of
changes in norms.

Second, in maintaining the degree of operationalism of the transaction
cost theory of contractual choice, one must be careful to avoid rendering
the results tautological by merely *assuming* that the contracts which exist
are efficient. When the issue was probed in the case studies, however, it
turned out that in only one of the case studies was there any serious reason
for believing existing contracts to be inefficient. This was the case of tax
collection contracts where it would seem that, if appropriate safeguards were
employed, the fixed rent or tax farming contracts could be more efficient than

wage contracts in taxing, at least some, additional forms of economic activity in which, as in the case of weekly markets, the activities to be taxed are rather difficult to monitor. In view of the rather poor record that Tunisia and other LDCs have in collecting the revenues justified by law, this is an important conclusion. In other cases, however, and especially in the case of agriculture and fishing, the dominant forms of contract seem to be advantageous to both the demanders and suppliers of such contracts.

Third, with respect to institutional rigidity, in none of the case studies was there any evidence of institutional rigidity or inflexibility. Indeed, considerable evidence to the contrary was provided, at least in the sense that various forms of contract were either in practice simultaneously in the same activities, or had been in use in the recent past. Especially in the case study of agriculture, the interviews demonstrated that there has been a remarkable amount of changing in contractual form in the recent past and very considerable willingness to consider alternative forms. The reason for the unusual degree of contractual flexibility in the case of agricultural contracts may be attributable to the fact that these are the simplest contracts, generally between two individuals, often with respect to a single crop during a single season of the year. Fishing, manufacturing and tax collection activities, on the other hand, involve more agents of different types and therefore the contractual forms used in them seem to be more costly to change, especially in the short run.

Fourth, perhaps as a result of its breadth, flexibility and generality, the transaction cost approach may be insufficiently precise to explain some of the interesting institutional details revealed in the case studies. For example, with respect to tax farming contracts for collecting taxes in Tunisia's periodic markets, it would seem difficult to explain the choice of auction types or the use of non-refundable deposits among alternative bidders with reference to transaction cost theory alone. In these respects, it would seem desirable that the looser transaction cost analyses be supplemented with more rigorous, though less flexible, principal-agent analyses. In this respect, we wind up in agreement with recent directions in the literature and one of the criticisms of the transaction cost framework identified in Chapter 2.

II. The Theory of Collective Action

The variety of sectors and issues investigated from the perspective of the theory of collective action in Part III bears witness to the fruitfulness of the approach in dealing with a wide range of issues in LDCs. Indeed, considerable evidence has been provided for several of the different elements of the theory.

For example, strong evidence has been provided for several Olsonian hypotheses concerning the importance and positive influence on the prospects of collective action of group characteristics such as homogeneity of background, heterogeneity of goals, geographic concentration, size inequality, and small numbers. Indeed, homogeneity of background and geographic concentration seem to have been crucial factors in explaining the remarkable strength of the porters in the wholesale market of Tunis, labor unions in public enterprises, and the relative strength of certain producer organizations.

Homogeneity in background would also seem to have been important in explaining the success of the ulama in resisting proposals for reform of the educational system of Tunisia. Heterogeneity of goals seems to have played a very important role in explaining both the greater success of industrialists and urban-based commercial farmers *vis-à-vis* other agriculturalists in obtaining institutional credit and recently (subsequent to the entry of the development banks) that of the banks in raising interest rates. Equality in size seems to have had a significant negative influence on collective action and interest group strength among Tunisian farmers, and members of the individual craft guilds of the city of Tunis. Small numbers would seem to have been important in explaining the relative strength of the ulama in the 19th century, and of bureaucrats, hotel owners, chemical producers, banks and union officers in contemporary Tunisia.

Strong evidence for other (non-Olsonian) elements in the theory of collective action has also been provided in the case studies. For example, Hirschman's concept of "exit" also seems to be extremely relevant. The relatively low cost of exit to the impoverished small farmers in Tunisia compared to the high cost of exit to the relatively well-paid and job-secure employees of public enterprises helps explain why the former are much less likely to engage in "voice" and collective action than the latter. The high cost of exit would also seem to have contributed to the longevity of power and influence of the Tunisian ulama over the educational and other institutions in the face of tremendous pressures for change and to the large and growing influence of capital-intensive industrialists and hotel owners who have sunk large investments in fixed assets which cannot easily be transferred for use in other activities. The relative weakness of retailers and of farmers in resisting the monopolistic pressures of the porters' cooperative (COOPMAG) in the wholesale market of Tunis can also be attributed to the fact that they can relatively easily satisfy their needs through alternative channels of exchange. The recent success of taxicabs of very different types and location in gaining tax exemptions on imported automobiles is attributable to the taxi organization's use of Olson's "federation" principle and Hirschman's "tunnel effect" principle.

A little reflection on the various case studies reveals two important underlying similarities. First, in all of them the success or failure of collective action hinges not on the action of a single group but rather on the relative importance of several different groups and the interactions among them. Second, the state itself is an important and relatively active group whose activity significantly affects the outcome of collective action in all the case studies of Part III. This highlights the limited usefulness and relevance of the Olsonian partial equilibrium, single group type of analysis which forms the overwhelming proportion of collective action theory.

As explained in Chapter 3, the existing theory of collective action does not take us very far in explaining the choice among the different instruments available for achieving collective action, i.e., why some groups favor protection, others subsidized inputs, etc. Nevertheless, the case studies would seem to suggest that the cost of exit, which in a sense may be regarded as a specific manifestation of the more general concept of opportunity cost, may also be of use in explaining a given group's choices in this regard. For example, in those activities in which it is relatively costless to pass on the costs of producer (employer or employee) group benefits to consumers, as in the case of manufactures for the domestic market, producer groups may prefer to push for tariff protection and non-tariff barriers to imports. On the other hand, in sectors in which this is not possible, as in the case of farmers, exporters, hotel owners and taxis, producer groups seem to turn their attention to the subsidization of inputs such as credit, imported equipment and energy.

As has been noted in Chapter 3 above, much of the theory of collective action and its applications have been devoted to DCs and hence to countries characterized by representative governments, freedom of the press and freedom of association. In much of this literature the state has been viewed as a mere bystander or at most a rather passive mediator of intergroup competition in the practice of collective action. The state is usually seen as simply responding by supplying the various different interest groups with what they demand in proportion to the relative strength of those demands.

However, again as suggested in Chapter 3, in LDCs which are generally characterized by considerably less freedom of the press and of association, and by autocratic governments more continuously concerned for their own security, one might expect the state itself to take a more active role in interest group activities and indeed to try to control them. As a result, interest groups may be more corporatist in LDCs than in the DCs. These expectations have been fulfilled by the findings of virtually all the case studies.

Even if it may have started as a weak state, by the late 19th century the Tunisian state had come to be rather strong [Anderson (1986)] and hence able to exercise considerable influence over the character of the craft guilds by virtue of the state's assignment of various state functions to the amins. More recently, through the dominant political party and its allies in the bureaucracy, the legislature, and throughout society, the state has become by no means an innocent bystander with respect to unions, producer organizations, public enterprises, and banks. Indeed, three of the case studies — those on wage rate and interest rate determination and public enterprise formation — have shown the state itself to have been a prime actor. In the case of interest rate determination, the state's interest is in part motivated by the fact that (as the country's most important debtor) the state has considerable self-interest in low interest rates. But also, because of its continuing fiscal deficits, the state continues to need assurance of continued access to credit from the banking system. In the case of state enterprise formation, the power of patronage seems to be an important motive for state participation. In the case of worker and producer organizations, the state's interest would seem to have been partly that of keeping them under control. In both these cases also, the state seems to have taken to heart the implication of Olson's hypothesis that encompassing groups would be less distortionary and more favorable to growth than narrow groups by encouraging or even forcing these organizations to assume an encompassing character. Nevertheless, to date the Tunisian experience with encompassing labor and producer organizations provides little evidence suggesting that their influence has been growth-enhancing. Indeed, because of the importance of growth-retarding selective incentives in encompassing groups, this orientation may have hindered rather than encouraged economic growth and efficiency.

Most but not all of the collective action observed in the case studies has resulted in the creation of formal organizations capable of applying selective incentives. Exceptions seem to have been (a) the historical case of the ulama which, although remarkably strong, never became a formal organization and (b) the contemporary example of public enterprises which, given their remarkably good access to the highest levels of state decision-making and their strong backing by organized labor, have always managed to engage in collective action without the benefit of formal organizations of their own. The selective incentives practiced by these groups — both formal and informal — have contributed very substantially to their success in collective action.

With respect to producers and consumers, the relative weakness, or even total absence, of their collective action would seem to have had a deleterious effect on welfare and growth. Given the aforementioned common characteristic of the case studies, namely for collective action to be the resultant of many different group forces, the natural result is that one group's success is at the same time another group's failure. The fact that collective action often results from an imbalance of forces may help explain how many of the examples of collective action in the case studies would seem to have exerted negative influences on the growth and development of the Tunisian economy. The success of the ulama in delaying the introduction of modern secular education until well into the 20th century is perhaps the most outstanding example. The failure of the guilds to innovate in the face of external competition until more than a century after guilds had been replaced by modern manufacturing enterprises virtually everywhere in Europe is another important example. The same can be said, though perhaps to a lesser extent, of the porters organization and wholesale market of Tunis.

III. Interactions among the Two Approaches, Common Shortcomings and Future Research Needs

Besides the aforementioned conclusions that transaction cost considerations can be important and useful in analyzing the kinds of institutional issues to which they are typically applied, namely contracts and organizational forms, and that the principles of collective action can be useful in explaining the level and character of collective action, even more fundamentally the case studies demonstrate the complementarities between the two approaches. For example, collective action frequently requires the creation of formal organizations, but organizations, the forms they assume and their qualitative character are affected by transaction cost considerations. The past experience in collective action can influence both the magnitude and the nature of transaction costs. The relevance of these interactions is most clearly demonstrated in the case study on Tunisia's labor organization.

Each approach is not without its shortcomings; in particular, the transaction cost framework fails to explain how the various alternative contracts and organizations are instituted, and collective action theory fails to explain the choice among alternative organizational forms and selective incentives. Notably, however, each of these approaches can help overcome the shortcomings of the other. As a result, by taking advantage of their potential complementarities, the two approaches together can explain institutions more successfully than either could individually. As one example of these complementarities, in Chapter 3 it was seen that changes in norms, which occur only very slowly over time, are extremely important determinants of both transaction costs (and hence of contractual choice and contractual efficiency) and the level of economic development. But also, it was shown that changes in transaction costs can help bring about changes in norms. In many cases, however, changes in norms cannot be accomplished without collective action which in turn, may be either aided or impeded by changes in transaction costs. For this reason it would seem that changes in norms may result from dynamic interactions between transaction costs and collective action. Given the dearth of case studies on changes in norms, these considerations would seem to imply that it would be desirable that such case studies should be undertaken and that allowances for such interactions should be made in their design.

A shortcoming of most studies of transaction costs and collective action, including the case studies presented in Parts II and III of this volume, is that most of the determinants of institutional forms and collective action have offsetting influences. For example, while larger group size may make it more difficult to achieve collective action for the reasons given by Olson (as summarized in Chapter 3 above), in some respects at least, group size may also attract political entrepreneurs whose existence may make it more likely that a critical mass of resources can be obtained, thereby enhancing the chances of success in collective action. For any single factor exerting influences in different directions, it becomes difficult to know *a priori* from qualitative studies the expected direction of the net effects. Furthermore, even if the net effects of a single factor were unambiguous, different factors would be likely to exert offsetting influences, once again rendering ambiguous the direction of their combined effect. One or even a few case studies of qualitative character like those reported in this volume are not likely to resolve this issue and yield clear-cut policy implications. In fact, unless appropriate precautions are taken, studies of this type can easily degenerate into exercises of the "functionalist" or ex-post rationalization type in which any outcome can be explained by appealing to an appropriate constellation of effects. Clearly, such exercises do not constitute tests of the theory in any meaningful sense of the term.

This shortcoming greatly limits the usefulness for policy of existing theory and case studies inasmuch as qualitative information about the expected direction of the effects of individual policy changes generally will also be insufficient for predicting the net impact of policy changes in circumstances when (as is usually the case) several exogenous variables and policy instruments are likely to change at the same time. For the same reason, even quantitative information on the extent of the anticipated policy changes will not allow the policy maker to know whether such changes will be sufficient for changing contracts or engaging in specific kinds of collective action.

Therefore, an important implication for future research is that future case studies need to be more quantitative in nature, more along the lines of the case study of Chapter 7 but each based on the examination of many different cases which would vary both across countries and over time. Given the importance of changes that occur only slowly over time, it is clear that at least some of these studies should be historical in character. But, future research should also give more emphasis to identifying the necessary and sufficient conditions for institutional change.

Future case studies along these lines should also give more attention be given to the dynamic interaction between collective action and transaction costs and to understanding the dynamics of collective action success and failure. To be more useful, collective action theory cannot remain a theory about static conditional probabilities but rather, as Kuran (1989) argues, it needs to develop into a dynamic theory of how these probabilities may change over time as a result of historical antecedents, and of how critical thresholds for change can be operationalized, identified and then explained.

References

Anderson, Lisa, 1986, *State and Society in the Third World.* Cambridge: Cambridge University Press.

Crawford, Vincent P., 1988, "Long-term Relationships Governed by Short-term Contracts," *American Economic Review*, 78 (June): 485-499.

Kuran, Timur, 1989, "Sparks and Prairie Fires: A Theory of Unanticipated Political Revolution." *Public Choice*, 60, in press.

Williamson, Oliver E., 1985, *The Economic Institutions of Capitalism.* New York: Free Press.

INDEX